# ISSUES IN RACE AND ETHNICITY

# ISSUES IN RACE
# AND ETHNICITY

## SELECTIONS FROM CQ RESEARCHER

**7TH EDITION**

Los Angeles | London | New Delhi
Singapore | Washington DC

Los Angeles | London | New Delhi
Singapore | Washington DC

FOR INFORMATION:

CQ Press

An Imprint of SAGE Publications, Inc.

2455 Teller Road

Thousand Oaks, California 91320

E-mail: order@sagepub.com

SAGE Publications Ltd.

1 Oliver's Yard

55 City Road

London EC1Y 1SP

United Kingdom

SAGE Publications India Pvt. Ltd.

B 1/I 1 Mohan Cooperative Industrial Area

Mathura Road, New Delhi 110 044

India

SAGE Publications Asia-Pacific Pte. Ltd.

3 Church Street

#10-04 Samsung Hub

Singapore 049483

Acquisitions Editor:   Sarah Calabi

Editorial Assistant: Davia Grant

Production Editor: Kelly DeRosa

Copy Editor: Karin Rathert

Typesetter: C&M Digitals (P) Ltd.

Cover Designer: Candice Harman

Marketing Manager: Amy Whitaker

Printed in the United States of America

Library of Congress Control Number: 2014948475

ISBN 978-1-4833-1704-5

This book is printed on acid-free paper

SFI° Certified Sourcing
www.sfiprogram.org
SFI-00453

SFI label applies to text stock

14 15 16 17 18 10 9 8 7 6 5 4 3 2 1

# Contents

# Annotated Contents

## CHANGING DEMOGRAPHICS

### Voting Controversies

Election laws and voting procedures have been a major source of controversy in the United States ever since the stunted recount in Florida that determined the outcome of the 2000 presidential contest. Republicans and Democrats have clashed fiercely in state after state over GOP-backed proposals to require government-approved photo IDs for voters to cast ballots. Republicans say the laws prevent fraud; Democrats say the laws are aimed at vote suppression. Court rulings on the laws are mixed. The Supreme Court added to the controversies with a decision in June to disable a major provision of the federal Voting Rights Act that required some states and localities with a history of discrimination to obtain permission from the government before instituting any change in voting procedures. A bill to restore the provision has been introduced in Congress, but no hearings have been scheduled yet. Election officials are also looking at recommendations from a presidential commission for online registration, more early voting and costly replacement of technologically obsolescent voting machinery.

### Changing Demographics

The nation is undergoing one of the most important demographic transitions in its history. For the first time, minority babies outnumbered white newborns in 2011, and Census estimates predict that by 2042 non-Hispanic whites will no longer be in the majority. Already, more than a third of Americans are minorities, and non-whites accounted for 92 percent of population growth between 2000 and 2010, a trend driven by rising Hispanic immigration.

Meanwhile, as millions of baby boomers retire, the nation is growing older. More than a fifth of Americans will be 65 or older by 2030, compared with one in eight today. Seismic changes also are occurring on the religious front: Protestants are no longer in the majority, and millions have abandoned religion altogether. And, in a striking trend of reverse migration, millions of blacks are moving back to the South.

## Redistricting Debates

The once-every-decade process of redrawing legislative and congressional districts is getting under way in state capitals around the country. To start, Sun Belt states will gain and Rust Belt states will lose seats in the U.S. House of Representatives. But win or lose, states have to redraw lines to make sure that legislative and congressional districts have equal populations and give fair opportunities to minority groups. The process is intensely political, with parties maneuvering for advantage and incumbents seeking to hold on to friendly territory. Republicans are in a good position after gaining control of legislatures in a majority of states last November. But demographic trends, especially the growth of Latino populations in some states, may limit the GOP's opportunities. In addition, California and Florida will be operating under new rules pushed by good-government groups that seek to limit "gerrymandering," line-drawing for purely partisan reasons. After redistricting plans are completed, many will be challenged in court, where outcomes are difficult to predict.

## Changing U.S. Electorate

Demographics played nearly as large a role in the 2008 presidential race as health care, war and the economy. The Democratic field came down to an African-American man dominating voting among blacks, the young and highly educated voters and a white woman winning older voters, Hispanics and the white working class.

# ETHNICITY AND IMMIGRATION

## Border Security

The United States has poured unprecedented resources into securing its borders, spending billions of dollars on surveillance technology, fencing and personnel. Today more than 21,000 federal agents guard the borders, nearly 10 times the total in 1980. The buildup, particularly strong along the 1,933-mile-long Mexican border, also includes new measures at so-called ports of entry — authorized border-crossing points, seaports and airports. Concerns about illegal immigration initially spurred the buildup, but it accelerated after the 9/11 terrorist attacks. Immigration reform legislation under consideration by Congress includes additional measures, including doubling the Border Patrol and allocating billions more for fencing and surveillance. But critics question the additional spending, saying existing border-security measures have not deterred illegal immigration or made the nation safer from terrorism. Supporters, however, point to a reduction in illegal crossings as proof the buildup is working.

## Immigration Conflict

Americans are very concerned about illegal immigration but ambivalent about what to do about it — especially the 11 million aliens currently in the United States illegally. Frustrated with the federal government's failure to secure the borders, several states passed laws allowing state and local police to check the immigration status of suspected unlawful aliens. Civil rights organizations warn the laws will result in ethnic profiling of Latinos. The Obama administration sued to block several of the laws for infringing on federal prerogatives. Advocates of tougher enforcement say undocumented workers are taking jobs from U.S. citizens, but many business and agricultural groups say migrant workers are needed to fill jobs unattractive to U.S. workers. In 2010, the U.S. Supreme Court upheld an Arizona law providing stiff penalties for employers that knowingly hire illegal aliens. In 2012, the justices heard arguments on the controversial, new Arizona law that inspired other states to crack down on illegal immigration.

## Immigration Debate

The number of illegal immigrants in the country has topped 12 million, making immigration once again a central topic of debate. Moreover, with undocumented workers spreading far beyond traditional "gatekeeper" states such as California and Texas, complaints about illegal immigrants have become a daily staple of talk radio. Enacting tougher enforcement policies has become a dominant theme in the 2008 presidential campaign, particularly on the Republican side. Just in the past year, states and localities have passed hundreds of bills to crack down on employers and illegal immigrants seeking public benefits. But Congress has been unable to act, despite a bipartisan deal brokered last year by the Bush administration. A new administration and the next Congress will likely face what has proved so far an impossible task — curbing the number of immigrants without causing labor shortages in key economic sectors such as agriculture and hospitality.

### American Indians

Winds of change are blowing through Indian Country, improving prospects for many of the nation's 4.4 million Native Americans. The number of tribes managing their own affairs has increased dramatically, and an urban Indian middle class is quietly taking root. The booming revenues of many Indian-owned casinos seem the ultimate proof that Indians are overcoming a history of mistreatment, poverty and exclusion. Yet most of the gambling houses don't rake in stratospheric revenues. And despite statistical upticks in socioeconomic indicators, American Indians are still poorer, more illness-prone and less likely to be employed than their fellow citizens. Meanwhile, tribal governments remain largely dependent on direct federal funding of basic services — funding that Indian leaders and congressional supporters decry as inadequate. But government officials say they are still providing essential services despite budget cuts.

## RACE AND EDUCATION

### Racial Profiling

Civil liberties and minority groups are pressuring police departments to eliminate racial and ethnic profiling in pedestrian and traffic stops, while police groups and some experts insist the complaints about the practice are exaggerated. African-Americans have long complained of traffic stops seemingly for "driving while black," and many — including President Obama and Oprah Winfrey — said recently they have felt profiled by store clerks for "shopping while black." Hispanics and Muslims also feel singled out as suspected immigration violators or terrorists. Two big law enforcement agencies — the New York City Police Department and the Maricopa County Sheriff's Office, which covers Phoenix — are under court

order to eliminate the practice. In New York, Mayor-elect Bill de Blasio is expected to change the NYPD's aggressive stop-and-frisk policies after he takes office on Jan. 1.

### Affirmative Action

Since the 1970s, affirmative action has played a key role in helping minorities get ahead. But many Americans say school and job candidates should be chosen on merit, not race. In November 2008, ballot initiatives in Colorado and Nebraska would have eliminated race as a selection criterion for job or school candidates but would have allowed preferences for those trying to struggle out of poverty, regardless of their race. It's an approach endorsed by foes of racial affirmative action. Big states, meanwhile, including California and Texas, are still struggling to reconcile restrictions on the use of race in college admissions designed to promote diversity. Progress toward that goal has been slowed by a major obstacle: Affirmative action hasn't lessened the stunning racial disparities in academic performance plaguing elementary and high school education. Still, the once open hostility to affirmative action of decades ago has faded. Even some race-preference critics don't want to eliminate it entirely but seek ways to keep diversity without eroding admission and hiring standards. In the fall of 2012, the Supreme Court will revisit the issue of affirmative action and will hear arguments in the Texas case, *Fisher v. University of Texas*.

### Racial Diversity in Public Schools

Fifty years after the Supreme Court outlawed racial segregation in public schools, a 2007 ruling raised doubts about how far local school boards can go to integrate classrooms. The court's 5-4 ruling in cases from Seattle and Louisville bars school districts from using race as a factor in individual pupil assignments. Like many other school districts, the two school systems used racial classifications to promote diversity in the face of segregated housing patterns. But parents argued the plans improperly denied their children their school of choice because of race. Dissenting justices said the ruling was a setback for racial equality. In a pivotal concurrence, however, Justice Anthony M. Kennedy said schools still have some leeway to pursue racial diversity. Meanwhile, some experts argue that socioeconomic integration — bringing low-income and middle-class students together — is a more effective way to pursue educational equity.

### Fixing Urban Schools

African-American and Hispanic students — largely in urban schools — lag far behind white students, who mostly attend middle-class suburban schools. Critics argue that when Congress reauthorizes the 2002 No Child Left Behind Act (NCLB), it must retarget the legislation to help urban schools tackle tough problems, such as encouraging the best teachers to enter and remain in high-poverty schools, rather than focusing on tests and sanctions. Some advocates propose busing students across district lines to create more socioeconomically diverse student bodies. But conservative analysts argue that busing wastes students' time and that permitting charter schools to compete with public schools will drive improvement. Meanwhile, liberal analysts point out that successful charter programs are too costly for most schools to emulate, and that no one has yet figured out how to spread success beyond a handful of schools, public or private.

# Preface

As minority populations continue to grow apace, and concerns about U.S. border security and immigration intensify, issues in race and ethnicity resonate ever more profoundly with Americans. These topics confound even well-informed citizens and often lead to cultural and political conflicts, because they raise the most formidable public policy questions: Are U.S. elections being conducted fairly? Can politicians find a way to curb illegal immigration? Is it time to end racial preferences? To promote change and hopefully reach viable resolution, scholars, students, and policymakers must strive to understand the context and content of each of these issues, as well as how these debates play out in the public sphere.

With the view that only an objective examination that synthesizes all competing viewpoints can lead to sound analysis, this seventh edition of *Issues in Race and Ethnicity* provides comprehensive and unbiased coverage of today's most pressing policy problems. It enables instructors to fairly and comprehensively uncover opposing sides of each issue, and illustrate just how significantly they impact citizens and the government they elect. This book is a compilation of twelve recent reports from *CQ Researcher*, a weekly policy backgrounder that brings into focus key issues on the public agenda. *CQ Researcher* fully explains complex concepts in plain English. Each article chronicles and analyzes past legislative and judicial action as well as current and possible future maneuvering. Each report addresses how issues affect all levels of government, whether at the local, state, or federal level, and also the lives and futures of all citizens. *Issues in Race and Ethnicity* is designed to promote in-depth discussion, facilitate further research, and help readers think critically and formulate their own positions on these crucial issues.

This collection is organized into three sections: Changing Demographics; Ethnicity and Immigration; and Race and Education. Each section spans a range of important public policy concerns. These pieces were chosen to expose students to a wide range of issues, from affirmative action to illegal immigration. We are gratified to know that *Issues in Race and Ethnicity* has found a following in a wide range of departments in political science and sociology.

## CQ RESEARCHER

*CQ Researcher* was founded in 1923 as *Editorial Research Reports* and was sold primarily to newspapers as a research tool. The magazine was renamed and redesigned in 1991 as *CQ Researcher*. Today, students are its primary audience. While still used by hundreds of journalists and newspapers, many of which reprint portions of the reports, *Researcher*'s main subscribers are now high school, college and public libraries. In 2002, *Researcher* won the American Bar Association's coveted Silver Gavel Award for magazine excellence for a series of nine reports on civil liberties and other legal issues.

*Researcher* writers — all highly experienced journalists — sometimes compare the experience of writing a *Researcher* report to drafting a college term paper. Indeed, there are many similarities. Each report is as long as many term papers — about 11,000 words — and is written by one person without any significant outside help. One of the key differences is that the writers interview leading experts, scholars and government officials for each issue.

Like students, the writers begin the creative process by choosing a topic. Working with *Researcher*'s editors, the writer identifies a controversial subject that has important public policy implications. After a topic is selected, the writer embarks on one to two weeks of intense research. Newspaper and magazine articles are clipped or downloaded, books are ordered and information is gathered from a wide variety of sources, including interest groups, universities and the government. Once the writers are well informed, they develop a detailed outline and begin the interview process. Each report requires a minimum of ten to fifteen interviews with academics, officials, lobbyists and people working in the field. Only after all interviews are completed does the writing begin.

## CHAPTER FORMAT

Each issue of *CQ Researcher*, and therefore each selection in this book, is structured in the same way. A selection begins with an introductory overview, which is briefly explored in greater detail in the rest of the report.

The second section chronicles the most important and current debates in the field. It is structured around a number of key issues questions, such as "Has the border security buildup made the United States more secure?" and "Should employers be penalized for hiring illegal immigrants?" This section is the core of each selection. The questions raised are often highly controversial and usually the object of much argument among scholars and practitioners. Hence, the answers provided are never conclusive, but rather detail the range of opinion within the field.

Following those issue questions is the "Background" section, which provides a history of the issue being examined. This retrospective includes important legislative and executive actions and court decisions to inform readers on how current policy evolved.

Next, the "Current Situation" section examines important contemporary policy issues, legislation under consideration and action being taken. Each selection ends with an "Outlook" section that gives a sense of what new regulations, court rulings and possible policy initiatives might be put into place in the next five to ten years.

Each report contains features that augment the main text: sidebars that examine issues related to the topic, a pro/con debate by two outside experts, a chronology of key dates and events and an annotated bibliography that details the major sources used by the writer.

## CUSTOM OPTIONS

Interested in building your ideal CQ Press Issues book, customized to your personal teaching needs and interests? Browse by course or date, or search for specific topics or issues from our online catalog of over 500 *CQ Researcher* issues at http://custom.cqpress.com.

## ACKNOWLEDGMENTS

We wish to thank many people for helping to make this collection a reality. Thomas J. Billitteri, managing editor of *CQ Researcher,* gave us his enthusiastic support and cooperation as we developed this edition. He and his talented staff of editors have amassed a first-class collection of *Researcher* articles, and we are fortunate to have access to this rich cache. We also thankfully acknowledge the advice and feedback from current readers and are gratified by their satisfaction with the book.

Some readers may be learning about *CQ Researcher* for the first time. We expect that many readers will want regular access to this excellent weekly research tool. For subscription information or a no-obligation free trial of *Researcher,* please contact CQ Press at www.cqpress.com or toll-free at 1-866-4CQ-PRESS (1-866-427-7737).

We hope that you will be pleased by the seventh edition of *Issues in Race and Ethnicity.* We welcome your feedback and suggestions for future editions. Please direct comments to Sarah Calabi, Acquisitions Editor for Political Science, CQ Press, 2300 N St, NW, Suite 800, Washington, DC 20037; or send e-mail to *scalabi@ cqpress.com.*

—The Editors of CQ Press

# Contributors

**Charles S. Clark** is a veteran Washington freelancer who writes for *The Washington Post, National Journal,* and other publications. He previously served as a staff writer at the *CQ Researcher* and writer-researcher at Time-Life Books. He graduated in political science from McGill University.

Staff writer **Marcia Clemmitt** is a veteran social-policy reporter who previously served as editor in chief of *Medicine & Health* and staff writer for *The Scientist.* She has also been a high school math and physics teacher. She holds a liberal arts and sciences degree from St. John's College, Annapolis, and a master's degree in English from Georgetown University. Her recent reports include "Genes and Health" and "Animal Intelligence."

**Alan Greenblatt** covers foreign affairs for National Public Radio. He was previously a staff writer at *Governing* magazine and *CQ Weekly,* where he won the National Press Club's Sandy Hume Award for political journalism. He graduated from San Francisco State University in 1986 and received a master's degree in English literature from the University of Virginia in 1988. For the *CQ Researcher,* his reports include "Confronting Warming," "Future of the GOP" and "Immigration Debate." His most recent *CQ Global Researcher* reports were "Attacking Piracy" and "Rewriting History."

**Kenneth Jost** has written more than 160 reports for *CQ Researcher* since 1991 on topics ranging from legal affairs and social policy to national security and international relations. He is the author of *The Supreme Court Yearbook* and *Supreme Court From A to Z* (both CQ Press). He is an honors graduate of Harvard College and Georgetown Law School, where he teaches media law as an adjunct professor. He also writes the blog Jost on Justice (http://jostonjustice.blogspot.com). His previous reports include "Racial Profiling" (2013) and "Supreme Court Controversies" (2012).

**Peter Katel** is a *CQ Researcher* staff writer who previously reported on Haiti and Latin America for *Time* and *Newsweek* and covered the Southwest for newspapers in New Mexico. He has received several journalism awards, including the Bartolomé Mitre Award for coverage of drug trafficking, from the Inter-American Press Association. He holds an A.B. in university studies from the University of New Mexico. His recent reports include "Prisoner Reentry" and "Downsizing Prisons."

**Reed Karaim**, a freelance writer in Tucson, Ariz., has written for *The Washington Post, U.S. News &World*

*Report, Smithsonian, American Scholar, USA Weekend* and other publications. He is the author of the novel, *If Men Were Angels*, which was selected for the Barnes & Noble Discover Great New Writers series. He is also the winner of the Robin Goldstein Award for Outstanding Regional Reporting and other journalism honors. Karaim is a graduate of North Dakota State University in Fargo.

**Patrick Marshall** is a freelance writer in Seattle, Wash., who writes about public policy and technology issues. He is a computer columnist for *The Seattle Times* and holds a BA in anthropology from the University of California at Santa Cruz and a master's in international studies from the Fletcher School of Law & Diplomacy at Tufts University.

**Bill Wanlund** is a freelance writer in the Washington, D.C., area. He is a former foreign service officer, with service in Europe, Asia, Africa, and South America. He holds a journalism degree from The George Washington University and has written for *CQ Researcher* on drone warfare and downtown development.

# 1

# Voting Controversies

Kenneth Jost

Voters in Miami wait to cast ballots in the presidential election on Nov. 6, 2012. A bipartisan commission that President Obama created, partly in response to overlong delays at some polling places, recommended on Jan. 22, 2014, that states upgrade voting machines to keep pace with technological change. The commission also wants more states to adopt online voter registration and allow voting before Election Day — either in person or by absentee ballots.

From *CQ Researcher*, February 21, 2014.

With the 2012 presidential campaign underway, Republican legislators in the battleground state of Pennsylvania pushed through a new law requiring voters to show a photo ID before casting their ballots. GOP lawmakers minimized the likely impact of the law, approved on a party-line vote, saying that only 90,000 Pennsylvanians lacked the kind of government-issued photo identification required by the law.

In a damning decision two years later, however, a state court judge found that the law — on hold pending a legal challenge — could disenfranchise up to 5 percent of the state's electorate, or as many as 400,000 otherwise qualified voters. In a 103-page ruling issued on Jan. 17, Judge Bernard McGinley faulted state agencies for doing little to tell voters about the new requirement or the procedures for obtaining a qualifying identification.

McGinley also said the state had failed to show the need for the photo-ID procedure, which GOP legislators said would help prevent voter fraud at polling places. The state "wholly failed to show any evidence of in-person voter fraud," McGinley wrote.[1]

The Pennsylvania law is one of more than 20 state measures establishing or tightening voter-ID requirements passed since 2005. The issue has split the two major political parties. In sponsoring these measures, Republicans say they are needed to prevent fraud and protect the integrity of elections. Democrats say the laws are not needed and are being pushed in order to reduce voting among groups that skew Democratic in elections, especially Latinos and African Americans.[2]

## Nearly Three Dozen States Have Voter-ID Laws

Thirty-five states have passed voter-ID laws, although some laws are not currently in effect, either because they are too new or because they are being challenged in court. State laws vary widely as to the kinds of identification accepted, with 13 states — since 2005 — requiring photo IDs and others accepting such items as a Social Security card, a birth certificate or a utility bill. State laws also vary as to voters who show up without identification. In some states, for instance, a voter can cast a ballot, but it won't be counted until the voter returns with a qualifying ID.

### States That Have Enacted Voter-ID Laws

Source: "Voter Identification Requirements," National Conference of State Legislatures, Feb. 12, 2014, www.ncsl.org/research/elections-and-campaigns/voter-id.aspx #al

The two parties are also divided for the most part on a new issue created by the Supreme Court's June 2013 decision to nullify a key provision of the federal Voting Rights Act used to police racially discriminatory election practices in some parts of the country. The decision in *Shelby County v. Holder* effectively nullified a requirement that eight states and localities in four others had to obtain "preclearance" from the Justice Department or a federal court in Washington before instituting any change in election law, procedure or practice.

A bipartisan bill cosponsored by Senate Judiciary Committee Chairman Patrick J. Leahy, D-Vt., and former House Judiciary Committee Chairman James Sensenbrenner, R-Wis., would reimpose the preclearance requirement on states or localities with a recent history of racial discrimination in voting procedures. The bill is aimed at meeting the court's objection that the use of a "coverage formula" dating from the 1960s to determine the jurisdictions subject to preclearance was unconstitutional. Voter-ID laws, however, would be exempt from the new preclearance provision.[3]

Traditional civil rights and civil liberties groups are strongly supporting the proposed rewrite, as are many Democrats on Capitol Hill. Despite Sensenbrenner's role, some of his leading Republican colleagues oppose the bill, as do some conservative election law experts and advocates.

Elections in the United States have been under intense scrutiny ever since the presidency was awarded to George W. Bush in 2000 on the basis of a highly disputed vote count in the pivotal state of Florida. Two years later, Congress passed and Bush signed into law the Help America Vote Act, aimed at helping states upgrade voting machines and improve vote-counting procedures.[4]

A decade later a bipartisan commission that President Obama created in part as a response to reports of overlong delays at some polling places in the 2012 presidential election says states need to upgrade voting machines again to keep pace with technological change. The Presidential Commission on Election Administration, which released its recommendations on Jan. 22, also wants more states to adopt online voter registration and allow voters to cast ballots before Election Day — either in person or by absentee ballots.

As a new benchmark, the commission recommends that no voter should have to wait in line more than 30 minutes to cast a ballot. The 15-member group was cochaired by experienced election lawyers from both major parties: Democrat Robert Bauer and Republican Benjamin Ginsberg, who served as chief lawyers for the Obama and Romney presidential campaigns, respectively, in 2012.[5]

By deliberately sidestepping the politically contentious issues of voter-ID laws and the Voting Rights Act rewrite, the commission is winning applause for striking a bipartisan chord. "The commission's report is an indication that in a huge core [of election issues] there isn't a split," says David Becker, director of the elections initiative at the Pew Charitable Trusts.

"There's only a split on these highly volatile issues," says Becker, formerly an attorney with the Justice Department's voting rights section. There is "wide agreement," he adds, on "a large core of reform that could have a huge impact on our democracy."

The partisan divide continues, however, in Pennsylvania and other states over voter-ID laws. Pennsylvania's Republican governor, Tom Corbett, who signed the measure into law on March 14, 2012, says the state will appeal McGinley's ruling even as Democrats are urging him not to.

McGinley's ruling cheered opponents of the new crop of voter-ID laws after challenges in several other states had fallen short. The decision may have limited impact, however, because McGinley based it on provisions of Pennsylvania law and the state's constitution guaranteeing equal voting rights.

The judge rejected claims by the plaintiffs, individual voters, the League of Women Voters and the Pennsylvania conference of the NAACP, that the law violated equal-protection clauses in the Pennsylvania and U.S. constitutions. McGinley also found no impermissible partisan motivation in enactment of the law despite the remark by the Republican leader in the Pennsylvania House of Representatives three months after the measure was adopted that it would help Republican Mitt Romney carry the state in November 2012. With the law blocked from taking effect, Obama carried the state with about 52 percent of the vote.

Voting issues are in play in courts and legislatures in several states as well as on Capitol Hill in Washington. Voter ID laws are being challenged in at least four other

## Most States Have Expanded Voting Laws

Twenty-seven states and the District of Columbia allow voters to cast ballots before Election Day and to get an absentee ballot without giving a reason, called "no-excuse" balloting. Six states, mostly in the South, allow only early voting, and Minnesota has adopted only no-excuse absentee voting.

### States with Early Voting and No-Excuse Absentee Voting

*Source:* "Absentee and Early Voting," National Conference of State Legislatures, www.ncsl.org/research/elections-and-campaigns/absentee-and-early-voting.aspx#no_excuse

states — Kansas, North Carolina, Texas and Wisconsin — while legislatures in some states are gearing up to consider tightening voter identification procedures.

"It's definitely an ongoing battle," says Tova Wang, a senior fellow and election reform expert at the liberal advocacy group Demos headquartered in New York City.

Myrna Pérez, deputy director of election programs at the Brennan Center for Justice, a liberal think tank at New York University School of Law, thinks the wave of new voter ID laws may have crested. "Our hope is that given how much outrage there has been over attempts at voter suppression, some folks will think twice before engaging in such efforts," she says.

Conservative election law experts bristle at the accusation that new ID laws are aimed at voter suppression. "That's ridiculous," says Hans von Spakovsky, a senior fellow at the conservative Heritage Foundation in Washington and a former member of the Federal Election Commission (FEC). "We've had election after election" in states with voter ID laws, von Spakovsky says, "and turnout did not go down after those laws went into effect."

Pérez, one of Obama's two pending nominees to the U.S. Election Assistance Commission (EAC), the agency created in 2002 to help states upgrade voting machines, also says some state legislatures are likely to move toward easing voting requirements. A new Brennan Center report finds more bills to expand voting rights introduced in state legislatures for 2014 than measures to narrow access to voting.[6]

Von Spakovsky, who has criticized Pérez as "a radical, left-wing activist with absolutely no experience in election administration," says civil rights litigation hampers election officials' efforts to improve voting procedures. "They are constantly being sued in what I consider to be unwarranted lawsuits, particularly by civil rights organizations," he says.[7]

Meanwhile, the partisan divide in Washington over election issues is so deep that it threatens the very existence of the EAC. The four-member commission has been short of a quorum — which requires three members — since 2010 and has had no members at all since 2011. Pérez and a second Obama nominee, Thomas Hicks, appear headed toward likely Senate confirmation after protracted delays, but Republicans are refusing to offer

Experienced election lawyers from both major parties, Republican Benjamin Ginsberg, right, and Democrat Robert Bauer, are co-chairs of the Presidential Commission on Election and Administration. As a new benchmark, the commission recommends that no voter should have to wait in line more than 30 minutes to cast a ballot.

candidates for seats reserved for GOP members because they believe the agency should be abolished.

As voting and election issues percolate in Washington and around the country, here are some of the questions being debated:

### Should Congress revive the Voting Rights Act's preclearance requirement for some states and localities?

With the Voting Rights Act's preclearance requirement in effect, Texas was denied permission in 2012 to put into effect its strict photo-ID voting law enacted the year before. Both the Justice Department and a three-judge federal court said the state had failed to prove that the law would not have a "retrogressive" effect on voting by Latinos and African-Americans.

When the Supreme Court effectively nullified the preclearance requirement in June 2013, however, Texas officials immediately announced they would put the law into effect. The Justice Department responded just two months later with a suit, still pending, seeking to block the law under the Voting Rights Act's general prohibition — found in Section 2 — against racial discrimination.

Civil rights advocates seeking to reinstate the preclearance requirement say the Supreme Court's decision has weakened efforts to prevent racial discrimination in voting. The ruling eliminated "a very effective mechanism of preventing states from enacting restrictions that take away voting rights from minorities," says Wang, the election law expert at Demos.

The Brennan Center's Pérez agrees. "Section 2 is an important and helpful tool, but it does not have the scope or the functions of Section 5," she says, referring to the preclearance provision.

Conservative groups that applauded the Supreme Court's decision see no need to revive a preclearance process. "There is no need for preclearance because there are powerful remedies in the rest of the Voting Rights Act that provide remedies for discrimination," says the Heritage Foundation's von Spakovsky.

Roger Clegg, president and general counsel of the Center for Equal Opportunity, which opposes racial preferences, agrees. "The only difference between Section 2 and Section 5 is that under Section 5 the defendant has to prove his innocence before he's allowed to make a voting change," Clegg says. "Now, if someone doesn't like a voting change, they have to come into court and prove a civil rights violation, which is the way every other civil rights statute works."

The Supreme Court decision did not outlaw preclearance; it only invalidated the coverage formula set out in the act's Section 4, which was based on minority voting turnout during the 1960s. To meet the court's objections, sponsors of the proposed rewrite crafted a new formula based on recent Voting Rights Act violations.

Under the proposed formula, a state would be subject to preclearance if it had five voting rights violations within the most recent 15-year period, at least one of which was committed by the state itself. A local jurisdiction would be covered if it had three voting rights violations within the most recent 15-year period or one such violation along with "persistent and extremely low minority voter turnout." Initially, only four states would be covered under that formula: Georgia, Louisiana, Mississippi and Texas.

The bill also would continue to allow a court to impose a preclearance requirement on a jurisdiction under the so-called bail-in procedure, but under a relaxed burden of proof. The existing bail-in procedure requires proof of intentional racial discrimination; the bill would allow preclearance to be imposed based on so-called disparate impact on minorities without proof of intentional discrimination.

Supporters of the bill say some form of preclearance is still needed. "We know that there are still efforts to restrict voting rights in our country," says Pérez.

Conservative groups disagree. "There's no case to be made that we need Section 5 at all," says Clegg.

The bill also includes a new provision requiring jurisdictions to disclose, among other items, any changes in voting procedures within 180 days of a federal election. And it retains the attorney general's existing authority to assign federal observers to elections. But in a concession to political reality sponsors decided to protect photo-ID laws from any need to obtain preclearance.

Civil rights groups supporting the bill regret the exemption for photo-ID laws. "Many of them are clearly discriminatory and do violate the Voting Rights Act and the Constitution for that matter," says Wang. From the opposite side, Clegg worries that even with a supposed exemption, the Justice Department could go after photo-ID laws by including them along with other

election law changes in a Section 2 suit or a bail-in procedure.

Richard Hasen, an election law expert at the University of California-Irvine Law School and publisher of the influential *Election Law Blog*, disagrees with the Supreme Court's decision and calls the proposed rewrite "sensible." He also regrets that Congress did not revise the coverage formula after the Supreme Court raised constitutional doubts about the law in an earlier ruling in 2009.

The formula in the new bill might be upheld, Hasen says, but some other parts might not be — specifically, extending the bail-in procedure to unintentional discrimination. And, in any event, Hasen doubts that Congress will approve the bill in the current session.

### Should courts strike down voter photo-ID laws?

With Republicans controlling the legislature and governor's office for the first time in years, Indiana became the second state in 2005 (after Georgia) to enact a law requiring virtually all citizens to present a government-approved photo ID to vote. A legal challenge to the law, brought by Democrats and civil liberties advocates, reached the U.S. Supreme Court three years later.

The court's 6-3 decision in April 2008 upheld the law after finding the state's interest in detecting voter fraud to outweigh any burdens on voters. The ruling left the door open, however, to further challenges to the Indiana law.[8]

In the six years since the Supreme Court's decision, the number of states with similarly strict photo-ID voting requirements has grown to 11, according to the National Conference of State Legislatures. Legal challenges have proliferated, but the issues remain much the same. Supporters and opponents disagree sharply on the need for the laws in the first place and the resulting burdens on would-be voters as well as lawmakers' motives in adopting the measures.

Supporters of the laws depict the measures as self-evidently useful in preventing voter fraud at the polling place. To prove the point, the conservative guerrilla filmmaker James O'Keefe had an assistant use a hidden camera to record him posing as Attorney General Eric Holder at Holder's voting place in Washington, D.C., in April 2012. O'Keeefe offered to go get identification, but the election official said there was no need.

## Online Registration Gains in Popularity

Nineteen states have legislation allowing online voter registration, and six states offer limited online voter registration. For example, registered voters in New Mexico and Ohio can update an existing registration record online, but new applications still must be made on paper.

### States That Allow Online or Limited Online Registration
### (as of February 2014)

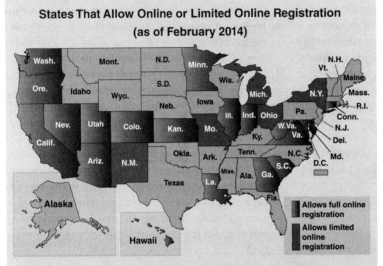

*Source:* "Online Voter Registration," National Conference of State Legislatures, www.ncsl.org/research/elections-and-campaigns/electronic-or-online-voter-registration.aspx

Curtis Gans, a longtime U.S. elections expert, faults advocates on both sides. "Those who say there's no fraud are just wrong," says Gans. "Those who say there's huge fraud in elections are also wrong."

Opponents also say the voter-ID laws impose significant burdens on citizens who lack the most common form of government-issued photo identification — a driver's license — and have to obtain an ID specifically for voting. "There's going to be some segment of the population for whom it will be difficult to get the kind of identification they need," says Wang, the election law expert at Demos.

In its decision refusing to preclear the Texas voter-ID law, the three-judge federal court in Washington noted that Texans in some rural counties would have to travel 100 miles or more to obtain a voter ID. Moreover, the court said, the burden "will fall most heavily on the poor."[11]

Supporters of the law counter with evidence that they say show voter-ID laws have not hurt turnout in states where they have been enacted and that few would-be voters have actually been turned away at the polls. "All the claims that they will suppress votes are just not true," says von Spakovsky. He calls the opponents' arguments "hysterical."

A statistical expert who testified for Texas in the voter-ID case agrees that voter-ID laws are unlikely to significantly affect turnout. "As a practical matter you're very unlikely to see voter-ID have substantive or demonstrable impact on aggregate turnout rates," says Daron Shaw, an associate professor of government at the University of Texas-Austin.

Matt Baretto, an associate professor of political science at the University of Washington in Seattle who has testified for plaintiffs in challenging voter-ID laws, says turnout depends on a host of factors other than identification requirements. But he says the laws definitely have an impact. "There are empirically millions of eligible voters who don't have photo IDs," he says.

O'Keefe stopped before asking for a ballot, but John Fund, a *National Review* columnist and co-author with the Heritage Foundation's von Spakovsky of a book on election fraud, wrote that the episode shows that it is "comically easy to commit voter fraud in person."[9] Von Spakovsky says voter-ID laws also can prevent other kinds of fraud, including voting by noncitizens, voting under false registration or casting ballots in more than one state.

Opponents of the law repeatedly emphasize the lack of evidence of any measurable amount of voter impersonation fraud. In the Pennsylvania case, lawyers from the office of Democratic Attorney General Kathleen Kane defended the law, but stipulated that there were "no specific incidents of voter ID fraud" leading up to its passage.

"The only fraud uncovered in this case is the ID law itself," Witold Walczak, legal director of the ACLU of Pennsylvania and one of the lawyers for the plaintiffs, said after the decision.[10]

Baretto says supporters of voter-ID laws are making "a circular argument" when they point to the low number of would-be voters turned away. "The effect happens before you show up at the polling place," he says. "If you don't have the ID, you don't go to the polling place."

Hasen, the election law expert at UC-Irvine, discounts the claimed rationales for voter-ID laws. "These laws are motivated by an interest in moderately depressing the vote and as a means of firing up the base by accusations of fraud," Hasen says. But Hasen, who favors a national voter-identification program, stops short of calling for the current laws to be struck down. "I can't make a blanket normative statement about what courts ought to do," he says.

## Should states make registration and voting easier?

Arizona was already a leader among states in using technology to improve government services in 2002 when it became the first state to allow online voter registration. A decade later, about 70 percent of voter registration in the state was done online instead of with paper forms, at a considerably lower cost and with fewer errors.

Experts are enthusiastic about the new procedure, which has now spread to around 20 states and could gain further ground now that the presidential commission has endorsed it. "Online registration is a no-brainer," says election law expert Hasen. The National Conference of State Legislatures calls online registration "the bipartisan trend in elections."[12]

Even so, some conservatives are raising red flags. The Heritage Foundation's von Spakovsky has no objections to online registration to change a voter's address or other information but opposes the practice for a voter's initial registration. "That is a recipe for voter fraud," von Spakovsky says. "You can't check identity online. You can't verify they are who they really are."

Von Spakovsky is also unenthusiastic about early voting and flatly opposes expanding so-called "no-excuse absentee voting" — two of the other steps recommended by the presidential commission. "I don't have a problem with more early voting if states want to devote the resources needed to do that, von Spakovsky says. "But you're making campaigns more expensive because campaigns have to mount get-out-the-vote efforts over a longer time."

A demonstrator in Columbia, S.C., on Feb. 26, 2013, urges the U.S. Supreme Court not to nullify Section 5 of the Voting Rights Act, which requires South Carolina and other states with histories of discriminatory voting practices to get federal preclearance before approving new voting laws. In June 2013, however, the high court effectively nullified the requirement. A bipartisan bill would reimpose preclearance. Civil rights and civil liberties groups strongly support the proposed rewrite; some leading Republicans oppose it, as do some conservative election law experts and advocates.

As for absentee balloting, von Spakovsky again sees the likelihood of increased fraud. "Fraud most often occurs with absentee ballot voting," he says. "They're the easiest ones to steal." In the book he co-authored, von Spakovsky labels absentee ballots the "tool of choice" of vote thieves.[13]

Some of von Spakovsky's concerns are seconded by Gans, the longtime U.S. voting expert. Eased rules for absentee voting are "an enhancement to fraud," Gans says. "You can buy votes and have proof that you bought something. It lends itself to the pressured vote. You can resist the pressure of peers in the voting booth. It's harder to do that in the living room."

Gans sees no risk of increased fraud in early, in-person voting, but he also questions the supposed benefit of increased turnout. "There's no evidence it enhances turnout," Gans says. The experience in states with early voting so far has been mixed, he says. As for eased absentee voting, Gans says the evidence indicates that the practice actually hurts turnout.

Becker, the Pew Trusts election expert, firmly rejects von Spakovsky's fears of fraud from online registration. "There isn't a shred of evidence to support that argument," Becker says.

"Online registration offers something paper registration does not," Becker continues. The process requires personal data from the voter that can be computer-checked against motor vehicle records or other government information. "That's something you can't do with a paper form," Becker says.

Pew has not studied early voting in detail, but Becker sees some benefits. "The research seems to support the view that early voting can reduce some of the burdens on Election Day," he says. And he says there is no evidence of increased risk of in-person voter fraud given the use of the same check-in procedure as on Election Day itself.

In presenting the commission's report, co-chairs Bauer and Ginsberg said elections ought to be viewed as a problem of professional administration and voters in effect as the government's customers. "There are a number of things that go to helping the voter experience and the way that they vote, an issue that both Republicans and Democrats agree on," Ginsberg said on the "PBS NewsHour," with Bauer seated beside him.[14]

Liberal advocacy groups generally applauded the commission's recommendations. Michael Waldman, president of the Brennan Center, said in a prepared statement that the commission's report "marks a significant advance in the way we think about voting."

Some liberal groups, however, also had reservations. Wang, the reform expert with Demos, is enthusiastic about online registration, but adds, "It's not going to do very much for the segments of the population who are left out." Katherine Culliton-Gonzalez, director of voter

protection at the New York-based Advancement Project, which is litigating voter-ID law challenges in Pennsylvania and Wisconsin, calls the commission's report "excellent" but complains it does not address issues of racial discrimination in voting. She favors a national "best practices" law that would prohibit any voting or election procedures shown to have a discriminatory impact on racial or ethnic minorities.

The commission also underscored what it calls the "impending crisis in voting technology." Voting machines bought 10 years ago are about to reach the end of their useful lives, the report says.

Despite praise for the commission's report, whether its recommendations are adopted depends on the actions of hundreds of state and local election officials. Costs also will be an issue for some of the recommendations, but Becker is optimistic that election administrators will make sure money is not a problem for some changes.

"I'm already hearing discussions [from officials] trying to find ways to have the best of both worlds," Becker says. "You can save money and improve performance. It doesn't have to cost money."

# BACKGROUND

## "Forces of Democracy"

Voting rights were very limited when the United States was founded and were determined by individual state governments, which for the most part allowed suffrage only to propertied white men. As states began to loosen wealth and property requirements in the 19th century, the French commentator Alexis de Tocqueville predicted that "forces of democracy" would result inexorably in an expanding suffrage. The further gains in voting rights — for freed slaves, immigrants, women, and young people — were won, however, only after long and hard-fought battles in the courts, Congress, state legislatures and streets.[15]

States began to dismantle colonial era property qualifications for voting soon after the Revolution. As the nation's population grew, states eased or eliminated the laws rapidly in the 19th century, often in response to demands by the new immigrants. Despite the liberalized voting rules, however, 12 states continued to bar "paupers" from voting until the late 1800s.

# CHRONOLOGY

**1960s-1970s** *Voting Rights Act changes election rules in South, elsewhere.*

**1965-1966** Voting Rights Act passed by Congress, signed by President Lyndon B. Johnson (Aug. 6, 1965); upheld by Supreme Court (March 7, 1966); preclearance provision (section 5) requires four Deep South states to get permission to make any voting, election law changes.

**1970** Congress reauthorizes Voting Rights Act, with preclearance provision.

**1971** Twenty-Sixth Amendment guarantees 18-year-olds right to vote.

**1975** Congress reauthorizes Voting Rights Act; adds provision to protect "language minorities;" extends preclearance provision.

**1980s-1990s** *Voting Rights Act reauthorized; "motor voter" bill adopted.*

**1980** Supreme Court limits nationwide Voting Rights Act provision (section 2) to intentional discrimination (April 22).

**1982** Voting Rights Act reauthorized for 25 years, amended to prohibit "disparate impact" discrimination (no proof of intent required).

**1992** President George H.W. Bush vetoes National Voter Registration Act — the so-called motor voter law — to require states to allow voter registration at driver's license offices, welfare agencies (July 2).

**1993** With Democrat Bill Clinton in White House, Congress again passes National Voter Registration Act; signed by Clinton (May 20); mandatory provision takes effect 1995.

**2000s-Present** *Voting procedures become partisan battleground.*

**2000** Supreme Court ends disputed recount of presidential ballots in Florida; ruling in *Bush v. Gore* ensures Electoral College victory for George W. Bush (Dec. 12).

**2002** Arizona is first state to allow voter registration online. . . . Help America Vote Act provides federal money, authorizes federal standards for upgrading election technology (signed Oct. 29).

**2005** Georgia, Indiana pass new voter-ID laws requiring government-approved photo identification to cast ballots.

**2006** Congress reauthorizes Voting Rights Act in near-unanimous votes; preclearance provision extended 25 years (signed July 27). . . . Missouri Supreme Court throws out state voter-ID law (Oct. 16).

**2008** Supreme Court upholds Indiana voter photo ID law (April 28). . . . Senate race in Minnesota between Republican incumbent Norm Coleman and Democratic challenger Al Franken goes to recount; after legal challenge, Franken declared winner in July 2009.

**2009** Supreme Court skirts challenge to Voting Rights Act; warns Congress to consider revising preclearance coverage formula (June 22); Congress fails to act.

**2011** Eight states adopt or strengthen voter ID laws; five others vetoed by Democratic governors. . . . U.S. Election Assistance Commission is left with no commissioners after remaining two members' terms expire.

**2012** Federal court delays South Carolina voter ID law until after 2012 elections (Oct. 10). . . . Minnesota voters reject voter ID law (Nov. 6).

**2013** Supreme Court throws out Voting Rights Act's coverage formula for preclearance (June 25); Senate, House Judiciary Committees hold hearing on restoring provision (July 17, 18). . . . Texas restores voter ID law; Justice Department sues to block (Aug. 22). . . . Justice Department sues to block North Carolina voter ID law, due to take effect in 2016 (Sept. 30). . . . Tennessee Supreme Court upholds voter ID law (Oct. 17).

**2014** Voting Rights Act rewrite introduced; bill would impose preclearance on four states (Jan. 16). . . . State court judge throws out Pennsylvania voter ID law (Jan. 17). . . . Presidential Commission on Election Administration calls for online registration, expanded early voting, election technology upgrades (Jan. 22). . . . Wisconsin Supreme Court to hear arguments on voter-ID law (Feb. 25); ruling in federal court case awaited.

# Outmoded Voting Machines Pose "Impending Crisis"

*Presidential commission says current technology no longer meets election needs.*

Barely 10 years ago, state and local election administrators used billions of federal dollars to upgrade the machines used to tabulate election results. But in today's world of high-tech products, a decade is a lifetime — or maybe two. So the state-of-the-art voting machinery bought before the smartphone and computer tablet era is now sadly out of date.

The situation amounts to an "impending crisis in voting technology," according to the Presidential Commission on Election Administration. Machines purchased 10 years ago "are now reaching the end of their natural life cycle," the commission said in its report issued Jan. 22, "and no comparable federal funds are in the pipeline to replace them." Besides fiscal constraints, election administrators face other obstacles in upgrading vote-counting technology, including out-of-date standards and a relatively small number of manufacturers.[1]

"Everything doesn't last as long as it used to," says Doug Lewis, executive director of the National Association of Election Officers. "Yet we've been locked into this thinking that election equipment should last eight to 10 to 12 years."

As Lewis recalls, the clunky lever machines that date from the late 19th century and remained in use through the 1950s and '60s are now museum pieces — although a few were pulled out of storage in the New York City mayoral primary in September. All but gone as well are the punch-card voting systems of the sort that malfunctioned so critically in Florida's presidential election in 2000.

The Help America Vote Act, enacted in 2002 in response to the *Bush v. Gore* fiasco, provided federal funds for state and local election agencies to replace the lever and punch-card devices with optical-scan or touch-screen machines. The act also created the Election Assistance Commission (EAC) and authorized it to establish voluntary certification standards for states to use in purchasing voting machines.

In its report, the presidential commission quoted state and local election officials as saying that available machines no longer meet their current needs and that voting machine manufacturers sympathize with the officials' problems. But manufacturers and election agencies alike are hampered by

African-American slaves were not allowed to vote, and so-called freedmen were allowed to vote in only five Northern states: Massachusetts, New Hampshire, New York, Rhode Island and Vermont. New York's property qualification, however, limited the impact of its provision. The 13th Amendment, ratified in 1865, freed the slaves but did not require states to grant them the right to vote. Nor did the 15th Amendment, narrowly ratified in 1870, which only prohibited states from using "race, color, or previous condition of servitude" to restrict whatever voting rights they granted in general.

Supreme Court decisions in the 1870s blunted enforcement of the 15th Amendment; a decade later, partisan divisions doomed a Republican-backed bill in Congress to authorize federal monitoring of state elections. Left alone, Southern and border states responded with an array

of measures and stratagems to keep African-Americans from voting, including literacy tests and poll taxes. So-called grandfather clauses allowed whites to bypass such requirements if they could show that their grandfathers had voted. In the same era, Northern and Western states threw up barriers to voting to immigrants.

Women's suffrage, deliberately omitted from both the 14th and 15th Amendments, made little headway until Western territories and states began allowing women to vote in the 1890s and early 1900s. By the 1910s, both parties supported women's suffrage, but Congress approved the eventual 19th Amendment only after an initial defeat and a special session convened by President Woodrow Wilson in 1919. Ratification was completed on Aug. 18, 1920, on the strength of a single-vote margin in the Tennessee House of Representatives.

EAC standards that have not been updated since 2005, in part because of the partisan impasse over the commission's role that has left the four-member commission without a quorum since 2010. Republicans in Congress want to abolish the EAC and are refusing to designate candidates for the two seats reserved for GOP nominees.

Election technology reformers envision a new world of tablet-like voting machines that 21st century voters will see as thoroughly familiar. "The device on which you record your choice would look like something you use every day," explains David Becker, director of the Pew Charitable Trusts' elections initiative.

The machines could use off-the-shelf software that could be updated without replacing the machines themselves. In addition, the machines could be used for multiple purposes instead of being stored in warehouses in two-year cycles.

For now, however, the EAC standards — voluntary but adopted by many states — are designed for the self-contained voting systems brought into service a decade ago. And the presidential commission said concerns about security among the computer science community have slowed manufacturers' interest in innovation.

Inevitably, cost is also a factor. "These things are not free," says Becker. Lewis says a new voting system can cost from $2 million for a small locality to $240 million for a major metropolitan jurisdiction.

Lewis laments that the United States tends to stay "behind the curve" on voting technology. "In the rest of

A woman votes on Nov. 6, 2012, in Manassas, VA. Voting machines were upgraded nationwide a decade ago, but the Presidential Commission on Election Administration says that they are now out of date and that there are no federal funds designated to replace them.

America, we go for the latest and greatest technology," he says. "In terms of voting we're stuck in the past."

— *Kenneth Jost*

[1]"The American Voting Experience: Report and Recommendations of the Presidential Commission on Election Administration," Jan. 22, 2014, pp. 11-13, 62-67, www.supportthevoter.gov/files/2014/01/Amer-Voting-Exper-final-draft-01-09-14-508.pdf. For coverage, see Martha T. Moore, "Digital voting machines are aging out of use," *USA Today*, Feb. 3, 2014, p. A4.

Women faced no special barriers to voting after ratification of the 19th Amendment, but blacks continued to be denied voting rights in practice in many Southern and border states. The Supreme Court in 1944 gave blacks an important victory by prohibiting all-white Democratic primaries or conventions in the one-party South. Literacy tests and poll taxes remained in place, however, even as the civil rights movement made progress on other fronts, including racial desegregation in schools and public accommodations.

Physical intimidation and violence also were used in the South to keep blacks from voting, notably on "Bloody Sunday" (March 7, 1965) when police in Selma, Ala., used nightsticks and tear gas to disperse a voting rights march as it set out toward the state capital in Montgomery. National outrage over the incident provided the catalyst for President Lyndon B. Johnson to propose and Congress to pass the strongest federal voting rights law in history. The Voting Rights Act of 1965 prohibited discrimination in voting nationwide and imposed the preclearance requirement on four Deep South states with histories of racial discrimination in voting: Alabama, Georgia, Louisiana and Mississippi. Upheld by the Supreme Court less than a year later, the act helped increase black registration by 1970 to more than 50 percent in all Deep South states.[16]

Congress reauthorized the Voting Rights Act in 1970 and included a provision extending the right to vote to 18-year-olds in all federal, state and local elections — a response to Vietnam War-era student activism. A constitutional challenge resulted in a split Supreme Court decision later that year limiting the provision to federal elections. The prospect of different voting rolls for federal

# Leadership Vacuum Stymies Election Agency

*Partisan infighting leaves Election Assistance Commission lacking a quorum.*

Arizona, Georgia and Kansas faced an unusual problem when they asked the federal Election Assistance Commission (EAC) for permission to revise a federally prescribed voter registration form to include a state law requirement for proof of citizenship. The problem: the EAC had no Senate-confirmed commissioners to act on the request, the result of a partisan impasse that has left the commission without a quorum for nearly four years and with no members at all for two.

When Congress created the four-member panel in 2002, it specified that the House and Senate majority and minority leaders should each nominate a commissioner to be appointed by the president. Republicans have refused to designate candidates since 2010 as commissioners' terms have expired and have been able to thwart Senate confirmation of Democratic nominees.

The Senate is trying to ease the impasse somewhat by getting ready to move the nominations of two Democratic voting-rights advocates toward a floor vote. But even if Thomas Hicks and Myrna Pérez are confirmed, the EAC will still be shy of the three members required for a quorum as long as Republicans refuse to submit candidates for the two seats reserved for GOP nominees.

House Republicans have waged a long campaign to abolish the agency, created in the Help America Vote Act, passed in 2002 after the *Bush v. Gore* presidential election

fiasco. GOP lawmakers, led by Rep. Gregg Harper of Mississippi, contend that the EAC has accomplished its original goal of helping states fund new voting technology. Harper calls the agency, with about 30 employees and an $11 million operating budget in 2013, a "bloated bureaucracy."[1]

Democrats say the commission is still needed. When the House Committee on Administration voted to kill the agency on June 5, the panel's top Democrat, Pennsylvania's Robert Brady, said the commission has "an important, valuable role" and was "worth reauthorizing."

Hicks, senior elections counsel for the House Administration Committee and a former staffer with the public interest group Common Cause, was nominated by President Obama in March 2010 on the recommendation of House Democratic Leader Nancy Pelosi. Pérez, senior counsel at the Brennan Center for Justice at New York University School of Law, was nominated in June 2011 on the recommendation of Senate Democratic Leader Harry Reid.

After his reelection, Obama renominated Hicks and Pérez on June 11, 2013, and they appeared before the Senate Rules Committee for a second confirmation hearing on Dec. 11. As acting chairman, Sen. Angus King, an independent from Maine who caucuses with Democrats, said both were "well qualified." The committee's top Republican,

versus state elections prompted state election administrators to join in urging adoption of what became the 26th Amendment, setting the minimum voting age at 18 nationwide.[17]

Congress reauthorized the act again in 1975 and expanded the preclearance provision to jurisdictions with low voting rates by "language minorities." The provision generally required bilingual voting materials in jurisdictions with significant language minorities and extended preclearance requirements to Texas and parts of six other states: Alaska and South Dakota (Native Americans) and Arizona, California, Florida and New York (Hispanics). As the decade ended, however, the Supreme Court intervened with a contentious decision that threatened to blunt the

usefulness of the act in expanding minorities' rights in voting and elections.

## Election Mechanics

Congress and two Republican presidents — Ronald Reagan and George W. Bush — approved long extensions and significant expansions of the Voting Rights Act in 1982 and 2006, respectively. Throughout that period, the Justice Department increasingly used the act's preclearance provision to affect election procedures in covered jurisdictions. Meanwhile, Congress twice turned to improving election mechanics: first with the Democratic-backed 1993 law to facilitate voter registration and then in 2002 with a bipartisan bill enacted after the *Bush v. Gore* controversy

Sen. Pat Roberts of Kansas, also acknowledged the nominees' qualifications, but reiterated the GOP goal of abolishing the agency. "The EAC has fulfilled its purpose and should be eliminated," Roberts said.[2]

The EAC rankled Republicans when a draft staff report prepared in 2006 cast doubt on allegations from GOP lawmakers about voting place fraud, which GOP lawmakers cite as the reason for stricter voter photo-ID laws. The draft report stated that there was "widespread but not unanimous agreement that there is little polling place fraud." The commission revised the final report, however, to state, in its executive summary, that "there is a great deal of debate on the pervasiveness of fraud."[3]

Election law watchers say the lack of leadership at the top has combined with turnovers in the major staff positions of executive director and general counsel to bring the EAC to a virtual standstill. Among other issues, the lack of a quorum is preventing the adoption of new certification standards for voting machines; the new standards are needed, according to the just-released report by the Presidential Commission on Election Administration, to allow replacement of technologically obsolescent equipment.[4]

Arizona, Georgia and Kansas encountered the agency's leadership vacuum when they asked for permission to revise the federally prescribed voter registration form for federal elections to include instructions to provide proof of U.S. citizenship to vote in state elections. The commission's 46-page memorandum rejecting the request, issued on Jan. 17, was signed by Alice Miller as chief operating officer and acting executive director.[5]

The leadership vacuum will continue for at least a little while. The Senate Rules Committee was due to vote on the Hicks and Pérez nominations on Feb. 12, but had to put off the action because of the lack of a quorum until after the Senate's Presidents Day recess. With a Democratic majority, the committee is certain to approve the nominations, but Republicans could use a number of parliamentary maneuvers to delay or possibly prevent a floor vote.

— *Kenneth Jost*

[1]See Deborah Barfield Berry, "House panel OKs ending Election Assistance Commission," *USA Today*, June 5, 2013, www.usatoday .com/story/news/politics/2013/06/04/house-panel-approves-eliminating-election-commission/2389737/; other background drawn from story. See also U.S. Election Assistance Commission, "2013 Activities Report," www.eac.gov/assets/1/Documents/2013%20 Activities_Report%20_FINAL%20website%20version,%201-31-14.pdf.

[2]The 59-minute hearing can be viewed at http://tinyurl.com/l9b8pfj.

[3]See Ian Urbina, "U.S. Panel Is Said to Alter Finding on Voter Fraud," *The New York Times*, April 11, 2007, p. A6.

[4]See "The American Voting Experience: Report and Recommendations of the Presidential Commission on Election Administration," Jan. 9, 2014, pp. 62-66, www.youtube.com/watch?v=xCUMXpU6N3k.

[5]"Memorandum of Decision Concerning State Requests to Include Additional Proof-of-Citizenship Instructions on the National Mail Voter Registration Form," U.S. Election Assistance Commission, Jan. 17, 2014, EAC-2013-0004, www.eac.gov/assets/1/Documents/20140117%20EAC%20Final%20Decision%20on%20Proof%20of%20Citizenship%20Requests%20-%20FINAL.pdf.

to establish and help states meet minimum standards for administration of elections.

Civil rights supporters were disappointed in 1980 when the Supreme Court ruled that the Voting Rights Act's nationwide provision, Section 2, prohibited only intentional racial discrimination.[18] After maneuvering between the Democratic-controlled House and Republican-controlled Senate, Congress expanded the definition of discrimination by prohibiting any voting practice that had the effect of denying a racial, ethnic or language minority an equal opportunity to participate in the political process.

The 1982 reauthorization also extended the preclearance provision, Section 5, for another 25 years. Congress

in 1992 extended the bilingual election assistance provisions — due to expire that year — until 2007 as well.

The Supreme Court blessed Section 2's expanded definition of racial discrimination in a 1986 decision that applied the provision to so-called "vote dilution" — defined as any election practice that reduced the ability of a cohesive racial or ethnic minority to elect candidates of their choice.[19] The Justice Department responded by applying this expanded definition to a growing number of election practices, both in suits initiated under Section 2 and in preclearance review under Section 5.

As one important consequence, the Justice Department began pressing states in the South to draw legislative and congressional districts with majority African-American or

Getty Images/Bloomberg/Paul Morris

Voters fill out ballots at a polling station in San Francisco on Nov. 6, 2012. Douglas Lewis, executive director of the National Association of Election Officials, sees a trend toward liberalizing voter access through online registration and early voting. Online registration "is coming one way or another," he says. Giving voters more opportunities to cast ballots early is "also of value."

Latino populations to facilitate election of minority legislators. The Supreme Court in the 1990s cut back on this use of the Voting Rights Act, however, by limiting the extent to which race could be considered in drawing district lines. But the expanded definition of racial discrimination also allowed the Justice Department to require preclearance of seemingly minor ground-level voting changes — such as moving a polling place away from a location convenient to minority voters.

In the meantime, Democrats in Congress had succeeded in enacting the so-called motor voter bill, formally the National Voter Registration Act. The law stemmed from efforts of two liberal college professor activists, Frances Fox Piven and Richard Cloward, who thought it possible to increase voter turnout by allowing registration at motor vehicle departments or other government agencies.

President George H. W. Bush vetoed the Democratic-backed legislation on July 2, 1992. With Democrat Bill Clinton in the White House, however, the Democratic-controlled Congress quickly passed the measure again and Clinton signed it into law on May 20, 1993. About half the states already allowed registration through motor vehicle departments, but Republicans arguing against the bill warned the measure would be expensive and invite fraud.

Congress's second major initiative on the mechanics of elections followed the embarrassing spectacle of Florida's disputed recount in the *Bush v. Gore* election in 2000.[20] Bush's 537-vote victory in the election-deciding state of Florida was certified and then left standing by the U.S. Supreme Court after a month of recounts and litigation that highlighted poorly designed ballots and inconsistent standards for tallying disputed votes. Responding to the controversy, a privately sponsored commission co-chaired by former presidents Jimmy Carter and Gerald R. Ford issued a report in July 2001 calling for, among other changes, creation of a new federal agency to oversee federal responsibilities for nationwide elections.[21]

Republicans and Democrats argued about provisions of the Help America Vote Act for more than a year until finally achieving strong bipartisan majorities for the version that Bush signed into law on Oct. 29, 2002.

As enacted, the law consigned punch card and lever voting machines to the waste heap and authorized $3.9 billion in federal money to help states and localities replace machinery, train poll workers and computerize registration lists. New identification requirements led major Latino groups and the American Civil Liberties Union (ACLU) to oppose the final bill, but the act required election officials to establish procedures for would-be voters challenged at the polls to cast provisional ballots and to have their votes counted after presenting sufficient evidence later.

Congress returned to the Voting Rights Act in 2005 as the act's preclearance provision was set to expire the next year. Fearing potential review by the Supreme Court, the House and Senate judiciary committees assembled up-to-date evidence on, among other factors, black vs. white turnout and registration in covered and uncovered jurisdictions. The evidence was ambiguous: African American turnout and registration had seemingly increased to comparable levels as whites; and the Justice Department was denying fewer requests to preclear election changes — only 92 objections in the previous 10 years.

Even so, the political difficulties entailed in rewriting the coverage formula led Congress in the end to leave it unchanged and extend the preclearance provision for another 25 years. Lawmakers in both chambers approved the bill by overwhelming margins — 390-33 in the House,

98-0 in the Senate — and President Bush signed it into law in a photo-op ceremony on July 27, 2006.[22]

## "Voting Wars"

The bipartisan support for extending the Voting Rights Act was not enough to deflect the constitutional challenge to the law or prevent the Supreme Court's eventual decision to neuter the preclearance provision by throwing out the act's coverage formula. In the meantime, voting controversies intensified as Republicans pushed and Democrats resisted new state voter-ID laws, eventually challenging them in court. In addition, some high-profile close elections were settled only after contentious and litigious recounts akin to *Bush v. Gore*. For his book chronicling the decade, election law expert Hasen chose an apt title: *The Voting Wars*.[23]

Laws requesting voters to present identification were on the books in 14 states as of 2001 but were lightly enforced, according to the National Conference of State Legislatures.[24] Would-be voters without identification were allowed to cast ballots after signing an affidavit or having an election official or other voter vouch for their identity. The strict laws pioneered by Georgia and Indiana in 2005 demanded a photo ID and required anyone without one to cast a provisional ballot that would be counted only if the citizen returned to the elections office with proper identification within a matter of days.

Indiana's law survived a legal challenge intact, but Georgia eased its enforcement provisions a bit to win preclearance from the Justice Department and eventually a favorable ruling in federal court. Meanwhile, however, the Missouri Supreme Court struck down a photo-ID law just as it was about to take effect for the November 2006 election.

Legislative activity spiked again in 2011 as eight states adopted new or strengthened identification requirements. In five other states, however, Democratic governors vetoed photo-ID bills. And in November 2012 Minnesota voters rejected a proposed constitutional amendment that would have required a photo ID to cast a ballot; the measure failed by about 100,000 votes out of nearly 3 million cast.

In the meantime, Minnesota had provided the country a rerun of sorts of the *Bush v. Gore* battle with its November 2008 contest between incumbent Republican Sen. Norm Coleman and his Democratic challenger, former television comedian Al Franken. As Hasen relates the story, Coleman held a 725-vote lead after an initial Election Night tabulation. The margin fell to 215 votes after a statewide canvass completed on Nov. 18 — so narrow as to trigger a mandatory recount under state law. After counting more than 900 wrongly rejected absentee ballots, the state's canvassing board certified Franken the winner by 225 votes, but Coleman contested the election in state court.

The Minnesota Supreme Court ruled for Franken, allowing him to be sworn in on July 2009. Hasen comments that the Minnesota rivals appeared to change positions as the vote count shifted. Coleman initially called for "a healing process" after the close vote before launching his court challenge once Franken was certified the winner. For his part, Franken switched from a "count every vote" position while he was behind to a "strict compliance" stance once he had gained the lead.[25]

By Franken's swearing in, the Supreme Court had added to election-related issues by sending a strong signal to Congress that the Voting Rights Act might be constitutionally defective. The court's June 22, 2009, decision in *Northwest Austin Municipal Utility District No. 1 v. Holder* stemmed from a challenge brought by a local utility district in suburban Austin, Texas, that chafed under the Justice Department's preclearance review of the relocation of a polling place. The utility district argued that Congress was wrong to subject Texas and other Southern states to preclearance requirements long after they had dropped the blatantly discriminatory practices in effect before 1965.

Conservative justices appeared sympathetic to the position in oral arguments, but the court skirted the issue in an 8-1 decision written by Chief Justice John G. Roberts Jr. The ruling merely gave local jurisdictions a greater opportunity to "bail out" of the preclearance provision. Roberts added, however, that the preclearance requirement raised "serious constitutional questions."[26]

Congress's failure to rewrite the coverage formula set the stage for a new challenge, this one by Shelby County, Ala., a predominantly white county in the Birmingham metropolitan area. As in the earlier case, a three-judge federal district court upheld the constitutionality of the preclearance requirement, but the

Supreme Court's 5-4 decision on June 26, 2013 — again written by Roberts — faulted Congress for an "irrational" decision to subject states and local jurisdictions to preclearance based on 40-year-old statistics.

With no coverage formula, the preclearance provision was reduced to a dead letter. Vermont's Sen. Leahy among others vowed to revive the provision, and committee hearings were held within the month in both the House and Senate. By the end of the year, however, lawmakers working on the issue were still talking behind the scenes about how to fashion a bill that might command bipartisan support in the Republican-controlled House and Democratic-controlled Senate.

## CURRENT SITUATION

### Court Cases

Civil rights groups are voicing optimism about legal challenges to state voter-ID laws, but supporters of the measures believe they will survive court tests.

With legal challenges pending in five states, opponents of photo-ID laws won the most recent round in Pennsylvania and are hopeful as suits in Wisconsin reach critical stages. Judges have yet to rule on pending suits in Texas and North Carolina brought separately by civil rights groups and the U.S. Justice Department or in a recently filed private suit in Kansas.

In Wisconsin, a federal judge is expected to rule soon on a challenge to the state's photo-ID law after presiding over a two-week trial in November. In the meantime, the Wisconsin Supreme Court decided to hear consolidated cases brought by the League of Women Voters and the state NAACP on Feb. 25 after a state appellate court upheld the law in one of the suits.

In Pennsylvania, lawyers for Gov. Corbett filed a motion before Judge McGinley on Jan. 27 urging him to reconsider his decision ruling the state's law unconstitutional. The lawyers argued that problems in making voter-ID cards available did not require the law to be struck down. But they also said that if McGinley does not change his mind, the law should be put on hold to avoid confusion in this year's primary and general elections.

The Justice Department and civil rights groups are separately challenging photo-ID requirements in both North Carolina and Texas. The Texas law will be in effect in the March 4 statewide party primaries because the Supreme Court's decision on the Voting Rights Act lifted the need for federal preclearance. The NAACP and Mexican American Legislative Caucus sued the state in federal court in Corpus Christi challenging the photo-ID requirement in September, the month after the Justice Department had filed its similar suit in the same court.

The department also filed suit in September challenging North Carolina's new voting law, shortly after the state's Republican governor, Pat McCrory, signed it into law. The government's suit challenges not only the photo-ID requirement, but also other provisions that reduce early voting by one week, limit same-day registration and tighten procedures for counting provisional ballots. The League of Women Voters and the North Carolina branch of the A. Philip Randolph Institute had filed a comparable suit in state court just days after McCrory signed the bill.

In Kansas, Topeka attorney Jim Lawing is representing two voters who are challenging the photo-ID requirement in state court after being prevented from casting ballots in 2012. Secretary of State Kris Kobach, a Republican known for promoting measures to require proof of citizenship for voting, moved to have the case tried in federal court instead. Lawing is opposing the move; the issue is pending.

In all of the cases, state officials are defending the laws, with the Wisconsin suits closest to resolution pending a possible appeal to the U.S. Supreme Court. In Wisconsin, as in Indiana in 2005, the photo-ID law was adopted in 2011 shortly after Republicans gained control of both legislative chambers and the governor's office. The law requires specified forms of government-issued photo IDs; a voter without qualifying identification may cast a provisional ballot, but must provide the right kind of identification by the end of the week for the vote to be counted.

The NAACP and League of Women Voters filed separate suits challenging the law and won rulings to strike it down. In the league's case, however, an intermediate appellate court upheld the law in March 2013. With the NAACP case pending at a different appellate court, the state's Supreme Court decided to hear both cases on Feb. 25. In the meantime, U.S. District Court Judge Lynn

**AT ISSUE**

# Should Congress pass the proposed Voting Rights Act rewrite?

## YES

**Sen. Chris Coons, D-Del.**
*Member, Senate Judiciary Committee*

Written for *CQ Researcher*, February 2014

We've come a long way since the Voting Rights Act was adopted in 1965, but we're not yet where we need to be. Discrimination still exists, and we'll never stop it by pretending it doesn't.

The Supreme Court's *Shelby County v. Holder* decision last June left a dangerous gap in our voter protections by gutting the preclearance system that allowed the Department of Justice to stop proposed discriminatory voting changes before they take effect. Since then, numerous jurisdictions have implemented voting changes that the preclearance system would have blocked. More are on the way, and together these changes serve as a sad reminder that Voting Rights Act protections are still critically necessary.

The Voting Rights Amendments Act of 2014 will restore the vitality of the law in jurisdictions where aggressive voting rights enforcement is still needed. The Supreme Court threw out the old formula for deciding which jurisdictions were subject to pre-clearance because it was based on 50-year-old data. This bill would base preclearance on a formula that looks clearly and soberly at the modern challenges facing voters.

Detractors criticized the old preclearance formula for applying only to the old South — even jurisdictions that no longer discriminate — while not covering states and counties in which race- or language-based discrimination has emerged over the past 50 years. This bill responds to those charges, as well. Jurisdictions with a history of discrimination but that no longer propose and enforce discriminatory practices will now no longer be subject to preclearance. Jurisdictions that enact new, discriminatory voting laws will be eligible for preclearance, whether or not they have been subject to preclearance in the past.

This bill also makes voting rights and elections more transparent, ensuring the public has access to basic information about polling places, election law changes and redistricting, so voters can feel confident elections are fair.

Under the leadership of Judiciary Chairman Patrick Leahy, Sen. Dick Durbin and Reps. James Sensenbrenner, John Conyers and John Lewis, we've crafted a bipartisan bill designed to be both effective and able to pass this Congress. It's practical, can become law and would survive future legal scrutiny.

It is a modern voting rights bill to confront modern voting rights challenges. It's time for Congress to pass this legislation and restore our democracy's fundamental promise of free and fair access to the ballot box.

## NO

**Rep. Lynn Westmoreland, R-Ga.**
*Member, Committee on Financial Services, Tea Party Caucus*

Written for *CQ Researcher*, February 2014

Everyone agrees that the significant burdens imposed by pre-clearance under the Voting Rights Act were desperately needed when they were passed in 1965. But that was nearly 50 years ago. Since its passage, we have seen dramatic changes across the country, especially in the South, that point to the fact that the law needed updating. Georgia has four African-American members of Congress and some of the highest minority voter turnout in the country. In fact, in November 2012, a higher percentage of registered African-American women turned out to vote than registered white women or men.

Because of the major changes since the dark days of the 1960s, the Supreme Court's ruling in *Shelby County v. Holder* last year that the preclearance formula used under Section 5 of the Voting Rights Act was unconstitutional should not have come as a surprise. This law used outdated information to set the formula for preclearance and punished certain areas of the country for the sins of their fathers and grandfathers. To put it in perspective, a person who became eligible to vote the year the law was adopted became eligible for Medicare last year.

I pushed hard to update the coverage formula — the portion the court struck down — when the law was reauthorized in 2006. Unfortunately, my pleas fell on deaf ears. I applaud my colleague from Wisconsin Rep. Jim Sensenbrenner for attempting to update the law, but unfortunately cannot agree with his method.

First and foremost, the proposed update doesn't change the scope of preclearance, which is a huge burden to jurisdictions and was a major consideration in the Supreme Court's decision on the old formula. Second, it continues to punish entire states for the actions of counties — even if the state government has no control over its counties, as is the case in Georgia. Third, it backdates coverage to include any election changes made since the formula was overturned last year, punishing states at a time when they didn't realize they would be punished. Fourth, it defines which races will be the "majority" and "minority" for all time, even if that is not true in a particular state or jurisdiction, making the law less able to account for changing conditions. Finally, it disproportionately punishes states that were under the unconstitutional formula because all existing objections raised under the old preclearance system still count toward coverage — something that is not true for other states.

Adelman has under advisement a comparable suit, filed by the League of United Latin American Citizens, among other groups, after a two-week trial in November and filing of briefs in December.[27]

The Advancement Project is providing lawyers in the Pennsylvania case and the federal case in Wisconsin. Culliton-Gonzalez calls the ruling in Pennsylvania "a great victory" and feels optimistic about Wisconsin. "I feel like the tide has turned," she says.

The Heritage Foundation's von Spakovsky, however, feels the challengers will come up short. "We're going to have years and years of experience with states, which will show that claims against [photo-ID laws] are hot air," he says.

## Shift in Legislation?

State lawmakers are throwing more bills into the hopper this legislative season to ease access to voting than measures to make it harder to participate in elections, according to a compilation by the Brennan Center for Justice.

The center, which strongly backs moves to increase access to voting, counts 190 bills introduced in 31 states in that direction so far in 2014, nearly four times greater than the 49 bills to restrict access to voting introduced or carried over from the previous year.

The trend is less pronounced, however, when counting only bills that the center considers "active" — based on hearings or other action. The center counts 12 "expansive" bills active in seven states on such topics as modernizing voter registration and increasing early voting opportunities. The center counts five "restrictive" bills active in four states, primarily bills to establish or tighten photo-ID requirements.[28]

"The beginning of 2014 shows real momentum toward improving our elections, both in the states and nationally," the center says in introducing the report. At the federal level, the report notes the introduction of the bipartisan Leahy-Sensenbrenner measure in the House and the Senate to revive the Voting Rights Act provision requiring some states and localities to obtain preclearance before any voting or election law change.

Using the Brennan Center's terminology, however, the proposed rewrite of the Voting Rights Act was not "active" as of early February. Despite the photo-op introduction of the bill in January, neither the House nor Senate Judiciary panel has scheduled hearings on the bill.

The Heritage Foundation's von Spakovsky discounts the center's reading of the political climate on the issues. "They're declaring victory before they've achieved victory," he says after quickly reviewing the center's report. "I actually don't think that they're winning momentum."

The apparent trend toward liberalizing voting laws comes after a year when the opposing election-law camps swapped victories, according to the National Conference of State Legislatures. In its report for 2013, the group noted the enactment of strict photo-ID laws in Arkansas and North Carolina offset by adoption of online registration in Illinois and West Virginia. Virginia enacted laws adopting both practices.

Same-day registration was adopted in Colorado, the conference reports, but eliminated as part of North Carolina's omnibus election law overhaul. Colorado also moved toward all-mail elections, while Florida restored early-voting opportunities to what had been available before a restrictive 2010 enactment.

The head of the organization for local election administrators also sees a trend toward liberalizing voter access through online registration and early voting, as recommended by the Bauer-Ginsberg election law reform commission. Online registration "is coming one way or another," says Doug Lewis, executive director of the National Association of Election Officials. Giving voters more opportunities to cast ballots early is "also of value," he says.

In addition to online registration and early voting, the Brennan Center favorably notes bills introduced in 11 states to allow students under age 18 to preregister so they are registered as soon as they reach voting age. The center also applauds introduction of bills in seven states to make it easier for felons to regain voting rights.

The center's list of restrictive bills include proposals to require proof of citizenship for voting, to limit voter registration mobilization drives and to make it easier to remove voters from registration rolls.

Lewis applauds the presidential commission for "a credible job of looking at a limited number of issues" in its report. Like the commission, Lewis says long wait times are a problem for some voters—though he says 97 percent of voters cast ballots within 14 minutes. He says the commission's recommendation that no voter should wait more than 30 minutes to cast a ballot is "not a bad goal," but says election administrators think a one-hour limit is more achievable.

Like the commission, Lewis sees a "looming crisis" in voting technology. "The biggest danger to American elections today is state and local governments trying to force equipment to be used longer than it was designed for," Lewis says. But he fears that fiscally strapped state and local governments may continue to defer needed replacement of outdated equipment.

# OUTLOOK:

## Continuing Debates

When Texans go to the polls in party primaries on March 4 to choose candidates for congressional and state offices, it will be the biggest test to date of a strict voter photo-ID law. And Republicans and Democrats in Texas are differing on the likely impact of the law just as the two major parties disagree nationwide on the need for such measures.

Texas, second in population to California, is the nation's biggest state to require voters to present a government-approved photo identification before casting a ballot. Democrats in Texas are warning the law will confuse voters and dampen turnout, while Republicans are discounting the fears.

As evidence, GOP leaders, including Greg Abbott, state attorney general and leading contender for the party's gubernatorial nomination, point to the turnout in the November 2013 statewide balloting on constitutional amendments. With the ID law in effect, turnout averaged about 1.1 million votes on nine measures, around 50 percent higher than the average turnout of 672,000 in a comparable election two years earlier with 11 amendments to be voted on.

Still, the Democratic majority on the Dallas County Commissioners Court was concerned enough about voter turnout to approve $145,000 in October for an informational mailing to explain the new law. The court was debating a second appropriation of $165,000 in February as the primaries approached. The court's lone Republican opposed the expenditures.

Whatever the turnout may be in the March 4 races, the arguments over the impact of voter-ID laws in Texas and elsewhere appear likely to continue, unresolved. Shaw, the University of Texas political scientist, notes that turnout can be affected by any number of factors — from the level of interest in the contests themselves to Election Day weather and transportation conditions. "It's hard to disentangle" the effect of any single factor, Shaw says.

The parties are also likely to continue to fight over proposals to enact or to tighten ID requirements, according to election law expert Hasen. "There are fundamental disputes over whether to make voting easier," he says. "Democrats want to make voting easier. They see voting as about the allocation of power among equals. Republicans see voting more as a test to determine the best candidate — in which case imposing hurdles weeds out voters who are least informed."

The opposing camps also differ on the likely course of court rulings on voter-ID laws. Supporters, such as the Heritage Foundation's von Spakovsky, predict most laws will be upheld, while the Advancement Project's Culliton-Gonzalez and other opponents expect more victories like the one in Pennsylvania.

The Pennsylvania ruling, however, gives the state government a chance to revive the law if sufficient resources are provided to help voters obtain qualifying identification. For his part, Baretto, the University of Washington professor who testified for the plaintiffs in the Pennsylvania case, expects courts to examine ID laws with "more scrutiny," even in cases where the laws are not struck down.

In Washington, supporters of the proposed rewrite of the federal Voting Rights Act are working behind the scenes to try to muster Republican support that the bill will need to advance in the GOP-controlled House. Without referring specifically to the bill, Vice President Joe Biden used a Martin Luther King Day appearance to call for reviving the Voting Rights Act in the wake of the Supreme Court's decision last year. For his part, Attorney General Holder went before a criminal justice reform symposium at Georgetown Law School in Washington to call for restoring voting rights for felons.[29]

As for the rest of the nation's election machinery and procedures, more attention is on the agenda, but the prospects for concrete action are cloudy. Online registration may advance, given its claimed advantages of greater accuracy at less expense. But the parties' opposing views on whether to make voting easier raise doubts about the presidential commission's recommendations for more early and no-excuse absentee voting. And fiscal realities threaten the commission's urgent recommendation to upgrade vote-counting technology.

The nation got a wake-up call on the problems of administering elections in 2000, according to Becker, head of the Pew elections initiative. Despite the mixed forecast for changes, he sees the past decade-plus of debates as necessary and useful.

"America should be a model for the world in democracy," Becker says, "and that means harnessing technology to build an election system that is as accurate, convenient, cost-effective and efficient as possible."

## NOTES

1. See *Applewhite v. Commonwealth*, 330 M.D. 2012 (Jan. 17, 2014), www.pacourts.us/assets/files/setting-647/file-3490.pdf?cb=a5ec29. For coverage, see Karen Langley, "Judge Declares Voter ID Law is Invalid," *Pittsburgh Post-Gazette*, Jan. 18, 2014, p. A-1; Amy Worden, "Pa. voter ID law struck down," *The Philadelphia Inquirer*, Jan. 18, 2014, p. A1; Rick Lyman, "Pennsylvania Voter ID Law Struck Down as Judge Cites Burdens on Citizens," *The New York Times*, Jan. 18, 2014, p. A12. Some background drawn from Charles Thompson, "State nears requiring that voters show IDs," *Patriot News* (Harrisburg, Pa.), March 13, 2012, p. A1.

2. For a detailed list and chronology, see "Voter Identification Requirements," National Conference of State Legislatures (regularly updated), www.ncsl.org/research/elections-and-campaigns/voter-id.aspx. For previous coverage, see these *CQ Researcher* reports by Peter Katel: "Voter Rights," May 18, 2012, pp. 449-476; "Voting Controversies," Sept. 15, 2006, pp. 745-768.

3. The case is *Shelby County v. Holder*, 570 U.S. — (June 25, 2013), www.supremecourt.gov/opinions/12pdf/12-96_6k47.pdf. For coverage, see Kenneth Jost, *Supreme Court Yearbook 2012-2013*.

4. See Kathy Koch, "Election Reform," *CQ Researcher*, Nov. 2, 2001, pp. 897-920.

5. "The American Voting Experience: Report and Recommendations of the Presidential Commission on Election Administration," Presidential Commission on Election Administration, Jan. 22, 2014, www.supportthevoter.gov. For coverage, see Scott Wilson,

"Election commission recommends changes," *The Washington Post*, Jan. 23, 2014, p. A4.

6. "Voting Laws Roundup 2014," Brennan Center for Justice, Feb. 6, 2014, www.brennancenter.org/analysis/voting-laws-roundup-2014#ftn4.

7. Von Spakovsky's earlier quote from Lachlan Markay, "Critics Blast Obama Nominee for Election Assistance Commissioner," *The Washington Free Beacon*, June 11, 2013, http://freebeacon.com/critics-blast-obama-nominee-for-election-assistance-commissioner/.

8. The decision is *Crawford v. Marion County Board of Elections*, 533 U.S. 188 (2008). For an account, see Kenneth Jost, *Supreme Court Yearbook 2007-2008*.

9. John Fund, "Why We Need Voter-ID Laws Now," *National Review Online*, April 9, 2012, www.nationalreview.com/articles/295431/why-we-need-voter-id-laws-now-john-fund. Fund stresses that O'Keefe did not violate the law because he did not explicitly identify himself as Holder or request a ballot. The book co-authored by Fund and von Spakovsky is *Who's Counting? How Fraudsters and Bureaucrats Put Your Vote at Risk* (2012).

10. Quoted in "Democracy Prevails in Pennsylvania Voter ID Trial," Advancement Project, Jan. 17, 2014, www.advancementproject.org/news/entry/democracy-prevails-in-pennsylvania-voter-id-trial.

11. *Texas v. Holder*, 12-cv-128, U.S. Dist. Ct.-Dist. Col., (Aug. 30, 2012), pp. 46-47, www.scribd.com/doc/104429876/Texas-v-Holder.

12. See "Online Voter Registration," National Conference of State Legislatures, November 2013, www.ncsl.org/research/elections-and-campaigns/electronic-or-online-voter-registration.aspx. The report includes a link to the 55-minute Nov. 12 webinar, "Online Voter Registration: The Bipartisan Trend in Elections."

13. Fund and von Spakovsky, *op. cit.*, chap. 6.

14. "Reforming the voting process to improve access," "PBS NewsHour," Jan. 23, 2014, http://video.pbs.org/video/2365162592/.

15. Historical background drawn in part from Alexander Keyssar, *The Right to Vote: The Contested History of Democracy in the United States* (rev. ed, 2010). See also Katel, "Voter Rights," *op. cit.*

16. The Supreme Court decision is *South Carolina v. Katzenbach*, 383 U.S. 301 (1966).

17. The Supreme Court decision is *Oregon v. Mitchell*, 400 U.S. 112 (1970).

18. The decision is *Mobile v. Bolden*, 446 U.S. 55 (1980). The ruling threw out a lower court order that found the city of Mobile, Ala., had violated the Voting Rights Act by changing from a district to an at-large system for electing members of the city's governing body.

19. The decision is *Thornburg v. Gingles*, 478 U.S. 30 (1986). The decision sustained a lower court decision that threw out several multimember legislative districts in North Carolina.

20. For background, see Koch, *op. cit.*

21. "To Assure Pride and Confidence in the Electoral Process," National Commission on Federal Election Reform, August 2001, http://web1.millercenter.org/commissions/comm_2001.pdf. The commission was co-sponsored by the University of Virginia's Miller Center on Public Affairs and the Century Foundation; the report was presented to President Bush at the White House on July 31, 2001.

22. For a detailed dissection of the reauthorization, see Nathaniel J. Persily, "The Promise and Pitfalls of the New Voting Rights Act," *Yale Law Journal*, Vol. 117, No. 2 (November 2007), pp. 174-253, http://yalelawjournal.org/images/pdfs/606.pdf.

23. Richard L. Hasen, *The Voting Wars: From Florida 2000 to the Next Election Meltdown* (2012).

24. "Voter ID: Where Are We Now?" The Canvass, National Conference of State Legislatures, April 2012, www.ncsl.org/documents/legismgt/elect/Canvass_Apr_2012_No_29.pdf.

25. Hasen, "Margin of Litigation," *op. cit.*, pp. 131-133.

26. For an account, see Kenneth Jost, *Supreme Court Yearbook 2008-2009*.

27. See Patrick Marley, "High court to take up cases on voter ID," *Milwaukee Journal Sentinel*, Nov. 21, 2013, p. B1; Bruce Vielmetti, "Legal filings hone voter ID arguments," *Milwaukee Journal Sentinel*, Dec. 25, 2013, p. B1.

28. "Voting Laws Roundup 2014," *op. cit.* States with active "expansive" bills are California, Colorado, Kentucky, Massachusetts, Nebraska, New York and Washington; states with active "restrictive" bills are Nebraska, New Hampshire, Washington and Wisconsin. Also see "2013 Election Legislation Enacted by State Legislatures," National Conference of State Legislatures, Jan. 14, 2014, www.ncsl.org/research/elections-and-campaigns/wrap-up-2013-election-legislation-enactments.aspx.

29. See Dave Boyer, "Biden hits voter ID laws at event to honor King," *The Washington Times*, Jan. 21, 2014, A3; Matt Apuzzo, "Holder Urges States to Lift Ban on Felons' Voting," *The New York Times*, Feb. 12, 2014, p. A17.

# BIBLIOGRAPHY
## Selected Sources
### Books

**Fund, John H., and Hans von Spakovsky, *Who's Counting? How Fraudsters and Bureaucrats Put Your Vote at Risk, Encounter Books*, 2012.**
Fund, a columnist with *National Review Online*, and von Spakovsky, a senior fellow with the conservative Heritage Foundation and former Federal Election Commission member, contend that voting fraud is spreading in the United States. They call for voter-ID laws, among other steps, to safeguard the integrity of elections, and they criticize liberal-backed proposals such as same-day voter registration as invitations to fraud. Includes notes. Fund also is author of *Stealing Elections: How Voting Fraud Threatens Our Democracy* (2d ed.), Encounter Books, 2008.

**Hasen, Richard L., *The Voting Wars: From Florida 2000 to the Next Election Meltdown, Yale University Press*, 2012.**
A nationally prominent election law expert at the University of California-Irvine School of Law details the controversies over administration of elections beginning with the presidential vote recount in Florida in 2000 and continuing through the 2010 election cycle. Includes notes. Hasen also publishes the comprehensive *Election Law Blog* (http://electionlawblog.org/).

**Keyssar, Alexander, *The Right to Vote: The Contested History of Democracy in the United States* (rev. ed.), *Basic Books*, 2010 (originally published 2000).**

A professor of history and public policy at Harvard University's Kennedy School of Government traces the history of voting issues from the limited suffrage in the country's early history through the hard-fought battles over expanding voting rights from the mid-19th century to the present day. Includes appendix material, detailed notes.

**May, Gary, *Bending Toward Justice: The Voting Rights Act and the Transformation of American Democracy*, Basic Books, 2013.**
A professor of history at the University of Delaware details the events leading to the enactment of the Voting Rights Act of 1965. Includes notes.

**Wang, Tova Andrea, *The Politics of Voter Suppression: Defending and Expanding Americans' Right to Vote*, Cornell University Press, 2012.**
An election-law expert at the liberal advocacy group Demos criticizes voter-ID laws among other proposals as attempts at "voter suppression."

## Articles

**Lee, Suevon, "Everything You've Ever Wanted to Know About Voter ID Laws," *Pro Publica*, Nov. 5, 2012, www.propublica.org/article/everything-youve-ever-wanted-to-know-about-voter-id-laws.**
A question-and-answer format provides a thorough explanation of the origin of and controversy over voter-ID laws.

**Toobin, Jeffrey, "Annals of Law: Holder v. Roberts," *The New Yorker*, Feb. 17, 2014, www.newyorker.com/reporting/2014/02/17/140217fa_fact_toobin.**
A legal analyst depicts Attorney General Eric Holder as deeply committed to using suits against Texas and North Carolina to restore the power of the Voting Rights Act to prevent discriminatory voting practices.

## Hearings

**"From Selma to Shelby County: Working Together to Restore the Protections of the Voting Rights Act," *U.S.* Senate Judiciary Committee, July 17, 2013, www.judiciary.senate.gov/hearings/hearing.cfm?id=6ae289b2466e2489f90d6b42c9d8d78f.**
The hearing included testimony by two of the House co-sponsors of the proposed rewrite of the Voting Rights Act and three private witnesses.

**"The Voting Rights Act After the Supreme Court's Decision in Shelby County," U.S. House Judiciary Subcommittee on the Constitution and Civil Justice, July 18, 2013, http://judiciary.house.gov/index.cfm/hearings?ID=3798FE70B5F1-C18F-30C6-70FAF7EBCA5C.Committee.**
The hearing included testimony by four private individuals.

## Reports and Studies

**"The American Voting Experience: Report and Recommendations of the Presidential Commission on Election Administration," January 2014, www.supportthevoter.gov/files/2014/01/Amer-Voting-Exper-final-draft-01-09-14-508.pdf.**
The bipartisan, 10-member commission called for online registration, expanded early or absentee voting and improved voting technology; commissioners were unanimous in the 112-page report, but did not address photo-ID proposals.

**"Building Confidence in U.S. Elections: Report of Commission on Federal Election Reform," September 2005, www1.american.edu/ia/cfer/report/full_report.pdf.**
The private commission called for photo IDs for all voters, verifiable paper trails for election results and impartial administration of elections.

## On the Web

**Election Law @ Moritz, http://moritzlaw.osu.edu/electionlaw/.**
The Ohio State University's Moritz College of Law maintains a website with "information and insights on the laws governing federal, state, and local elections."

# For More Information

**Advancement Project**, 1220 L St., N.W., Suite 850, Washington, DC 20005; 202-728-9557; www.advancement project.org. The multiracial civil rights organization works with community organizations on election reform and other issues.

**American Civil Liberties Union**, 125 Broad St., New York, NY 10004; 212-549-2500; www.aclu.org/voting-rights. The ACLU's Voting Rights Project participates in litigation against photo-ID laws and other election issues; also provides news, analysis and research reports.

**Brennan Center for Justice at New York University School of Law**, 161 Avenue of the Americas, New York, NY 10013; 646-292-8310; www.brennancenter.org. The nonpartisan law and policy institute publishes research, analysis and litigation documents on major election law issues.

**Election Assistance Commission**, 1335 East West Highway, Suite 4300, Silver Spring, MD 20910; 301-563-3919; www .eac.gov. The federal agency is an independent bipartisan commission established in 2002 to assist states and localities in improving election administration and implementing provisions of the Help America Vote Act.

**Fair Elections Legal Network**, 1825 K St., N.W., Suite 450, Washington, DC 20006; 202-331-0114; http://fairelec tionsnetwork.com. The network of lawyers works to remove barriers to voting and improve election administration across the United States.

**Heritage Foundation**, 214 Massachusetts Ave., N.E., Washington, DC 20002; 202-546-4999; www.heritage.org/ issues/legal. The conservative think tank advocates stricter ID requirements for voting.

**Mexican American Legal Defense and Educational Fund (MALDEF)**, 634 S. Spring St., Los Angeles, CA 90014; 213-629-2512; www.maldef.org. The longtime civil rights organization works on voting rights issues affecting Latinos.

**NAACP**, 4805 Mt. Hope Drive, Baltimore, MD 21215; 877-622-2798; www.naacp.org. The longtime civil rights organization participates in voting rights advocacy at the federal, state and local levels.

**NAACP Legal Defense and Educational Fund**, 99 Hudson St., 16th floor, New York, NY 10013; 212-219-1900; www.naacpldf.org. The organization — separate from the NAACP — litigates on voting rights issues in federal and state courts.

**National Association of Election Officials**, 21946 Royal Montreal Drive, Suite 100, Katy, TX 77450; 281-396-4309; http://electioncenter.org. The professional association represents government employees who serve in voter registration and elections administration.

**National Association of Secretaries of State**, 444 North Capitol St., N.W., Suite 401, Washington, DC 20001; 202-624-3525; www.nass.org. The association represents secretaries of state from the 50 states, the District of Columbia, Puerto Rico and American Samoa, most of whose offices have responsibility for administering elections in their jurisdictions.

**National Conference of State Legislatures**, 7700 East First Pl., Denver, CO 80230; 303-364-7700; www.ncsl.org. The nonpartisan organization furnishes the most complete and up-to-date information on states' voter-ID laws and other election-related measures.

**Project on Fair Representation**, c/o Project Liberty, 109 N. Henry St., Alexandria, VA 22314; 703-505-1922; www .projectonfairrepresentation.org/. The project sponsored the litigation that resulted in the Supreme Court's decision to invalidate the Voting Rights Act's preclearance coverage formula.

**True the Vote**, P.O. Box 27368, Houston, TX 77227; http:// truethevote.org. The Web-based organization supports photo-ID laws and organizes a nationwide network of election-watchers.

**U.S. Department of Justice**, 950 Pennsylvania Ave., N.W., Washington, DC 20530; 202-514-2000; www.justice.gov. The Justice Department's Voting Section is responsible for enforcing federal laws regarding voting rights.

# 2

# Changing Demographics

Bill Wanlund

Hundreds of older Americans rally in Chicago on Nov. 7, 2011, against cuts in programs that benefit the elderly. Each day for the next 19 years, 10,000 baby boomers will reach the traditional retirement age of 65. By 2030, more than one in five Americans will be 65 or older, compared with about one in eight today. The number of older Americans is expected to more than double between now and 2050, to about 84 million.

From *CQ Researcher*,
November 16, 2012.

The nation is undergoing a profound population makeover, a transformation so sweeping that just about every aspect of American life will be affected in coming years, from economic growth and electoral politics to social-welfare policies and religious affiliation.

Growing ethnic and racial diversity is the most striking sign of change. For the first time in U.S. history, minority babies outnumbered white newborns last year, a trend driven by rising Hispanic immigration.[1] By 2042, non-Hispanic whites will cease to be in the majority. Already, more than a third of Americans are minorities, and non-whites accounted for 92 percent of population growth between 2000 and 2010.[2]

The pace of demographic change in the nation, whose population has grown to about 315 million, has stunned even the experts. "It was always predicted that we would be diverse, but it's happened faster than anyone predicted," said Cheryl Russell, former editor in chief of *American Demographics* magazine and now editorial director of New Strategist Publications. "Diversity and the rapid growth in diversity is one of the reasons we have a black president today. That's one thing that would never have been predicted."[3]

Nowhere have the effects of diversity been more evident than in this month's presidential election. In his Nov. 6 victory over GOP contender Mitt Romney, President Obama garnered an estimated 71 percent of the Hispanic vote, according to election day polling by the Pew Hispanic Center.[4] Asian-Americans, who supported Obama by about 47 percentage points, made up 3 percent of the 2012 electorate, up a full point from 2008.[5] "The nonwhite vote has been growing — tick,

## More Americans Religiously Unaffiliated

The percentage of Americans who classify themselves as religiously unaffiliated has steadily increased since 2007, to nearly 20 percent, and Protestants comprise less than half the population for the first time in U.S. history. Experts say fewer and fewer young adults are embracing the religious traditions of their elders and that more Americans are choosing to remain unaffiliated with any faith group.

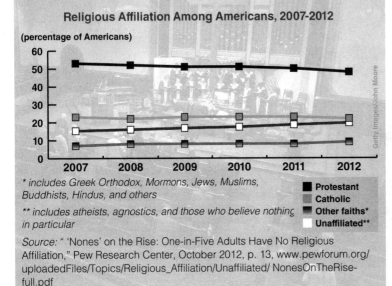

**Religious Affiliation Among Americans, 2007-2012**

(percentage of Americans)

■ Protestant
▨ Catholic
■ Other faiths*
□ Unaffiliated**

* includes Greek Orthodox, Mormons, Jews, Muslims, Buddhists, Hindus, and others

** includes atheists, agnostics, and those who believe nothing in particular

Source: " 'Nones' on the Rise: One-in-Five Adults Have No Religious Affiliation," Pew Research Center, October 2012, p. 13, www.pewforum.org/uploadedFiles/Topics/Religious_Affiliation/Unaffiliated/ NonesOnTheRise-full.pdf

- For the first time, Protestants are a minority in the United States: Only 48 percent of Americans identify themselves as Protestants — down from 53 percent in 2007.[8]

The nation's shifting demographic profile has huge implications for many facets of American life, noted Laura B. Shrestha and Elayne J. Heisler, researchers for the Congressional Research Service, which advises Congress on policy issues. "There is ample reason to believe that the United States will be able to cope with the current and projected demographic changes if policy makers accelerate efforts to address and adapt to the changing population profile as it relates to . . . work, retirement and pensions, private wealth and income security — and the health and well-being of the aging population," they wrote.[9]

Indeed, the rise in the average age of the U.S. population is among the benchmarks demographers and economists are watching most closely. The number of Americans 65 or older is expected to more than double between now and 2050 — from 40 million to 84.5 million. On Jan. 1, 2011, the first of the 78 million Americans born between 1946 and 1964 — the baby boomers — reached the traditional retirement age of 65. For the next 19 years, 10,000 more will cross that threshold every day, according to the Pew Research Center.[10]

Experts note that as a nation's citizens age out of the workforce, its tax base declines, reducing the amount of money available for pensions and publicly supported medical and residential needs. What's more, older people generally spend less on consumer goods, putting less money into the economy.

Yet, while an aging U.S. population poses challenges for social-welfare programs targeted at the elderly, including Medicare and Social Security, experts say the nation retains an economic advantage over Europe,

tick, tick — slowly, steadily," said Paul Taylor, executive vice president of the nonpartisan Pew Research Center. "Every four-year cycle the electorate gets a little bit more diverse. And it's going to continue."[6]

That diversity extends to Capitol Hill. Next year's 113th Congress will include 28 Latinos in the House of Representatives, the largest Latino class in U.S. history, and a third Latino will join the U.S. Senate.[7]

The nation's demographic evolution goes far beyond ethnicity, race and politics, however. For example:

- By 2030, more than one in five Americans will be age 65 or older, compared with about one in eight today.
- More than one-fourth of Americans have left the religious denomination of their childhood and either joined a different faith or abandoned organized religion altogether.

Japan and China, all of which are aging faster than the United States.[11] The reason for the U.S. edge, they say, is immigration. The Census Bureau estimates that 14 million immigrants came legally or illegally to the U.S. between 2000 and 2010 — the largest decennial influx in history. Some 40 million Americans — about one in eight — are foreign-born.[12]

"If the U.S. depended on white births alone, we'd be dead," said Dowell Myers, a professor of policy, planning and demography at the University of Southern California. "Without the contributions from all these other groups, we would become too top-heavy with old people."[13]

Myers noted that countries with low immigration rates, such as Japan, can end up with young, working-age populations too small to support the larger group of aging citizens.

Along with immigration, birth rates also are keeping America younger than other industrialized countries. Between 2000 and 2010, the Hispanic population — now the nation's largest minority — grew 43 percent, to more than 50 million, partly because the birth rate among Hispanics is 60 percent higher than among whites. The Asian-American population grew at about the same rate, reaching 17 million, while the black population rose 15.4 percent, to 42 million.

For some whites, predictions that minorities will grow to more than half of the U.S. population come as a jolt. They feel as though they had gone "from being a privileged group to all of a sudden becoming whites, the new victims," said Charles Gallagher, a sociologist at La Salle University in Pennsylvania who researches racial attitudes among whites.[14] In fact, a 2011 joint survey by the Brookings Institution and the Public Religion Research Institute, both in Washington, found that nearly half of whites believe discrimination against them is now as big a problem as discrimination against minorities.[15]

## Religion and the 2012 Election

White evangelicals and white Catholics largely backed GOP contender Mitt Romney in this year's presidential election, as did most members of his Mormon faith. Black Protestants and Hispanic Catholics largely supported President Obama's re-election. Experts say the ethnic identity of minority voters, who traditionally support Democratic candidates, often trumps religious affiliation at the polls. Religiously unaffiliated voters overwhelmingly backed Obama.

### Presidential Vote by Religious Affiliation and Race, 2012
(by percentage of voters)

| Religion | Barack Obama | Mitt Romney |
|---|---|---|
| **Total Percentage** | **50%** | **48%** |
| **Protestant/other Christian** | **42** | **57** |
| White Protestant/other Christian | 30 | 69 |
| Born-again/evangelical | 20 | 79 |
| Non-evangelical | 44 | 54 |
| Black Protestant/other Christian | 95 | 5 |
| **Catholic** | **50** | **48** |
| White Catholic | 40 | 59 |
| Hispanic Catholic | 75 | 21 |
| **Jewish** | **69** | **30** |
| **Mormon** | **21** | **78** |
| **Other faiths** | **74** | **23** |
| **Religiously unaffiliated** | **70** | **26** |

Source: "How the Faithful Voted: 2012 Preliminary Analysis," Pew Forum on Religion and Public Life, November 2012.

Meanwhile, "non-affiliated" is now the fastest-growing category in the nation's religious profile. Twenty percent of Americans say they have no church affiliation — up from 15 percent five years ago, according to a study by the Pew Forum on Religion and Public Life released in October. "Young people today are coming of age at a time when they are less religious than at any time before in our polling," says Greg Smith, a lead researcher on the study.

In what Smith calls a "churn" taking place in American religion, 28 percent of adults have left the faith in which they were raised to join another religion — or to practice no religion at all. Roughly 44 percent have either switched religious affiliation, rejoined a church after being unaffiliated or dropped out of organized religion altogether.[16]

AFP/Getty Images/Nicholas Kamm

Worshippers at the First Church of Seventh-day Adventists in Washington, D.C., on March 31, 2012, pray for the families of slain Florida teenager Trayvon Martin and the neighborhood watch volunteer who killed him. More than a fourth of Americans have left the religious denomination of their childhood and either joined a different faith or abandoned organized religion.

The Protestant decline marks an important transition point, says Randall Balmer, chairman of the religion department at Dartmouth College. But he adds, "The U.S. has always been a pluralistic country in terms of religion, and this is simply another indication that we are a religiously diverse people."

The Catholic Church has lost the most followers of any major denomination in the United States: Four Catholics leave the Church for every individual who converts to the faith.[17]

Nevertheless, about 25 percent identify themselves as Catholic, a proportion that has remained steady for decades, Smith notes. "Immigration from Latin America is boosting the size of the Catholic population, and it's mostly responsible for the Catholic share of the population holding steady," he says.

As demographic changes bring sweeping changes to American society, here are some of the questions being debated:

## Will changing demographics affect American values?

The late Harvard University political scientist Samuel P. Huntington feared that America was losing its way. He was particularly concerned about the influx of Hispanic immigrants, specifically from Mexico. Huntington feared that their sheer numbers and the rise of multiculturalism in the United States would be a challenge to America's "core culture."[18]

But Joel Kotkin, distinguished presidential fellow in urban futures at Chapman University in Orange, Calif., took a different view of immigrants. "America's ability to absorb newcomers represents . . . a new paradigm, where race itself begins to matter less than culture, class and other factors," he wrote. "Rather than a source of national decline, the new Americans represent the critical force that can provide the new markets, the manpower, and, perhaps most important, the youthful energy to keep our country vital and growing.[19]

Attitudes toward abortion and gay marriage are often seen as a yardstick of religious values. Hispanics — many of whom are Catholic — are more conservative than the U.S. population overall on abortion, according to a 2012 survey by the Pew Hispanic Center. Slightly more than half of Hispanics believe abortion should be illegal in all or most cases, compared to 41 percent of the general population.

Americans' support for same-sex marriage has been gradually increasing, and in 2011, according to the Pew Research Center, the public was evenly divided on whether gay and lesbian couples should be allowed to marry. A slim majority of Hispanics believes same-sex marriage should be legal.[20]

Pew also found that Asian-Americans' views on abortion and homosexuality largely mirror those of the nation at large. Like Hispanics, Asians are more likely to call themselves liberal — 31 percent do so — and less likely than the overall population to describe themselves as conservative.[21]

"Another measure of Americans' acceptance of diversity is the increase in interracial marriage, which demographers typically interpret to mean that race relations are improving, says Cornell University sociology professor Daniel Lichter. "It means the things that promote intimacy between racial and ethnic groups — for example, residential proximity or economic equality or similar levels of education — have taken place," Lichter says.

A 2012 study by the Pew Research Center showed that about 15 percent of all new marriages in the United States in 2010 were between spouses of different races or ethnicity, more than double the 6.7 percent share in 1980.[22]

However, "This doesn't mean that we're in a post-racial society," Lichter says. "We've made great strides, but we have an awfully long way to go before race doesn't matter in this culture."[23]

Twenty-eight percent of Asians married people of another race, the highest percentage of all ethnic groups. "The rate of intermarriage in the Asian-American, especially the Japanese-American, community is definitely having a cultural impact," says Lane Hirabayashi, a professor of Asian-American studies at the University of California, Los Angeles.

However, Hirabayashi also notes that the rate of increase of Asian interracial marriage has slowed. "Increasing immigration from Asia gives immigrants a larger pool of potential partners from the same ethnic group," he says.

John Nieto-Phillips, a history professor at Indiana University who specializes in Latino studies, says, "Latinos are comfortable with marrying a person of another heritage or background. Latinos are less comfortable, however, defining their own identity by existing racial categories. The 'browning of America' by way of intermarriage portends the blurring of conventional racial boundaries, though it may not mitigate the social or structural inequalities that tend to sustain boundaries."

Pew found that 43 percent of Americans feel that having more interracial marriages has been a change for the better, and nearly two-thirds say it "would be fine" with them if a member of their own family were to marry someone outside their own racial or ethnic group. In 1986, only one-third viewed intermarriage as acceptable.[24]

Pew Research Center researcher Kim Parker, who worked on the intermarriage study, says increased immigration over the past 40 years has helped spur the attitudinal change. "With greater diversity, there's more opportunity for people of different ethnic backgrounds to interact," Parker says. "As people get to know each other, the pool of 'candidates' becomes larger. And as an individual gains familiarity with people from different backgrounds, the degree of acceptance may rise."

It's difficult to generalize about baby boomers' impact on values. Some formed their political consciousness during the turbulent anti-Vietnam War movement, while many others were influenced by the conservative "Reagan Rebellion" of the early 1980s.

In general, however, according to a 2011 Pew survey, boomers appear to be nudging the values needle leftward. On issues such as abortion and same-sex marriage, they are somewhat less conservative than their parents' generation but less liberal than their children. Still, Pew found, in recent years "more boomers have come to call themselves conservatives [and] many . . . express reservations about the changing face of America. . . . Boomers' current attitudes bear little imprint from coming of age in an era of great social change."[25]

American University communications professor Leonard Steinhorn, author of *The Greater Generation: In Defense of the Baby Boom Legacy*, believes embracing diversity may be the boomers' chief lasting contribution to America. "It used to be that the white men who ran our businesses could exclude women and minorities with a wink and a nod," he says. "That's no longer acceptable. [Boomers] have made diversity a moral value. And they have created a cultural norm that says prejudice and discrimination are immoral; they have created new norms, and the children they have raised under those norms have internalized them."

Still, says Brookings Institution demographer William Frey, "Demography marches on. It's the younger population that [will] be living, working and building communities with each other in a very different kind of America. They are developing a different set of values, in terms of their acceptance of diversity — from having more mixed race and racially diverse friends, dating partners, spouses — and are generally more accepting of new social trends including same-sex couples, alternative religions, etc. They will also be more globally conscious due to their associations with more new Americans and their greater ability to "network" across the country and globally through social media. . . . [A]s we move into the next decade or two we're going to be much more about the people who are under age 30 than the people who are over age 50."

## Will the nation's demographic changes benefit the U.S. economy?

As the U.S. population ages, economists see both trouble and opportunity ahead.

The number of Americans 65 or older is expected to more than double by 2050, to about 84 million, and today's 65-year-old can expect to live another 20 years, up from 13 years in 1950.[26]

Increased longevity and a desire to remain active are spurring many older workers to remain in the labor

## Older Population on Rise

The number of Americans age 65 or older is projected to surpass 70 million by 2030. Experts cite two key reasons for the rise: the aging of the post-World War II baby boom generation and medical advances that have increased average life expectancy.

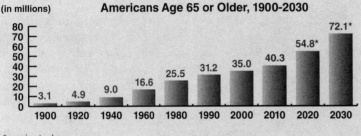

**Americans Age 65 or Older, 1900-2030**
(in millions)

*projected (72.1*, 54.8*)*

Bar values: 1900: 3.1, 1920: 4.9, 1940: 9.0, 1960: 16.6, 1980: 25.5, 1990: 31.2, 2000: 35.0, 2010: 40.3, 2020: 54.8*, 2030: 72.1*

\* projected

*Source:* "A Profile of Older Americans: 2011," Administration on Aging, U.S. Department of Health and Human Services, 2011, p. 3, www.aoa.gov/aoaroot/aging_statistics/Profile/2011/docs/2011profile.pdf

force. But so too are economic pressures, stemming in part from the loss of trillions of dollars in retirement assets during the recent recession.

Researchers Frank W. Heiland and Zhe Li of Boston College's Center for Retirement Research found that nearly 23 percent of men over age 65 were working in 2010, compared to 16.8 percent in 1994. The participation rate for women over 65 nearly doubled, from 7.4 percent in 1988 to 13.8 percent.[27]

As more older workers remain on the job, some experts believe they may be preventing younger workers from finding employment. One of the reasons [that young people can't find jobs is] because older people are not leaving the workforce," said Sung Won Sohn, an economist at California State University-Channel Islands.[28] But others disagree with the view that older workers are hurting the prospects of younger ones. There is "no evidence that increasing the employment of older persons reduces the job opportunities or wage rates of younger persons," said Alicia Munnell, director of the Center for Retirement Research. In fact, she said, "greater employment of older persons leads to better outcomes for the young in the form of reduced unemployment, increased employment and a higher wage."[29]

"Younger workers come into the labor force with a different vintage of education, and they don't have

work experience. So, you don't often find old and young workers clamoring for the same low-wage McDonald's job," said Jeffrey Zax, a professor at the University of Colorado who specializes in labor economics. Moreover, Zax said, "A senior worker with experience might allow a company to hire more junior employees because you have someone who can manage them."[30]

Inevitably, aging Americans will require medical care and specialized living and transportation accommodations — which will open up job opportunities for younger workers, says Sara Rix, senior strategic policy adviser at the AARP Public Policy Institute.

"The proportion of older people living in nursing homes is declining, but we are going to see a substantial increase in the 'very, very old' — people in their upper 90s and 100s — many of whom . . . will need assisted-living facilities." As a result, Rix says, construction workers will be needed to build and upgrade assisted-living facilities, and doctors, nurses and home health care workers will be needed to care for the elderly.

Even so, America's aging population poses deep challenges for the health care system. For example, a projected nursing shortage is expected to grow worse as baby boomers grow older and care needs grow.[31]

As policy makers debate the implications of America's aging population, they also are studying the impact of immigration — particularly the influx of undocumented workers — on the economy.

The Federation for American Immigration Reform (FAIR), a group in Washington that promotes reduced immigration, argues that by curbing illegal immigration, "there would be many more jobs available to native workers — jobs that paid higher wages and offered better working conditions."[32]

Pia Orrenius, an assistant vice president and senior economist with the Federal Reserve Bank of Dallas, says illegal immigration might have some adverse effects on employment among specific groups — native-born teenagers, for example. "It looks like if employers have the choice of an undocumented, somewhat higher-skilled 23- or 24-year-old, they'll take that person over a 16- to 19-year-old." But, she adds, "the effects are modest."

Julie Hotchkiss, a research economist and policy adviser at the Federal Reserve Bank of Atlanta, researched undocumented workers in Georgia. "Our research shows that newly arriving undocumented workers appear to displace only earlier-arriving undocumented workers," she said. "This makes sense since undocumented workers are going to be the closest substitutes for each other."[33]

Many economists say that immigrant workers have a positive effect on the economy. "There is no evidence that immigrants crowd out U.S.-born workers in either the short or long run," wrote Giovanni Peri, an economics professor at the University of California-Davis. "The economy absorbs immigrants by expanding opportunities rather than by displacing U.S.-born workers. Data show that, on net, immigrants expand the U.S. economy's productive capacity, stimulate investment and promote specialization that in the long run boosts productivity."[34]

Moreover, Peri says in an interview, in the short run the loss of immigrant workers would cause an economic contraction. And while the economy might recover, the loss of immigrant labor could turn out to be "quite costly.

"If we don't have people picking vegetables and fruit in California, for example, we'll end up importing [those products]. Other jobs can't be outsourced — such as construction workers or waiters. We have seen very few natives taking these jobs, especially at the low end . . . a lot of businesses will have to slim down or substitute with imports or pay more wages."

## Will changing demographics affect future U.S. elections?

Obama's victory in this year's presidential election was due, in the words of *The Hill*, a Washington newspaper that covers national politics, to "at least three concrete, demographic reasons" — the president's "broad advantage among female voters," his negation of the erroneous view "that black enthusiasm for Obama would taper off this year" and the fact that "Latinos went for Obama by even bigger margins than they did in 2008."[35]

While Obama may be particularly popular among female, black and Latino voters, many experts view the influence of those demographic groups in the 2012

Pedestrians pass an American flag mural in San Francisco's Chinatown on June 19, 2012. In 2011, the number of Asian immigrants who came to the United States outnumbered Hispanics for the first time: 438,000 came from East and South Asia and the Middle East, compared with 404,000 who arrived from Central or South America or the Caribbean.

election as a harbinger of how demographics might shape political destiny in campaigns of the future.

Ruy Teixeira, a senior fellow at the Center for American Progress, a liberal think tank in Washington, says a growing minority population and a shrinking white working class — a traditionally Republican-voting demographic — point to growing minority influence in future elections, a force he said would favor liberal candidates. However, he cautioned, "There is no guarantee that demographic trends will automatically lead to [electoral] dividends. . . . Parties always have to deliver."[36]

While the expected majority-minority tipping point for the general population is still 30 years off, it will come by 2023 for the younger sector of the population, primarily because of the rapid growth in the Hispanic population, according to Census Bureau estimates. Among children under age 17, about 17 million, or 23 percent, were Latinos, a rise of 39 percent in a decade, according to the Pew Hispanic Center. [37]

Brookings Institution demographer Frey said minorities' electoral influence is just becoming apparent. He pointed to the relative youth of the minority population: Currently, only 44 percent of Hispanics, 69 percent of African-Americans and 53 percent of Asians are eligible to vote, compared with 78 percent of whites. "It's because they are disproportionately below age 18, and among Hispanics and Asians, are less likely to be citizens," he says.

Whites still comprise 71 percent of the electorate, Frey pointed out, and will outnumber minority voters "well beyond" the 2012 election. Nevertheless, he added, "the handwriting is on the wall." In coming elections, as today's minority children reach the voting age of 18, "minority votes will matter, and both parties need to pay attention," Frey observed.[38]

Alan Abramowitz, a political science professor at Emory University in Atlanta, predicts that the minority electorate, which stood at 13 percent in 1992, will comprise more than a third of voters by the 2020 election.[39]

Cornell University's Lichter, who also directs the Cornell Population Center, believes the divide between older and younger voters is an issue to watch. He says, "In the 2012 elections, we saw a large, aging, mostly white population voting in one direction, and a mostly minority population voting differently. The question is, how will an older, aging, white population vote and what will it support? When older people vote, are they going to vote to support children of people who might not share the same culture?"

"In 15 or 20 years, today's minorities are going to be America's taxpayers and leaders," Lichter points out. "They're going to be replacing the white baby boom generation. Will they vote to support pension and health care programs for older, American, white baby boomers? And will boomers support the kind of education, employment and social programs that help make these groups good citizens?"

Raw numbers aren't the only measure of minority voters' influence; another is location. Teixeira and Frey wrote that minorities are strongly influencing election outcomes in "swing states," where races are particularly hotly contested. Between 2008 and 2012, the minority share of eligible voters rose 9 percent in Nevada, 4 percent in Florida and North Carolina, 3 percent in Colorado and Wisconsin, 2 percent in Pennsylvania and Michigan, and 1 percent in Virginia. At the same time, the share of white voters in those states declined by between 1 and 3 percent.[40] And of those states, all but North Carolina voted for Obama in 2012. As for the electorate's changing religious makeup, some scholars say that just because Hispanic immigrants are predominantly Catholic does not mean they constitute a Catholic voting bloc. Indeed, said presidential scholar John Kenneth White, a professor of politics at Catholic University (CU) in Washington, the "Catholic vote" has effectively vanished. "For Hispanics, ethnic identity trumps Catholic identity," he said at a Sept. 27, 2012, forum at the university.

In 2004 more Catholics voted for George W. Bush, an evangelical Christian, than for Catholic John Kerry. William Dinges, a CU professor of religion and culture, agrees there is no such thing as a Catholic vote any more. "People are becoming more independent," he said at the CU forum. "They can support a candidate or party who supports ideas not consistent with teachings of the faith. And, the church hierarchy can't force votes the way it once could."

For example, the tide appears to be changing with regard to gay marriage, which Catholic leaders and evangelical Protestants have strongly opposed. After voters rejected same-sex marriage in 32 state referendums since the late 1990s, a measure to legalize it passed on Nov. 6 in three states (Maine, Maryland and Washington), and a constitutional amendment to define marriage as between a man and a woman failed in Minnesota.[41]

According to a Pew Forum on Religion & Public Life analysis of exit polls, traditionally Republican groups such as white evangelicals and weekly churchgoers strongly backed Republican Mitt Romney, while traditionally Democratic groups such as black Protestants, Hispanic Catholics, Jews and the religiously unaffiliated backed Obama by large margins. Obama's support among white Catholics fell 7 percentage points from 2008 but gained 3 points among Hispanic Catholics. Meanwhile, his support among white evangelicals fell by 6 percentage points.[42]

The apparent growing electoral support for same-sex marriage indicates to some analysts that the political power of white evangelicals may be on the wane. Dartmouth's Balmer, an evangelical himself, says that while the religious right will continue to be a force in U.S. politics, its influence may be less apparent in coming elections.

"I think it's going to be a bit less forceful, less dramatic than it was in the 1980s and '90s and the first decade of the 21st century," Balmer says.

# BACKGROUND

## Pioneering Blacks

The first blacks who came to North America hundreds of years ago were not slaves — far from it.

In 1613, João Rodrigues — son of a Portuguese sailor and an African woman — served as a translator on a Dutch trading ship that had sailed to the North American island known as Manhatta. When the ship returned to Europe, Rodrigues stayed behind to start a trading post selling hatchets and knives provided by the ship's captain. He also served as an interpreter and facilitator for Dutch merchants who came to the island to trade with the Indians. That's how a black man became the first non-native American to live and do business in what was to become New York City.

A little over 150 years later, Jean Baptiste Point Sable — son of a French father and African mother and probably born in the Caribbean in what is now the Dominican Republic — established himself in North America as a trader at the mouth of a river in an area called Eschecagou. Point Sable, a black man, is regarded as the first non-Indian to set up permanent residence in present-day Chicago.

And in 1781, 26 full or mixed-race blacks were among the 44 Mexicans who settled the little pueblo that would become Los Angeles.

Far better known, of course, is the tragic history of the blacks who came to North America under extreme duress. England began taking captured Africans to serve as slaves in its Carolina colony in 1670. During the colonial period, an estimated 600,000 African slaves were brought to America. In 1808, Congress banned the importation of slaves, but the law was not seamlessly enforced. It did effectively end the transatlantic slave trade — though not the practice of slavery in the colonies. By 1860, the slave population in the United States was about 4 million.

With the end of the Civil War and ratification in 1865 of the 13th amendment abolishing slavery, blacks were granted citizenship. Black males gained the right to vote with ratification of the 15th Amendment in 1870. The postwar Reconstruction period saw improved educational and economic opportunities for Southern blacks, and many even were elected to public office. In the Carolinas alone, nearly 100 black legislators were elected during

Reconstruction, including 22 who were elected to Congress between 1870 and 1901.[43] Tens of thousands of African-Americans living in the North moved south to become teachers or farmers or just to reunite with families.

By 1876, however, the federal government's commitment to protect the rights of black citizens was wavering. States enacted harsh "Jim Crow" laws that institutionalized racial segregation in schools and other public places, and black voting was blocked by fraud, intimidation or worse. In 1896, a nearly unanimous U.S. Supreme Court, in the infamous *Plessy v. Ferguson* decision, upheld the concept that state laws could require separate facilities for blacks and whites, as long as the facilities were equivalent. But equivalence was left undefined. The ruling in effect conferred constitutionality to the South's Jim Crow caste system.

## Early Immigrants

In the first years of the democracy, immigration to the United States was relatively slight; even so, one of the early legislative acts of the cautious Founding Fathers was the Naturalization Act of 1790, which limited naturalized citizenship to "free white persons" of "good moral character."

Immigration gathered momentum in the early 19th century. During the 1820s, 143,000 immigrants were reported; in the following decade, immigration — mostly by Irish and Germans — more than quadrupled. The 1840s recorded 1,713,000 immigrants, nearly half of them from Ireland escaping the 1845-49 potato famine. Politics also helped swell the immigrant tide, as unsuccessful European revolutions in 1848 spurred large numbers of intellectuals and political activists to flee their homelands. By 1850 foreign-born residents made up 9.7 percent of America's 23 million population.

While early post-colonial America was largely a Protestant nation, large numbers of Catholics were absorbed with the acquisition of the Louisiana Purchase from France in 1803, Florida from Spain in 1819, and territory in what is now New Mexico and California in 1847 as a result of the Mexican-American War.

The second half of the century saw the Catholic population triple, in large part the result of immigration from Europe — notably Ireland, Italy, and Poland. By 1906, there were 14 million Catholics in America, 17 percent of the total population.[44]

Asian immigrants were rare in North America until 1849, when Chinese workers were recruited to work in the California gold fields, and later to help build the transcontinental railway system and work in other, mostly menial, jobs. As the Chinese population grew, racial prejudice and distrust increased among whites, and in 1882 Congress passed the Chinese Exclusion Act, which ended immigration by Chinese laborers. The law also made Chinese immigrants already in the country ineligible for citizenship.

## Expanding Equality

The 20th century saw the United States experience major demographic changes. The start of World War I (1914-1918) helped spark the mass South-to-North movement of African-Americans, and the end of World War II (1939-1945) led to the birth of the baby boom generation — the largest population bulge in the nation's history. In addition, after the United States loosened immigration restrictions, a flood of new citizens dramatically altered the country's ethnic mixture. All these forces began to come together around the middle of the 20th century, ultimately changing the way Americans perceived each other and their own values.

Meanwhile, the black population, which had reached 8.8 million by 1900 — 90 percent of whom lived in the South — began to change rapidly in the early to mid-1900s. Jobs were being created in the rapidly industrializing North, while the South's oppressive Jim Crow laws were spurring a mass exodus known as the Great Migration. Over six decades, an estimated 6 million blacks left the South for new lives in the North and West.

Mexican migration also began to accelerate in the early to mid-20th century. It had begun in the late 1800s with the building of the railroads across the American Southwest. By 1900, half a million Mexicans were living in the United States. Though they weren't treated as well as Northern European immigrants, Mexicans didn't experience the same exclusion as Asians. All Mexicans living in territories acquired from Mexico were granted citizenship. In 1897, a U.S. district court ruled that the skin color of Mexicans should not be a factor in determining eligibility for citizenship.

The vast majority, however, had no interest in citizenship. "Why bother to become an American citizen when the land one loved, the land of family, language and

*la raza* (the people or race), was so close by?," wrote historian Lawrence H. Fuchs.[45]

But eligibility for citizenship didn't stop discrimination, of course. "The Mexican-American has been the black man of the Southwest," wrote Ronnie Lopez, executive assistant to former Arizona Democratic Gov. Bruce Babbitt. "There have been rapings and lynchings. . . . People's land was taken from them."[46]

The immigrant waves of the first quarter of the century brought another 750,000 legal immigrants from Mexico. The flow ebbed during the Great Depression, when many recent Mexican arrivals voluntarily returned to their homeland, and the United States tightened its immigration policy. Some 400,000 Mexicans — including many born in the United States — were deported. Mexican immigration to the United States picked up again — though slightly — in the 1940s, spurred by wartime labor shortages. In 1942, the nation initiated the "Bracero" guestworker program, under which large numbers of temporary workers were transported north. The program was supposed to end with the war but lasted until Congress refused to renew it in 1964. The Mexican guestworkers — 4.8 million over the life of the program — worked in at least 38 states, mostly picking fruit and vegetables in the Southwest.[47]

By the 1960s, public sympathy for the Civil Rights Movement was spreading across the country, giving President Lyndon B. Johnson (1963-1969) the support he needed to push through the 1964 Civil Rights Act, which outlawed segregation in public places. A year later, Johnson signed the Voting Rights Act of 1965, significantly improving blacks' access to the polls.

The new laws were the crowning legislative achievements of the Civil Rights Movement and reflected its successful effort to mobilize public support for its cause. The movement's success also inspired other groups that felt they were treated unfairly. Feminist scholar Jo Freeman wrote, "During the fifties and early sixties, the Civil Rights Movement captured the public imagination and educated it on the immorality of discrimination and the legitimacy of mass protest . . . . For women, it provided not only a model for action but a very different world view from that of the 'separate spheres' [for women and men], which had been the reigning ideology for the previous century."[48]

# CHRONOLOGY

**1600s-1700s** *Slavery is introduced to North America.*

**1670-1783** England begins importing African slaves to its Carolina colony. Some 600,000 African slaves are brought to America during the colonial period.

**1790** Congress restricts naturalized citizenship to "free white persons" of "good moral character."

**1800s** *Slavery is abolished, and new rights are granted to African-Americans.*

**1808** Congress bans the transatlantic slave trade but not slavery.

**1849** Chinese laborers recruited for California gold fields.

**1863** President Abraham Lincoln issues the Emancipation Proclamation, declaring slaves in the Confederate states to be free.

**1865** Thirteenth Amendment to Constitution is ratified Dec. 1, freeing all slaves.

**1866** Congress enacts legislation giving blacks full citizenship.

**1870** Fifteenth Amendment gives black men the right to vote.

**1876** First "Jim Crow" laws in South mandate segregated public facilities.

**1882** Chinese Exclusion Act forbids immigration by Chinese laborers.

**1896** Supreme Court upholds "separate but equal" doctrine for whites and blacks in *Plessy v. Ferguson.*

**1900s-1945** *Congress seeks "homogeneity" by favoring immigrants from northern and western Europe while severely restricting everyone else. U.S. blacks migrate northward for jobs and rights.*

**1915** Blacks begin "Great Migration" from the South to the North.

**1924** Immigration Act of 1924 essentially limits citizenship to immigrants from northern and western Europe.

**1943** Congress repeals Chinese Exclusion Act (but 1924 Immigration Act is still in force).

**1946-2000** *Post-war baby boom creates huge population "bulge." Immigrant pool expands. Civil Rights Movement makes major advances.*

**1946** First of 78 million post-World War II baby boomers are born.

**1963** March for Jobs and Freedom attracts up to 300,000 demonstrators to Washington in pivotal moment for the Civil Rights Movement.

**1964** President Lyndon B. Johnson signs Civil Rights Act, outlawing segregation in public places.

**1965** Immigration and Nationality Act opens citizenship to Asians, Hispanics, Africans and others largely excluded by the 1924 Immigration Act. The Supreme Court, in *Loving v. Virginia*, unanimously rules that restrictions on interracial marriage are unconstitutional."

**1970s** Rev. Jerry Falwell and other leaders call on conservative Christians to become politically active; the Religious Right becomes political force.

**2000s–Present** *America contemplates "majority-minority" status. Baby boomers enter old age.*

**2001** U.S. Hispanic population reaches 37 million, making Latinos the largest ethnic minority.

**2008** Census Bureau projects that by 2042 whites will no longer be majority in the United States.

**2011** Minority births outnumber white newborns. . . . Net Mexican immigration to United States falls to zero, mostly in response to Great Recession that began in 2007. First baby boomers reach retirement age of 65.

**2012** Religion survey indicates that for the first time Protestants comprise less than half of Americans.

# Black Migration Makes a U-Turn

*Millions fled the South, but many are returning.*

Demographers and historians call it the "Great Migration," an extraordinary exodus of blacks from the South to the urban North throughout much of the 20th century. Now that epic shift is reversing, bringing millions of African-Americans back to a region that once shunned or tormented them and their ancestors.

Between 1916 and 1975, an estimated 6 million African-Americans left the South in search of greater economic opportunity and social freedom in cities such as Chicago, Detroit, Cleveland and New York. But in the 1990s demographers began to notice something remarkable: Millions of black Americans were leaving their homes and jobs in the North and returning to their roots in the South.

Census data released in 2011 show that 57 percent of American blacks now live in the South, the highest percentage since 1960. Michigan and Illinois, home to large concentrations of African-Americans, both lost black population for the first time, according to the 2010 census, and Atlanta replaced Chicago as the city with the second-largest African-American population, after New York. More than one million blacks now living in the South were born in the Northeast, a 10-fold increase since 1970.[1]

"This is the decade of black flight," Brookings Institution demographer William Frey told *The New York Times* last year.[2]

Frey credited the return of many blacks to the South to an improved racial and economic climate there, along with "the strong cultural and economic ties that the South holds for blacks." Even so, he noted that "blacks, by and large, are not settling in the Deep South states that registered the greatest out-migration of blacks in the 1960s" and where discriminatory "Jim Crow" laws restricted blacks' freedom.[3]

That out-migration began in earnest in the second decade of the 20th century, driven by the demand for workers in Northern munitions factories during World War 1.

Between 1916 and 1919, half a million African-Americans came North.

Yet, jobs were far from the only lure for Southern blacks. Isabel Wilkerson, author of the Pulitzer Prize-winning portrait of the Great Migration, *The Warmth of Other Suns*, frames the migration as a flight from racial hatred and abuse.

"This was . . . a defection from a system that had held [black] Americans in an artificial hierarchy that restricted their every move . . .," Wilkerson told *CQ Researcher* in an e-mail interview. "They were, in effect, seeking political asylum from a caste system that limited every aspect of their lives and [that] was enforced with such brutality that, in the two decades leading up to the Migration, an African-American was lynched in a public spectacle every four days for some perceived breach of that caste system."

The economic impact the South faced from the exodus of blacks wasn't apparent at first. Some Southerners gloated: "As the North grows blacker, the South grows whiter," the New Orleans *Times-Picayune* wrote.[4]

Then, as the implications of the loss of so much of the South's agricultural workforce became clear, worry set in. Southern authorities tried to stem the hemorrhaging of cheap farm labor by invoking "anti-enticement" laws to discourage agents from northern companies from recruiting blacks.[5] But it was too late: The Great Migration was on. And it kept going long after the lure of Northern jobs ended following World War I.

"Those in the World War I-era wave of the Great Migration didn't see their move as permanent — they thought when the war was over, they'd go back home," says Lorenzo Morris, a political science professor at Howard University in Washington. "But when the war ended, although it was difficult to stay [in the North], to return was intolerable."

Lessons from the Civil Rights Movement also helped to frame the push for gay rights. Bayard Rustin, a civil rights leader and a key organizer of the landmark 1963 March on Washington, later turned the lessons he had learned to promoting gay rights. "Today, blacks are no longer the litmus paper or the barometer of social change," he said in 1986. "The new 'niggers' are gays. . . . It is in this sense that gay people are the new barometer for social change."[49]

## The New Newcomers

The Exclusion Act, which prohibited Chinese and most other Asians from immigrating to the United States,

During the post-war 1920s, the industrial economy kept booming, and so did the migration: Nearly a million more blacks headed North during the decade, and nearly half a million more left the South during the Depression era of the 1930s. The exodus continued — 1.6 million in the 1940s, 1.4 million in the '50s, another million in the '60s. When the Great Migration began, one in 10 American blacks lived outside the South; by the 1970s, nearly one in two did.[6] Within the migration statistics is evidence of an evolution in American society, culture and politics. "Many leading figures in American culture — from [writers] Toni Morrison and August Wilson to [performers] Miles Davis and Aretha Franklin to [sports figures] Jesse Owens and Jackie Robinson — are people whose names we likely would never have known had there been no Great Migration," Wilkerson said in the e-mail interview. "Each one of them was a child of this Migration, whose life chances were altered because their parents or grandparents chose to escape the restrictions of the South."

The Great Migration came to a close in the 1970s after its over-arching catalyst — a caste system sanctioned by law — ended with passage of landmark civil rights legislation during the previous decade. By the 1990s, the Great Migration had turned around. But its legacy lives on.

"Perhaps one of the least recognized effects of the migration was its role, unintended though it was, in helping bring the South into mainstream culture and ultimately helping it open up to the rest of the country," Wilkerson said in the e-mail interview. "The upending of the caste system brought the South more in line with the rest of the country and made it a more welcoming place for white Northerners and for immigrants who might never have considered living there under the old regime, as well as for the children and grandchildren of black Southerners who had fled in previous generations.

"The return migration of many of the children and grandchildren of the Great Migration is, in my view, one of the legacies of the Great Migration itself," Wilkerson continued. "The people who left, by their heartbreaking decision

An estimated 6 million African-Americans left the South between 1916 and 1975 in search of greater economic opportunity and social freedom, settling in such cities as Chicago, Detroit, Cleveland and New York. Today, many blacks are leaving the North and returning to their Southern roots.

to leave, helped to change the region they had been forced to flee and make it a more welcoming place for everyone, including immigrants from other parts of the world, for white Northerners who might never have considered living in the South and for the migrants' own descendants."

*— Bill Wanlund*

[1] Sabrina Tavernise and Robert Gebeloff, "Many U.S. Blacks Moving to South, Reversing Trend," *The New York Times*, March 24, 2011, www.nytimes.com/2011/03/25/us/25south.html?pagewanted=all.

[2] Quoted in *ibid.*

[3] William Frey, "The New Great Migration: Black Americans' Return to the South, 1965-2000", The Brookings Institution, May 2004, www.brookings.edu/~/media/research/files/reports/2004/5/demographics%20frey/20040524_frey.

[4] Isabel Wilkerson, *The Warmth of Other Suns: The Epic Story of America's Great Migration* (2010), p. 162.

[5] *Ibid.*

[6] *Ibid.*, p. 8.

was repealed in 1943, when China was an American ally in World War II. However, another strict law — the Immigration Act of 1924, which put annual quotas on the number of immigrants from each country who could be accepted into the United States — was still in effect.

In a later analysis, the State Department historian's office wrote, "The most basic purpose of the 1924 Immigration Act was to preserve the ideal of American homogeneity."[50] To do so, the act tied the quotas to numbers from the 1890 census, in a thinly disguised attempt to limit a new flood of immigrants — many of

# Boomers More Conservative but Still Feisty

*Mistrust of government still spurs '60s generation.*

Forty years ago, the anti-establishment protests of the baby boom generation helped end the Vietnam War. Today, many of those same boomers form the core of the conservative Tea Party movement.

The Tea Party phenomenon reflects a general move to the right by many of the 78 million Americans born between 1946 and 1964, pollsters and demographers say. In 2008, 12 percent of boomers identified themselves as liberal, compared with 30 percent in 1972, according to the American National Election Survey. Meanwhile, the percentage calling themselves conservative more than doubled, from 21 percent to 46 percent.[1]

Still, many experts say the ideological transformation of the boomer generation is not inconsistent with its formative ideals in the 1960s.

"Tea Partiers are mistrustful of authority," says Leonard Steinhorn, a communications professor at American University in Washington who has studied the boomers. "In many ways that distrust of any sort of power or authority is not so dissimilar to what so many boomers throughout the years have expressed against either unchecked power or illegitimate authority, which many felt was exercised during the Vietnam War."

The Pew Research Center, which tracks Americans' social and political attitudes, says many boomers who pushed for sweeping societal change in the '60s are feeling uncomfortable with demographic and cultural shifts occurring in society today.

"Many boomers express reservations about the changing face of America," the Pew Research Center said in a report outlining the results of a survey on political views. "Boomers' current attitudes bear little imprint from coming of age in an era of great social change."[2]

Citing the Pew report, William Frey, a demographer at the Brookings Institution, a Washington think tank, noted boomers' attitudes on immigration. "[Twenty-three] percent of baby boomers regard the country's growing population of immigrants as a change for the better," he wrote. "Forty-three percent saw it as a change for the worse. Almost half of white boomers said the growing number of newcomers from other countries represented a threat to traditional U.S. customs and values."[3]

The conservative shift belies boomers' popular image — honed by the counterculture of the 1960s — as left-wing idealists whose motto was "don't trust anyone over 30."

Under that banner, boomers challenged the "establishment" over issues such as the Vietnam War, racial and sexual equality and matters of faith. More than 60 percent left organized religion, most while in their teens or early 20s, though about a third of those eventually returned.[4]

them poor and uneducated — from Eastern and Southern Europe. So, while the law allowed immigration by about 51,000 Germans and 62,000 people from Great Britain and Ireland, it permitted fewer than 4,000 Italians and around 2,000 Russians to enter. In fact, 86.5 percent of the yearly immigrant quota of 164,667 was to come from northwest Europe and Scandinavia.[51]

With only minor modifications, the act remained in force for 40 years. Then, reflecting the growing atmosphere of tolerance in the 1960s, Congress passed the Immigration and Nationality Act of 1965, which abolished the national origins quota system. The new law limited to 170,000 the total number of immigrants allowed into the country but eliminated regional quotas and tied immigration to immigrants' skills and family relationships with citizens or U.S. residents.

"This is not a revolutionary bill," President Johnson said at the time. "It does not affect the lives of millions. . . . It will not reshape the structure of our daily lives or add importantly to either our wealth or our power."[52]

Johnson may have underestimated the impact of the law, or he may have been understating the case to ease the fears of nervous nationalists. In any event, 30 years after the law went into effect, the United States had admitted more than 18 million new immigrants, more than three times the number who had entered over the previous three decades.

This time, instead of northern Europeans, immigrants from Latin America topped the list. While European immigrants made up nearly 60 percent of the United States' total foreign population in 1970,

A 2009 survey by pollster John Zogby found that 36 percent of boomers thought their generation would be remembered for its self-indulgence, compared with 31 percent who said its legacy would be social change.[5]

Still, in gauging the boomer generations' legacy, it's important to see the nation's transformation in the past four decades in a positive light, Steinhorn says.

"We are a far better, more inclusive, more equal, more free, more environmentally conscious and less bigoted and prejudiced society than we have ever been in our nation's history," he says. "And given that our nation's original sin was built on bigotry and discrimination . . ., we have come a very long way in just a few decades."

— *Bill Wanlund*

[1]Survey cited by Karlyn Bowman and Andrew Rugg, "As the Baby Boomers Turn," *Los Angeles Times*, Sept. 12, 2011, www.latimes/news/opinion/commentary/la-oe-bowman-baby-boomers-more-conservative-20010912,0,4867587.story.

[2]"The Generation Gap and the 2012 Election," Pew Research Center for the People and the Press, Nov. 3, 2011, p. 11, www.people-press.org/2011/11/03/the-generation-gap-and-the-2012-election/3.

[3]William Frey, "Baby Boomers Had Better Embrace Change," *The Washington Post*, June 8, 2012, www.brookings.edu/research/opinions/2012/06/08-baby-boomers-frey.

[4]Research by Prof. Wade Clark Roof, cited in Leonard Steinhorn, *The Greater Generation* (2006).

[5]John Zogby, "The Baby Boomers' Legacy," *Forbes.com*, July 23, 2009, www.forbes.com/2009/07/22/baby-boomer-legacy-change-consumer-opinions-columnists-john-zogby.html.

AFP/Getty Images/Kimihiro Hoshino

Some 78 million Americans, known as the baby boom generation, were born between 1946 and 1964. In 2008, 12 percent of boomers identified themselves as liberal, compared with 46 percent who said they were conservative.

they accounted for only 15 percent by the end of the century. The percentage of immigrants from Latin America, however, grew from less than 19 percent to more than 50 percent in the same period.[53]

In recent years the United States has admitted more than a million new immigrants annually. Today, Hispanics make up the lion's share of the immigrant population. Nearly 22 million, or around 55 percent of foreign-born Americans, came from Central or South America or the Caribbean; about 404,000 arrived in 2011 alone, or about 37 percent of the total.

However, in 2011, for the first time, Asian immigrants outnumbered Hispanics: Some 438,000 came from East and South Asia and the Middle East, representing 41 percent of new immigrants. About 8.4 percent of American immigrants came from Europe, another 9.1 percent from Africa and the remainder, around 5.1 percent, from "other regions" — principally, Canada and Oceania.[54]

Overall, the U.S. population is aging. In 1950, when the baby boom was just getting under way, 8.2 percent of Americans were 65 or older; now, with the boomers reaching that age, 13.3 percent are in that age bracket.[55] Meanwhile, the birth rate is declining: The United States recorded 4 million births in 2010, down 3 percent from the previous year, continuing a recent trend.[56]

These factors, along with increasing longevity (expected life span in the United States now is about 78.5 years), pushed the median age of Americans to 37.2 in 2010 — up from 35.3 in 2000. "The aging of the baby boom population, along with stabilizing birth rates and longer life expectancy, have contributed to the increase in median age," according to the Census Bureau.[57]

# CURRENT SITUATION

## Immigration Standstill

Once a flood, the flow of immigrants from Mexico into the United States has come to a halt.

In April, the Pew Hispanic Center reported that since 2007 net immigration from Mexico — the single largest source of immigrants to the United States — had dropped to zero. Mexicans are still emigrating to the United States, the center said, but just as many, and maybe more, are returning home.

"The standstill appears to be the result of many factors, including the weakened U.S. job and housing construction markets, heightened border enforcement, a rise in deportations, the growing dangers associated with illegal border crossings, the long-term decline in Mexico's birth rates and broader economic conditions in Mexico," Pew said.[58]

Audrey Singer, a senior fellow at the Metropolitan Policy Program at the Brookings Institution, believes the decline is due largely to developments in Mexico. "They've been sending labor to the U.S. for one or two generations, but now they have a shrinking supply themselves. Fertility rates are dropping, and they have a birthrate close to ours. Moreover, Mexican education levels are rising, and people are deciding not to come who may have taken a chance before."

The immigration pause is not likely to continue, however, she says. "We can probably assume that when our economy begins to pick up, immigration from Mexico will resume."

Even with the recent slowdown, America has about 12 million Mexican immigrants — more immigrants than from all other countries combined. Roughly 10 percent of people born in Mexico currently reside in the United States.[59]

However, more than half of the Mexicans in the United States are undocumented, according to the Department of Homeland Security, a fact that stirs heated debate, especially in the Border States.[60] Cities and states have adopted a variety of measures to deal with illegal immigration, including a controversial law adopted by Arizona in 2010 aimed at driving illegal immigrants away. Known as SB 1070, the measure requires law enforcement officials to check the immigration papers of suspected undocumented workers.[61]

Under challenge in the courts, SB 1070 is regarded as at least partly responsible, along with high unemployment rates, for a sharp decline in the number of undocumented immigrants in Arizona, from 560,000 in 2008 to 360,000 in 2011.[62]

"The greatest effect of the bill is its deterrent effect," said Republican state Rep. John Kavanagh, a sponsor of SB 1070. "It probably scared a lot of illegal immigrants from coming here in the first place or staying if they were here." Kavanagh said the loss of illegal immigrants opened up job opportunities for U.S. citizens and legal immigrants at a time when the state's unemployment rate is 9.5 percent. "So losing 100,000 or 200,000 workers who were undercutting legal workers and depressing wages is a big plus, as far as I am concerned," he said. "Good riddance."[63]

But the Center for American Progress, a liberal Washington, D.C., research organization that opposes the legislation, estimates that if all undocumented workers were expelled from Arizona, the state would lose $29.5 billion in pre-tax salary and wage earnings, $4.2 billion in tax revenue and more than 500,000 jobs for both legal and undocumented workers.[64]

## Dayton Model

In some places, especially cities far removed from the Border States, public officials are encouraging immigration instead of discouraging it.

For instance, the once-thriving manufacturing center of Dayton, Ohio, started losing population in the 1970s after businesses began relocating to Sun Belt states with cheaper, non-union labor. General Motors closed a large assembly plant in 2008, eliminating 2,400 jobs; NCR, born in Dayton in 1884 as the National Cash Register Co., moved to Atlanta in 2009, eliminating another 1,000 jobs. Dayton's population plunged 42 percent between 1970 and 2010, sinking to 141,000. Unemployment is currently over 10 percent.

Hoping to end the downward spiral, civic leaders in 2011 introduced the "Welcome Dayton" initiative to attract immigrant entrepreneurs and workers. Welcome Dayton serves as a catalyst for public institutions such as police, libraries and community-service organizations to help brand the city as immigrant-friendly. For instance, the city's teachers are offered classes in Spanish, Arabic, Turkish and Swahili to make it easier for them to work with immigrant students.

Dayton also helped to establish a center to provide education, recreation and other services to immigrants for the region's Ahiska Turkish community. Officials plan to authorize grants to help immigrants establish businesses, and the city's First Annual World Soccer Tournament, held in September, featured local adult and youth teams representing the international community.

Tom Wahlrab, who retired in January as director of the city's Office of Human Rights, says, "Two things are fueling Welcome Dayton: The need for economic development and the human factor. Many of those who are coming are refugees with a lot of needs. Unless we recognize those needs and do what we can to help them gain a foothold in our community, they're going to be a burden. They won't be productive, and they're going to cost the community in terms of the social services we'll need to provide."

It's too early to measure concrete results, although Dayton in 2011 added 600 new residents, Wahlrab says — a small gain, but the first population increase after 40 years of steady decline. Still, other localities are taking notice. Financially strapped Detroit, which launched "Global Detroit" in 2010 with the slogan, "Welcoming and Connecting the World to Our City," invited Wahlrab to come and discuss Dayton's experiences. "There is a certain elegance and opportunity in the plan that Dayton has put together," said Steve Tobocman, director of Global Detroit. "They've done certain things so profoundly right that I think we have a lot to learn from it."[65]

## Aging in Place

As cities and states try to adjust to immigration trends, they also are beginning to taking steps — albeit haltingly in some cases — to accommodate the transportation, housing, health and other needs of the aging population. In eight years, one-fourth of residents in half of Ohio's counties will be at least 60 years old, and Arizona and Pennsylvania are projecting that a quarter of their residents will top age 60 by 2020.[66]

Some cities are stepping up to the challenge. For example:

• New York City, where more than one in eight residents are over 60, established Age-Friendly New York City, which officials describe as "promoting an 'age-in-everything' lens across all aspects of city life. The initiative asks the city's public agencies, businesses, cultural, educational and religious institutions, community

Young people at the Coalition for Humane Immigrant Rights of Los Angeles on Aug. 15, 2012, hear about a new federal program under which eligible undocumented young people can avoid deportation and obtain work permits. Many economists argue that immigrant workers have a positive effect on the economy, but others contend that curbing immigration would leave more jobs for U.S.-born workers.

*Getty Images/Kevork Djansezian*

groups and individuals to consider how changes to policy and practice can create a city more inclusive of older adults and more sensitive to their needs." The effort, formed in 2009, is part of a broader Age-friendly Cities project sponsored by the World Health Organization.[67]

• In Atlanta, where one-fifth of residents will be over age 60 by 2030, the Atlanta Regional Commission created a Lifelong Communities Initiative aimed at promoting housing and transportation options, encouraging healthy lifestyles and expanding information and access to services tailored to older residents.[68]

Still, many localities are ill-prepared to accommodate the coming wave of older residents, experts say. A 2005 survey of communities by the National Association of Area Agencies on Aging found that while many communities had some programs for older people, "few had undertaken a comprehensive assessment to create a 'livable community' for all ages." A 2011 follow-up survey found "only limited progress" toward that goal, the group said. Indeed, as a result of the recent recession, "most communities have been able only to 'hold the line' — maintaining policies, programs and services already established," the association said. "They have not been able to move

# Is large-scale immigration good for the U.S. economy?

## YES
**Audrey Singer**
*Senior Fellow,*
*The Brookings Institution*

Written for *CQ Global Researcher*, November 2012

The typical way of viewing immigration's impact on the economy is through costs and benefits derived from their presence in the labor market.

While economists debate how best to address this issue, there is some agreement that immigrants are a net benefit as measured by national GDP.

A benefit of a steady flow of immigrant workers to the United States is that they are responsive to labor-market changes and can go where workers are needed. This is especially so for newcomers, who tend to be most flexible on where to locate. The plateauing of immigration to the United States in response to declining jobs following the recession is an important illustration at the national level; many local areas mirror this trend.

It is not surprising, then, that the greatest economic impact of immigrants is at the state and local levels, where the brunt of costs to schools, health care systems and law enforcement is borne.

In the past two decades, immigrant settlement patterns have shifted significantly. Between 1930 and 1990, half of all immigrants in the United States lived in just five metropolitan areas, primarily in the Northeast and Midwest. Since then, the share in the top five places has declined to 40 percent, as immigrants have found opportunities in new places, particularly in the South and West.

Areas with new immigrant streams are more focused on the costs of immigration because, at least in the pre-recession economy, these areas attracted low-wage undocumented workers at a fast pace.

Estimates summarized by the Congressional Budget Office in 2007 show that in the aggregate and over the long term, tax revenues paid by immigrants are greater than the services they use. However, unauthorized immigrants use more state and local services than they pay for because of the types of services provided and because of the eligibility rules.

For example, while the percentage of school-age children of unauthorized immigrants is small nationally, this population tends to be concentrated at the very local level, and thus its impact can be swift.

The long-term view brings an important economic benefit into focus. Most of the future growth of the U.S. labor force will come from immigrants and their offspring. This next generation of workers will support the large cohort of baby boom retirees that now looms large. This is a reward that the United States should reap — with proper investments — as the next economy and workforce take shape.

## NO
**Madeleine Sumption**
*Senior Policy Analyst,*
*Migration Policy Institute*

Written for *CQ Global Researcher*, March 2012

The assertion that large-scale immigration is good for the U.S. economy implies that more immigration is inherently better than less. This is not necessarily true. The types of immigrants a country has — and whether their skills meet U.S. labor market needs — arguably matters much more than raw numbers.

Most economists believe that immigration to the United States has raised average incomes (albeit recognizing the gains are not universal), and that immigrants — through their tax contributions — make it easier to provide public services without raising tax rates. Other research suggests immigrants have contributed disproportionately to innovation and productivity. But these findings come with caveats.

First, not all immigration is the same, and the benefits of some types of immigration are more clear-cut than others. The greatest economic gains come from highly skilled immigrants, many of whom compete for the tiny share of permanent visas available for employment-based immigration. (Most U.S. green cards are issued on the basis of family ties, not prospective economic value.)

Low-skilled immigrants bring some economic benefits, such as lower prices for goods and services like food and child care. But these overwhelmingly low-paid workers also draw on public services such as education. More selective policies to admit and retain the low-skilled workers best able to support themselves might help shift this calculus. Balancing current costs and benefits, the overall economic impact of low-skilled workers today is probably close to zero.

The green card lottery, known as the diversity visa, is also likely to have a low economic return, since its annual 50,000 beneficiaries fare relatively poorly in the U.S. labor market. A similar argument applies to some refugees and to the parents and adult siblings of U.S. citizens. These types of immigration are almost certainly not economically detrimental, and there are plenty of noneconomic arguments in their favor (like the value of family unity and the moral obligation to protect people fleeing persecution). The economic arguments, however, are not particularly compelling.

Immigration policies are adopted with more than economic benefit in mind — and for good reason. But if the goal is purely economic gain, simply opening the immigration spigot is not the best strategy. Rather than a bottom-line focus on numbers, a more reliable approach for making immigration an engine for economic growth would be to create more thoughtful, predictable and transparent policies to select the immigrant workers who will succeed here.

forward to the degree needed to address the nation's current 'age wave.'"[69]

"The bottom line is, the baby boomers are hitting," Charles Gehring, president and CEO of LifeCare Alliance, an agency that serves seniors in central Ohio, told the *Columbus Dispatch*. "Are communities prepared for this? No."[70]

# OUTLOOK:

## Political Changes

The 2012 presidential election underscored in dramatic fashion the crucial role that demographic changes are having in political and policy circles. Experts expect that role to grow even stronger in coming years as the profile of the electorate continues to evolve.

Many analysts believe the Republican Party fared poorly in this year's election in part because it did not do enough to address the interests of the nation's burgeoning Hispanic population. "The Hispanic population will grow faster than any other demographic, meaning this political problem is growing for Republicans," GOP strategist Matt Mackowiak told *The Hill* after the Nov. 6 elections. "We need more Hispanic candidates, more Hispanic outreach and less bellicose language on immigration."[71]

Former Secretary of State Condoleezza Rice, who served in the administration of Republican George W. Bush, said Republicans had sent "mixed messages" on immigration and women's issues and must do a better job of adapting to changing U.S. demographics.

"Right now for me, the most powerful argument is that the changing demographics in the country really necessitate an even bigger tent for the Republican Party," she said. "But when you look at the composition of the electorate, clearly we are losing important segments of that electorate, and what we have to do is to appeal to those people not as identity groups but understanding that if you can get the identity issues out of the way, then you can appeal on the broader issues that all Americans share concerns for."[72]

The demographic challenges facing policy makers in coming years cross party lines, however. Dealing with the burgeoning ranks of seniors and adequately funding Social Security, Medicare and Medicaid — which pays

for nursing home care for low-income elderly people — are among the biggest challenges.

More than 56 million Americans now receive Social Security benefits, and 23 percent of married couples and about 46 percent of unmarried persons who are 65 years old or older rely on Social Security for 90 percent or more of their income.[73]

In 2010, for the first time, Social Security collected less in taxes than it paid out in benefits. The Social Security Board of Trustees told Congress that the combined assets of the two trust funds from which Social Security benefits are paid will be exhausted in 2033.[74]

Meanwhile, some question whether Obama's re-election, along with the growing prominence of minorities in the nation's demographic profile, means that policy makers no longer need to pay the same degree of attention to race and ethnicity as in the past.

Brian Smedley, vice president of the Joint Center for Political and Economic Studies, a Washington-based research organization dealing with minority public policy issues, doesn't think so.

"One of the most significant challenges for the Civil Rights Movement today is to somehow tackle the notion that the United States is now color-blind or post-racial," he says. He fears the nation is in danger of leaving behind the ideals of racial equality.

"There are many who believe that because we have [elected] an African-American president, and people of color are leading *Fortune* 500 companies, etc., race no longer matters in our society. Of course, we've made tremendous progress in race relations in the United States over the past 50-plus years, and that should be celebrated," he says. "It's remarkable that we have created a society that is much more egalitarian, and we're moving closer to our ideal as a nation where people truly are judged by the content of their character and not by the color of their skin.

"However," he continues, "many people of color still face profound inequities across a host of dimensions . . . such as health, wealth, educational status, income, home ownership, you name it. It's more critical than ever that we focus the nation's attention on these problems because the demographic shifts that are coming suggest that we need to be very mindful of what our nation will look like and how the inequities will hurt everyone in this country unless we solve them."

# NOTES

1. "Most Children Younger Than Age 1 are Minorities, Census Bureau Reports", U.S. Census Bureau news release, May 17, 2012, www.census.gov/newsroom/releases/archives/population/cb12-90.html.

2. "An Older and More Diverse Nation by Midcentury", U.S. Census Bureau news release, Aug. 14, 2008, www.census.gov/newsroom/releases/archives/population/cb08-123.html.

3. Haya El Nasser and Paul Overberg, "Census tracks 20 years of sweeping change," *USA Today*, Aug. 10, 2011, http://usatoday30.usatoday.com/news/nation/census/2011-08-10-census-20-years-change_n.htm.

4. Mark Hugo Lopez and Paul Taylor, "Latino Voters in the 2012 Election," Pew Hispanic Center, Nov. 7, 2012, www.pewhispanic.org/2012/11/07/latino-voters-in-the-2012-election/.

5. Michael D. Shear, "Demographic Shift Brings New Worry for Republicans," *The New York Times*, Nov. 7, 2012, www.nytimes.com/2012/11/08/us/politics/obamas-victory-presents-gop-with-demographic-test.html?ref=politics.

6. "Obama Win Shows Demographic Shifts," *op. cit.*

7. Press release, "Latino Candidates Make History on Election Night," National Association of Latino Elected and Appointed Officials Education Fund, Nov. 7, 2012, www.prnewswire.com/news-releases/latino-candidates-make-history-on-election-night-177729141.html.

8. " 'Nones' on the Rise: One-in-Five Adults Have No Religious Affiliation", Report by the Pew Research Center Forum on Religion & Public Life, Oct. 9, 2012, www.pewforum.org/Unaffiliated/nones-on-the-rise.aspx.

9. Laura B. Shrestha and Elayne J. Heisler, "The Changing Demographic Profile of the United States", Congressional Research Service, March 31, 2011, www.fas.org/sgp/crs/misc/RL32701.pdf.

10. D'Vera Cohn and Paul Taylor, "Baby Boomers Approach Age 65 — Glumly," Pew Research Center, Dec. 20, 2010, http://pewresearch.org/pubs/1834/baby-boomers-old-age-downbeat-pessimism.

11. For background see Alan Greenblatt, "The Graying Planet," *CQ Global Researcher*, March 15, 2011, pp. 133-156.

12. 2010 Census Data, U.S. Census Bureau, http://2010.census.gov/2010census/data/.

13. Sabrina Tavernise, "Whites Account for Under Half of Births in U.S.," *The New York Times*, May 17, 2012, www.nytimes.com/2012/05/17/us/whites-account-for-under-half-of-births-in-us.html?pagewanted=all.

14. John Blake, "Are Whites Racially Oppressed?", CNN, March 4, 2011, www.cnn.com/2010/US/12/21/white.persecution/index.html.

15. Daniel Cox; E.J. Dionne, Jr.; William A. Galston; Robert P. Jones, "What it Means to be an American," Brookings Institution, Sept. 6, 2011, www.brookings.edu/research/reports/2011/09/06-american-attitudes.

16. "U.S. Religious Landscape Survey", Pew Forum on Religion and Public Life, February 2008, http://religions.pewforum.org/pdf/report-religious-landscape-study-full.pdf.

17. *Ibid.*

18. Samuel P. Huntington, *Who Are We? The Challenges to America's National Identity* (2004), p. 18.

19. Joel Kotkin, "Minority America," Newgeography.com, Aug. 20, 2008, www.newgeography.com/content/00175-minority-america.

20. Paul Taylor, Mark Hugo Lopez, Jessica Hamar Martinez and Gabriel Velasco, "When Labels Don't Fit: Hispanics and Their Views of Identity," Pew Hispanic Center, April 4, 2012, "Two-Thirds of Democrats Now Support Gay Marriage," Poll, Pew Forum on Religion and Public Life, July 31, 2012, www.pewforum.org/Politics-and-Elections/2012-opinions-on-for-gay-marriage-unchanged-after-obamas-announcement.aspx.

21. "The Rise of Asian Americans," Pew Research Center, June 19, 2012, www.pewsocialtrends.org/2012/06/19/the-rise-of-asian-americans/.

22. Wendy Wang, "The Rise of Intermarriage," Pew Research Center, Feb. 16, 2012, www.pewsocialtrends.org/2012/02/16/the-rise-of-intermarriage/?src=prc-headline.

23. For background, see Haya El Nasser, "Black-white marriages on the rise," *USA Today*, Sept. 20, 2011, http://usatoday30.usatoday.com/news/nation/story/2011-09-19/interracial-marriages/50469776/1.

24. Wang, *op. cit.*

25. "The Generation Gap and the 2012 Election," The Pew Research Center, Nov. 3, 2011, www.people-press.org/2011/11/03/the-generation-gap-and-the-2012-election-3/.

26. Linda A. Jacobsen, *et al.*, "America's Aging Population," *Population Bulletin 66*, no. 1 (2011), Population Reference Bureau.

27. Frank W. Heiland and Zhe Li, "Changes in Labor Force Participation of Older Americans and Their Pension Structures: A Policy Perspective," Boston College Center for Retirement Research, August 2012, http://crr.bc.edu/working-papers/changes-in-labor-force-participation-of-older-americans-and-their-pension-structures-a-policy-perspective-2.

28. Don Lee, "More older workers making up labor force," *Los Angeles Times*, Sept. 4, 2012, http://articles.latimes.com/2012/sep/04/business/la-fi-labor-seniors-20120903.

29. Alicia H. Munnell and April Yanyuan Wu, "Will Delayed Retirement by the Baby Boomers Lead to Higher Unemployment Among Younger Workers?", Center for Retirement Research at Boston College, October 2012, http://crr.bc.edu/working-papers/will-delayed-retirement-by-the-baby-boomers-lead-to-higher-unemployment-among-younger-workers/.

30. Mark Miller, "Are Older Workers Getting in the Way of the Young?," Reuters, Jan. 6, 2012, www.reuters.com/article/2012/01/06/retirement-jobs-idUSN1E80507520120106.

31. Press release, American Association of Colleges of Nursing, "Nursing Shortage," www.aacn.nche.edu/media-relations/fact-sheets/nursing-shortage.

32. "Immigration, Poverty and Low-Wage Earners: The Harmful Effects of Unskilled Immigrants on American Workers," Federation for American Immigration Reform, July 2010 (revised Feb. 2011), www.fairus.org/publications/immigration-poverty-and-low-wage-earners-the-harmful-effects-of-unskilled-immigrants-on-american-wor.

33. "Georgia Data Quantify Impact of Undocumented Workers," Southwest Economy, Federal Reserve Bank of Dallas, second quarter 2012, www.dallasfed.org/assets/documents/research/swe/2012/swe1202e.pdf.

34. Giovanni Peri, "The Effect of Immigrants on U.S. Employment and Productivity," Federal Reserve Bank of San Francisco Economic Letter, August 30, 2010, www.frbsf.org/publications/economics/letter/2010/el2010-26.html.

35. Niall Stanage, "Women, minorities propel Obama victory," *The Hill*, Nov. 7, 2012, http://thehill.com/homenews/campaign/266485-women-minorities-propel-obama-victory.

36. Quoted in Dylan Scott, "Political Demographic Trends Brighter for Democrats," *Governing*, April 11, 2012, www.governing.com/blogs/politics/gov-political-demographic-trends-brighter-for-democrats.html.

37. Jeffrey Passell, D'Vera Cohn and Mark Hugo Lopez, "Hispanics Account for More than Half of Nation's Growth in Past Decade," Pew Hispanic Center, March 24, 2011, www.pewhispanic.org/2011/03/24/hispanics-account-for-more-than-half-of-nations-growth-in-past-decade/.

38. William H. Frey, "Will 2012 be the Last Hurrah for Whites?," *National Journal*, "The Next America," June 13, 2012, http://nationaljournal.com/thenextamerica/demographics/will-2012-be-the-last-hurrah-for-whites—20120613.

39. Alan I. Abramowitz, "Beyond 2010: Demographic Change and the Future of the Republican Party," University of Virginia Center for Politics, "Larry J. Sabato's Crystal Ball," March 11, 2010, www.centerforpolitics.org/crystalball/articles/aia2010031101/.

40. Ruy Teixeira and William Frey, "New Data on Obama's Massive Demographic Advantage," *The New Republic*, July 9, 2012, www.tnr.com/blog/plank/104746/how-much-will-demographic-changes-help-obama-in-swing-states.

41. Lila Shapiro, "Gay Marriage Victory In Maine, Maryland; Minnesota Votes Down 'Traditional' Amendment (UPDATE)," *The Huffington Post*, Nov. 7, 2012, www.huffingtonpost.com/2012/11/07/gay-marriage-victory_n_2085900.html.

42. "How the Faithful Voted: 2012 Preliminary Analysis," Pew Forum on Religion & Public Life, Nov. 7, 2012, www.pewforum.org/Politics-and-Elections/How-the-Faithful-Voted-2012-Preliminary-Exit-Poll-Analysis .aspx.

43. "Black Americans in Congress," Office of the Clerk, U.S. House of Representatives, http://baic.house.gov/ historical-essays/essay.html?intID=1&intSectionID=11.

44. Roger Finke and Rodney Starke, *The Churching of America, 1776-2005: Winners and Losers in Our Religious Economy* (2002), p. 123.

45. Lawrence H. Fuchs, *The American Kaleidoscope: Race, Ethnicity, and the Civic Culture* (1990), p. 134.

46. Rodman D. Griffin, "Hispanic Americans," *CQ Researcher*, Oct. 30, 1992.

47. For background, see Congressional Quarterly, *Congress and the Nation Vol. I* (1965), pp. 762-767.

48. Jo Freeman, "From Suffrage to Women's Liberation: Feminism in Twentieth Century America," published in Jo Freeman, ed., *Women: A Feminist Perspective* (5th ed., 1995), excerpted at www.uic.edu/orgs/ cwluherstory/jofreeman/feminism/suffrage.htm.

49. Rev. Osagyefo Uhuru Sekou, "Killing the Buddha" blog, http://killingthebuddha.com/mag/damnation/ gays-are-the-new-niggers/.

50. U.S. State Department, Office of the Historian, Milestones 1921-1936, http://history.state.gov/ milestones/1921-1936/ImmigrationAct.

51. "Who Was Shut Out?: Immigration Quotas, 1925-1927," History Matters, http://historymatters.gmu. edu/d/5078/.

52. Remarks by President Lyndon B. Johnson at the Signing of the Immigration Bill, Liberty Island, New York, Oct. 3, 1965, www.lbjlib.utexas.edu/johnson/ archives.hom/speeches.hom/651003.asp.

53. "U.S. Historical Immigration Trends," Migration Policy Institute, www.migrationinformation.org/ datahub/historicaltrends.cfm#source.

54. "The Newly Arrived Foreign-Born Population of the United States: 2010," American Community Survey Brief, U.S. Census Bureau, November 2011, www .census.gov/prod/2011pubs/acsbr10-16.pdf.

55. "USA Quick Facts", US Bureau of the Census, http://quickfacts.census.gov/qfd/states/00000.html.

56. "Births: Final Data for 2010", Joyce Martin, M.P.H., *et al.*, National Center for Health Statistics, August 2012, www.cdc.gov/nchs/births.htm.

57. "2010 Census Shows Nation's Population is Aging ", News Release, US Census Bureau, May 26, 2011, http://2010.census.gov/news/releases/operations/ cb11-cn147.html.

58. Jeffrey Passel, D'Vera Cohn and Ana Gonzalez-Barrera, "Net Migration from Mexico Falls to Zero-and Perhaps Less," Pew Hispanic Center, April 23, 2012, www.pewhispanic.org/2012/04/23/net-migra tion-from-mexico-falls-to-zero-and-perhaps-less/.

59. Jeffrey Passel, *et al.*, "Net Migration from Mexico Falls to Zero-and Perhaps Less", Pew Hispanic Center, April 23, 2012, www.pewhispanic.org/2012/04/23/ net-migration-from-mexico-falls-to-zero-and-per haps-less/.

60. Michael Hoefer, Nancy Rytina and Bryan Baker, "Estimates of the Unauthorized Immigrant Population Residing in the United States: January 2011," Report of the Department of Homeland Security, March 2012, www.dhs.gov/files/statistics/publications/ estimates-unauthorized-immigrant-population.shtm.

61. For background, see Kenneth Jost, "Immigration Conflict," *CQ Researcher*, March 9, 2012, pp. 229-252.

62. Daniel González, "Arizona's illegal-immigration population plunges," *The Arizona Republic*, March 23, 2012, www.azcentral.com/arizonarepublic/news/arti cles/2012/03/23/20120323arizona-illegal-migrant-population-plunges.html.

63. Daniel Gonzalez, "Arizona immigration law: A look at bill's impact 1 year later," *The Arizona Republic*, April 23, 2011, www.azcentral.com/news/election/ azelections/articles/2011/04/23/20110423arizona-immigration-law-impact-year-later.html.

64. Raul Hinojsa-Ojeda and Marshall Fritz, "A Rising Tide or a Shrinking Pie: The Economic Impact of Legalization Versus Deportation in Arizona," Center for American Progress, March 2011, www.americanprogress.org/wp-content/uploads/issues/2011/03/pdf/rising_tide.pdf.

65. Andrew O'Reilly, "Dayton's Immigration Strategy for Growth is Drawing Notice", Fox News Latino, May 10, 2012, http://latino.foxnews.com/latino/ news/2012/05/10/dayton-immigration-strategy-for-growth-is-drawing-notice/.

66. "Few U.S. cities are ready for aging Baby Boomer population," Associated Press, March 25, 2012, http://usatoday30.usatoday.com/news/health/story/health/story/2012-03-25/Few-US-cities-are-ready-for-aging-baby-boomer-population/53765292/1.

67. "Age-Friendly NYC," Nov. 9, 2012 www.nyam.org/agefriendlynyc/.

68. "Lifelong Communities," Atlanta Regional Commission, Nov. 9, 2012, www.atlantaregional.com/aging-resources/lifelong-communities-llc.

69. "The Maturing of America: Communities Moving Forward for an Aging Population," National Association of Area Agencies on Aging, June 2011, pp. i, ii, www.n4a.org/files/MOA_FINAL_Rpt.pdf.

70. Quoted in "Few cities are ready . . .," *op. cit.*

71. Stanage, *op. cit.*

72. "Condoleezza Rice: GOP Sent 'Mixed Messages' On Immigration And Women's Issues," The Associated Press/ *The Huffington Post*, Nov. 9, 2012, www.huffingtonpost.com/2012/11/09/condoleezza-rice_n_2099505.html.

73. "Social Security Basic Facts," Social Security Administration fact sheet, July 30, 2012, www.ssa.gov/pressoffice/basicfact.htm.

74. "The 2012 Annual Report of the Board Of Trustees of the Federal Old-Age and Survivors Insurance and Federal Disability Insurance Trust Funds", April 25, 2012, U.S. Government Printing Office 73-947, Washington, DC.

# BIBLIOGRAPHY

## Selected Sources

### Books

Ehrenhalt, Alan, *The Great Inversion and the Future of the American City*, Alfred A. Knopf, 2012.
The executive editor of Stateline news service and former executive editor of *Governing* magazine explores how American cities are changing and the implications for the future.

Huntington, Samuel P., *Who Are We? The Challenges to America's National Identity*, Simon & Shuster, 2004.
The late Harvard University political scientist (1927-2008) examines the impact of immigrants and their cultural values on American society.

Putnam, Robert D., and David E. Campbell, *American Grace: How Religion Divides and Unites Us*, Simon & Schuster, 2010.
A professor of public policy at Harvard (Putnam) and a political science professor at the University of Notre Dame (Campbell) examine how religion, politics and culture intersect.

Steinhorn, Leonard, *The Greater Generation: In Defense of the Baby Boom Legacy*, Thomas Dunne Books, 2006.
A professor of communications at American University argues that the postwar generation shaped America for the better.

Wilkerson, Isabel, *The Warmth of Other Suns: The Epic Story of America's Great Migration*, Random House, 2010.
A journalist and Boston University professor provides a Pulitzer Prize-winning account of the exodus of 6 million African-Americans from the South to the urban North and West between 1915 and 1970.

### Articles

Brownstein, Ron, "Do Immigrants Threaten American Values?" *National Journal*, June 14, 2012, www.nationaljournal.com/thenextamerica/immigration/do-immigrants-threaten-american-values—20120614.
A journalist dissects a decade of Pew research polling that reveals consistent divides among whites over the impact of immigrants on American society.

Castañeda, Jorge G., and Douglas S. Massey, "Do-it-Yourself Immigration Reform," *The New York Times*, June 1, 2012, www.nytimes.com/2012/06/02/opinion/do-it-yourself-immigration-reform.html?_r=1&ref=jorgegcastaneda.
A former Mexican foreign minister (Castañeda) and a Princeton sociology and public affairs professor (Massey) discuss the causes and effects of the current stasis in immigration from Mexico.

"A Contentious Flock," *The Economist*, July 7, 2012, pp. 33-34.
The reporter examines polarization and diversity among American Catholics.

Frey, William, "Baby Boomers Had Better Embrace Change," *The Washington Post*, June 8, 2012,

www.brookings.edu/research/opinions/2012/06/08-baby-boomers-frey.
A demographer at the Washington, D.C.-based think tank discusses population and attitudinal trends.

Howe, Neal, "What Makes Boomers the Boomers?" *Governing.com*, September 2012, www.governing.com/generations/government-management/gov-what-makes-boomers.html.
A demographer, historian, author and consultant on generational transitions investigates the myths about and realities of the baby boom generation.

## Reports and Studies

"Immigration, Poverty and Low-Wage Earners: The Harmful Effect of Unskilled Immigrants on American Workers (2011)," Federation for American Immigration Reform, 2011, www.fairus.org/issue/immigration-poverty-and-low-wage-earners-the-harmful-effect-of-unskilled-immigrants-on-american-work.
A national nonprofit organization that seeks stricter limits on immigration argues that unskilled immigrant labor harms native-born Americans.

"State of Metropolitan America: On the Front Lines of Demographic Transformation," Metropolitan Policy Program, Brookings Institution, 2010.

The Washington-based public policy think tank analyzes the impact of recent demographic changes on U.S. metropolitan areas.

Funk, Cary, and Greg Smith, " 'Nones' on the Rise: One-in-Five Adults Have No Religious Affiliation," Pew Forum on Religion and Public Life, Oct. 9, 2012, www.pewforum.org/Unaffiliated/nones-on-the-rise.aspx.
A nonpartisan research organization examines trends in American religious belief and practice.

Jacobsen, Linda A., *et al.*, "America's Aging Population," Population Reference Bureau, 2011, www.prb.org/pdf11/aging-in-america.pdf.
The think tank report examines the costs and implications of an aging population.

Myers, Dowell, and John Pitkin, "Assimilation Tomorrow: How America's Immigrants will Assimilate by 2030," Center for American Progress, November 2011, www.americanprogress.org/issues/immigration/report/2011/11/14/10583/assimilation-tomorrow/.
A demographer/urban planner (Myers) and a demographer/economist from the University of Southern California (Pitkin) examine the outlook for American immigrants.

# For More Information

**American Association of Retired Persons**, 601 E St., N.W., Washington, DC 20009; 888-687-2277; www.aarp.org. Membership organization that advocates for people 50 years of age and older.

**Brookings Institution**, 1775 Massachusetts Ave., N.W., Washington, DC 20036; 202-797-6000; www.brookings.edu. Research organization focusing on wide range of issues, including economics, social policy, urban affairs and politics.

**Center for Immigration Studies**, 1629 K St., N.W., Suite 600, Washington, DC 20006; 202-466-8185; www.cis.org. Research organization that supports lower levels of immigration.

**Center for Retirement Research at Boston College**, Hovey House, 258 Hammond St., Chestnut Hill, MA 02467; 617-552-1762; www.crr.bu.edu. Research institution focusing on retirement issues.

**Pew Research Center**, 901 E St., N.W., Washington, DC 20004-2008; 202-552-2000; www.pew.org. Arm of the Pew Charitable Trusts that conducts research on such topics as Hispanics in America and the role of religion in public life.

**Urban Institute**, 2100 M St., N.W., Washington, DC 20037; 202-833-7200; www.urban.org. Non-partisan research organization focusing on social and economic issues.

**U.S. Social Security Administration**, Windsor Park Building, 6401 Security Blvd., Baltimore, MD 21235; 800-772-1213; www.ssa.gov. Federal agency that administers the Social Security retirement, disability and survivors' benefits programs.

# 3

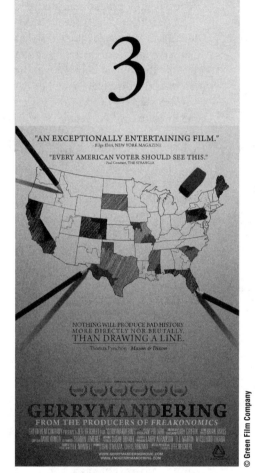

"AN EXCEPTIONALLY ENTERTAINING FILM."
Bilge Ebiri, NEW YORK MAGAZINE

"EVERY AMERICAN VOTER SHOULD SEE THIS."
Paul Constant, THE STRANGER

NOTHING WILL PRODUCE BAD HISTORY
MORE DIRECTLY NOR BRUTALLY,
THAN DRAWING A LINE.
Thomas Pynchon  *Mason & Dixon*

**GERRYMANDERING**
FROM THE PRODUCERS OF *FREAKONOMICS*

© Green Film Company

A poster promotes Gerrymandering, a documentary released last fall that sharply criticizes the controversial practice of drawing congressional districts to help political friends and hurt foes. Jeff Reichert, a self-described liberal who made the film, says he wants "more people involved in the redistricting process."

From *CQ Researcher*,
February 25, 2011.

# Redistricting Debates

Kenneth Jost

Meet Cynthia Dai: high-tech management consultant in San Francisco, Asian-American, outdoor adventurer, out lesbian, registered Democrat.

Meet Michael Ward: chiro-practor in Anaheim, Calif., disabled veteran, former polygraph examiner, Native American, registered Republican.

Dai has been interested in politics since 1984, when she helped register voters before reaching voting age herself. Ward has worked with college Republican groups since his undergraduate days.

Despite their interests, neither Dai nor Ward had ever held or sought public office until last year. For the next year, however, they and 12 other Californians, most with limited if any political experience, will be up to their necks in politics as members of the state's newly established Citizens Redistricting Commission.[1]

Along with the rest of the states, California must redraw its legislative and congressional maps in 2011 to make districts equal in population according to the latest U.S. Census Bureau figures. The every-10-year process is required to comply with the Supreme Court's famous "one person, one vote" rule, which requires districts to be divided according to population so each person is equally represented in government. The intricate line-drawing invites political maneuvering of all sorts, including the practice known as "gerrymandering" — irregularly shaping district maps specifically to help or hurt a political party or individual office-holder or candidate.

With the redistricting cycle just getting under way, California's citizens commission provides a high-profile test of the latest idea

## GOP Has Grip on Redistricting Authority

Republicans control 23 of the state legislatures that draw either state or congressional districts or both, including Nebraska's nominally nonpartisan legislature; Democrats control only 12. Legislatures in seven states with redistricting authority are split, with each of the major parties having a majority in one of the chambers. Eight states use commissions to draw both legislative and congressional lines; five others use commissions just for congressional redistricting.

### Congressional Redistricting Authority by State

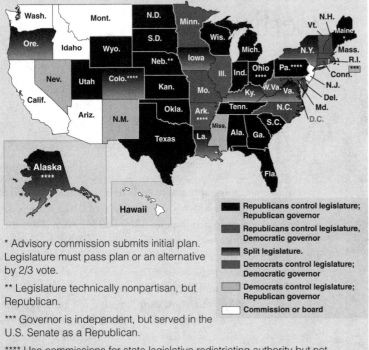

Republicans control legislature; Republican governor

Republicans control legislature, Democratic governor

Split legislature.

Democrats control legislature; Democratic governor

Democrats control legislature; Republican governor

Commission or board

\* Advisory commission submits initial plan. Legislature must pass plan or an alternative by 2/3 vote.

\*\* Legislature technically nonpartisan, but Republican.

\*\*\* Governor is independent, but served in the U.S. Senate as a Republican.

\*\*\*\* Use commissions for state legislative redistricting authority but not congressional.

*Sources:* National Conference on State Legislatures; U.S. Department of Justice Civil Right Division; U.S. House of Representatives

Democrats on the partisan-balanced commission. "Part of the problem is the politicians have had the right to pick the voters instead of voters picking politicians, which seems like a very big myth in our democracy."

Ward, one of the five registered Republican commissioners, agrees. "The condition of California is evidence that politicians draw districts that serve their own interests and not necessarily first and foremost the communities that they serve," he says.

Completing the commission's membership are four people unaffiliated with either of the two major parties. The maps to be drawn by the commission, due to be completed by Aug. 15, must meet a series of criteria, including "to the extent practicable" compactness. But the commission is specifically prohibited from "favoring or discriminating against" any incumbent, candidate or political party. The final maps must be approved by a bipartisan supermajority of the commission, with votes from at least three Democrats, three Republicans and three independents.

No one knows how the experiment will work. "It's fair to say that the mechanism that we came up with is not simple, but we're hopeful that it will work out," says Derek Cressman, Western regional director for the public interest group Common Cause. Along with the state's former Republican governor, Arnold Schwarzenegger, California's Common Cause chapter was the driving force behind Proposition 11, which in 2008 created the new commission to redraw state legislative districts.

With approval of the measure, California became the second state, after Arizona, to establish a citizens redistricting commission. Arizona's commission, created through a ballot initiative approved in 2000, has responsibility for legislative and congressional districts.

for reforming the often-discredited process. By taking the job away from the state legislature through ballot measures approved in 2008 and 2010, California voters sought to cut out the bizarre maps and unsavory deal-making that good-government groups say prevent the public from ousting incumbents or holding them accountable for their performance in office.

"There's a fair amount of cynicism about how California is being run now," says Dai, one of five

California voters in 2010 approved a second measure, Proposition 20, that gave the commission power over congressional districts too.*

Redistricting is an arcane process that stirs more interest among political junkies than the general public. But experts say the decennial line-drawing helps shape voters' relationships with their elected officials and can affect the balance of power between rival political parties. "This is one of the most important events in our democracy," says Kristen Clarke, co-director of the political participation group for the NAACP Legal Defense and Educational Fund, a major advocacy group for African-American interests.[2]

The redistricting cycle flows out of the Constitution's requirement that seats in the U.S. House of Representatives be "apportioned" among the states according to an "enumeration" of the population — the census — to be conducted every 10 years (Article I, Section 2). Under the figures released by the U.S. Census Bureau in December, eight states will gain and 10 will lose House seats to be filled in the 2012 election.

The new apportionment has the potential to strengthen the Republican majority that the GOP gained in November 2010. States gaining seats are mostly in the Republican-leaning Sun Belt in the South and West, while states losing seats are mostly in the Democratic-leaning Rust Belt in the Northeast and Midwest.

Thanks to gains in state elections in November, Republicans are positioned to take control of the micro-level line-drawing of congressional and state legislative districts in a near majority of the states. Among states where legislatures draw either congressional or legislative maps or both, Republicans have undivided control

## Twelve Seats Shift in Reapportionment Process

Ten states will lose a total of 12 seats in the U.S. House of Representatives during reapportionment. Those seats will be reallocated among eight other states, with Texas and Florida the big winners. They will gain four and two seats, respectively.

### States Gaining or Losing House Seats in Reapportionment Process

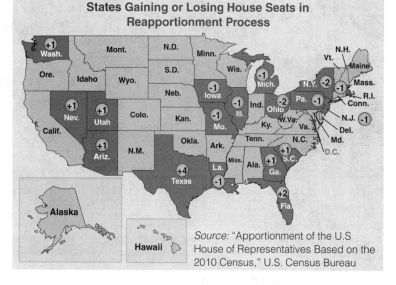

*Source:* "Apportionment of the U.S House of Representatives Based on the 2010 Census," U.S. Census Bureau

---

*The commission is also charged with drawing the four districts for the state's Board of Equalization, which administers the state's tax laws.

in 19, including Nebraska's nominally nonpartisan unicameral legislature; Democrats in only eight. "Republicans are in the best position ever in the modern era of redistricting," says Tim Storey, a veteran redistricting expert with the National Conference of State Legislatures.

Democrats are disadvantaged not only because they lost ground at the polls in November but also because some states with Democratic-controlled legislatures — most notably, California — assign redistricting to non-legislative boards or commissions. "Democrats are going to have less influence [in California] than they had in the past," says Charles Bullock, a professor of political science at the University of Georgia in Athens.

In fact, California's post-2000 redistricting is Exhibit No. 1 in the reformers' case against the prevailing practice of allowing state lawmakers to draw their own districts as well as those of members of Congress. In the reformers' view, Democrats and Republicans in the state legislature agreed on district lines aimed at protecting incumbents of both parties — a so-called bipartisan gerrymander.

Over the next year, 14 Californians, all with post-graduate degrees but most with limited if any political experience, will redraw the state's legislative and congressional maps as members of the state's newly established Citizens Redistricting Commission. Here they pose for an official photograph midway through a three-day public meeting Feb. 10-12. Michael Ward, a chiropractor, presided as rotating chair; Connie Galambos Malloy, a community organizer, is to his right. Others standing, left to right, are Jodie Filkins Webber (attorney), Gabino Aguirre (city councilman; retired high school principal), Vincent Barabba (online-commerce consultant), Michelle DiGuilo (stay-at-home mom), Maria Blanco (foundation executive), Peter Yao (ex-city council member; retired engineer), Cynthia Dai (management consultant), Libert "Gil" Ontai (architect), Jeanne Raya (insurance agent), Angelo Ancheta (law professor), Stanley Forbes (bookstore owner) and M. Andre Parvenu (urban planner). The panel includes four Asian-Americans, three Hispanic-Americans, one African-American, one Native American and five whites.

Supporters of the new citizens commission say the legislative plan worked as the lawmakers intended. In the five elections from 2002 through 2010, only one of the state's 53 congressional seats changed hands. The districts "represent the legislators' interest, not the voters,'" says Cressman of Common Cause.

Some redistricting experts, however, discount the reformers' complaints about self-interested line-drawing. "The effect of redistricting in the incumbency advantage is unclear," says Nathan Persily, director of the Center for Law and Politics at Columbia University Law School in New York City. "Incumbents win not only because they draw the district lines, but for all kinds of reasons."

Political calculations in redistricting are also limited by legal requirements dating from the Supreme Court's so-called reapportionment revolution in the 1960s. In a series of decisions, the justices first opened federal courts to suits to require periodic redistricting by state legislatures and then mandated congressional and legislative districts to be equal in population within each state.

The Voting Rights Act, passed in 1965, has also played a major role in redistricting. In particular, the act's Section 5 requires that election law changes in nine states and local jurisdictions in seven others be "pre-cleared" with the Justice Department or a federal court in Washington, D.C. Beginning with the post-1990 redistricting cycle, the Justice Department used its leverage to pressure states into drawing "majority-minority" districts to protect African-Americans' and Latinos' voting rights, with some of the districts very irregularly shaped. The Supreme Court limited the practice somewhat, however, with rulings in the 1990s that bar the use of race or ethnicity as the "predominant" factor in a district's boundaries.[3]

African-American and, in particular, Latino groups are looking for more "minority opportunity" districts in the current redistricting cycle. "I hope we will have an increase in the number of districts where Latinos can elect candidates of their choice," says Arturo Vargas, executive director of the National Association of Latino Elected and Appointed Officials (NALEO). Among the states being closely watched is Texas, which will gain four House seats in large part because of the state's growing Hispanic population.

The Supreme Court decisions limiting racial line-drawing came in suits filed by white voters and backed by groups opposed to racial preferences, including the Washington-based Project on Fair Representation. Edward Blum, the group's president, says it will bring similar legal challenges if it sees "evidence of unconstitutional racial gerrymandering" in the current redistricting.

As Blum acknowledges, however, the Voting Rights Act requires some consideration of race, nationwide, to prevent what is termed "retrogression" — new districts that reduce the ability of minority groups to elect their preferred candidate. "Race must be one factor among many that line drawers use," says Clarke with the Legal Defense Fund. It has joined with the Mexican American Legal Defense and Educational Fund (MALDEF) and the Asian American Justice Center in publishing a 78-page booklet aimed at educating and mobilizing minority communities on redistricting issues.

Increased public participation is also the goal of good-government groups, including Common Cause and the League of Women Voters. "There are a lot of opportunities for greater public participation and better maps," says Nancy Tate, the league's executive director.

In addition, two reform-minded academics — George Mason University political scientist Michael McDonald and Harvard University quantitative social scientist Micah Altman — have formed the straightforwardly named Public Mapping Project to put mapping data and software into the hands of interest groups, community organizations and even students to propose redistricting plans. The goal, McDonald says, "is to allow redistricting to be done out of people's homes."

Despite the reformers' hopes, one longtime redistricting expert doubts that public or media pressure will carry much weight as state legislatures go about their work. "I don't see state legislatures buckling much to that," says Peter Galderisi, a lecturer in political science at the University of California, San Diego. "In most situations, they don't have the direct ability to influence this at all."

As state legislatures and redistricting commissions get down to work, here are some of the major questions being debated:

## Should partisan gerrymandering be restricted?

Texas Republicans chafed for more than a decade under the post-1990 congressional redistricting, a Democratic-drawn plan that helped Democrats hold a majority of the House seats through the decade. When Republicans gained control of both houses of the state legislature and the governorship in 2002, it was payback time.

Despite an attempted boycott by outnumbered Democrats, the GOP majorities approved an artful plan aimed at giving Republicans an edge wherever possible. In the first election under the new map, the GOP in 2004 gained 21-11 control of the state's congressional delegation. Democrats cried foul and argued all the way to the U.S. Supreme Court that the plan was a partisan gerrymander that violated Democratic voters' constitutional rights. The justices could not agree on a legal rule to govern gerrymandering, however, and left the map intact except to require redrawing a majority Latino district in the Rio Grande Valley.

The ruling in the Texas case marked the third time that the Supreme Court had entertained a constitutional claim against gerrymandering — and the third time that the justices failed to give any guidance on when, if ever, federal courts could strike down a partisan power-grab as going too far.[4]

Legal experts say the judicial impasse is likely to continue. Justice Anthony M. Kennedy straddles the divide between four conservatives uncomfortable with or opposed to gerrymandering challenges altogether and four liberals unable to agree on a standard to police the practice. "Four-and-a-half justices have demonstrated that they don't want to deal with this, and the other four-and-a-half cannot agree on how to deal with it," says Justin Levitt, an associate professor at Loyola Law School in Los Angeles who formerly worked on redistricting issues at the Brennan Center for Justice at New York University School of Law.

For many political scientists, the effort to control gerrymandering through the courts is simply at war with U.S. political traditions dating back to the 19th century.

"We've gotten used to the fact that when one party controls, you get partisan gerrymanders," says Galderisi at UC San Diego.

With courts on the sidelines, the critics of partisan gerrymandering are looking to two approaches in the current redistricting cycle to control the practice. The California citizens commission — and the citizens commission created in Arizona for the post-2000 cycle — take the job away from legislators and establish guidelines, including geographically compact districts. In Florida, reform groups, allied with major Democratic interest groups, won adoption of constitutional amendments in November that prohibit the legislature from drawing districts "with the intent to favor or disfavor a political party or an incumbent."

Bullock, the University of Georgia professor, says the commission approach has the potential to create more competitive districts, one of the main goals of the gerrymandering critics. (Competitiveness is one of the criteria in Arizona, though not in California.) But longtime political expert Thomas Mann, a senior fellow in governance studies at the Brookings Institution in Washington, says geographically compact districting schemes do not necessarily increase competitiveness because like-minded voters often live in the same neighborhood. "In some states, you've got to do real gerrymandering to create more competitive districts," Mann says.

In Florida, even supporters of the anti-gerrymandering amendment acknowledge doubts about how faithfully the Republican-controlled legislature will comply with the provision. "Your guess is as good as mine," says Ellen Freidin, a Miami attorney-activist who headed the Fair Districts Florida campaign for the amendments. Meanwhile, some political scientists see the command not to favor or disfavor an incumbent in drawing district lines as a logical impossibility. "Either it's going to favor them or disfavor them," says Thomas Brunell, a professor of political science at the University of Texas at Dallas. "It's got to be one of those things."

Brunell, in fact, takes the contrarian position of opposing the maximization of competitive districts. In his book *Redistricting and Representation*, Brunell argues that competitive elections are not essential for good government and in fact increase voter discontent. "The more competitive the district, the more upset voters you have," he says.[5]

For incumbents, partisan gerrymandering may actually have a downside, according to UC-San Diego's Galderisi, if likely party voters in one district are spread around to enhance the party's chances of winning in others. "Incumbents don't feel well off unless they have a comfortable margin of victory," he says.

In fact, cutting political margins too thin in a particular district can result in a party's loss of a once-safe seat — a process that redistricting expert Bernard Grofman at the University of California-Irvine calls "a dummymander." In the current cycle, Galderisi thinks Republicans may take that lesson to heart and concentrate on protecting the gains they made in November. "A lot of efforts are going to be to shore up new incumbents rather than engage in traditional partisan gerrymanders," he says.

McDonald, the George Mason University political scientist in the Public Mapping Project, says that with so much political volatility in the last few elections, Democrats and Republicans alike will be more interested in political security than partisan advantage. "Incumbents are going to want safer districts," he says.

## Should district lines be drawn to help minorities get elected to office?

Rep. Luis Gutierrez, a Chicago Democrat, has represented since 1993 a congressional district that only a redistricting junkie could love. Dubbed the "ear muff" district, Illinois-4 includes predominantly Latino neighborhoods from close-in suburbs along the city's southern border and other Latino neighborhoods in Chicago itself that are connected only by a stretch of the Tri-State Tollway.

The district was drawn that way in 1991 not to help or hurt an individual officeholder or candidate but to comply with the federal Voting Rights Act. In a city with a history of racially polarized voting and a state with no previous Hispanic member of Congress, Latinos were entitled to a majority Latino district, a federal court ruled. But the new map had to avoid carving up the majority African-American districts that lay between Latino neighborhoods. "This is not gerrymandering," the Mexican American Legal Defense and Educational Fund explains, "but rather protecting voting rights."[6]

Latino and African-American groups will be working again in the current redistricting cycle to try to protect minority incumbents and increase opportunities for minority candidates. "We know that Latinos have increased significantly in population," says Nina Perales, MALDEF's litigation director. "We hope to see a redistricting that fairly reflects that growth."

With the African-American population growing less rapidly, Clarke says the NAACP Legal Defense Fund will first be "looking to ensure that existing opportunities are not taken away." In particular, Clarke says LDF wants to guard against the possibility that the Supreme Court's most recent decision on racial redistricting is not "misinterpreted" to call for dismantling so-called crossover or influence districts — districts where a racial or ethnic minority comprises less than a majority of the population but can form coalitions with white voters to elect a candidate.

For their part, critics of racial redistricting would like to see less attention to race and ethnicity in map-drawing. Blum, with the Project on Fair Representation, says district maps should be drawn without access to racial and ethnic data and checked only at the end to see whether redistricters had "inadvertently" reduced minority voting rights.

The Supreme Court has played the lead role in shaping the current law on racial redistricting. In a trio of decisions in the 1990s, the court struck down oddly shaped, majority-minority congressional districts in Georgia, North Carolina and Texas on the grounds that race or ethnicity was the predominant factor in drawing them. But the court in 1998 upheld the Illinois redistricting with the majority-Latino "earmuff" district. And in 2001 the court ruled in effect that redistricters may draw a majority-minority district if done for a partisan purpose — in the specific case, to make the district Democratic.[7]

The post-2000 redistricting generated fewer major decisions on racial redistricting, but the court's 2009

---

## Rules of the Road for California Redistricting

Ballot measures creating the California Citizens Redistricting Commission to redraw the state's legislative and congressional maps set out mandatory criteria and prohibited districts aimed at helping or hurting an incumbent, candidate or political party.

*Districts must:*

- Have "reasonably equal population," except where "deviation" is required to comply with the federal Voting Rights Act.
- Comply with the Voting Rights Act. The law prohibits race- or ethnicity-based interference with voting rights
- Be "geographically contiguous."
- Respect the "geographic integrity" of any county, city, neighborhood or "community of interest" to the extent possible. "Communities of interest" do not include "relationships with political parties, incumbents or political candidates."
- Be "drawn to encourage geographical compactness" to the extent practicable.
- Be drawn, to the extent practicable, so that each state Senate district encompasses precisely two Assembly districts.
- The commission is prohibited from considering an incumbent's or candidate's residence in drawing district lines. Districts "shall not be drawn for the purpose of favoring or discriminating against an incumbent, political candidate, or political party."

*Source:* California Citizens Redistricting Commission, http://wedrawthelines.ca.gov/downloads/voters_first_act.pdf

---

ruling on a North Carolina legislative map troubles minority groups. The decision, *Bartlett v. Strickland*, required the redrawing of a once majority-black legislative district that had been reconfigured in a way to prevent the African-American population from falling below the threshold needed to form a "crossover" district. In a splintered 5-4 decision, the Supreme Court said a racial or ethnic minority could not challenge a redistricting map as impermissible "vote dilution" under the Voting Rights Act unless it comprised a majority of the district's population.[8]

The ruling "is not an invitation to dismantle existing influence districts," says Clarke. "Majority-minority districts along with influence and crossover districts continue to represent some of the most diverse constituencies in our country."

Minority groups bristle at the criticism of racial line-drawing as gerrymandering. They argue that oddly shaped districts are often the only way to bring together "communities of interest." "People don't live in squares, circles and triangles," says Vargas, with the Latino office-holders' group. "So it's hard to draw districts that have nice geometric shapes."

Blum counters that the dispersal of ethnic and racial minorities from central cities into suburbs forces redistricters to ignore geographic communities in order to create majority-minority districts. "What you have to do is draw a district that basically harvests African-Americans block by block, neighborhood by neighborhood, all across the county or across multiple counties," Blum says. "That breaks up communities of interest that are far more powerful in America today than cobbling together these racially apartheid homelands."

As in Chicago, some of the line-drawing may come in areas with Latino, African-American or Asian-American neighborhoods in close, sometimes overlapping, proximity. Both Clarke and Perales acknowledge the potential for cross-racial tensions but say their groups aim to work cooperatively.

In any event, redistricting experts say minority groups have a huge stake in the maps to be drawn. "Racial and ethnic minorities have historically been disadvantaged by deliberate efforts to mute their voices in redistricting cycles," says Costas Panagopoulos, an assistant professor of political science at Fordham University in New York City and executive editor of the magazine *Campaigns and Elections.* "Minority groups want to be sure that that does not happen this time."

## Should redistricting be done by independent commissions instead of state legislatures?

As head of Arizona's first citizens' redistricting commission, Steve Lynn spent thousands of hours over the past decade redrawing legislative and congressional districts in Arizona and defending the new maps in federal and state courts. Lynn, a utility company executive in Tucson who says he is both a former Democrat and former Republican, counts the commission's work a success: no judicial map-drawing, more opportunities for minorities and — in his view at least — more competitive districts.

Surprisingly, however, Lynn voted against Proposition 106 when it was on the Arizona ballot in 2000. Back then, he had no quarrel with the state legislature doing the job. Today, Lynn endorses independent commissions,

but somewhat equivocally. "It's one way to do it," Lynn told a redistricting conference sponsored by the National Conference of State Legislatures in late January. "It's not the only way to do it. Either way can work."[9]

Thirteen states now have redistricting commissions or boards with primary responsibility for drawing legislative districts; seven of those also have responsibility for drawing congressional districts.* Apart from the Arizona and California citizen commissions, the other bodies consist of specifically designated officeholders or members chosen in various ways by political officeholders with an eye to partisan balance. Five other states have backup commissions that take over redistricting in the event of a legislative impasse; two others have advisory commissions.

Two of the non-legislative bodies are long-standing: Ohio's, created in 1850; and the Texas backup commission, established in 1947. McDonald, the George Mason professor with the Public Mapping Project, says those commissions and others created in the 1960s and since were designed to make sure that redistricting was completed on time, not to divorce the process from politics. Indeed, McDonald says, there is "no evidence" that the commissions, despite their description as "bipartisan," have reduced the kind of self-interested or partisan line-drawing that gives redistricting a bad name.

By contrast, the Arizona and California commissions consist of citizens who apply for the positions in screening processes somewhat akin to college admissions. Candidates must specify that they have not served within a specified time period in any party position or federal or state office.

In Arizona, applicants for the five-member commission are screened by the appellate court nominating commission, which approves a pool of 25 candidates: 10 Republicans, 10 Democrats and five independents. From that pool, the majority and minority leaders of the state House of Representatives and Senate each pick one member; those four then pick one of the independents to serve as chair.

California's process is even more complex. The state auditor's office screens candidates, forming a pool of 60,

---

*The number includes Montana, which currently has one House member, elected at large; Montana lost its second House seat after the 1990 census.

equally divided among Republicans, Democrats and independents. Those lists are provided to legislative leaders, who can strike a total of 24 applicants. The auditor's office then chooses the first eight commissioners by randomly pulling names from a spinning basket: three from each of the major parties and two independents. Those eight then pick six more: two Democrats, two Republicans and two independents.

Cressman, with Common Cause, acknowledges the complexity of the process. "It is challenging to come up with a system that gives you a combination of expertise and diversity and screens out conflict of interest and self-interest," he says.

Opponents of California's Proposition 11 cited the complexity in campaigning against the ballot measure in 2008. They also argued the commission would be both costly and politically unaccountable. In 2010, opponents qualified an initiative to abolish the commission, which appeared on the same ballot with the measure to expand the commission's role to congressional redistricting. The repealer, Proposition 27, failed by a 40 percent to 60 percent margin.

Political veterans in California continue to complain about the commission — in private. But longtime redistricting expert Bruce Cain, a professor of political science at the University of California-Berkeley and now executive director of the university's Washington, D.C., program, publicly challenged the commission approach in a presentation to the state legislators' group in January.

Cain told the legislators that commissions result in added costs because of the need to train commission members, hire additional staff and consultants and hold extra rounds of public hearings. In any event, Cain said that reformers "oversell" the likely benefits of commissions. Commissions "cannot avoid making political judgments" and are as likely as legislatures to run afoul of legal requirements, he says.

"It doesn't matter whether you have a pure heart," Cain concludes. "If you wind up with a plan that's unfair to one group or another, you're going to have trouble."

Cressman is optimistic about the California commission, which heard from a series of experts in training sessions in January and held its first public hearing in February. "They have a lot of expertise," Cressman says. "They strongly reflect the diversity of California. And they are quite ready to attack their job quite seriously."

Still, experts across the board profess uncertainty about whether the California commission will deliver on the supporters' promise of a fairer redistricting plan. "It's a very open question whether those hopes will be realized," says Douglas Johnson, president of the National Demographics Corporation, which consults on redistricting issues for governments and public interest groups. Johnson himself helped draft the initiative.

## BACKGROUND
### Political Thickets

The modern era of redistricting began in the 1960s when the Supreme Court intervened to force an end to state legislatures' decades-long neglect of the obligation to redraw legislative and congressional districts to reflect population changes. In a series of decisions, the court first opened the federal courts to redistricting suits and then laid down the famous "one person, one vote" requirement of mathematical equality — strict for congressional districts, slightly relaxed for legislative lines. The rulings redressed the underrepresentation of urban and suburban voters, but they also forced legislatures and the courts into the political thicket of redistricting every 10 years.[10]

The political uses of redistricting date back more than two centuries. Patrick Henry engineered district lines in an unsuccessful effort to prevent the election of his adversary James Madison to the House of Representatives in the nation's first congressional vote in 1788. The salamander-shaped district that Gov. Elbridge Gerry crafted for an 1812 legislative election in Massachusetts gave birth to the pejorative term "gerrymander" for politically motivated line-drawing.*

Through the 19th century, Congress passed laws requiring representatives to be elected in contiguous, single-member districts. A 1901 act — re-enacted in 1911 — specified that districts also be compact and contain "as nearly as practicable an equal number of inhabitants." The provisions went unenforced, however. Most notably, the House failed to act on a committee's recommendation

---

*Gerry pronounced his name with a hard "g," but "gerrymander" came to be pronounced with a soft "g."

## CHRONOLOGY

**Before 1960,** *Congress, courts take hands-off approach to reapportionment, redistricting lapses.*

**1908** House of Representatives refuses to enforce equal-population requirement, allows seating of member chosen from malapportioned district in Virginia.

**1932** Supreme Court rejects voters' suit challenging malapportioned Mississippi congressional districts.

**1946** Supreme Court rejects voters' suit challenging malapportioned Illinois congressional districts.

**1960s-1970s** *Supreme Court's "one-person, one-vote" revolution forces states to redraw legislative and congressional districts.*

**1962-1964** Supreme Court says federal courts can entertain suits to challenge state legislature's failure to reapportion (1962). . . . Adopts "one-person, one-vote" requirement for state legislative districts (1963). . . . Applies equal-population requirement to House seats, both chambers of state legislatures (1964).

**1965** Voting Rights Act prohibits interference with right to vote based on race (Section 2); imposes "preclearance" requirements for election law changes on nine states, local jurisdiction in seven others (Section 5).

**1969-1973** Supreme Court strikes down congressional districting plan because of 3 percent population variation (1969), but later allows nearly 10 percent variation for state legislative districts (1973).

**1980s-1990s** *Supreme Court allows suits to challenge partisan gerrymanders, racial line-drawing.*

**1980-1982** Supreme Court says Section 2 of Voting Rights Act prohibits only intentional discrimination; two years later, Congress adds "effects" test to prohibit any election law changes that abridge right to vote because of race.

**1983** Supreme Court strikes down congressional map with 1 percent variation between districts.

**1986** Supreme Court, in Indiana case, says federal courts can entertain suits to challenge legislative districting as partisan gerrymander; on remand, Republican-drawn plan is upheld against Democratic challenge.

**1993-1996** Supreme Court allows white voters' suit to challenge majority African-American congressional district in North Carolina (1993). . . . Later rulings strike down majority-minority districts in Georgia (1995), North Carolina (1996), Texas (1996).

**2000s–Present** *Redistricting reform proposals advance.*

**2000** Arizona voters approve creation of independent citizens' redistricting commission (Prop. 106).

**2001** Supreme Court upholds creation of majority African-American district in North Carolina; motivation was partisan, not racial, court finds.

**2001-2004** Republican-controlled Pennsylvania legislature redraws congressional districts to GOP's benefit (2001); Republicans gain 12-7 majority in state delegation (2002); Supreme Court rejects Democrats' challenge to plan; in splintered ruling, Justice Kennedy leaves door open to gerrymandering suits (2004).

**2003-2006** Republican-controlled Texas legislature reopens congressional districts, draws new map to GOP's benefit (2003); Republicans gain 21-11 majority in state delegation (2004); Democrats' challenge rejected by Supreme Court (2006).

**2008-2010** California voters approve citizens' commission to redraw state legislative districts (Prop. 11); two years later, add congressional redistricting to commission's responsibility (Prop. 20).

**2009** Supreme Court says states may reduce minority voters' influence if they constitute less than majority of voters in district.

**2010** Florida voters approve anti-gerrymandering constitutional amendments (Nov. 2). . . . House seats shift from Northeast, Midwest to South, West (Dec. 21).

**2011** States begin work on redistricting. . . . Louisiana, Mississippi, New Jersey, Virginia to hold legislative elections in November.

to bar a representative elected in 1908 from a malapportioned Virginia district redrawn earlier in the year to his benefit.[11]

Twice in the first half of the 20th century, the Supreme Court also balked at enforcing reapportionment requirements. In 1932, the court rejected a suit by Mississippi voters challenging the congressional district map drawn by the state legislature on the ground that it violated the 1911 act's requirements. The majority opinion held that the 1911 law had lapsed; four justices went further and said the federal courts should not have entertained the suit. The high court adopted that latter position in 1946 in turning aside a suit by Illinois voters challenging a congressional map as violating a state law requiring equal-population districts. Writing for a three-justice plurality in *Colegrove v. Green*, Justice Felix Frankfurter sternly warned against judicial review. "Courts ought not to enter this political thicket," Frankfurter wrote. A fourth justice joined in a narrower opinion, while three justices said in dissent they would have allowed the suit to go forward.[12]

The Supreme Court reversed direction in its landmark ruling in a Tennessee case, *Baker v. Carr*, in 1962. With Frankfurter in dissent, the court detailed Tennessee's failure to reapportion state legislative districts since 1901 and found urban voters entitled to use the Equal Protection Clause to challenge the malapportionment in federal court. The ruling went only so far as to send the case back to a lower court for a full trial, but in short order the Supreme Court went further. In 1963, it struck down Georgia's county-unit system for apportioning state legislative seats on the grounds that it disadvantaged large urban counties. "The concept of political equality," Justice William O. Douglas wrote in the 8-1 ruling, "can mean only one thing — one person, one vote." A year later, the court applied the equal-population requirement to congressional districts and to both chambers of bicameral state legislatures.[13]

The Supreme Court's rulings opened the door to a flood of reapportionment and redistricting lawsuits in the states. By one count, more than 40 states faced legal challenges by the time of the 1964 decisions. State legislatures across the country became more representative of the growing urban and suburban populations. In Tennessee, for example, both the House of Representatives and the Senate elected urban members as speakers at the turn of the decade. The rulings also affected membership in

the U.S. House of Representatives, if somewhat less dramatically. After the 1970 reapportionment, one study found that the number of members from rural districts had dropped from 59 to 51 while the number from urban and suburban districts rose from 147 to 161.[14]

In further cases, the court confronted how close to equal districts had to be to meet the one-person, one-vote test. For Congress, the court required strict and later stricter equality. In 1969, the justices rejected a Missouri redistricting plan because it resulted in as much as a 3.1 percent variation from perfectly equal population districts. Years later, the court in 1983 rejected, on a 5-4 vote, a New Jersey plan with less than 1 percent variation in population because the state had offered no justification for the discrepancies. States were given somewhat more leeway. In a pair of decisions in 1973, the court upheld Connecticut and Texas plans with variances, respectively, of 7.8 percent and 9.9 percent. And in 1983, on the same day as the ruling in the New Jersey case, the court upheld a Wyoming plan that gave each county at least one member in the state House of Representatives despite the large variation in district population that resulted.[15]

## Legal Puzzlers

The Supreme Court in the 1980s and '90s confronted but gave only puzzling answers to two second-generation redistricting issues: whether to open federal courts to challenges to partisan or political gerrymandering or to racially or ethnically based line-drawing. On the first issue, the court ostensibly recognized a constitutional claim against partisan gerrymandering, but gave such little guidance that no suits had succeeded in federal courts by the turn of the 21st century — or, indeed, have since. On the second issue, the court in a series of decisions in the 1990s allowed white voters to challenge racially or ethnically based districting plans and eventually barred using race or ethnicity as the "predominant" motive in redrawing districts.

The political gerrymandering issue reached the Supreme Court in a challenge by Indiana Democrats to a state legislative redistricting plan drawn by Republicans after the 1980 census that helped fortify GOP majorities in the 1982 elections. A federal district court agreed with the Democrats that the plan violated the Equal Protection Clause because it was intentionally designed to preserve Republicans' dominance. The Supreme Court ruled, 6-3,

# "Underrepresented" Voters Get No Help in Court

*"It's pretty clear that this is not equal and it's not as equal as practicable."*

The Constitution created the House of Representatives with 65 members, each representing no more than 30,000 people. Today, the House has 435 members, and their districts average about 710,000 constituents, according to the 2010 census.

That average conceals a wide variation from one state to another. Delaware's only congressman, freshman Democrat John Carney, represents about 900,000 people. In Wyoming, the state's only member of Congress, two-term Republican Cynthia Lummis, represents about 563,000 people.[1]

"One person, one vote" requires congressional districts to be equal in population within each state so that each person is equally represented in government. But the constitutional provision allotting one seat to each state combines with the need to round some fractions up and others down to make mathematical equality impossible from state to state.

Plaintiffs from five of the states disadvantaged in House seats under the 2000 census — Delaware, Mississippi, Montana, South Dakota and Utah — filed suit in federal court in Mississippi to challenge the disparities as a violation of their rights to equal representation in Congress. At the time, Montana had more than 900,000 people, just below the threshold then needed for a second House seat.

"We believe that it's pretty clear that this is not equal and it's not as equal as practicable," says Michael Farris, a constitutional lawyer in Northern Virginia and well-known conservative activist. Farris, a home-schooling advocate, recruited the plaintiffs for the case after being approached by another home-schooling father in the area.

In defending the suit, the government argued that complete elimination of the interstate disparities would require "an astronomical increase" in the size of the House. The number of House seats has been fixed since 1911 except for temporary increases to accommodate new states: Arizona and New Mexico in 1912, Alaska and Hawaii in the late 1950s.

Farris countered that an increase of as few as 10 seats would have reduced state disparities by half. And he noted that the British House of Commons has more than 500 members for a country with 62 million residents — one-fifth of the U.S. population of 308 million.

in *Davis v. Bandemer* (1986) that the suit presented a "justiciable" claim — that is, one that federal courts could hear. Only two of the six justices, however, agreed that the Indiana Democrats had proved their case. As a result, the case was sent back to the lower court, with no guidelines and for an eventual ruling against the Democrats. Challengers in gerrymandering cases over the next two decades were similarly unsuccessful.[16]

The Supreme Court first encountered a racial gerrymander in the late 1950s in a case brought by African-American voters who, in effect, had been carved out of the city of Tuskegee, Ala., by new, irregular municipal boundaries. The court in 1960 ruled unanimously that district lines drawn only to disenfranchise black voters violated the 15th Amendment.[17] The Voting Rights Act,

passed and signed into law five years later, went further by specifically prohibiting interference with the right to vote (Section 2) and forcing states and counties with a history of discrimination against minorities to preclear any election or voting changes with the Justice Department or a federal court in Washington (Section 5).

The Supreme Court upheld the act, but in 1980 held that Section 2 barred election law changes only if shown to be intentionally discriminatory. Two years later, Congress amended Section 2 by adding a "results" or "effects" test that prohibits any voting or election law change, nationwide, that denies or abridges anyone's right to vote on account of race or color. In applying the law to a North Carolina legislative redistricting case, the court crafted a three-part test for a so-called vote dilution claim. Under

The government also contended that the suit raised a "political question" that, in effect, was none of the federal courts' business. Ruling last summer, the three-judge district court hearing the case held that the plaintiffs had no right to equal representation in the House. "We see no reason to believe that the Constitution as originally understood or long applied imposes the requirements of close equality among districts in different States that the Plaintiffs seek here," the court wrote in the July 8 ruling.[2]

On appeal, the Supreme Court rejected the suit even more firmly by setting aside the district court's ruling with instructions to dismiss the case altogether. The court gave no explanation, but Farris says he assumed the justices decided the case on political-question grounds.

Farris is not the only advocate for increasing the size of the House. In an op-ed essay in *The New York Times*, two professors argued that a significantly larger House would allow representatives to be closer to their constituents, reduce the cost of campaigns and limit the influence of lobbyists and special interests. "It's been far too long since the House expanded to keep up with population growth," New York University sociologist Dalton Conley and Northwestern University political scientist Jacqueline Stevens wrote. As a result, Conley and Stevens contended, the House "has lost touch with the public and been overtaken by special interests."[3]

Farris also believes a larger House would be politically more responsive — and, in his view, more conservative. "Bigger districts create more liberal legislators," he says.

"The more it costs to campaign, the more beholden you are to people who want something from government."

Farris also warns that the disparities in the size of districts will increase over time. But he acknowledges that another court challenge may meet the same fate as his and that House members are unlikely to vote, in effect, to reduce their power by increasing the body's size. "The foxes have been given complete control of the henhouse," he says.

In the meantime, however, one of the states with the greatest underrepresentation under the 2000 apportionment — Utah — will be picking up a seat in the 2012 election. Under the new apportionment, Utah's four representatives will have about 692,000 constituents each, slightly below the national average. Delaware, Montana and South Dakota each remains well above the average district size, while Mississippi's four districts have about 744,000 people each, only slightly above the national average.

— *Kenneth Jost*

[1] For an interactive map showing average size of House districts state by state, see the Census Bureau's website: http://2010.census.gov/2010census/data/.

[2] *Clemons v. Department of Commerce*, No. 3:09-cv-00104 (U.S.D.C. — N.D. Miss.), July 8, 2010, www.apportionment.us/DistrictCourtOpinion.pdf. For coverage, see Jack Elliott Jr., "Judges reject lawsuit to increase size of House," The Associated Press, July 9, 2010.

[3] Dalton Conley and Jacqueline Stevens, "Build a Bigger House," *The New York Times*, Jan. 24, 2011, p. A27.

the so-called *Gingles* test, a plaintiff must show a concentrated minority voting bloc, a history of racially polarized voting and a change that diminishes the minority voters' effective opportunity to elect a candidate of their choice.[18]

Under President George H. W. Bush, the Justice Department interpreted the act in advance of the 1990 redistricting cycle to require states in some circumstances to draw majority-minority districts. Along with other factors, including incumbent protection and partisan balance, the requirement resulted in some very irregularly shaped districts. White voters challenged the district plans in several states, including North Carolina, Georgia and Texas, and won favorable rulings from the Supreme Court in each. The 1993 ruling in *Shaw v. Reno* reinstated a challenge to a majority-black district created by stitching

together African-American neighborhoods in three North Carolina cities. Subsequent rulings threw out majority-black districts in Georgia in 1995 and in Texas in 1996. In the Georgia case, the court declared that a district map could be invalidated if race was shown to be "the predominant factor motivating the legislature's decision to place a significant number of voters within or without a particular district."[19]

With a new decade beginning, however, the court recognized an escape hatch of sorts for states drawing majority-minority districts. In *Hunt v. Cromartie*, the court in 2001 upheld North Carolina's redrawing of the disputed majority-black 12th Congressional District in the center of the state. A lower federal court had found the district lines still to be "facially race driven," but the Supreme

Court instead said the state's motivation was "political rather than racial" — aimed at putting "reliably Democratic," African-American voters in the district. The message of the ruling, as *New York Times* reporter Linda Greenhouse wrote at the time, "was that race is not an illegitimate consideration in redistricting as long as it is not the 'dominant and controlling' one."[20]

The racial line-drawing combined with demographics to increase minority representatives in Congress. The number of African-Americans in the House of Representatives increased from 26 in 1991 to 37 in 2001, and the number of Hispanics from 11 to 19.[21] Minority groups hoped to continue to make gains in the new cycle.

Meanwhile, states braced for more litigation as the new redistricting cycle got under way. In the 1990s, 39 states were forced into court to defend redistricting plans on substantive grounds.[22] Most were upheld, but some legislatures were forced to redraw lines. And courts took over the process altogether in a few states, most notably California. There, a Democratic-controlled legislature and a Republican governor deadlocked at the start of the decade, forcing the California Supreme Court to appoint a team of special masters to draw the legislative and congressional maps.

## Crosscurrents

The post-2000 redistricting cycle brought a new round of political fights and legal challenges along with the nation's first experience in Arizona with an independent citizens redistricting commission. As in the previous decade, state or federal courts in many states forced legislatures to redraw redistricting plans or drew redistricting plans themselves after legislative impasses. Arizona's independent commission itself faced protracted litigation over its plans but ended with its maps left largely intact. The Supreme Court, meanwhile, retreated somewhat from its activist posture of the 1990s. The court declined twice to crack down on partisan gerrymandering, while its rulings on racial line-drawing gave legislatures somewhat more discretion to avoid drawing favorable districts for minorities.[23]

Arizona's Proposition 106 grew out of discontent with a Republican-drawn redistricting plan in 1992 that solidified GOP control of the legislature while giving little help to the state's growing Hispanic population. The ballot measure gained approval on Nov. 7, 2000, with 56 percent of the vote after a campaign waged by good-government groups, including Common Cause and the League of Women Voters, and bankrolled by a wealthy Democratic activist. The congressional and legislative plans drawn by the five-member commission were challenged in court by Democrats and minority groups for failing to create enough competitive districts. In state court, the congressional map was upheld, while the legislative map was initially ordered redrawn. In a second ruling, however, the state court in 2008 found the commission had given sufficient consideration to competitiveness along with the other five criteria listed in the measure.

In other states, redistricting was still being played as classic political hardball. In Pennsylvania, a GOP-controlled legislature and Republican governor combined in 2001 to redraw a congressional map after the loss of two House seats that helped the GOP win a 12-7 edge in the state's delegation in the 2002 election. The Democratic challenge to the Pennsylvania plan went to the Supreme Court, where the justices blinked at the evident partisan motivation. Justice Kennedy's refusal to join four other conservatives in barring partisan gerrymandering suits left the issue for another day. But the four liberals' failure to agree on a single standard for judging such cases gave little help to potential challengers in future cases.[24]

Two years later, the Texas redistricting case produced a similarly disappointing decision for critics of partisan gerrymandering. Preliminarily, the court found no bar to Texas's mid-decade redistricting. On the gerrymandering claim, Kennedy wrote for three justices in finding that the new map better corresponded to the state's political alignment than the previous districts; two others — Antonin Scalia and Clarence Thomas — repeated their call for barring gerrymandering challenges altogether. Kennedy also led a conservative majority in upholding the breaking up of African-American voters in Dallas and Houston, but he joined with the liberal bloc to find the dispersal of Latino voters in the Rio Grande Valley a Voting Rights Act violation.[25]

In other Voting Rights Act cases, the Supreme Court and lower federal courts generally moved toward giving state legislators more leeway on how to draw racial and ethnic lines. In 2003, the high court upheld a Democratic-drawn plan in Georgia that moved African-American voters out of majority-black legislative districts to create adjoining "influence" districts where they could form majorities with like-minded voters. In the North Carolina

# Bringing Redistricting to the Big Screen

*"I would like to see more people involved in the redistricting process."*

Jeff Reichert, a self-described left-wing political junkie, remembers being both fascinated and outraged at the political shenanigans that Texas Republicans carried out to redraw congressional districts to their benefit in 2003. Reichert, who was working with a film-distribution company at the time, began to think of going behind the camera himself to bring the somewhat arcane subject of redistricting to the big screen.

"I just couldn't shake it," Reichert says today of his urge to make *Gerrymandering*, an 81-minute documentary released to theaters in fall 2010. "I thought there was a way of making a movie out of this."

Documentary filmmaker Jeff Reichert defends *Gerrymandering's* one-sided examination of redistricting practices. "A lot of people feel that redistricting isn't working," he says.

© Green Film Company

The film cost "mid-six figures" to produce, Reichert says, with much of that money coming from "folks in California who had worked on the reform effort." The reformers made good use of the investment. In 2010, supporters of the 2008 ballot initiative put their weight behind a new effort — Proposition 20 — to give the citizens' commission responsibility for congressional redistricting as well. The supporters bought 660,000 copies of Reichert's DVD to send to California voters before the November midterm elections. Proposition 20 passed, with a better margin than its predecessor two years earlier.

The film drew some attention when shown in festivals in spring and summer 2010. The reviews on *Rotten Tomatoes*, a popular movie-fan website, are mixed.

True to its origins, the film takes a hard and mostly critical look at legislators' time-dishonored practice of drawing district lines to help one's friends and hurt one's foes. [1] Presidents of both parties — Democrats John F. Kennedy and Barack Obama and Republicans Ronald Reagan and George H. W. Bush — denounce the practice in the film's opening. The Texas story is told at length, with semicomic efforts by outvoted Democrats to decamp to Oklahoma to deny Republicans a quorum needed to complete their legislative coup.

The film gains more structure and immediacy from the successful effort in 2008 to pass California's Proposition 11, a ballot initiative to create an independent citizens redistricting commission charged with drawing state legislative boundaries. Gov. Arnold Schwarzenegger, the face of the initiative, and state Common Cause Executive Director Kathay Feng, the organizational mastermind, are presented as crusaders for the public good. "Pass Proposition 11," placards read, "to hold politicians accountable."

"Sincere but slick," one commenter writes. *New York Times* film critic Stephen Holden faulted the Proposition 11 story as "sloppily told" and took Reichert to task for failing to show anyone in defense of redistricting practices. [2]

Reichert makes no apologies for the film's one-sided critique of gerrymandering. "Documentary filmmakers aren't journalists," he says. "I have a perspective. I would like to see more people involved in the redistricting process."

Still, Reichert takes a time-will-tell attitude toward California's experiment with citizen-drawn district lines and reform efforts in other states. Some will succeed, he says, and some won't. For now, however, "a lot of people feel that redistricting isn't working."

*— Kenneth Jost*

---

[1] For background, see the film's website: www.gerrymanderingmovie.com.

[2] Stephen Holden, "The Dark Art of Drawing Political Lines," *The New York Times*, Oct. 15, 2010, p. C18.

case six years later, however, the court made plain that legislators were also free to decide not to create such "crossover" or "influence" districts. In that case, a lower state court had interpreted the Voting Rights Act to require concentrating minority voters even if they did not constitute a majority in the district.[26]

As the decade neared an end, new attention was focused on reform proposals. In California, Gov. Schwarzenegger had made redistricting reform a major issue since taking office in 2003. In 2005, voters rejected by a 3-2 margin his ballot measure, Proposition 77, to give redistricting authority to a panel of retired judges. Three years later, Schwarzenegger worked closely with Common Cause and the League of Women Voters to push the more complex citizens' commission proposal, Proposition 11. In a crucial decision, supporters sought to neutralize potential opposition from members of Congress by leaving congressional redistricting in the legislature's hands. The plan won approval by fewer than 200,000 votes out of 12 million cast (51 percent to 49 percent). Two years later, with House Democrats focused on midterm elections, the measure to add congressional redistricting to the commission's authority, Proposition 20, passed easily.

In Florida, reformers suffered a setback mid-decade when the state supreme court barred a redistricting proposal in 2005 as violating the state's "single-subject rule" for initiatives. The redrawn proposals, on the ballot in November 2010 as Amendments 5 and 6, set out parallel criteria for the legislature to follow in redrawing legislative and congressional districts: contiguous, compact where possible, "not drawn to favor or disfavor an incumbent or political party" and "not drawn to deny racial or language minorities the equal opportunity to participate in the political process and elect representatives of their choice." Fair Districts Florida received major contributions from teachers' unions; the opposition group, Protect Our Vote, got the bulk of its money from the state's Republican Party. The measure passed with 62.6 percent of the vote.

## CURRENT SITUATION

### Advantage: Republicans

Republican control of congressional redistricting machinery in major states adding or losing House seats puts the GOP in a favorable position to gain or hold ground in the 2012 elections. But Democrats will try to minimize partisan line-drawing and lay the groundwork for court challenges later.

The November 2010 elections gave Republicans undivided control of 25 state legislatures plus Nebraska's nominally nonpartisan unicameral body. Democrats control 16, while eight other states have divided party control between two chambers. "Republicans control more legislatures," says Columbia law professor Persily. "They are in the driver's seat when it comes to drawing lines."

But Jeffrey Wice, a Democratic redistricting attorney in Washington, says pressure by good-government groups for greater transparency and public participation adds a new element that may reduce partisan gerrymandering. "We're too early in the game to predict winners and losers," Wice says. "There's no simplicity in this process."

Out of eight states picking up House seats in the current reapportionment, Republicans control both houses of the state legislature and the governor's offices in five, including the two biggest gainers: Texas, with four new seats, and Florida, with two. The GOP also has undivided control in Georgia, South Carolina and Utah, each picking up one seat. All five states currently have majority-Republican delegations.

Republicans also have undivided control in three states to lose seats: Ohio, giving up two seats, as well as Michigan and Pennsylvania. In those states, Republican lawmakers are likely to draw maps to try to avoid losing House seats in the currently majority-GOP delegations.

Democrats start the congressional redistricting process with significantly less leverage. They have undivided control of redistricting machinery in none of the three other states to gain seats. Arizona and Washington both use bipartisan commissions to redraw congressional districts. In Nevada, Democrats have majorities in both legislative chambers, but Republican Gov. Brian Sandoval could veto a redistricting plan approved by the legislature.

Among states losing seats, Democrats have undivided control only in Illinois, where Republicans currently have an 11-8 majority in the House delegation, and Massachusetts, where Democrats hold all nine current House seats. In New York, which loses two seats, Democrats control the Assembly and Republicans the Senate — setting the stage for a likely deal in which each party yields one House district.

# Should redistricting be done by independent commissions?

## YES

**Derek Cressman**
*Western regional director,*
*Common Cause*

Written for *CQ Researcher*, February 2011

Throughout 2011, states will redraw their political districts in a process usually controlled either directly or indirectly by state legislators, the very people with the most to gain or lose from the outcome. The process will almost always cater to incumbent or partisan self-interests. Too often, it also will divide communities, dilute the political strength of ethnic voters and virtually guarantee re-election for the vast majority of incumbents. Unable to hold politicians accountable, too many voters will be left feeling powerless, and citizen participation in politics will suffer.

Reforming this dysfunctional process is fundamental to restoring both a truly representative government and one that can solve societal problems. When voters are disengaged and stay home on election day, legislators have little incentive to act, whatever the issue.

Gerrymandering — manipulating district lines in a way that essentially predetermines election results — has been with us since the early days of our republic. Today, it's more sophisticated, and more sinister, than ever.

Using powerful computer-mapping software, legislators and their political consultants can draw boundaries that remove a potential opponent from a district, add or subtract voters of a certain ethnicity, bring in big donors or concentrate members of an opposing party in a single district to reduce their overall representation. Elections in the ensuing decade are so predetermined that there is little left for voters to choose.

This is a mess best addressed by turning over redistricting to independent, citizen commissions whose members have no stake in where the lines are drawn. California recently made this move, creating a citizens commission of five Democrats, five Republicans and four independent or minor-party voters. The new law requires the panel to make compliance with the federal Voting Rights Act a priority and avoid splitting communities. The commission is prohibited from drawing districts to aid any incumbent legislator off-the-record. Most important, the commission has to conduct all hearings in public, with no off-record conversations about maps allowed.

Other states have created similar panels, though none go as far as California to wring partisanship and self-interest from the redistricting process. And while no commission can be expected to produce maps that please everyone, any effort that shifts the focus of redistricting toward the voters' interest in accountable, effective government and away from the politicians' interest in self-preservation and partisan advantage is a step in the right direction.

## NO

**Bruce E. Cain**
*Heller Professor of Political Science, University*
*of California, Berkeley, and Executive Director,*
*UC Washington Center*

Written for *CQ Researcher*, February 2011

Replacing legislative redistricting with independent commissions is high on the reform agenda, but is it really so obviously irrational or shameful for a state to resist this trend?

Even the most independent commissions, such as those in Arizona and California, have peculiar issues. Most basically, there is the composition problem. Legislatures are imperfectly reflective of state populations, but they are at least democratically elected and relatively large. Commissions are both appointed (in California's case by an odd, convoluted mix of jury selection and college application-style procedures) and small (making it harder to reflect population diversity). If there is controversy over the lines, as there usually is, these composition disputes can figure prominently in the ensuing litigation.

For good and bad reasons, commissions tend to be more expensive. There are high costs associated with being more open and independent. Greater transparency means more hearings and outreach efforts, which are costly and time consuming to set up, and the yield in terms of broad public participation as opposed to the usual interested groups will likely be low. And given that any association with political parties or elected officials is grounds for exclusion by virtue of excessive political interest, commissions cannot borrow from legislative and political staff. They must hire consultants instead.

Commissions are also no less likely to end up in lawsuits or political controversies. Redistricting is inherently political, involving choices and trade-offs related to race, communities of interest, the integrity of city and county boundaries, the number of competitive seats and so on. However one chooses, someone is going to feel aggrieved. Commissioners cannot be sequestered like jury members or insulated from political influences. Doing without political or incumbency data only means making controversial decisions blindly, not avoiding them. The losers in redistricting disputes will derive little consolation from the commission's efforts at impartiality by empirical blindness, which is why commissions to date have been no more successful in avoiding legal challenges.

On the other side, the sins of legislative redistricting have been grossly exaggerated. Partisan redistricting is rare, and in states with term limits, redistricting is less important than it used to be. Studies show that effects of redistricting on competition and party polarization are marginal at best, casting doubt on the hyperventilated assertions of commission advocates.

So adopt a commission if you must, but expect no miracles. Just be prepared to pay the consultants' bills.

Ed Cook, legal counsel for the Iowa Legislative Services Agency, displays a map Feb. 9 that is being used to help draw new congressional district lines in the state. Iowa is losing a seat in the U.S. House of Representatives during reapportionment. Unique among the states, Iowa essentially assigns legislative and congressional redistricting to professional staff, subject to legislative enactment and gubernatorial approval.

Louisiana's legislature is also divided, with Republicans in control in the House and the two parties tied with one vacancy in the Senate. Democrats hold only one of the state's current seven House seats. In Missouri, a Republican-controlled legislature will draw congressional districts, but Democratic Gov. Jay Nixon has to sign or veto any plan approved by lawmakers.

New Jersey, the one other state losing a House seat, uses a bipartisan commission. Democrats have a 7-6 majority in the state's current congressional delegation, but the state is losing population in the predominantly Democratic north and gaining population in Republican areas to the west and south.

California poses the biggest question mark for the 2012 congressional districts. The state's current congressional map favors Democrats, who hold 35 of the 53 House seats. Democrats also hold a nearly 2-to-1 majority in both legislative chambers.

A chart presented to the Citizens Redistricting Commission in an early training session shows that congressional districts in predominantly Democratic Los Angeles and San Francisco are now underpopulated, while districts in some Republican areas — such as the so-called Inland Empire to the east of Los Angeles — are overpopulated.[27] As a result, Los Angeles and San Francisco

could lose seats or at least shed voters to adjoining districts.

The commission has pointedly avoided deciding so far whether — or to what extent — to use the existing legislative and congressional districts as a starting point for the new maps. But commission members Ward and Dai both stressed that the ballot measures creating the commission specifically prohibit any consideration of protecting incumbents. "The idea of creating competitive districts," Ward adds, "seems to be unanimous among the commissioners."

In some Republican-controlled states, demographics may limit the GOP's opportunity to gain ground. In particular, Latino advocacy groups believe that Texas will be required to make two of the four new congressional districts majority Latino. That would benefit Democrats since Latinos in Texas and elsewhere have been voting predominantly Democratic in recent elections.

In Virginia, a different demographic change — the growth of the Northern Virginia suburbs surrounding Washington, D.C. — is seen as a possible benefit for Democrats in redrawing the existing 11 House seats despite the GOP's control of the redistricting machinery. Northern Virginia is seen as more liberal than rural counties in the state's south and west, some of which are losing population, according to the Census Bureau.

### Forecast: Cloudy

California's new Citizens Redistricting Commission is just getting organized even as a midsummer deadline looms for the 14 map-drawing neophytes to complete the nation's largest legislative and congressional redistricting.

The commission spent two-and-a-half days in mid-February working on housekeeping matters without touching on any of the politically sensitive issues members will face in redrawing lines for 53 congressional districts, 40 state Senate districts and 80 state Assembly districts in the nation's most populous state

"We do believe we're behind schedule," says Ward, the Anaheim chiropractor who held the rotating position of chair for the commission's Feb. 10-12 sessions. "Given the compressed time line, I don't believe you can ever be on schedule."

As in California, redistricting is still in initial stages in most states, but is moving faster in the four that must redraw legislative lines quickly because of general elections scheduled this fall and primary elections beginning this summer. Besides New Jersey, the others are Louisiana, Mississippi and Virginia — Southern states with divided legislatures and significant African-American populations. Under the Voting Rights Act, all three must have redistricting maps precleared by either the Justice Department or a federal court in Washington.

The California commission is working on an ambitious series of four public sessions in each of nine regions in the state, with informational or educational workshops to explain the redistricting process hoped to begin in March. Plans then call for more formal public-input meetings to be held before maps are drawn, as they are being drawn and again after the maps are completed.

Proposition 20, the 2010 ballot measure, established an Aug. 15 deadline for the maps to be certified to the state's secretary of state. But commission member Dai explains that to allow time for public notice and for preclearance — five of the state's counties are subject to the Voting Rights Act's Section 5 — the commission's target date for completion is July 25.

The four states with legislative elections this year are all moving to get redistricting maps up for decisions in March or April.

In New Jersey, the 10-member legislative redistricting commission — with five members appointed by each of the Democratic and Republican state chairs — is holding a series of public hearings aimed at submitting a map by an early April deadline. "The two delegations have been working on tentative maps," says Alan Rosenthal, a professor of political science at Rutgers University in Newark, who is a likely candidate to be named by the state's chief justice as a tie-breaker if the commission reaches an impasse. The separate commission to redraw New Jersey's congressional districts — to be reduced from 13 to 12 — has not been appointed yet.

In Louisiana, the legislature's governmental affairs committees were due to complete eight public hearings around the state by March 1; the legislature was then to convene on March 20 in special session to redraw legislative and congressional districts. Mississippi's Standing Joint Committee on Reapportionment also held public hearings in February, with an announced plan to bring redistricting proposals to the floor of each chamber in early March.

In Virginia the General Assembly's Joint Reapportionment Committee set up an Internet site in December for public comment on redistricting proposals and then laid plans for a special session to begin April 6. Meanwhile, Republican Gov. Bob McDonnell fulfilled a campaign pledge on Jan. 9 by appointing a bipartisan, 11-member advisory commission on redistricting. The commission plans to propose legislative and congressional redistricting plans by April 1, but the legislature will not be bound to follow the recommendations.

Meanwhile, political skirmishes are breaking out in other states. Litigation is already under way in Florida over the newly passed anti-gerrymandering ballot measures. Two minority-group members of Congress filed a federal court suit immediately after the election challenging Amendment 6 on congressional redistricting as a violation of the Constitution and the Voting Rights Act. Reps. Mario Diaz-Balart, a Hispanic Republican, and Corrine Brown, an African-American Democrat, argue standards for congressional district-drawing are up to Congress, not the states; in addition, they say the Voting Rights Act requires protection for already-elected minority legislators. Separately, supporters of the amendment have filed suit against Republican Gov. Rick Scott for failing to submit Amendment 6 to the Justice Department for preclearance.[28]

In other states, Democratic legislators in New York are pressing the GOP-controlled state Senate to stick to pre-election campaign pledges by Republican members and candidates to support an independent commission to redraw lines. In Michigan, a coalition of reform groups is urging the GOP-controlled legislature to allow more public input by posting any redistricting maps on the Internet at least 30 days before taking action. And in Illinois, Democratic Gov. Pat Quinn is weighing whether to sign a bill approved by the Democratic-controlled legislature to require four public hearings on any redistricting proposal and, significantly, to require creation of minority group-protective "crossover" and "influence" districts where feasible.

# OUTLOOK:

## Not a Pretty Picture?

The 20 "most gerrymandered" congressional districts in the United States selected by the online magazine *Slate* present an ugly picture of the redistricting process. The boundaries of the districts — 16 of them represented by

Democrats as of 2009 — zig and zag, twist and turn and jut in and out with no apparent logic.[29]

To redistricting expert Storey, however, many of the districts amount to marvels of political-representation engineering. As one example, Storey points to Arizona-2, which stretches from the Phoenix suburbs to the state's northwestern border and then connects only by means of the Colorado River to a chunk of territory halfway across the state to the east.

As Storey explains, the safely Republican district was drawn in the post-2000 cycle to include a Hopi reservation while placing the surrounding reservation of the rival Navajo nation in an adjoining district. And the districting scheme was crafted not by a politically motivated legislature but by the then brand-new independent citizens redistricting commission.

Among *Slate's* list of worst districts are others drawn to connect minority communities, such as Illinois-4 (majority Hispanic) and several majority African-American districts in the South (Alabama-7, Florida-23, North Carolina-12). "Lines that look funny may represent real communities without any partisan motivation," says Loyola law professor Levitt.

"There are reasons why districts aren't pretty," adds Cynthia Canary, director of the Illinois Campaign for Political Reform. "But people want pretty."

The people who "want pretty" may well be disappointed again with the post-2010 redistricting cycle despite the concerted efforts of reform-minded groups and experts to improve the process. "This is going to be hardball politics," Sherri Greenberg, a professor at the University of Texas Lyndon B. Johnson School of Public Affairs in Austin and a former Texas legislator, says of the state's redistricting process just now under way. "This is a process that creates enemies, not friends."

In California, however, members of the Citizens Redistricting Commission are professing optimism that they can reach a bipartisan agreement on maps that are both fairer and more competitive than the existing legislative and congressional districts. "There really has been no evidence of partisanship among the commissioners," says Dai, one of the Democratic members. Asked whether a bipartisan agreement is "doable," Republican commissioner Ward replies simply: "Undoubtedly, yes, it is doable."

Reformers are similarly hopeful about the likely outcome of the anti-gerrymandering measures in Florida.

"It's going to stop the most egregious gerrymanders," says MacDonald, the professor who co-founded the Public Mapping Group. But John Ryder, the Tennessean who heads the Republican National Committee's redistricting committee, says the Florida measures — with the stated prohibition against helping or hurting a political party or candidate — defy logic. "It's simply an unenforceable standard," he says.

Latino advocacy groups have high hopes — and expectations — for the current round of redistricting. MALDEF president Thomas Saenz predicts nine new majority-Hispanic districts, including two in Texas. Perales, the group's litigation director, makes clear that MALDEF is prepared to go to court to defend plans that increase Latinos' political influence and challenge any that do not.

For her part, the NAACP Legal Defense Fund's Clarke declines to predict whether the redistricting cycle will help elect more African-Americans to the next Congress. "We don't have quotas," Clarke says. But she stresses that the Legal Defense Fund is closely monitoring developments in states to try to prevent dismantling existing influence districts as well as those with majority black population.

Politically, experts are predicting Republican gains in the 2012 congressional elections, thanks to geographic shifts as well as political control of redistricting machinery in close to half the states. Galdaresi, the UC-Irvine professor, expects the GOP to pick up seven to 15 House seats.

Political pros profess uncertainty. "I think it takes a pretty good crystal ball to predict what the net effect of redistricting is," the RNC's Ryder says. Democratic attorney Wice thinks public pressure may reduce Republicans' ability to engineer favorable plans. "It's not over by any means to give the Republicans the final word," he says.

Whatever happens in the first round, many, perhaps most, of the redistricting plans will be headed for a second round in the courts. "It's hard not to predict litigation in redistricting," says Perales. "Somebody's always unhappy after the plan is done."

Increased public participation may influence the process not only in legislatures and commissions but also in the courts, according to Norman Ornstein, a longtime Congress watcher now at the conservative American Enterprise Institute think tank. "Courts will have more information to use in evaluating or drawing maps," he says.

But the calls for more public participation will be a challenge to citizen groups. "This is an incredibly complex topic," says Canary. "Nobody out in the public knows why it is so complicated."

## NOTES

1. Dai's and Ward's background taken in part from their application for the positions, posted on the California Citizens Redistricting Commission's website: http://wedrawthelines.ca.gov//.

2. For previous *CQ Researcher* coverage, see Kenneth Jost, "Redistricting Disputes," March 12, 2004, pp. 221-248; Jennifer Gavin, "Redistricting," Feb. 16, 2001, pp. 113-128; Ronald D. Elving, "Redistricting: Drawing Power With a Map," Feb. 15, 1991, pp. 98-113.

3. For background, see Nadine Cohodas, "Electing Minorities," *CQ Researcher*, Aug. 12, 1994; pp. 697-720.

4. The Texas case is *League of United Latin American Citizens (LULAC) v. Perry*, 548 U.S. 399 (2006). The previous cases are *Vieth v. Jubelirer*, 541 U.S. 267 (2004); and *Davis v. Bandemer*, 478 U.S. 109 (1986).

5. Thomas Brunell, *Redistricting and Representation: Why Competitive Elections Are Bad for America* (2008).

6. The quote is from a power-point presentation, "Redistricting 101," by the Brennan Center for Justice and MALDEF, dated Feb. 23, 2010, www.midwestredistricting.org/. The court case is *Hastert v. State Board of Elections*, 777 F.Supp. 634 (N.D. Ill. 1991). For coverage, see Thomas Hardy, "GOP in clover as federal judges approve congressional remap," *Chicago Tribune*, Nov. 7, 1991, p. 2.

7. The first three decisions are *Miller v. Johnson*, 515 U.S. 900 (1995) (Georgia); *Shaw v. Hunt*, 517 U.S. 889 (1996) (North Carolina); and *Bush v. Vera*, 517 U.S. 952 (1996) (Texas). The Supreme Court summarily upheld the Illinois plan in *King v. Illinois Board of Elections*, 522 U.S. 1087 (1998). The final ruling is *Hunt v. Cromartie*, 532 U.S. 234 (2001). For a summary compilation, see "Redistricting Disputes," *op. cit.*, p. 228.

8. The citation is 556 U.S. 1 (2009).

9. The Arizona Independent Redistricting Commission's website is at www.azredistricting.org/?page=.

10. For a comprehensive overview, see "Reapportionment and Redistricting" in *Guide to Congress* (6th ed., 2008), pp. 1039-1072. See also "The Right to an Equal Vote" in David G. Savage, *Guide to the U.S. Supreme Court* (5th ed., 2010), Vol. 1, pp. 640-653.

11. Edward W. Saunders was elected from Virginia's 5th congressional district in 1908 after Floyd County was transferred to the adjoining 6th district. The transfer left the 5th district with significantly less population than the 6th. Saunders' opponent, who would have won the election in the district as previously drawn, challenged Saunders' seating on the ground of the 1901 apportionment act; a committee recommended the challenger be seated, but the House did not act on the recommendation. See "Reapportionment and Redistricting," *op. cit.*, p. 1049.

12. The Mississippi case is *Wood v. Broom*, 287 U.S. 1 (1932). The citation for *Colegrove v. Green* is 327 U.S. 549 (1946). The dissenting justices were Hugo L. Black, William O. Douglas and Francis Murphy.

13. See *Baker v. Carr*, 369 U.S. 186 (1962); *Gray v. Sanders*, 372 U.S. 368 (1963); *Wesberry v. Sanders*, 376 U.S. 1 (1964); *Reynolds v. Sims*, 377 U.S. 533 (1964).

14. Jack L. Noragon, "Congressional Redistricting and Population Composition, 1964-1970," *Midwest Journal of Political Science*, Vol. 16, No. 2 (May 1972), pp. 295-302, www.jstor.org/pss/2110063.

15. The cases are detailed in Savage, *op. cit.*, pp. 646-650.

16. The citation is 478 U.S. 109 (1986).

17. The case is *Gomillon v. Lightfoot*, 364 U.S. 339 (1960).

18. The decision is *Thornburg v. Gingles*, 478 U.S. 30 (1986); the earlier ruling is *Mobile v. Bolden*, 446 U.S. 55 (1980).

19. For a summary compilation, with citations, see "Redistricting Disputes," *op. cit.*, p. 228.

20. See Linda Greenhouse, "Justices Permit Race as a Factor in Redistricting," *The New York Times*, April 19, 2001, p. A1.

21. "Redistricting Disputes," *op. cit.*, p. 233.

22. *Outline of Redistricting Litigation: The 1990s*, National Conference of State Legislatures, www.sen ate.mn/departments/scr/redist/redout.htm.

23. Coverage drawn in part from *Outline of Redistricting Litigation: The 2000s, National Conference of State Legislatures*, www.senate.mn/departments/scr/redist/redsum2000/redsum2000.htm.

24. The case is *Vieth v. Jubelirer, op. cit.* For a comprehensive account, see Kenneth Jost, *Supreme Court Yearbook 2003-2004*.

25. The case is *LULAC v. Perry, op. cit.* For a comprehensive account, see Kenneth Jost, *Supreme Court Yearbook 2005-2006*. See also Steve Bickerstaff, *Lines in the Sand: Congressional Redistricting in Texas and the Downfall of Tom DeLay* (2007).

26. The decisions are *Georgia v. Ashcroft*, 539 U.S. 461 (2003); *Bartlett v. Strickland, op. cit.*

27. Karin MacDonald and Nicole Boyle, "Redistricting California: An Overview of Data, Processes and GIS," Statewide Database_Berkeley Law, p. 53, http://wedrawthelines.ca.gov/downloads/crc_pub lic_meeting_20101130_training_karin_mac_donald_nicole_boyle.pdf.

28. See Marc Caputo and Lee Logan, "Redistricting Amendment Challenged," *St. Petersburg Times*, Nov. 4, 2010, p. 4B; Steve Bousquet, "Scott's Action May Stall Ban on Gerrymandering," *ibid.*, Jan. 26, 2011, p. 1B.

29. See "The 20 Most Gerrymandered Districts," *Slate*, www.slate.com/id/2274411/slideshow/2208554/fs/0//entry/2208555/. The unsigned, undated slide show was apparently posted in 2009.

## BIBLIOGRAPHY

### Books

**Brunell, Thomas, *Redistricting and Representation: Why Competitive Elections Are Bad for America*, Routledge, 2008.**

A professor at the University of Texas at Dallas argues that competitive elections are not vital for effective representation, but in fact increase the number of people who "are left unrepresented in Congress." Includes notes, references.

**Bullock, Charles S. III, *Redistricting: The Most Political Activity in America*, Rowman & Littlefield, 2010.**

A professor at the University of Georgia summarizes background information on congressional and legislative redistricting and examines the strategies and tactics of a process that he says is inevitably political if in control of elected officials. Includes notes.

**Cox, Gary W., and Jonathan N. Katz, *Elbridge Gerry's Salamander: The Electoral Consequences of the Reapportionment Revolution*, Cambridge University Press, 2002.**

The authors argue that, contrary to conventional wisdom, the reapportionment revolution of the 1960s onward was not without political consequence but had two lasting effects: strengthening the Democratic advantage in the U.S. House of Representatives and the advantage of incumbents over challengers. Cox is a professor emeritus at the University of California-San Diego, Katz a professor at the California Institute of Technology. Includes notes, references

**Galderisi, Peter F. (ed.), *Redistricting in the New Millennium*, Lexington Books, 2005.**

The 14 essays by 18 contributors include overviews of events through the turn of the 21st century, detailed examination of race and redistricting and case studies of redistricting in several states. Editor Galderisi is a lecturer at the University of California-San Diego. Includes notes, 12-page bibliography.

**Winburn, Jonathan, *The Realities of Redistricting: Following the Rules and Limiting Gerrymandering in State Legislative Redistricting*, Lexington Books, 2008.**

A professor at the University of Mississippi examines the "realities" of redistricting as seen in four institutional settings: unified partisan control of the state legislature; divided partisan control; partisan commission; and bipartisan commission. Includes selected bibliography.

**Yarbrough, Tinsley, *Race and Redistricting: The Shaw-Cromartie Cases*, University Press of Kansas, 2002.**

A professor at East Carolina University chronicles the decadelong fight over congressional redistricting in

North Carolina that first recognized constitutional objections to racially drawn district lines but ended with upholding a plan with district lines drawn to take race into account to some degree. Includes chronology, short bibliographical essay.

## Articles

**"Reapportionment and Redistricting," in *Guide to Congress* (6th ed.), CQ Press, 2007, pp. 1039-1072, http://library.cqpress.com/congressguide/toc.php?mode=guides-toc&level=3&values=Part+VII%3A+Congress+and+the+Electorate~Ch.+33++Reapportionment+and+Redistricting (purchase required).**
The chapter provides a comprehensive overview of developments in regard to congressional reapportionment and redistricting from the Constitutional Convention through the mid-2000's. Includes select bibliography.

## Reports and Studies

**"The Impact of Redistricting in YOUR Community: A Guide to Redistricting," NAACP Legal Defense and Educational Fund/Asian American Justice Center/ Mexican American Legal Defense and Educational Fund, 2010.**
The 78-page guide covers redistricting practices and policies as they affect racial and ethnic minorities.

Includes state-by-state listing of contact information for redistricting authorities.

**Levitt, Justin, "A Citizen's Guide to Redistricting," Brennan Center for Justice at New York University School of Law, 2010, http://brennan.3cdn.net/7182a 7e7624ed5265d_6im622teh.pdf.**
The 127-page guide published by the nonpartisan public policy and law institute covers from an often critical perspective the basics of current redistricting practices and outlines current reform proposals. Includes additional resources, notes, other appendix materials. Levitt is now an associate professor at Loyola Law School in Los Angeles.

**"Redistricting Law 2010," National Conference of State Legislatures, 2009.**
The 228-page guide covers current redistricting practices, step by step and subject by subject. Includes notes, extensive appendix materials.

## On the Web

**GovTrack, www.govtrack.us/congress/findyourreps .xpd.**
This private, unofficial website includes well-organized, state-by-state information and maps on congressional districts and current members of Congress.

*Note: For earlier works, see "Bibliography" in Kenneth Jost, "Redistricting Debates," CQ Researcher, March 12, 2004, p. 243.*

# For More Information

**Asian America Justice Center**, 1140 Connecticut Ave., N.W., #1200, Washington, DC 20036; (202) 296-2300; www.advancingequality.org. Organization founded in 1991 to advance human and civil rights of Asian Americans.

**Brennan Center for Justice**, New York University Law School, 161 Sixth Ave., 12th Floor, New York, NY 10013; (646) 292-8310; www.brennancenter.org. Nonpartisan public policy and law institute founded in 1995 that focuses in part on voting rights and campaign and election reform.

**Common Cause**, 1250 Connecticut Ave., N.W., #600, Washington, DC 20036; (202) 833-1200; www.commoncause.org. Nonpartisan public-interest advocacy organization founded in 1970.

**League of United Latin American Citizens**, 2000 L St., N.W., Suite 610, Washington, DC 20036; (202) 833-6130; www.lulac.org. Organization founded in 1929 to advance the economic condition, educational attainment, political influence, housing, health and civil rights of the U.S. Hispanic population.

**League of Women Voters**, 1730 M St., N.W., Suite 1000, Washington, DC 20036-4508; (202) 429-1965; www.lwv .org. Nonpartisan organization founded in 1920 to promote government reform through education and advocacy.

**Mexican American Legal Defense and Educational Fund**, 634 S. Spring St., Los Angeles, CA; (213) 629-2512; www .maldef.org. Leading Latino civil rights advocacy organization, founded in 1968.

**NAACP Legal Defense and Educational Fund**, 99 Hudson St., 6th Floor, New York, NY 10013-6289; (212) 965-2200; http://naacpldf.org. Nonprofit civil rights law firm founded in 1940.

**National Association of Latino Elected and Appointed Officials**, 600 Pennsylvania Ave., S.E., Suite 230, Washington, DC 20003; (202) 546-2536; www.naleo.org. Organization founded in 1976 as a national forum for Latino officials.

**National Conference of State Legislatures**, 7700 E. First Place, Denver, CO 80230; (303) 364-7700; www.ncsl.org. Bipartisan organization that provides research, technical assistance and other support for legislators and legislative staff in the states, commonwealths and territories.

**Project on Fair Representation**, 1150 17th St., N.W., #910, Washington, DC 20036; (703) 505-1922; www.projecton-fairrepresentation.org. Legal defense fund founded in 2005 to support litigation that challenges racial and ethnic classifications and preferences in state and federal courts.

**Public Mapping Project**, Prof. Michael MacDonald, George Mason University, Department of Public and International Affairs, 4400 University Drive — 3F4, Fairfax, VA 22030-4444; www.publicmappingproject. A project founded for the post-2010 redistricting cycle to make census data and redistricting software available to general public.

*The two major political parties' national committees:*

**Democratic National Committee**, 430 South Capitol St., S.E., Washington, DC 20003; (202) 863-8000; www.dnc .org.

**Republican National Committee**, 310 1st St., S.E., Washington, DC 20003; (202) 863-8500; www.rnc.org.

# 4

# Changing U.S. Electorate

Alan Greenblatt and Patrick Marshall

White, working-class Americans like this Ford worker in Wayne, Mich., have helped New York Sen. Hillary Clinton beat Barack Obama in California, Pennsylvania and other large states. Since the Great Depression, working-class whites had been loyal Democrats, but many of them defected in the 1970s and '80s due to liberal Democratic policies. Sen. John McCain, the presumptive Republican presidential nominee, may appeal to working-class voters, who sometimes support GOP candidates because of their conservative social stances.

From *CQ Researcher*,
May 30, 2008 (updated June 29, 2014).

AFP/Getty Images/Bill Pugliano

Given the historic nature of the Democratic presidential primary contest — with the nomination coming down to a battle between a white woman and an African-American man — perhaps it's not surprising that there have been splits among voters along racial, geographic, age, income and educational divides.[1]

"I don't think there's any way this election could have been anything but demographically focused, given the candidates left standing," says Scott Keeter, associate director of the Pew Research Center for People & the Press.

The Democrats' internal splits have them nervous about repairing the breaches in order to get all party supporters on board for the fall contest against Arizona Sen. John McCain, the presumptive Republican nominee. McCain might well appeal to white, working-class voters, including the so-called Reagan Democrats, who have sometimes supported GOP candidates because of their relatively conservative stances on social issues.

New York Sen. Hillary Rodham Clinton has repeatedly pointed out that, thanks to working-class support, she has beaten Illinois Sen. Barack Obama in the largest states — California, New York, Ohio, among others — which a Democrat would need to carry in order to win in November against McCain.

In an interview with *USA Today* conducted the day after the May 6 Indiana and North Carolina primaries, Clinton cited an Associated Press report "that found how Sen. Obama's support among working, hard-working Americans, white Americans, is weakening again, and how whites in both states who had not completed college were supporting me."[2]

## More Americans Moving to the Suburbs

Half of all Americans lived in suburbs in 2000, a sevenfold increase from 90 years earlier. The Democratic Party has been making significant inroads into the traditional GOP turf in the suburbs. Meanwhile, the percentage of Americans in central cities has remained at around 30 percent since 1930, also favoring Democrats.

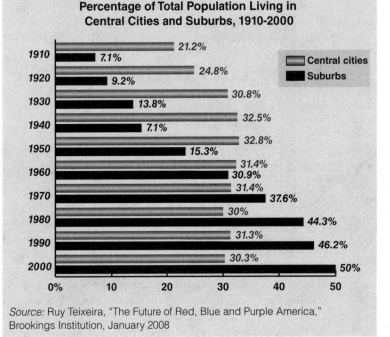

**Percentage of Total Population Living in Central Cities and Suburbs, 1910-2000**

| Year | Central cities | Suburbs |
|------|------|------|
| 1910 | 21.2% | 7.1% |
| 1920 | 24.8% | 9.2% |
| 1930 | 30.8% | 13.8% |
| 1940 | 32.5% | 7.1% |
| 1950 | 32.8% | 15.3% |
| 1960 | 31.4% | 30.9% |
| 1970 | 31.4% | 37.6% |
| 1980 | 30% | 44.3% |
| 1990 | 31.3% | 46.2% |
| 2000 | 30.3% | 50% |

*Source:* Ruy Teixeira, "The Future of Red, Blue and Purple America," Brookings Institution, January 2008

In exit polls conducted during the April 22 Pennsylvania Democratic primary, 16 percent of white voters said that race had influenced their decision, with almost half of these saying they would not support Obama in the fall. Only 60 percent of Catholics said they would vote for him in November.

"Mr. Obama was supposed to be a transformational figure, with an almost magical ability to transcend partisan difference," writes Paul Krugman, a *New York Times* columnist who has been supporting Clinton. "Well, now he has an overwhelming money advantage and the support of much of the Democratic establishment — yet he still can't seem to win over large blocs of Democratic voters, especially among the white working class. As a result, he keeps losing big states."[3]

Obama supporters, meanwhile, are concerned that his supporters — particularly young people and African-Americans — will feel disenfranchised if Clinton wins the nomination through a coronation by party officials, because it seems certain she will trail Obama in delegates and overall popular vote support after all the primaries are concluded on June 3.

"We keep talking as if it doesn't matter, it doesn't matter that Obama gets 92 percent of the black vote, [that] because he only got 35 percent of the white vote he's in trouble," House Majority Whip James E. Clyburn, D-S.C., the highest-ranking African-American in Congress, told *The Washington Post* following the Pennsylvania primary.

"Well, Hillary Clinton only got 8 percent of the black vote. . . . It's almost saying black people don't matter. The only thing that matters is how white people respond."[4]

Whatever the outcome, Obama's candidacy has already highlighted many of the ways in which the American electorate is starting to shift — as well as the ways that it hasn't changed quite yet.

"The biggest trend is that the U.S. is no longer going to be a majority-white country," says Scott Page, a University of Michigan political scientist. Given the growth of the Asian and, particularly, the Hispanic share of the population, most demographers predict that whites will no longer comprise a majority by 2050.

"Within 40 years, no single racial group will be a majority," Page says. "Second, interracial marriage is increasing, and many of these marriages are in the upper-income groups, which means that many of our future leaders will be multiracial," like Obama.

In leading the battle for Democratic delegates and total votes, Obama has forged a coalition unlike any seen before in his party. It's typical for one candidate to appeal to educated elites, as Obama does, while a rival appeals to "beer track" blue-collar voters, as Clinton does.

What Obama has done differently is wed African-Americans, who typically vote along with lower-income whites in Democratic primaries, to his base among elites. "This is the first time African-Americans have sided with the educated class," says David Bositis, an elections analyst at the Joint Center for Political and Economic Studies.

Referring to the leading contenders of the 1984 Democratic primary race, Bositis continues, "Obama is Gary Hart, but with the black vote. Hillary Clinton is Walter Mondale but without any black support. Obama's going to be the first nominee who represents the more educated and higher-income Democrats."

Assuming he does ultimately win the nomination, an Obama victory will be the result not only of this historic shift in black voting but also the fact that educated and upper-income voters are both growing in number and becoming more Democratic. He has also benefited from unusually high levels of support among young voters of all races.

But the white working-class vote, while shrinking as a share of the total electorate, is still a predominant factor in American politics. Many Democrats — as well as Republicans — believe that Obama's inability to appeal to this group will prove an Achilles' heel.

"Hillary supporters are going to be very unhappy," says Herbert I. London, president of the conservative Hudson Institute. London predicts that McCain will do very well in the fall among the older Democrats who have supported Clinton — and could make inroads into other Democratic constituencies as well.

"This age gap [between Clinton and Obama] is so persistent that I would be concerned about it," says Robert David Sullivan, managing editor of *CommonWealth* magazine, "especially because McCain might have a particular appeal to older independents."

"Older whites are really going to stick with McCain," echoes Dowell Myers, a University of Southern California demographer. "They're going to think that he speaks to their interests."

William H. Frey, a demographer at the Brookings Institution, suggests that Obama's candidacy does represent

## Whites Moving to More Republican Areas

The percentage of whites living in what are considered Republican counties has steadily increased since 1970. Thirty and 29 percent lived in what are considered "Republican landslide" and "Republican competitive" counties, respectively, in 2000, compared to 24 and 25 percent three decades earlier. By contrast, the number of whites living in what are considered "Democratic landslide" counties has decreased by 7 percentage points during the 30-year span.

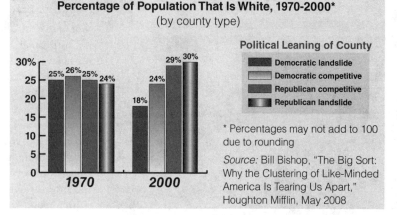

**Percentage of Population That Is White, 1970-2000***
(by county type)

Political Leaning of County
- Democratic landslide
- Democratic competitive
- Republican competitive
- Republican landslide

* Percentages may not add to 100 due to rounding

Source: Bill Bishop, "The Big Sort: Why the Clustering of Like-Minded America Is Tearing Us Apart," Houghton Mifflin, May 2008

a possible future for American politics. His candidacy has been "post-ethnic" in terms of his appeal to upper-income whites, as well as other white voters in states such as Wisconsin and Virginia. It's also "post-boomer," with Obama appealing to millions of "millennial" voters (referring to the generation born since 1982) and seeking, not entirely successfully, to move politics beyond the culture clashes that have marked American politics since the 1960s.

"Obama got a lot of initial support from people who liked his post-boomer sensibility — a way to get beyond moralistic politics," says Pew's Keeter. But as for a post-boomer period, he adds, "I don't think we're there yet."

Frey also cautions that Obama's candidacy may represent the shape of a political future that hasn't yet fully arrived. The trends that have benefited Obama — the rise of the youth vote, the increasing size of the upscale Democratic electorate — will continue, but may not yet be sufficiently in place to overcome the type of traditional, white working-class voters who have long dominated American politics and have fueled Clinton's campaign.

"Maybe 20 years down the road there will be more of the Obama group overall, but for now everything is split," Frey says. "It's not 2030 yet."

**The Candidates**

Sens. Hillary Rodham Clinton, D-N.Y., and Barack Obama, D-Ill., have carved out distinct groups of voters as they battle for the Democratic presidential nomination. Sen. John McCain, R-Ariz., the presumptive Republican nominee, is seeking to appeal to conservatives, blue-collar workers and religious fundamentalists.

Many demographic trends appear to be moving more generally in the Democrats' favor, including support from voters in their 20s, the increasing number of unmarried adults and secular-minded voters, the party's inroads into traditional GOP turf in the suburbs and the support of a majority of Hispanics — the nation's largest and fastest-growing minority group, who have been put off by the hard line many Republicans have taken on illegal immigration.

In seven states that held primaries in March and April alone, 1 million new voters registered as Democrats, while Republican numbers mostly "ebbed or stagnated." In Indiana and North Carolina, which held their Democratic primaries on May 6, the rate of new registrants tripled from 2004.[5]

Ruy Teixeira, another Brookings scholar and coauthor of the 2002 book *The Emerging Democratic Majority*, not surprisingly suggests that all these trends should help his party. But he concedes that Republicans still have some potent arrows in their quiver.

"The good news for the Republicans is that despite some of these various demographic factors that are moving against them, they have held the loyalties of lower-income white voters pretty well," he says.

Other structural advantages that Republicans have enjoyed in recent years — dominance of the South and the interior West, the rock-solid support of regular churchgoers, large margins of victory in the nation's fastest-growing communities — also remain in place.

And McCain's candidacy may dash Democratic hopes of running up a bigger margin among Hispanics that could help them prevail in states President Bush has carried, such as Nevada, New Mexico and Colorado. McCain has famously taken a more conciliatory stance toward immigrants than much of his party. "McCain takes Democrats out of their Western strategy entirely," says John Morgan, a Republican demographer.

With Democrats not quite settled on a candidate, it's premature to guess how the persistent demographic differences that have played out in the primaries will manifest themselves in the fall. Bositis suggests that Clinton's performance has been an indication of support for her among white women, in particular — not of white antipathy toward Obama. White working-class Democrats will mainly "come home" to support Obama in the fall, he suggests.

McCain's candidacy also has engendered some concerns on the Republican side that evangelicals — the conservative Christians who have been the party's most loyal supporters of late — will not support him with any enthusiasm. McCain consistently trailed among evangelical white Protestants during his primary race against former Govs. Mike Huckabee of Arkansas and Mitt Romney of Massachusetts.

How all these crosscurrents of support — or lack thereof — will play out in the fall remains to be seen, of course. What this year's election season has indicated more than anything, however, is that the nature and shape of the American electorate is in a state of flux just now, with the allegiances of various groups shifting between and within the two major parties — and with new constituencies making their presence very much felt.

"We're seeing more people registering now than we've ever seen before," says Kimball Brace, a Democratic consultant. "How that is going to change the demographics and nature of voting is one of the larger questions coming into play."

As the election season wears on, here are some of the other questions being asked about America's changing electorate:

### Are whites losing political clout?

After the release of the 2000 census figures, some Republican strategists recognized that their party faced a serious long-term demographic challenge. Rich Bond, a former Republican National Committee chairman, told *The Washington Post*, "We've taken white guys about as far as that group can go. We are in need of diversity, women, Latino, African-American, Asian . . . That is where the future of the Republican Party is."[6]

Republicans count on a disproportionate share of the white vote. Even in 2006, as Democrats regained control of Congress, white males supported GOP candidates by an eight-percentage-point margin.[7] The overall white vote that year favored Republicans by 4 percentage points — although that was down from a 15 percent margin in 2004. Whites were, in effect, outvoted by

## Hispanic Population Grew Rapidly

The number of Hispanics in the United States has grown by nearly a third since 2000. By contrast, blacks and whites have only grown by 9 and 2 percent, respectively. Democrats are favored by a majority of Hispanics — the nation's largest and fastest-growing minority group — who have been put off by the hard line many Republicans have taken on illegal immigration.

### Growth in U.S. Population by Ethnicity, 2000-2008

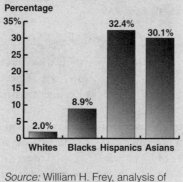

*Source:* William H. Frey, analysis of U.S. Census estimates

Hispanics, blacks and Asians, who gave massive margins to Democratic candidates (favoring Democrats by 39-, 79- and 25-point margins, respectively).[8]

Obama, the leading Democratic candidate, appears to be prevailing despite his inability to win a majority among white voters. He's doing well among young and well-educated whites and has carried 9 out of 10 black voters. But Clinton has carried the overall white vote in many states. In an analysis of the primary vote through the end of April, former *Los Angeles Times* editor Bill Boyarsky concluded that Obama's share of the white vote was "short [of] a majority, but still substantial."[9]

So if Democrats can nominate a candidate who fails to receive a majority of the white vote, and if whites' share of the total vote is shrinking, does that mean that white voters are losing influence?

Ronald Walters, a University of Maryland political scientist, believes that white influence will decline, given the growth in both immigration and naturalization. "I would think in the future you're going to have substantial demographic shifts bringing in more Hispanics and African-Americans," he says. "What it will mean in terms of whites is that they will have to adjust to the loss of political power."

Walters estimates that 13 states — comprising 43 percent of the Electoral College — have combined black and Hispanic populations topping 25 percent of their total. "You really have to have those votes in order to win," he says.

During the 1950s, whites made up more than 90 percent of the electorate (95 percent in 1952).[10] During the decades since then, blacks have secured their place in the voting booth through passage of voting-rights laws, and the Latino share of the population has skyrocketed. White males alone made up nearly half of the

## Hispanics' Share of U.S. Electorate Increasing

The number of Hispanics living in the United States is expected to total about 48 million in 2010, or about 16 percent of the total U.S. population. This represents a fivefold increase compared to 1970. By 2050, a quarter of the electorate is projected to be Hispanic, numbering just over 100 million people.

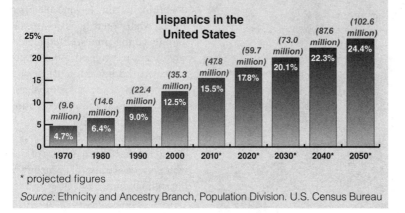

**Hispanics in the United States**

* projected figures

*Source:* Ethnicity and Ancestry Branch, Population Division. U.S. Census Bureau

electorate in 1952, according to Emory University political scientist Alan Abramowitz. Their share had dropped to 33.1 percent by 2004.

"Thanks to the recent growth in the Latino population . . . the white male share is now dropping about a percentage point a year, accelerating a decline that began with the increased enfranchisement of African-Americans in the civil rights era," Thomas F. Schaller wrote in *Salon* last September. "In [this] year's election, white males may account for fewer than one out of three voters. Bubba is no longer a kingmaker."[11]

But not everyone is convinced that whites are in any danger of losing their sway over elections. Karlyn Bowman, a senior fellow at the American Enterprise Institute (AEI), points out that "the black share of the electorate doesn't appear to be growing. That could change if Obama's the nominee, but at least at this point it doesn't appear to be growing. Asians are growing, but they are still a small percentage."

Despite the rapid growth and spread of Hispanics, their political power does not yet mirror their numbers, which, after all, includes millions of non-citizens. And the median age of Hispanics in the U.S. is just 27 compared to 39 for Anglos, meaning that a much higher percentage of Hispanics don't vote simply because they're too young.[12]

"White people are going to have less power," says Teixeira at the Brookings Institution, "but it's not going to be as fast as you think because of the lack of eligible voters" among Latinos.

Fernando Guerra, a political scientist at Loyola Marymount University in Los Angeles, also disputes the notion that growing minority populations will translate either into monolithic voting patterns or influence exceeding that of Anglos.

"Whites continue to be the majority or plurality everywhere, with the exception of some cities and counties," Guerra says. "There are states where African-Americans and Latinos make up more than 30 percent of the population, but none are above 50 percent."

It's become conventional wisdom in the South, where the black share of the vote tops 35 percent in some states — and is a share that votes heavily Democratic — that Republicans have to take at least 60 percent of the white vote in order to prevail in statewide elections. But they've had no apparent problem doing so.

Guerra notes that whites represent a majority of the electorate even in states with exceptionally large minority populations, such as California, New Mexico and Hawaii. Myers, the USC demographer, has reached a similar conclusion about his own state.

"In California, whites are already down to 45 percent of the population, but they're about 70 percent of the voters," Myers says. "Whites will remain a majority [of the state electorate] until 2031. Despite their shrinking numbers, they're older, and older people tend to vote. Also, they're all citizens."

Nationwide, whites still make up a large and disproportionate share of the electorate. According to Brookings demographer Frey, whites' share of the population is down to 66 percent, but they still make up 74 percent of eligible voters and 78 percent of actual voters.

"The role of whites is diminishing," says Clark Bensen, a Republican demographer and consultant.

"Whether it actually reaches a critical mass where it doesn't matter is another story."

### Are suburbs shifting to the Democrats?

The vote in most states splits along predictable geographic lines. Big cities are primarily Democratic, while rural areas are reliably Republican. The suburbs have become the most important battlegrounds, the biggest trove of votes nationwide, with enough numbers to sway most statewide elections.

Because of their success in fast-growing counties — President Bush carried 97 of the nation's 100 fastest-growing counties in 2004 — Republicans have been hopeful that their appeal to suburban voters on issues such as tax rates and national security would be enough to assure victory in most presidential contests for the foreseeable future.[13]

"Suburban and exurban areas . . . were central to Republican political guru Karl Rove's grand scheme for cementing GOP dominance for decades in the wake of President Bush's 2004 re-election victory," writes political journalist David Mark.[14]

Voters in exurban areas — counties on the fringe of metropolitan areas — seem naturally receptive to the GOP's overarching message about the need to limit government spending. They tend to be highly sensitive to tax increases and have sought out areas where the private sector, rather than local governments, provides services — from privately owned cars for transportation to homeowners' associations for parks and gated communities for maintenance of streetscapes.

Joel Kotkin, an expert on development and living patterns at Chapman University in Anaheim, Calif., told Minnesota Public Radio in February that for the past 40 years cities have lost middle-class white people with children who moved to suburbs seeking better schools,

## Young Voters Trending Democratic

Three out of every five voters ages 18 to 29 voted Democratic in 2006, an 11-percentage-point increase from 2000. Republican votership declined by a similar amount during the same period.

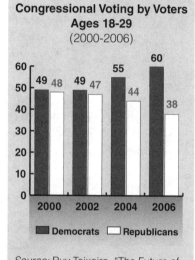

**Congressional Voting by Voters Ages 18-29**
(2000-2006)

*Source:* Ruy Teixeira, "The Future of Red, Blue and Purple America," Brookings Institution, January 2008

more space and increased security. That left cities with what Kotkin calls an array of demographic "niches."

"And that niche tends to be either minorities, poor people, young people or people without children — all of whom tend to be much more liberal."

Democratic author and researcher Teixeira agrees "there's a density gradient for Democratic voting. The question is, where does it tip?" Teixeira argues that, despite the long-standing notion that suburban voters are more conservative than city folks, voters in older, more established "inner-ring" suburbs are increasingly favoring Democrats.

Democrats carried nearly 60 percent of the 2006 U.S. House vote in the inner-ring suburbs of the nation's 50 largest metropolitan areas — up from 53 percent in 2002 — according to an analysis by the Metropolitan Institute at Virginia Tech. They won nearly 55 percent of the next ring of "mature" suburbs, up from 50 percent four years earlier.[15]

In Virginia, Republicans pinned their hopes for retaining control of the state Senate last fall on campaigns that stressed a hard line against illegal immigration. They lost the chamber and lost state House seats by ceding Northern Virginia suburbs that had once been firm GOP territory.

In Minnesota in 2006, Republicans lost 19 state House seats, and control of that chamber, largely in suburban districts around the Twin Cities, where voters were skeptical of the GOP's emphasis on social issues. And, in a particularly painful symbolic loss in March, Democrat Bill Foster picked up the suburban Chicago House seat formerly occupied by Republican Speaker Dennis Hastert.

"I doubt the Karl Roves of the world would disagree with the fact that the Democrats have been able to push

Nascar fans stand during the prayer before a race at the California Speedway in Fontana. Nascar fans tend to be blue-collar, patriotic, and Republican. In recent elections, candidatesof all stripes have sought to "microtarget" voters — tailoring messages to appeal to particular demographic niches, such as "Nascar dads," "soccer moms" and "angry white males."

out more into the suburbs, and Republicans have to push them back," says AEI's Bowman.

Demographer Robert Lang of Virginia Tech says that population growth rates are highest in Republican-leaning emerging suburbs — about 17 percent, he says, compared with just 4 percent growth in the inner-ring and mature suburbs. But the existing population in the latter category is so much greater that their growth in absolute numbers is about the same as the outer suburbs.

"The outer suburbs are not gaining everything," he says. "The rural and exurban growth cannot offset urbanizing suburbs much longer."

Republican demographer Morgan agrees that the older suburbs are filling up with people coming out from cities — including immigrants increasingly drawn to suburbs. But he says Republicans are moving to outer suburbs and exurban areas.

"The main county [in a metropolitan area] is no longer Republican, or it breaks about even," he says. "But what we have is hundreds of counties becoming exurban Republican. Around Atlanta, all of North Georgia is exurban and all Republican."

What's happening is that some inner-ring suburbs are coming to resemble center cities in their population density and makeup. Morgan says, "The older suburbs aren't genuinely suburbs, so many people are coming out from the cities."

Michael Barone, an AEI resident fellow and senior writer for *U.S. News & World Report*, notes that Arlington, Va., just outside Washington, was once "family territory, with young families and was Republican. In Arlington now, most people live in apartments, it's full of singles and it's become very heavily Democratic." Barone notes that similar changes have happened in other metropolitan areas as well.

The key to suburban control, as Teixeira suggests, is determining how far the line of Democratic dominance extends out from the core city. Republicans concede they are losing the inner suburbs, while Teixeira notes that "the exurbs are likely to remain solidly Republican.

"The question," he says, "is will the emerging suburbs" — the areas growing in population but closer to the city than the exurbs on the fringe — "remain competitive, as they were in 2006, or will they be solidly Republican? If the GOP can't keep the emerging suburbs solidly Republican, the math suggests they'll lose the suburbs overall."

Others are not willing to concede the suburbs to the Democrats quite yet. "This trend of the close-in suburbs becoming more Democratic seems to have started in the North, but there's still some question of whether it will happen in the South," says Robert David Sullivan, managing editor of *CommonWealth* magazine.

"If the suburbs of Atlanta act in the same way as the suburbs of Boston and Chicago, that is good news for the Democrats, but it hasn't started happening yet. That's a question for this fall."

### Are young voters more liberal?

In April, the Pew Research Center for the People & the Press released survey data that suggested voters in their 20s strongly identified with the Democratic Party. More than half — 58 percent — identified with the Democrats, compared with 33 percent who affiliated with the GOP.[16] "This makes Generation Next the least Republican generation," according to the center.[17]

The findings received a good deal of attention, with some observers speculating that the unpopular presidency of George W. Bush and the war in Iraq might cost the Republicans a generation's support. The overwhelming preference for Obama among young voters in this year's Democratic primaries and caucuses also spoke to the party's hopes for winning over this fresh cohort of voters.

Voters ages 18 to 29 gave 60 percent of their support to Democrats in 2006, giving the party a 22-point margin, compared with a closer 55-to-44 percent split in 2004.[18]

"Clearly, George Bush does not appeal to them positively," says Barone, the political commentator and AEI fellow. "Unlike Presidents Reagan and Clinton, he has not attracted young voters to his party.

"Certainly, they did not go through the experiences of the 1970s — stagflation, the overregulation of the economy — that left a lot of Americans skeptical about big-government policies," Barone continues. "That's been a help to Republicans in preceding years. It's not now."

Morley Winograd and Michael D. Hais, the Democratic authors of the new book *Millennial Makeover: MySpace, YouTube and the Future of American Politics*, go so far as to suggest that the party capturing the White House this year has "a historic opportunity to become the majority party for at least four more decades."[19]

But even though many conservatives such as Barone — and even some Republican political consultants — are willing to concede an advantage for Democrats among young voters today, they argue that such an advantage could prove fleeting. Today's young may be sour on the Republican "brand," but that doesn't mean they'll be life-long liberals who will remain loyal to the Democrats.

"This is a generation that's up for grabs," says Bowman, Barone's AEI colleague. She concedes that "they're leaning very heavily Democratic today" but argues that their attitudes toward both big government and big business could "tip them Republican as they start their careers."

"Democrats may have the young for a couple of elections," Republican demographer Morgan says.

Bowman also argues that, although today's young people tend to be more tolerant toward gays than their forebears, "attitudes on abortion and drugs have not become more liberal over time. They're not so much liberal or conservative," she says. "They're just different."

James Gimpel, a political scientist and expert on demographics at the University of Maryland, says that young voters are skewing more liberal on social and cultural issues, but he suggests that the Democrats' current success among them has as much to do with the party's active recruitment and appeal to these voters as ideology.

"The Democrats and progressive forces have been much more aggressive," he says. "Republicans have been

very slow at recruiting younger people. The Republicans are maybe hanging back and hoping when people get into their 30s, they'll switch."

Gimpel suggests that the potential for intergenerational warfare — with younger voters resentful about having to pay high payroll taxes to support Social Security and health benefits for aging boomers — could redound to the GOP's benefit. "The opportunity is there for Republican candidates who offer lower taxes and smaller government," he says.

But not everyone believes that waiting for changing conditions will prove a winning strategy for the GOP. Myers, the USC demographer, says that each younger generation tends to exaggerate the political climate of the time in which they came to maturity. He argues that despite the fact people's voting habits change to some extent due to their place in the "life cycle" — people with children tend to become more conservative, for instance — "these cohorts tend to hold their orientations for the rest of their lives."

Mark Grebner, a Democratic consultant based in Michigan, agrees. He says that people who came of age under Reagan were heavily Republican and have remained so. "The people born around 1962, 1964, they're about as Republican as any age cohort that we've seen in a long time," he says.

But the people who are coming up under the Bush presidency, Grebner argues, are strongly Democratic. "People who are now 18 to 28 are much more Democratic — dramatically," he says.

A poll of 18-to-24-year-olds conducted in March and April for Harvard University's Institute of Politics found that they favor Obama over McCain, 53 percent to 32 percent, while giving Clinton a much smaller margin over McCain (44 to 39 percent).[20]

"Certainly the Bush presidency has not been a big plus for the Republican Party," Grebner says.

## BACKGROUND

### After the New Deal

American politics in recent decades has been a massive square dance, with regions and demographic groups switching parties. The Northeast, for example, was the most solidly Republican part of the country into the

# CHRONOLOGY

**1950s-1960s** *Democratic dominance of American politics starts to ebb.*

**1952** Dwight D. Eisenhower is elected president — the only Republican president from 1933 to 1969.

**1954** Supreme Court's *Brown v. Board of Education* ruling overturns "separate but equal" segregation policies in schools, leading to "white flight" from cities. . . . Democrats gain House and Senate majorities that endure for decades.

**1965** President Lyndon B. Johnson signs Voting Rights Act, guaranteeing suffrage for black Americans. . . . Johnson also signs an immigration law that moves away from quotas favoring Western Europeans, signaling the beginning of enormous Latino immigration.

**1966** In response to Johnson's Great Society programs, Republicans gain 47 House seats, three Senate seats and eight governorships.

**1968** Assassination of Rev. Martin Luther King Jr. sparks riots in more than 100 cities. . . . Richard M. Nixon wins the presidency by pursuing a "Southern strategy" that addresses whites' concerns about law and order and changing social mores. His is the first of five Republican wins out of six elections.

**1970s-1980s** *Republicans dominate voting for the White House, but Democratic majorities in Congress mostly endure.*

**1970** For the first time, suburban residents outnumber city dwellers.

**1973** Supreme Court's *Roe v. Wade* decision legalizing abortion spurs evangelicals to greater political involvement.

**1974** President Nixon resigns amidst the Watergate scandal; 75 new Democrats, "known as Watergate babies," are elected to the House, compared to just 17 Republicans.

**1980** Ronald Reagan addresses 20,000 evangelicals at a gathering later called "the wedding ceremony of evangelicals and the Republican Party"; in his first election, Reagan moves millions of white working-class voters and much of the South into the GOP's column.

**1990s-2000s** *Political parity and increasing polarization lead to close competition between the two parties.*

**1992** Democrat Bill Clinton wins the White House by appealing on economic issues to working-class voters who "play by the rules."

**1994** Republicans win House for first time in 40 years, along with the Senate, through the support of "angry white males."

**2000** Church attendance becomes a predictor of Republican voting; George W. Bush carries 74 percent of evangelical vote.

**2004** Record 40 percent of Latinos vote for President Bush. . . . Nearly 50 percent of Americans live in "landslide counties" where one of the presidential candidates won by 20 percent or more; the figure in 1976 was 27 percent.

**2005** Republican Party Chairman Ken Mehlman apologizes to African-American voters for seeking "to benefit politically from racial polarization." . . . House Republicans pass an immigration bill that would reclassify illegal immigrants as felons, angering Hispanics. . . . Twenty-eight percent of adults hold college degrees, compared with 5 percent in 1940.

**2006** Democrats regain control of Congress; whites give marginal support to Republicans but are outvoted by heavy Democratic voting among blacks, Hispanics and Asians.

**2008** Christian leader James Dobson says he would not vote for Sen. John McCain, R-Ariz., "under any circumstances" (Jan. 13). . . . Sen. Hillary Clinton, D-N.Y., carries 67 percent of the Hispanic vote in Texas (March 4). . . . Answering criticism about the Rev. Jeremiah Wright, his former pastor, Sen. Barack Obama gives widely praised speech on race in America (March 18). . . . Obama tells San Francisco fundraiser that working-class voters are "bitter" and "cling to guns or religion" for solace (April 4). . . . Bush's disapproval rating hits 69 percent (April 22). . . . Voters in Montana, South Dakota close out Democratic primary season (June 3).

**November 2008** Barack Obama becomes first African-American to be elected president. . . . Since 2004, the share of blacks voting Democratic rises 7 percent, youths 13 percent and Hispanics 14 percent, with the latter the largest shift toward the left by any group in history.

**2009**

Republican Scott Brown of Massachusetts is elected to the U.S. Senate, the first time the seat is held by a Republican in 38 years. . . . National Popular Vote, a California-based group, advocates presidential elections based on the popular vote rather than the Electoral College system. . . . The House passes a popular-vote bill and sends it to the Senate.

**2010**

States redraw congressional districts based on the 2010 census.

**January —** On January 21, the Supreme Court rules in *Citizens United v. FEC* (2010) that the government cannot limit political spending by corporations.

**February —** The National Tea Party Convention is held in Nashville, Tenn.

**April —** Tea Party supporters protest tax day and hold rallies nationwide to spread their message.

**May —** Tea Party candidate Rand Paul wins the Republican Senate nomination in Kentucky.

**2012**

**November** Barack Obama wins reelection, defeating Republican candidate Mitt Romney 51 to 47 percent. Obama won 93 percent of black votes, while Romney won 59 percent of white votes.

Republicans won control of the House of Representatives by a margin of 234-201, despite the fact that Democratic candidates received 1.8 million more votes than Republican candidates.

**2014**

**June** The Supreme Court holds in *Shelby County v. Holder* (2013) that the federal government cannot require states to preclear changes to voting laws, at least until Congress addresses the issue again based on more recent data.

1960s but now is the Democrats' strongest base. Conversely, the "solid South" is no longer wholly Democratic but mostly Republican.

Roman Catholics, once predominantly Democratic in their voting habits, now divide their votes evenly between the parties. African-Americans in the North, for whose allegiance both parties competed effectively up until about 1960, are now the most loyal voting bloc for Democrats. The list of groups shifting loyalties between the parties goes on and on and will remain a crucial factor this year, as Democrats struggle to hold onto a sizable share of the white working-class vote, which will likely prove decisive.

White working-class voters for decades comprised the majority of the Democratic vote as the largest bloc within the New Deal coalition, which dominated U.S. politics from 1932, with the election of Franklin D. Roosevelt as president, until 1968.

Republicans had enjoyed near-permanent occupancy of the White House since the Civil War, winning 14 of

the 18 presidential elections since 1860. But in 1932, in response to the federal government's weak response to the Great Depression, Roosevelt not only won big but put together an enduring political coalition that included members of labor unions, big-city political machines in the North, farm groups, intellectuals, minority groups including Jews and the South.

The New Deal coalition propelled Democrats to victory in all but two of the nine presidential elections from 1932 to 1964. "The Republicans were the party of the Northeast, of business, of the middle classes and of white Protestants, while the Democrats enjoyed a clear majority among the working classes, organized labor, Catholics and the South" at all political levels, wrote pollster Everett Carll Ladd Jr.[21]

Even during the Democrats' years in the wilderness — the two-term presidency of Dwight D. Eisenhower — New Deal-style politics and programs continued to dominate the national agenda, with the expansion of government

# The Gap between Blacks and Hispanics

*Will racial politics affect the Democratic nomination?*

One of the most notable racial divides in voting this year has been the gap between African-Americans and Hispanics during the Democratic primary campaign. Blacks have been supporting Illinois Sen. Barack Obama by margins as great as 9-to-1, while Hispanics have given New York Sen. Hillary Clinton a 2-to-1 advantage in multiple states.

Is this just a fluke, or does it speak to some underlying enmity between the nation's two largest minority groups? There does appear to be evidence of tension between blacks and Hispanics in some areas, based on economic and political competition. But many observers say that claims of a deep divide are overblown.

A widely cited comment by Sergio Bendixen, Clinton's Hispanic pollster, set the template for debate about this issue on the presidential campaign trail. "The Hispanic voter — and I want to say this very carefully — has not shown a lot of willingness or affinity to support black candidates," Bendixen told *The New Yorker* in January.[1]

There have been some schisms between the two groups. Traditionally black areas such as South Los Angeles and Compton have become majority Latino, and Hispanics have also made strong inroads in Southern states such as North Carolina and Georgia, "bringing change to communities where blacks had gained economic and political power after years of struggle against Jim Crow laws," writes Stephan Malanga, a senior fellow at the Manhattan Institute.[2]

Studies of Southern cities conducted by Duke University political scientist Paula D. McClain have found that blacks believe Latinos have robbed them of jobs, while Hispanics regard blacks as "slothful and untrustworthy."[3]

"There is considerable anger among African-Americans about the immigrant labor force that has taken over whole sections of the economy and excluded African-Americans from those jobs," says Ronald Walters, director of the University of Maryland's African American Leadership Center. Walters notes that Hispanics sometimes complain in turn that black mayors or members of Congress don't do much for them in areas where black and brown residents live together.

In local elections, there have been examples both of coalitions built between the two groups, and of one constituency's refusal to vote for candidates drawn from the other. In Democratic primary campaigns over the years in New York and Texas, Hispanics have tended to vote for whites over blacks, and blacks have returned the favor when it comes to contests between Anglos and Hispanics.[4] On the other hand, Hispanics have lent overwhelming support to several black big-city mayors, while at least eight African-American congressmen currently represent areas that are heavily Latino.[5]

In Los Angeles, Latinos now represent 46.5 percent of the population — up from just 18.5 percent 30 years ago. The black share of the population, in the meantime, has shrunk from 17 percent to 11.2 percent, fueling some animosity from both sides as blacks continue to enjoy disproportionate sway.[6] Antonio Villaraigosa, a Latino politician, carried just 20 percent of the black vote in his first race for mayor of Los Angeles against James Hahn, who is Anglo.

social-welfare programs continuing unabated. Eisenhower, for instance, oversaw the creation of the Department of Health, Education and Welfare.[22] In addition, during Eisenhower's second year in office, Democrats won majorities in the House and Senate that would endure for 40 and 26 years, respectively.

The high-water mark for Democrats came with the election of 1964, when Lyndon B. Johnson won the largest share of the popular presidential vote in modern times, and the party took two-thirds of the House and Senate seats. Their landslide led to the passage of a slew of domestic legislation known as the Great Society, including the creation of Medicare, the Voting Rights Act of 1965 and a rewrite of the nation's immigration law, abolishing a system of quotas that had limited immigration mainly to newcomers from Western Europe.

The price tag and policy directions of many of these bills prompted a backlash in 1966, when Republicans gained 47 House seats, three Senate seats and eight governorships, including the election of Ronald Reagan in California. Notably, the election represented a breakthrough for the GOP in the South, which had given

But Villaraigosa carried blacks during his successful rematch against Hahn in 2005. "When people say to me, African-Americans didn't vote for you in your first race, I say, well, they didn't know me," Villaraigosa told the *Chicago Tribune*. "In my second race, they did, and they voted for me overwhelmingly." [7]

Hahn's family had enjoyed a long history of support from L.A.'s black community. Such personal ties, as opposed to racial preferences, may go a long way toward explaining Clinton's performance among Hispanics this year.

Hispanics were big supporters of Bill Clinton and have proven to be a key constituency for Hillary Clinton as well. According to exit polling, she took 64 percent of the Latino vote in the Nevada caucuses, to Obama's 26 percent. Her share of the Hispanic vote in California was 67 percent, while in Texas it was 64 percent.

"If you look at the demographics of Latinos — working class, lower educational attainment — it's very similar to the demographics of whites who are supporting Hillary," says Loyola Marymount University political scientist Fernando Guerra.

Guerra adds that, "African-Americans would be supporting Hillary overwhelmingly, if everything about Obama's background and platform were the same, but he was white."

Los Angeles Mayor Antonio Villaraigosa.

Getty Images/Neilson Barnard

David Bositis, an expert on black voting behavior at the Joint Center for Political and Economic Studies, says that Hispanics are choosing to support Clinton, as opposed to voting against Obama. Taken as a group, Hispanics did well economically during her husband's time in the White House.

Although that is also true about African-Americans, the latter group has been motivated by Obama's historic candidacy but put off by the Clinton campaign's occasional injection of his race as an issue. "If Hillary hadn't blown it with them, she would have been receiving at least a third of the black vote, instead of none," Bositis says.

[1] Ryan Lizza, "Minority Reports," *The New Yorker*, Jan. 21, 2008.

[2] Stephen Malanga, "The Rainbow Coalition Evaporates," *City Journal*, winter 2008, p. 35.

[3] Arian Campo-Flores, "Everything to Everyone," *Newsweek*, Feb. 4, 2008, p. 33.

[4] James Traub, "The Emerging Minority," *The New York Times Magazine*, March 2, 2008, p. 15.

[5] Clarence Page, "Clinton's Hispanic Edge Over Obama," *Chicago Tribune*, Jan. 30, 2008, p. 21.

[6] Susan Anderson, "The Clout That Counts," *Los Angeles Times*, Nov. 11, 2007, p. M4.

[7] Clarence Page, "When the Melting Pot Boils Over," *Chicago Tribune*, Feb. 6, 2008, p. 25.

virtually all of its support to Democrats since the Civil War. Several Southern states were among the few to support Arizona Sen. Barry M. Goldwater over Johnson in 1964. Further breaking with tradition, about a third of the South's House districts elected Republicans in 1966.

The South began to turn mainly for one reason — the passage of federal civil rights laws granting equal opportunity and voting privileges to African-Americans. The share of Southern blacks registered to vote rose from 29 percent in 1960 to 62 percent in 1970, but their presence on the voter rolls was not enough to offset the conservative and increasingly Republican voting patterns of white Southerners. [23]

Other demographic patterns began to work in the GOP's favor, including the explosive growth during the post-World War II era of the suburbs, triggered by a combination of factors that included the nationwide construction of new highways and the postwar "baby boom." The suburbs also gained population due to "white flight," with white parents taking their children out of urban school districts that were undergoing integration by race.

# Diversity Blamed for "Social Isolation"

*Do Obama's problems in mixed states prove the point?*

One of the many striking features of this year's Democratic presidential primary contest has been the difference in the kinds of states Illinois Sen. Barack Obama has won and lost. He easily carried states with large African-American populations such as Mississippi and South Carolina, as well as nearly all-white states such as Maine, Vermont and Idaho, yet he lost nearly all the states with a broader demographic mix, including Pennsylvania, California, Ohio and New York.

"As some bloggers have shrewdly pointed out, Obama does best in areas that have either a large concentration of African-American voters or hardly any at all, but he struggles in places where the population is decidedly mixed," writes political reporter Matt Bai in *The New York Times Magazine*. "What this suggests, perhaps, is that living in close proximity to other races — sharing industries and schools and sports arenas — actually makes Americans less sanguine about racial harmony rather than more so."[1]

If that is indeed the case, the Obama campaign may serve as an important illustration of a point made last year by Robert D. Putnam, a Harvard University political scientist. In a study that attracted widespread attention and engendered a good deal of controversy despite its appearance in a journal called *Scandinavian Political Studies*, Putnam posited that diversity — despite its near-universal approbation as one of America's major strengths — actually causes significant social harm, at least in the near-term.

Putnam and his team conducted detailed telephone interviews with 30,000 Americans — a far larger sample than usual in such surveys — and dug more deeply into 41 communities across the country. Even controlling for factors such as income disparities and local crime rates, Putnam found that residents of diverse communities are less likely to trust their neighbors — even those of their own race — than people who live in more homogenous areas.

"Diversity seems to trigger . . . social isolation," Putnam writes in the study. "In colloquial language, people living in ethnically diverse settings appear to 'hunker down' — that is, to pull in like a turtle. . . ."

"Inhabitants of diverse communities tend to withdraw from collective life, to distrust their neighbors, regardless of the color of their skin, to withdraw even from close friends, to expect the worst from their community and its leaders, to volunteer less, give less to charity and work on community projects less often, to register to vote less, to agitate for social reform more, but have less faith that they can actually make a difference and to huddle unhappily in front of the television."[2]

Other social scientists have reached similar conclusions. A pair of Harvard economists found that about half the difference in social-welfare spending between Europe and the U.S. could be attributed to greater ethnic diversity in America. Two other economists reviewed 15 recent studies and concluded that ethnic diversity was linked to lower school funding and trust, as well as declines in other measures of "social capital" (a phrase Putnam helped popularize with his 2000 best-seller *Bowling Alone*).[3]

Putnam's work on diversity was soon seized upon by conservatives who saw it as a necessary corrective to the "Politically Correct Police" who had championed diversity

During this era, the Supreme Court issued numerous rulings that did not sit well with conservatives, including requirements that white families send their children by bus to schools dominated by blacks; a ban on prayer in public schools; the lifting of restrictions on contraception; and increased protections for criminal defendants. The Republican Party platform began to complain about "moral decline and drift."

Cultural ferment extended well beyond the reach of the court, with peaceful civil rights marches giving way to riots in hundreds of cities in 1967 and 1968. Republican Richard M. Nixon played to the fears of the "silent majority," promising in 1968 to restore law and order — a message that had particularly strong partisan resonance after rioting took place at that year's Democratic National Convention in Chicago.

Nixon also devised a "Southern strategy" of appealing to the fears of whites in response to the growing political power and demands of African-Americans. Nixon strategist Kevin Phillips popularized the phrase, explaining that

as an unquestionable virtue — and as a warning against the effects of immigration, both legal and illegal. "I'm not at all surprised by what Mr. Putnam has found in his study," says Herbert I. London, president of the Hudson Institute. "[Diversity's] going to breed resentment and, to some extent, hostility."

*The Orange County Register* ran an editorial called "Greater Diversity Equals More Misery," while Putnam's work was favorably cited on the Web site of former Ku Klux Klan leader David Duke. [4] This sort of response clearly left Putnam uncomfortable. "It certainly is not pleasant when David Duke's Web site hails me as the guy who found out racism is good," the liberal Putnam said.[5]

More important than his discomfort, though, was Putnam's frustration that the second half of his argument was often left out of the commentary — that both immigration and diversity, over the long term, would prove to be pluses. We forget, he suggested in an interview, that there were similar levels of discomfort among communities receiving European immigrants a century or more ago.

He maintains that the current waves of immigrants can be successfully assimilated over time if social divisions are subsumed within the sort of shared identity that has always unified Americans. The areas that are attracting immigrants today are among the nation's most economically vibrant, Putnam points out.

"Immigration policies may at first seem tangential to productivity, but they are not," says Scott Page, a University of Michigan political scientist and author of a 2007 book about diversity called *The Difference.* "Diversity is crucial to the development of a nation, especially economically. Diverse people bring diverse skills, which prove invaluable for innovation and growth."

"Chief diversity officers" have become a staple of *Fortune* 500 companies, not to please the P.C. Police but to keep abreast of demographic trends that are changing the makeup of the skilled workforce. "If you define the global talent pipeline as all those individuals around the world who have at least a college degree, only 17 percent of this pipeline comprises white males," says Sylvia Ann Hewlett, an economist at the New York-based Center for Work-Life Policy. "Increasingly, talent management is diversity management."

As Putnam himself argues, diversity may be uncomfortable, but it's beneficial — and inevitable — over the long haul. "The most certain prediction that we can make about almost any modern society is that it will be more diverse a generation from now than it is today," he writes in his study.

In the short term, however, one of the most important political questions of the year is whether Obama, assuming he's the Democratic nominee, will be able to win over the white working-class voters who have largely supported New York Sen. Hillary Clinton in the more mixed states that she has won.

"Rather than serving to heal America's racial wounds," writes conservative columnist Jonah Goldberg, "maybe Obama's campaign is more like a dye marker that helps us better diagnose the complexity of the problem."[6]

---

[1] Matt Bai, "What's the Real Racial Divide?," *The New York Times Magazine*, March 16, 2008, p. 15.

[2] Robert D. Putnam, "E Pluribus Unum: Diversity and Community in the Twenty-First Century," *Scandinavian Political Studies*, June 2007, p. 137.

[3] Michael Jonas, "The Downside of Diversity," *The Boston Globe*, Aug. 5, 2007, p. D1.

[4] Ilana Mercer, "Greater Diversity Equals More Misery," *The Orange County Register*, July 22, 2007; available at www.ocregister.com/opin ion/putnam-diversity-social-1781099-racial-greater.

[5] Jonas, *op. cit.*

[6] Jonah Goldberg, "Obama: Winning White Votes in White States," *The Kansas City Star*, Feb. 14, 2008, p. B9.

---

Republicans would never get more than 20 percent of "the Negro vote" but nevertheless would enforce the Voting Rights Act. "The more Negroes who register as Democrats in the South, the sooner the Negrophobe whites will quit the Democrats and become Republicans," he explained to *The New York Times.*[24]

The Democratic share of the presidential vote plummeted from a record 61 percent in 1964 to just 43 percent in 1968, with third-party candidate George Wallace appealing even more directly to voter anxiety than Nixon. In his 1969 book *The Emerging Republican Majority,* Phillips wrote, "This repudiation visited upon the Democratic Party for its ambitious social programming, and inability to handle the urban and Negro revolutions, was comparable to that given conservative Republicanism in 1932 for its failures to cope with the economic crisis of the Depression."[25]

## Reagan Democrats

Republicans would go on to win all but one of the next six presidential elections. (The one exception came in

1976, when the party was punished for the Watergate scandal that ended the Nixon presidency.) The GOP appeared to have a lock on the Electoral College, with victory virtually assured throughout the South, the Rocky Mountain West and the Plains states. The Sun Belt, which had about as many electoral votes as Snow Belt states in the 1970s, continues to pick up votes with each census.[26]

Underlying Republican success, however, was the fracturing of the New Deal coalition and the GOP's ability to tap into white working-class votes that had long been denied its candidates. Reagan's presidential campaigns of 1980 and 1984 moved the South further into the GOP corner. Despite his antagonism toward unions, Reagan's hard line on foreign policy appealed to working-class voters, as did his economic optimism — which was borne out by a lengthy period of economic expansion on his watch.

The white working class had been loyal to Democrats in previous decades largely because of economic policies the party pursued that redistributed income toward lower-income voters. But many of them were put off by Democratic platforms during the 1970s and '80s that seemed to emphasize liberal stances on social and cultural issues. Blue-collar voters had been 12 percent more Democratic than the electorate as a whole in 1948, but by 1972 they were 4 percent less. (There was a similar drop in Democratic support among urban Catholics).[27]

In 1972, when the National Election Survey asked who composed the Democratic Party, respondents still made it sound like it was still the party of the New Deal — the poor, working class, blacks, Catholics and unions. By 1984, responses to the same survey painted a different picture, saying the party was made up of black militants, feminists, civil rights leaders, people on welfare, gays and unions.[28]

Even as Democrats were losing some of their traditional supporters, Republicans were benefiting from the re-emergence of an important force — white evangelical Protestants. They had largely retreated from politics following the battles during the 1920s and '30s over Prohibition and evolution. As late as 1965, the Rev. Jerry Falwell said that pastors should win souls, not concern themselves with fighting communism and political reform.

The liberal decisions of the Supreme Court, particularly in the 1973 *Roe v. Wade* case that legalized abortion,

> **With the rapid growth of Hispanics and other minority groups, some GOP strategists were concerned that their party's dependence on white male voters, in particular, was too limiting. In 2000, Bush sought to portray himself as an inclusive candidate, featuring many black and Hispanic speakers at his nominating convention.**

angered evangelicals, however. In May 1979, secular conservative leaders met with Falwell and urged him to form an organization that would mobilize fundamentalists. He did so a month later, founding the Moral Majority.

The following year, Reagan appealed for their support directly, addressing a gathering of 20,000 evangelicals, praising their efforts and questioning evolution. Ralph Reed, later the executive director of the Christian Coalition, which would supersede the Moral Majority as the leading force among Christian-right groups during the 1990s, called the meeting "the wedding ceremony of evangelicals and the Republican Party."[29] Evangelicals in recent election cycles have generally been estimated to represent 40 percent of the GOP primary vote.

### Clinton and Bush

Bill Clinton in 1992 would become the only Democratic presidential candidate of the post-Reagan era to carry any Southern states. He won back a larger share of the white working-class vote by emphasizing economic issue (his campaign's unofficial slogan was "it's the economy, stupid") and signaled a shift away from "identity politics" by promising to "end welfare as we know it."

But Clinton's success did not translate into victories for his party. Democrats relinquished their 40-year hold

# Do demographic trends favor Democrats?

## YES
**Ruy Teixeira**
*Visiting fellow, The Brookings Institution*

From "The Future of Red, Blue and Purple America," The Brookings Institution, January 2008

A new wave of demographic and geographic change is currently washing over the United States and is sure to have profound effects on our future politics, just as earlier changes helped give birth to the politics we know today. Here is a quick outline of several of the political and demographic trends that are leading to a Democratic and center-left majority in the United States:

- **Immigration and minorities.** Immigration and differential fertility have driven minority voters from about 15 percent of voters in 1990 to 21 percent today, and will produce a voting electorate that is about one-quarter minority by the middle of the next decade. Presently, with some exceptions — such as President Bush's 40 percent support among Hispanics in the 2004 election — these rising constituencies tend to give the Democrats wide margins (69-30 percent among Hispanics and 62-37 percent among Asians in the 2006 congressional elections).
- **Family changes.** Changes in household structure and differences in fertility are reshaping American families. Consider these dramatic trends: Married couples with children now occupy fewer than one in four households. Single women have recently become a majority of all adult women. These trends intersect in increasingly important ways with political behavior. Married voters are far more likely to vote Republican than are unmarried voters, eclipsing the effects of the celebrated gender gap. In the 2006 congressional election, married voters slightly favored Republicans (50-48 percent), while unmarried voters favored Democrats (64-34 percent).
- **Suburbs.** Much will ride on how the changing mix of residents votes in the different parts of suburbia. In 2006, Democratic House pickups in areas like suburban Denver, suburban Philadelphia, Connecticut and southern Florida were powered by coalitions where professionals and minorities took a leading role. Jim Webb's Senate victory in Virginia was largely due to his margin in Northern Virginia's high-tech suburbs.
- **Young voters.** According to one standard definition, 80 million Americans today are Millennials (birth years 1978-1996). By 2008, the number of citizen-eligible Millennial voters will be nearing 50 million. Now they seem to be leaning Democratic. In the 2006 congressional election, the first election in which almost all 18-to-29-year-olds were Millennials, they supported Democrats by a 60-38 percent margin.

## NO
**Michael J. New**
*Assistant Professor, University of Alabama*

Written for *CQ Researcher*, May 2008

In recent years, many observers have argued that the rising Hispanic population in America will do serious damage to the electoral prospects of the Republican Party. However, these analysts overlook a number of other trends that bode favorably for Republicans. For instance, investors are a reliable Republican constituency. In 1980 only 20 percent of American households owned stock. Today that number is up to 50 percent, and rising. Other groups that consistently vote for Republicans, including gun owners and home-schoolers, are growing rapidly as well. Better yet, many policies that have been advanced by the Republican Party, including concealed carry laws and expanded IRAs, have successfully expanded these Republican constituencies.

Furthermore, the membership trends of various religions should give serious pause to those who think that demographic trends favor Democrats. Indeed, many religious groups whose members are likely to support Republicans, including Evangelical Protestants, Mormons and Orthodox Jews, are seeing their memberships grow. Conversely, religious groups whose memberships are mostly Democrats, including mainline Protestants and Reform Jews, are actually getting smaller. It should also be noted that other important Democratic constituencies, including labor unions, are seeing their memberships shrink in absolute terms as well.

These demographic trends will strengthen a number of political trends that already favor Republicans. For instance, in close presidential elections in 2000 and 2004, President Bush won 30 and 31 states, respectively. Since Republican Senate candidates should be at an advantage in these states, Republicans should eventually accumulate over 60 Senate seats — good for a filibuster-proof majority. The rise of the Internet and talk radio has given conservatives greater ability to promote their ideas, free of interference from the mainstream media.

Finally, there is evidence to suggest that Hispanics may not be a lost cause for the Republican Party. First, Hispanics who are evangelical Protestants and those from Cuba are already likely to support Republican candidates. Furthermore, Republicans have been successful in capturing a large percentage of the Hispanic vote in states like Florida and Texas, which have pro-immigrant governors and less generous welfare benefits.

The best strategy might be to follow the lead of these governors and implement policies that will create and expand Republican constituencies among Hispanic voters. One way this can be done is to continue to pursue policies that will make Hispanics more sensitive toward taxes and less supportive of government programs.

A poll worker in New Orleans signs up a voter last February. Barack Obama has added African-Americans, who typically vote along with lower-income whites in Democratic primaries, to his base among elites. If Obama wins the nomination, it will reflect this historic shift in black voting and also the fact that educated and upper-income voters are growing in number and becoming more Democratic.

on the House in 1994 and lost the Senate as well, as white male voters turned against the party, particularly in the South. By 2004, Clinton's home state of Arkansas was unique among Southern states in sending more Democrats than Republicans to Congress. There were 16 Republican senators from the region that year, compared with just four Democrats.[30]

Although he lost the popular vote in 2000, George W. Bush benefited from the demographic trends that had been moving voters into the Republican column. He carried every Southern state, as well as 74 percent of the evangelical vote.[31] The most certain predictor of support for Bush in both his elections was regular church attendance.

With the rapid growth of Hispanics and other minority groups, some GOP strategists were concerned that their party's dependence on white male voters, in particular, was too limiting. In 2000, Bush sought to portray himself as an inclusive candidate, featuring many black and Hispanic speakers at his nominating convention. He was also careful not to take as hard a line against immigrants as some members of his party.

But many suburban and highly educated voters began to turn against the GOP, concerned about the party's stances on social issues, such as opposition to stem-cell research, skepticism about evolution and political interference with the decision about keeping alive Terri Schiavo, a brain-dead Florida woman.

Bush's attempts to reach beyond his political base proved futile during his second term, as when the Republican-controlled House in 2006 refused to vote on a moderate Senate-passed immigration bill that had been negotiated with his administration. But what drove down Bush's approval ratings and cost his party control of Congress in 2006 was, primarily, the war in Iraq.

Bush's widely criticized handling of the devastation in New Orleans wrought by Hurricane Katrina erased any small gains his party had made among African-Americans, while a tougher immigration bill passed by the House drove down GOP support among Hispanics from 40 percent in 2004 to 30 percent or less in 2006.[32]

Brother political scientists Earl Black and Merle Black wrote last year, "In modern American politics, a Republican Party dominated by white Protestants faces a Democratic Party in which minorities plus non-Christian whites far outnumber white Protestants."[33]

## CURRENT SITUATION

### "The Big Sort"

Despite the close balance between the parties in recent years — neither party has enjoyed a large majority in either congressional chamber for years, and no presidential candidate received a majority of the popular vote from 1992 until 2004 — comparatively few geographical areas remain in close contention.

Nationwide, the parties might be nearly tied, but candidates on either side can count on blowouts one way or the other within most counties. Compare the results of the presidential elections of 1976 and 2004, both of which were extremely close. In 1976, fewer than 25 percent of Americans lived in "landslide counties" that one candidate or the other carried by a margin of 20 points or greater. By 2004, nearly half the country — 48.3 percent — lived in a landslide county.[34]

Today, suggests journalist Bill Bishop in his new book *The Big Sort*, "Zip codes have political meaning. . . . As Americans have moved over the past three decades, they have clustered in communities of sameness, among people with similar ways of life, beliefs and, in the end, politics."[35]

It's not that liberals or conservatives ask their real-estate agents for printouts of precinct voting data when they're shopping for houses, but they do make lifestyle choices that place them among people who tend to live — and vote — much the way they do.

"There are lifestyle differences between liberals and conservatives that there weren't 30 years ago," says Notre Dame political scientist David Campbell. "The parties are well sorted ideologically, and we live in an era when it's easy to signal where you stand on these things by the type of car you drive and whether you shop at the farmer's market or Sam's Club. It's a way of constructing an identity, and those identities are playing out in politics."

Political analyst Charles Cook sometimes jokes that Democratic candidates have trouble carrying any district that doesn't include a Starbucks.[36] Rural areas are strongly Republican, cities are Democratic and the two parties fight their major turf wars in the suburbs, with fast-growing outer suburbs favoring the GOP and inner-ring suburbs becoming denser and more Democratic.

Such generalizations have long carried an element of truth, but some experts think the truth grows more compelling with each passing election year. "Even if you drop below the broad regional level, you find that neighborhoods and communities are looking more homogeneous than they ever have before," says Gimpel at the University of Maryland. "You have Republicans settling in around Republicans and Democrats settling around Democrats."

## Lack of Competition

Although it's something of a myth that there are Republican "red" or Democratic "blue" states — plenty of states vote one way for president and the opposite for senator or governor — increasingly there are red and blue counties. That's why there are so few competitive House or state legislative seats.

Redistricting has been widely blamed for the fact that few legislative seats — perhaps less than 10 percent — are competitive at either the congressional or state level. It's become normal for a major state such as California to pass through an entire election cycle with none of its legislative seats — U.S. House, state Assembly or state Senate — changing partisan hands.

It's true that partisan redistricting, in which lines are generally drawn by state legislators for both Congress and their own seats, lumps together as many Republicans or Democrats together into districts that heavily favor one party or another. But most political scientists seem to believe that such partisan mapmaking simply exaggerates the natural ideological or partisan sorting that people are already doing by settling within like-minded communities.

In 2004, a third of U.S. voters lived in counties that had voted for the same party in each presidential election dating back all the way to 1968; just under half hadn't switched allegiances since 1980; and 73 percent lived in counties that had voted the same way in every election since 1992 — four in a row.[37]

Along with the geographical sorting, there is also an ideological sorting in terms of media choices, with citizens turning to media that gibe with their established worldview. Conservatives watch Fox News Channel and read blogs such as Instapundit, while liberals tune into National Public Radio and leave comments at DailyKos.com.

Journalist Bishop argues in his book that all this self-sorting amplifies people's natural preferences — that progressives grow more liberal in the exclusive company of left-leaning neighbors and media outlets, with the same "echo chamber" effect pushing conservatives further to the right. He contends it's one of the major reasons for today's heated partisan bickering and lack of interparty cooperation.

"Like-minded, homogeneous groups squelch dissent, grow more extreme in their thinking and ignore evidence that their positions are wrong," Bishop writes. "As a result, we now live in a giant feedback loop."[38]

## Picking Out Raisins

Candidates and consultants are well aware of the way counties or districts are likely to favor one party or another. In recent election years, they have sought to "microtarget" voters — tailoring messages to appeal to particular groups of voters within a community, rather than the community as a whole.

Every recent election cycle seems to bring about talk of new niche demographic groups who are being courted by candidates and consultants, such as "angry white males," "soccer moms" and "Nascar dads." Microtargeting represents an effort to appeal to dozens of different demographic groups, generally defined by their lifestyle and consumer choices.

Only a few years ago, party databases still targeted voters solely by precinct. Now they crack open each subdivision and make a good guess about which residents are socially liberal and which ones are anti-tax conservatives.

Sophisticated campaigns are trying to become more precise with their messages, as well. Rather than sending out six or seven pieces of mail districtwide, they may send 20 different mailings to five different groups, such as veterans, seniors or gun owners.

How do they know which voter should get which piece of mail — and, more important, which swing voters should have the candidate show up personally on their doorsteps? Consultants such as Mark Grebner, an Ingham County commissioner in Michigan, look at every piece of information they can find about each voter — their ethnicity; whether they live in a precinct that turns out for hot Democratic primaries but not Republican ones; which magazines they subscribe to; and whether they ever have signed a petition to put an initiative or a candidate on a ballot. (To learn more about voters for his clients in Wisconsin, where he has less data, Grebner pays a fellow in Bangladesh to read every letter to the editor in state papers via the Web and code them according to likely party preference.)

Grebner takes all this information, runs a bunch of statistical analyses and assigns a percentage to each voter's likelihood of voting Democratic. Further narrowing the universe of potentially receptive voters is what winning close campaigns is all about. "If you don't want raisins in your cereal," Grebner says, "buy cereal that doesn't have raisins — don't pick them out one at a time."

## OUTLOOK:

### Creating a New Map

In Bishop's analysis, it's Republicans who "were the winners in the big sort." From 1980 to 2006, Republican counties outgrew Democratic ones, on average, by more than 1 million people a year. Nearly all of that was due to people moving in, not natural population growth. "From 1990 to 2006 alone, 13 million people moved from Democratic to Republican counties."[39]

Republicans have taken advantage of the fact that much recent domestic migration has been toward the South and West, lending them added advantages in the Electoral College. Brookings demographer Frey predicts that the states that voted for Bush in 2004 will gain an additional 17 electoral votes (and House seats) by 2030.[40]

"In 2012, we gain a 15-electoral-vote advantage over the Democrats, on top of the earlier advantage," says GOP consultant Morgan. "That leaves the Dems really scrambling, like 270 [electoral votes] would be out of reach for them."

That is based on two assumptions. The first is that recent state population trends will continue through the rest of the decade, which is not necessarily the case. "The increase we've had in population growth in a lot of areas has just evaporated, except for Arizona and Texas," says Clark Bensen, another Republican consultant.

The other assumption is that states will continue to vote the way they have in the past. That has seemed like a good bet through the early part of this decade, with only three small states — New Hampshire, Iowa and New Mexico — switching their votes between 2000 and 2004. But nothing in politics is static.

Although Brookings scholar and author Teixeira is optimistic that demographic trends favor Democrats, including increasing support from Hispanics and "millennials" now in their 20s, the fact that parts of the electorate are changing can cause an opposite reaction in other parts. Republicans benefited from the rise of the Christian Right and their gains in the South, but these gains cost them support among moderate voters in the Northeast and suburbs in general.

"The very fact that the Democrats are benefiting from demographic trends, such as the rise of single women, could drive other voters into the arms of Republicans," he says. "They might not like Democrats as the party of single people."

Teixeira and other Democrats believe that this year's election represents a chance for their party not only to consolidate the demographic trends that have been breaking their way but also to capitalize on the unpopularity of President Bush, the war in Iraq and uncertainty about the economy.

"Even though McCain was probably the best person Republicans could nominate, I think the Democrats win no matter who ends up being the nominee, Clinton or Obama," says Guerra, the Loyola Marymount political scientist. "It's not only the changing demographics that is going to reward Democrats. We get tired of a certain party, and we're going to punish Republicans for their policies, even if McCain was not always on their side."

But as they wrap up the primary season, even Democrats are debating whether they might blow an election in which they appear to have many advantages. A lot of that debate comes down to the question of demographics. If Clinton is the nominee, African-Americans and the young will not be as motivated as they would be by an Obama candidacy. But Obama has yet to prove he can carry white working-class voters in the preponderance of swing states.

Head-to-head polls have shown as many as 14 states breaking different ways, depending on the Democratic nominee. Political analyst Rhodes Cook suggests that Clinton would likely carry 18 to 22 states — roughly the same group that Al Gore carried in 2000 and John Kerry won in 2004. Cook predicts that Obama, however, might win as many as 30 states — or as few as 10.

Although Obama lost the Pennsylvania primary, he carried the state's 300,000 newly registered Democrats by about 20 points. Republican registrations in the state were down by 70,000. Obama has launched a voter-registration effort that seeks to replicate such new-minted support in all 50 states.

"Hillary goes deeper and stronger in the Democratic base than Obama, but her challenge is that she doesn't go as wide," said Peter Hart, a Democratic pollster. "Obama goes much further reaching into the independent and Republican vote, and has a greater chance of creating a new electoral map for the Democrats."[41]

# 2010 UPDATE

Voting patterns in the election of Barack Obama to the presidency in November 2008 reflected several major changes in the U.S. electorate, according to experts and exit polls.

The presence of a black candidate, not surprisingly, generated expectations for a huge turnout of black voters. But according to exit polls, while more blacks voted than in recent years, their share of the voting electorate did not increase significantly. Indeed, while black voters accounted for 11 percent of the votes in 2004 they accounted for 13 percent in 2008, an increase of only 2 percentage points.[42]

And while some analysts expected Obama to bring out the youth vote in unprecedented numbers, the share of the votes cast by those ages 18-29 rose only a single percentage point between 2004 and 2008, from 17 percent to 18 percent.

Although Obama didn't bring out significantly greater numbers of black and young voters, however, he did attract more of those voters to the Democratic Party. From 2004 to 2008, the Democrats' share of the black vote rose seven points, while the party's share of the youth vote jumped 13 points.[43]

The biggest shift took place among Latino voters. Latinos moved to Obama from the Republican Party in large numbers, ensuring an Obama victory in the battleground states of Colorado, New Mexico and Nevada. Obama also attracted a majority of the Latino vote in Florida, the first time a Democrat has done that since 1988.

## Hispanic Power

Indeed, Obama's support among Hispanic voters increased by 14 points compared with support for the Democratic nominee, Sen. John Kerry of Massachusetts, in 2004 — the biggest shift toward the Democrats by any voter group. Nationwide, Hispanics favored Obama over the Republican candidate, Sen. John McCain of Arizona, 61 percent to 38 percent.[44]

"They really delivered," says Efrain Escobedo, director of civic engagement at the National Association of Latino Elected Officials, a bipartisan group that ran voter-registration drives across the country. "This is an electorate that now understands the importance of voting, and they made a significant shift in the political landscape."[45]

Obama also did well with white voters. McCain attracted a majority in only one category of voters: those over age 60. Although whites made up just under three-quarters of the voters, it was their smallest share ever in a presidential election.[46]

Obama attracted significant support from voters, particularly in the Midwest, who generally align with conservative candidates but who voted for the Democratic candidate primarily out of frustration with the Bush administration. But some commentators believe voting patterns in the 2008 race reflect more far-reaching changes than short-term misgivings about the prior administration.

"Even though Obama's victory was nowhere near as numerically lopsided as Franklin D. Roosevelt's in 1932, his margins among decisive and growing constituencies make clear that this was a genuinely realigning election," wrote *Washington Post* columnist Harold Meyerson.[47]

Republican presidential candidate John McCain and his running mate, then-Alaska Gov. Sarah Palin, attend a campaign event at Van Dyke Park in Fairfax, Va., on Sept. 10, 2008.

## Government's Role

In addition to the growing Latino vote, Meyerson pointed to Obama's strong support among the growing ranks of well-educated professionals. "The final element of this realignment is the shift in public sentiment toward governmental activism — a shift in good measure occasioned by our long-term economic decline and short-term economic collapse," wrote Meyerson, noting exit polls that showed that 51 percent of Americans believed government "should do more" than it is doing — a reversal of the Reagan-era majorities that believed government should do less.

While Obama's campaign may have realigned the electorate, there already has been a strong counter-reaction from the right in the form of a loosely knit political movement known as the Tea Party.

Even before the 2008 election, apparently unorganized conservatives evoked the rebelliousness of the Boston Tea Party and used "tea party" symbols and labels at political rallies protesting policy positions of Obama and Sen. Hillary Rodham Clinton, his primary competitor for the Democratic presidential nomination. This year, one analyst described the Tea Party as being comprised of "hundreds of local groups, three loose national networks with Tea Party in their titles and allied conservative groups."[48]

"Members of the professional political class in Washington are uncertain whether they're observing a loud-mouthed flash in the pan or the birth of an important and lasting national movement," wrote Joseph J. Schatz in *CQ Weekly*. "Either way, the tea partiers' vituperative and vocal activism has accumulated into the strongest new force on the electoral landscape for this year and for both parties."[49]

Indeed, the Tea Party movement was credited with the biggest political upset since 2008, the election of Republican Scott P. Brown to the Senate seat left empty by the death of Sen. Edward M. Kennedy in August 2009. Brown's victory marked the first time in 38 years the seat had been held by a Republican.

Although members of the Tea Party movement generally favor Republican candidates, they tend to support policies even more conservative than many Republicans, and they are not disposed to compromise. For that reason, the Tea Party has proved problematic for the GOP.

"Urged on by prominent conservative commentators such as Glenn Beck and courted by Sarah Palin and other national Republican figures, tea party-affiliated groups have the mainstream GOP looking over its collective shoulder, more concerned than ever about the price of dealing with Democrats," wrote Schatz.[50]

## Tea Party Influence

While Tea Party supporters tend to have more politically conservative views than the general public, they are demographically very much in the mainstream. According to the Gallup Poll News Service, "compared with average Americans, supporters are slightly more likely to be male and less likely to be lower-income. In several other respects, however — their age, educational background, employment status, and race — Tea Partiers are quite representative of the public at large."[51]

Despite the Tea Party movement's growing numbers and influence, some analysts say that diffuse nature may prevent it from having a lasting impact.

"It's like an amoeba. Its strength is there isn't a structure to collapse. Their strength is that they're coming at you in all different directions and different ways, and if there's a crack they're going to work their way into it and try to get what they want done," said Charles Zelden, a professor of history and legal studies at Nova Southeastern University in South Florida. "The weakness is they don't have a structure. Amoebas don't stand up very well. Without a skeleton, a structure, they just sort of sit there."[52]

Indeed, as those supported by the Tea Party have experienced political success and have had to endure media scrutiny and take specific positions on issues, they have generated controversy both within the movement and in broader Republican circles.

When Rand Paul, a Tea Party candidate, won the Republican senate nomination in Kentucky in May 2010, his suggestion that the Civil Rights Act of 1964 shouldn't apply to private businesses generated controversy within his own party. "The case of Mr. Paul . . . shows the risks that have emerged as new figures move to the forefront of conservative politics, as candidates with little experience and sometimes unorthodox policy positions face the kind of scrutiny and pressure that could trip up even the most experienced politicians," wrote Adam Nagourney and Carl Hulse of *The New York Times*.[53]

Similarly, when Sen. Brown joined four other Republicans in voting to remove procedural hurdles blocking a $15 billion job-creation package being pushed by Democrats, he was called "Benedict Brown" by some in the movement. "Brown, whose prospects for winning a full term in two years will almost surely require him to toe a moderate line, tried to play down his apparent apostasy, urging his critics to 'read the bill' and learn that it wouldn't raise taxes," wrote Schatz.[54]

### Mid-Term Pressure

As the Democratic and Republican parties approach the mid-term election in November 2010, they face an electorate that is to an unusual degree feeling pressed by multiple issues.

"The generation-high jobless rate, coupled with the erosion of the financial safety net over some years, is elevating middle-class voter anxiety and raising doubts with the public about Washington's ability to help," wrote Clea Benson of *CQ Weekly*. "Between now and Election Day on Nov. 2, jobs and the economy will be the defining issue for voters, but it isn't evident there is much lawmakers and government officials can do to change things anytime soon."[55]

Analysts also expect that, as is common with mid-term elections, local issues will have more impact on the voting electorate than national issues.

"For a voter sitting out there, there is not just one focal point to this election. There are lots of things that are making people angry right now," Democratic pollster Geoff Garin said. "It's clear that there are lots of moving parts to this election that have and will affect individual races. It's not a neat, simple story line."[56]

One trend, however, is expected to continue: Despite significant shifts in the electorate since the election of 2008, poor and minority groups will remain underrepresented at the polls.

"The unregistered and non-voting populations remain disproportionately composed of low-income and minority Americans," concluded a recent report of Project Vote, a nonprofit voter advocacy group.[57] And that's especially true for mid-term elections, which don't attract the same level of media attention as presidential elections, says the report.

## 2014 UPDATE

### Key Events since the Last Update in 2010

The reelection of President Barack Obama in 2012 demonstrated the growing influence of minority voters.

Indeed, between the presidential elections of 2008 and 2012 there were increases in votes cast by black (9.4%), Asian (14%), and Hispanic (12.9%) voters, while the votes cast by white voters actually dropped by more than 2 million or 2 percent over the same period.[58]

What's more, the demographic changes in voting were not just in raw numbers but also as a percentage of eligible voters in each group, which some analysts see as a shift of engagement by groups in the electoral process. While a slightly higher percentage of eligible voters in each minority group actually turned out to vote in 2012, the percentage of eligible white voters fell a little more than 2 percent over the same period.[59]

In a milestone, 66.2 percent of eligible blacks voted in the 2012 presidential election, exceeding the participation rate of eligible non-Hispanic white voters (64.1%) for the first time since the U.S. Census Bureau began tracking that statistics in 1996.[60]

On election day, Republican candidate Mitt Romney won 59 percent of white votes. And white voters still represented 71.1 percent of eligible voters in 2012—down

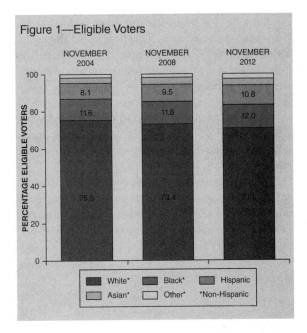

Figure 1—Eligible Voters

from 73.4 percent in 2012. But Obama's overwhelming share of minority votes assured him of victory. Obama won 93 percent of black votes, 71 percent of Hispanic votes, and 73 percent of Asian votes.[61]

The age of voters was another significant factor in deciding the 2012 election. Though young voters did not turn out in the numbers they did in 2008, Obama won the votes of those under 30 by 23 points over Romney, while Romney won the senior vote by 12 points.[62]

Although some analysts expected religion to be a significant issue in the 2012 election, with some on the right casting Obama as a Muslim and some on the left questioning the influence of Republican candidate Mitt Romney's Mormonism, judging from exit polls, it did not appear to have a significant role in voters' decisions.

"In the end, religion was relegated to a supporting role, dwarfed mainly by economic issues," writes Robert Jones, CEO of Public Religion Research Institute, a non-profit, nonpartisan group.[63]

While Obama prevailed over Romney 51 to 47 percent, the percentage of eligible citizens who voted declined from 63.6 percent in 2008 to 61.8 percent in 2012.[64]

## Redistricting

Although demographic changes in the electorate over recent decades have tended to favor Democrats, at least at the national level, the effects of those changes have been mitigated by a number of factors, including notably the political redistricting that took place in the states after the 2010 census.

Even as Obama won reelection to the presidency in 2012, Republicans won control of the House of Representatives by a margin of 234 to 201, this despite the fact that Democratic candidates received 1.8 million more votes than Republican candidates.

"Through artful drawing of district boundaries, it is possible to put large groups of voters on the losing side of every election," writes Sam Wang, founder of the Princeton Election Consortium.[65]

Wang points to the success of the Republican State Leadership Committee's REDMAP (REDistricting Majority Project) as the major factor in the shift. The Republican State Leadership Committee describes the program as "dedicated to winning state legislative seats that will have a critical impact on congressional redistricting in 2011."[66]

## Supreme Court Decisions

Two Supreme Court decisions—one in 2010 and one in 2013—have already had significant impacts on the influence of various sectors of the electorate.

In *Citizens United v. Federal Election Commission* (2010) the court held 5-4 that the government couldn't limit political spending by corporations.

At the time, President Obama called the ruling, "a major victory for big oil, Wall Street banks, health insurance companies and the other powerful interests that marshal their power every day in Washington to drown out the voices of everyday Americans."[67]

And in fact, according to the nonpartisan and non-profit Center for Political Responsiveness, the amount of outside spending on campaigns roughly tripled between 2010 and 2012, amounting to more than $300 million.[68]

While the complex nature of campaign contribution and reporting laws make it impossible to determine just how much increased spending on the part of corporations is because of Citizens United, even analysts who believe the impact of the ruling has been overstated do not deny that there has been an impact.

"What the new rulings did, as the experts like to put it, was to 'lift the cloud of uncertainty' that hung over such expenditures, and the effect of this psychological shift should not be underestimated," writes Matt Bai, political editor for the *New York Times Magazine*. "It almost certainly accounts for some rise in political money this year, both from individuals and companies."[69]

In June 2014, the Supreme Court held in *Shelby County v. Holder* (2013)—also by a 5-4 decision—that it was improper to require certain states to clear changes in voting laws in advance.

Under Section 5 of the Voting Rights Act of 1965, states and localities with a history of racial discrimination were required to get permission from the federal government to enact any changes to their voting laws. As of June 2013, nine states—Alabama, Alaska, Arizona, Georgia, Louisiana, Mississippi, South Carolina, Texas and Virginia—needed to get any new voting laws preapproved.

The court did not strike down the law, but it ruled that Congress must base its decisions on more recent data about discrimination in order to require preclearance. With the currently divided state of Congress, however, analysts see new legislation addressing the issue as unlikely to pass.

Effectively, the ruling means that states are free to pass laws affecting voting rights—such as requiring government-issued identification—and that citizens or the Department of Justice would have to file suit after the fact to argue that there is a discriminatory impact.

Attorney General Eric H. Holder Jr., called the decision a "serious setback for voting rights," and said his department will "continue to carefully monitor jurisdictions around the country for voting changes that may hamper voting rights."[70]

According to a report by the Brennan Center for Justice, a nonpartisan institute, since the 2010 election new voting restrictions are scheduled to be in place in 22 states before the 2014-midterm elections.[71]

In addition, according to Project Vote, a nonpartisan, nonprofit research group, so far this year at least 11 states have introduced bills to pass strict voter ID laws or add further restrictions to existing voter ID requirements.[72]

## Republican Party Divided

In the wake of the Republican loss in the 2012 presidential election, divisions within the Republican Party have been growing. Approaching the 2014-midterm elections, a number of Republican incumbents—most notably in Kentucky and Mississippi—were faced with primary challenges by ultra-conservative Tea Party candidates. In most cases, the incumbents won their primaries, but questions remain as to the support those candidates will have in the general election if Tea Party supporters are disaffected.

"Throughout the early part of this year, there has been one political narrative above all others: tea party [*sic*] vs. Republican establishment, or a Republican Party at war with itself," writes Dan Balz, chief correspondent at *The Washington Post*. "It is both a real and a flawed concept, as the first rounds of primaries have shown. Real because there are key differences between hard-charging tea party conservatives who believe there is still too much business as usual, even among Republicans in Washington, and the more cautious establishment types. Flawed because the Republican Party of 2014 is still more united by its deep dislike of President Obama and his policies, and by the prospect of winning control of the Senate in the fall, than by those differences."[73]

As much as the Republican Party might be united in its opposition to Obama, however, it is divided on many issues that reflect a demographic quandary for the party. Party leaders question whether the party can succeed if it doesn't attract more minority voters, young voters, and women, yet it's not apparent how the party can back policies that will attract those demographics without alienating Tea Party voters.

"Our demographics are changing, and we have to change," former Florida Governor Jeb Bush told the Republican convention in 2012. "Not necessarily our core beliefs, but the tone of our message and the message and the intensity of it for sure. Long-term, conservative principles, if they're to be successful and implemented, there has to be a concerted effort to reach out to a much broader audience than we do today."[74]

## Approaching the 2014 Midterm Election

As the 2014 midterm elections approach, according to a recent study by the Pew Research Center, "Republicans and Democrats are more divided along ideological lines —and partisan antipathy is deeper and more extensive—than at any point in the last two decades."[75]

Based on extensive survey data, the report found that the percentage of Americans who express "consistently conservative or consistently liberal" opinions has doubled over the past two decades, rising from 10 percent to 21 percent. And the two major parties are moving farther apart as well. "Ideological overlap between the two parties has diminished: Today, 92% of Republicans are to the right of the median Democrat, and 94% of Democrats are to the left of the median Republican."[76]

At the same time, candidates and voters alike face uncertainty as challenges to states' changes in voting laws wind their way through the courts. Most recently, on June 11 a federal judge ordered Ohio's election commissioner to restore early voting hours on the three days before election day.

"The court decisions have gone both ways, but several have provided a new round of judicial rebukes to the wave of voting restrictions, nearly all of them introduced since 2011 in states with Republican majorities," writes Lizette Alvarez of *The New York Times*. "The decisions have ensured that challenges will remain a significant part of the voting landscape, perhaps for years. And, with challenges still going through the courts, voting rules and requirements remain uncertain in several states before the midterm elections."[77]

## NOTES

1. Alan Greenblatt, "The Partisan Divide," *CQ Researcher*, April 30, 2004, pp. 373-396.

2. Kathy Kiely and Jill Lawrence, "Clinton Makes Case for Staying In," *USA Today*, May 8, 2008, p. 1A.

3. Paul Krugman, "Self-Inflicted Confusion," *The New York Times*, April 25, 2008, p. A27.

4. Jonathan Weisman and Matthew Mosk, "Party Fears Racial Divide," *The Washington Post*, April 26, 2008, p. A1.

5. Eli Saslow, "Democrats Registering in Record Numbers," *The Washington Post*, April 28, 2008, p. A1.

6. Thomas B. Edsall, "Census a Clarion Call for Democrats, GOP," *The Washington Post*, July 8, 2001, p. A5.

7. Susan Page, "GOP Coalition Fractured by Opposition to War," *USA Today*, Nov. 8, 2006, p. 1A.

8. Larry J. Sabato, *The Sixth-Year Itch* (2008), p. 22. For background, see the following *CQ Researcher* reports: David Masci, "Latinos' Future," Oct. 17, 2003, pp. 869-892; Alan Greenblatt, "Race in America," July 11, 2003, pp. 593-624, and Nadine Cohodas, "Electing Minorities," Aug. 12, 1994, pp. 697-720.

9. Bill Boyarsky, "Courting the White Vote," *Truthdig*, April 24, 2008, www.truthdig.com/report/item/20080425_courting_the_white_vote/.

10. Earl Black and Merle Black, *Divided America* (2007), p. 10.

11. Thomas F. Shaller, "So Long, White Boy," *Salon*, Sept. 17, 2007, www.salon.com/opinion/feature/2007/09/17/white_man/.

12. Alan Greenblatt, "Slow March to the Polls," *Governing*, June 2006, p. 17.

13. Ronald Brownstein and Richard Rainey, "GOP Plants Flag on New Voting Frontier," *Los Angeles Times*, Nov. 22, 2004, p. A1.

14. David Mark, "The Battle Over Suburban, Exurban Vote," *Politico*, Dec. 4, 2007. Mary H. Cooper, "Smart Growth," *CQ Researcher*, May 28, 2004, pp. 469-492.

15. Jill Lawrence, "Democratic Gains in Suburbs Spell Trouble for GOP," *USA Today*, Nov. 26, 2006, p. 6A.

16. Scott Keeter *et al*, "Gen Dems: The Party's Advantage Among Young Voters Widens," Pew Research Center for the People & the Press, April 28, 2008.

17. "A Portrait of 'Generation Next': How Young People View Their Lives, Futures and Politics," Pew Research Center for the People & the Press, Jan. 9, 2007; available at http://people-press.org/reports/pdf/300.pdf.

18. Sabato, *op. cit.*, p. 22.

19. Michiko Kakutani, "Why Are These Democrats Smiling? It's Cyclical," *The New York Times*, April 22, 2008, p. E7.

20 . "Obama Dominating Highly-Charged Youth Vote in Presidential Race, Harvard Poll Finds," Harvard Institute of Politics, news release April 24, 2008.

21. Everett Carll Ladd Jr., "The Shifting Party Coalitions, 1932 to 1976," in Seymour Martin Lipset, ed., *Emerging Coalitions in American Politics* (1978), p. 83.

22. Kenneth S. Baer, *Reinventing Democrats* (2000), p. 14.

23. Barbara Sinclair, *Party Wars* (2006), p. 17.

24. James Boyd, "Nixon's Southern Strategy," *The New York Times*, May 17, 1970, p. 215.

25. Kevin Phillips, *The Emerging Republican Majority* (1969), p. 25.

26. Kenneth Jost and Greg Giroux, "Electoral College," *CQ Researcher*, Dec. 8, 2000, pp. 977-1008.

27. Ladd, *op. cit.*, p. 94.

28. Baer, *op. cit.*, p. 35.

29. Sinclair, *op. cit.*, p. 49.

30. *Ibid.*, p. 14.

31. *Ibid.*, p. 51.

32. "Latinos and the 2006 Midterm Election," Pew Hispanic Center, Nov. 27, 2006.

33. Black and Black, *op. cit.*, p. 29.

34. Bill Bishop, *The Big Sort* (2008), p. 6.

35. *Ibid.*, p. 5.

36. Alan Greenblatt, "Whatever Happened to Competitive Elections?", *Governing*, October 2004, p. 22.

37. Bishop, *op. cit.*, p. 45.

38. *Ibid.*, p. 39.

39. *Ibid.*, p. 56.

40. William H. Frey, "The Electoral College Moves to the Sun Belt," The Brookings Institution, May 2005, p. 4.

41. Patrick Healy, "For Democrats, Questions Over Race and Electability," *The New York Times*, April 24, 2008, p. A1.

42. Chris Cillizza, "Myths About One Mythic Election," *The Washington Post*, Nov. 16, 2008, p. B3.

43. *Ibid.*

44. Julia Preston, "What Got Obama Elected," *The New York Times*, Nov. 7, 2008, p. A24.

45. *Ibid.*

46. Marjorie Connelly, "Dissecting the Changing Electorate," *The New York Times*, Nov. 9, 2008, WK5.

47. Harold Meyerson, "A Real Realignment," *The Washington Post*, Nov. 7, 2008, p. A19.

48. Joseph J. Schatz, "Reading the Tea Leaves at the Capitol," *CQ Weekly*, Feb. 28, 2010.

49. *Ibid.*

50. *Ibid.*

51. Lydia Saad, "Tea Partiers Are Fairly Mainstream in Their Demographics; Skew right politically, but have typical profile by age, education, and employment," Gallup Poll News Service, April 5, 2010, www.gallup.com/poll/ 127181/Tea-Partiers-Fairly-Mainstream-Demo graphics.aspx?utm_source=alert &utm_medium= email&utm_campaign=syndi cation&utm_con tent=morelink&utm_term= All+Gallup+Head lines+-+Politics#1.

52. Anthony Man, "November or Beyond? Tea Party Faces Choices; As Grassroots Movement Grows, So Do Questions About Direction," *Fort Lauderdale Sun-Sentinel*, July 4, 2010, p. 1B.

53. Adam Nagourney and Carl Hulse, "Tea Party Pick Causes Uproar on Civil Rights," *The New York Times*, May 21, 2010, p. A1.

54. Schatz, *op. cit.*

55. Clea Benson, "The Price of Perception," *CQ Weekly*, Jan. 17, 2010.

56. Dan Balz, " 'Angry electorate' could be unpredictable at polls this fall," *The Washington Post*, June 13, 2010, p. A2.

57. Douglas R. Hess and Jody Herman, "Representational Bias in the 2008 Electorate," Project Vote, November 2009, http://projectvote.org/ reports-on-the-electorate-/ 440.html.

58. Thom File, "The Diversifying Electorate—Voting Rates by Race and Hispanic Origin in 2012 (and Other Recent Elections)." *Current Population Survey Reports, 2013*, U.S. Census Bureau, Washington, D.C., p. 2.

59. William H. Frey, "Minority Turnout Determined the 2012 Election," The Brookings Institution, May 10, 2013, http://www.brookings.edu/research/ papers/2013/05/10-election-2012-minority-voter-turnout-frey.

60. Thom File, "The Diversifying Electorate—Voting Rates by Race and Hispanic Origin in 2012 (and Other Recent Elections)." *Current Population Survey Reports*, 2013, U.S. Census Bureau, Washington, D.C., p. 8.

61. "U.S. Elections: How Groups Voted in 2012," The Roper Center, University of Connecticut, http://www.ropercenter.uconn.edu/elections/how_groups_voted/voted_12.html.

62. *Ibid.*

63. Robert P. Jones, "How Values, Demographics and the Economy Helped Shape the Election," *The Washington Post*, Nov. 9, 2012, http://www.faithstreet.com/onfaith/2012/11/07/how-values-demographics-and-the-economy-helped-shape-the-election/10703.

64. U.S. Census Bureau, http://www.census.gov/newsroom/releases/archives/voting/cb13-84.html.

65. Sam Wang, "The Great Gerrymander of 2012," *The New York Times*, February 2, 2013, http://www.nytimes.com/2013/02/03/opinion/sunday/the-great-gerrymander-of-2012.html?pagewanted=all&module=Search&mabReward=relbias%3Ar.

66. http://www.redistrictingmajorityproject.com/?page_id=2.

67. Adam Liptak, "Justices, 5-4, Reject Corporate Spending Limit," *The New York Times*, January 21, 2010, http://www.nytimes.com/2010/01/22/us/politics/22scotus.html?pagewanted=all&_r=0.

68. http://www.opensecrets.org/outsidespending/index.php?cycle=2012&view=Y&chart=N#viewpt.

69. Matt Bai, "How Much Has Citizens United Changed the Political Game?" *New York Times Magazine*, July 17, 2012, http://www.nytimes.com/2012/07/22/magazine/how-much-has-citizens-united-changed-the-political-game.html?pagewanted=all&_r=0.

70. Robert Barnes, "Supreme Court stops use of key part of Voting Rights Act," *The Washington Post*, June 25, 2013, http://www.washingtonpost.com/politics/supreme-court-stops-use-of-key-part-of-voting-rights-act/2013/06/25/26888528-dda5-11e2-b197-f248b21f94c4_story.html.

71. Wendy R. Weiser and Erik Opsal, "The State of Voting in 2014," Brennan Center for Justice, June 17, 2014, http://www.brennancenter.org/analysis/state-voting-2014.

72. Erin Ferns Lee, "Election Legislation 2014: Legislative Threats and Opportunities," *Project Vote*, p. 7, http://projectvote.org/component/content/article/110-reports-and-analysis/1084-election-legislation-2014-legislative-threats-and-opportunities.html.

73. Dan Baltz, "Will the tea party rally behind the Republican establishment?" *The Washington Post*, May 21, 2014, http://www.washingtonpost.com/politics/will-the-tea-party-rally-behind-gop-establishment/2014/05/21/9f9a7a30-e0f0-11e3-810f-764fe508b82d_story.html.

74. Phil Oreskes, "Can Democracies Shift an Election?" *The New York Times*, August 31, 2012, <http://www.nytimes.com/2012/09/01/us/01iht-letter01.html?module=Search&mabReward=relbias%3Ar>.

75. Pew Research Center, June 2014, "Political Polarization in the American Public," p. 5, http://www.people-press.org/2014/06/12/political-polarization-in-the-american-public/.

76. *Ibid.*

77. Lizette Alvarez, "Court Rulings on Voter Restrictions Create Limbo as Midterms Near," *The New York Times*, June 16, 2014, <http://www.nytimes.com/2014/06/17/us/court-rulings-on-voter-restrictions-create-limbo-as-midterms-near.html?hp&_r=0>.

# BIBLIOGRAPHY

## Books

**Bishop, Bill, with Robert G. Cushing, *The Big Sort: Why the Clustering of Like-Minded America is Tearing Us Apart*, Houghton Mifflin, 2008.**
A journalist shows how many more Republicans and Democrats are moving into communities that are partisan enclaves, contributing to the polarization of U.S. politics.

**Bowman, Karlyn, and Ruy Teixeira, eds., *Red Blue and Purple America; The Future of Election Demographics*, Brooking Institution Press (forthcoming).**
In a book coming this fall, a group of political scientists and demographers examine how trends in religion, geography, immigration and income and class are affecting voting habits.

Fisher, Claude S., and Michael Hout, *Century of Difference: How America Changed in the Last Hundred Years*, Russell Sage Foundation, 2006.
University of California, Berkeley sociologists draw on census data and polling surveys to present a comprehensive description of demographic, economic and cultural changes since 1900.

Singer, Audrey, Susan W. Hardwick and Caroline B. Brettell, eds., *Twenty-First Century Gateways: Immigrant Immigration in Suburban America*, Brookings Institution Press, 2008.
Academic authors examine the impact of immigrants no longer settling in urban cores so much as the suburbs.

## Articles

Brownstein, Ron, "The Warrior and the Priest," *Los Angeles Times*, March 25, 2007, p. M1.
An influential column argues Barack Obama would appeal to upscale voters while Hillary Clinton would assume the role of "warrior" defending the interests of blue-collar voters.

Curry, Tom, "How Reagan Hobbled the Democrats," MSNBC.com, June 7, 2004, www.msnbc.msn.com/id/5151912/.
Curry examines how the Republican president captured lower- and middle-income whites and the South through clear economic and foreign policies.

Frum, David, "Why the GOP Lost the Youth Vote," *USA Today*, April 9, 2008, p. 12A.
A former speechwriter for President George W. Bush says Republicans must pay more attention to payroll taxes and environmental and social issues to woo young voters.

Healy, Patrick, "For Democrats, Questions Over Race and Electability," *The New York Times*, April 24, 2008, p. A1.
The split among Democratic primary voters has party leaders debating who has the best chance to prevail in the fall.

Malanga, Steven, "The Rainbow Coalition Evaporates," *City Journal*, Winter 2008.
A conservative author examines tensions between African-Americans and immigrants in urban neighborhoods.

Mark, David, "The Battle Over Suburban, Exurban Vote," *Politico*, Dec. 4, 2007.
A political journalist looks at how emerging suburbs have become a contested battleground.

Schaller, Thomas F., "So Long, White Boy," *Salon*, Sept. 17, 2007.
White males have abandoned the Democrats, so party candidates should learn to win without their support.

## Reports and Studies

Frey, William H., "The Electoral College Moves to the Sun Belt," The Brookings Institution Research Brief, May 2005.
Sun Belt states, which had a nearly equal amount of electoral votes as the Northeast and Midwest in 1972, will have 146 more by 2030.

Keeter, Scott, Juliana Horowitz and Alex Tyson, "Gen Dems: The Party's Advantage Among Young Voters Widens," Pew Research Center for the People & the Press, April 28, 2008, http://pewresearch.org/pubs/813/gen-dems.
Fifty-eight percent of voters under 30 are leaning toward the Democrats, fueling party growth much as young voters drove GOP growth during the 1990s.

Marcelo, Karlo Barrios, *et al.*, "Young Voter Registration and Turnout Trends," Rock the Vote and the Center for Information & Research on Civic Learning and Engagement, February 2008.
The turnout of young voters — typically low since 18-year-olds got the vote in 1972 — rose in both the 2004 and 2006 elections and is likely to increase again this year.

McKee, Seth C. and Daron S. Shaw, "Suburban Voting in Presidential Elections," *Presidential Studies Quarterly*, March 2003.
The decisive suburban vote edged away from Republican candidates during the 1990s in the North, but not in the South.

Putnam, Robert D., "E Pluribus Unum: Diversity and Community in the Twenty-First Century," *Scandinavian Political Studies*, June 2007, p. 137.
Based on a nationwide survey, the Harvard political scientist finds decreased levels of trust and social participation in communities that are more diverse.

# For More Information

**American Enterprise Institute**, 1150 17th St., N.W., Washington, DC 20036; (202) 862-5800; www.aei.org. A conservative public policy think tank that conducts research and education on politics, economics and social welfare.

**Atlas of U.S. Elections**; uselectionatlas.org. A Web site providing comprehensive mapping of election results by state, city and county.

**Brookings Institution**, 1775 Massachusetts Ave., N.W., Washington, DC 20036; (202) 797-6000; www.brookings .edu. A centrist think tank that issues regular reports on politics, immigration and demographics through its Metropolitan Policy and Governance Studies programs.

**Joint Center for Political and Economics Studies**, 1090 Vermont Ave., N.W., Suite 1100, Washington, DC 20005; (202) 789-3500; (202) 789-3500; www.jointcenter.org. Studies issues of importance to African-Americans.

**Patchwork Nation Project**, *The Christian Science Monitor*, 210 Massachusetts Ave., Boston, MA 02115; (617) 450-2300; www.csmonitor.com/patchworknation. Tracks political demographic information and hosts blogs by residents of 11 representative types of communities.

**Pew Research Center for The People & The Press**, 1615 L St., N.W., Suite 700, Washington, DC 20036; (202) 419-4350; people-press.org. Conducts public opinion polls and research on media and political issues.

**UCLA Higher Education Research Institute**, 3005 Moore Hall/Box 951521, Los Angeles, CA 90095; (310) 825-1925; www.gseis.ucla.edu/heri/. Has conducted nationwide surveys of college freshmen for more than 40 years.

**U.S. Census Bureau**, 4600 Silver Hill Rd., Suitland, MD 20746; (202) 501-5400; www.census.gov. The primary source for information about the U.S. population.

**William C. Velásquez Institute**, 206 Lombard St., First Floor, San Antonio, TX 78226; (210) 992-3118; www .wcvi.org. Conducts research as part of its mission of improving the level of political participation among Latinos.

# 5

# Border Security

Reed Karaim

Hundreds of motorists from Mexico wait to enter the United States at the Nogales, Ariz., border crossing. Many are Mexicans who work in the United States or are visiting relatives there. Such scenes have been common along the 1,933-mile U.S.-Mexican border — and to a lesser extent along the 4,000-mile Canadian border — since the United States began intensifying security, especially after the Sept. 11, 2001, terrorist attacks.

From *CQ Researcher*,
September 27, 2013.

Less than 30 yards from the U.S.-Mexican border outside Nogales, Ariz., new, 80-foot concrete poles rise into the desert air. They will soon be topped with the latest in surveillance hardware, including infrared and radar-directed cameras that can be controlled remotely from the U.S. Border Patrol station in Nogales, the nation's biggest.

"It's going to make a tremendous difference," says Leslie Lawson, chief of the Nogales station, standing beneath one of the surveillance towers. "It's going to extend our view several more miles, and it's going to be stuffed with the newest technology."

Already running along the border is a new 18-foot-tall fence made with concrete-filled posts that extend six to eight feet underground.[1]

In addition, agents have an array of sophisticated personal surveillance gear, including Recon, a $135,000 portable device that looks like a giant pair of binoculars but features infrared and thermal vision. It can read heat signatures of people and objects and then bounce a laser off the target to get an exact reading of its location.

Back in the station's windowless control room in Nogales, agents monitor 30 screens linked to cameras, along with alarms connected to ground sensors along the border. Also watching the border from above are tethered radar blimps, surveillance aircraft and unarmed Predator drones.[2] About 25 miles farther into the United States, a Border Patrol checkpoint on the major highway in the area provides another layer of security.

"We've built a new road or had a new piece of technology installed every month, or so it seems," says Lawson, who credits the new infrastructure and technology with helping her agents effectively patrol more than 1,000 square miles of country.

## Illegal Crossings Fall to Record Low

The number of people apprehended after crossing the U.S.-Mexican border illegally hit a 30-year low in 2012, with most apprehensions occurring near Tucson, Ariz. After the United States began beefing up security along the border in 1980, apprehensions rose sharply, reaching 1.6 million in 1986 — the year Congress enacted landmark immigration reform. Subsequently, apprehensions fell and rose unevenly, hitting 1.5 million in 1996, when Congress passed another immigration law. Apprehensions reached a record 1.6 million in 2000 before falling well below 400,000 in 2011 and 2012, in part because of poor job prospects in the U.S.

**Illegal Crossings on the Southwest Border, by Sectors, FY1980-2012**

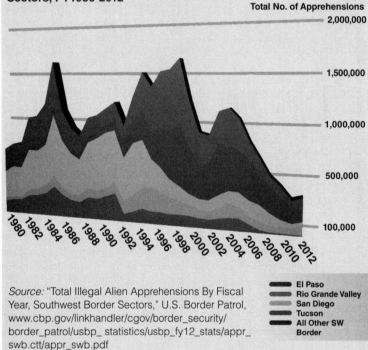

*Source:* "Total Illegal Alien Apprehensions By Fiscal Year, Southwest Border Sectors," U.S. Border Patrol, www.cbp.gov/linkhandler/cgov/border_security/ border_patrol/usbp_ statistics/usbp_fy12_stats/appr_ swb.ctt/appr_swb.pdf

El Paso
Rio Grande Valley
San Diego
Tucson
All Other SW Border

2,500 in the early 1980s to more than 21,000, doubling in just the last eight years.[3] Since 1986, the United States has spent more than $219 billion in today's dollars on border and immigration enforcement, building some 650 miles of fencing along the Southern border while beefing up high-tech surveillance along both borders and at so-called ports of entry, including authorized land crossings, seaports and airports.[4]

The buildup began in response to concerns about rising illegal immigration from Mexico but accelerated after the Sept. 11, 2001, terrorist attacks, which created a new sense of urgency concerning national security and led to a new surge in spending along both borders.

The reaction to 9/11 "provided a stimulus package for border control," says Peter Andreas, a professor of political science and international studies at Brown University. Border Patrol agents now "were supposed to be the front line in the war on terror. They never really had that job before, and it was added to their mission — not just added, but put up front."

In addition to beefing up the Border Patrol, "about 5,000 ICE [Immigration and Customs Enforcement] agents are deployed to [the] U.S. border, along with numerous other federal law enforcement agents . . . and various state and local law enforcement agents," Marc R. Rosenblum, an immigration policy specialist with the Congressional Research Service, told a House committee this year.[5]

Nevertheless, political debate continues to rage about the effectiveness and focus of the nation's border security programs. Some analysts question the need for the buildup and how resources have been allocated, while others believe it still falls far short of what is needed to completely secure America's borders.

The situation in Nogales is representative of a vastly intensified security effort along the 1,933-mile U.S.-Mexican border, and to a lesser degree along the 4,000-mile U.S.-Canadian border. Since the mid-1980s, the United States has poured more personnel and resources into policing its borders than at any other time in history.

Since the buildup began, the number of Border Patrol agents on the Mexican border has jumped from less than

Other observers claim the federal government is still too concerned about the rights of undocumented border crossers, is not prosecuting enough to deter illegal crossing and unnecessarily restricts Border Patrol operations in environmentally sensitive areas and on Native American lands.

"The effort, the additional agents, that's all been tempered by the fact that the administration — the current one or the prior one — would not allow the agents out in the field to go out and do their job," says Jeffery L. Everly, vice chairman of the National Association of Former Border Patrol Officers. "We say one thing, but we have policies and procedures that water it down."

But others say the border buildup is eroding civil rights. "It's been called a Constitution-lite, or even a Constitution-free zone, [because] agencies have greater rights to stop and question people than they do elsewhere in the country," says Brian Erickson, a policy advocate at the American Civil Liberties Union (ACLU) Regional Center for Border Rights in Las Cruces, N.M.

The Constitution's Fourth Amendment prohibits "unreasonable" searches and seizures of American citizens, but within 100 miles of the border the U.S. Supreme Court's longstanding "border search exception" rule gives authorities the right to stop and search individuals or vehicles without probable cause or a warrant.[6]

That's only one way federal authority is exercised to a greater degree close to the border. In 2005, for example, the Real ID Act gave the Department of Homeland Security the power to sweep aside environmental regulations and other legal impediments to speed the building of the border security fence.[7]

Some human-rights activists blame the fence and personnel buildup for a 27 percent jump in deaths among migrants since last year, even as the number of border crossings fell.[8] Activists say border crossers are diverting to more remote and dangerous terrain, making them more dependent on violent smugglers.

There also have been more charges of harassment or brutality by the swelling force of Border Patrol agents.

## One-third of Mexican Border Is Fenced

The United States has built 636 miles of fencing along the nation's 1,933-mile Southwestern border since 1996, when only 14 miles were fenced. Much of the expansion was financed by the Secure Fencing Act of 2006, which initially required construction of about 800 miles of fencing. A subsequent law reduced the requirement, but the recently passed Senate immigration reform bill would mandate another 50 miles of fence, bringing the total to 700 miles.

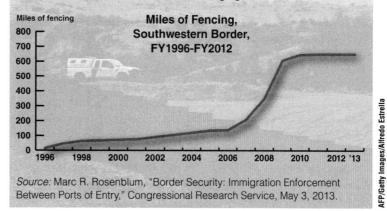

Miles of fencing

**Miles of Fencing, Southwestern Border, FY1996-FY2012**

Source: Marc R. Rosenblum, "Border Security: Immigration Enforcement Between Ports of Entry," Congressional Research Service, May 3, 2013.

AFP/Getty Images/Alfredo Estrella

The Department of Homeland Security has received hundreds of complaints of rights violations, and at least 15 people have been killed by Border Patrol agents in the last three years.[9]

The debate over border security has become entangled in the larger controversy over immigration policy.[10] In June the Senate passed an immigration reform package that would provide a path to citizenship for many of the estimated 11.7 million unauthorized immigrants in the United States in 2012.[11] To broaden support for the bill, provisions were added that would further boost border security, including the addition of another 20,000 Border Patrol agents, essentially doubling the number of agents. House Republicans strongly oppose the Senate measure, however, arguing the bill does not clearly establish measurable standards for securing the border from further illegal immigration.

Although blocking terrorists now tops Border Patrol agents' agenda, Andreas says, "in practice, the day-to-day activity is the same old same old: drug smuggling, customs work and illegal immigration."

As a reflection of that reality, the vast majority of Border Patrol agents and most resources remain concentrated on the U.S. border with Mexico.[12] But some security experts believe America's coastlines and its main Canadian border, which is nearly twice as long at about 4,000 miles and more lightly patrolled than the Mexican border, pose the greater threats of terrorist incursion.*

President Obama and administration officials often cite a sharp decline in the number of people crossing the U.S.-Mexico border illegally as proof that the border buildup is working. "We put more boots on the ground on the Southern border than at any time in our history," Obama said in a speech on immigration this year in Las Vegas. "And today, illegal crossings are down nearly 80 percent from their peak in 2000."[13]

But critics of the administration's efforts say proof of success is still lacking. "Every day, everything from humans to illicit drugs are smuggled across our borders," Rep. Michael McCaul, R-Texas, chairman of the House Homeland Security Committee, said shortly after Obama's speech. "While the administration claims it has spent more funds to secure the border than ever before, the fact remains that the Department of Homeland Security still does not have a comprehensive plan to secure the border that includes a reasonable definition of operational control we can measure."[14]

As the debate continues on nearly all aspects of border security, here are some of the questions being discussed:

### Has the border security buildup made the United States more secure?

Analysts point out that the effort to secure America's borders is a reaction to three challenges: international terrorism, drug smuggling and illegal immigration.

Most border security analysts say there is little evidence the buildup has significantly reduced the availability of illegal narcotics in the United States. The U.S. Drug Enforcement Administration (DEA) has cited reduced use of some drugs, especially cocaine, as proof the buildup is working. But other drugs have grown in popularity, and smugglers have proved adept at shifting their methods and locations in response to interdiction efforts.[15] "I don't think the U.S. has gotten fundamentally better at stopping drugs," says Brown

University's Andreas. "I don't think there's anybody who argues otherwise."

The debate over the effectiveness of border security centers on terrorism and illegal immigration. Although much public attention has focused on immigration, counterterrorism is the focus of many security analysts, some of whom believe the bolstered security on the border has made the United States safer.

"The U.S. has tripled the size of the Border Patrol, so there's a higher probability of detection of anybody coming across the border illegally, whether they're a terrorist or anybody. So in that sense, yes, we've reduced the likelihood of terrorists coming across the border," says Seth M. M. Stodder, who served as director of policy and planning at U.S. Customs and Border Protection during the George W. Bush administration.

But Stodder, a senior associate with the Center for Strategic and International Studies, adds that effectively fighting international terrorism requires a layered approach that includes working closely with other nations. Land borders, he says, should be seen as "the last line of defense in regard to terrorism."

However, other experts say the U.S.-Mexico border has never been a likely avenue for terrorists. "Mexico is not a hotbed of international terrorism, and to say it is is just not to understand the facts," says Erik Lee, executive director of the North American Research Partnership, a think tank in San Diego that focuses on the relationship between the United States, Mexico and Canada.

Lee thinks the border is an illogical route for terrorists from outside Mexico to choose. "People who want to do harm to the United States will choose the paths of least resistance, and the ports of entry will be among those paths," he says. "Crossing the U.S.-Mexico border is much more logistically difficult. These are remote areas, dangerous and hard to cross."

Even more dismissive is Scott Nicol, a member of the No Border Wall Coalition, a grassroots group opposed to the construction of the fence separating the United States and Mexico. The idea of terrorists crossing the Mexican border is "a total red herring. A terrorist has never come across the Southern border," says Nicol, who lives near the border in McAllen, Texas. "There may be some people who really believe it's a threat. But I think a lot of it is, when you're going to militarize something so heavily, you have to have a big excuse for it."

---

*The Canadian border with the Lower 48 states is about 4,000 miles long. The border with Alaska is about 1,500 miles long, but that border is nearly all wilderness and has not been a focus of security concerns.

But Paul Rosenzweig, who served as deputy assistant secretary for policy in the Department of Homeland Security in the George W. Bush administration, says, "The best evidence we have is that there haven't been seizures of terrorists on the Southern border. On the other hand, we did have at least one case of a seizure on the Northern border." However, terrorists might have been seized on the Southern border without the government disclosing it, he says. "It could be classified."

The Northern border case occurred before 9/11, when a U.S. customs agent in December 1999 stopped Ahmed Ressam, an Algerian who had received training from al Qaeda, trying to enter the United States from Canada in Port Angeles, Wash., with a rental car full of explosives. Ressam, dubbed the "Millennium Bomber," had planned to detonate a bomb at Los Angeles International Airport on New Year's Eve.

Rosenzweig, now a visiting fellow with the Heritage Foundation, a conservative think tank in Washington, says any potential terrorist today faces more challenges on both borders. "If the question is, have we done a better job of preventing terrorist incidents in the United States through a ramp-up in border security, I think the answer is clearly yes," he says.

Whether the border buildup is curbing illegal immigration is also a subject of strong debate. Speaking this August, outgoing Homeland Security Secretary Janet Napolitano said the effort is having a significant impact. "Over the past four-and-a-half years, we have invested historic resources to prevent illegal cross-border activity," Napolitano said. "And because of these investments in manpower, and technology, and infrastructure, our borders are now better staffed and better protected than any time in our nation's history, and illegal crossings have dropped to near 40-year lows."[16]

The claim that illegal crossings have fallen is based largely on the sharp decline in the number of apprehensions along the Mexican border in recent years — from more than 1.6 million in 1986 to about 357,000 last year.[17] But some analysts believe the decline says more about the slowdown in the U.S. economy than increased

*Getty Images/John Moore*

*Getty Images/Joe Raedle*

***Methods of Detection***

U.S. Border Patrol cameras along the Niagara River monitor the U.S.-Canadian border in Grand Island, N.Y. (top). Customs agents in Miami X-ray incoming bags of charcoal to prevent undeclared goods, including drugs, from entering the country (bottom). Controversy over immigration policy has complicated the debate over border security. In June, the Senate passed an immigration reform package that would provide a path to citizenship for the estimated 11.7 million unauthorized immigrants in the United States. The bill also would add 20,000 Border Patrol agents.

border protection: Fewer available jobs draw fewer undocumented workers.

Wayne Cornelius, director emeritus of the Center for Comparative Immigration Studies at the University of California, San Diego, says the security buildup may have had some effect on illegal migration levels, primarily by

## Border Patrol Concentrated in Southwest

Far more U.S. Border Patrol agents guard the Mexican border than monitor coastal ports or the Canadian border. The number of agents patrolling the Southwestern border rose fivefold between 1993 and 2012, to 18,546. The Canadian border has only about one-eighth the Border Patrol force as the Mexican border but saw a more than sevenfold rise in the number of agents — from 310 to 2,206.

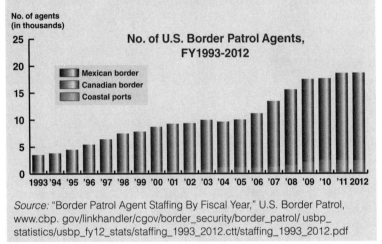

**No. of agents (in thousands)**

**No. of U.S. Border Patrol Agents, FY1993-2012**

- Mexican border
- Canadian border
- Coastal ports

*Source:* "Border Patrol Agent Staffing By Fiscal Year," U.S. Border Patrol, www.cbp. gov/linkhandler/cgov/border_security/border_patrol/ usbp_ statistics/usbp_fy12_stats/staffing_1993_2012.ctt/staffing_1993_2012.pdf

driving up smugglers' fees. But the center's interviews with unauthorized border crossers indicate that 85 percent still eventually make it into the country. "It has yet to be proven that it's an effective way of keeping people out of the country," Cornelius says.

Others doubt the reported falloff in attempted border crossings. Janice Kephart, research fellow at the Center for Immigration Studies, a Washington think tank that favors low immigration, says her analysis and observations by citizens' groups along the Southern border indicate the opposite, especially since President Obama issued a policy directive last year allowing young immigrants who had arrived illegally — many brought by their parents — and who were of "good moral character" and doing well in school to avoid deportation.

"At least over the central Arizona border, there has been a tremendous surge in the amount of illegal border crossing activity from August to December of last year," Kephart, a former counsel to the 9/11 Commission that investigated the 2001 terrorist attacks, said in Senate testimony last April.[18]

Some experts, in fact, believe that the "militarization" of the border, as they refer to it, has made the border less

secure. "The Mexican drug war and the U.S. border security crackdown have given rise to a new wave of criminality at the border in the form of highly armed bandits who seize drug loads and rob immigrants and their guides," wrote policy analyst Tom Barry in his book *Border Wars*. "In other words, thanks in part to U.S. government attempts to secure the border . . . the border has grown more violent."[19]

But federal statistics indicate that U.S. communities along the Southern border have some of the lowest crime rates in the nation. And Lawson says her 19 years of experience in the Border Patrol, including in Nogales, which was once besieged by unauthorized migrants, leave her no doubt that the agency is making a positive difference.

"We've come a long way," she says. "You talk to anybody in this Nogales area, and there aren't aliens running through their back yards anymore."

### Is it possible to "seal" the U.S. borders?

Calls to secure or even "seal" the nation's borders have become a rallying cry among some conservative politicians and members of the public who feel the nation is being overwhelmed by undocumented immigrants.

Defining what a secure border would look like remains a subject of debate, however. "It's a very subjective, highly politicized question," says Mike Slaven, a policy analyst for the Morrison Institute Latino Public Policy Center at Arizona State University, Tempe, and the author of a new report, "Defining Border Security in Immigration Reform."[20]

"Most experts agree that preventing 100 percent of unlawful entries across U.S. borders is an impossible task," Rosenblum, the Congressional Research Service policy analyst, concluded.[21]

Other analysts also say it's an unrealistic expectation. "Sure, if you want to stop all trade and set up minefields, make it like the DMZ between North and South Korea, yeah, you could stop it. But I don't think that's what most Americans want," says Rey Koslowski, a political science professor who directs the Program on Border Control and Homeland Security at the University at Albany, part of the State University of New York system. "That kind of absolutism — that if we don't stop everybody, it's not good enough — isn't really useful."

The more realistic question, say border experts, is whether security at the legal land border crossing points and airports and seaports can be built up to the point that almost all migrants wishing to cross illegally are either caught or deterred from trying. Some analysts believe that is possible. "Given the right resources, it's realistic to think about stopping the vast majority of people attempting to cross," says Koslowski.

However, experts estimate that around 40 percent of the undocumented workers already in the United States entered the country legally through ports of entry and then overstayed their visas.[22] Thus, Koslowski says, halting illegal immigration would also require a system that not only tracks the entry of visitors into the United States but also accurately records the exit of every visitor. Currently, the United States does not have such a system at all its ports of entry.[23]

But Koslowski says the experience of Australia, where such as system exists, indicates it can be a powerful tool to identify those overstaying their visas.

Another crucial part of the effort, he adds, would be to impose stiff penalties for businesses that hire undocumented workers. "There are a lot of businesses whose business model is to employ undocumented workers," he says. "And until that changes there's going to be people coming through."

But Tony Payan, a political science professor at the University of Texas, El Paso, who has done extensive cross-border research, says the sheer volume of legal traffic along the border and the economic significance of that traffic for both countries means it is unrealistic to try to halt all illegal traffic.

"Every year you have 400 million trips across the [Southern] border at the ports of entry. Say, at the peak, there were about 1 million people who crossed without legal papers or overstayed," Payan says. "In the end, illegality on the border is a very small part of border crossing. . . . People who say [you can stop it] have never lived on the border."

However, Everly, of the Association of Former Border Patrol Officers, believes the primary problem has been the refusal of the government to give those policing the border the resources, authority and backing they need to succeed. Government policies that make it easy for those who arrived illegally to escape prosecution or remain in the United States, he says, encourage illegal migration, making it difficult to stem the flow of undocumented border crossers.

"It's never going to be possible to stop all of it, but having an effective process where we can go down there and enforce the laws, using the right technology with the right intel, I think it can be really reduced," Everly says. With those changes, he says, illegal crossings could be diminished so much that most Americans would feel the border was secure.

But Brown University's Andreas argues that porous borders are a part of American and world history. "Sealing the border is a complete utopian fantasy because sealing the border wasn't actually achieved with the Iron Curtain or the Berlin Wall," he says. "Even there, even then, there was leakage. I can guarantee you there will always be a leaky border. The question is how many leaks? Where is it flowing? . . . You can imagine a lot more tunnels; you can imagine a lot more people coming through the ports of entry. It's going to be leaky; it's just a question of where."

### Is the United States paying enough attention to security at its ports of entry, Canadian border, and coasts?

With the debate about border security focused primarily on America's boundary with Mexico, the Southern border has received most of the resources and personnel committed to building up security along the nation's perimeter.

As of January 2013, a total of 18,462 Border Patrol agents were posted at the Southwestern border compared with only 2,212 on the Northern border with Canada, according to the Congressional Research Service.[24] Most federal spending on border security also has gone to the Southwestern border.

Some experts believe the focus on the vast open spaces in the Southwest has led the country to neglect other parts of its border infrastructure. "Much more attention needs to be placed on what is happening at the ports of entry," says the North American Research Partnership's Lee.

Failure to upgrade and expand the infrastructure at ports of entry — which include authorized land crossing points, seaports and airports — not only increases the security risk, it exacts an economic toll by slowing down legal crossings between nations that are economically interdependent, notes Lee.

The resources the United States has dedicated to its ports of entry have expanded, but not as dramatically as for the rest of the border, according to the Migration Policy Institute, a Washington think tank that studies the movement of people worldwide. "Border Patrol resources have doubled since 2005, while port-of-entry increases have grown about 45 percent," the institute concluded.[25]

But former Homeland Security official Stodder thinks security gains at the ports of entry have been among the most significant, particularly when it comes to thwarting potential terrorist incursions. He cited deployment of radiation detectors and other equipment to improve cargo inspections, better training of personnel and greater collaboration between the Border Patrol and other law enforcement agencies. "A big part of the buildup is actually at the ports of entry," says Stodder.

In addition to concerns about the ports of entry, some political leaders and security analysts say the United States needs to devote more resources to protecting the Canadian border and coastlines.

Rosenzweig, the former Homeland Security assistant secretary, says the Coast Guard is in "desperate need" of more money for modernizing and upgrading its fleet. "One of the key reasons to recapitalize the Coast Guard is precisely because we have three borders — a Northern, a Southern and a maritime border," he says. "A speedboat can get to the U.S. from the Bahamas in 60 to 90 minutes. I tell you truthfully, if I had a nuclear device I wanted to sneak into the United States, I wouldn't try to drive it into the U.S. because we've got the land borders pretty locked up. I would bring it on a boat."

But in testimony before a House subcommittee, Coast Guard Rear Adm. William Lee said the Coast Guard is working closely with other U.S. security entities and nations to position its ships to protect the United States. "The Coast Guard's mix of cutters, aircraft and boats — all operated by highly proficient personnel — allows the Coast Guard to exercise layered and effective security through the entire maritime domain," he said.[26]

The Obama administration has made $93 million available this year through the Port Security Grant Program to help the nation's ocean ports improve their security.[27] However, in its 2014 budget request the administration called for $909 million more to modernize the Coast Guard fleet.[28]

Everly, of the Association of Former Border Patrol Officers, believes the United States could use more personnel for both the Northern and maritime borders. "The Canadian border, there are not a lot of folks assigned up there," he says. "We have them at the ports of entry, but there's so many places you can cross up there, and with the geography, it's so hard to get at some of the spots. It's the same with the coastline. We've got marine and air units, but it's not uncommon for a boatload of people to go from Tijuana beyond detection and then come inshore down the California coast."

The number of Border Patrol agents on the Northern border increased by nearly 550 percent, from 340 in 2001 to more than 2,200 in 2013, or roughly one agent for every two miles of border.[29] But that's still far fewer than the nearly 10 agents per mile along the U.S.-Mexican border.

Stodder, however, says that disparity simply reflects the difference between the two borders. "There's a reason why we haven't put tons and tons of border patrol agents on the Northern border," he says, "Number one is that they would be really, really bored."

The issue along the Northern border, Stodder says, isn't mass illegal migration but the possibility that terrorists would come through Canada to the United States. Stodder argues that good intelligence and police work are more effective in countering that threat. "The Royal Canadian Mounted Police plus the Canadian intelligence service are really quite good," he says.

Other analysts note the high level of cooperation between Canadian and U.S. border agents, intelligence agencies and immigration officials. "There are a lot of good things that have been happening along the Northern border in terms of cooperation, with [joint patrolling] teams and a few other things," including more sharing of information about travelers and potential threats, says the University at Albany's Koslowski. "I think it's addressed the most glaring kinds of holes."

# CHRONOLOGY

1980s *U.S. grants amnesty to some undocumented immigrants; Border Patrol, a small agency since its creation in 1924, begins to expand.*

**1980** U.S. Border Patrol has 2,268 agents, 1,975 of them assigned to the Southern border.

**1986** Nearly 1.7 million illegal aliens are apprehended nationwide, the highest one-year total on record. . . . Immigration Reform and Control Act of 1986 grants amnesty under certain conditions to illegal immigrants who have been in the United States since 1982.

**1987** The first of six helium-filled balloons with radar capability is deployed along the Southwestern border to track illegal crossers.

1990s *United States turns to fences and other barriers along the U.S.-Mexico border, while continuing to expand the number of Border Patrol agents.*

**1990** Border Patrol begins erecting 14-mile fence to deter illegal entries and drug smuggling in the San Diego sector.

**1994** After the fence proves ineffective, the Border Patrol launches Operation Gatekeeper, which greatly increases the number of border agents.

**1995** The number of Border Patrol agents reaches 5,000.

**1996** Illegal Immigration Reform and Immigrant Responsibility Act gives the U.S. attorney general broad authority to construct border barriers.

2000s *Terrorist attacks heighten U.S. concerns about openness of its borders.*

**September 11, 2001** Terrorist attacks on the World Trade Center, Pentagon and United Airlines Flight 93 kill nearly 3,000 people. All 19 airline hijackers entered the U.S. legally.

**October 2001** USA Patriot Act gives more law enforcement authority to Immigration and Naturalization Service and provides $50 million for expanded security on the U.S.-Canadian border.

**2002** The number of Border Patrol agents tops 10,000.

**2003** New Department of Homeland Security takes over functions of Immigration and Naturalization Service.

**2004** Intelligence Reform and Terrorism Prevention Act of 2004 requires U.S., Mexican and Canadian citizens to have a passport or other accepted document to enter United States.

**2005** REAL ID Act authorizes Homeland Security secretary to expedite the construction of border barriers.

**2006** Secure Fence Act of 2006 directs Homeland Security to construct 850 miles of additional fencing along border.

**2007** Consolidated Appropriations Act gives Homeland Security secretary greater freedom to build the border fence and changes the requirement to not less than 700 miles of fencing along the Southern border.

**2007** Illegal immigration begins to plummet as worst economic downturn since the Great Depression hits United States.

**2010** Gov. Jan Brewer, R-Ariz., signs hardline immigration enforcement law (SB1070) designed to catch illegal border crossers (April). Other states adopt similar measures.

**2011** Apprehension of illegal aliens nationwide falls to below 350,000, the lowest one-year total since 1971.

**2012** U.S. Supreme Court rules parts of Arizona SB1070 illegal, but says police can investigate the immigration status of a person they have stopped if they have reasonable cause for suspicion. . . . Pew Hispanic Center estimates the United States may be seeing a net outflow of undocumented migrants because they can't find jobs.

**2013** Border Patrol has 21,370 agents, with 18,462 posted at the Southwest border and 2,212 on the Northern border. The number of agents has more than doubled since 2001. . . . Senate passes immigration reform bill in June that calls for hiring 20,000 more border agents, completing 700 miles of border fence and spending $40 billion over 10 years on border security. Many Republicans denounce the bill as inadequate.

# BACKGROUND

## Two-Way Street

For most of U.S. history, the nation's land borders have been relatively unguarded, reflecting the country's sense of security about its relationships with its neighbors to the north and south and its tradition of being an open society where people are largely free to come and go as they please.

Although mounted patrols were conducted sporadically along the borders earlier, the U.S. Border Patrol wasn't created until 1924. It began with 450 officers responsible for patrolling 6,000 miles of U.S. borders.[30] The patrol was created in conjunction with the Immigration Act of 1924, which stiffened requirements for entering the United States and established quotas for immigration from different countries.

More than half a century later, in 1980, the number of agents had increased to 2,268, or about one agent for every three miles of border.[31] Informal crossings remained common on both borders, but security was almost nonexistent along the 4,000-mile boundary with Canada, which was often referred to as the "world's longest undefended border."[32]

Illegal trade also has moved across the Canadian border over time. During Prohibition it was the favorite route of illegal alcohol shipments into the United States.[33] In more recent years, Canadians have worried about illegal gun trafficking into Canada from the United States, says Emily Gilbert, director of the Canadian Studies Program at the University of Toronto.

Historically, the U.S.-Mexican border was even more lawless and wide open. The remoteness of much of the region made it a popular place for people — or smugglers — to slip from one country to the other undetected. "The popular notion that the U.S.-Mexico border is out of control falsely assumes that there was once a time when it was truly under control," Brown University's Andreas writes in *Border Games: Policing the U.S.-Mexico Divide*.[34]

Today's illegal border activities are "part of an old and diverse border smuggling economy that thrived long before drugs and migrants were being smuggled," Andreas notes.[35] In the 19th century, he writes, much of the smuggling was from the United States into Mexico, to avoid Mexico's high tariffs.

Illegal immigration, too, initially followed a north-to-south route, as Americans moved without authorization into Mexico's northern regions in the early 1800s. "The so-called Mexican Decree of 3 April 1830 had prohibited immigration from the United States, and Mexico deployed garrisons to try to enforce the law," Andreas writes.[36]

## Changing Attitudes

The flow of illegal border traffic began to shift the other way in the early 20th century, as migrant workers traveled north to U.S. agricultural fields. Attitudes toward the workers swung back and forth, with Americans welcoming them when labor was short and rounding them up and shipping them home when they weren't needed.

Facing a labor shortage during World War I, the United States temporarily admitted 77,000 "guest" workers from Mexico. But when the Great Depression led to a steep rise in joblessness, thousands of Mexican immigrants were deported. With the U.S. entry into World War II in December 1941, the country again found itself short of workers and created the Bracero Program — bracero being Spanish for laborers — which eventually brought more than 400,000 Mexicans into the United States for jobs.[37]

The program was controversial, with many unions, religious groups and other critics citing cases of abuses of workers by employers. The initial effort ended in 1947, but it continued under various laws for agricultural workers until 1964.[38]

By the 1950s, illegal immigration was accelerating as more Mexicans sought to take advantage of America's postwar boom. In 1954, the U.S. Immigration and Naturalization Service (INS) initiated "Operation Wetback," choosing a name that had become a derogatory way to refer to migrants, who often swam or wadded across the Rio Grande River to reach the United States. Immigration officers swept through Mexican *barrios* (neighborhoods) in U.S. cities looking for immigrants living in the United States illegally. At least 1 million people were deported in 1954 alone.[39]

Although American attitudes toward Mexican labor have shifted back and forth, depending on whether U.S. companies needed workers, the Southern border remained relatively unguarded. Even in the late 1990s, in many remote parts of Arizona, New Mexico and Texas the border was protected by only a waist-high wire fence, with occasional stone markers denoting the international line.[40]

In cross-border communities such as Nogales, which straddles Arizona and Mexico, and El Paso (Texas) and Cuidad Juarez (Mexico), many families had members on both sides of the line and crossed back and forth casually. "People don't understand how a border community works. In my case, I live in Mexico. I cross every day to the United States to go to work, and then I go back again," says Astrid Dominguez, advocacy coordinator for the American Civil Liberties Union of Texas. "It's not just them and us — you have friends and relatives on both sides."

Dominguez lives in Matamoros, Mexico, and works across the border in Brownsville, Texas. She says she has heard stories from her parents and grandparents about how much easier it used to be to cross and how much casual interaction existed between the two communities. Now, she says, "Every time I go across the border I get questioned by Border Patrol agents."

The American Civil Liberties Union and other groups have criticized U.S. border and customs enforcement personnel for using excessive force, both with migrants in custody and in the field. Since 2010, at least eight people have been killed by the Border Patrol while throwing rocks at agents, including six who were on the Mexican side of the border.[41]

In one of the most publicized cases, agents shot and killed José Antonio Elena Rodriguez, a 16-year-old Mexican, in October 2012, just across the border from Nogales, Ariz. Agents said a group of men were throwing rocks at them while others tried to bring drugs across the border. But a witness in Mexico said Rodriguez was simply walking down the street and not involved in the confrontation. An autopsy found he had been shot multiple times, with five of the shots hitting his back at an angle that indicated he was already lying on the ground.[42] While not responding directly to this case, Border Patrol officials have noted that agents frequently come under dangerous assault from people throwing rocks from Mexico.[43]

On the Canadian border, too, in sister cities such as Detroit and Windsor, Ontario, social and economic exchanges between Canada and the United States were casual. Before the 9/11 terrorist attacks led to changes, half the crossings between Canada and the United States were unguarded at night, with traffic cones simply set out to close the roads.[44] "The level of openness that existed was unbelievable, if you think about it," says the University at Albany's Koslowski, given how heavily guarded many international borders are around the world.

But security has tightened. In an article earlier this year in *Mother Jones*, Americans of Arab descent reported being subjected to lengthy interrogations and even handcuffed by the U.S. Border Patrol when crossing into the United States from Canada.[45] "Previously, there was this sense of community there," says the University of Toronto's Gilbert, speaking of the cross-border culture. "Even though there was a border, there was a sense of generosity across it. Now, it's one of belligerence."

### Security Buildup

Through most of the 1960s, the Border Patrol apprehended fewer than 50,000 undocumented immigrants a year. The total began to climb in the late 1960s as more Mexicans turned to the prospering U.S. economy for work. The pace quickened further in the 1970s, and by 1983 apprehensions topped 1.1 million for the first time since 1954, during Operation Wetback.[46]

Still a relatively small agency with fewer than 3,000 agents, the Border Patrol by the early 1980s found itself overwhelmed at the most popular crossings, mostly in border cities.[47] In March 1986 alone, more migrants were caught crossing illegally in San Diego than had been caught there in three years in the mid-1960s. Alan E. Eliason, the chief Border Patrol agent in the area at the time, said that on a Sunday night, agents could see as many as 4,000 people gathering on the Mexican side, preparing to rush across the border.[48]

By then, public impatience with the immigrant surge was growing.[49] At the same time, protecting the border was given new urgency by the Reagan administration. It supported anti-Communist insurgencies in Central America, most notably an effort by so-called Contra rebels to overthrow the ruling Sandinista government in Nicaragua. Tying border security to national security, President Ronald Reagan said in 1986 that failure to overthrow the Sandinistas would leave "terrorists and subversives just two days' driving time from Harlingen, Texas."[50]

# Robots May Soon Help Guard the Border

*"We can get more reliability and cut down on the manpower needed."*

The U.S. border agent has brushed-back hair, sculpted cheekbones and a somewhat distant gaze. Politely but persistently he questions you. "Have you ever used any other names? Do you live at the address you listed on your application? Have you visited any foreign countries in the last five years?"

It's a fairly routine interview aimed at checking whether you qualify for a preferred-traveler program that will allow you easier entry into the United States. Routine, that is, except for one thing. The agent isn't really an agent at all but a human face on a kiosk screen, and this virtual agent is watching you more closely than any human ever could to determine the truthfulness of your responses.

The Automated Virtual Agent for Truth Assessment in Real Time, or AVATAR, is one of several projects at the National Center for Border Security and Immigration at the University of Arizona, Tucson. The center is part of BORDERS, a consortium of 18 research institutions, primarily universities, working on innovative technologies and procedures to protect the nation's borders.[1] Taken together, the projects are a snapshot of the next wave of border security.

For example, AVATAR's cameras, microphone and sensors quietly measure a variety of stress indicators as a person speaks to it: how your body is shifting, how much and where your eyes move, the changing timbre of your voice.

The data are run through computer algorithms that combine the different responses to develop a risk assessment for every person interviewed.

In limited field tests last year, AVATAR has been accurate between 70 percent and 100 percent of the time, better than human screeners, who are generally about as reliable as flipping a coin, says Nathan Twyman, the project's lead researcher.

Twyman stresses that human agents will always be needed to follow up on cases identified as high risk. But an average of 1.1 million people are processed at the nation's borders daily.[2] By automating the first level of screening, Twyman says, "We can get a lot more reliability . . . and cut down on the manpower needed at the border."

BORDERS also is working on a project at the University of Washington, Seattle, designed to locate people hiding behind boulders or other objects by triangulating radio waves and other signals. Another project is aimed at determining what combination of fingerprints, retina scans and other biometric data provides the fastest and most accurate way to identify an individual.

BORDERS also has looked at the role of dogs used at many border ports of entry to sniff for illegal drugs and people hidden in trucks or other vehicles. "We had a project that was a favorite of mine — developing an [electronic] sniffer that could do what a dog does," says Jay Nunamaker Jr.,

Congress addressed the border security issue with the 1986 Immigration Reform and Control Act. For the first time, the law made it illegal to recruit or hire undocumented workers, while also allowing approximately 3 million unauthorized immigrants who had arrived before 1982 and who met certain other conditions to remain legally in the United States.[51] Lawmakers hoped the combination would sharply reduce illegal border crossings.[52]

The number of apprehensions along the border did fall — by more than 700,000 from 1986 to 1988 — but then resumed an uneven climb. The Border Patrol responded with a series of targeted efforts, such as Operation

Hold the Line in El Paso, Texas, and Operation Gatekeeper in San Diego, to shut down illegal crossings in the worst areas.[53]

But the flow of migrants tended to shift quickly from one spot to another. In California, for example, the Border Patrol built a fence that ran from the Pacific Ocean to the port of entry in San Ysidro, Calif., a land-border crossing between Tijuana, Mexico, and San Diego. The Border Patrol also greatly increased the number of agents behind the fence. But illegal migration shifted to San Ysidro itself, with illegal crossers making "bonzai runs," racing through traffic at the border in an effort to escape into the community.

director and principal researcher at the center. "But we had an awful time getting the drugs to test the sniffer with." The project was finally shelved, he says.

In addition, Twyman says the center has experimented with even more advanced ways to measure human reaction, including a laser that measures the carotid artery for an increased heart rate. Researchers found, however, that beards interfere with the process.

In the future, thermal cameras could detect the opening of the pores on a person's face, providing information similar to how a lie detector measures sweat to detect stress, Twyman says. The idea, he says, is "a polygraph that works without having to hook people up."

Another part of BORDERS research involves developing the best procedures and training for agents operating at the border. For example, researchers have examined the process by which agents record where they find migrants crossing illegally and have noted a high degree of error, probably caused by manual entry at the end of work shifts. Creating a digital data-entry system, which BORDERS is working on, and training agents to use it properly could result in a more accurate picture of crossing patterns, which should help agents operate more effectively.

While it's not as eye-catching as the technology under development, researcher Jeff Proudfoot says it's as important. "Just buying gadgets isn't going to make any difference," he says. "They have to be used properly."

— *Reed Karaim*

AVATAR, an innovative screening device developed by the National Center for Border Security and Immigration, allows for speedier border-security checks.

[1] A list of the participating institutions, along with more information about research projects, is at www.borders.arizona.edu.

[2] Rey Koslowski, "The Evolution of Border Controls as a Mechanism to Prevent Illegal Immigration," Migration Policy Institute, February 2011, p. 1 www.migrationpolicy.org/pubs/bordercontrols-koslowski.pdf.

Through the 1990s, both the Clinton and George W. Bush administrations responded to public concern about unauthorized immigration by further increasing border personnel, equipment and barriers. The 1996 Illegal Immigration Reform and Immigration Responsibility Act included provisions for more border security but also increased interior enforcement of immigration laws and barred deportees from returning for from three to 10 years, depending on the length of their illegal stay.[54]

The security buildup and other measures had an impact on the routes chosen by border crossers. As it became more difficult to cross in urban areas, illegal immigration moved into remote areas, such as the Arizona desert, where it formerly had been less of a problem.

Migrant deaths in the desert and other remote areas rose steeply. But apprehensions indicated that as many, or more, people were still trying to cross. In 2000, the Border Patrol apprehended 1.68 million illegal crossers — close to the 1.69 million apprehended during the previous peak in 1986.[55]

Experts generally agree that the Sept. 11, 2001, terrorist attacks placed border security in a different light. Even though all the 9/11 terrorists had entered the United States legally, the nation's land borders were seen as potential routes for further terrorist incursions. Border security "used

# Senate Considers Mandatory E-Verify System

*Backers see workplace as a key to border security; critics say the system hurts businesses.*

The United States has deployed thousands of Border Patrol agents along its border with Mexico and spent billions of dollars in an effort to halt illegal immigration. But some policy analysts believe the focus on the border has led government to neglect one of the most effective places to curb illegal immigration: the American workplace.

Surveys of immigrants who arrived illegally by the Center for Comparative Immigration Studies at the University of California, San Diego, and others have found that most undocumented border crossers come to the United States for work. Yet, while it has been illegal to hire an unauthorized immigrant since passage of the Immigration and Control Act in 1986, many businesses have ignored the law.

The act, which requires employers to attest to their employees' residency status and fines employers who hire undocumented workers, "has never been enforced to the letter of the law," says Mike Slaven, a policy analyst with the Morrison Institute Latino Public Policy Center at Arizona State University, Tempe.

In 1996, Congress attempted to make it easier for businesses to abide by the law by creating E-Verify, a Web-based system that allows employers voluntarily to check the immigration status of newly hired employees. The program has grown steadily and was being used by 424,000 employers nationwide at the start of 2013.[1] But a comprehensive immigration reform act, which passed the Senate in June and is awaiting action in the House, would make E-Verify mandatory for almost all businesses within five years.[2]

Some analysts see it as a key to ending unauthorized border crossings. "Effective employer verification must be the linchpin of comprehensive immigration reform legislation if new policies are to succeed in preventing future illegal immigration," concluded immigration policy experts Marc R. Rosenblum and Doris Meissner, a former commissioner of the Immigration and Naturalization Service, in an early study of the E-Verify system.[3]

But other analysts are skeptical E-Verify alone can solve the problem of illegal immigration. E-Verify "could be very effective when it comes to formal employment, but I think it partially loses sight of the big problem, which is that there are labor demands by U.S. businesses that have to be met by immigrants," says Slaven. Effective immigration reform must include a way for those workers to enter the United States legally, he contends.

to be a labor-enforcement issue," says Payan, the University of Texas professor. "Now it becomes a national security issue," a view that echoed the earlier Reagan administration attempt to tie the border to international threats. In the years since 9/11, Payan adds, "It's been transformed and swallowed by the national security agenda."

The post-9/11 change was dramatic. Besides the growth of the Border Patrol, which doubled from 2002 to 2012, the United States assigned thousands of National Guard troops to the U.S.-Mexico border, along with officers from a variety of other agencies.[56]

U.S. Customs and Border Protection became part of the newly created Department of Homeland Security, which was given broad authority to secure the border.

In 2006, the Secure Fencing Act required construction of about 800 miles of fencing along the Southern border. Subsequent legislation modified the length required, but by 2012 the United States had some 650 miles of fencing along the border with Mexico.

Some projects were failures. An initial effort to create a "virtual fence" along the border using a coordinated system of sensors, radar, cameras and other technology was plagued with enough problems when installed in a 53-mile section along the border in Arizona that the government did not deploy it more widely.[57]

But the government has proceeded with a wide range of roads, surveillance towers, lights and other security measures, according to the Congressional Research Service, including, as of December 2012:

- 35 permanent interior checkpoints and 173 tactical checkpoints;
- 12 forward-operating bases in remote areas to house personnel in close proximity to illegal-crossing routes;

Rey Koslowski, a political science professor at the University at Albany (SUNY), New York, points out that many unauthorized migrants work in the cash-based shadow economy. "As long as there's a way for someone to come to the United States and go to work cutting people's lawns for 10 bucks an hour cash, I'm sorry, but young guys will try to do it," he says, "and they'll take the risk to do it."

Some conservative commentators have argued that E-Verify will expand into a national identification system that could be used more broadly by government.[4] In addition, some business groups believe it will unfairly hamper their ability to hire qualified workers.

Todd McCracken, president and CEO of the National Small Business Association, writing in *The Washington Post*, said results from E-Verify, so far, indicate that as many as 420,000 legal job hunters a year could receive an initial non-approval from the database, requiring them to file an appeal if they wish to keep working. "Those authorized, perfectly legal workers will then be forced — along with their employers — to navigate a bureaucratic morass," McCracken wrote. "It currently takes several months, on average, to resolve database mistakes, leaving both the employer and employee in legal and business limbo."[5]

But Rep. Lamar Smith, R-Texas, author of House legislation to expand E-Verify, said it has proved to be quick and effective while confirming 99.7 percent of employees checked by the system. Nationwide use of E-Verify, he said, will reduce illegal immigration "by shutting off the jobs magnet that draws millions of illegal workers to the U.S."[6]

— *Reed Karaim*

[1] "E-Verify Celebrates 2012!" *The Beacon*, the Official Blog of USCIS, March 28, 2013, http://blog.uscis.gov/2013/03/e-verify-celebrates-2012.html.

[2] "A Guide to S.744: Understanding the 2013 Senate Immigration Bill," Immigration Policy Center, July 20, 2013, www.immigrationpolicy.org/special-reports/guide-s744-understanding-2013-senate-immigration-bill.

[3] Doris Meissner and Marc R. Rosenblum, "The Next Generation of E-Verify: Getting Employment Verification Right," Migration Policy Institute, July 2009, p. i, www.migrationpolicy.org/pubs/verification_paper-071709.pdf.

[4] Jim Harper, "E-Verify Wrong for America," CATO Institute, May 23, 2013, www.cato.org/publications/commentary/e-verify-wrong-america.

[5] Todd McCracken, "Verification for job applicants is needed, but mandating E-Verify is not the answer," *The Washington Post*, May 13, 2012, www.washingtonpost.com/blogs/on-small-business/post/verification-for-job-applicants-is-needed-but-mandating-e-verify-is-not-the-answer/2012/05/11/gIQAD3KwMU_blog.html.

[6] "Smith Bill to Expand E-Verify Approved by Committee," press release, office of Rep. Lamar Smith, June 26, 2013, http://lamarsmith.house.gov/media-center/press-releases/smith-bill-to-expand-e-verify-approved-by-committee.

- 337 remote video surveillance systems (up from 269 in 2006);
- 198 short and medium range mobile vehicle surveillance systems; 41 long-range mobile surveillance systems (up from zero in 2005);
- 15 portable medium range surveillance systems (up from zero in 2005);
- 15 fixed towers with surveillance gear;
- 13,406 unattended ground sensors (up from about 11,200 in 2005); and
- 10 unmanned aerial vehicle systems (drones), up from zero in 2006.[58]

Since 9/11 the government "has built a formidable immigration enforcement machinery," said a Migration Policy Institute report.[59]

## CURRENT SITUATION

### Deep Divisions

Congress faces sharp divisions over immigration reform and border security.

A Senate immigration reform bill that passed with bipartisan support on June 27 offers a path to citizenship for some unauthorized immigrants. The bill also would bolster border security even further, most notably by adding 20,000 Border Patrol agents. It also would require completing 700 miles of new fence along the U.S.-Mexico line and deploying $3.2 billion in additional security technology.[60]

The Department of Homeland Security would have to certify that these provisions were in place before laws providing a path to citizenship for undocumented immigrants went into effect.

Pedestrians wait to enter the United States at the San Ysidro, Calif., immigration station, across the border from Tijuana, Mexico. Although blocking terrorists from entering the country is now considered the Border Patrol's top priority, agents continue to focus on drug smuggling, customs work and illegal immigration.

The border security measures were stiffened in a late amendment by Sens. Bob Corker, R-Tenn., and John Hoeven, R-N.D., in an effort to garner more Republican support and allay concerns about the measure among immigration hardliners.[61]

Nevertheless, House Republicans remain opposed to the legislation, particularly in the Tea Party caucus. The primary objection centers on allowing unauthorized immigrants a path to citizenship, which opponents have denounced as "amnesty." But several Republicans also have called for placing border security front and center, ahead of immigration concerns. "The first step right now is to secure the border," said Rep. Pete Olson, R-Texas.[62]

Yet, several experts question the bill's increased border security provisions. "All of this becomes less a matter of a thorough planning process and much more driven by symbolic politics," says the University at Albany's Koslowski.

The proposal to add 20,000 more Border Patrol agents draws particular skepticism. A comprehensive study examining conditions along the border concluded that current staff levels are already "at or past a point of diminishing returns."[63] "We absolutely stand by that analysis," says the North American Research Partnership's Lee, the study's principal author. He cites the El Paso sector as an example. "If you do the math there, we're talking about not quite three apprehensions per agent per year," he says. "El Paso is a clear case of overstaffing."

Whether either comprehensive immigration reform legislation or a narrower bill targeting border security will make it out of the House remained an open question as lawmakers returned in September. President Obama had originally called on Congress to pass immigration reform by the end of the summer.[64] But many observers believe it's unlikely the House will deal with comprehensive legislation this fall, and the final timetable for any vote on a bill remains unclear.[65]

## State Efforts

Policing the borders is generally recognized as a federal responsibility, but in recent years frustration with what some state leaders considered the U.S. government's failure to halt illegal crossings has led to aggressive action in some border states, particularly Texas and Arizona.

The most highly publicized legislative effort was a 2010 Arizona law, SB1070, allowing police to ask anyone they stopped to produce proof they were in the United States legally if the police suspected otherwise. The law also contained provisions designed to deter unauthorized migrants from entering Arizona.

Defending the law, Arizona Republican Gov. Jan Brewer painted a picture of a violent border. "Our law enforcement agencies have found bodies in the desert, either buried or just lying out there, that have been beheaded," Brewer told a local television station.[66] Brewer recanted her claim after local law enforcement officials said they had no cases of beheadings in the desert.[67] The U.S. Supreme Court eventually declared much of SB1070 unconstitutional, but not before five states had passed similar laws.[68]

Arizona recently has concentrated on cooperative efforts with authorities in the Mexican state of Sonora, directly to the south, to increase border security, according to the governor's office.

Texas has taken a more aggressive approach. "The Texas legislature, with the support of state leaders, has dedicated substantial funding over the last several years, and the DPS [Department of Public Safety] has dedicated a significant amount of resources, technology, equipment and personnel for border security," Texas Department of Public Safety Director Steven McCraw stated in an email interview. Staff for a state legislative board estimated total spending on border security at $452 million from 2008-2013.[69]

Texas has sent Ranger Reconnaissance Teams to gather intelligence, conduct interdictions and disrupt drug cartel criminal activity in remote border areas where conventional law enforcement cannot operate, according to the DPS.

# Should the United States tighten its border security?

## YES
**Janice Kephart**
*Special Counsel, Senate Judiciary Committee, during consideration of Immigration Reform in 2013; Former Border Counsel, 9/11 Commission*

Written for *CQ Researcher*, September 2013

Do we need more border security? Yes. Specifically, we need more efficient and cost-effective measures that identify those who seek to do us harm and keep them out or apprehend them. This can be achieved by defining a secure border, creating a secure border system and adopting measures to determine success.

A "secure border" should be capable of blocking those who pose a threat or attempt illegal entry via visas, ports-of-entry or immigration-benefit processing. That's in addition to the interdiction work of our 20,000 Border Patrol agents. It is essential to verify visitors' identities and ensure they abide by the terms of their entry. Creating secure borders requires Congress to support a balance of resources, law and policy so that we can:

- Maintain and expand visa investigations to prevent those with nefarious intentions from entering.
- Install, where feasible, fencing across the Southern border that can't be stepped over, cut, tunneled under or ramped over.
- Use technology to achieve 100 percent detection and safer, more efficient operations without increasing Border Patrol staff.
- Deploy cost-effective, feasible biometrics at airports and seaports of entry to ensure that holders of expired visas depart on time.
- Empower states and localities to support federal immigration enforcement and enable local agents to retain certain powers that the Obama administration has severely curtailed by invoking "prosecutorial discretion."
- Discourage inadequate review of immigration-benefit applications and reward proper vetting.
- Expand E-Verify, the worker authorization program.

Congress must exercise its authority in measuring success. A Senate immigration bill allows the Department of Homeland Security to exercise discretion or grant waivers in more than 200 types of immigration cases, enabling the department — not Congress — to measure success.

Nearly all of the 550,000 individuals on the terrorist watch list are foreign-born, and up to 20,000 of them are U.S. residents. In addition, every major U.S. city is infiltrated by violent drug cartels. Illegal-entry numbers for the January-April period increased substantially between 2012 and 2013, after the administration recommended immunity from deportation for young illegal immigrants brought here as children. So yes, we need more border security. But mostly, we need better border security.

## NO
**Wayne A. Cornelius**
*Director, Mexican Migration Field Research and Training Program, Division of Global Public Health, University of California-San Diego; Co-Author, Budgeting for Immigration Enforcement*

Written for *CQ Researcher*, September 2013

Spending taxpayer dollars on more border security has reached the point of diminishing returns. With attempts at illegal entry down to 1971 levels, no appreciable additional deterrence can be wrung from more investments in Border Patrol agents, fencing, drones and high-tech surveillance systems.

The key statistic for measuring the effectiveness of border enforcement is migrants' "eventual success rate." In other words, on a given attempt to cross the border, what percentage of unauthorized migrants, even if apprehended initially, can get through if they keep trying? Each year since 2005, my research team has interviewed hundreds of undetected and returned migrants on both sides of the border. In every study we have found that nine out of 10 people apprehended on the first try were able to re-enter undetected on the second or third try — impressive testimony to the near impossibility of stopping migrants determined to feed their families or reunite with relatives in the United States.

The recent decline in attempted entries is driven by weak U.S. labor demand and recession-related declines in wages. Among migrants who returned from the United States since 2008, four of five of those interviewed this year said their U.S. wages had declined — on average, by $428 per week — during the period before they returned to Mexico. Diminished economic returns, coupled with greater physical risks of border crossings and drug-related violence in border areas, have strongly discouraged new migrations.

Spending up to another $46 billion on border enforcement, as the Senate-approved immigration reform bill would authorize, will only enable people-smugglers to charge more for their services, increase the death toll among migrants crossing in ever-more dangerous areas and induce more permanent settlement among those already here.

If Congress were serious about reducing future growth of the nation's undocumented population, it would direct more resources to screening people passing through our legal ports of entry — where a third of unauthorized entries occur — and at U.S. embassies and consulates, which issue tourist and other short-term visas. That would be far more cost-effective than spending more to fortify remote stretches of the Southwestern border.

We should declare victory at that border and move on to the hard work of ensuring that future flows of migrants will be predominantly legal and creating a meaningful path to legalization for undocumented immigrants already here.

Texas also has created a Tactical Marine Unit that uses special shallow-water interceptor boats to patrol the state's intracoastal waterways and the Rio Grande River.

In a collaboration called Operation Drawbridge, the DPS, U.S. Border Patrol and border-county sheriffs have installed motion detectors and surveillance cameras along the border. Since its launch in January 2012, the operation has resulted in the apprehension of more than 16,000 individuals and seizure of 35 tons of narcotics, according to DPS. Texas also has increased collaborative efforts with Mexican authorities in communities across the border.

McCraw says the state had to take action. "Due to the increasingly confrontational nature of ruthless and powerful Mexican cartels and transnational gangs and the lack of sufficient federal resources on the Texas border, the Texas-Mexico border remains unsecure," he says.

But some Texas border residents disagree with that characterization. "I live in McAllen," says border activist Nicol, "and McAllen is one of the quietest places I've ever lived in my life. I think the hysteria that comes out of the 'border wars' view of the borders is absolutely misplaced."

The vision of the border as a lawless zone also does not square with government crime statistics, at least for urban areas. "As measured by Federal Bureau of Investigation crime statistics, U.S. border cities rank among the safest in the United States," according to "The State of the Border Report" published earlier this year by the Wilson Center, a Washington think tank that fosters dialogue in the social sciences.[70]

El Paso, which sits across the border from Cuidad Juarez, the scene of much drug cartel violence, has been rated the safest large city in America for the last three years by CQ Press's *City Crime Rankings*.[71] Still, the report notes there is a split in perceptions between urban and rural areas, with many rural residents who live near the border in Texas, New Mexico and Arizona concerned about illegal crossings.

Earlier this year, Gary Thrasher, a veterinarian and rancher in southern Arizona, told NBC News he feels the border is now more dangerous because there are more armed smugglers. "The border statistically is securer than ever. That means nothing," Thrasher said. "That's like saying we fixed this whole bucket, except for this hole down here."[72]

## Cooperative Efforts

Little noticed amid the border security buildup and the immigration debate has been the level of increased cooperation between U.S. officials and those in Mexico and Canada in the post 9/11 era.

During a visit to Brownsville, Texas, last July, Homeland Security Secretary Napolitano announced an agreement with Mexico on a border communications network that would include increased sharing of intelligence on drug smuggling and other illegal activities.[73] She also announced the start of coordinated patrols by the Mexican Federal Police and the U.S. Border Patrol.

"The United States and Mexico have taken unprecedented steps in recent years to deepen our cooperation along our shared border," Napolitano said.[74]

Cooperation may be even closer with Canada. Besides sharing intelligence and traveler watch lists, the two nations already operate Integrated Border Enforcement Teams (IBET) on land and station officers on each other's vessels through the Shiprider Program, effectively strengthening the border security efforts of both nations.

In addition, since 9/11 Canada has tightened its visa and immigration system, which previously was more open than the U.S. system to refugees and foreign travelers, bringing it closer in line with U.S. requirements.

In December 2011, the United States and Canada announced the Beyond the Border Action Plan, which pursues "a perimeter approach to security" in which the nations share more intelligence and work in greater collaboration along the border.[75] "I think that's the most effective thing we've done since 9/11 — sharing more information," say Stodder, the former Homeland Security official, adding the effort has made the United States and its borders less vulnerable.

But the effort to harmonize Canada's immigration and border security policies with those of the United States has been controversial in some Canadian circles, according to the University of Toronto's Gilbert. She says Canadians have questioned the necessity for the changes and wondered whether the country is surrendering too much sovereignty as it tries to accommodate concerns. "I think the amount of money we're putting toward border security isn't really justified," she says.

## OUTLOOK:

### "Drone Recycling"

The United States has been building up security along its Southern border for more than 25 years. For analysts, the question is whether the trend will continue into the next quarter-century or is nearing its end.

"I don't anticipate a rollback or de-escalation. Very rarely do you have buildups of this kind that are dismantled," says Brown University's Andreas. "The real question is, at what point does it sort of plateau? How militarized does it become?"

He adds that the recent end of the war in Iraq and the winding down of the war in Afghanistan could lead to an expanded use of military technology on the border.[76] "All these drones are going to come home from Iraq and Afghanistan looking for work," he says. "Homeland Security would like to beef up its fleet of drones. To what extent does the border become a drone recycling center?"

Gilbert, the director of the Canadian studies program at the University of Toronto, believes a fundamental change has occurred along the U.S.-Canadian border. "The Canadian government keeps pushing this idea that the more we work with the U.S. the more we'll get back. Canadians keep saying we can return to that mythical moment where we have this open border between us," Gilbert says. "But I don't see the border between Canada and the U.S. ever going back to that moment."

Slaven, the Morrison Institute policy analyst, believes the future of security on the U.S.-Mexican border depends on the ability of the United States to adopt effective immigration reform that provides a legal avenue for immigrants to fill U.S. labor needs. "It's a matter of whether the political will is going to be there to do it," he says.

But in the longer term, the University of Texas' Payan says, demographic shifts in Mexico and Latin America could change the situation drastically. He notes that the Mexican population is aging, and since most unauthorized migrants are young men, that should reduce the pressure on the border. Fertility rates in Mexico and El Salvador, another source of unauthorized border crossers, are also forecast to drop significantly.[77]

"I suspect that the great wave of Mexican migration is over," says Payan, "and I suspect that the great wave of

Central American migration is not going to come in the numbers that some predicted."

If the United States does not change its immigration policies, Payan says, it could eventually face a labor shortage. "If they don't pass the immigration reform they're considering now," he says, "they're going to have to pass another immigration reform 10 or 15 years down the road. They're going to have to pass a law that says: 'Please come.' "

## NOTES

1. For background, see Reed Karaim, "America's Border Fence," *CQ Researcher*, Sept. 19, 2008, pp. 745-768.

2. Bob Ortega, "Border technology remains flawed," *The Arizona Republic*, June 3, 2013, www.azcentral .com/news/politics/articles/20130524border-tech nology-flawed.html.

3. Marc R. Rosenblum, "Border Security: Immigration Enforcement Between Ports of Entry," Congressional Research Service, May 3, 2013, p. 13, http://fpc .state.gov/documents/organization/180681.pdf.

4. Doris Meissner, *et al.*, "Immigration Enforcement in the United States: The Rise of a Formidable Machinery," Migration Policy Institute, January 2013, p. 9, www.migrationpolicy.org/pubs/enforce mentpillars.pdf.

5. Customs agents generally work at official ports of entry while immigration agents deal with immigrants already in the country illegally, not just along the border. See in addition, Marc R. Rosenblum, "What Would a Secure Border Look Like?" Congressional Research Service, Feb. 26, 2013, p. 8, http://docs .house.gov/meetings/HM/HM11/20130226/1003 00/HHRG-113-HM11-Wstate-RosenblumM-20130226.pdf.

6. "Fact Sheet on U.S. 'Constitution Free Zone,'" American Civil Liberties Union, Oct. 22, 2008, www.aclu.org/technology-and-liberty/fact-sheet-us-constitution-free-zone. For background, see Chuck McCutcheon, "Government Surveillance," *CQ Researcher*, Aug. 30, 2013, pp. 717-740.

7. "Emergency Supplemental Appropriation Act for Defense, the Global War on Terror, and Tsunami

Relief of 2005 (Pub. L. No. 109-13)," House Committee on Oversight and Government Reform, http://oversight-archive.waxman.house.gov/bills.asp?ID=36.

8. Alan Gomez, "Big surge in border-crossing deaths reported," *USA Today*, March 18, 2013, www.usatoday.com/story/news/nation/2013/03/18/immigrant-border-deaths/1997379/.

9. Todd Miller, "War on the Border," *The New York Times*, April 17, 2013, www.nytimes.com/2013/08/18/opinion/sunday/war-on-the-border.html?pagewanted=all&_r=0.

10. For background, see Reed Karaim, "Immigration," "Hot Topic," *CQ Researcher*, June 15, 2013; and Kenneth Jost, "Immigration Conflict," *CQ Researcher*, March 9, 2012, pp. 229-252.

11. Jeffrey S. Passel, D'Vera Cohn and Ana Gonzalez-Barrera, "Population Decline of Unauthorized Immigrants Stalls, May Have Reversed," Pew Research Hispanic Trends Project, Sept. 23, 2013, www.pewhispanic.org/2013/09/23/population-decline-of-unauthorized-immigrants-stalls-may-have-reversed/.

12. About 18,000 of the Border Patrol's 21,000 agents are assigned along the Southern border, according to Rosenblum, "What Would a Secure Border Look Like?" *op. cit.*, p. 8.

13. "Remarks by the President on Comprehensive Immigration Reform," The White House, Jan. 29, 2013, www.whitehouse.gov/the-press-office/2013/01/29/remarks-president-comprehensive-immigration-reform.

14. "DHS Cmte: McCaul: Border Security Must Come First," website of Rep. Michael McCaul, U.S. House of Representatives, Feb. 2, 2013, http://mccaul.house.gov/press-releases/dhs-cmte-mccaul-border-security-must-come-first/. For background, see Martin Kady II, "Homeland Security," *CQ Researcher*, Sept. 12, 2003, pp. 749-772.

15. Claire O'Neill McCleskey, "Will Meth Overtake Cocaine on the Southwest Border?" *inSight Crime*, April 3, 2013, www.insightcrime.org/news-analysis/meth-cocaine-trafficking-mexico-us-southwest-border.

16. "Remarks by Secretary of Homeland Security Janet Napolitano at the National Press Club," Department of Homeland Security, Aug. 27, 2013, www.dhs.gov/news/2013/08/27/remarks-secretary-homeland-security-janet-napolitano-national-press-club.

17. "Southwest Border Sectors, Total Illegal Alien Apprehensions by Fiscal Year," U.S. Border Patrol, www.cbp.gov/linkhandler/cgov/border_security/border_patrol/usbp_statistics/usbp_fy12_stats/appr_swb.ctt/appr_swb.pdf.

18. Janice L. Kephart, "The Border Security, Economic Opportunity, and Immigration Modernization Act, S.744," testimony before the Senate Committee on the Judiciary, April 22, 2013.

19. Tom Barry, "Border Wars," Kindle Edition (Locations 35-37) (2011). For background, see Peter Katel, "Mexico's Drug War," *CQ Researcher*, Dec. 12, 2008, pp. 1009-1032.

20. Mike Slaven, "Defining Border Security in Immigration Reform," ASU Morrison Institute, July 2013, http://morrisoninstitute.asu.edu/publications-reports/2013-defining-border-security-in-immigration-reform.

21. Rosenblum, "Border Security: Immigration Enforcement Between Ports of Entry," *op. cit.*, p. 29.

22. Sara Murray, "Many in U.S. illegally overstayed their visas," *The Wall Street Journal*, April 7, 2013, http://online.wsj.com/article/SB10001424127887323916304578404960101110032.html.

23. For background, see Pamela M. Prah, "Port Security," *CQ Researcher*, April 21, 2006, pp. 337-360.

24. Rosenblum, "Border Security: Immigration Enforcement Between Ports of Entry," *op. cit.*, p. 13.

25. Meissner, *et al.*, *op. cit.*, p. 18.

26. "Written testimony of U.S. Coast Guard Deputy for Operations Policy and Capabilities Rear Admiral William Lee," House Committee on Homeland Security Subcommittee on Border and Maritime Security, Department of Homeland Security, June 18, 2012, www.dhs.gov/news/2012/06/18/written-testimony-us-coast-guard-house-homeland-security-subcommittee-border-and.

27. "DHS Announces Grant Allocation for Fiscal Year (FY) 2013 Preparedness Grants," Department of

Homeland Security, Aug. 23, 2013, www.dhs.gov/news/2013/08/23/dhs-announces-grant-allocation-fiscal-year-fy-2013-preparedness-grants.

28. "Fact Sheet, Fiscal Year 2014 President's Budget," U.S. Coast Guard, April 10, 2013, www.uscg.mil/posturestatement/docs/fact_sheet.pdf.

29. Chad Haddal, "Border Security: The Role of the U.S. Border Patrol," Congressional Research Service, Aug. 11, 2010, p. 25, www.fas.org/sgp/crs/homesec/RL32562.pdf. For the 2012 figures, see Rosenblum, "What Would a Secure Border Look Like?" *op. cit.*, p. 14.

30. "Border Patrol History," CBP.gov, Jan. 5, 2010, www.cbp.gov/xp/cgov/border_security/border_patrol/border_patrol_ohs/history.xml.

31. Rosenblum, "Border Security: Immigration Enforcement Between Ports of Entry," *op. cit.*, p. 13.

32. "Legacy of 9/11: the world's longest undefended border is now defended," *The Globe and Mail*, Sept. 9, 2011, www.theglobeandmail.com/commentary/editorials/legacy-of-911-the-worlds-longest-undefended-border-is-now-defended/article593884/.

33. Peter Andreas, *Smuggler Nation: How Illicit Trade Made America* (2013), p. 243.

34. Peter Andreas, *Border Games: Policing the U.S. Mexico Divide*, Second Ed. (2009), p. 29.

35. *Ibid.*

36. *Ibid.*, p. 32.

37. Karaim, "America's Border Fence," *op. cit.*

38. For background, see William Triplett, "Migrant Farmworkers," *CQ Researcher*, Oct. 8, 2004, pp. 829-852.

39. *Ibid.*

40. Reed Karaim, "The Mexican Border: Crossing a Cultural Divide," *American Scholar*, summer 2011, http://theamericanscholar.org/the-mexican-border-crossing-a-cultural-divide/#.UiOTuOArzww.

41. Ted Robbins, "Border Killings Prompt Scrutiny Over Use Of Force," NPR, Nov. 24, 2012, www.npr.org/2012/11/24/165822846/border-killings-prompt-scrutiny-over-use-of-force.

42. Bob Ortega, "New details in Mexico teenager's death," *The Arizona Republic*, April 11, 2013, www.azcentral.com/news/arizona/articles/20130410border-patrol-new-details-mexico-teens-death.html.

43. "Border Patrol under scrutiny for deadly force," *USA Today*, Nov. 14, 2012, www.usatoday.com/story/news/nation/2012/11/14/border-patrol-probe/1705737/.

44. *Ibid.*

45. Todd Miller, "U.S. Quietly Ramps Up Security Along the Canadian Border," *Mother Jones*, Feb. 7, 2013, www.motherjones.com/politics/2013/02/US-canada-border-constitution-free-zone.

46. "Nationwide Illegal Alien Apprehensions Fiscal Years 1925-2012," *op. cit.*

47. Figure 3, "U.S. Border Patrol Agents, Total and by Region, FY 1980-FY2013," in Rosenblum, "Border Security: Immigration Enforcement Between Ports of Entry," *op. cit.*, p. 14.

48. Robert Lindsey, "The Talk of San Diego: as flow of illegal aliens grows, complaints mount in the West," *The New York Times*, April 27, 1986, www.nytimes.com/1986/04/27/us/talk-san-diego-flow-illegal-aliens-grows-complaints-mount-west.html.

49. *Ibid.*

50. Eleanor Clift, "With Rebel Leaders at his Side, Reagan Presses for Contra Aid," *Los Angeles Times*, March 4, 1986, http://articles.latimes.com/1986-03-04/news/mn-15033_1_contra-aid.

51. "Immigration Reform and Control Act of 1986," U.S. Citizenship and Immigration Services, www.uscis.gov/portal/site/uscis/menuitem.5af9bb95919f35e66f614176543f6d1a/?vgnextchannel=b328194d3e88d010VgnVCM10000048f3d6a1RCRD&vgnextoid=04a295c4f635f010VgnVCM1000000ecd190aRCRD.

52. "A Reagan Legacy: Amnesty For Illegal Immigrants," NPR, July 10, 2010, www.npr.org/templates/story/story.php?storyId=128303672.

53. "Southwest Border Security Operations," National Immigration Forum, December 2010, www.immigrationforum.org/images/uploads/SouthwestBorderSecurityOperations.pdf.

54. "Illegal Immigration Reform and Immigration Responsibility Act," Legal Information Institute,

Cornell University Law School, www.law.cornell .edu/wex/illegal_immigration_reform_and_immi gration_responsibility_act.

55. "Nationwide Illegal Alien Apprehensions Fiscal Years 1925-2012," *op. cit.*

56. Rosenblum, "Border Security: Immigration Enforcement Between Ports of Entry," *op. cit.*, p. 14.

57. "After SBINet: DHS' New Border Control Strategy," FCW: The Business of Federal Technology, Jan. 14, 2011, http://fcw.com/articles/2011/01/14/dhs-can cels-rest-of-sbinet-and-plans-mix-of-new-technolo gies-at-border.aspx; and, Rey Koslowski, "The Evolution of Border Controls as a Mechanism to Prevent Illegal Immigration," Migration Policy Institute, February 2011, www.migrationpolicy.org/ pubs/bordercontrols-koslowski.pdf.

58. Rosenblum, "What Would a Secure Border Look Like?" *op. cit.*, p. 9.

59. Meissner, *op. cit.*

60. Alan Silverleib, "Senate passes sweeping immigra- tion bill," CNN, June 28, 2013, www.cnn .com/2013/06/27/politics/immigration.

61. Ashley Parker and Jonathan Martin, "Senate, 68 to 32, Passes Overhaul for Immigration," *The New York Times,* June 27, 2013, www.nytimes.com/2013/06/28/ us/politics/immigration-bill-clears-final-hurdle-to- senate-approval.html?pagewanted=all&_r=0.

62. Todd J. Gillman, "House Republicans dig in on demand for border security fix before citizenship in immigration bill," *The Dallas Morning News*, July 10, 2013, www.dallasnews.com/news/politics/ headlines/20130710-house-republicans-dig-in-on- demand-for-border-security-fix-before-citizenship- in-immigration-bill.ece.

63. Erik Lee, "The State of the Border Report: A com- prehensive analysis of the U.S.-Mexico border," Wilson Center, May 2013, www.wilsoncenter.org/ publication/the-state-the-border-report.

64. Steven T. Dennis, "Obama Urges Congress to Pass Immigration Bill by End of Summer," *Roll Call*, June 11, 2013, www.rollcall.com/news/obama_ urges_congress_to_pass_immigration_bill_by_end_ of_summer-225504-1.html.

65. Matt Canham, "House GOP to take it slow on immigration," *The Salt Lake Tribune*, July 10, 2013, www.sltrib.com/sltrib/politics/56579284-90/ bishop-chaffetz-citizenship-immigrants.html.csp.

66. "Brewer says she was wrong about beheadings in the desert," Fox News, Sept. 3, 2010, www.foxnews .com/politics/2010/09/03/brewer-says-wrong-be headings-arizona/.

67. *Ibid.*

68. The five states were Alabama, Georgia, Indiana, South Carolina and Utah. The case is *Arizona v. United States*, 11-182. Background and legal filings compiled on SCOTUSblog, www.scotusblog.com/_ case-files/_cases/_arizona-v-united-states/_?wpmp_ switcher=desktop.- For background see Kenneth Jost, "Immigration Conflict," *CQ Researcher*, March 9, 2012, pp. 229-252.

69. "Texas Border Security Funding Overview," Legislative Board Budget Staff, April 2013, www .lbb.state.tx.us/Issue_Briefs/420_Texas_Border_ Security_Funding_Overview.pdf.

70. Lee, *et al.*, *op. cit.*, p. 90.

71. *CQ Press City Crime Rankings*, 2012-2013, 2011- 2012, and 2010-2011, www.cqpress.com/pages/ cc1213. See also, Daniel Borunda, "El Paso ranked safest large city in America for third straight year," *The El Paso Times*, Feb. 6, 2013, www.elpasotimes .com/tablehome/ci_22523903/el-paso-ranked- safest-large-city-u-s.

72. Mark Potter, "Despite safer border cities, undocu- mented immigrants flow through rural areas," NBC News, May 2, 2013, http://dailynightly.nbcnews .com/_news/2013/05/02/17708115-despite-safer- border-cities-undocumented-immigrants-flow- through-rural-areas?lite.

73. "Readout of Secretary Napolitano's Trip to Mexico and Texas," Department of Homeland Security, July 23, 2013, www.dhs.gov/news/2013/07/23/readout- secretary-napolitano's-trip-mexico-and-texas.

74. *Ibid.*

75. "United States-Canada Beyond the Border: A shared vision for perimeter security and economic competi- tiveness," The White House, December 2011,

www.whitehouse.gov/sites/default/files/us-canada_btb_action_plan3.pdf.

76. For background, see Thomas J. Billitteri, "Drone Warfare," *CQ Researcher*, Aug. 6, 2010, pp. 653-676.

77. "The U.S.-Mexico Border: Secure enough," *The Economist*, June 22, 2013, www.economist.com/news/united-states/21579828-spending-billions-more-fences-and-drones-will-do-more-harm-good-secure-enough.

## BIBLIOGRAPHY

### Selected Sources

### Books

**Andreas, Peter,** *Smuggler Nation: How Illicit Trade Made America,* **Oxford University Press, 2013.**
A political science professor at Brown University argues that the current battles over border security are part of a historic tradition of smuggling and federal attempts to control it.

**Barry, Tom,** *Border Wars,* **MIT Press, 2011.**
The director of the TransBorder Project at the Center for International Policy concludes that federal and state border security policies have made U.S. borders more dangerous, rather than safer.

**Brewer, Jan,** *Scorpions for Breakfast: My Fight Against Special Interests, Liberal Media, And Cynical Politicos To Secure America's Border,* **Broadside Books, 2011.**
Arizona's governor explains the threat she sees to the country and her state posed by unauthorized border crossers and the need for Arizona's law allowing police to ask people to produce papers showing legal residency.

**Payan, Tony,** *The Three U.S.-Mexico Border Wars,* **ABC-Clio, 2006.**
A political science professor at the University of Texas, El Paso, looks at the social and economic costs of America's three border "wars" on terrorism, drug smuggling and undocumented migration.

### Articles

**"Secure Enough: spending billions more on fences and drones will do more harm than good,"** *The Economist,* **June 22, 2013, www.economist.com/news/united-states/21579828-spending-billions-more-fences-and-drones-will-do-more-harm-good-secure-enough.**
Increasing security along the U.S.-Mexico border in Arizona could lead undocumented crossers to take more desperate risks, leading to more deaths, the British newsweekly concludes.

**"US border security data not reliable, government reports show,"** FOXNews.com, Aug. 16, 2013, www.foxnews.com/politics/2013/08/16/us-border-security-data-not-reliable-government-watchdog-groups-say.
The Obama administration says a steep decline in apprehensions along the U.S.-Mexican border shows the border is more secure, but Fox News cites analyses by independent government agencies concluding apprehensions alone are a flawed measure of border security.

**Castillo, Mariano, "For those living on border, security is complicated subject,"** CNN, July 21, 2013, www.cnn.com/2013/07/21/us/immigration-border-security.
CNN examines the various, sometimes contradictory, reactions to increased border security.

**Miller, Todd, "US Quietly Ramps Up Security Along the Canadian Border,"** *Mother Jones,* **Feb. 7, 2013, www.motherjones.com/politics/2013/02/US-canada-border-constitution-free-zone.**
The 4,000-mile U.S.-Canadian border was once largely unpatrolled, and citizens could pass freely between the two countries, but that has changed since the 9/11 attacks, particularly for Muslims.

**Ortega, Bob, "Border Technology Remains Flawed,"** *The Arizona Republic,* **June 3, 2013, www.azcentral.com/news/politics/articles/20130524border-technology-flawed.html.**
Despite $106 billion spent on militarizing U.S. borders over the past five years, much of the surveillance technology used in catching migrants crossing illegally is unreliable, Ortega writes.

### Reports and Studies

**Martin, Jack, "Ten Years Later: We Will Not Forget,"** **Federation for American Immigration Reform**

**(FAIR), September 2011, www.fairus.org/publica tions/ten-years-later-we-will-not-forget-2011.**
The director of special projects for a group supporting increased border security and lower immigration levels surveys U.S. policies a decade after the 9/11 terrorist attacks and concludes the nation has failed to secure its borders and ports.

**Meissner, Doris, *et al.*, "Immigration Enforcement in the United States: The Rise of a Formidable Machinery," Migration Policy Institute, January 2013, www.migra tionpolicy.org/pubs/enforcementpillars.pdf.**
A former commissioner of the U.S. Immigration and Naturalization Service and now a senior fellow at a Washington think tank focused on international migration says the main challenge of the massive increases in U.S. border security resources is determining how they can be used most effectively.

**Rosenblum, Marc R., *et al.*, "Border Security: Understanding Threats at U.S. Borders," Congressional Research Service, Feb. 21, 2013, www.fas.org/ sgp/crs/homesec/R42969.pdf.**
An analysis prepared for members of Congress reviews the threats along U.S. borders, including terrorists, drug smugglers and undocumented border crossers.

**Slaven, Mike, "Defining Border Security in Immigration Reform," Arizona State University, Morrison Institute, Latino Public Policy Center, July 2013, http://morrisoninstitute.asu.edu/publications-reports/2013-defining-border-security-in-immigra tion-reform.**
A university researcher looks at the twin difficulties of defining what constitutes a secure border and measuring how effective various security measures are in the current, polarized political environment.

# For More Information

**American Immigration Council**, 1331 G St., N.W., Suite 200, Washington, DC 20005-3141; 202-507-7500; www .americanimmigrationcouncil.org. Supports a path to citizenship for immigrants who arrived illegally and de-emphasizes "enforcement first" as an approach.

**Center for Comparative Immigration Studies**, University of California, San Diego, 9500 Gilman Dr., Mail Code 0548, La Jolla, CA 92093-0548; 858-822-4447; http://ccis .ucsd.edu. Studies worldwide migration. Conducts extensive field interviews with migrants crossing the border illegally into the United States.

**Migration Policy Institute**, 1400 16th St., N.W., Suite 300, Washington, DC 20036; 202-266-1940; www.migrationpol icy.org. An independent, nonpartisan think tank that analyzes the movement of people worldwide. Publishes *The Migration Information Source*, an online resource providing current migration and refugee data and analysis.

**National Center for Border Security and Immigration**, University of Arizona, McClelland Hall, Room 427, P.O. Box 210108, Tucson, AZ 85721-0108; 520-621-7515; http://

borders.arizona.edu/cms/. A consortium of 18 institutions dedicated to the development of technologies, processes and policies designed to protect the nation's borders, foster international trade and enhance understanding of immigration.

**The National Immigration Forum**, 50 F St., N.W., Suite 300, Washington, DC 20001; 202-347-0040; www.immi grationforum.org. Promotes "responsible and humane" federal immigration policies that address the nation's economic and security needs while "respecting the rights of workers and employers, families and communities."

**NumbersUSA**, 1601 N. Kent St., Suite 1100, Arlington, VA 22209; https://www.numbersusa.com/content/. Advocates for significantly lower immigration levels and stepped-up enforcement of immigration laws.

**U.S. Customs and Border Protection**, 1300 Pennsylvania Ave., N.W., Washington, DC 20229; 877-227-5511; www .cbp.gov. Section of the Department of Homeland Security that is charged with securing the border, enforcing drug and immigration laws and facilitating legal international trade and travel.

# 6

# Immigration Conflict

Kenneth Jost

Arizona residents rally in Phoenix on July 31, 2010, in support of the state's hard-hitting immigration law, which gives police new responsibilities to look for immigration law violators. Five states last year followed Arizona's lead. The U.S. Supreme Court will hear arguments on the disputed Arizona measure on April 25.

Getty Images/John Moore

From *CQ Researcher*,
March 9, 2012.

**M**icky Hammon minced no words when he urged his fellow Alabama legislators to enact what would become the toughest of a batch of new state laws cracking down on illegal immigrants. "This bill is designed to make it difficult for them to live here so they will deport themselves," Hammon, leader of the Alabama House of Representatives' Republican majority, said during the April 5, 2011, debate on the bill.[1]

Immigrant-rights groups say the law, which took effect Sept. 28 after partly surviving a court challenge, is as tough as Hammon hoped — and more. "It's been pretty devastating," says Mary Bauer, legal director of the Southern Poverty Law Center in Montgomery, Alabama's capital. "Tens of thousands of people have left, and the people who remain are completely terrorized by this law."

Among other provisions, Alabama's law requires state and local law enforcement officers to determine the immigration status of anyone arrested, detained or stopped if there is a "reasonable suspicion" that the person is an alien "unlawfully present" in the United States. Failure to carry alien-registration papers is made a state crime, punishable by up to 30 days in jail for a first offense.

Alabama, with an estimated 120,000 unlawful aliens living within its borders as of 2010, was one of five states that last year followed Arizona's lead a year earlier in giving police new responsibilities to look for immigration law violators.* Republican-controlled legislatures in each of the states said they were forced to

_____

* The others were Utah, Indiana, Georgia and South Carolina.

## West Has Highest Share of Unlawful Aliens

Undocumented immigrants comprise at least 6 percent of the population of Arizona, California, Nevada and Texas and at least 3.8 percent of the population of New Mexico, Oregon and Utah. Unlawful immigrants also make up sizable percentages of several other states' populations, including New Jersey and Florida. The nationwide average is 3.7 percent.

### Unauthorized Immigrants as a Share of State Population, 2010

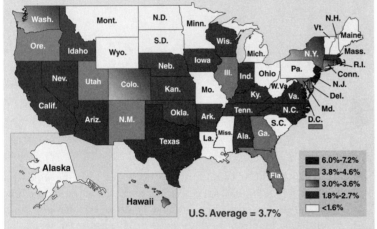

U.S. Average = 3.7%

Legend:
- 6.0%–7.2%
- 3.8%–4.6%
- 3.0%–3.6%
- 1.8%–2.7%
- <1.6%

*Source:* Jeffrey Passel and D'Vera Cohn, "Unauthorized Immigrant Population: National and State Trends, 2010," Pew Research Center, February 2011, p. 29, www.pewhispanic.org/files/reports/133.pdf

act because the federal government was not doing enough to control illegal immigration at the border or in U.S. workplaces. Opponents warned the laws risked profiling Latinos, including U.S. citizens and aliens with legal status.

All six of the laws are being challenged in federal court, with the "stop and check" provisions blocked except in Alabama's case. In the most important case, the Arizona measure is scheduled to be argued before the U.S. Supreme Court on April 25 after a federal appeals court struck some of the law enforcement provisions as interfering with federal immigration policy.[2]

Alabama's law includes a unique provision that prohibits unlawful aliens from entering into any "business transaction" with state or local governments. Some public utilities in the state interpreted the provision to require proof of immigration status for water or electricity service. Until a federal judge's injunction on Nov. 23, some counties were applying the law to prevent unlawful

immigrants from renewing permits for mobile homes.[3]

Once the law went into effect, school attendance by Latino youngsters dropped measurably in response to a provision — later blocked — requiring school officials to ascertain families' immigration status. The fear of deportation also led many immigrants in Alabama to seek help in preparing power-of-attorney documents to make sure their children would be taken care of in case the parents were deported, according to Isabel Rubio, executive director of the Hispanic Interest Coalition of Alabama. "You have to understand the sheer terror that people fear," Rubio says.

The law is having a palpable effect on the state's economy as well, according to agriculture and business groups. With fewer migrant workers, "some farmers have planted not as much or not planted at all," says Jeff Helms, spokesman for the Alabama Farmers Federation. Jay Reed, president of Associated Builders and Contractors of Alabama, says it has been harder to find construction workers as well.

Reed, co-chair of the multi-industry coalition Alabama Employers for Immigration Reform, wants to soften provisions that threaten employers with severe penalties, including the loss of operating licenses, for hiring undocumented workers. He and other business leaders also worry about the perception of the law outside the state's borders. "Some of our board members have expressed concern about our state's image and the effect on economic-development legislation," Reed says.

Reed says the state's Republican governor, Robert Bentley, and leaders in the GOP-controlled legislature are open to some changes in the law. But the two chief sponsors, Hammon and state Sen. Scott Beason, are both batting down any suggestions that the law will be repealed or its law enforcement measures softened.

"We are not going to weaken the law," Hammon told reporters on Feb. 14 as hundreds of opponents of the measure demonstrated outside the State House in Montgomery. "We are not going to repeal any section of the law."[4]

On the surface, Alabama seems an improbable state to take a leading role in the newest outbreak of nativist concern about immigration and immigrants. Alabama's unauthorized immigrant population has increased nearly fivefold since 2000, but the state still ranks relatively low in the proportion of unauthorized immigrants in the population and in the state's workforce.

Alabama's estimated 120,000 unauthorized immigrants comprise about 2.5 percent of the state's total population. Nationwide, the estimated 11.8 million unauthorized immigrants represent about 3.7 percent of the population. Alabama's estimated 95,000 unauthorized immigrants with jobs represent about 4.2 percent of the workforce. Nationwide, 8 million undocumented workers account for about 5.2 percent of the national workforce.[5]

Nationwide, the spike in anti-immigrant sentiment is also somewhat out of synch with current conditions. Experts and advocates on both sides of the immigration issues agree that the total unauthorized immigrant population has fallen somewhat from its peak in 2007, mainly because the struggling U.S. economy offers fewer jobs to lure incoming migrant workers.

"The inflow of illegals has slowed somewhat," says Mark Krikorian, executive director of the Center for Immigration Studies (CIS) in Washington. The center describes its stance as "low-immigration, pro-immigrant."[6]

Jobs were a major focus of the debate that led to Alabama's passage of the new law. "This is a jobs bill," Beason said as the measure, known as HB 56, reached final passage in June. "We have a problem with an illegal workforce that displaces Alabama workers. We need to put those people back to work."[7]

Today, Beason, running against an incumbent congressman for the U.S. House seat in the Birmingham area, credits the law with helping Alabama lower its

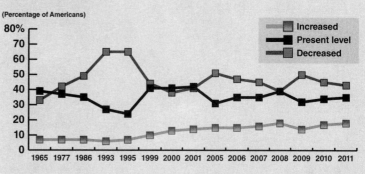

**Americans Want Less Immigration**

More than 40 percent of Americans say they favor a lower level of immigration, reflecting a view that has prevailed over most of the past half-century. About one in six want immigration to increase, while about one-third favor the current level.

*Should immigration be kept at its present level, increased or decreased?*

(Percentage of Americans)

Legend: Increased, Present level, Decreased

*Sources*: Jeffrey M. Jones, "Americans' Views on Immigration Holding Steady," Gallup, June 2011, www.gallup.com/poll/148154/americans-views-immigration-holding-steady.aspx; Roger Daniels, Guarding the Golden Door, Hill and Wang Press, December 2004, p. 233

unemployment rate from 9.8 percent in September to 8.1 percent in December. "I promised that the anti-illegal immigration law would open up thousands of jobs for Alabamians, and it has done that," Beason said in a Jan. 26 statement.

A University of Alabama economist, however, doubts the law's claimed effect on unemployment. Samuel Addy, director of the university's Center for Business and Economic Research in Tuscaloosa, notes that unemployment actually has increased, rather than declined, in the four sectors in the state viewed as most dependent on immigrant labor: agriculture, construction, accommodation and food and drinking places.[8]

In a nine-page study released in January, Addy contends instead that the immigration law is likely to hurt the state's economy overall. After assuming that 40,000 to 80,000 workers leave the state, Addy calculated that the law could reduce the state's gross domestic product by $2.3 billion to $10.8 billion. State income and sales taxes could take a $56.7 million to $265.4 million hit, Addy projected, while local sales tax revenue could decline by $20.0 million to $93.1 million. Hammon dismissed the report as "baloney."[9]

# Immigration Law Basics

*Even experts find it confusing.*

Immigrating legally to the United States is difficult at best for those who fit into categories defined in mind-numbing detail by federal law and impossible for those who do not. Here is a primer on a body of law that is complex and confusing even to immigration experts, and all the more so for would-be Americans.

**The Immigration and Nationality Act** — sets an overall limit of 675,000 permanent immigrants each year. The limit does not apply to spouses, unmarried minor children or parents of U.S. citizens, but the sponsoring U.S. citizen must have an income above the U.S. poverty level and promise to support family members brought to the United States.

**Who gets visas** — Out of the 675,000 quota, 480,000 visas are made available under family-preference rules, and up to 140,000 are allocated for employment-related preferences. Unused employment-related visas may be reallocated to the family-preference system.

The family-sponsored visas are allocated according to a preference system with numerical limits for each category. Unmarried adult children of U.S. citizens are in the first category, followed, in this order, by spouses and minor children of lawful permanent residents; unmarried adult children of lawful permanent residents; married adult children of U.S. citizens; and brothers and sisters of U.S. citizens. No other relatives qualify for a family preference. Again, the sponsor must meet financial and support requirements.

**Visa categories** —The employment-based preference system also sets up ranked, capped categories for would-be immigrants. The highest preference is given to "persons of extraordinary ability" in the arts, science, education, business or athletics; professors and researchers; and some multinational executives. Other categories follow in this order: persons with professional degrees or "exceptional" abilities in arts, science or business; workers with skills that are in short supply and some "unskilled" workers for jobs not temporary or seasonal; certain "special immigrants," including religious workers; and, finally, persons who will invest at least $500,000 in a job-creating enterprise that employs at least 10 full-time workers.

In addition to the numerical limits, the law sets a cap of 7 percent of the quota for immigrants from any single country. The limit in effect prevents any immigrant group from dominating immigration patterns.

**Refugees** — Separately, Congress and the president each year set an annual limit for the number of refugees who can be admitted based on an inability to return to their home country because of a fear of persecution. Currently, the overall ceiling is 76,000. The law also allows an unlimited number of persons already in the United States, or at a port of entry, to apply for asylum if they were persecuted or fear persecution in their home country. A total of 21,113 persons were granted asylum in fiscal 2010. Refugees and asylees are eligible to become lawful permanent residents after one year.

**Debate over the rules** — An immigrant who gets through this maze and gains the coveted "green card" for lawful permanent residents is eligible to apply for U.S. citizenship after five years (three years for the spouse of a U.S. citizen). An applicant must be age 18 or over and meet other requirements, including passing English and U.S. history and civics exams. About 675,000 new citizens were naturalized in 2010, down from the peak of slightly more than 1 million in the pre-recession year of 2008.

**Applying for citizenship** — Immigration advocates say the quotas are too low, the rules too restrictive and the waiting periods for qualified applicants too long. Low-immigration groups say the record level of legal and illegal immigration over the past decade shows the need to lower the quotas and limit the family-reunification rules.

*— Kenneth Jost*

Five months after it took effect, however, the law's impact may be ebbing. Police appear not to have enforced the law vigorously, perhaps stung by the nationwide embarrassment when a visiting Mercedes-Benz executive from Germany carrying only a German identification card was held after a traffic stop until he could retrieve his passport. With police enforcement lagging, some of the immigrants who left appear to be coming back. "Some people have returned," Rubio says.[10]

Meanwhile, attorneys for the Obama administration and the state were preparing for arguments on March 1 before the federal appeals court in Atlanta in the government's suit challenging the state law on grounds of federal pre-emption, the doctrine used to nullify state laws that conflict with U.S. laws and policies. The Hispanic Interest Coalition had challenged the law on broader grounds in an earlier suit, represented by the American Civil Liberties Union and other national groups.

In a massive, 115-page ruling, U.S. District Court Judge Sharon Blackburn upheld major parts of the law on Sept. 28 and then allowed the upheld parts to go into effect even as the government and civil rights groups appealed. Blackburn blocked half a dozen provisions on pre-emption grounds but found no congressional intent to prevent states from checking the immigration status of suspected unlawful aliens.[11]

With the legal challenges continuing, the political debates over immigration are intensifying. Republican presidential candidates generally agree on criticizing the Obama administration for failing to control illegal immigration even though the administration has increased the number of immigrants deported to their home countries. The Republican hopefuls disagree among themselves on the steps to deal with the problem.

For his part, Obama concedes that Congress will not approve a broad immigration overhaul in this election year. But he used his State of the Union speech to call for passage of a bill — the so-called DREAM Act — to allow legal status for some immigrants who have served in the U.S. military or completed college.

As the immigration debates continue, here are some of the major questions being considered:

## Major State Immigration Laws in Court

Five states have followed Arizona's lead in giving state and local police a role in enforcing federal immigration law. With some variations, the laws authorize or require police after an arrest, detention or stop to determine the person's immigration status if he or she is reasonably suspected of being unlawfully in the United States. In legal challenges, federal courts have blocked major parts of five of the laws; the Supreme Court is set to hear arguments on April 25 in Arizona's effort to reinstate the blocked portions of its law.

| State | Bill, date signed | Legal challenge |
|-------|------------------|-----------------|
| Arizona | S.B. 1070: April 23, 2010 | *United States v. Arizona* Major parts enjoined; pending at Supreme Court |
| Utah | H.B. 497: March 15, 2011 | *Utah Coalition of La Raza v. Herbert* Major parts blocked; suit on hold pending Supreme Court ruling in Arizona case |
| Indiana | SB 590: May 10, 2011 | *Buquer v. City of Indianapolis* Major parts blocked; suit on hold pending Supreme Court ruling in Arizona case |
| Georgia | HB 87: May 13, 2011 | *Georgia Latino Alliance v. Deal* Major parts blocked; on hold at 11th Circuit |
| Alabama | HB 56: June 9, 2011 | *United States v. Alabama* Major parts upheld; on hold at 11th Circuit |
| South Carolina | S20: June 27, 2011 | *United States v. South Carolina* Major parts blocked; suit on hold pending Supreme Court ruling in Arizona case |

*Sources*: National Conference of State Legislatures, http://www.ncsl.org/issues-research/immig/omnibus-immigration-legislation.aspx; American Civil Liberties Union; news coverage.

## Is illegal immigration an urgent national problem?

As the anti-illegal immigration bill HB 56 was being signed into law, Alabama's Republican Party chairman depicted the measure as needed to protect the state's taxpayers and the state's treasury. "Illegal immigrants have become a drain on our state resources and a strain on our taxpaying, law-abiding citizens," Bill Armistead declared as Republican governor Bentley signed it into law on June 9, 2011.[12]

Today, Republican officials continue to defend the law in economic terms. "Unemployment was sky high, especially in areas where there's high concentration of these undocumented workers," says Shana Kluck, the party's spokeswoman. Kluck also points to the cost on

## Unlawful Immigration High Despite Dip

Despite a dip beginning in 2007, an estimated 11.2 million unauthorized immigrants live in the United States, one-third more than a decade ago (top graph). An estimated 8 million are in the civilian labor force, a 45 percent increase since 2000 (bottom graph).

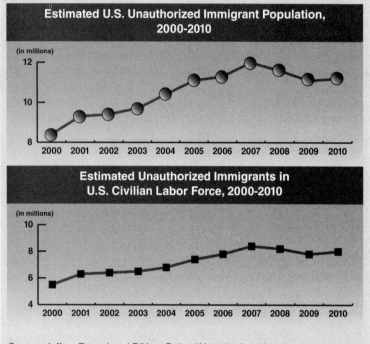

**Estimated U.S. Unauthorized Immigrant Population, 2000-2010**

(in millions)

**Estimated Unauthorized Immigrants in U.S. Civilian Labor Force, 2000-2010**

(in millions)

*Source*: Jeffrey Passel and D'Vera Cohn, "Unauthorized Immigrant Population: National and State Trends, 2010," Pew Research Center, February 2011, pp. 1, 17, www.pewhispanic.org/files/reports/133.pdf

everyone is left scrambling for crumbs at the bottom."

"The longer this economic doldrum continues, the more likely you are to see some real pushback on immigration levels as such, not just illegal immigration," says Krikorian with the low-immigration group Center for Immigration Studies. The group's research director, Steven Camarota, said if illegal immigrants are forced to go back to their home countries, there is "an ample supply of idle workers" to take the jobs freed up.[13]

Pro-immigration groups say their opponents exaggerate the costs and all but ignore the benefits of immigrant labor. "They never take into account the contributions that undocumented immigrants make," says Mary Giovagnoli, director of the American Immigration Council's Immigration Policy Center.

"We've had an economy that depends on immigration," says Ali Noorani, executive director of the National Immigration Forum. "It would be an economic and social disaster for 11 million people to pick up and leave."

Madeleine Sumption, a senior labor market analyst with the pro-immigration Migration Policy Institute in Washington, acknowledges that immigration may have what she calls a "relatively small" impact on employment and wages for citizen workers. But the costs are more than offset, she says, by the benefits to employers, consumers and the overall economy.

The benefits can be seen particularly in sectors that employ large numbers of immigrants, according to Sumption. "The United States has a large agriculture industry," she says. "Without immigration labor, it would almost certainly not be possible to produce the same volume of food in the country." The health care industry also employs a high number of immigrants, especially in low-end jobs, such as home-health aides and hospital orderlies. "These are jobs for which there is

public treasuries. "The public-assistance budgets were bursting at the seams," she says. "That's why HB 56 was necessary."

Nationally, groups favoring tighter immigration controls make similar arguments about immigrants' economic impact, especially on jobs and wages for citizen workers. "We need to slow down immigration," says Dan Stein, president of the Federation for American Immigration Reform (FAIR), pointing to the current high levels of unemployment and underemployment.

"Immigration helps to decimate the bargaining leverage of the American worker," Stein continues. "If you use a form of labor recruitment that bids down the cost of labor, that leads you to a society where a small number are very, very rich, there's nobody in the middle, and

a growing demand and an expectation of an even more rapidly growing demand in the future," Sumption says.

In Alabama, Rubio with the Hispanic coalition and the leaders of the agriculture and construction groups all discount Camarota's contention that citizen workers are available to take the jobs currently being filled by immigrants. "We did not have a tomato crop [last] summer because the immigrants who pick that crop weren't there," Rubio says. "This is hard work, and many people don't want to do it."

Reed, president of the state's builders and contractors' organization, says construction companies similarly cannot find enough workers among the citizen labor force. "Traditionally, in our recruitment efforts we have unfortunately not found those that are unemployed are ready and willing to perform these kinds of jobs that require hard labor in extreme weather conditions," Helms says.

The claimed costs and benefits from immigration for public treasuries represent similarly contentious issues. Low- or anti-immigration groups emphasize the costs in government services, especially education and medical care. Pro-immigration groups point to the taxes that even unlawful aliens pay and the limits on some government benefits under federal and state laws. In an independent evaluation of the issue, the nonpartisan Congressional Budget Office in 2007 found a net cost to state and local governments but called the impact "most likely modest."[14]

The cost-benefit debates are more volatile in stressed economic times, according to David Gerber, a professor of history at the University of Buffalo and author of a primer on immigration. "People get angry when they feel that immigrants are competing for jobs of people in the United States or when they feel that immigrants are getting access to social benefits that the majority is paying for," Gerber says. "In harder times, it makes people angrier than in times of prosperity."[15]

Even so, David Coates, a professor at Wake Forest University in Winston-Salem, N.C., and co-editor of a book on immigration issues, notes that fewer undocumented workers are entering the United States now than in the peak year of 2007, and the Obama administration has been deporting unlawful aliens in significantly greater numbers than previous administrations. Asked whether illegal immigration should be less of an issue for

AP Photo/Montgomery Advertiser/Mickey Welsh

Republican Alabama Gov. Robert Bentley addresses lawmakers at the state capitol on June 9, 2011, before signing the state's new immigration law. Republican cosponsors of the law, Sen. Scott Beason (left), and state Rep. Micky Hammon (right), both oppose softening or repealing the law. But state business interests want to ease provisions that threaten employers with severe penalties for hiring undocumented workers. They also worry about the perception of the law outside the state.

state legislators and national politicians, Coates replies simply: "Yes, in terms of the numbers."

## Should state and local police enforce immigration laws?

Alabama's HB 56 was stuffed with more provisions for state and local governments to crack down on illegal immigrants than the Arizona law that inspired it or any of the copy-cat laws passed in four other states. Along with the stop-and-check section, the law includes provisions making it a state crime for an unauthorized alien to apply for work and barring unauthorized aliens from court enforcement of any contracts. Another provision made it illegal to conceal, harbor or rent to an illegal immigrant or even to stop in a roadway to hire workers.

Opponents harshly criticized the enforcement provisions as they were signed into law. "It turns Alabama into a police state where anyone could be required to show their citizenship papers," said Cecillia Wang, director of the ACLU's Immigrant Rights Project. Noorani, with the National Immigration Forum, called the law "a radical departure from the concepts of fairness and equal treatment under the law," adding, "It makes it a crime, quite literally, to give immigrants a ride without checking their legal status."[16]

Today, even with the harboring provision and several others blocked from taking effect, opponents say the law is having the terrorizing effect that they had predicted on immigrants both legal and illegal as well as U.S. citizens of Hispanic background. "We've heard numerous accounts of people who have been stopped under very suspicious circumstances, while driving or even while walking on the street," says Justin Cox, an ACLU staff attorney in Atlanta working on the case challenging the law.

The law "has had the effect that it was intended to have," Cox says, "which was to make immigration status a pervasive issue in [immigrants'] everyday lives."

Supporters of the law are defending it, but without responding to specific criticisms. "We've seen an awful lot of illegal immigrants self-deport," House Majority Leader Hammon said as opponents rallied in Montgomery on Feb. 14. "We're also seeing Americans and legal immigrants taking these jobs."[17]

When questioned by a Montgomery television station about critical documentaries prepared for the progressive group Center for American Progress, Hammon declined to look at the films but attacked the filmmaker. "We don't need an activist director from California to come in here and tell us whether this law is good or not," Hammon said. "The people in Alabama can see it for themselves."[18]

Nationally, immigration hawks view the new state laws as unexceptional. "They're helping the feds to enforce immigration laws," says Center for Immigration Studies executive director Krikorian. "The question is [whether] local police use immigration laws as one of the tools in their tool kit to help defend public safety."

"Every town is a border town, every state is a border state," Krikorian continues. "Immigration law has to be part of your approach, part of your strategy in dealing with some kind of a significant problem."

FAIR president Stein strongly objects to the Obama administration's legal challenges to the state laws. "It should be a massive, industrial-strength issue that the Obama administration" has attacked the laws on grounds of federal pre-emption. But Giovagnoli with the pro-immigration American Immigration Council says the state laws should be struck down. "Congress has established that immigration enforcement is a federal matter," she says. "The more states get into the mix, the more you create a real patchwork of laws that don't make sense together."

As Krikorian notes, federal law already provides for cooperative agreements between the federal government and state or local law enforcement agencies to enforce immigration laws. U.S. Immigration and Customs Enforcement (ICE), the successor agency to the Immigration and Naturalization Service, touts the so-called 287(g) program on its website as one of the agency's "top partnership initiatives." The program, authorized by an immigration law overhaul in 1996, permits the federal agency to delegate enforcement power to state or local law enforcement after officers have received training on federal immigration law.[19]

Pro-immigration groups say the training requirement distinguishes 287(g) programs from the broader roles being given state and local police by the new state laws. "State and local law enforcement officers are not trained to do this kind of work," says Cox. "Inevitably, they're going to rely on pernicious stereotypes about what an undocumented immigrant looks like." The result, Cox continues, "is a breakdown of trust between the immigrant community and law enforcement, which ultimately affects all of us. It undermines public safety."

Alabama Republicans, however, insist that the state law fulfills a 2010 campaign pledge that helped the GOP gain control of both houses of the state legislature and that it remains popular despite the criticisms and legal challenges. "We've definitely been criticized," party spokeswoman Kluck acknowledges, but she blames the criticisms on "misinformation." As for possible changes in the law, Hammon and other legislative leaders are guarding details until a bill with proposed revisions can be completed by late March.

## Should Congress make it easier for illegal immigrants to become citizens?

With many Republican primary and caucus voters viewing illegal immigration as a major issue, presidential candidate and former Massachusetts Gov. Mitt Romney says he has a simple solution: Get undocumented immigrants to "self-deport" to their home countries and then get in the legal waiting line for U.S. citizenship. But one of his rivals for the Republican nomination, former House speaker Newt Gingrich, pushing stronger enforcement at the border, mocks Romney's belief that 11 million unlawful aliens will go back home voluntarily. Speaking to a Spanish-language television network in late January on the eve of the Florida presidential primary, Gingrich called Romney's plan "an Obama-level fantasy."[20]

Pro-immigration groups agree that Romney's stance is unrealistic. "It's a fantasy to think that people are going to self-deport," says the National Immigration Forum's Noorani. Unlike border-control advocates, however, Noorani and other pro-immigration advocates and experts say the solution is "a path to legal citizenship" for the undocumented.

"We need a functioning legal immigration system, a system that has the necessary legal channels for a person to immigrate here whether for a job or his family," Noorani says. "That doesn't exist here." Without "a solution," Noorani says, "the only ones who are winning are the crooked employer who is more than happy to exploit the undocumented, poor third-country worker."

Immigration hawks quickly denounce any broad legalization proposal as an "amnesty" that they say is neither workable nor deserved. "All amnesties attract future immigration," says the CIS's Krikorian. "All amnesties reward lawbreakers." As evidence, immigration critics point to the broad amnesty granted under the 1986 immigration act to some 3 million immigrants — and its evident failure within a matter of years to stem the flow of illegal immigrants from across the country's Southern borders.

As an alternative to broader proposals, pro-immigration groups are pushing narrower legislation that in its current form would grant conditional legal status to immigrants who came to the United States before age 16 and have lived in the United States for at least five years. The so-called DREAM Act — an acronym for the Development, Relief and Education for Alien Minors Act — had majority support in both chambers of the Democratic-controlled Congress in 2010 but failed to get a Senate floor vote in the face of Republican opposition.

The DREAM Act starts with the assumption that immigrants who came to the United States as children have grown up as Americans and are innocent of any intentional immigration violations. They would be eligible for a conditional permanent residency and could then earn a five-year period of temporary residency by completing two years in the U.S. military or two years in a four-year college or university.

"The intent of the DREAM Act is to provide legal status for individuals who are enlisting in our armed services or pursuing higher education," says Noorani. "Whether they came here at age 5 or 15, I think we only stand to benefit."

"It's a good way to show that if you provide legal status to folks like this, the world is not going to fall apart," says Giovagnoli with the American Immigration Council. "In fact, the country would be better off if these people were in the system."

Similar proposals have been introduced in Congress since 2001. Immigration hawks acknowledge the proposals' appeal and argue over details. "The concept that people who have been here from childhood, that it might be prudent to legalize people in that position, is a plausible one," says Krikorian. But, he adds, "As it exists, it is not a good piece of legislation."

As one change, Krikorian says the eligibility age should be lowered, perhaps to age 10 or below. "The reason they pick 16 is it legalizes more," he says. Paradoxically, Krikorian also says the bill is too narrow by allowing temporary residency only by joining the military or going to college. "What if you're not college material?" he asks.

Krikorian also dismisses the idea of absolving those who arrived as youngsters of any responsibility for immigration violations. "The parents . . . did know what they were doing," he says. The bill needs to be changed, he says, "to ensure that no parent would ever be able to benefit" under family-reunification rules.

Gingrich and some GOP lawmakers favor a narrower version of the DREAM Act that would extend legal status for serving in the military but not for going to college. Supporters oppose the narrower version. "If you read the bill carefully, it would actually allow a fewer number of immigrants to enlist in the military than the original," Noorani says. Krikorian also dismisses the alternative. He calls it "phony," adding that it would help "only a few thousand people a year."

The White House pushed hard for the bill in the Democratic-controlled Congress's lame-duck session in December 2010 but fell short in the Senate. Obama continues to speak out for the bill, most prominently in his State of the Union address. "[I]f election-year politics keeps Congress from acting on a comprehensive plan, let's at least agree to stop expelling responsible young people who want to staff our labs, start new businesses, defend this country," Obama said near the end of the Jan. 24 speech. "Send me a law that gives them the chance to earn their citizenship. I will sign it right away."[21]

## BACKGROUND

### Constant Ambivalence

The United States is a nation of immigrants that has been ambivalent toward immigration through most of its history. Immigrants are alternately celebrated as the source of diversity and criticized as agents of disunity. Immigrants were recruited to till the soil, build the cities and labor in the factories, but often criticized for taking jobs from and lowering wages for the citizen workforce. The federal government reflected popular sentiment in restricting immigration in the late 19th and early 20th century, only to draw later criticism for exclusionary policies. Today, the government is drawing criticism for liberalized policies adopted in the 1960s and for ineffective border enforcement from the 1980s on.[22]

African slaves were the first source of immigrant labor in America, but Congress banned importation of slaves in 1808. Otherwise, the United States maintained an open-door policy on immigration until the late 19th century. Europe's mid-century agricultural crisis drove waves of German and Irish peasants to the United States in the 1840s and '50s. Many were met by ethnic and anti-Catholic hostility, embodied in the first nativist political movement: the American or so-called Know-Nothing Party. The party carried one state in the 1856 presidential election and then faded from history.

Significant Chinese immigration began with the California Gold Rush of 1849 and increased with the post-Civil War push to complete the transcontinental railroad. Stark warnings of the "Yellow Peril" led to a series of restrictions at the federal level — most notably, the Chinese Exclusion Act of 1882, which suspended immigration of Chinese laborers and barred citizenship for those already in the United States. Significantly for present-day debates, efforts to deport those in the country or to seal the borders against new Chinese immigrants were no more than partly successful.[23]

Congress laid the basis for present-day immigration law and policy in a series of increasingly restrictive enactments from the 1890s through the early 1920s that coincided with the great waves of immigration from Europe, including regions previously unrepresented in the American polity. The Immigration Act of 1891 established the Bureau of Immigration, then under the Treasury Department, and provided for border inspections and deportation of unlawful aliens. Additional laws prescribed admission procedures, created categories of inadmissible immigrants and tightened the exclusion of immigrants from Asia.

The restrictive policies drew support from nativists worried about assimilation, pro-labor groups concerned about the impact on jobs and wages and progressive leaders fearful of the impact on the urban environment. The restrictions culminated in the passage of the first and second Quota Acts in 1921 and 1924, which established the first quantitative limitation on immigration (350,000, lowered to 150,000) and a national-origins system that favored immigrants from Northern and Western Europe. In reporting the bill in 1924, a House committee stated: "If the principle of liberty . . . is to endure, the basic strain of our population must be preserved."[24]

The Quota Acts' exception for Western Hemisphere immigrants combined with the unrest associated with the Mexican Revolution (1910-1929) to produce what Stanford historian Albert Camarillo calls "a tsunami" in immigration across the United States' Southern border. Camarillo says 1.5 million Mexicans — one-tenth of the country's population — relocated to the United States by the end of the 1930s.[25] The influx fueled ethnic prejudice embodied in the derogatory term "wetback" to refer to the Mexican immigrants, most of whom actually entered by crossing arid regions rather than fording the Rio Grande River.

During the Great Depression of the 1930s, the federal and state governments — concerned about the impact on jobs for Anglo workers — sent tens of thousands of Mexicans back to their home country, sometimes with force and little regard for due process. During World War II, however, the government worked with Mexico to establish the so-called bracero program to use temporary immigrant labor for agricultural work. The "temporary" program continued into the 1960s.

## CHRONOLOGY

Before 1960 *Congress establishes immigration quotas.*

**1920s** Quota Act (1921), Johnson-Reed Act (1924) establish national-origins quota system, favoring Northern European immigrants over those from Southern Europe, elsewhere.

**1952** McCarran-Walter Act retains national-origins system but adds small quotas for some Asian countries.

1960s *Congress opens door to immigration from outside Europe.*

**1965** Immigration and Nationality Act of 1965 abolishes national-origins quota system dating from 1920s; allows dramatic increase in immigration from Central and South America, Asia.

1980s-1990s *Illegal immigration increases, becomes major public issue.*

**1986** Immigration Reform and Control Act allows amnesty for many unlawful aliens, prohibits employers from employing undocumented workers; enforcement proves elusive.

**1996** Illegal Immigration Reform and Immigrant Responsibility Act seeks to strengthen border security, streamline deportation proceedings; creates optional E-Verify system for employers to electronically check immigration status of workers and job applicants.

2000-Present *Illegal immigration increases; immigration reform falters in Congress; state laws to crack down on illegal immigration challenged in court.*

**2001** Al Qaeda 9/11 attacks on U.S. soil underscore national security threat from failure to track potential terrorists entering United States (Sept. 11); USA Patriot Act gives immigration authorities more power to exclude suspected terrorists (Oct. 26).

**2005-2006** Immigration reform measures fail in GOP-controlled Congress despite support from Republican President George W. Bush; Congress approves Secure Fence Act, to require double-layer fence on U.S.-Mexico border.

**2007** Immigration reform measure dies in Senate; three motions to cut off debate fail (June 7). . . . Arizona legislature passes employer-sanctions law; companies threatened with loss of operating license for knowingly hiring undocumented aliens, required to use federal E-Verify system; signed into law by Democratic Gov. Janet Napolitano (July 2). . . . Unauthorized immigrant population in United States peaks near 12 million.

**2008** Democrat Barack Obama elected president after campaign with little attention to immigration issues (Nov. 4); Obama carries Hispanic vote by 2-1 margin.

**2009** Obama endorses immigration reform, but without specifics; issue takes back seat to economic recovery, health care.

**2010** Arizona enacts law (S.B. 1070) to crack down on illegal immigrants; measure requires police to check immigration status if suspect or detainee is reasonably believed to be unlawful alien; makes it a crime to fail to carry alien registration papers; signed by Republican Gov. Jan Brewer (April 23); federal judge blocks parts of law (July 28). . . . DREAM Act to allow legal status for unlawful aliens who entered U.S. as minors approved by House of Representatives (Dec. 8) but fails in Senate: 55-41 vote is short of supermajority needed for passage (Dec. 18).

**2011** Utah, Indiana, Georgia follow Arizona's lead in giving state, local police immigration-enforcement powers (March, May). . . . Federal appeals court upholds injunction against parts of Arizona's S.B. 1070 (April 11). . . . Supreme Court upholds Arizona's employer-sanctions law 5-3 (May 21). . . . Alabama enacts nation's toughest state law on illegal immigrants, HB 56 (June 9). . . . Federal judge blocks some parts of HB 56, allows others to take effect (Sept. 28).

**2012** Immigration is flashpoint for Republican presidential candidates. . . . Obama urges passage of DREAM Act (Jan. 24). . . . Alabama, Georgia laws argued before U.S. appeals court (March 1). . . . Supreme Court to hear arguments on Arizona's S.B. 1070 (April 25); ruling due by end of June.

# Journalist Reveals His Immigration Secret

*"There's nothing worse than being in limbo."*

When journalist-turned-immigration rights activist Jose Antonio Vargas traveled to Alabama with a documentary filmmaker, he found a Birmingham restaurant patron who strongly supported the state law cracking down on undocumented aliens. "Get your papers or get out," the patron said.

"What if I told you I didn't [have papers]?" Vargas is heard asking off camera. "Then you need you get your ass home then," the patron rejoined. [1]

Vargas says he is home — in America, where he has lived since his Filipina mother sent him, at age 12, to live in California with his grandparents in 1993. "I'm an American without papers," says Vargas, who came out as an undocumented immigrant in dramatic fashion in a 4,300-word memoir in *The New York Times Magazine* in June 2011. [2]

In the story, Vargas recounts how he learned at age 16 that he was carrying a fake green card when he applied for a driver's license. The DMV clerk let him go. Back home, Vargas confronted his grandfather, who acknowledged the forgery and told Vargas not to tell anyone else.

For the next 14 years, Vargas kept his non-status secret from all but a handful of enablers as he completed high school and college and advanced rapidly from entry-level newspaper jobs to national-impact journalism at *The Washington Post*, *Huffington Post* and glossy magazines. His one attempt at legal status ended in crushing disappointment in 2002 when an immigration lawyer told him he would have to return to the Philippines and wait for 10 years to apply to come back.

Vargas was inspired to write about his life by the example of four undocumented students who walked from Miami to Washington, D.C., in 2010 to lobby for the DREAM Act, the status-legalizing proposal for immigrants who came to the United States as minors. Vargas's story, published by *The Times* after *The Washington Post* decided not to, quickly went viral in old and new media alike.

In the eight months since, Vargas has founded and become the public face for a Web-based campaign, Define American (www .defineamerican.org). "Define American brings new voices into the immigration conversation, shining a light on a growing 21st century Underground Railroad: American citizens who are forced to fill in where our broken immigration system fails," the mission statement reads. "Together, we are going to fix a broken system."

The DREAM Act fell just short of passage in Congress in December 2010 and has gotten little traction since. Broader proposals to give legal status to some of the 11 million unlawful

Journalist Jose Antonio Vargas disclosed in *The New York Times* in June 2011 that he was an undocumented immigrant.

aliens are far off the political radar screen. Vargas is critical of Alabama's law cracking down on illegal immigration but acknowledges the states' frustration with federal policies. "At the end of the day, the federal government hasn't done anything on this issue," he says.

In the meantime, Vargas waits. "There's nothing worse than being in limbo," he says. In the story, he cited some of the hardships for the undocumented. As one example, he cannot risk traveling to the Philippines, so he has yet to meet his 14-year-old brother. But Vargas says he has no plan to "self-deport." "I love this country," he says.

— *Kenneth Jost*

---

[1] "The Two Faces of Alabama," http://isthisalabama.org/. The films by director Chris Weitz were prepared under the auspices of the Center for American Progress. Some comments from Vargas are from a Feb. 15, 2012, screening of the videos at the center.

[2] Jose Antonio Vargas, "Outlaw," *The New York Times Magazine*, June 26, 2011, p. 22. Disclosure: the author is a professional acquaintance and Facebook friend of Vargas.

Congress liberalized immigration law with a 1952 statute that included restrictionist elements as well and then, dramatically, with a 1965 law that scrapped the Eurocentric national-origins system and opened the gate to increased immigration from Latin America and Asia.

The 1952 law preserved the national-origins system but replaced the Chinese Exclusion Act with very small quotas for countries in the so-called Asia-Pacific Triangle. The act also eliminated discrimination between sexes. Over the next decade, immigration from European countries declined, seemingly weakening the rationale for the national-origins system. Against the backdrop of the civil rights revolution, the national-origins system seemed to many also to be antithetical to American values. The result was the Immigration Act of 1965, which replaced the national-origins system with a system of preferences favoring family reunification or to lesser extents admissions of professionals or skilled or unskilled workers needed in the U.S. workforce.

Quickly, the demographics of immigration shifted — and dramatically. Immigration increased overall under the new law, and the new immigrants came mostly from Latin America and Asia. By 1978, the peak year of the decade, 44 percent of legal immigration came from the Americas, 42 percent from Asia and only 12 percent from Europe.[26]

## Cracking Down?

Immigration to the United States increased overall in the last decades of the 20th century, and illegal immigration in particular exploded to levels that fueled a public and political backlash. Congress and the executive branch tried to stem the flow of undocumented aliens first in 1986 by combining employer sanctions with an amnesty for those in the country for several years and then a decade later by increasing enforcement and deportations.

Then, in the wake of the Sept. 11, 2001, terrorist attacks on the United States, Congress and President George W. Bush joined in further efforts to tighten admission procedures and crack down on foreigners in the country without authorization.

Estimates of the number of immigrants in the United States illegally are inherently imprecise, but the general upward trend from the 1980s until a plateau in the 2000s is undisputed. As Congress took up immigration bills in

the mid-1980s, the Census Bureau estimated the number of those undocumented at 3 million to 5 million; many politicians used higher figures. The former Immigration and Naturalization Service put the number at 3.5 million in 1990 and 7.0 million a decade later. Whatever the precise number, public opinion polls registered increasing concern about the overall level of immigration. By the mid-1990s, Gallup polls found roughly two-thirds of respondents in favor of decreasing the level of immigration, one-fourth in favor of maintaining the then-present level and fewer than 10 percent for an increase.[27]

The congressional proposals leading to the Immigration Reform and Control Act in 1986 sought to stem illegal immigration while recognizing the reality of millions of undocumented immigrants and the continuing need for immigrant labor, especially in U.S. agriculture. The law allowed legal status for immigrants in the country continuously since 1982 but aimed to deter unauthorized immigration in the future by forcing employers to verify the status of prospective hires and penalizing them for hiring anyone without legal status. Agricultural interests, however, won approval of a new guest worker program. Some 3 million people gained legal status under the two provisions, but illegal immigration continued to increase even as civil rights groups warned that the employer sanctions would result in discrimination against Latino citizens.

The backlash against illegal immigration produced a new strategy for reducing the inflows: state and federal laws cutting off benefits for aliens in the country without authorization. California, home to an estimated 1.3 million undocumented aliens at the time, blazed the path in 1994 with passage of a ballot measure, Proposition 187, that barred any government benefits to illegal aliens, including health care and public schooling. The education provision was flatly unconstitutional under a 1982 ruling by the U.S. Supreme Court that guaranteed K-12 education for school-age alien children.[28]

The measure mobilized Latino voters in the state. They contributed to the election of a Democratic governor in 1998, Gray Davis, who dropped the state's defense of the measure in court in his first year in office. In the meantime, however, Congress in 1996 had approved provisions — reluctantly signed into law by President Bill Clinton — to deny unauthorized aliens most federal benefits, including food stamps, family assistance and Social Security. The law allows states to deny state-provided benefits

A Maricopa County deputy arrests a woman following a sweep for illegal immigrants in Phoenix on July 29, 2010. The police operation came after protesters against Arizona's tough immigration law clashed with police hours after the law went into effect. Although the most controversial parts of the law have been blocked, five other states — Utah, Indiana, Georgia, Alabama and South Carolina — last year enacted similar laws.

as well; today, at least a dozen states have enacted such further restrictions.

The centerpieces of the 1996 immigration law, however, were measures to beef up enforcement and toughen deportation policy. The Illegal Immigration Reform and Immigrant Responsibility Act authorized more money for the Border Patrol and INS, approved more funding for a 14-mile border fence already under construction and increased penalties for document fraud and alien smuggling. It sought to streamline deportation proceedings, limit appeals and bar re-entry of any deportee for at least five years. And it established an Internet-based employer verification system (E-Verify) aimed at making it easier and more reliable for employers to check legal status of prospective hires. The law proved to be tougher on paper, however, than in practice. The border fence remains incomplete, deportation proceedings backlogged and E-Verify optional and — according to critics — unreliable. And illegal immigration continued to increase.

The 9/11 attacks added homeland security to the concerns raised by the nation's porous immigration system. In post-mortems by immigration hawks, the Al Qaeda hijackers were seen as having gained entry into the United States with minimal scrutiny of their visa applications and in many cases having overstayed because of inadequate follow-up.[29] The so-called USA Patriot Act, enacted in October 2001 just 45 days after the attacks, gave the INS — later renamed the U.S. Citizenship and Immigration Service and transferred to the new Department of Homeland Security — greater authority to exclude or detain foreigners suspected of ties to terrorist organizations. The act also mandated information-sharing by the FBI to identify aliens with criminal records. Along with other counterterrorism measures, the act is viewed by supporters today as having helped prevent any successful attacks on U.S. soil since 2001. Illegal immigration, however, continued to increase — peaking at roughly 12 million in 2007.

## Getting Tough

Congress and the White House moved from post-9/11 security issues to broader questions of immigration policy during Bush's second term, but bipartisan efforts to allow legal status for unlawful aliens fell victim to Republican opposition in the Senate. As a presidential candidate, Democrat Obama carried the Hispanic vote by a 2-1 margin over Republican John McCain after a campaign with limited attention to immigration issues. In the White House, Obama stepped up enforcement in some respects even as he urged Congress to back broad reform measures. The reform proposals failed with Democrats in control of both the House and the Senate and hardly got started after Republicans regained control of the House in the 2010 elections.

Bush lent support to bipartisan reform efforts in the Republican-controlled Congress in 2005 and 2006 and again in the Democratic-controlled Congress in his final two years in office. Congress in 2006 could agree only on authorizing a 700-mile border fence after reaching an impasse over a House-passed enforcement measure and a Senate-approved path-to-citizenship bill. Bush redoubled efforts in 2007 by backing a massive, bipartisan bill that would have allowed "earned citizenship" for aliens who had lived in the United States for at least eight years and met other requirements. As in the previous Congress, many Republicans rejected the proposal as an unacceptable amnesty. The bill died on June 7 after the Senate rejected three cloture motions to cut off debate.[30]

Immigration played only a minor role in the 2008 presidential campaign between Obama and McCain,

Senate colleagues who had both supported reform proposals. Both campaigns responded to growing public anger over illegal immigration by emphasizing enforcement when discussing the issue, but the subject went unmentioned in the candidates' three televised debates. McCain, once popular with Hispanics in his home state of Arizona, appeared to have paid at the polls for the GOP's hard line on immigration. Exit polls indicated that Obama won 67 percent of a record-size Hispanic vote; McCain got 31 percent — a significant drop from Bush's 39 percent share of the vote in 2004.[31]

With Obama in office, Congress remained gridlocked even as the president tried to smooth the way for reform measures by stepping up enforcement. The congressional gridlock had already invited state lawmakers to step into the vacuum. State legislatures passed more than 200 immigration-related laws in 2007 and 2008, according to a compilation by the National Conference on State Legislatures; the number soared to more than 300 annually for the next three years.[32]

The numbers included some resolutions praising the country's multi-ethnic heritage, but most of the new state laws sought to tighten enforcement against undocumented aliens or to limit benefits to them. Among the earliest of the new laws was an Arizona measure — enacted in June 2007, two weeks after the Senate impasse in Washington — that provided for lifting the business licenses of companies that knowingly hired illegal aliens and mandated use of the federal E-Verify program to ascertain status of prospective hires. Business and labor groups, supported by the Obama administration, challenged the law on federal preemption grounds. The Supreme Court's 5-3 decision in May 2011 to uphold the law prompted several states to enact similar mandatory E-Verify provisions.[33]

The interplay on immigration policy between Washington and state capitals is continuing. In Obama's first three years in office, the total number of removals increased to what ICE calls on its website "record levels." Even so, Arizona lawmakers and officials criticized federal enforcement as inadequate in the legislative debate leading to SB 1070's enactment in April 2010. Legal challenges followed quickly — first from a Latino organization; then from a broad coalition of civil rights and civil liberties groups; and then, on July 6, from the Justice Department. The most controversial parts of the law have been blocked,

first by U.S. District Court Judge Susan Bolton's injunction later that month and then by the Ninth Circuit's decision affirming her decision in April 2011. The legal challenges did not stop five other states — Utah, Indiana, Georgia, Alabama and South Carolina — from enacting similar laws in spring and early summer 2011. Civil rights groups and the Justice Department followed with similar suits challenging the new state enactments.

As the 2012 presidential campaign got under way, immigration emerged as an issue between Republican candidates vying for the party's nomination. The issue posed difficulties for the GOP hopefuls as they sought to appeal to rank-and-file GOP voters upset about illegal immigration without forfeiting Latino votes in the primary season and in the general election. Presumed front-runner Mitt Romney took a hard stance against illegal immigration in early contests but softened his message in advance of winning the pivotal Jan. 31 primary in Florida with its substantial Hispanic vote.

Despite differences in details and in rhetoric, the three leading GOP candidates — Romney, Newt Gingrich and Rick Santorum — all said they opposed the DREAM Act in its present form even as Obama called for Congress to pass the bill in his State of the Union speech.

## CURRENT SITUATION

### Obama's Approach

The Obama administration is claiming success in increasing border enforcement and removing unlawful aliens while injecting more prosecutorial discretion into deportation cases. But the mix of firm and flexible policies is resulting in criticism from both sides of the issue.

U.S. Immigration and Customs Enforcement (ICE) counted a record 396,906 "removals" during fiscal 2011, including court-ordered deportations as well as administrative or voluntary removals or returns. The number includes a record 216,698 aliens with criminal convictions.[34]

Meanwhile, Homeland Security Secretary Janet Napolitano says illegal border-crossing attempts have decreased by more than half in the last three years. In a Jan. 30 speech to the National Press Club in Washington, Napolitano linked the decline to an increase in the number of Border Patrol agents to 21,000, which she said was more than double the number in 2004.

"The Obama administration has undertaken the most serious and sustained actions to secure our borders in our nation's history," Napolitano told journalists. "And it is clear from every measure we currently have that this approach is working."[35]

Immigration hawk Krikorian with the Center for Immigration Studies gives the administration some, but only some, credit for the removal statistics. "They're not making up the numbers," Krikorian says. But he notes that immigration removals increased during the Bush administration and that the rate of increase has slowed under Obama.

In addition, Krikorian notes that new figures compiled by a government information tracking service indicate the pace of new immigration cases and of court-processed deportations slowed in the first quarter of fiscal 2012 (October, November and December 2011). A report in early February by Syracuse University's Transactional Records Access Clearinghouse (TRAC) shows 34,362 court-ordered removals or "voluntary departures" in the period, compared to 35,771 in the previous three months — about a 4 percent drop.

A separate TRAC report later in the month showed what the service called a "sharp decline" in new ICE filings. ICE initiated 39,331 new deportation proceedings in the nation's 50 immigration courts during the first quarter of fiscal 2012, according to the report, a 33 percent decline from the 58,639 new filings in the previous quarter.[36]

"The people in this administration would like to pull the plug on enforcement altogether," Krikorian complains. "They refuse to ask for more money for detention beds and then plead poverty that they can't do more."

From the opposite perspective, some Latino officials and organizations have been critical of the pace of deportations. When Obama delivered a speech in favor of immigration reform in El Paso, Texas, in May 2011, the president of the National Council of La Raza tempered praise for the president's position with criticism of the deportation policy.

"As record levels of detention and deportation continue to soar, families are torn apart, innocent youth are being deported and children are left behind without the protection of their parents," Janet Murguía said in a May 10 press release. "Such policies do not reflect American values and do little to solve the problem. We can do better."[37]

Latinos disapprove of the Obama administration's handling of deportations by roughly a 2-1 margin, according to a poll by the Pew Hispanic Center in December 2011. Overall, the poll found 59 percent of those surveyed opposed the administration's policy while 27 percent approved. Disapproval was higher among foreign-born Latinos (70 percent) than those born in the United States (46 percent).[38]

Napolitano and ICE Director John Morton are both claiming credit for focusing the agency's enforcement on the most serious cases, including criminal aliens, repeat violators and recent border crossers. Morton announced the new "prosecutorial discretion" policy in an agency-wide directive in June 2011.[39]

TRAC, however, questions the claimed emphasis on criminal aliens. The 39,331 new deportation filings in the first quarter of fiscal 2012 included only 1,300 against aliens with convictions for "aggravated felonies," as defined in immigration law. "Even this small share was down from previous quarters," the Feb. 21 report states. Aliens with aggravated felony convictions accounted for 3.3 percent of deportations in the period, compared to 3.8 percent in the previous quarter.[40]

The administration is also being questioned on its claim — in Obama's El Paso speech and elsewhere — to have virtually completed the border fence that Congress ordered constructed in the Secure Fence Act of 2006.[41] The act called for the 652-mile barrier to be constructed of two layers of reinforced fencing but was amended the next year — with Bush still in office — to give the administration more discretion in what type of barriers to use.

As of May 2011, the barrier included only 36 miles of double-layer fencing, according to PolitiFact, the fact-checking service of the *Tampa Bay Times*. The rest is single-layer fencing or vehicle barriers that critic Krikorian says are so low that a pedestrian can step over them. PolitiFact calls Obama's claim "mostly false."[42]

Meanwhile, the administration is preparing to extend nationwide its controversial "Secure Communities" program, which tries to spot immigration law violators by matching fingerprints of local arrestees with the database of the Department of Homeland Security (DHS). A match allows U.S. Immigration and Customs Enforcement (ICE)

# Should Congress pass the DREAM Act?

## YES
**Walter A. Ewing**
*Senior Researcher, Immigration Policy Center American Immigration Council*

Written for *CQ Researcher*, March 2012

The Development, Relief and Education for Alien Minors Act is rooted in common sense. To begin with, it would benefit a group of unauthorized young people who, in most cases, did not come to this country of their own accord. Rather, they were brought here by their parents. The DREAM Act would also enable its beneficiaries to achieve higher levels of education and obtain better, higher-paying jobs, which would increase their contributions to the U.S. economy and American society. In short, the DREAM Act represents basic fairness and enlightened self-interest.

More than 2 million young people would benefit from the DREAM Act, and their numbers grow by roughly 65,000 per year. They came to the United States before age 18, many as young children. They tend to be culturally American and fluent in English. Their primary ties are to this country, not the countries of their birth. And the majority had no say in the decision to come to this country without authorization — that decision was made by the adult members of their families. Punishing these young people for the actions of their parents runs counter to American social values and legal norms. Yet, without the DREAM Act, these young people will be forced to live on the margins of U.S. society or will be deported to countries they may not even know.

Assuming they aren't deported, the young people who would benefit from the DREAM Act face enormous barriers to higher education and professional jobs because of their unauthorized status. They are ineligible for most forms of college financial aid and cannot work legally in this country. The DREAM Act would remove these barriers, which would benefit the U.S. economy.

The College Board estimates that over the course of a working lifetime, a college graduate earns 60 percent more than a high school graduate. This higher income translates into extra tax revenue flowing to federal, state and local governments.

The DREAM Act is in the best interest of the United States both socially and economically. It would resolve the legal status of millions of unauthorized young people in a way that is consistent with core American values. And it would empower these young people to become better-educated, higher-earning workers and taxpayers. Every day that goes by without passage of the DREAM Act is another day of wasted talent and potential.

## NO
**Mark Krikorian**
*Executive Director, Center for Immigration Studies*

Written for *CQ Researcher*, March 2012

The appeal of the DREAM Act is obvious. People brought here illegally at a very young age and who have grown up in the United States are the most sympathetic group of illegal immigrants. Much of the public is open to the idea of amnesty for them.

But the actual DREAM Act before Congress is a deeply flawed measure in at least four ways:

• Rather than limiting amnesty to those brought here as infants and toddlers, it applies to illegal immigrants who arrived before their 16th birthday. But if the argument is that their very identity was formed here, age 7 would be a more sensible cutoff. That is recognized as a turning point in a child's psychological development (called the "age of reason" by the Catholic Church, hence the traditional age for First Communion). Such a lower-age cutoff, combined with a requirement of at least 10 years' residence here, would make a hypothetical DREAM Act 2.0 much more defensible.

• All amnesties are vulnerable to fraud, even more than other immigration benefits. About one-fourth of the beneficiaries of the amnesty granted by Congress in 1986 were liars, including one of the leaders of the 1993 World Trade Center bombing. But the DREAM Act specifically prohibits the prosecution of anyone who lies on an amnesty application. So you can make any false claim you like about your arrival or schooling in America without fear of punishment. A DREAM Act 2.0 would make clear that any lies, no matter how trivial, will result in arrest and imprisonment.

• All amnesties send a signal to prospective illegal immigrants that, if you get in and keep your head down, you might benefit from the next amnesty. But the bill contains no enforcement provisions to limit the need for another DREAM Act a decade from now. That's why a serious proposal would include measures such as electronic verification of the legal status of all new hires, plus explicit authorization for state and local enforcement of immigration law.

• Finally, all amnesties reward illegal immigrants — in this case including the adults who brought their children here illegally. A credible DREAM Act 2.0 would bar the adult relatives of the beneficiaries from ever receiving any immigration status or even a right to visit the United States. If those who came as children are not responsible, then those who are responsible must pay the price for their lawbreaking.

to issue a so-called detainer against violators, sending their cases into the immigration enforcement system. The administration touts the program as "a simple and common sense" enforcement tool. Critics note, however, that it has resulted in wrongful detention of U.S. citizens in a considerable but unknown number of cases. One reason for the mistakes: The DHS database includes all immigration transactions, not just violations, and thus could show a match for an immigrant with legal status.[43]

## Supreme Court Action

All eyes are on the Supreme Court as the justices prepare for arguments on April 25 in Arizona's effort to reinstate major parts of its trend-setting law cracking down on illegal immigrants.

The Arizona case is the furthest advanced of suits challenging the six recently enacted state laws that give state and local police responsibility for enforcing federal immigration laws. After winning an injunction blocking major parts of the Arizona law, the Obama administration filed similar suits against Alabama's HB 56 as well as the Georgia and South Carolina measures.

The ACLU's Immigrants Rights Project, along with Hispanic and other civil rights groups, has filed separate challenges on broader grounds against all six laws. Federal district courts have blocked parts of all the laws, though some contentious parts of Alabama's law were allowed to take effect.

District court judges in the Indiana, South Carolina and Utah cases put the litigation on hold pending the Supreme Court's decision in the Arizona case. Alabama and Georgia asked the Eleventh U.S. Circuit Court of Appeals to postpone the scheduled March 1 arguments in their cases, but the court declined.

Judge Charles R. Wilson opened the Atlanta-based court's March 1 session, however, by announcing that the three-judge panel had decided to withhold its opinion until after the Supreme Court decides the Arizona case. "Hopefully, that information will help you in framing your arguments today," Wilson told the assembled lawyers.[44]

Wilson and fellow Democratic-appointed Circuit Judge Beverly B. Martin dominated the questioning during the three hours of arguments in the cases. Both judges pressed lawyers defending Alabama and Georgia on the effects of their laws on the education of children, the ability of illegal aliens to carry on with their lives while immigration courts decided their cases and what would happen if every state adopted their approach to dealing with immigration violations. The third member of the panel, Richard Voorhees, a Republican-appointed federal district court judge, asked only three questions on technical issues.

Opening the government's argument in the Alabama case, Deputy Assistant U.S. Attorney General Beth Brinkmann said the state's law attempts to usurp exclusive federal authority over immigration. "The regulation of immigration is a matter vested exclusively in the national government," Brinkman said. "Alabama's state-specific regulation scheme violates that authority. It attacks every aspect of an alien's life and makes it impossible for the alien to live."

Alabama Solicitor General John C. Neiman Jr. drew sharp challenges from Wilson and Martin even before he began his argument. Wilson focused on the law's Section 10, which makes it a criminal misdemeanor for an alien unlawfully present in the United States to fail to carry alien registration papers.

"You could be convicted and sent to jail in Alabama even though the Department of Homeland Security says, 'You're an illegal alien, but we've decided you're going to remain here in the United States?'" Wilson asked.

Neiman conceded the point. "If the deportation hearing occurred after the violation of Section 10, then yes," Neiman said. "Someone could be held to be in violation of Section 10 and then later be held not removable."

Wilson also pressed Neiman on the potential effects on the federal government's ability to control immigration policy if states enacted laws with different levels of severity. "These laws could certainly have the effect of making certain states places where illegal aliens would be likely to go," the state's attorney acknowledged.

Representing the ACLU in the separate challenge, Immigrants Rights Project director Wang sharply attacked the motive behind the Alabama law. The law, she said, was written to carry out the legislature's stated objective "to attack every aspect of an illegal immigrant's life so that they will deport themselves."*

---

*The appeals court on March 8 issued a temporary injunction blocking enforcement of two provisions, those prohibiting unlawful aliens from enforcing contracts in court or entering into business transactions with state or local government agencies.

In Washington, lawyers for Arizona filed their brief with the Supreme Court defending its law, SB 1070, in early February. Among 20 *amicus* briefs filed in support of Arizona's case is one drafted by the Michigan attorney general's office on behalf of 16 states similarly defending the states' right to help enforce federal immigration law. A similar brief was filed by nine states in the Eleventh Circuit in support of the Alabama law.

The government's brief in the Arizona case is due March 19. Following the April 25 arguments, the Supreme Court is expected to decide the case before the current term ends in late June.

Meanwhile, legal challenges to other parts of the state's law are continuing in federal court in Arizona. In a Feb. 29 ruling, Bolton blocked on First Amendment grounds a provision prohibiting people from blocking traffic when they offer day labor services on the street.[45]

## OUTLOOK:

### A Broken System

The immigration system is broken. On that much, the pro- and low-immigration groups agree. But they disagree sharply on how to fix it. And the divide defeats any attempts to fix it even if it can be fixed.

Pro-immigration groups like to talk about the "three-legged stool" of immigration reform: legal channels for family- and job-based immigration; a path to citizenship for unlawful aliens already in the United States; and better border security. Low-immigration groups agree on the need for better border controls but want to make it harder, not easier, for would-be immigrants and generally oppose legal status for the near-record number of unlawful aliens.

Public opinion is ambivalent and conflicted on immigration issues even as immigration, legal and illegal, has reached record levels. The nearly 14 million new immigrants, legal and illegal, who came to the United States from 2000 to 2010 made that decade the highest ever in U.S. history, according to the low-immigration Center for Immigration Studies. The foreign-born population reached 40 million, the center says, also a record.[46]

Some public opinion polls find support for legal status for illegal immigrants, especially if the survey questions specify conditions to meet: 66 percent

supported it, for example, in a Fox News poll in early December 2011. Three weeks earlier, however, a CNN poll found majority support (55 percent) for concentrating on "stopping the flow of illegal immigrants and deporting those already here" instead of developing a plan for legal residency (42 percent).[47]

Other polls appear consistently to find support for the laws in Arizona and other states to crack down on illegal immigrants — most recently by a 2-1 margin in a poll by Quinnipiac University in Connecticut.[48] "Popular sentiment is always against immigration," says Muzaffar Chishti, director of the Migration Policy Institute's office at New York University School of Law and himself a naturalized U.S. citizen who emigrated from his native India in 1974.

Pro-immigration groups say the public is ahead of the politicians in Washington and state capitals who are pushing for stricter laws. State legislators "have chosen to scapegoat immigration instead of solving tough economic challenges," says Noorani with the National Immigration Forum. "There are politicians who would rather treat this as a political hot potato," he adds, instead of offering "practical solutions."

From the opposite side, the Federation for American Immigration Reform's Stein says he is "pessimistic, disappointed and puzzled" by what he calls "the short-sighted views" of political leaders. Earlier, Stein says, "politicians all over the country were touting the virtues of engagement in immigration policy." But now he complains that even Republicans are talking about "amnesty and the DREAM Act," instead of criticizing what he calls the Obama administration's "elimination of any immigration enforcement."

Enforcement, however, is one component of the system that, if not broken, is at least completely overwhelmed. In explaining the new prosecutorial discretion policy, ICE director Morton frankly acknowledged the agency "has limited resources to remove those illegally in the United States."[49] The nation's immigrant courts have a current backlog of 300,225 cases, according to a TRAC compilation, double the number in 2001.[50]

Employers' groups say the system's rules for hiring immigrants are problematic at best. In Alabama, Reed with the contractors' group says employers do their best to comply with the status-verification requirements but find the procedures and paperwork difficult. The farm federation's Helms says the same for the rules for temporary guest workers. "We're working at the national level to have a more effective way to hire legal migrant workers to do those jobs that it's hard to find local workers to do," he says.

The rulings by the Supreme Court on the Arizona law will clarify the lines between federal and state enforcement responsibilities, but the Center for Immigration Studies' Krikorian says the decision is likely to increase the politicization of the issue. A ruling to uphold the law will encourage other states to follow Arizona's lead, he says, but would also "energize the anti-enforcement groups." A ruling to find the state laws pre-empted, on the other hand, will mobilize pro-enforcement groups, he says.

The political and legal debates will be conducted against the backdrop of the nation's rapidly growing Hispanic population, attributable more to birth rates than to immigration.[51] "Whoever the next president is, whoever the next Congress is, will have to address this issue," says Giovagnoli with the American Immigration Council. "The demographics are not going to allow people to ignore this issue.

"I do believe we're going to reform the immigration system," Giovagnoli adds "It's going to be a lot of work. Even under the best of circumstances, it's a lot of work."

## NOTES

1. Quoted in Kim Chandler, "Alabama House passes Arizona-style immigration bill," *The Birmingham News*, April 6, 2011, p. 1A.

2. The case is *Arizona v. United States*, 11-182. Background and legal filings compiled on SCOTUSblog, www.scotusblog.com/case-files/cases/arizona-v-united-states/?wpmp_switcher=desktop.-

3. See Human Rights Watch, "No Way to Live: Alabama's Immigration Law," December 2011, www.hrw.org/news/2011/12/13/usalabama-no-way-live-under-immigrant-law.

4. Quoted in David White, "Hundreds rally at State House seeking immigration law repeal," *The Birmingham News*, Feb. 15, 2012, p. 1A.

5. See "Unauthorized Immigrant Population: State and National Trends, 2010," Pew Hispanic Center, Feb. 1, 2011, pp. 23, 24, www.pewhispanic.org/files/reports/133.pdf. The U.S. Department of Homeland Security estimates differ slightly; for 2010, it estimates nationwide unauthorized immigrant population at 10.8 million.

6. For previous *CQ Researcher* coverage, see: Alan Greenblatt, "Immigration Debate," pp. 97-120, updated Dec. 10, 2011; Reed Karaim, "America's Border Fence," Sept. 19, 2008, pp. 745-768; Peter Katel, "Illegal Immigration," May 6, 2005, pp. 393-420; David Masci, "Debate Over Immigration," July 14, 2000, pp. 569-592; Kenneth Jost, "Cracking Down on Immigration," Feb. 3, 1995.

7. Quoted in David White, "Illegal immigration bill passes," *The Birmingham News*, June 3, 2011, p. 1A.

8. See Dana Beyerle, "Study says immigration law has economic costs," *Tuscaloosa News*, Jan. 31, 2012, www.tuscaloosanews.com/article/20120131/news/120139966. For Beason's statement, see http://scottbeason.com/2012/01/26/beason-statement-on-the-impact-of-hb-56-on-alabama-unemployment-rate/.

9. Samuel Addy, "A Cost-Benefit Analysis of the New Alabama Immigration Law," Center for Business and Economic Research, Culverhouse College of Commerce and Business Administration, University of Alabama, January 2012, http://cber.cba.ua.edu/New%20AL%20Immigration%20Law%20-%20Costs%20and%20Benefits.pdf; Hammon quoted in Brian Lyman, "Studies, surveys examine immigration law's impact," *The Montgomery Advertiser*, Feb. 1, 2012.

10. See Alan Gomez, "Immigrants return to Alabama," *USA Today*, Feb. 22, 2012, p. 3A; Jay Reeves, "Immigrants trickling back to Ala despite crackdown," The Associated Press, Feb. 19, 2012.

11. The decision in *United States v. Alabama*, 2:11-CV-2746-SLB, U.S.D.C.-N.D.Ala. (Sept. 28, 2011), is available via *The New York Times*: http://graphics8.nytimes.com/packages/pdf/national/112746memopnentered.pdf. For coverage, see Brian Lyman, "Judge allows key part of immigration

law to go into effect," *The Montgomery Advertiser*, Sept. 29, 2011; Brian Lawson, "Judge halts part of immigration law," *The Birmingham News*, Sept. 29, 2011, p. 1A. The Alabama Office of the Attorney General has a chronology of the legal proceedings: www.ago.state.al.us/Page-Immigration-Litigation-Federal.

12. Quoted in Eric Velasco, "Immigration law draws praise, scorn," *The Birmingham News*, June 10, 2011, p. 1A.

13. Steven A. Camarota, "A Need for More Immigrant Workers?," Center for Immigration Studies, June 2011, http://cis.org/no-need-for-more-immigrant-workers-q1-2011.

14. "The Impact of Unauthorized Immigrants on the Budgets of State and Local Governments," Congressional Budget Office, Dec. 6, 2007, p. 3, / www.cbo.gov/sites/default/files/cbofiles/ftp docs/87xx/doc8711/12-6-immigration.pdf.

15. David Gerber, *American Immigration: A Very Short Introduction* (2011).

16. Quoted in Velasco, *op. cit.*

17. Quoted in White, *op. cit.* Hammon's office did not respond to several *CQ Researcher* requests for an interview.

18. "Alabama's Illegal Immigration Law Gets Hollywood's Attention," WAKA/CBS8, Montgomery, Feb. 21, 2012, www.waka.com/home/top-stories/Alabamas-Illegal-Immigration-Law-Gets-Attention-From-Hollywood-139937153.html. The four separate videos by Chris Weitz, collectively titled "Is This Alabama?" are on an eponymous website: http://isthisalabama.org/.

19. See "Delegation of Immigration Authority 287(g) Immigration and Nationality Act," www.ice.gov/287g/ (visited February 2012).

20. See Sandhya Somashekhar and Amy Gardner, "Immigration is flash point in Fla. Primary," *The Washington Post*, Jan. 26, 2012, p. A6.

21. Text available on the White House website: www.whitehouse.gov/the-press-office/2012/01/24/remarks-president-state-union-address.

22. General background drawn from Gerber, *op. cit.*; Otis L. Graham Jr., *Unguarded Gates: A History of America's Immigration Crisis* (2004). Some country-by-country background drawn from Mary C. Waters and Reed Ueda (eds.), *The New Americans: A Guide to Immigration Since 1965* (2007).

23. Roger Daniels, *Guarding the Golden Door: American Immigration Policy and Immigrants Since 1882* (2004), pp. 19-22.

24. Quoted in Graham, *op. cit.*, p. 51.

25. Albert M. Camarillo, "Mexico," in Waters and Ueda, *op. cit.*, p. 506.

26. Figures from *INS Statistical Yearbook*, 1978, cited in Daniels, *op. cit.*, p 138.

27. Polls cited in Daniels, *op. cit.*, p. 233.

28. See *Plyler v. Doe*, 452 U.S. 202 (1982).

29. See Graham, *op. cit.*, Chap. 17, and sources cited therein.

30. "Immigration Rewrite Dies in Senate," *CQ Almanac 2007*, pp. 15-9 — 15-11, http://library.cqpress.com/cqalmanac/cqal07-1006-44907-2047763.

31. See Julia Preston, "Immigration Cools as Campaign Issue," *The New York Times*, Oct. 29, 2008, p. A20, www.nytimes.com/2008/10/29/us/politics/29immig.html; Mark Hugo Lopez, "How Hispanics Voted in the 2008 Election," Pew Hispanic Research Center, Nov. 5, 2008, updated Nov. 7, 2008, http://pewresearch.org/pubs/1024/exit-poll-analysis-hispanics.

32. "Immigration Policy Report: 2011 Immigration-Related Laws and Resolutions in the States (Jan. 1-Dec. 7, 2011)," National Conference of State Legislatures, www.ncsl.org/issues-research/immigration/state-immigration-legislation-report-dec-2011.aspx.

33. The decision is *Chamber of Commerce v. Whiting*, 563 U.S. — (2011). For coverage, see Kenneth Jost, *Supreme Court Yearbook 2010-2011*, http://library.cqpress.com/scyb/document.php?id=scyb10-1270-72832-2397001&type=hitlist&num=0.

34. See "ICE Removals, Fiscal Years 2007-2011," in Mark Hugo Lopez, *et al.*, "As Deportations Rise to Record Levels, Most Latinos Oppose Obama's Policy," Pew Hispanic Center, Dec. 28, 2011, p. 33, http://pewresearch.org/pubs/2158/

latinos-hispanics-immigration-policy-deportations-george-bush-barack-obama-administration-democrats-republicans. The report notes that ICE's statistics differ somewhat from those released by DHS, its parent department.

35. "Secretary of Homeland Security Janet Napolitano's 2nd Annual Address on the State of America's Homeland Security: Homeland Security and Economic Security," Jan. 30, 2012, www.dhs.gov/ynews/speeches/napolitano-state-of-america-home-land-security.shtm.

36. "Share of Immigration Cases Ending in Deportation Orders Hits Record Low," *TRAC Reports*, Feb. 7, 2012, http://trac.syr.edu/immigration/reports/272/; "Sharp Decline in ICE Deportation Filings," Feb. 21, 2012, http://trac.syr.edu/immigration/reports/274/. For coverage, see Paloma Esquivel, "Number of deportation cases down by a third," *Los Angeles Times*, Feb. 24, 2012, p. AA2, http://articles.latimes.com/2012/feb/24/local/la-me-deportation-drop-20120224.

37. Text of La Raza statement, www.nclr.org/index.php/about_us/news/news_releases/janet_murgua_president_and_ceo_of_nclr_responds_to_president_obamas_speech_in_el_paso_texas/. For coverage of the president's speech, see Milan Simonich, "In El Paso, President Obama renews national immigration debate, argues humane policy would aid national economy," *El Paso Times*, May 11, 2011.

38. Lopez, *op. cit.*, p. 16.

39. U.S. Immigration and Customs Enforcement: Memorandum, June 17, 2011, www.ice.gov/doclib/secure-communities/pdf/prosecutorial-discretion-memo.pdf. For coverage, see Susan Carroll, "ICE memo urges more discretion in immigration changes," *Houston Chronicle*, June 21, 2011, p. A3.

40. "Sharp Decline," *op. cit.*

41. For background, see Reed Karaim, "America's Border Fence," *CQ Researcher*, Sept. 19, 2008, pp. 745-768.

42. "Obama says the border fence is 'now basically complete,' " PolitiFact, www.politifact.com/truth-o-meter/statements/2011/may/16/barack-obama/obama-says-border-fence-now-basically-complete/.

The original rating of "partly true" was changed to "mostly false" on July 27, 2011.

43. See "Secure Communities," on the ICE website: www.ice.gov/secure_communities/; Julia Preston, "Immigration Crackdown Snares Americans," *The New York Times*, Dec. 14, 2011, p. A20, www.nytimes.com/2011/12/14/us/measures-to-capture-illegal-aliens-nab-citizens.html?pagewanted=all.

44. Coverage of the hearing by contributing writer Don Plummer. For additional coverage, see Brian Lawson, "11th Circuit won't rule on Alabama/Georgia laws until after Supreme Court rules on Arizona," *The Huntsville Times*, March 2, 2012; Jeremy Redmon, "Court to rule later on Georgia, Alabama anti-illegal immigrant laws," *The Atlanta Journal-Constitution*, March 2, 2012.

45. See Jacques Billeaud, "Judge blocks day labor rules in AZ immigration law," The Associated Press, March 1, 2012.

46. Steven A. Camarota, "A Record-Setting Decade of Immigration, 2000-2010," Center for Immigration Studies, October 2011, www.cis.org/articles/2011/record-setting-decade.pdf.

47. Fox News poll, Dec. 5-7, 2011, and CNN/ORC International poll, Nov. 18-20, 2011, cited at www.PollingReport.com/immigration.htm.

48. Quinnipiac University poll, Feb. 14-20, 2011, cited *ibid.*

49. ICE memo, *op. cit.*

50. "Immigration Court Backlog Tool," Transactional Records Access Clearinghouse, http://trac.syr.edu/phptools/immigration/court_backlog/ (visited March 2012).

51. "The Mexican-American Boom: Births Overtake Immigration," Pew Hispanic Center, July 24, 2011, www.pewhispanic.org/files/reports/144.pdf. The report depicts the phenomenon as "especially evident" among Mexican-Americans; it notes that Mexican-Americans are on average younger than other racial or ethnic groups and that Mexican-American women have more children than their counterparts in other groups. For background, see David Masci, "Latinos' Future," *CQ Researcher*, Oct. 17, 2003, pp. 869-892.

# BIBLIOGRAPHY

## Books

**Coates, David, and Peter M. Siavelis (eds.),** *Getting Immigration Right: What Every American Needs to Know*, **Potomac, 2009.**
Essays by 15 contributors representing a range of backgrounds and views examine, among other issues, the economic impact of immigration and proposed reforms to address illegal immigration. Includes notes, two-page list of further readings. Coates holds a professorship in Anglo-American studies at Wake Forest University; Siavelis is an associate professor of political science there.

**Daniels, Roger,** *Guarding the Golden Door: American Immigration Policy and Immigrants Since 1882*, **Hill and Wang, 2004.**
A professor of history emeritus at the University of Cincinnati gives a generally well-balanced account of developments and trends in U.S. immigration policies from the Chinese Exclusion Act of 1882 through the immediate post-9/11 period. Includes detailed notes, 16-page bibliography.

**Gerber, David,** *American Immigration: A Very Short Introduction*, **Oxford University Press, 2011.**
A professor of history at the University of Buffalo gives a compact, generally positive overview of the history of immigration from colonial America to the present. Includes two-page list of further readings.

**Graham, Otis L. Jr.,** *Unguarded Gates: A History of America's Immigration Crisis*, **Rowman & Littlefield, 2004.**
A professor emeritus at the University of California-Santa Barbara provides a critical account of the United States' transition from an open-border policy with relatively small-scale immigration to a system of managed immigration that he views today as overwhelmed by both legal and illegal immigration. Includes notes.

**Reimers, David M.,** *Other Immigrants: The Global Origins of the American People*, **New York University Press, 2005.**
A New York University professor of history emeritus brings together new information and research about the non-European immigration to the United States, emphasizing the emergence of "a new multicultural society"

since 1940. Individual chapters cover Central and South America, East and South Asia, the Middle East, "new black" immigrants and refugees and asylees. Includes extensive notes, six-page list of suggested readings.

**Waters, Mary C., and Reed Ueda (eds.),** *The New Americans: A Guide to Immigration Since 1965*, **Harvard University Press, 2007.**
The book includes essays by more than 50 contributors, some covering broad immigration-related topics and others providing individual portraits of immigrant populations by country or region of origin. Includes detailed notes for each essay, comprehensive listing of immigration and naturalization legislation from 1790 through 2002. Waters is a professor of sociology at Harvard University, Ueda a professor of history at Tufts University.

## Articles

**"Reap What You Sow,"** *This American Life*, **Jan. 27, 2012, www.thisamericanlife.org/radio-archives/episode/456/reap-what-you-sow.**
The segment by reporter Jack Hitt on the popular public radio program found that Alabama's law to encourage undocumented immigrants to self-deport was having unintended consequences.

**Kemper, Bob, "Immigration Reform: Is It Feasible?,"** *Washington Lawyer*, **October 2011, p. 22, www.dcbar.org/for_lawyers/resources/publications/washington_lawyer/october_2011/immigration_reform.cfm.**
The article gives a good overview of recent and current immigration debates, concluding with the prediction that any "permanent resolution" will likely prove to be "elusive."

## Reports and Studies

**"No Way to Live: Alabama's Immigrant Law,"** Human Rights Watch, December 2011, www.hrw.org/reports/2011/12/14/no-way-live-0.
The highly critical report finds that Alabama's law cracking down on illegal immigrants has "severely affected" the state's unlawful aliens and their children, many of them U.S. citizens, as well as "the broader community linked to this population."

**Baxter, Tom, "Alabama's Immigration Disaster: The Harshest Law in the Land Harms the State's Economy**

and Society," Center for American Progress, February 2012, www.americanprogress.org/issues/2012/02/pdf/alabama_immigration_disaster.pdf.
The critical account by journalist Baxter under the auspices of the progressive Center for American Progress finds that Alabama's anti-illegal immigration law has had "particularly harsh" social and economic costs and effects.

Passel, Jeffrey S., and D'Vera Cohn, "Unauthorized Immigrant Population: National and State Trends, 2010," Pew Hispanic Center, Feb. 1, 2011, www.pewhispanic.org/files/reports/133.pdf.
The 32-page report by the Washington-based center provides national and state-by-state estimates of the unauthorized immigrant population and the number of unauthorized immigrants in the workforce.

# For More Information

**American Civil Liberties Union**, Immigrant Rights Project, 125 Broad St., 18th floor, New York, NY 10004; 212-549-2500; www.aclu.org/immigrants-rights. Seeks to expand and enforce civil liberties and civil rights of immigrants.

**American Immigration Council**, 1331 G St., N.W., 2nd floor, Washington, DC 20005; 202-507-7500; www.americanimmigrationcouncil.org. Supports sensible and humane immigration policies.

**America's Voice**, 1050 17th St., N.W., Suite 490, Washington, DC 20036; 202-463-8602; http://americasvoiceonline.org/. Supports "real, comprehensive immigration reform," including reform of immigration enforcement practices.

**Center for Immigration Studies**, 1522 K St., N.W., Suite 820, Washington, DC 20005-1202; 202-466-8185; www.cis.org. An independent, nonpartisan research organization that supports what it calls low-immigration, pro-immigrant policies.

**Define American**, www.defineamerican.com/. Founded by journalist and undocumented immigrant Jose Antonio Vargas, the web-based organization seeks to fix what it calls a "broken" immigration system.

**Federation for American Immigration Reform**, 25 Massachusetts Ave., N.W., Suite 330, Washington, DC 20001; 202-328-7004; www.fairus.org. Seeks "significantly lower" immigration levels.

**Migration Policy Institute**, 1400 16th St., N.W., Suite 300, Washington, DC 20036; 202-266-1940; www.migrationpolicy.org. A nonpartisan, nonprofit think tank dedicated to analysis of the movement of people worldwide.

**National Council of La Raza**, 1126 16th St., N.W., Suite 600, Washington, DC 20036-4845; 202-785-1670; www.nclr.org. The country's largest national Hispanic advocacy and civil rights organization.

**National Immigration Forum**, 50 F St., N.W., Suite 300, Washington, DC 20001; 202-347-0040; www.immigrationforum.org. Advocates for the values of immigration and immigrants to the nation.

**Pew Hispanic Center**, 1615 L St., N.W., Suite 700, Washington, DC 20036; 202-419-4300; www.pewhispanic.org/. Seeks to improve understanding of the U.S. Hispanic population and to chronicle Latinos' growing impact on the nation.

7

# Immigration Debate

Alan Greenblatt

A Mexican farmworker harvests broccoli near Yuma, Ariz. With the number of illegal immigrants in the U.S. now over 12 million — including at least half of the nation's 1.6 million farmworkers — tougher enforcement has become a dominant theme in the 2008 presidential campaign. Meanwhile, with Congress unable to act, states and localities have passed hundreds of bills cracking down on employers and illegal immigrants seeking public benefits.

From *CQ Researcher*, February 1, 2008. (updated December 10, 2010).

John McCain, the senior senator from Arizona and the leading Republican candidate for president, has been hurt politically by the immigration issue.

McCain would allow illegal immigrants to find a way eventually to become citizens. The approach is seen by many Republican politicians and voters (and not a few Democrats) as akin to "amnesty," in effect rewarding those who broke the law to get into this country. Legislation that he helped craft with Sen. Edward M. Kennedy, D-Mass., and the White House went down to defeat in both 2006 and 2007.

McCain rejects the approach taken by House Republicans during a vote in 2005 and favored by several of his rivals in the presidential race — namely, classifying the 12 million illegal immigrants already in this country as felons and seeking to deport them. This wouldn't be realistic, he says, noting not only the economic demands that have brought the foreign-born here in the first place but also the human cost such a widespread crackdown would entail.

On the stump, McCain talks about an 80-year-old woman who has lived illegally in the United States for 70 years and has a son and grandson serving in Iraq. When challenged at Clemson University last November by a student who said he wanted to see all illegal immigrants punished, McCain said, "If you're prepared to send an 80-year-old grandmother who's been here 70 years back to some other country, then frankly you're not quite as compassionate as I am."[1]

As the issue of illegal immigrants reaches the boiling point, however, and as he gains in the polls, even McCain sounds not quite so

## California Has Most Foreign-Born Residents

California's nearly 10 million foreign-born residents represented about one-quarter of the national total in 2006 and more than twice as many as New York.

### Foreign-Born Individuals by State, 2006 *

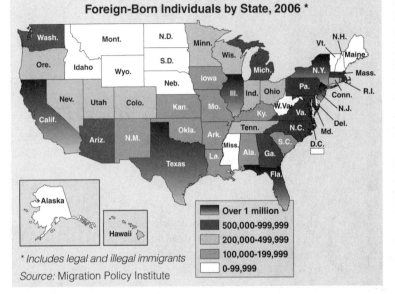

Over 1 million
500,000-999,999
200,000-499,999
100,000-199,999
0-99,999

\* Includes legal and illegal immigrants

Source: Migration Policy Institute

staple of talk radio programs, as well as CNN's "Lou Dobbs Tonight."

In a high-profile speech in August 2007, Newt Gingrich, a former Republican House Speaker, railed about two suspects in a triple murder in New Jersey who turned out to be illegal immigrants. He argued that President Bush should call Congress into special session to address the matter, calling himself "sickened" by Congress being in recess "while young Americans are being massacred by people who shouldn't be here."

Gingrich said Bush should be more serious about "winning the war here at home, which is more violent and more dangerous to Americans than Iraq or Iran."[4]

Concerns about terrorism have also stoked fears about porous borders and unwanted intruders entering the country.

"Whenever I'm out with a [presidential] candidate at a town hall meeting, it's the exception when they do not get a question about immigration — whether it's a Democratic event or a Republican event," says Dan Balz, a veteran political reporter at *The Washington Post*.

With no resolution in sight to the immigration debate in Congress, the number of immigrant-related bills introduced in state legislatures tripled last year, to more than 1,500. Local communities are also crafting their own immigration policies.

In contrast to the type of policies pursued just a few years ago, when states were extending benefits such as in-state tuition to illegal immigrants, the vast majority of current state and local legislation seeks to limit illegal immigrants' access to public services and to crack down on employers who hire them.

"For a long time, the American public has wanted immigration enforcement," says Ira Mehlman, media director of the Federation for American Immigration Reform (FAIR), which lobbies for stricter immigration limits.

"Is there a rhetorical consensus for the need for immigration control? The answer is clearly yes," Mehlman

compassionate as before. In response to political pressures, McCain now shares the point of view of hard-liners who say stronger border security must come before allowing additional work permits or the "path to citizenship" that were envisioned by his legislation.

"You've got to do what's right, OK?" McCain told *The New Yorker* magazine recently. "But, if you want to succeed, you have to adjust to the American people's desires and priorities."[2]

Immigration has become a central concern for a significant share of the American public. Immigrants, both legal and illegal, are now 12.6 percent of the population — more than at any time since the 1920s.

Not only is the number of both legal and illegal immigrants — now a record 37.9 million — climbing rapidly but the foreign-born are dispersing well beyond traditional "gatekeeper" states such as California, New York and Texas, creating social tensions in places with fast-growing immigrant populations such as Georgia, Arkansas and Iowa.[3]

Complaints about illegal immigrants breaking the law or draining public resources have become a daily

says. "When even John McCain is saying border security and enforcement have to come first before the amnesty he really wants, then there is really a consensus."

While most of the Republican presidential candidates are talking tougher on immigration today than two or three years ago, Democrats also are espousing the need for border security and stricter enforcement of current laws. But not everyone is convinced a majority of the public supports the "enforcement-only" approach that treats all illegal immigrants — and the people that hire them — as criminals.

"All through the fall, even with the campaign going on, the polls consistently showed that 60 to 70 percent of the public supports a path to citizenship," says Tamar Jacoby, a senior fellow at the Manhattan Institute who has written in favor of immigrant absorption into U.S. society.

There's a core of only about 20 to 25 percent of Americans who favor wholesale deportation, Jacoby says. "What the candidates are doing is playing on the scare 'em territory."

But over the last couple of years, in the congressional and state-level elections where the immigration issue has featured most prominently, the candidates who sought to portray themselves as the toughest mostly lost.

Some analysts believe that, despite the amount of media attention the issue has attracted, anti-immigrant hard-liners may have overplayed their hand, ignoring the importance of immigrant labor to a shifting U.S. economy.

"To be energized we need new workers, younger workers, who are going to be a part of the whole economy. We don't have them here in the United States," Sen. Kennedy told National Public Radio in 2006.

"We need to have the skills of all of these people," he continued. "The fact is, this country, with each new

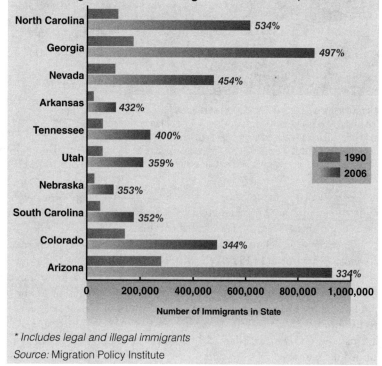

## Fastest-Growing Foreign-Born Populations

Foreign populations at least tripled in 10 states since 1990. In North Carolina foreign-born residents increased by a record 534 percent.

### Percentage Increases in Foreign-Born Individuals, 1990-2006

- North Carolina — 534%
- Georgia — 497%
- Nevada — 454%
- Arkansas — 432%
- Tennessee — 400%
- Utah — 359%
- Nebraska — 353%
- South Carolina — 352%
- Colorado — 344%
- Arizona — 334%

1990
2006

**Number of Immigrants in State**
0    200,000    400,000    600,000    800,000    1,000,000

*\* Includes legal and illegal immigrants*

*Source:* Migration Policy Institute

wave of immigrants, has been energized and advanced, quite frankly, in terms of its economic, social, cultural and political life. I don't think we ought to fear it, we ought to welcome it."[5]

Polls have made it clear that the Republican Party, which is seen as generally tougher on the issue, is losing support among Hispanics — the fastest-growing segment of the population.

"The Bush strategy — enlightened on race, smart on immigration — developed in Texas and Florida with Jeb Bush — has been replaced by the Tancredo-Romney strategy, which is demonizing and scapegoating immigrants," said Simon Rosenberg, a Democratic strategist, "and that is a catastrophic event for the Republican Party."[6] Jeb Bush, the president's brother, served two terms as governor of Florida, while Colorado Rep. Tom

A prospective employer in Las Vegas holds up two fingers indicating how many day laborers he needs. One of the few pieces of immigration legislation still considered to have a chance in Congress this year is the SAVE Act, which would require all employers to use an electronic verification system to check the legal status of all workers.

Tancredo and former Massachusetts Gov. Mitt Romney each sought this year's GOP presidential nomination.*

There is a well-known precedent backing up Rosenberg's argument. In 1994, Pete Wilson, California's Republican governor, pushed hard for Proposition 187, designed to block illegal immigrants from receiving most public services. The proposition passed and Wilson won reelection, but it turned Hispanic voters in California against the GOP — a shift widely believed to have turned the state solidly Democratic.

"While there might be some initial appeal to trying to beat up on immigrants in all different ways, it ultimately isn't getting to the question of what you do with 12 million people," says Angela Kelley, director of the Immigration Policy Center at the American Immigration Law Foundation, which advocates for immigrants' legal rights. "It isn't a problem we can enforce our way out of."

But it's not a problem politicians can afford to ignore. There will be enormous pressure on the next president and Congress to come up with a package that imposes practical limits on the flow of illegal immigrants into the United States. Doing so while balancing the economic interests that immigrant labor supports will remain no less of a challenge, however.

---

*Tancredo dropped out in December, and Romney has been trailing McCain in the primaries.

That's in part because the immigration debate doesn't fall neatly along partisan lines. Pro-GOP business groups, for example, continue to seek a free flow of labor, while unions and other parts of the Democratic coalition fear just that.

"The Democrats tend to like immigrants, but are suspicious of immigration, while the Republicans tend to like immigration but are suspicious of immigrants," says Frank Sharry, executive director of the National Immigration Forum, a pro-immigration lobby group.

"Republicans want to deport 12 million people while starting a guest worker program," he says. "With Democrats, it's the reverse."

During a Republican debate in Florida last December, presidential candidate and former Massachusetts Gov. Mitt Romney took a less draconian position, moving away from his earlier calls to deport all illegals. "Those who have come illegally, in my view, should be given the opportunity to get in line with everybody else," he said. "But there should be no special pathway for those that have come here illegally to jump ahead of the line or to become permanent residents or citizens."[7]

One of the loudest anti-immigration voices belongs to Republican Oklahoma state Rep. Randy Terrill, author of one of the nation's toughest anti-immigration laws, which went into effect in December 2007. "For too long, our nation and our state have looked the other way and ignored a growing illegal immigration crisis," he said. "Oklahoma's working families should not be forced to subsidize illegal immigration. With passage of House bill 1804, we will end that burden on our citizens."[8] Among other things, the law gives state and local law enforcement officials the power to enforce federal immigration law.

As the immigration debate rages on, here are some of the specific issues that policy makers are arguing about:

## Should employers be penalized for hiring illegal immigrants?

For more than 20 years, federal policy has used employers as a checkpoint in determining the legal status of workers. It's against the law for companies to knowingly hire illegal immigrants, but enforcement of this law has been lax, at best.

Partly as a result — but also because of the growing attention paid to illegal immigrants and the opportunities that may attract them to this country — the role of business in enforcing immigration policy has become a major concern.

"I blame 90 percent on employers," says Georgia state Sen. Chip Rogers. "They're the ones that are profiting by breaking the law."

The Immigration and Customs Enforcement agency has pledged to step up its efforts to punish employers who knowingly hire undocumented workers. In response, an Electrolux factory in Springfield, Tenn., fired more than 150 immigrant workers in December after Immigration and Customs Enforcement (ICE) agents arrested a handful of its employees.

Last year, ICE levied $30 million in fines and forfeitures against employers, but arrested fewer than 100 executives or hiring managers, compared with 4,100 unauthorized workers.[9]

One of the few pieces of immigration legislation still considered to have a chance in Congress this year is the SAVE Act (Secure America With Verification Enforcement), which would require all employers to use an electronic verification system to check the legal status of all workers. The House version of the bill boasts more than 130 cosponsors.

Employers are also being heavily targeted by state and local lawmakers. More than 300 employment-related laws addressing illegal immigrants have been recently passed by various levels of government, according to the U.S. Chamber of Commerce.

"There is still this general consensus that although the current employer-sanctions regime hasn't worked, the point of hire is the correct place to ensure that the employee before you is legally here," says Kelley, of the American Immigration Law Foundation.

But for all the efforts to ensure that businesses check the legal status of their workers — and to impose stiffer

## Immigration Is on the Rise

The number of foreign-born people in the United States has nearly quadrupled since 1970, largely because of changes in immigration laws and increasing illegal immigration (top). The increase has pushed the foreign-born percentage of the population to more than 12 percent (bottom).

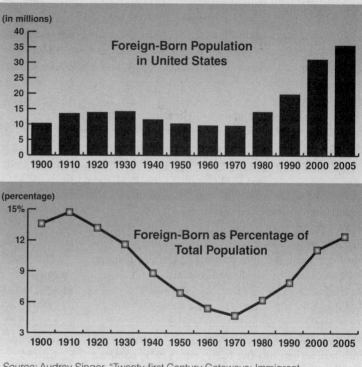

*Number and Percentage of Foreign-Born Individuals in the U.S., 1900-2005*

*Source:* Audrey Singer, "Twenty-first Century Gateways: Immigrant Incorporation in Suburban America," Metropolitan Policy Program, Brookings Institution, April 2007

penalties on those who knowingly hire illegal immigrants — there is still considerable debate about whether such measures will ultimately resolve the problem.

Critics contend there is no easy way for employers to determine legal status. For one thing, documents often are faked. Dan Pilcher, spokesman for the Colorado Association of Commerce and Industry, notes that during a high-profile ICE raid on the Swift meatpacking plant in Greeley in December 2006, many of the arrests were for identity theft, not immigration violations, since so many illegal immigrants were using Social Security numbers that belonged to other people.

"Even when those numbers are run through the system, the computers didn't pick up anything," Pilcher says. "Until that system [of verification] is bulletproof, it doesn't work to try to mandate that businesses be the front line of enforcement."

Concerns about the verification systems in place are shared across the ideological spectrum. "We're now 21 years after the enactment of employer sanctions, and we still haven't come up with a system that allows for instant verification," says Mehlman, at the Federation for American Immigration Reform. "If Visa and MasterCard can verify literally millions of transactions a day, there's no reason we can't have businesses verify the legal status of their employees."

"When you look to employers to be the ones that are going to have damages imposed for hiring someone who is not properly documented, the first thing you have to do is give me a program so I can make sure the person is legal for me to hire," says Bryan R. Tolar, director of marketing, education and environmental programs for the Georgia Agribusiness Council.

So far, though, there is no such system. The Department of Homeland Security's E-Verify system, which grew out of a pilot program, is the new checking point of choice. In fact, federal contractors will soon be required to check the residency status of employees using E-Verify. As of Jan. 1, a new state law requires all employers in Arizona to use the E-Verify system.

But such requirements have drawn lawsuits from both business groups and labor unions, who complain that E-Verify is based on unreliable databases. Tom Clark, executive vice president of the Denver Metro Chamber of Commerce, complains that E-Verify is not accurate and worries therefore that the employer sanctions contained in the Arizona law could lead to serious and unfair consequences.

Under the law, companies found guilty of hiring an illegal worker can lose their business licenses for 10 days; for second offenses they are at risk of forfeiting their licenses entirely. "Do you know the [power] that gives you to take out your competitors?" Clark asks.

Supporters of tougher employer sanctions say the databases are getting better all the time. Mark Krikorian, executive director of the Center for Immigration Studies,

says E-Verify needs to be made into a requirement for all American employers. Once they are handed a working tool, he says, all businesses need to follow the same rules.

"Legal status is a labor standard that needs to be enforced just like other labor standards," he says. "Holding business accountable to basic labor standards is hardly revolutionary."

The National Immigration Forum's Sharry agrees that employers "need to be held to account for who they hire." But he warns that imposing stiff penalties against them at a juncture when verification methods remain in doubt could create greater problems.

"Until you create an effective verification system, employer sanctions will drive the problem further underground and advantage the least scrupulous employers," Sherry says.

## Can guest worker programs be fixed?

The United States has several different programs allowing foreigners to come into the country for a limited time, usually to work for specific "sponsoring" employers, generally in agriculture. But most of these programs have been criticized for being ineffective — both in filling labor demands and ensuring that temporary workers do not become permanent, illegal residents.

The best-known guest worker program, the H-2A visa program for visiting agricultural workers, has been derided by farmers as cumbersome and time-consuming, preventing them from timing their hiring of workers to growing and harvesting seasons. Farmers use H-2A visas only to cover an estimated 2 percent of farmworkers.

Instead, growers turn to the black market for undocumented workers. At least half of the nation's 1.6 million farmworkers — and as many as 70 percent by some estimates — are immigrants lacking documentation.[10]

Still, growers' groups have complained about labor shortages as border security and regulation of employers are tightening. Some growers in the Northwest last fall let cherries and apples rot because of a shortage of workers, and some in North Carolina did not plant cucumbers because of a fear they wouldn't find the workers to harvest them.[11]

Three federal agencies — Homeland Security, State and Labor — have been working in recent months to craft regulations to speed the H-2A visa process. But farmworker advocates worry that the sort of changes the administration has been contemplating could weaken labor protections for workers. Some critics of lax immigration policy complain, meanwhile, that the H-2A changes would allow employers to skirt a process designed to limit the flow of immigrant workers.

Changes adopted by or expected from the administration could weaken housing and wage standards that have traditionally been a part of temporary-worker programs, which date back to World War II, according to Bruce Goldstein, executive director of Farmworker Justice, a group that provides legal support to migrant workers.

Those changes would make a bad situation for farmworkers worse, Goldstein contends. "The government has failed to adopt policies that adequately protect workers from abuses and has failed to enforce the labor protections that are on the books," Goldstein says.

The Federation for American Immigration Reform's Mehlman criticizes the proposed changes for "trying to tip the balance in favor of employers. "There's no evidence that we have a labor shortage in this country," Mehlman says. "You have businesses that have decided they don't want to pay the kind of wages American workers want in order to do these kinds of jobs."

Whether there is an overall labor shortage or not, clearly the numbers don't add up in agriculture. Officials with several immigration-policy groups note that the number of people coming to work in this country outnumber the visas available to new, full-time workers by hundreds of thousands per year.

"The only way we can provide for the labor needs of a growing and very diverse agriculture industry is to make sure there's an ample workforce to do it," says Tolar, at the Georgia Agribusiness Council. "Americans have proven that they're not willing to provide the work that needs doing at a wage agriculture can support."

## Legal Immigration Has Steadily Increased

The number of legal immigrants has risen steadily since the 1960s, from about 320,000 yearly to nearly 1 million. The largest group was from Latin America and the Caribbean. (In addition to legal entrants, more than a half-million immigrants arrive or remain in the U.S. illegally each year.)

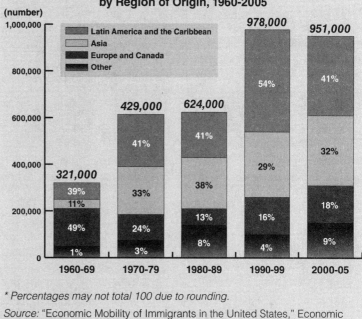

**Average Annual Number of Legal U.S. Immigrants by Region of Origin, 1960-2005**

Legend:
- Latin America and the Caribbean
- Asia
- Europe and Canada
- Other

| Period | Total | Latin America and the Caribbean | Asia | Europe and Canada | Other |
|---|---|---|---|---|---|
| 1960-69 | 321,000 | 39% | 11% | 49% | 1% |
| 1970-79 | 429,000 | 41% | 33% | 24% | 3% |
| 1980-89 | 624,000 | 41% | 38% | 13% | 8% |
| 1990-99 | 978,000 | 54% | 29% | 16% | 4% |
| 2000-05 | 951,000 | 41% | 32% | 18% | 9% |

*\* Percentages may not total 100 due to rounding.*

*Source:* "Economic Mobility of Immigrants in the United States," Economic Mobility Project, Pew Charitable Trusts, 2007

Five years ago, a bipartisan group of congressmen, working with farmworkers, growers and church groups, proposed a piece of legislation known as the AgJobs bill. The attempt at a compromise between the most directly interested players has been a part of the guest worker and immigration debates ever since.

The bill would allow some 800,000 undocumented workers who have lived and worked in the U.S. for several years to register, pay a fine and qualify for green cards (proof of legal residency) by working in agriculture for three to five more years. It would also streamline the H-2A visa application process.

Although it won Senate passage as part of a larger immigration bill in 2006, the current version of AgJobs has not gained traction due to complaints that it would

## More Immigrants Moving to Suburbs

The gap between the number of immigrants who live in inner cities and suburbs widened significantly from 1980-2005. By 2005 more than 15 million foreign-born people were in suburbs, or three times as many in 1980. The number in cities doubled during the same period. Demographers attribute the popularity of the suburbs to their relative lack of crime, lower cost and better schools.

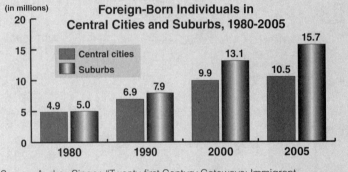

(in millions)

**Foreign-Born Individuals in Central Cities and Suburbs, 1980-2005**

Central cities
Suburbs

| | 1980 | 1990 | 2000 | 2005 |
|---|---|---|---|---|
| Central cities | 4.9 | 6.9 | 9.9 | 10.5 |
| Suburbs | 5.0 | 7.9 | 13.1 | 15.7 |

*Source:* Audrey Singer, "Twenty-first Century Gateways: Immigrant Incorporation in Suburban America," Metropolitan Policy Program, Brookings Institution, April 2007

reward illegal immigrants and employers with what amounts to "get out of jail free" cards.

In November 2007, Sen. Dianne Feinstein, D-Calif., announced that she would not seek to attach AgJobs as an amendment to a larger farm bill, due to strong opposition to legislation seen as helping illegal immigrants. "We know that we can win this," Feinstein said in a statement. But, she conceded, "When we took a clear-eyed assessment of the politics . . . it became clear that our support could not sustain these competing forces."

Feinstein vows to try again this year. But Krikorian, of the Center for Immigration Studies, which favors reduced immigration, counters that guest worker programs in any form are not the right solution. "They still imagine there's a way of admitting low-wage illegals and not have immigration consequences," he says. "It's a fantasy.

"Guest worker programs don't work anyway," he adds. "There's nothing as permanent as a temporary worker."

The American Immigration Law Foundation's Kelley speaks for many on the other side of the debate who argue that it's not enough to conclude that guest worker programs are problematic. Workers from other countries are going to continue to come into this country, she notes.

"We need somehow to replace what is an illegal flow with a legal flow," Kelley says. "We have a guest worker program now — it's called illegal immigration."

### Should illegal immigrants be allowed to attend public colleges and universities?

Miami college students Juan Gomez, 18, and his brother Alex, 20, spent a week in jail in Fort Lauderdale last summer. They were both students at Miami Dade College but faced deportation as illegal immigrants. They had come to the United States from Colombia when they were toddlers.

In handcuffs while riding to the detention center, Juan managed to type out a text message to a friend on his cell phone. The friend set up a Facebook group that in turn led 3,000 people to sign petitions lobbying Congress on the brothers' behalf.

In response, Rep. Lincoln Diaz-Balart, R-Fla., and Sen. Christopher Dodd, D-Conn., introduced legislation to prevent their deportation. As a courtesy to Congress, immigration officials delayed their deportation for two more years.[12]

But the brothers may still face deportation, because Congress failed to pass the DREAM (Development, Relief and Education for Alien Minors) Act. The bill would protect students from deportation and allow young adults (up to age 30) to qualify for permanent legal status if they completed high school and at least two years of college or military service.

On Oct. 24, 2007, the Senate voted 52-48 to end debate and move to a vote on final passage — eight votes short of the 60 needed under Senate rules to end a filibuster. Opponents of the measure claimed it was an unfair plan to grant amnesty to illegal immigrants.

The debate over illegal immigration has regularly and heatedly intersected with questions about education for illegal immigrants: Do young people deserve a break even if their parents skirted the law in bringing them to this country? Should illegal immigrants be barred from publicly supported colleges?

The courts have made it clear that states must provide elementary and secondary educations to all comers, including illegal immigrants. But higher education is another matter entirely.

Ten states have passed legislation in recent years granting in-state tuition to children of illegal immigrants. Most passed their laws during the early years of this decade, before immigration had become such a heated political topic.

Similar proposals in other states have died recently, with critics charging that it would be wrong to reward people who are in the country illegally with one of American society's dearest prizes.

"It is totally unfair if you're going to grant in-state tuition to illegal aliens in Georgia and charge out-of-state tuition to someone from Pennsylvania," says Phil Kent, national spokesman for Americans for Immigration Control.

Katherine "Kay" Albiani, president of the California Community Colleges board, stepped down last month along with two other board members in response to criticism from Republican legislators. The board had voted unanimously last year to support legislation that would have allowed illegal immigrants to qualify for student financial aid and community-college fee waivers.

"We have the best benefit package of any state for illegal immigrants, so they come here," complained California Senate GOP leader Dick Ackerman.[13]

Some argue that illegal immigrants should be barred not only from receiving tuition breaks but also from attending public colleges and universities altogether. Public institutions of higher education, after all, are subsidized by taxpayers, and therefore all students — including illegal immigrants — receive an indirect form of aid from state or local governments.

"Every college student is subsidized to the tune of thousands of dollars a year," says Krikorian, of the Center for Immigration Studies. "They are taking slots and huge amounts of public subsidies that would otherwise go to Americans or legal immigrants."

"Our view is that they shouldn't be there in the first place, and they certainly shouldn't be subsidized by taxpayers," says Mehlman of FAIR. "The typical illegal immigrant isn't coming to the U.S. for higher education.

But once you're here, if the state says we'll subsidize your college education, that's a pretty good incentive to stay here."

Others argue that banning students because their parents chose to break the law would be a mistake. "We are a better country than to punish children for what their parents did," former Arkansas Gov. Mike Huckabee said during the Nov. 28 CNN/YouTube GOP presidential debate. Huckabee says he opposes the congressional DREAM Act, but his opponents in the primary campaign have pointed out his former support as governor for in-state tuition for longtime illegal residents.

Beyond the question of whether it's fair to punish students for decisions their parents made, some argue it would be a mistake to deprive illegal immigrants of educational opportunities. A college education may be an extra inducement for them to stay in this country, but the vast majority are likely to remain in this country anyway.

"If these are people who are going to live here for the rest of their lives, we want them to be as educated as possible," says the Manhattan Institute's Jacoby.

The American Immigration Law Foundation's Kelley agrees. She describes the DREAM Act as a reasonable compromise, saying it would protect students but wouldn't give illegal immigrants access to scholarships or grants. She argues that states that do offer in-state tuition rates to illegal immigrant students have not seen "a huge influx" of them.

"Saying to students who have been raised here and by all accounts are American and are graduating in high numbers and are doing well — 'You can't advance and go any further' — doesn't make sense," Kelley says. "It would be helpful to our economy to have these kids get college degrees."

## BACKGROUND

### Earlier Waves

The United States was created as a nation of immigrants who left Europe for political, religious and economic reasons. After independence, the new nation maintained an open-door immigration policy for 100 years. Two great waves of immigrants — in the mid-1800s and the late-19th and early-20th centuries — drove the

After living in Clarion, Iowa, for nine years, undocumented Mexican immigrant Patricia Castillo, right, and her family were deported for entering the country illegally. Townspeople like Doris Holmes and her daughter Kelli threw a fund-raiser to help the Castillos pay their legal bills.

nation's westward expansion and built its cities and industrial base.[14]

But while the inscription on the Statue of Liberty says America accepts the world's "tired . . . poor . . . huddled masses," Americans themselves vacillate between welcoming immigrants and resenting them — even those who arrive legally. For both legal and illegal immigrants, America's actions have been inconsistent and often racist.

In the 19th century, thousands of Chinese laborers were brought here to build the railroads and then were excluded — via the Chinese Exclusion Act of 1882 — in a wave of anti-Chinese hysteria. Other Asian groups were restricted when legislation in 1917 created "barred zones" for Asian immigrants.[15]

The racist undertones of U.S. immigration policy were by no means reserved for Asians. Describing Italian and Irish immigrants as "wretched beings," *The New York Times* on May 15, 1880, editorialized: "There is a limit to our powers of assimilation, and when it is exceeded the country suffers from something very like indigestion."

Nevertheless, from 1880 to 1920, the country admitted more than 23 million immigrants — first from Northern and then from Southern and Eastern Europe. In 1890, Census Bureau Director Francis Walker said the country was being overrun by "less desirable" newcomers from Southern and Eastern Europe, whom he called "beaten men from beaten races."

In the 1920s, public concern about the nation's changing ethnic makeup prompted Congress to establish a national-origins quota system. Laws in 1921, 1924 and 1929 capped overall immigration and limited influxes from certain areas based on the share of the U.S. population with similar ancestry, effectively excluding Asians and Southern and Eastern Europeans, such as Greeks, Poles and Russians.[16]

But the quotas only swelled the ranks of illegal immigrants — particularly Mexicans, who needed only to wade across the Rio Grande River. To stem the flow, the United States in 1924 created the U.S. Border Patrol to guard the 6,000 miles of U.S. land bordering Canada and Mexico.

After World War II, Congress decided to codify the scores of immigration laws that had evolved over the

# CHRONOLOGY

**1920s** *Hard economic times and public concern about the nation's changing ethnic makeup prompt Congress to limit immigration.*

**1921-1929** Congress establishes immigration quota system, excluding Asians and Southern and Eastern Europeans.

**1924** U.S. Border Patrol is created to block illegal immigrants, primarily Mexicans.

**1940s-1950s** *Expansion of U.S. economy during World War II attracts Mexican laborers. U.S. overhauls immigration laws, accepts war survivors and refugees from communist countries.*

**1942** Controversial Bracero guest worker program allows Mexicans to work on American farms.

**1952** Landmark Immigration and Nationality Act codifies existing quota system favoring Northern

Europeans but permitting Mexican farmworkers in Texas.

## 1960s-1970s *Civil Rights Movement spurs U.S. to admit more Asians and Latin Americans.*

**1965** Congress scraps national quotas, gives preference to relatives of immigrants.

**1980s** Rising illegal immigration sparks crackdown.

**1986** Apprehension of a record 1.7 million illegal Mexican immigrants prompts lawmakers to legalize undocumented workers and for the first time impose sanctions on employers.

## 1990s-2000s *Congress again overhauls immigration laws amid national-security concerns.*

**1993** Middle Eastern terrorists bomb World Trade Center; two had green cards.

**1994** California voters pass Proposition 187, blocking illegal immigrants from receiving most public services; three years later it is largely declared unconstitutional.

**1996** Number of illegal immigrants in U.S. reaches 5 million.

**September 11, 2001** Attacks on World Trade Center and Pentagon focus new attention on porous U.S. borders.

**2004** The 9/11 Commission points to "systemic weaknesses" in border-control and immigration systems.

**2005** Congress passes Real ID Act, requiring proof of identity for driver's licenses. . . . President Bush calls for a "temporary worker" program excluding "amnesty" for illegal immigrants. . . . House passes bill to classify illegal immigrants as felons and deport them.

**2006** On April 20, Homeland Security Secretary Michael Chertoff announces a federal crackdown on employers who hire illegal aliens. . . . On May 1, hundreds of thousands of immigrants demonstrate across the country to call for legal status. . . . On Nov. 7, 69 percent of Hispanic voters support Democrats in congressional races, according to exit polls.

**2007** On May 9, churches in coastal cities provide "sanctuaries" for undocumented families. . . . On May 17, President Bush and a bipartisan group of senators announce agreement on a comprehensive bill to strengthen border protection and allow illegal

immigrants eventual access to citizenship. . . . On Aug. 10, the administration calls for more aggressive law enforcement, screening of new employees by federal contractors and firing of workers whose Social Security numbers don't match government databases. . . . On Oct. 24, the Senate fails to end debate on a proposal to protect illegal immigrants who are attending college from deportation. . . . On Dec. 26, Bush signs spending bill calling for 700 miles of "reinforced fencing" along U.S.-Mexico border.

**January 1, 2008** Arizona law holding employers responsible for checking legal status of workers is the most recent of hundreds of punitive, new state immigration laws. . . . On Jan. 22, Michigan stops issuing driver's licenses to illegal immigrants. . . . Implementation of Real ID Act, slated to go into effect in May, is postponed.

**December 15, 2009** — Congressional Hispanic Caucus joins 100 House cosponsors to introduce Comprehensive Immigration Reform for America's Security and Prosperity Act of 2009. It goes nowhere.

## 2010

**April 23** — Arizona enacts tough immigration law, prompting worldwide protests and boycotts of state economy.

**July 6** — U.S. Attorney General Eric Holder files suit challenging Arizona law.

**July 27** — U.S. District Judge Susan Bolton blocks portions of Arizona's law.

**August 24** — Sen. John McCain, R-Ariz., wins primary after moving to the right on immigration enforcement.

**August 26** — Arizona Gov. Jan Brewer appeals district court's rejection of parts of immigration crackdown law. Judges hear appeal on Nov. 1 and give indications of a possible reinstatement.

**November 2** — Republicans win House in a landslide, gaining 63 seats. Anti-immigrant Tea Party candidates make huge gains.

**December 8** — House of Representatives passes DREAM Act favoring citizenship for young immigrants. Senate tables vote amid doubts over passage.

## 2011

**January 5** — Republicans assume control of the House of Representatives.

# States Racing to Pass Restrictive Immigration Laws

*Arizona, Georgia and Oklahoma seek to outdo Colorado.*

Andrew Romanoff, the speaker of the Colorado House, offers a simple explanation for why his state enacted a sweeping immigration law in 2006.

"The immigration system is, by all accounts, broken," he says, "and the federal government has shown very little appetite for either enforcing the law or reforming the law."

In the absence of federal action on immigration, in 2007 every state in the nation considered legislation to address the issue, according to the National Conference of State Legislatures (NCSL). It released a study in November showing that states considered "no fewer than 1,562 pieces of legislation related to immigrants and immigration," with 244 passed into law in 46 states. [1] Both the number of bills and the number of new laws were three times higher than the totals in 2006.

When Colorado's law was enacted in 2006, it was considered perhaps the toughest in the country. It requires anyone older than 18 who is seeking state benefits to show identification proving legal status and requires employers to verify the legal status of workers. But it provides exemptions for certain types of medical care and was designed to hold harmless the children of illegal immigrants.

Colorado's approach has since been superseded by states such as Arizona, Georgia and Oklahoma, which have taken an even harder line. In fact, if there's one clear trend in state and local legislation, it's toward a stricter approach.

In Hazelton, Pa., a controversial set of laws has been held up by the courts. The ordinances would require businesses to turn employee information over to the city, which would then verify documents with the federal government. Prospective tenants would have to acquire a permit to rent by proving their legal right to be in the country.

"It used to be that state and local activity was all over the map," says Mark Krikorian, executive director of the Center for immigration Studies, which advocates reduced immigration. "Those that are loosening the rules now are the exception."

Georgia's law touches on every facet of state policy that relates to illegal immigrants. Under its provisions, state and local government agencies have to verify the legal residency of benefit recipients. Many employers will have to do the same whenever they make a hiring decision. And law enforcement agencies are given authority to crack down on human trafficking and fake documents.

Thousands of immigrants, both legal and illegal, have left Oklahoma following the November enactment of a law (HB 1804) that makes it a felony to knowingly transport illegal immigrants and requires employers to verify the immigration status of workers. It also limits some government benefits to those who can produce proof of citizenship.

---

years. The landmark Immigration and Nationality Act of 1952 retained a basic quota system that favored immigrants from Northern Europe — especially the skilled workers and relatives of U.S. citizens among them. At the same time, it exempted immigrants from the Western Hemisphere from the quota system — except for the black residents of European colonies in the Caribbean.

## Mass Deportation

The 1952 law also attempted to address — in the era's racist terms — the newly acknowledged reality of Mexican

workers who crossed the border illegally. Border Patrol agents were given more power to search for illegal immigrants and a bigger territory in which to operate.

"Before 1944, the illegal traffic on the Mexican border . . . was never overwhelming," the President's Commission on Migratory Labor noted in 1951, but in the past seven years, "the wetback traffic has reached entirely new levels. . . . [I]t is virtually an invasion."[17]

In a desperate attempt to reverse the tide, the Border Patrol in 1954 launched "Operation Wetback," transferring nearly 500 Immigration and Naturalization

Employers in numerous sectors, including hotels, restaurants and agriculture, have complained about labor shortages. But Republican state Rep. Randy Terrill, who wrote the law, says it will save the state money due to the abolition of public subsidies for illegal immigrants. "There's significant evidence that HB 1804 is achieving its intended purpose," he said.[2]

States just a few years ago were debating the expansion of benefits for illegal immigrants, such as in-state tuition rates for college. But now politicians in most locales who appear to be aiding illegal immigrants in any way are widely castigated.

New York Gov. Eliot Spitzer, a Democrat, proposed in fall 2007 that illegal immigrants should be eligible for driver's licenses, arguing that would make them more likely to buy insurance. But the idea touched off a political firestorm not only in his state but also within the Democratic presidential campaign and he quickly backed down.

Early this year, Maryland Democratic Gov. Martin O'Malley called for his state to stop issuing driver's licenses to undocumented immigrants. (It's one of seven that currently do so.) "When you've got a New York governor getting clubbed over the head for trying to institute what Maryland has . . . you realize we are out of sync with the rest of the nation," said state House Republican leader Anthony J. O'Connell.[3]

A demonstrator in Tucson supports Proposition 200 on Dec. 22, 2004. The voter-approved Arizona law denies some public benefits to illegal immigrants.

Legislatures in at least a dozen states are already considering bills modeled on the get-tough approaches taken elsewhere. Legislators in states neighboring Oklahoma, for instance, say that they feel pressure to introduce restrictive legislation, particularly from constituents in areas where immigrants who had lived in Oklahoma have relocated.

The fact that there's a sort of legislative arms race going on, with states trying to outdo each other on the immigration issue, has many people worried. A patchwork approach, with tough laws in scattered places driving some immigrants toward more lenient jurisdictions, is clearly not the way to resolve a national or even international issue such as immigration.

"Obviously, 50 different state immigration policies is ultimately unworkable," says Romanoff. "All of us much prefer a federal solution.

"The question is, how long should we wait? In Colorado we decided we could wait no longer."

[1] "2007 Enacted State Legislation Related to Immigrants and Immigration," National Conference of State Legislatures, Nov. 29, 2007, www.ncsl.org/print/ immig/2007Immigrationfinal.pdf.

[2] Emily Bazar, "Strict Immigration Law Rattles Okla. Businesses," *USA Today*, Jan. 10, 2008, p. 1A.

[3] Lisa Rein, "Immigrant Driver ID Rejected by O'Malley," *The Washington Post*, Jan. 16, 2008, p. B1.

Service (INS) officers from the Canadian perimeter and U.S. cities to join the 250 agents policing the U.S.-Mexican border and adjacent factories and farms. More than 1 million undocumented Mexican migrants were deported.

Although the action enjoyed popular support and bolstered the prestige — and budget — of the INS, it exposed an inherent contradiction in U.S. immigration policy. The 1952 law contained a gaping loophole — the Texas Proviso — a blatant concession to Texas agricultural interests that relied on cheap labor from Mexico.

"The Texas Proviso said companies or farms could knowingly hire illegal immigrants, but they couldn't harbor them," said Lawrence Fuchs, former executive director of the U.S. Select Commission on Immigration and Refugee Policy. "It was a duplicitous policy. We never really intended to prevent illegals from coming."

## Immigration Reform

The foundation of today's immigration system dates back to 1965, when Congress overhauled the immigration rules, scrapping national-origin quotas in favor of

# Are Voters Ignoring Immigration?

*Iraq War, other issues, may resonate more.*

Immigration has emerged as a pervasive political issue, a part of seemingly every state and local campaign and presidential debate. "No issue has dominated the Republican presidential nomination fight the way illegal immigration has," The Washington Post reported in January.[1]

A poll conducted by the Post and ABC News in December found that more Republican voters in Iowa picked immigration as the first or second most important issue to them — 30 percent — than any other issue. Only 6 percent of Iowa Democrats rated the issue so highly.[2]

Yet illegal immigration has also emerged as a key concern in the Democratic contest. After Sen. Hillary Rodham Clinton, D-N.Y., gave conflicting answers during an October debate about her opinion of Democratic New York Gov. Eliot Spitzer's abortive plan to issue driver's licenses to illegal immigrants, her opponents attacked her. That moment has been widely characterized as opening up the first crack in the façade of her "inevitability" as the Democratic nominee.

"This is a real wedge issue that Democrats need to get right," wrote Stan Greenberg and James Carville, two prominent Democratic Party strategists.[3]

Despite the attention that the issue gets from both candidates and the media, however, there's as yet scant evidence that illegal immigration resonates as strongly with voters as other issues such as the economy, health care or the war in Iraq. "The bottom line is, to most people it's not a pocketbook issue," says Arizona pollster Jim Haynes, "and the pocketbook tends to be seminal in determining how somebody's going to end up voting."

In 2006, several House incumbents and candidates who made tough stances against illegal immigration the centerpiece of their campaigns went down to defeat, including Reps. J.D. Hayworth, R-Ariz., and Jim Ryun, R-Kan.

The track record for gubernatorial candidates who focused their campaigns on immigration was no better that year. Len Munsil in Arizona, Ernest Istook in Oklahoma and Jim Barnett in Kansas all ran against Democratic incumbents and tried to take advantage of their opponents' seeming vulnerability on the immigration issue. None won more than 41 percent of the vote.

Rep. Tom Tancredo, R-Colo., based his presidential campaign on his strong support for tougher immigration measures, but never broke out of the low single digits in polls before dropping out of the race in December.

It was also difficult for candidates to make immigration decisive at the ballot box during the off-year elections of 2007. Even in contests where the issue played a prominent role, it didn't have the influence many observers had predicted. In local contests in New York, for example, Democrats did not pay the predicted price for Spitzer's idea of issuing driver's licenses to illegal immigrants. Instead, they fared better.

In Virginia, Republicans made tough talk on immigration central to their plans for holding on to their threatened majority in the state Senate this past November. They ended up losing control of that body after a decade in power. Local Virginia elections told much the same story.

In Loudoun County, where arguments about illegal newcomers have been intense for several years, Sheriff Stephen Simpson lost a primary bid for renomination but came back to win as an independent against an opponent who had accused him of being soft on immigration. "I think it was hyped up quite a bit in the election, not

immigration limits for major regions of the world and giving preference to immigrants with close relatives living in the United States. By giving priority to family reunification as a basis for admission, the amendments repaired "a deep and painful flaw in the fabric of American justice," President Lyndon B. Johnson declared at the time.

However, the law also dramatically changed the immigration landscape. Most newcomers now hailed from the developing world — about half from Latin America. While nearly 70 percent of immigrants had come from Europe or Canada in the 1950s, by the 1980s that figure had dropped to about 14 percent. Meanwhile, the percentage coming from Asia, Central America and the

just in my race but in the area," Simpson says.

In numerous other local contests in Virginia, the injection of immigration as a central concern not only failed to change the outcome but barely shifted the winner's share of the vote from previous elections.

There were some races where opposition to illegal immigration was an effective political tactic. Tom Selders, the mayor of Greeley, Colo., lost after expressing sympathy for illegal immigrants snared in a federal raid on a local meatpacking plant. By showcasing immigration concerns, Republican Jim Ogonowski ran a surprisingly close race in an October special election in a Massachusetts congressional district that has long favored Democrats, although ultimately he lost.

Rep. Tom Tancredo, R-Colo., based his presidential campaign on his strong support for tougher immigration measures but got little traction and dropped out of the race in December 2007.

NBC NewsWire via AP Photo/Paul Drinkwater

"This issue has real implications for the country. It captures all the American people's anger and frustration not only with immigration but with the economy," said Rep. Rahm Emanuel of Illinois, chairman of the House Democratic Caucus and chief strategist for his party's congressional candidates in 2006. "It's self-evident. This is a big problem."[4]

But it has become surprisingly hard to outflank most candidates on this contentious subject. Last November's challenger to Charles Colgan, a Democratic state senator in Virginia, tried to paint him as soft, going so far as to distribute cartoons depicting Colgan helping people over the wall at the border. But Colgan countered by pointing out his votes in opposition to extending various benefits to illegal immigrants. "The first thing this nation must do is seal the border," he says. "We cannot let this influx continue." Colgan won reelection easily.

Why hasn't immigration, which is getting so much attention, proved to be a central concern when voters cast their ballots? For one thing, not everyone agrees on every proposal to make life tougher for illegal immigrants. And the GOP's hard line on immigration threatens to push Hispanic voters over to the Democratic Party.

But illegal immigration may be failing to take off as a voting issue not because of opposition to the hard-line proposals but because something like a consensus in favor of them has already emerged. It's a simple matter for any candidate to communicate a belief that border security should be tightened and that current laws should be more strictly enforced.

The emergence of that kind of consensus suggests that hardliners have in fact won a good portion of their argument. In his statement announcing he was leaving the presidential race, Tancredo said, "Just last week Newsweek declared that 'anti-immigrant zealot' [Tancredo] had already won. 'Now even Dems dance to his no mas salsa tune.' "

---

[1] Jonathan Weisman, "For Republicans, Contest's Hallmark Is Immigration," *The Washington Post*, Jan. 2, 2008, p. A1.

[2] "What Iowans Care About," *The Washington Post*, Jan. 3, 2008, p. A11.

[3] Perry Bacon Jr. and Anne E. Kornblut, "Issue of Illegal Immigration Is Quandary for Democrats," *The Washington Post*, Nov. 2, 2007, p. A2.

[4] Jonathan Weisman, "GOP Finds Hot Button in Illegal Immigration," *The Washington Post*, Oct. 23, 2007, p. A7.

Caribbean jumped from about 30 percent in the 1950s to 75 percent during the '70s.

In 1978, the select commission concluded that illegal immigration was the most pressing problem facing immigration authorities, a perception shared by the general public.[18] The number of border apprehensions peaked in 1986 at 1.7 million, driven in part by a deepening economic crisis in Mexico. Some felt the decade-long increase in illegal immigration was particularly unfair to the tens of thousands of legal petitioners waiting for years to obtain entry visas.

"The simple truth is that we've lost control of our own borders," declared President Ronald Reagan, "and no nation can do that and survive."[19]

In the mid-1980s, a movement emerged to fix the illegal-immigration problem. Interestingly, the debate on Capitol Hill was marked by bipartisan alliances described by Sen. Alan K. Simpson, R-Wyo., as "the goofiest ideological-bedfellow activity I've ever seen."[20] Conservative, anti-immigration think tanks teamed up with liberal labor unions and environmentalists favoring tighter restrictions on immigration. Pro-growth and business groups joined forces with longtime adversaries in the Hispanic and civil rights communities to oppose the legislation.

After several false starts, Congress passed the Immigration Reform and Control Act (IRCA) in October 1986 — the most sweeping revision of U.S. immigration policy in more than two decades. Using a carrot-and-stick approach, IRCA granted a general amnesty to all undocumented aliens who were in the United States before 1982 and imposed monetary sanctions — or even prison — against employers who knowingly hired undocumented workers for the first time.

## Changes in 1996

In the 1990s nearly 10 million newcomers — the largest influx ever — arrived on U.S. shores, with most still coming from Latin America and Asia.

Bill Clinton realized early in his presidency that the so-called amnesty program enacted in 1986 had not solved the illegal-immigration problem. And in the Border States, concern was growing that undocumented immigrants were costing U.S. taxpayers too much in social, health and educational services. On Nov. 8, 1994, California voters approved Proposition 187, denying illegal immigrants public education or non-essential public-health services. Immigrants'-rights organizations immediately challenged the law, which a court later ruled was mostly unconstitutional. But the proposition's passage had alerted politicians to the intensity of anti-illegal immigrant sentiment.[21]

House Republicans immediately included a proposal to bar welfare benefits for legal immigrants in their "Contract with America," and in 1995, after the GOP had won control of the House, Congress took another stab at reforming the rules for both legal and illegal immigration. But business groups blocked efforts to reduce legal immigration, so the new law primarily focused on curbing illegal immigration.

The final legislation, which cleared Congress on Sept. 30, 1996, nearly doubled the size of the Border Patrol and provided 600 new INS investigators. It appropriated $12 million for new border-control devices, including motion sensors, set tougher standards for applying for political asylum and made it easier to expel foreigners with fake documents or none at all.[22] The law also severely limited — and in many cases completely eliminated — non-citizens' ability to challenge INS decisions in court.[23]

But the new law did not force authorities to crack down on businesses that employed illegal immigrants, even though there was wide agreement that such a crackdown was vital. As the Commission on Immigration Reform had said in 1994, the centerpiece of any effort to stop illegal entrants should be to "turn off the jobs magnet that attracts them."

By 1999, however, amid an economic boom and low unemployment, the INS had stopped raiding work sites to round up illegal immigrant workers and was focusing on foreign criminals, immigrant-smugglers and document fraud. As for cracking down on employers, an agency district director told *The Washington Post*, "We're out of that business." The idea that employers could be persuaded not to hire illegal workers "is a fairy tale."[24]

Legal immigration, however, has been diminished by the government response to the terrorist attacks of Sept. 11, 2001. In fiscal 2002-2003, the number of people granted legal permanent residence (green cards) fell by 34 percent; 28,000 people were granted political asylum, 59 percent fewer than were granted asylum in fiscal 2000-2001.[25] But the growth of illegal immigration under way before 9/11 continued, with 57 percent of the illegal immigrants coming from Mexico.[26]

Due to the family-reunification provision in immigration law, Mexico is also the leading country of origin for legal immigrants — with 116,000 of the 705,827 legal immigrants in fiscal 2002-2003 coming from Mexico.[27] No Middle Eastern or predominantly Muslim countries have high numbers of legal immigrants, although Pakistan was 13th among the top 15 countries of origin for legal immigrants in 1998.[28]

## Public Opinion

The combination of concerns about terrorism and the growing number of illegal immigrants — and their movement into parts of the country unused to dealing with foreign newcomers — made illegal immigration a top-tier issue.

In 2005, Congress passed the Real ID Act, which grew out of the 9/11 Commission investigations into how Arab terrorists burrowed into American society to carry out the Sept. 11, 2001. Of the 19 hijackers, 13 had obtained legitimate driver's licenses, said Rep. F. James Sensenbrenner Jr., R-Wis., author of the legislation. The commission called for national standards for the basic American identification documents: birth certificates, Social Security cards and driver's licenses. In states that adopt the strict requirements of the law — which begins to go into effect in May 2008 — license applicants will have to present ironclad proof of identity, which will be checked against federal and state databases.[29]

After the House in 2005 passed a punitive bill that would have classified illegal immigrants as felons, demonstrations in cities across the country drew hundreds of thousands of marchers during the spring of 2006. On May 1, hundreds of thousands more participated in what some billed as "the Great American Boycott of 2006." The idea was for immigrants, legal and illegal, to demonstrate their economic contribution to the country by staying away from their jobs on May Day.

In terms of numbers alone, the demonstrations of April and May were impressive. But they may also have spurred a backlash among some sectors of the public. "The size and magnitude of the demonstrations had some kind of backfire effect," John McLaughlin, a Republican pollster, told reporters after the first round of marches. "The Republicans that are tough on immigration are doing well right now."[30]

That turned out not to be the case come election-time, however. Some prominent critics of current immigration policy, including Republican Reps. Jim Ryun of Kansas and J.D. Hayworth of Arizona, went down to defeat in November 2006. Republicans in general paid a clear price among Hispanics for their tough stand. Exit polling in 2006 suggested that 30 percent of Hispanics voted for Republicans in congressional races that year, while Democrats garnered 69 percent. President Bush had taken 40 percent of the Hispanic vote in his reelection race two years earlier.[31] "I don't think we did ourselves any favors when we engaged the public in a major topic and didn't

A pro-immigrant rally in Atlanta draws a crowd on May 1, 2006. The nation's rapidly rising foreign-born population is dispersing well beyond "gatekeeper" states such as California and Texas to non-traditional destinations like Georgia, Arkansas and Iowa.

AP Photo/John Bazemore, file

pass the legislation to deal with it," said Sen. Sam Brownback, R-Kan., who dropped out of the GOP presidential primary in October 2007.[32]

Perhaps partly in response, Republicans just after the 2006 elections selected as their new national chairman Florida Sen. Mel Martinez, a prominent Cuban-American who had served in the Bush Cabinet. The Federation for American Immigration Reform's Mehlman, then the outgoing party chairman, told reporters that he was concerned about where the party stood with Hispanics. "Hispanics are not single-issue voters, but GOP officials said the tone of the immigration debate hurt the party's

# Would tighter border security curb illegal immigration?

## YES
**Mark Krikorian**
*Executive Director, Center for Immigration Studies*

Written for *CQ Researcher*, Jan. 23, 2008

## NO
**Douglas S. Massey**
*Professor of Sociology, Princeton University*

From testimony before House Judiciary Subcommittee on Immigration, April 20, 2007

Border security is one piece of the very large controlling-immigration puzzle. But policing borders, including the use of physical barriers where necessary, has been integral to the preservation of national sovereignty for centuries. In our country, some two-thirds of the illegal population has snuck across the border with Mexico; the rest entered legally — as tourists, students, etc. — and never left.

As part of the development of a modern, national immigration system, Congress in 1924 created the U.S. Border Patrol. As illegal immigration grew to massive proportions in the late 1970s, the Border Patrol's work became something of a charade, with a handful of officers returning whatever Mexican border-jumpers they could nab and then watching them immediately turn around and try again.

The first step in closing that revolving door came in 1993 and 1994, when new strategies were implemented in San Diego and El Paso, where most illegal immigration occurred, to deter crossings altogether rather than simply chase after people through streets and alleys after they'd already crossed.

Over the past decade-and-a-half, the enforcement infrastructure at the border has grown immensely, but it is still laughably inadequate. Although the number of agents at the Southern border has tripled, to some 12,000, that still represents an average of no more than two agents per mile per shift.

Expanded fencing has also been part of this build-up. In the past, when the region on both sides of our Southern border was essentially empty, the limited fencing in place was intended simply to keep cattle from wandering off. Now, with huge metropolises on the Mexican side, serious fencing is being built — first in San Diego, where illegal crossings have plummeted as a result, and now along more than 800 additional miles of the border, though this is still a work in progress. In addition to these physical barriers, we have had for years additional security measures (deceptively labeled "virtual fencing"), such as motion sensors, stadium lighting and remote-controlled cameras.

But while border enforcement is a necessary element of immigration control, it is not sufficient. There are three layers of immigration security — our visa-issuing consulates abroad, the border (including legal entry points) and the interior of the country. Improvements at the border are essential, and many are already under way. The weakest link today is the interior, where efforts to deny illegal immigrants jobs, driver's licenses, bank accounts, etc., are being fought at every turn by the business and ethnic lobbyists who benefit from open borders.

As envisioned under [the North American Free Trade Agreement], the economies of the U.S. and Mexico are integrating, and the rising cross-border movement of goods and services has been accompanied by migration of all sorts of people. Since 1986, the number of exchange visitors from Mexico has tripled, the number of business visitors has quadrupled and the number of intra-company transferees has grown 5.5 times.

Within this rapidly integrating economy, however, U.S. policy makers have somehow sought to prevent the cross-border movement of workers. We have adopted an increasingly restrictive set of immigration and border-enforcement policies. First, the Immigration Reform and Control Act of 1986 granted $400 million to expand the size of the Border Patrol. Then the 1990 Immigration Act authorized hiring another 1,000 officers. In 1993, these new personnel were deployed as part of an all-out effort to stop unauthorized border crossing in El Paso, a strategy that was extended to San Diego in 1994. Finally, the 1996 Illegal Immigration Reform and Immigrant Responsibility Act provided funds to hire an additional 1,000 Border Patrol officers per year through 2001.

In essence, the U.S. militarized the border with its closest neighbor, a nation to which it was committed by treaty to an ongoing process of economic integration. Rather than slowing the flow of immigrants into the U.S., however, this policy yielded an array of unintended and very negative consequences.

The most immediate effect was to transform the geography of border crossing. Whereas undocumented border crossing during the 1980s focused on San Diego and El Paso, the selective hardening of these sectors after 1993 diverted the flows to new and remote crossings. Undocumented Mexican migration was thus nationalized. The migrants got wise and simply went around built-up sectors. As a result, the probability of apprehension plummeted to record low levels. American taxpayers were spending billions more to catch fewer migrants.

And, rather than returning home possibly to face the gauntlet at the border again, Mexicans without documents remained longer in the U.S. The ultimate effect of restrictive border policies was to double the net rate of undocumented population growth, making Hispanics the nation's largest minority years before Census Bureau demographers had projected.

At this point, pouring more money into border enforcement will not help the situation, and in my opinion constitutes a waste of taxpayer money. We must realize that the solution to the current crisis does not lie in further militarizing the border with a friendly trading nation that poses no conceivable threat.

standing with the fastest-growing minority group," *The Washington Post* reported.[33]

## CURRENT SITUATION

### Difficult Fix

Currently, immigration is the subject of countless legislative proposals at all levels of government. Congress under the new Democratic majority ushered in with the 2006 elections has generally considered more lenient legislation, but any proposal that seems to offer any sort of aid to illegal immigrants has failed to gain traction. In states and in many localities, meanwhile, hundreds of punitive bills have passed into law.

Amid much fanfare, President Bush and a bipartisan group of 10 senators announced an agreement on May 17, 2007, on a comprehensive compromise plan to tighten border security and address the fate of the nation's 12 million illegal immigrants. "The agreement reached today is one that will help enforce our borders," Bush said. "But equally importantly, it will treat people with respect. This is a bill where people who live here in our country will be treated without amnesty, but without animosity."[34]

The 380-page plan was worked out just in time to meet a deadline for the beginning of Senate debate on the issue. "The plan isn't perfect, but only a bipartisan bill will become law," said Sen. Kennedy.[35]

But immigration is the rare issue that cuts across partisan lines. Despite the backing of most Democrats, the Bush administration and conservative Republicans such as Kennedy's negotiating partner, Sen. Jon Kyl, R-Ariz., the package went down to defeat. Supporters were unable to muster the support of 60 senators necessary even to bring it to a vote in the face of determined opposition.

The agreement would have granted temporary legal status to virtually all illegal immigrants, allowing them to apply for residence visas and citizenship through a lengthy process. They would have to wait for eight years before applying for permanent resident status and pay fines of up to $5,000; in addition, heads of households would be forced to leave the country and reenter legally.

But the process could not begin for any illegal aliens — and a new guest worker program would also be put on hold — until after a tough border crackdown had gone into effect. The deal called for the deployment of

President George W. Bush announces the bipartisan compromise immigration deal he struck with Congress on May 17, 2007. The agreement would have granted temporary legal status to virtually all illegal immigrants. Despite the backing of most Democrats and several conservative Republicans, the package was defeated. Bush is flanked by Homeland Security Secretary Michael Chertoff, left, and Commerce Secretary Carlos Gutierrez.

18,000 new Border Patrol agents and extensive new physical barriers, including 200 miles of vehicle barriers, 370 miles of fencing and 70 ground-based camera and radar towers. In addition, funding would be provided for the detention of 27,500 illegal immigrants, and new identification tools would be developed to help screen out illegal job applicants.

Conservative opponents of the package in the Senate — as well as most of the 2008 GOP presidential hopefuls — derided it as an "amnesty" bill, giving an unfair citizenship advantage to people who had come into the country illegally.

But liberals and immigration advocacy groups also questioned the terms of the Senate proposal, particularly a change in visa applications. In contrast to the current system, which stresses family ties, a new, complex, point system would favor skilled, educated workers. About 50 percent of the points would be based on employment criteria, with just 10 percent based on family connections.

Even if the Senate had passed the bill, its prospects in the House would have been dim. Despite the change in partisan control of Congress, there was still less sentiment in the House than in the Senate for any bill that was perceived as giving a break to illegal aliens. "Unless the White House produces 60 or 70 Republican votes in the House, it will be difficult to pass an immigration bill similar to the Senate proposal," Rep. Rahm Emanuel,

D-Ill., chairman of the House Democratic Caucus, said in May 2007.[36]

Those votes would have been tough to get. Some staunch critics of immigration policy were defeated in the 2006 elections, but for the most part they were replaced by newcomers who also took a hard line against illegal immigration. "This proposal would do lasting damage to the country, American workers and the rule of law," said Lamar Smith of Texas, ranking Republican on the House Judiciary Committee, in response to the deal between senators and the White House. "Just because somebody is in the country illegally doesn't mean we have to give them citizenship."[37] The House did not vote at all on comprehensive immigration legislation in 2007.

## Federal Inaction

Not long after the Senate's comprehensive bill failed, the attempt to extend legal status to immigrants attending college also failed. The DREAM Act would have protected students from deportation and allowed young adults (up to age 30) to qualify for permanent legal status if they completed high school and at least two years of college or military service.

On Oct. 24, Senate supporters fell eight votes short of the 60 needed to end debate on the bill and bring it to a final vote. The following month, supporters of legislation to address the issue of temporary guest workers — the AgJobs bill — announced that the political climate had turned against them, and they would drop their efforts at least until 2008.

"Amnesty for illegal immigrants is dead for this Congress," says Krikorian of the Center for Immigration Studies. "When the pro-amnesty side couldn't even pass small measures like the DREAM Act and the AgJobs bill, there's little doubt that legalizing illegal immigrants is dead in the water at least until 2009."

Given the pressure on Congress to do something to address the topic, those lobbying for tougher restrictions remain optimistic that this year could see passage of the Secure America With Verification Enforcement Act. The SAVE Act would require all employers to use an electronic verification system to check the legal status of all workers.

In the absence of successful congressional action thus far, the Bush administration last August unveiled a package designed to break the stalemate. The strategy includes stepped-up work-site raids and arrests of fugitive illegal immigrants. The administration also created a new requirement for federal contractors to use the E-Verify system for screening the legal status of new employees.

In October, a federal judge issued a temporary injunction blocking a part of the Homeland Security package that would have required employers to fire workers whose Social Security numbers do not match information in government databases.

The Immigrations and Customs Enforcement agency in January announced a plan to speed the deportation of foreign-born criminals. Under current law, immigrants convicted of crimes are only deported after serving their sentences. ICE intends to work with states to create parole programs that would allow for the early release of non-violent offenders if they agreed to immediate deportation. The program would place a strain on federal detention centers but provide fiscal relief and bed space to state and local governments housing such prisoners. Last year, ICE sent 276,912 people back to their home countries, including many who were not arrested for crimes but had violated civil immigration statutes.[38]

# OUTLOOK:

## Tough Talk

Immigration will clearly remain an important part of the political conversation in this country. The factors that have made it so prominent — the record number of immigrants, both legal and illegal, and their dispersal into parts of the country that had not seen large influxes of immigrants in living memory — show little sign of abating.

The course that any policy changes will take will depend on who wins the presidency. Attempts at addressing the issue in a comprehensive way in Congress failed, due to concerted opposition to the compromise package brokered between the Bush White House and a bipartisan group of senators. Since that time, more modest bills have not been able to advance.

That means the issue will not be resolved as a policy matter until 2009, at the earliest. Instead, it will remain a major theme of the presidential campaign. Immigration has become, perhaps, the dominant issue among the Republican candidates, as well as one that Democrats have had to address in several particulars.

In a December interview with *The Boston Globe*, Illinois Sen. Barack Obama, one of the Democratic front-runners, predicted that any Republican candidate, save for McCain, would center his race on two things — fear of terrorism and fear of immigration.[39]

But the immigration issue has not broken along strictly partisan lines. Krikorian of the Center for Immigration Studies predicts that even if the election results in a Democratic president and Congress, the broad policy trajectory will be toward further tightening of immigration policy.

"I don't care whether it's a new Democratic or a new Republican president, they're going to have to address it," says Kent, of Americans for Immigration Control. "The new president will have to toughen up the border."

Politicians of all stripes indeed now pay homage to the idea that border security must be tightened and that current laws need more rigorous enforcement. But debate is still hot over questions of how much to penalize illegal immigrants and employers — and whether efforts to do just that may ultimately prove counterproductive.

Mehlman of the Federation for American Immigration Reform says "the forces that have been trying to promote amnesty and lots of guest workers are not going to go away." Mehlman says that even if current campaign rhetoric generally supports the tough approach his organization favors, the dynamic of actually changing policies in 2009 and after may not change that much.

"It wouldn't be the first time a politician said one thing during the campaign and acted differently once in office," he says.

He notes that the business groups that encourage immigration have deep pockets, but he believes that "this is an issue that the American public is making a stand on."

The National Immigration Forum's Sharry counters that the policy debate has been hijacked by heated political rhetoric and that it's become difficult to discuss what would be the best solutions without accusations being hurled if a proposal sounds at all "soft" on illegal immigrants.

Nevertheless, he notes, most people do not support the toughest proposals that would treat illegal immigrants as felons and seek their mass deportation. "I suspect it's going to take one or perhaps two election cycles to figure out who does it help and who does it hurt," Sharry says.

"My prediction is that the Republican embrace of the extreme anti-immigrant groups will be seen in retrospect as an act of slow-motion suicide."

Douglas S. Massey, a Princeton University sociologist, agrees that the politics of this issue may play out poorly over the long term for those proposing a serious crackdown. He notes that there have been many occasions in American history when "beating on immigrants" has been an expedient strategy, but he argues it's never played well successfully as a sustained national issue.

"It's not a long-term strategy for political success, if you look at the future composition of America," Massey says, alluding in particular to the growth in foreign-born populations.

The political debate clearly will have a profound influence on the policy decisions made on immigration in the coming years. But the underlying demographic trends are likely to continue regardless. "With the baby boomers retiring, we will need barely skilled workers more than ever," says Jacoby, of the Manhattan Institute, referring in part to health-care aides.

She argues that growth in immigration is simply an aspect of globalization. Although people are uncomfortable with change and tend to see its downsides first, she believes that people will eventually realize large-scale migration is an inevitable part of the American future.

"We're in a bad time, and our politics are close to broken," she says, "but eventually American pragmatism will come to the surface."

# UPDATE

For illegal immigrants in the United States, 2010 has not been a good year, and it appears likely to end on a particularly sour note. On Dec. 8, the House passed its version of the much-vaunted Development, Relief and Education of Alien Minors (DREAM) Act, which would create a path to citizenship for young undocumented immigrants brought into the United States as children. But Senate Democrats promptly tabled the bill, making its passage this year highly unlikely. Immigrants saw similar lack of support throughout the year.

"People come here to have babies," Sen. Lindsey Graham, R-S.C., declared on Fox News in July 2010 during a summer when immigration controversies swirled through the country. Graham introduced to the national discourse the term "drop and leave," a practice he says is common among illegal immigrants who enter the country and proceed to the nearest emergency room to give birth to their family's "anchor baby," who is automatically a U.S. citizen.[40]

### Constitutional Amendment

Graham joined other Republicans who have been agitating for a constitutional amendment to alter the 14th Amendment to remove "birthright citizenship" for children of immigrants. Many of them know it would be an uphill battle to change a 142-year-old amendment designed primarily to ensure freedom for children of slaves. The Supreme Court has twice rejected similar proposals.[41]

Politically, however, the proposal put wind in the sails of conservatives calling for stepped-up enforcement of immigration laws to seal porous U.S. borders, restore respect for the law and reduce the financial burden they say undocumented workers impose on state and local social programs.

But to immigrants' advocates, the proposal is a xenophobic distraction. "Our nation cannot revert to the shameful 'separate but equal' doctrine that justified segregation in America for over 50 years," said Ali Noorani, executive director of the National Immigration Forum, a

Critics of Arizona's tough immigration law protest at the state capitol in Phoenix in April after Gov. Brewer signed the law. President Obama said it threatened "to undermine basic notions of fairness that we cherish as Americans." The Ninth U.S. Circuit Court of Appeals is weighing a lower court order freezing several of the law's provisions.

*Getty Images/John Moore*

Washington-based group that advocates on behalf of immigrants. "By denying the right to citizenship to children born on American soil, we will not only stifle the potential of success for countless Americans, but we will betray the basic principles of equality envisioned by our Founding Fathers."[42]

About 340,000 of the 4.3 million babies born in the United States in 2008 — about 8 percent of the total — have at least one undocumented immigrant as a parent, according to a study released in August by the Pew Hispanic Center.[43]

The proposal to change the 14th Amendment is opposed by 56 percent of Americans, according to a national poll by the Pew Research Center for People and the Press, while 41 percent favor it.

### Arizona's New Law

Whether or not the anchor-baby issue endures or fades, it encapsulates the national divisions over proposed crackdowns on illegal immigration. These fissures have been on noisy display this year in Arizona, where Republican Gov. Jan Brewer in April signed the nation's toughest immigration enforcement law.

It makes the failure to carry immigration documents a crime and gives police broad powers to detain anyone suspected of being in the country illegally. "We have to trust our law enforcement," said Brewer, responding to demands from Arizonans fearful of being overrun by illegal immigrants committing crimes in their communities while the politically stalemated federal government sits idly by.[44]

"What part of illegal don't you understand?" read countless protest signs carried by Arizonans supporting the crackdown when President Obama pounced on the law, saying it threatened "to undermine basic notions of fairness that we cherish as Americans, as well as the trust between police and our communities that is so crucial to keeping us safe."[45]

The controversy only intensified. Foreign governments, including Mexico, protested, and entertainers and civil rights groups began a boycott of Arizona businesses. U.S. Attorney General Eric Holder filed a lawsuit to block the law, and on July 27 — two days before they would have taken effect — U.S. District Judge Susan Bolton froze several of the law's provisions. In August, Gov. Brewer filed an appeal to the Ninth U.S.

Circuit Court of Appeals.[46] On November 1, the three-judge panel heard arguments and gave indications that it might reinstate — but strike down some components of — the law.[47]

National polls showed a majority of Americans backing the Arizona crackdown, by 55 percent according to a July CNN/Opinion Research poll.

## State Immigration Bills

The Arizona debate, coupled with Congress' failure to take up immigration legislation, prompted an uptick in proposed state immigration bills around the country. As of November 10, bills similar to Arizona's had been introduced in South Carolina, Pennsylvania, Minnesota, Rhode Island, Michigan and Illinois, according to the National Conference of State Legislatures.[48]

The political import of the issue was demonstrated in the August primary election for the Senate seat held by Sen. John McCain, R-Ariz. McCain in 2007 had worked with Democrats and the George W. Bush administration in an unsuccessful attempt at comprehensive immigration reform. In 2010 he moved sharply to the right in his ultimately successful re-election campaign against conservative former U.S. Rep. J.D. Hayworth. McCain abandoned his past support for guest worker programs and stressed the enforcement approach.[49]

What is happening, according to Ira Mehlman, media director of the Federation for American Immigration Reform, which favors strict immigration enforcement, is that "the enforcement of immigration law has become a higher priority for the public, as evidenced by the public support for the Arizona law and opposition to" the lawsuit by Attorney General Holder. "His suit is directed at other states in an attempt to intimidate them" so they won't follow Arizona's path, Mehlman says. "He's saying, 'We don't want immigration law enforced.' "

Noorani of the National Immigration Forum says that what stands out from the polling is that "the country is asking why Congress hasn't fixed the broken immigration system."

Congress, however, has been unable to muster consensus even to take up omnibus immigration reform, and the Obama administration has not offered its own bill. The only recent action of note came on August 12, when the Senate convened in a special session and passed by acclamation a bill just passed by the House providing $600 million for "emergency supplemental appropriations for border security."

## DREAM Act

Proponents had hoped for better luck with the DREAM Act, introduced by Sen. Richard Durbin, D-Ill., and Rep. Howard Berman, D-Calif. Backed by many colleges and universities, it would help children of undocumented immigrants who have attended American public schools go on to higher education and emerge on a path to citizenship. Eligible immigrants would have to prove that they entered the United States prior to age 18 and would be required to complete at least two years of college or military training, among other requisites.

The American Association of Community Colleges said in an April 26 statement: "We call upon Congress to pass the DREAM Act and to further fulfill its responsibility to enact a national immigration policy that is clear, that is fair and that upholds our nation's founding principles as a land of sanctuary and opportunity."

Opponents of the bill, who are organized at the noamericandreamact.org website, call it amnesty for illegal immigrants who will compete with native-born Americans for scarce slots at public universities. Furthermore, critics say, the bill would increase illegal immigration by allowing undocumented individuals to pin their hopes on eventual citizenship for their children, as well as for themselves through sponsorships.

The House passed the measure, 216 to 198, on December 9. Senate Democrats, however, tabled the DREAM Act amid a lack of support, jeopardizing its chances of passage before the lame-duck session ends in early January.[50]

Moreover, Rep. Lamar Smith, R-Texas, the likely chairman of the House Judiciary Committee in the new Congress, has been labeled a hard-liner on immigration policy and a proponent for nationwide laws similar to the one enacted in Arizona.[51] The passage of the DREAM Act, analysts say, would become impossible after the conclusion of the lame-duck.

## Border Enforcement

The administration, meanwhile, has stepped up border enforcement, committing in May to send several hundred Army National Guard troops to Arizona. To help employers comply with the law on hiring, the

Department of Homeland Security has launched a free, voluntary program called E-Verify, an Internet-based system that allows an employer, using information reported on an employee's Employment Eligibility Verification form, to determine the eligibility of that employee to work in the United States. More than 216,000 employers are enrolled in the program, and more than 13 million queries have gone through the system in fiscal 2010, as of July 31.[52]

Meanwhile, the Department of Justice has filed a lawsuit against Arizona's hard-line Maricopa County Sheriff's Office for refusing to provide access to records and facilities in connection to charges that the office violates federal civil rights laws. The lawsuit, which names tough-talking Sheriff Joe Arpaio, alleges discriminatory jailing practices on the basis of national origin. His attorney says the lawsuit is merely an attempt to exact retribution on Arpaio for enforcing the state's controversial immigration law. In a separate suit, the sheriff's office settled for $600,000 with a man who accused an officer of abuse and racial discrimination at a traffic stop in 2009.[53]

More controversially, Homeland Security's Immigration and Customs Enforcement (ICE) in August embarked on a systematic review of pending cases of immigration-law violations and moved to dismiss a backlog of thousands that do not involve immigrants with serious criminal records.[54] An ICE spokesman said the review is part of the agency's national strategy to prioritize the deportations of illegal immigrants who pose a threat to security and public safety. Critics, however, assailed the plan as another sign that the administration is trying to create a backdoor "amnesty" program.

Criticism of the Obama approach is not confined to conservatives. In July, lawyers at the pro-immigration American Immigration Council sued Homeland Security seeking public release of enforcement records for the H-1B visa program, which allows businesses temporarily to hire foreign workers with high-level skills. The concern is over a perceived increase in unannounced workplace visits by federal agents, as well as whether the Obama administration is holding to its announced "open government" initiative, which pledged to make the operations of federal agencies more transparent.

Meanwhile, hopes have faded that Congress, following the November midterm elections, will overcome political fractiousness and take up a bill that addresses key questions, such as what to do about the estimated 11.1 million undocumented immigrants living in the United States.[55] The questions also include how to stanch the continuing influx of foreigners illegally penetrating U.S. borders and how legally to meet the needs of industries such as agriculture, construction and domestic services that depend on immigrant workers.

"All indicators are that Congress' makeup will be different, with less likelihood for amnesty," Mehlman said in August, foreshadowing the Republicans' takeover of the House. "Then the 2012 election starts, and there will likely be some pressure for more enforcement. Amnesty [for those who entered the country illegally] as a precondition [for a deal] is unacceptable," he says.

But Noorani predicts more compromise. "Early in 2011, before the presidential primaries, Republicans will be faced with a decision on whether to sue for peace on immigration," he says. "Only the most delusional political operative will think they can win the White House without significant numbers of Hispanic voters."

## NOTES

1. Quoted in Ryan Lizza, "Return of the Nativist," *The New Yorker*, Dec. 17, 2007, p. 46. For more on immigrant families that face being split up, see Pamela Constable, "Divided by Deportation: Unexpected Orders to Return to Countries Leave Families in Anguish During Holidays," *The Washington Post*, Dec. 24, 2007, p. B1.

2. Quoted in Lizza, *op. cit.*

3. Ellis Cose, "The Rise of a New American Underclass," *Newsweek*, Jan. 7, 2008, p. 74.

4. William Neikirk, "Gingrich Rips Bush on Immigration," *Chicago Tribune*, Aug. 15, 2007, p. 3.

5. Jennifer Ludden, "Q&A: Sen. Kennedy on Immigration, Then & Now," May 9, 2006, NPR.org, www.npr.org/templates/story/story. php?storyId= 5393857.

6. Lizza, *op. cit.*

7. "GOP Hopefuls Debate Immigration on Univision," www.msnbc.msn.com/id/22173520/.

8. David Harper, "Terrill Leads Way on Issue," *Tulsa World*, Oct. 30, 2007, www.Tulsa World.com.

9. Julia Preston, "U.S. to Speed Deportation of Criminals Behind Bars," *The New York Times*, Jan. 15, 2008, p. A12.

10. "Rot in the Fields," *The Washington Post*, Dec. 3, 2007, p. A16.

11. Steven Greenhouse, "U.S. Seeks Rules to Allow Increase in Guest Workers," *The New York Times*, Oct. 10, 2007, p. A16.

12. Kathy Kiely, "Children Caught in the Immigration Crossfire," *USA Today*, Oct. 8, 2007, p. 1A.

13. Patrick McGreevy, "Gov's Party Blocks His College Board Choice," *Los Angeles Times*, Jan. 15, 2008, p. B3.

14. Unless otherwise noted, material in the background section comes from Rodman D. Griffin, "Illegal Immigration," April 24, 1992, pp. 361-384; Kenneth Jost, "Cracking Down on Immigration," Feb. 3, 1995, pp. 97-120; David Masci, "Debate Over Immigration," July 14, 2000, pp. 569-592; and Peter Katel, "Illegal Immigration," May 6, 2005, pp. 393-420, all in *CQ Researcher*.

15. For background, see Richard L. Worsnop, "Asian Americans," *CQ Researcher*, Dec. 13, 1991, pp. 945-968.

16. For background, see "Quota Control and the National-Origin System," Nov. 1, 1926; "The National-Origin Immigration Plan," March 12, 1929; and "Immigration and Deportation," April 18, 1939, all in *Editorial Research Reports*, available from *CQ Researcher Plus Archive*, http://cqpress.com.

17. Quoted in Ellis Cose, *A Nation of Strangers: Prejudice, Politics and the Populating of America* (1992), p. 191.

18. Cited in Michael Fix, ed., *The Paper Curtain: Employer Sanctions' Implementation, Impact, and Reform* (1991), p. 2.

19. Quoted in Tom Morganthau, *et al.*, "Closing the Door," *Newsweek*, June 25, 1984.

20. Quoted in Dick Kirschten, "Come In! Keep Out!" *National Journal*, May 19, 1990, p. 1206.

21. Ann Chih Lin, ed., *Immigration*, CQ Press (2002), pp. 60-61.

22. William Branigin, "Congress Finishes Major Legislation; Immigration; Focus is Borders, Not Benefits," *The Washington Post*, Oct. 1, 1996, p. A1.

23. David Johnston, "Government is Quickly Using Power of New Immigration Law," *The New York Times*, Oct. 22, 1996, p. A20.

24. William Branigin, "INS Shifts 'Interior' Strategy to Target Criminal Aliens," *The Washington Post*, March 15, 1999, p. A3.

25. Deborah Meyers and Jennifer Yau, "US Immigration Statistics in 2003," Migration Policy Institute, Nov. 1, 2004, www.migrationinformation.org/USfocus/display.cfm?id=263; and Homeland Security Department, "2003 Yearbook of Immigration Statistics," http://uscis.gov/graphics/shared/statistics/yearbook/index.htm.

26. Jeffrey S. Passel, "Estimates of the Size and Characteristics of the Undocumented Population," Pew Hispanic Center, March 21, 2005, p. 8.

27. Meyers and Yau, *op. cit.*

28. Lin, *op. cit.*, p. 20.

29. For background, see Peter Katel, "Real ID," *CQ Researcher*, May 4, 2007, pp. 385-408.

30. David D. Kirkpatrick, "Demonstrations on Immigration are Hardening a Divide," *The New York Times*, April 17, 2006, p. 16.

31. Arian Campo-Flores, "A Latino 'Spanking,'" *Newsweek*, Dec. 4, 2006, p. 40.

32. Rick Montgomery and Scott Cannon, "Party Shift Won't End Immigration Debate," *The Washington Post*, Dec. 17, 2006, p. A11.

33. Jim VandeHei, "Florida Senator Will Be a Top RNC Officer," *The Washington Post*, Nov. 14, 2006, p. A4.

34. Karoun Demirjian, "Bipartisan Immigration Deal Reached," *Chicago Tribune*, May 18, 2007, p. 1.

35. *Ibid.*

36. Robert Pear and Jim Rutenberg, "Senators in Bipartisan Deal on Broad Immigration Bill," *The New York Times*, May 18, 2007, p. A1.

37. Demirjian, *op. cit.*

38. Julia Preston, "U.S. to Speed Deportation of Criminals Behind Bars," *The New York Times*, Jan. 15, 2008, p. A12.

39. Foon Rhee, "Obama Says He Wants a Mandate for Change," www.boston.com/news/politics/politicalintelligence/2007/12/obama_says_he_w.html.

40. Elise Foley, "Graham Wants To Deny American-Born Babies Citizenship," *Washington Independent*, July 29, 2010.

41. For a legal and historical discussion on birthright citizenship, see www.immigrationpolicy.org/perspectives/made-america-myths-facts-about-birthright-citizenship.

42. "Immigration Detour: GOP Attacks American Children Instead of Fixing Broken Immigration System," press release, National Immigration Forum, Aug. 11, 2010.

43 "Unauthorized Immigrants and Their U.S.-Born Children," Pew Hispanic Center, Aug. 11, 2010, http://pewhispanic.org/reports/report.php? Report ID=125.

44. Randal C. Archibold, "Arizona Enacts Stringent Law on Immigration," *The New York Times*, April 23, 2010.

45. *Ibid.*

46. Warren Richey, "Why Judge Susan Bolton blocked key parts of Arizona's SB 1070," *The Christian Science Monitor*, July 28, 2010.

47. Bob Egelko, "Court Signals Backing for Arizona Immigration Law," *The San Francisco Chronicle*, Nov. 2, 2010, www.sfgate.com/cgi-bin/article.cgi?f=/c/a/2010/11/01/MNDP1G54K0.DTL.

48. "Arizona's Immigration Enforcement Laws," National Conference of State Legislatures, 2010, www.ncsl.org/?tabid=20263.

49. Robert Rische, "The 'Maverick' survives Arizona Primary, but incumbency is still frowned upon from Florida to Alaska," *San Diego Examiner*, Aug. 25, 2010.

50. Julia Preston, "House Backs Legal Status for Many Young Immigrants," *The New York Times*, Dec. 8, 2010, www.nytimes.com/2010/12/09/us/politics/09immig.html.

51. Simmi Aujla, "Immigration Hard-liners Poised to Lead Judiciary," *Politico*, Oct. 26, 2010, p. 10.

52. See Department of Homeland Security, www.dhs.gov/files/programs/gc_1185221678150.shtm.

53. Yvonne Wingett and J. J. Hensley, "Abuse Lawsuit Against Sheriff Joe Arpaio's Office Settled for $600,000," *AZCentral*, Oct. 6, 2010, www.azcentral.com/news/election/azelections/articles/2010/10/06/20101006joe-arpaio-office-discrimination-suit-settlement06-ON.html.

54. Susan Carroll, "Feds moving to dismiss some deportation cases," *Houston Chronicle*, Aug. 24, 2010.

55. Hope Yen, "Illegal Immigration Population Down for 1stst Time in 2 Decades," *Detroit Free Press*, Sept. 2, 2010.

# BIBLIOGRAPHY

## Selected Sources

### Books

**Massey, Douglas S., ed., *New Faces in New Places: The Changing Geography of American Immigration*, Russell Sage Foundation, 2008.**
A collection of academic pieces shows how the waves of recent immigrants have been dispersed across America by shifts in various economic sectors and how their presence in areas outside traditional "gateways" has led to social tension.

**Myers, Dowell, *Immigrants and Boomers: Forging a New Social Contract for the Future of America*, Russell Sage Foundation, 2007.**
A demographer suggests that rates of immigration already may have peaked and argues that rather than being stigmatized immigrants need to be embraced as a replacement workforce for an aging Anglo population.

**Portes, Alejandro, and Ruben G. Rumbaut, *Immigrant America: A Portrait*, 3rd ed., University of California Press, 2006.**
This updated survey by two sociologists offers a broad look at where immigrants settle, what sort of work they do and how well they assimilate.

## Articles

**Bacon, Perry Jr., and Anne E. Kornblut, "Issue of Illegal Immigration Is Quandary for Democrats," *The Washington Post*, Nov. 2, 2007, p. A4.**
Immigration is a wedge issue that can work against Democratic presidential candidates and is perhaps the strongest card in the GOP's deck.

**Bazar, Emily, "Strict Immigration Law Rattles Okla. Businesses," *USA Today*, Jan. 10, 2008, p. 1A.**
Numerous business sectors in Oklahoma are complaining about worker shortages in the wake of a new state law that makes transporting or sheltering illegal immigrants a felony.

**Goodman, Josh, "Crackdown," *Governing*, July 2007, p. 28.**
States are reacting to immigration pressures largely by enacting new restrictions on illegal immigrants and the employers who hire them.

**Greenhouse, Steven, "U.S. Seeks Rules to Allow Increase in Guest Workers," *The New York Times*, Oct. 10, 2007, p. A16.**
Bush administration officials say they will allow farmers to bring in more foreign labor.

**Kiely, Kathy, "Children Caught in the Immigration Crossfire," *USA Today*, Oct. 8, 2007, p. 1A.**
A million young, illegal immigrants in the United States face potential deportation since the failure of a bill designed to grant permanent legal status to those who finish high school and at least two years of higher education.

**Lizza, Ryan, "Return of the Nativist," *The New Yorker*, Dec. 17, 2007, p. 46.**
How a hard line on immigration became central to the GOP Republican debate, taken even by candidates who had previously favored a more conciliatory approach.

**Preston, Julia, "U.S. to Speed Deportation of Criminals Behind Bars," *The New York Times*, Jan. 15, 2008, p. A12.**
A federal agency pledges to step up arrests of employers who knowingly hire illegal immigrants, while speeding deportation of immigrants who have committed crimes.

**Sandler, Michael, "Immigration: From the Capitol to the Courts," *CQ Weekly*, Dec. 10, 2007, p. 3644.**
The lack of action on Capitol Hill has encouraged scores of state and local jurisdictions to step in with immigrant-related legislation.

**Weisman, Jonathan, "For Republicans, Contest's Hallmark Is Immigration," *The Washington Post*, Jan. 2, 2008, p. A1.**
Illegal immigration has been a dominant issue in the GOP presidential primary contests.

## Reports and Studies

**"2006 Yearbook of Immigration Statistics," *Department of Homeland Security*, Sept. 2007, www.dhs.gov/xlibrary/assets/statistics/yearbook/2006/OIS_2006_Yearbook.pdf.**
A wealth of statistical information about immigrant populations is presented, as well as enforcement actions.

**"2007 Enacted State Legislation Related to Immigrants and Immigration," *National Conference of State Legislatures*, Nov. 29, 2007, www.ncsl.org/print/immig/2007Immigrationfinal.pdf.**
Last year, every state considered legislation related to immigration, with more than 1,500 bills introduced and 244 enacted into law. The amount of activity "in the continued absence of a comprehensive federal reform" was unprecedented and represented a threefold increase in legislation introduced and enacted since 2006.

**"2007 National Survey of Latinos: As Illegal Immigration Issue Heats Up, Latinos Feel a Chill," *Pew Hispanic Center*, Dec. 19, 2007; available at http://pewhispanic.org/files/reports/84.pdf.**
The poll finds that the prominence of the illegal-immigration issue has Hispanics more concerned about deportation and discrimination but generally content with their place in U.S. society.

# For More Information

**American Immigration Law Foundation**, 918 F St., N.W., 6th Floor, Washington, DC 20004; (202) 742-5600; www .ailf.org. Seeks to increase public understanding of immigration law and policy, emphasizing the value of immigration to American society.

**Center for Comparative Immigration Studies**, University of California, San Diego, La Jolla, CA 92093-0548; (858) 822-4447; www.ccis-ucsd.org. Compares U.S. immigration trends with patterns in Europe and Asia.

**Center for Immigration Studies**, 1522 K St., N.W., Suite 820, Washington, DC 20005-1202; (202) 466-8185; www .cis.org. The nation's only think tank exclusively devoted to immigration-related issues advocates reduced immigration.

**Federation for American Immigration Reform**, 25 Massachusetts Ave., NW, Suite 330; Washington, DC 20001; (202) 328-7004; http://fairus.org. A leading advocate for cracking down on illegal immigration and reducing legal immigration.

**Metropolitan Policy Program**, The Brookings Institution, 1775 Massachusetts Ave., N.W., Washington, DC 20036; (202) 797-6000; www.brookings.edu/metro.aspx. The think tank produces numerous reports on both immigration and broader demographics, including geographical mobility.

**Migration Dialogue**, University of California, Davis, 1 Shields Ave., Davis, CA 95616; (530) 752-1011; http:// migration.ucdavis.edu/index.php. A research center that focuses on immigration from rural Mexico and publishes two Web bulletins.

**Migration Policy Institute**, 1400 16th St., N.W., Suite 300, Washington, DC 20036; (202) 266-1940; www.migration-policy.org. Analyzes global immigration trends and advocates fairer, more humane conditions for immigrants.

**National Immigration Forum**; 50 F St., N.W., Suite 300, Washington, DC 20001; (202) 347-0040; www.immigra tionforum.org. A leading advocacy group in support of immigrants' rights.

# 8

# American Indians

Peter Katel and Charles S. Clark

Jerolyn Fink lives in grand style in the housing center built by Connecticut's Mohegan Tribe using profits from its successful Mohegan Sun casino. Thanks in part to booming casinos, many tribes are making progress, but American Indians still face daunting health and economic problems, and tribal leaders say federal aid remains inadequate.

From *CQ Researcher*,
April 28, 2006 (updated August 5, 2010).

It's not a fancy gambling palace, like some Indian casinos, but the modest operation run by the Winnebago Tribe of Nebraska may just help the 2,300-member tribe hit the economic jackpot.

Using seed money from the casino, it has launched 12 businesses, including a construction company and an Internet news service. Projected 2006 revenues: $150 million.

"It would be absolutely dumb for us to think that gaming is the future," says tribe member Lance Morgan, the 37-year-old Harvard Law School graduate who runs the holding company for the dozen businesses. "Gaming is just a means to an end — and it's done wonders for our tribal economy."

Indian casinos have revived a myth dating back to the early-20th-century Oklahoma oil boom — that Indians are rolling in dough.[1] While some of the 55 tribes that operate big casinos indeed are raking in big profits, the 331 federally recognized tribes in the lower 48 states, on the whole, endure soul-quenching poverty and despair.

Arizona's 1.8-million-acre San Carlos Apache Reservation is among the poorest. The rural, isolated community of about 13,000 people not only faces devastating unemployment but also a deadly methamphetamine epidemic, tribal Chairwoman Kathleen W. Kitcheyan, told the Senate Indian Affairs Committee in April.

"We suffer from a poverty level of 69 percent, which must be unimaginable to many people in this country, who would equate a situation such as this to one found only in Third World countries," she said. Then, speaking of the drug-related death of one of her own grandsons, she had to choke back sobs.

## Conditions on Reservations Improved

Socioeconomic conditions improved more on reservations with gambling than on those without gaming during the 1990s, although non-gaming reservations also improved substantially, especially compared to the U.S. population. Some experts attribute the progress among non-gaming tribes to an increase in self-governance on many reservations.

### Socioeconomic Changes on Reservations, 1990-2000*
(shown as a percentage or percentage points)

| | Non-Gaming | Gaming | U.S. |
|---|---|---|---|
| Real per-capita income | +21.0% | +36.0% | +11.0% |
| Median household income | +14.0% | +35.0% | +4.0% |
| Family poverty | -6.9 | -11.8 | -0.8 |
| Child poverty | -8.1 | -11.6 | -1.7 |
| Deep poverty | -1.4 | -3.4 | -0.4 |
| Public assistance | +0.7 | -1.6 | +0.3 |
| Unemployment | -1.8 | -4.8 | -0.5 |
| Labor force participation | -1.6 | +1.6 | -1.3 |
| Overcrowded homes | -1.3 | -0.1 | +1.1 |
| Homes lacking complete plumbing | -4.6 | -3.3 | -0.1 |
| Homes lacking complete kitchen | +1.3 | -0.6 | +0.2 |
| College graduates | +1.7 | +2.6 | +4.2 |
| High school or equivalency only | -0.3 | +1.8 | -1.4 |
| Less than 9th-grade education | -5.5 | -6.3 | -2.8 |

* The reservation population of the Navajo Nation, which did not have gambling in the 1990s, was not included because it is so large (175,000 in 2000) that it tends to pull down Indian averages when it is included.

Source: Jonathan B. Taylor and Joseph P. Kalt, "Cabazon, The Indian Gaming Regulatory Act, and the Socioeconomic Consequences of American Indian Governmental Gaming: A Ten-Year Review, American Indians on Reservations: A Databook of Socioeconomic Change Between the 1990 and 2000 Censuses," Harvard Project on American Indian Economic Development, January 2005

- Nearly one in five Indians age 25 or older in tribes without gambling operations had less than a ninth-grade education. But even members of tribes with gambling had a college graduation rate of only 16 percent, about half the national percentage.[5]
- Death rates from alcoholism and tuberculosis among Native Americans are at least 650 percent higher than overall U.S. rates.[6]
- Indian youths commit suicide at nearly triple the rate of young people in general.[7]
- Indians on reservations, especially in the resource-poor Upper Plains and West, are the nation's third-largest group of methamphetamine users.[8]

The immediate prognosis for the nation's 4.4 million Native Americans is bleak, according to the Harvard Project on American Indian Economic Development. "If U.S. and on-reservation Indian per-capita income were to continue to grow at their 1990s' rates," it said, "it would take half a century for the tribes to catch up."[9]

Nonetheless, there has been forward movement in Indian Country, though it is measured in modest steps. Among the marks of recent progress:

- Per-capita income rose 20 percent on reservations, to $7,942, (and 36 percent in tribes with casinos, to $9,771), in contrast to an 11 percent overall U.S. growth rate.[10]
- Unemployment has dropped by up to 5 percent on reservations and in other predominantly Indian areas.[11]
- Child poverty in non-gaming tribes dropped from 55 percent of the child population to 44 percent (but the Indian rate is still more than double the 17 percent average nationwide).[12]

"Our statistics are horrific," says Lionel R. Bordeaux, president of Sinte Gleska University, on the Rosebud Sioux Reservation in South Dakota. "We're at the bottom rung of the ladder in all areas, whether it's education levels, economic achievement or political status."[2]

National statistics aren't much better:

- Indian unemployment on reservations nationwide is 49 percent — 10 times the national rate.[3]
- The on-reservation family poverty rate in 2000 was 37 percent—four times the national figure of 9 percent.[4]

More than two centuries of court decisions, treaties and laws have created a complicated system of coexistence between tribes and the rest of the country. On one level, tribes are sovereign entities that enjoy a government-to-government relationship with Washington. But the sovereignty is qualified. In the words of an 1831 Supreme Court decision that is a bedrock of Indian law, tribes are "domestic dependent nations."[13]

The blend of autonomy and dependence grows out of the Indians' reliance on Washington for sheer survival, says Robert A. Williams Jr., a law professor at the University of Arizona and a member of North Carolina's Lumbee Tribe. "Indians insisted in their treaties that the Great White Father protect us from these racial maniacs in the states — where racial discrimination was most developed — and guarantee us a right to education, a right to water, a territorial base, a homeland," he says. "Tribes sold an awful lot of land in return for a trust relationship to keep the tribes going."

Today, the practical meaning of the relationship with Washington is that American Indians on reservations, and to some extent those elsewhere, depend entirely or partly on federal funding for health, education and other needs. Tribes with casinos and other businesses lessen their reliance on federal dollars.

Unlike other local governments, tribes don't have a tax base whose revenues they share with state governments. Federal spending on Indian programs of all kinds nationwide currently amounts to about $11 billion, James Cason, associate deputy secretary of the Interior, told the Senate Indian Affairs Committee in February.

But the abysmal conditions under which many American Indians live make it all too clear that isn't enough, Indians say. "This is always a discussion at our tribal leaders' meetings," says Cecilia Fire Thunder, president of the Oglala Sioux Tribe in Pine Ridge, S.D. "The biggest job that tribal leaders have is to see that the government lives up to its responsibilities to our people. It's a battle that never ends."

Indeed, a decades-old class-action suit alleges systematic mismanagement of billions of dollars in Indian-owned assets by the Interior Department — a case that has prompted withering criticism of the department by the judge.

Government officials insist that, despite orders to cut spending, they've been able to keep providing essential services. Charles Grim, director of the Indian Health

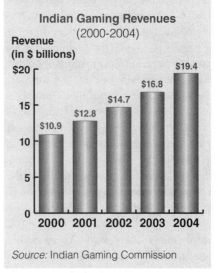

### Revenues From Casinos Almost Doubled

Revenue from Indian gaming operations nearly doubled to $19.4 billion from 2000-2004. The number of Indian casinos increased from 311 to 367 during the period.

**Indian Gaming Revenues**
(2000-2004)

Revenue
(in $ billions)

- 2000: $10.9
- 2001: $12.8
- 2002: $14.7
- 2003: $16.8
- 2004: $19.4

*Source:* Indian Gaming Commission

Service, told the Indian Affairs Committee, "In a deficit-reduction year, it's a very strong budget and one that does keep pace with inflationary and population-growth increases."

In any event, from the tribes' point of view, they lack the political muscle to force major increases. "The big problem is the Indians are about 1 percent of the national population," says Joseph Kalt, co-director of the Harvard Project. "The voice is so tiny."

Faced with that grim political reality, Indians are trying to make better use of scarce federal dollars through a federally sponsored "self-governance" movement. Leaders of the movement say tribes can deliver higher-quality services more efficiently when they control their own budgets. Traditionally, federal agencies operate programs on reservations, such as law enforcement or medical services.

But since the 1990s, dozens of tribes have stepped up control of their own affairs both by building their own businesses and by signing self-governance "compacts" with the federal government. Compacts provide tribes with large chunks of money, or block grants, rather than individual grants for each service. Then, with minimal federal oversight, the tribes develop their own budgets and run all or most services.

The self-governance trend gathered steam during the same time that Indian-owned casinos began booming. For many tribes, the gambling business provided a revenue stream that didn't flow from Washington.

According to economist Alan Meister, 228 tribes in 30 states operated 367 high-stakes bingo halls or casinos in 2004, earning an estimated $19.6 billion.[14]

The gambling houses operate under the 1988 Indian Gaming Regulatory Act (IGRA), which was made possible by a U.S. Supreme Court ruling upholding tribes' rights to govern their own activities.[15] A handful of tribes are doing so well that $80 million from six tribes in 2000-2003 helped fuel the scandal surrounding one-time Washington super-lobbyist Jack Abramoff, whose clients were among the most successful casino tribes.[16]

If the Abramoff scandal contributed to the notion of widespread Indian wealth, one reason may be the misimpression that tribes don't pay taxes on their gambling earnings. In fact, under the IGRA, federal, state and local governments took in $6.3 billion in gambling-generated tax revenues in 2004, with 67 percent going to the federal government. In addition, tribes paid out some $889 million in 2004 to state and local governments in order to get gambling operations approved.[17]

The spread of casinos has prompted some cities and counties, along with citizens' groups and even some casino-operating tribes, to resist casino-expansion plans.

The opposition to expansion is another reason tribal entrepreneur Morgan doesn't think gaming is a good long-range bet for Indians' future. His vision involves full tribal control of the Indians' main asset — their land. He argues for ending the "trust status" under which tribes can't buy or sell reservation property — a relic of 19th-century protection against rapacious state governments.

Indian Country needs a better business climate, Morgan says, and the availability of land as collateral for investments would be a big step in that direction. "America has a wonderful economic system, probably the best in the world, but the reservation tends to be an economic black hole."

As Indians seek to improve their lives, here are some of the issues being debated:

## Is the federal government neglecting Native Americans?

There is wide agreement that the federal government bears overwhelming responsibility for Indians' welfare, but U.S. and tribal officials disagree over the adequacy of the aid Indians receive. Sen. John McCain, R-Ariz., chairman of the Senate Indian Affairs Committee, and Vice Chairman Byron L. Dorgan, D-N.D., have been leading the fight for more aid to Indians. "We have a full-blown crisis . . . particularly dealing with children and elderly, with respect to housing, education and health care," Dorgan told the committee on Feb. 14. He characterized administration proposals as nothing more than "nibbling around the edges on these issues . . . making a few adjustments here or there.'"

Administration officials respond that given the severe federal deficit, they are focusing on protecting vital programs. "As we went through and prioritized our budget, we basically looked at all of the programs that were secondary and tertiary programs, and they were the first ones on the block to give tradeoffs for our core programs in maintaining the integrity of those," Interior's Cason told the committee.

For Indians on isolated reservations, says Bordeaux of the Rosebud Sioux, there's little alternative to federal money. He compares tribes' present circumstances to those after the buffalo had been killed off, and an Army general told the Indians to eat beef, which made them sick. "The general told them, 'Either that, or you eat the grass on which you stand.'"

But David B. Vickers, president of Upstate Citizens for Equality, in Union Springs, N.Y., which opposes Indian land claims and casino applications, argues that accusations of federal neglect are inaccurate and skirt the real problem. The central issue is that the constitutional system is based on individual rights, not tribal rights, he says. "Indians are major recipients of welfare now. They're eligible. They don't need a tribe or leader; all they have to do is apply like anybody else."

Pat Ragsdale, director of the Bureau of Indian Affairs (BIA), acknowledges that Dorgan's and McCain's criticisms echo a 2003 U.S. Commission on Civil Rights report, which also called underfunding of Indian aid a crisis. "The government is failing to live up to its trust responsibility to Native peoples," the commission concluded. "Efforts to bring Native

Americans up to the standards of other Americans have failed in part because of a lack of sustained funding. The failure manifests itself in massive and escalating unmet needs."[18]

"Nobody in this government disputes the report, in general," says Ragsdale, a Cherokee. "Some of our tribal communities are in real critical shape, and others are prospering."

The commission found, for example, that in 2003 the Indian Health Service appropriation amounted to $2,533 per capita — below even the $3,803 per capita appropriated for federal prisoners.

Concern over funding for Indian programs in 2007 centers largely on health and education. Although 90 percent of Indian students attend state-operated public schools, their schools get federal aid because tribes don't pay property taxes, which typically fund public schools. The remaining 10 percent of Indian students attend schools operated by the BIA or by tribes themselves under BIA contracts.

"There is not a congressman or senator who would send his own children or grandchildren to our schools," said Ryan Wilson, president of the National Indian Education Association, citing "crumbling buildings and outdated structures with lead in the pipes and mold on the walls."[19]

Cason told the Indian Affairs Committee the administration is proposing a $49 million cut, from $157.4 million to $108.1 million, in school construction and repair in 2007. He also said that only 10 of 37 dilapidated schools funded for replacement by 2006 have been completed, with another 19 scheduled to finish in 2007. Likewise, he said the department is also behind on 45 school improvement projects.

McCain questioned whether BIA schools and public schools with large Indian enrollments would be able to meet the requirements set by the national No Child Left Behind Law.[20] Yes, replied Darla Marburger, deputy assistant secretary of Education for policy. "For the first time, we'll be providing money to . . . take a look at how students are achieving in ways that they can tailor their programs to better meet the needs of students." Overall, the Department of Education would spend about $1 billion on Indian education under the administration's proposed budget for 2007, or $6 million less than in 2006.

Controversial Whiteclay, Neb., sells millions of cans of beer annually to residents of the nearby Pine Ridge Reservation in South Dakota. Alcohol abuse and unemployment continue to plague the American Indian community.

*AP Photo/William Lauer*

McCain and Dorgan are also among those concerned about administration plans to eliminate the Indian Health Service's $32.7 million urban program, which this year made medical and counseling services available to some 430,000 off-reservation Indians at 41 medical facilities in cities around the nation. The administration argues that the services were available through other programs, but McCain and Dorgan noted that "no evaluation or evidence has been provided to support this contention."[21]

Indian Health Service spokesman Thomas Sweeney, a member of the Citizen Potawatomi Nation of Oklahoma, says only 72,703 Indians used urban health centers in 2004 and that expansion of another federal program would pick up the slack.[22]

In Seattle, elimination of the urban program would cut $4 million from the city's Indian Health Board budget, says Executive Director Ralph Forquera. "Why pick on a $33 million appropriation?" he asks. In his skeptical view, the proposal reflects another "unspoken" termination program. You take a sub-population — urban Indians — and eliminate funding, then [you target] tribes under 1,000 members, and there are a lot of them. Little by little, you pick apart the system."

The IHS's Grim told the Senate committee on Feb. 14 the cuts were designed to protect funding that "can be used most effectively to improve the health status of American Indian and Alaskan Native people."

## Have casinos benefited Indians?

Over the past two decades, Indian casinos have become powerful economic engines for many tribal economies. But the enthusiasm for casinos is not unanimous.

"If you're looking at casinos in terms of how they've actually raised the status of Indian people, they've been an abysmal failure," says Ted Jojola, a professor of planning at the University of New Mexico and a member of Isleta Pueblo, near Albuquerque. "But in terms of augmenting the original federal trust-responsibility areas — education, health, tribal government — they've been a spectacular success. Successful gaming tribes have ploughed the money either into diversifying their economies or they've augmented funds that would have come to them anyway."

Tribes with casinos near big population centers are flourishing. The Coushatta Tribe's casino near Lake Charles, La., generates $300 million a year, enough to provide about $40,000 to every member.[23] And the fabled Foxwoods Resort Casino south of Norwich, Conn., operated by the Mashantucket Pequot Tribe, together with Connecticut's other big casino, the Mohegan Tribe's Mohegan Sun, grossed $2.2 billion just from gambling in 2004.[24]

There are only about 830 Coushattas, so their benefits also include free health care, education and favorable terms on home purchases.[25] The once poverty-stricken Mashantuckets have created Connecticut's most extensive welfare-to-work program, open to both tribe members and non-members. In 1997-2000, the program helped 150 welfare recipients find jobs.[26]

Most tribes don't enjoy success on that scale. Among the nation's 367 Indian gambling operations, only 15 grossed $250 million or more in 2004 (another 40 earned $100 million to $250 million); 94 earned less than $3 million and 57 earned $3 million to $10 million.[27]

"We have a small casino that provides close to $3 million to the tribal nation as a whole," says Bordeaux, on the Rosebud Sioux Reservation. The revenue has been channeled into the tribe's Head Start program, an emergency home-repair fund and other projects. W. Ron Allen, chairman of the Jamestown S'Klallam Tribe in Sequim, Wash., says his tribe's small casino has raised living standards so much that some two-dozen students a year go to college, instead of one or two.

Efforts to open additional casinos are creating conflicts between tribes that operate competing casinos, as well as with some of their non-Indian neighbors. Convicted lobbyist Abramoff, for example, was paid millions of dollars by tribes seeking to block other tribal casinos.[28]

Some non-Indian communities also oppose casino expansion. "We firmly believe a large, generally unregulated casino will fundamentally change the character of our community forever," said Liz Thomas, a member of Tax Payers of Michigan Against Casinos, which opposes a casino planned by the Pokagon Band of Potawotami Indians Tribe in the Lake Michigan town of New Buffalo, where Taylor and her husband operate a small resort.

"People are OK with Donald Trump making millions of dollars individually," says Joseph Podlasek, executive director of the American Indian Center of Chicago, "but if a race of people is trying to become self-sufficient, now that's not respectable."

Nevertheless, some American Indians have mixed feelings about the casino route to economic development. "I don't think anyone would have picked casinos" for that purpose, says the University of Arizona's Williams. "Am I ambivalent about it? Absolutely. But I'm not ambivalent about a new fire station, or Kevlar vests for tribal police fighting meth gangs."

"There's no question that some of the money has been used for worthwhile purposes," concedes Guy Clark, a Corrales, N.M., dentist who chairs the National Coalition Against Legalized Gambling. But, he adds, "If you do a cost-benefit analysis, the cost is much greater than the benefit." Restaurants and other businesses, for example, lose customers who often gamble away their extra money.

Even some Indian leaders whose tribes profit from casinos raise caution flags, especially about per-capita payments. For Nebraska's Winnebagos, payments amount to just a few hundred dollars, says CEO Morgan. What bothers him are dividends "that are just big enough that you don't have to work or get educated — say, $20,000 to $40,000."

But there's no denying the impact casinos can have. At a January public hearing on the Oneida Indian Nation's attempt to put 17,000 acres of upstate New York land into tax-free "trust" status, hundreds of the 4,500 employees of the tribe's Turning Stone Resort and Casino, near Utica, showed up in support. "When I was a kid, people worked for General Motors, General Electric, Carrier and Oneida Ltd.," said casino Human

Resources Director Mark Mancini. "Today, people work for the Oneida Indian Nation and their enterprises."[29]

For tribes that can't build independent economies any other way, casinos are appealing. The 225,000-member Navajo Nation, the biggest U.S. tribe, twice rejected gaming before finally approving it in 2004.[30] "We need that infusion of jobs and revenue, and people realize that," said Duane Yazzie, president of the Navajos' Shiprock, N.M., chapter.[31]

But the Navajos face stiff competition from dozens of casinos already in operation near the vast Navajo reservation, which spreads across parts of Arizona, New Mexico and Utah and is larger than the state of West Virginia.

## Would money alone solve American Indians' problems?

No one in Indian Country (or on Capitol Hill) denies the importance of federal funding to American Indians' future, but some Indians say it isn't the only answer.

"We are largely on our own because of limited financial assistance from the federal government," said Joseph A. Garcia, president of the National Congress of American Indians, in his recent "State of Indian Nations" speech.[32]

Fifty-two tribal officials and Indian program directors expressed similar sentiments in March before the House Appropriations Subcommittee on the Interior. Pleading their case before lawmakers who routinely consider billion-dollar weapons systems and other big projects, the tribal leaders sounded like small-town county commissioners as they urged lawmakers to increase or restore small but vital grants for basic health, education and welfare services.

"In our ICWA [Indian Child Welfare Act] program, currently we have a budget of $79,000 a year," said Harold Frazier, chairman of the Cheyenne River Sioux, in South Dakota. "We receive over 1,300 requests for assistance annually from 11 states and eight counties in South Dakota. We cannot give the type of attention to these requests that they deserve. Therefore, we are requesting $558,000."

To university President Bordeaux, federal funding is vital because his desolate reservation has few other options for economic survival. "What's missing is money," he says.

Money is crucial to improving Indians' health, says Dr. Joycelyn Dorscher, director of the Center of American Indian and Minority Health at the University of Minnesota-Duluth. Especially costly are programs to combat diabetes and other chronic diseases, says Dorscher, a Chippewa. While health programs have to be carefully designed to fit Indian cultural patterns, she says, "Everything comes down to time or money in the grand scheme of things."

But with funding from Washington never certain from year to year, says the Harvard Project's Kalt, "The key to economic development has not been federal funding" but rather "tribes' ability to run their own affairs."

For tribes without self-government compacts, growing demands for services and shrinking funding from Washington make keeping the dollars flowing the highest priority. "We're always afraid of more cutbacks," says Oglala Sioux President Fire Thunder.

But an Indian education leader with decades of federal budgetary negotiations acknowledges that problems go beyond funding shortfalls. "If you ask students why they dropped out, they say, 'I don't see a future for myself,'" says David Beaulieu, director of Arizona State University's Center for Indian Education. "Educators need to tie the purposes of schooling to the broad-based purposes of society. We're more successful when we tie education to the meaning of life."

The University of Arizona's Williams says a tribe's success and failure may be tied more to the way its government is organized than to how much funding it gets.

Williams says the first priority of tribes still using old-style constitutions should be reorganization, because they feature a weak executive elected by a tribal council. "That's what the BIA was used to," he explains. "It could play off factions and families, and the economic system would be based on patronage and taking care of your own family." Under such a system, he adds, "there's not going to be any long-term strategic planning going on."[33]

Yet other needs exist as well, says the American Indian Center's Podlasek. "It's so difficult for us to find a place to do a traditional ceremony," he says. "We had a traditional healer in town last month, and he wanted to build a sweat lodge. We actually had to go to Indiana. Doing it in the city wasn't even an option."

# BACKGROUND

## Conquered Homelands

Relations between Indian and non-Indian civilizations in the Americas began with the Spanish Conquistadors'

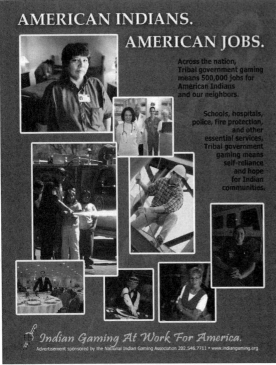

AMERICAN INDIANS.

AMERICAN JOBS.

Across the nation, Tribal government gaming means 500,000 jobs for American Indians and our neighbors.

Schools, hospitals, police, fire protection, and other essential services, Tribal government gaming means self-reliance and hope for Indian communities.

*Indian Gaming At Work For America.*

Advertisement sponsored by the National Indian Gaming Association 202.546.7711 • www.indiangaming.org

A National Indian Gaming Association advertisement touts the benefits of tribal gaming operations to American Indian communities. Some 228 tribes in 30 states operated 367 high-stakes bingo halls or casinos in 2004.

explorations of the 1500s, followed by the French and British. By turns the three powers alternated policies of enslavement, peaceful coexistence and all-out warfare against the Indians.[34]

By 1830, with the Europeans largely gone, white settlers moved westward into Georgia, Mississippi and Alabama. Unwilling to share the rich frontier land, they pushed the Indians out. President Andrew Jackson backed the strategy, and Congress enacted it into the Indian Removal Act of 1830, which called for moving the region's five big tribes into the Oklahoma Territory.

If the law didn't make clear where Indians stood with the government, the treatment of Mississippi's Choctaws provided chilling evidence. Under a separate treaty, Choctaws who refused to head for Oklahoma could remain at home, become citizens and receive land. In practice,

none of that was allowed, and Indians who stayed in Mississippi lived marginal existences.

Georgia simplified the claiming of Cherokee lands by effectively ending Cherokee self-rule. The so-called "Georgia Guard" reinforced the point by beating and jailing Indians. Jackson encouraged Georgia's actions, and when Indians protested, he said he couldn't interfere. The lawsuit filed by the Cherokees eventually reached the Supreme Court.

Chief Justice John Marshall's 1831 majority opinion, *Cherokee Nation v. Georgia*, would cast a long shadow over Indians' rights, along with two other decisions, issued in 1823 and 1832. "Almost all Indian policy is the progeny of the conflicting views of Jackson and Marshall," wrote W. Dale Mason, a political scientist at the University of New Mexico.[35]

In concluding that the court couldn't stop Georgia's actions, Marshall defined the relationship between Indians and the U.S. government. While Marshall wrote that Indians didn't constitute a foreign state, he noted that they owned the land they occupied until they made a "voluntary cession." Marshall concluded the various tribes were "domestic dependent nations." In practical terms, "Their relations to the United States resembles that of a ward to his guardian."[36]

Having rejected the Cherokees' argument, the University of Arizona's Williams writes, the court "provided no effective judicial remedy for Indian tribes to protect their basic human rights to property, self-government, and cultural survival under U.S. law."[37]

Along with the *Cherokee* case, the other two opinions that make up the so-called Marshall Trilogy are *Johnson v. M'Intosh* (also known as *Johnson v. McIntosh*), and *Worcester v. State of Georgia*.[38]

In *Johnson*, Marshall wrote that the European empires that "discovered" America became its owners and had "an exclusive right to extinguish the Indian title of occupancy, either by purchase or by conquest. The tribes of Indians inhabiting this country were fierce savages. . . . To leave them in possession of their country was to leave the country a wilderness."[39]

However, Marshall used the 1832 *Worcester* opinion to define the limits of state authority over Indian tribes, holding that the newcomers couldn't simply eject Indians.

"The Cherokee nation . . . is a distinct community occupying its own territory . . . in which the laws of Georgia can have no force," Marshall wrote. Georgia's conviction and sentencing of a missionary for not swearing allegiance to the state "interferes forcibly with the relations established between the United States and the Cherokee nation."[40] That is, the federal government — not states — held the reins of power over tribes.

According to legend, Jackson remarked: "John Marshall has made his decision — now let him enforce it." Between Jackson's disregard of the Supreme Court and white settlers' later manipulation of the legal system to vacate Indian lands, the end result was the dispossession of Indian lands.

## Forced Assimilation

The expulsions of the Native Americans continued in the Western territories — especially after the Civil War. "I instructed Captain Barry, if possible to exterminate the whole village," Lt. Col. George Green wrote of his participation in an 1869 campaign against the White Mountain Apaches in Arizona and New Mexico. "There seems to be no settled policy, but a general policy to kill them wherever found."[41]

Some military men and civilians didn't go along. But whether by brute force or by persuasion, Indians were pushed off lands that non-Indians wanted. One strategy was to settle the Indians on reservations guarded by military posts. The strategy grew into a general policy for segregating Indians on these remote tracts.

Even after the Indians were herded onto lands that no one else wanted, the government didn't respect reservation boundaries. They were reconfigured as soon as non-Indians saw something valuable, such as mineral wealth.

The strategy of elastic reservation boundaries led to the belief — or rationalization — that reservations served no useful purposes for Indians themselves. That doctrine led to a policy enshrined in an 1887 law to convert reservations to individual landholdings. Well-meaning advocates of the plan saw it as a way to inculcate notions of private property and Euro-American culture in general.

All tribal land was to be divided into 160-acre allotments, one for each Indian household. The parcels wouldn't become individual property, though, for 25 years.

Indian consent wasn't required. In some cases, government agents tried persuading Indians to join in; in others, the divvying-up proceeded even with many Indians opposed. In Arizona, however, the government backed off from breaking up the lands of the long-settled Hopis, who resisted attempts to break up their territory. The vast Navajo Nation in Arizona, Utah and New Mexico was also left intact.

While widely reviled, the "forced assimilation" policy left a benign legacy for the affected Indians: the grant of citizenship. Beyond that, the era's Indians were restricted to unproductive lands, and with little means of support many fell prey to alcoholism and disease.

The bleak period ended with President Franklin D. Roosevelt. In his first term he appointed a defender of Indian culture, John Collier, as commissioner of Indian affairs. Collier pushed for the Indian Reorganization Act of 1934, which ended the allotment program, financed purchases of new Indian lands and authorized the organization of tribal governments that enjoyed control over revenues.

## Termination

After World War II, a new, anti-Indian mood swept Washington, partly in response to pressure from states where non-Indians eyed Indian land.

Collier resigned in 1945 after years of conflict over what critics called his antagonism to missionaries proselytizing among the Indians and his sympathies toward the tribes. The 1950 appointment of Dillon S. Myer — fresh from supervising the wartime internment of Japanese-Americans — clearly reflected the new attitude. Myer showed little interest in what Indians themselves thought of the new policy of shrinking tribal land holdings. "I realize that it will not be possible always to obtain Indian cooperation. . . . We must proceed, even though [this] may be lacking."[42]

Congress hadn't authorized a sweeping repeal of earlier policy. But the introduction of dozens of bills in the late 1940s to sell Indian land or liquidate some reservation holdings entirely showed which way the winds were blowing. And in 1953, a House Concurrent Resolution declared Congress' policy to be ending Indians' "status as wards of the United States, and to grant them all of the rights and privileges pertaining to American citizenship." A separate law granted state jurisdiction over Indian reservations in

# C H R O N O L O G Y

1800s *United States expands westward, pushing Indians off most of their original lands, sometimes creating new reservations for them.*

**1830** President Andrew Jackson signs the Indian Removal Act, forcing the Cherokees to move from Georgia to Oklahoma.

**1832** Supreme Court issues the last of three decisions defining Indians' legal status as wards of the government.

**1871** Congress makes its treaties with tribes easier to alter, enabling non-Indians to take Indian lands when natural resources are discovered.

**December 29, 1890** U.S. soldiers massacre at least 150 Plains Indians, mostly women and children, at Wounded Knee, S.D.

1900-1950s *Congress and the executive branch undertake major shifts in Indian policy, first strengthening tribal governments then trying to force cultural assimilation.*

**1924** Indians are granted U.S. citizenship.

**1934** Indian Reorganization Act authorizes expansion of reservations and strengthening of tribal governments.

**1953** Congress endorses full assimilation of Indians into American society, including "relocation" from reservations to cities.

1960s-1980s *In the radical spirit of the era, Native Americans demand respect for their traditions and an end to discrimination; federal government concedes more power to tribal governments, allows gambling on tribal lands.*

**1969** American Indian Movement (AIM) seizes Alcatraz Island in San Francisco Bay to dramatize claims of injustice.

**July 7, 1970** President Richard M. Nixon vows support for Indian self-government.

**February 27, 1973** AIM members occupy the town of Wounded Knee on the Pine Ridge, S.D., Sioux Reservation, for two months; two Indians die and an FBI agent is wounded.

**1988** Indian Gaming Regulatory Act allows tribes to operate casinos under agreements with states.

1990s *Indian-owned casinos boom; tribal governments push to expand self-rule and reduce Bureau of Indian Affairs (BIA) supervision.*

**1994** President Bill Clinton signs law making experimental self-governance compacts permanent.

**March 27, 1996** U.S. Supreme Court rules states can't be forced to negotiate casino compacts, thus encouraging tribes to make revenue-sharing deals with states as the price of approval.

**June 10, 1996** Elouise Cobell, a member of the Blackfeet Tribe in Montana, charges Interior Department mismanagement of Indian trust funds cheated Indians out of billions of dollars. The case is still pending.

**November 3, 1998** California voters uphold tribes' rights to run casinos; state Supreme Court later invalidates the provision, but it is revived by a 1999 compact between the tribes and the state.

2000s *Indian advocates decry low funding levels, and sovereignty battles continue; lobbying scandal spotlights Indian gambling profits.*

**2000** Tribal Self-Governance Demonstration Project becomes permanent.

**2003** U.S. Commission on Civil Rights calls underfunding for Indians a crisis, saying federal government spends less for Indian health care than for any other group, including prison inmates.

**February 22, 2004** *Washington Post* reports on Washington lobbyist Jack Abramoff's deals with casino tribes.

**March 29, 2005** U.S. Supreme Court blocks tax exemptions for Oneida Nation of New York on newly purchased land simply because it once owned the property.

**2006** Congress passes Indian Gaming Regulatory Act Amendments to protect Indian casino operators from Indian tribes operating gaming facilities outside reservations. . . . American Indian Probate Reform Act (AIPRA) overhauls federal probate process for Indian trust property and helps to consolidate Indian land ownership across the nation.

**April 5, 2006** Tribal and BIA officials testify in Congress that methamphetamine addiction is ravaging reservations.

**2007** Cherokee Nation Principal Chief Chad Smith urges state lawmakers to quash proposed "English only" legislation that would make English Oklahoma's official language. . . . Department of Health and Human Services urges Senate to reauthorize Indian Health Care Improvement Act.

**2008** Revenues from Indian casinos in 30 states increase from $19.6 billion in 2004 to $26.7 billion in 2008. . . . Native American Housing Assistance and Self-Determination Reauthorization Act reauthorizes affordable housing programs for Native Americans and creates a promised loan program for economic development and community activities for Indian tribes. . . . President George W. Bush says he would veto the Indian Health Care Improvement Act of 2007 because of "cost and Medicaid documentation concerns," after Sen. Byron Dorgan, D-N.D., sponsors the bill for new funding for the Indian Health Service. . . . President Bush signs Emergency Economic Stabilization Act of 2008, allowing qualified Indian reservation property placed in service by Jan. 1, 2008, to be depreciated over shorter time periods.

**2009** Obama administration's economic stimulus package provides Indian Health Service with $500 million, including $227 million for construction of health facilities and $100 million for maintenance and improvements. . . . Supreme Court rules 7-2 against an Interior Department move to obtain 31 acres in Charlestown, R.I., for the Narragansett tribe that was to be used for a gambling facility. . . . Navajo Nation reports 225 youth gangs, many involving drug-trafficking, operate within its population of 250,000.

# 2010

**March** — Obama's health care reform legislation reauthorizes 1976 Indian Health Care Improvement Act.

**May** — National Indian Education Association requests $500 million for a deferred-maintenance backlog at almost 4,500 Indian schools and also seeks improved youth-violence prevention programs.

**June** — After the Mashpee Wampanoag tribe in Cape Cod, Mass., applies for a casino license to the Bureau of Indian Affairs, Interior Secretary Ken Salazar offers to give the tribe an exemption under the 1988 Federal Indian Gaming Regulatory Act, reviving the issue in the Massachusetts legislature and providing a licensing preference to Indian tribes. . . . At Sovereignty Symposium in Oklahoma City, National Indian Gaming Association Chairman Ernie Stevens Jr. praises local tribes for their improvements in education, transportation and health care and success at providing jobs.

**June 17** — Cherokee Nation Principal Chief Smith calls for more diverse curriculum in No Child Left Behind law, including emphasis on native culture and language, to help Indian students better face adversity and adaptation challenges.

**July** — Sen. Dorgan hosts summit meeting on suicide prevention among Native Americans, reports that the youth suicide rate on Indian lands is 70 percent higher than that of the general population. . . . On July 29 President Obama signs Tribal Law and Order Act giving tribal courts tougher sentencing powers, setting stricter rules to gather and collect more data on crimes and appointing special U.S. prosecutors to tackle what advocates of the law describe as an epidemic of violence on reservations.

# Budget Cuts Target Health Clinics

When Lita Pepion, a health consultant and a member of the Blackfeet Nation, learned that her 22-year-old-niece had been struggling with heroin abuse, she urged her to seek treatment at the local Urban Indian Clinic in Billings, Mont.

But the young woman had so much trouble getting an appointment that she gave up. Only recently, says Pepion, did she overcome her addiction on her own.

The clinic is one of 34 federally funded, Indian-controlled clinics that contract with the Indian Health Service (IHS) to serve urban Indians. But President Bush's 2007 budget would kill the $33-million program, eliminating most of the clinics' funding.

Indians in cities will still be able to get health care through several providers, including the federal Health Centers program, says Office of Management and Budget spokesman Richard Walker. The proposed budget would increase funding for the centers by nearly $2 billion, IHS Director Charles W. Grim told the Senate Indian Affairs Committee on Feb. 14, 2006.[1]

But Joycelyn Dorscher, president of the Association of American Indian Physicians, says the IHS clinics do a great job and that, "It's very important that people from diverse backgrounds have physicians like themselves."

Others, however, including Pepion, say the clinics are poorly managed and lack direction. Ralph Forquera, director of the Seattle-based Urban Indian Health Institute, says that while the clinics "have made great strides medically, a lack of resources has resulted in services from unqualified professionals." In addition, he says, "we have not been as successful in dealing with lifestyle changes and mental health problems."

Many Indian health experts oppose the cuts because Indians in both urban areas and on reservations have more health problems than the general population, including 126 percent more chronic liver disease and cirrhosis, 54 percent more diabetes and 178 percent more alcohol-related deaths.[2]

Indian health specialists blame the Indians' higher disease rates on history, lifestyle and genetics — not just on poverty. "You don't see exactly the same things happening to other poor minority groups," says Dorscher, a North Dakota Chippewa, so "there's something different" going on among Indians.

In the view of Donna Keeler, executive director of the South Dakota Urban Indian Health program and an Eastern Shoshone, historical trauma affects the physical wellness of patients in her state's three urban Indian clinics.

Susette Schwartz, CEO of the Hunter Urban Indian Clinic in Wichita, Kan., agrees. She attributes Indians' high rates of mental health and alcohol/substance abuse to their long history of government maltreatment. Many Indian children in the 19th and early 20th centuries, she points out, were taken from their parents and sent to government boarding schools where speaking native

---

five Midwestern and Western states and extended the same authority to other states that wanted to claim it.[43]

The following year, Congress "terminated" formal recognition and territorial sovereignty of six tribes. Four years later, after public opposition began building (spurred in part by religious organizations), Congress abandoned termination. In the meantime, however, Indians had lost 1.6 million acres.

At the same time, though, the federal government maintained an associated policy — relocation. The BIA persuaded Indians to move to cities — Chicago, Denver and Los Angeles were the main destinations — and opened job-placement and housing-aid programs. The BIA placed Indians far from their reservations to keep them from returning. By 1970, the BIA estimated that 40 percent of all Indians lived in cities, of which one-third had been relocated by the bureau; the rest moved on their own.[44]

## Activism

Starting in the late 1960s, the winds of change blowing through American society were felt as deeply in Indian Country as anywhere. Two books played a crucial role. In 1969, Vine Deloria Jr., member of a renowned family of Indian intellectuals from Oklahoma, published his landmark history, *Custer Died For Your Sins*, which portrayed American history from the Indians' viewpoint. The

languages was prohibited. "Taking away the culture and language years ago," says Schwartz, as well as the government's role in "taking their children and sterilizing their women" in the 1970s, all contributed to Indians' behavioral health issues.

Keeler also believes Indians' low incomes cause their unhealthy lifestyles. Many eat high-fat, high-starch foods because they are cheaper, Pepion says. Growing up on a reservation, she recalls, "We didn't eat a lot of vegetables because we couldn't afford them."

Opponents of the funding cuts for urban Indian health centers also cite a recent letter to President Bush from Daniel R. Hawkins Jr., vice president for federal, state and local government for the National Association of Community Health Centers. He said the urban Indian clinics and community health centers are complementary, not duplicative.

While Pepion does not believe funding should be cut entirely, she concedes that alternative health-care services are often "better equipped than the urban Indian clinics." And if American Indians want to assimilate into the larger society, they can't have everything culturally separate, she adds. "The only way that I was able to assimilate into an urban society was to make myself do those things that were uncomfortable for me," she says.

But Schwartz believes a great benefit of the urban clinics are their Indian employees, "who are culturally competent and sensitive and incorporate Native American-specific cultural ideas." Because of their history of cultural abuse, it takes a long time for Native Americans to trust non-Indian

Native Americans in downtown Salt Lake City, Utah, demonstrate on April 21, 2006, against the elimination of funding for Urban Indian Health Clinics.

health providers, says Schwartz. "They're not just going to go to a health center down the road."

Dorscher and Schwartz also say the budget cuts could lead to more urban Indians ending up in costly emergency rooms because of their reluctance to trust the community health centers. "Ultimately, it would become more expensive to cut the prevention and primary care programs than it would be to maintain them," Dorscher says.

*—Melissa J. Hipolit*

[1] Prepared testimony of Director of Indian Health Service Dr. Charles W. Grim before the Senate Committee on Indian Affairs, Feb. 14, 2006.

[2] Urban Indian Health Institute, "The Health Status of Urban American Indians and Alaska Natives," March 16, 2004, p. v.

following year, Dee Brown's *Bury My Heart at Wounded Knee* described the settling of the West also from an Indian point of view. The books astonished many non-Indians. Among young Indians, the volumes reflected and spurred on a growing political activism.

It was in this climate that the newly formed American Indian Movement (AIM) took over Alcatraz Island, the former federal prison site in San Francisco Bay (where rebellious Indians had been held during the Indian Wars), to publicize demands to honor treaties and respect Native Americans' dignity. The takeover lasted from Nov. 20, 1969, to June 11, 1971, when U.S. marshals removed the occupiers.[45]

A second AIM-government confrontation took the form of a one-week takeover of BIA headquarters in Washington in November 1972 by some 500 AIM members protesting what they called broken treaty obligations. Protesters charged that government services to Indians were inadequate in general, with urban Indians neglected virtually completely.

Another protest occurred on Feb. 27, 1973, when 200 AIM members occupied the village of Wounded Knee on the Oglala Sioux's Pine Ridge Reservation in South Dakota. U.S. soldiers had massacred at least 150 Indians at Wounded Knee in 1890. AIM was protesting what it called the corrupt tribal government. And a weak,

## Disease Toll Higher Among Indians

American Indians served by the Indian Health Service (IHS) — mainly low-income or uninsured — die at substantially higher rates than the general population from liver disease, diabetes, tuberculosis, pneumonia and influenza as well as from homicide, suicide and injuries. However, Indians' death rates from Alzheimer's disease or breast cancer are lower.

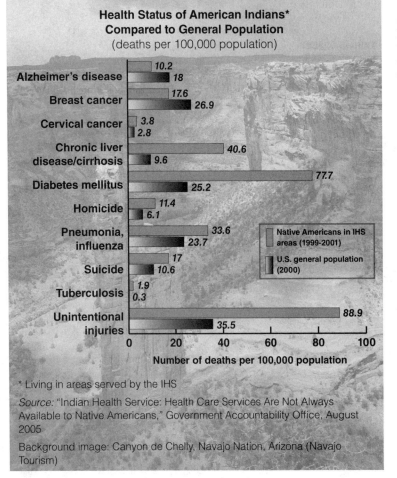

**Health Status of American Indians\***
**Compared to General Population**
(deaths per 100,000 population)

| Cause | Native Americans in IHS areas (1999-2001) | U.S. general population (2000) |
|---|---|---|
| Alzheimer's disease | 10.2 | 18 |
| Breast cancer | 17.6 | 26.9 |
| Cervical cancer | 3.8 | 2.8 |
| Chronic liver disease/cirrhosis | 40.6 | 9.6 |
| Diabetes mellitus | 77.7 | 25.2 |
| Homicide | 11.4 | 6.1 |
| Pneumonia, influenza | 33.6 | 23.7 |
| Suicide | 17 | 10.6 |
| Tuberculosis | 1.9 | 0.3 |
| Unintentional injuries | 88.9 | 35.5 |

Number of deaths per 100,000 population

\* Living in areas served by the IHS

*Source:* "Indian Health Service: Health Care Services Are Not Always Available to Native Americans," Government Accountability Office, August 2005

Background image: Canyon de Chelly, Navajo Nation, Arizona (Navajo Tourism)

involuntary manslaughter charge against a non-Indian who had allegedly killed an Indian near the reservation had renewed Indian anger at discriminatory treatment by police and judges.

The occupation soon turned into a full-blown siege, with the reservation surrounded by troops and federal law-enforcement officers. During several firefights two AIM members were killed, and an FBI agent was wounded. The occupation ended on May 8, 1973.

### Self-Determination

A mid the surging Indian activism, the federal government was trying to make up for the past by encouraging tribal self-determination.[46]

In 1975, Congress passed the Indian Self-Determination and Education Assistance Act, which channeled federal contracts and grants directly to tribes, reducing the BIA role and effectively putting Indian communities in direct charge of schools, health, housing and other programs.

And to assure Indians that the era of sudden reversals in federal policy had ended, the House in 1988 passed a resolution reaffirming the "constitutionally recognized government-to-government relationship with Indian tribes." Separate legislation set up a "self-governance demonstration project" in which eligible tribes would sign "compacts" to run their own governments with block grants from the federal government.[47]

By 1993, 28 tribes had negotiated compacts with the Interior Department. And in 1994, President Bill Clinton signed legislation that made self-governance a permanent option.

For the general public, the meaning of newly strengthened Indian sovereignty could be summed up with one word: casinos. In 1988, Congress enacted legislation regulating tribal gaming operations. That move followed a Supreme Court ruling (*California v. Cabazon*) that authorized tribes to run gambling operations. But tribes could not offer a form of gambling specifically barred by the state.

The law set up three categories of gambling operations: Class I, traditional Indian games, controlled exclusively by tribes; Class II, including bingo, lotto, pull tabs and some card games, which are allowed on tribal lands in states that allow the games elsewhere; and Class III, which takes in casino games such as slot machines, roulette and blackjack, which can be offered only under agreements with state governments that set out the size and types of the proposed casinos.

Limits that the Indian Gaming Regulatory Act put on Indian sovereignty were tightened further by a 1996 Supreme Court decision that the Seminole Tribe couldn't sue Florida to force negotiation of a casino compact. The decision essentially forced tribes nationwide to make revenue-sharing deals with states in return for approval of casinos.[48]

Meanwhile, particularly on reservations from Minnesota to the Pacific Northwest, a plague of methamphetamine addiction and manufacturing is leaving a trail of death and shattered lives. By 2002, Darrell Hillaire, chairman of the Lummi Nation, near Bellingham, Wash., said that members convicted of dealing meth would be expelled from the tribe.[49]

But the Lummis couldn't stop the spread of the scourge on other reservations. National Congress of American Indians President Garcia said early in 2006: "Methamphetamine is a poison taking Indian lives, destroying Indian families, and razing entire communities."[50]

## CURRENT SITUATION

### Self-Government

Some Indian leaders are advocating more power for tribal governments as the best way to improve the quality of life on reservations.

Under the Tribal Self-Governance Demonstration Project, made permanent in 1994, tribes can replace program-by-program grants by entering into "compacts" with the federal government, under which they receive a single grant for a variety of services. Some 231 tribes and Alaskan Native villages have compacts to administer a total of about $341 million in programs. Of the Indian communities now living under compacts, 72 are in the lower 48 states.[51]

Under a set of separate compacts, the Indian Health Service has turned over clinics, hospitals and health programs to some 300 tribes and Alaskan villages, 70 of them non-Alaskan tribes.

Native American children and adults in the Chicago area keep in touch with their cultural roots at the American Indian Center. About two-thirds of the nation's Indians live in urban areas.

*American Indian Center/Warren Perlstein*

The self-governance model has proved especially appropriate in Alaska, where the majority of the native population of 120,000 is concentrated in 229 villages, many of them remote, and compact in size, hence well-suited to managing their own affairs, experts say.

Another advantage of Alaska villages is the experience they acquired through the 1971 Alaska Native Claims Settlement Act, which granted a total of $962 million to Alaska natives born on or before Dec. 18, 1971, in exchange for giving up their claims to millions of acres of land. Villages formed regional corporations to manage the assets. In addition, all Alaska residents receive an annual dividend ($946 in 2005) from natural-resource royalty income.[52]

"The emergence of tribal authority is unprecedented in Indian Country's history," says Allen, of the Jamestown S'Klallam Tribe, one of the originators of the self-governance model. "Why not take the resources you have available and use them as efficiently as you can — more efficiently than currently being administered?"[53]

But the poorer and more populous tribes of the Great Plains and the Southwest have turned down the self-governance model. "They can't afford to do it," says Michael LaPointe, chief of staff to President Rodney Bordeaux of the Rosebud Sioux Tribe. "When you have a lot of poverty and not a lot of economic activity to generate tribal resources to supplement the unfunded mandates, it becomes impossible."

In contrast with the Jameston S'Klallam's tiny membership of 585 people, there are some 24,000 people on the Rosebud Siouxs' million-acre reservation. The tribe does operate law enforcement, ambulances and other services under contracts with the government. But it can't afford to do any more, LaPointe says.

A combined effect of the gambling boom and the growing adoption of the self-governance model is that much of the tension has gone out of the traditionally strained relationship between the BIA and tribes. "BIA people are getting pushed out as decision-makers," Kalt says. Some strains remain, to be sure. Allen says he senses a growing reluctance by the BIA to let go of tribes. "They use the argument that that the BIA doesn't have the money [for block grants]," he says.

BIA Director Ragsdale acknowledges that tougher financial-accounting requirements sparked by a lawsuit over Interior Department handling of Indian trust funds are slowing the compact-approval process. But, he adds, "We're not trying to hinder self-governance."

## Limits on Gambling

Several legislative efforts to limit Indian gaming are pending. Separate bills by Sen. McCain and House Resources Committee Chairman Richard Pombo, R-Calif., would restrict tribes' ability to acquire new land for casinos in more favorable locations.

More proposals are in the pipeline. Jemez Pueblo of New Mexico wants to build a casino near the town of Anthony, though the pueblo is 300 miles away.[54]

In eastern Oregon, the Warm Springs Tribe is proposing an off-reservation casino at the Columbia River Gorge. And in Washington state, the Cowlitz and Mohegan tribes are planning an off-reservation casino near Portland.[55] The process has been dubbed "reservation shopping."

Under the Indian Gaming Regulatory Act of 1988, a tribe can acquire off-reservation land for casinos when it is:

- granted as part of a land claim settlement;
- granted to a newly recognized tribe as its reservation;

- restored to a tribe whose tribal recognition is also restored; or
- granted to a recognized tribe that had no reservation when the act took effect.

The most hotly debated exemption allows the secretary of the Interior to grant an off-reservation acquisition that benefits the tribe without harming the community near the proposed casino location. Both Pombo and McCain would repeal the loophole created by this so-called "two-part test." Under Pombo's bill, tribes acquiring land under the other exemptions would have to have solid historic and recent ties to the property. Communities, state governors and state legislatures would have to approve the establishment of new casinos, and tribes would reimburse communities for the effects of casinos on transportation, law enforcement and other public services.

McCain's bill would impose fewer restrictions than Pombo's. But McCain would give the National Indian Gaming Commission final say over all contracts with outside suppliers of goods and services.

The bill would also ensure the commission's control over big-time gambling — a concern that arose from a 2005 decision by the U.S. Court of Appeals for the District of Columbia that limited the agency's jurisdiction over a Colorado tribe. The commission has been worrying that applying that decision nationwide would eliminate federal supervision of casinos.

McCain told a March 8 Senate Indian Affairs Committee hearing that the two-part test "is fostering opposition to all Indian gaming."[56]

If the senator had been aiming to soften tribal opposition to his bill, he didn't make much headway. "We believe that it grows out of anecdotal, anti-Indian press reports on Indian gaming, the overblown issue of off-reservation gaming, and a 'pin-the-blame-on-the-victim' reaction to the Abramoff scandal," Ron His Horse Is Thunder, chairman of the Standing Rock Sioux Tribe of North Dakota and South Dakota, told the committee. He argued that the bill would amount to unconstitutional meddling with Indian sovereignty.

But the idea of restricting "reservation-shopping" appeals to tribes facing competition from other tribes. Cheryle A. Kennedy, chairwoman of the Confederated Tribes of the Grand Ronde Community of Oregon, said

# Urban Indians: Invisible and Unheard

Two-thirds of the nation's 4.4 million American Indians live in towns and cities, but they're hard to find.[1] "Indians who move into metropolitan areas are scattered; they're not in a centralized geographical area," says New Mexico Secretary of Labor Conroy Chino. "You don't have that cohesive community where there's a sense of culture and language, as in Chinatown or Koreatown in Los Angeles."

Chino's interest is professional as well as personal. In his former career as a television journalist in Albuquerque, Chino, a member of the Acoma Pueblo, wrote an independent documentary about urban Indians. His subjects range from a city-loving San Franciscan who vacations in Hawaii to city-dwellers who return to their reservations every vacation they get. Their lives diverge sharply from what University of Arizona anthropologist Susan Lobo calls a "presumption that everything Indian is rural and long, long ago."[2]

Indian society began urbanizing in 1951, when the Bureau of Indian Affairs (BIA) started urging reservation dwellers to move to cities where — it was hoped — they would blend into the American "melting pot" and find more economic opportunity and a better standard of living.[3]

But many found the urban environment oppressive and the government assistance less generous than promised. About 100,000 Indians were relocated between 1951 and 1973, when the program wound down; unable to fit in, many fell into alcoholism and despair.[4]

Still, a small, urban Indian middle class has developed over time, partly because the BIA began systematically hiring Indians in its offices. Indians keep such a low profile, however, that the Census Bureau has a hard time finding them. Lobo, who consulted for the bureau in 1990, recalls that the agency's policy at the time was to register any household where no one answered the door as being in the same ethnic group as the neighbors. That strategy worked with urban ethnic groups who tended to cluster together, Lobo says, but not with Native Americans because theirs was a "dispersed population."

By the 2000 census that problem was resolved, but another one cropped up. "American Indians are ingenious at keeping expenses down — by couch-surfing, for instance," Lobo says. "There's a floating population that doesn't get counted because they weren't living in a standard residence."

But other urban Indians live conventional, middle-class lives, sometimes even while technically living on Indian land. "I am highly educated, a professor in the university, and my gainful employment is in the city of Albuquerque," says Ted Jojola, a professor of planning at the University of New Mexico (and a member of the Census Bureau's advisory committee on Indian population). "My community [Isleta Pueblo] is seven minutes south of Albuquerque. The reservation has become an urban amenity to me."

Some might see a home on Indian land near the city as a refuge from discrimination. "There have been years where you couldn't reveal you were native if you wanted to get a job," says Joseph Podlasek, executive director of the American Indian Center of Chicago.

Joycelyn Dorscher, president of the Association of American Indian Physicians, recalls a painful experience several years ago when she rushed her 6-year-old daughter to a hospital emergency room in Minneapolis-St. Paul, suspecting appendicitis. The young intern assigned to the case saw an Indian single mother with a sick child and apparently assumed that the daughter was suffering from neglect. "She told me if I didn't sit down and shut up, my daughter would go into the [child-protective] system," recalls Dorscher, who at the time was a third-year medical student.

Even Chino, whose mainstream credentials include an M.A. from Princeton, feels alienated at times from non-Indian city dwellers. He notes that Albuquerque officials ignored Indians' objections to a statue honoring Juan de Oñate, the 16th-century conqueror who established Spanish rule in what is now New Mexico. "Though native people protested and tried to show why this is not a good idea," Chino says, "the city went ahead and funded it."[5]

In the long run, Chino hopes a growing presence of Indian professionals — "we're not all silversmiths, or weavers" — will create more acceptance of urban Indians and more aid to combat high Indian dropout rates and other problems. "While people like having Indians in New Mexico and like visitors to get a feel for the last bastion of native culture," he says, "they're not doing that much for the urban Indian community, though we're paying taxes, too."

---

[1] Urban Indians were 64 percent of the population in 2000, according to the U.S. Census Bureau. For background, see, "We the People: American Indians and Alaska Natives in the United States," U.S. Census Bureau, 2000, p. 14, www.census.gov/prod/2006pubs/censr-28.pdf.

[2] "Looking Toward Home," *Native American Public Telecommunications*, 2003, www.visionmaker.org.

[3] Donald L. Fixico, *The Urban Indian Experience in America* (2000), pp. 9-11.

[4] *Ibid.*, pp. 22-25.

[5] Oñate is especially disliked at Acoma, Chino's birthplace, where the conqueror had the feet of some two-dozen Acoma men cut off in 1599 after Spanish soldiers were killed there. For background, see Wren Propp, "A Giant of Ambivalence," *Albuquerque Journal*, Jan. 25, 2004, p. A1; Brenda Norrell, "Pueblos Decry War Criminal," *Indian Country Today*, June 25, 2004.

**AT ISSUE**

# Should tribes open casinos on newly acquired land?

## YES — Ernest L. Stevens Jr.
*Chairman, National Indian Gaming Association*

From statement before U.S. House Committee on Resources, Nov. 9, 2005

Indian gaming is the Native American success story. Where there were no jobs, now there are 553,000 jobs. Where our people had only an eighth-grade education on average, tribal governments are building schools and funding college scholarships. Where the United States and boarding schools sought to suppress our languages, tribal schools are now teaching their native language. Where our people suffer epidemic diabetes, heart disease and premature death, our tribes are building hospitals, health clinics and wellness centers.

Historically, the United States signed treaties guaranteeing Indian lands as permanent homes, and then a few years later, went to war to take our lands. This left our people to live in poverty, often on desolate lands, while others mined for gold or pumped oil from the lands that were taken from us.

Indian gaming is an exercise of our inherent right to self-government. Today, for over 60 percent of Indian tribes in the lower 48 states, Indian gaming offers new hope and a chance for a better life for our children.

Too many lands were taken from Indian tribes, leaving some tribes landless or with no useful lands. To take account of historical mistreatment, the Indian Gaming Regulatory Act (IGRA), provided several exceptions to the rule that Indian tribes should conduct Indian gaming on lands held on Oct. 17, 1988.

Accordingly, land is restored to an Indian tribe in trust status when the tribe is restored to federal recognition. For federally recognized tribes that did not have reservation land on the date IGRA was enacted, land is put into trust. Or, a tribe may apply to the secretary of the Interior. The secretary consults with state and local officials and nearby Indian tribes to determine whether an acquisition of land in trust for gaming would be in the tribe's "best interest" and "not detrimental to the surrounding community."

Now, legislation would require "newly recognized, restored, or landless tribes" to apply to have land taken in trust through a five-part process. Subjecting tribes to this new and cumbersome process discounts the fact that the United States mistreated these tribes by ignoring and neglecting them, taking all of their lands or allowing their lands to be stolen by others.

We believe that Congress should restore these tribes to a portion of their historical lands and that these lands should be held on the same basis as other Indian lands.

## NO — State Rep. Fulton Sheen, R-Plainwell
*Michigan House of Representatives*

From statement to U.S. House Committee on Resources, April 5, 2006

The rampant proliferation of tribal gaming is running roughshod over states' rights and local control and is jeopardizing everything from my own neighborhood to — as the Jack Abramoff scandal has demonstrated — the very integrity of our federal political system.

In 1988, Congress passed the Indian Gaming Regulatory Act (IGRA) in an effort to control the development of Native American casinos and, in particular, to make sure that the states had a meaningful role in the development of any casinos within their borders. At that time, Native American gambling accounted for less than 1 percent of the nation's gambling industry, grossing approximately $100 million in revenue.

Since that time, the Native American casino business has exploded into an $18.5 billion industry that controls 25 percent of gaming industry revenue. Despite this unbridled growth, IGRA and the land-in-trust process remain basically unchanged.

When Congress originally enacted IGRA, the general rule was that casino gambling would not take place on newly acquired trust land. I believe Congress passed this general rule to prevent precisely what we see happening: a mad and largely unregulated land rush pushed by casino developers eager to cash in on a profitable revenue stream that is not burdened by the same tax rates or regulations that other businesses have to incur. "Reservation shopping" is an activity that must be stopped. And that is just one component of the full legislative overhaul that is needed.

IGRA and its associated land-in-trust process is broken, open to manipulation by special interests and in desperate need of immediate reform. It has unfairly and inappropriately fostered an industry that creates enormous wealth for a few select individuals and Las Vegas interests at the expense of taxpaying families, small businesses, manufacturing jobs and local governments.

Our research shows that while local and state governments receive some revenue-sharing percentages from tribal gaming, the dollars pale in comparison to the overall new costs to government and social-service agencies from increased infrastructure demands, traffic, bankruptcies, crime, divorce and general gambling-related ills.

I do not think this is what Congress had in mind. Somewhere along the way, the good intentions of Congress have been hijacked, and it is time for this body to reassert control over this process. It is imperative that Congress take swift and decisive steps today to get its arms around this issue before more jobs are lost and more families are put at risk.

her tribe's Spirit Mountain Casino could be hurt by the Warm Springs Tribes' proposed project or by the Cowlitz and Mohegan project.[57]

Pombo's bill would require the approval of new casinos by tribes that already have gambling houses up and running within 75 miles of a proposed new one.

The House Resources Committee heard another view from Indian Country at an April 5 hearing. Jacquie Davis-Van Huss, tribal secretary of the North Fork Rancheria of the Mono Indians of California, said Pombo's approval clause would doom her tribe's plans. "This provision is anti-competitive," she testified. "It effectively provides the power to veto another tribe's gaming project simply to protect market share."

## Trust Settlement

McCain's committee is also grappling with efforts to settle a decade-old lawsuit that has exposed longstanding federal mismanagement of trust funds. In 1999, U.S. District Judge Royce Lamberth said evidence showed "fiscal and governmental irresponsibility in its purest form."[58]

The alternative to settlement, McCain and Dorgan told the Budget Committee, is for the case to drag on through the courts. Congressional resolution of the conflict could also spare the Interior Department further grief from Lamberth. In a February ruling, he said Interior's refusal to make payments owed to Indians was "an obscenity that harkens back to the darkest days of United States-Indian relations."[59]

Five months later, Lamberth suggested that Congress, not the courts, may be the proper setting for the conflict. "Interior's unremitting neglect and mismanagement of the Indian trust has left it in such a shambles that recovery may prove impossible."[60]

The court case has its roots in the 1887 policy of allotting land to Indians in an effort to break up reservations. Since then, the Interior Department has been responsible for managing payments made to landholders, which later included tribes, for mining and other natural-resource extraction on Indian-owned land.

But for decades, Indians weren't receiving what they were owed. On June 10, 1996, Elouise Cobell, an organizer of the Blackfeet National Bank, the first Indian-owned national bank on a reservation, sued the Interior Department charging that she and all other trust fee recipients had been cheated for decades out of money that Interior was responsible for managing. "Lands and resources — in many cases the only source of income for some of our nation's poorest and most vulnerable citizens — have been grossly mismanaged," Cobell told the Indian Affairs Committee on March 1.

The mismanagement is beyond dispute, said John Bickerman, who was appointed to broker a settlement. Essentially, Bickerman told the Senate Indian Affairs Committee on March 28, "Money was not collected; money was not properly deposited; and money was not properly disbursed."

As of 2005, Interior is responsible for trust payments involving 126,079 tracts of land owned by 223,245 individuals — or, 2.3 million "ownership interests" on some 12 million acres, Cason and Ross Swimmer, a special trustee, told the committee.

Bickerman said a settlement amount of $27.5 billion proposed by the Indian plaintiffs was "without foundation." But the Interior Department proposed a settlement of $500 million based on "arbitrary and false assumptions," he added. Both sides agree that some $13 billion should have been paid to individual Indians over the life of the trust, but they disagree over how much was actually paid.

## Supreme Court Ruling

Powerful repercussions are expected from the Supreme Court's latest decision in a centuries-long string of rulings involving competing claims to land by Indians and non-Indians.

In 2005, the high court said the Oneida Indian Nation of New York could not quit paying taxes on 10 parcels of land it owns north of Utica.[61]

After buying the parcels in 1997 and 1998, the tribe refused to pay property taxes, arguing that the land was former tribal property now restored to tribal ownership, and thereby tax-exempt.[62]

The court, in an opinion written by Ruth Bader Ginsburg, concluded that though the tribe used to own the land, the property right was too old to revive. "Rekindling the embers of sovereignty that long ago grew cold" is out of the question, Ginsburg wrote. She invoked the legal doctrine of "laches," in which a party who waits too long to assert his rights loses them.[63]

Lawyers on both sides of Indian law cases expect the case to affect lower-court rulings throughout the country.

"The court has opened the cookie jar," Williams of the University of Arizona argues. "Does laches only apply to claims of sovereignty over reacquired land? If a decision favoring Indians is going to inconvenience too many white people, then laches applies — I swear that's what it says." Tribes litigating fishing rights, water rights and other assets are likely to suffer in court as a result, he argues.

In fact, only three months after the high court decision, the 2nd U.S. Circuit Court of Appeals in New York invoked laches in rejecting a claim by the Cayuga Tribe. Vickers of Upstate Citizens for Equality says that if the 2nd Circuit "thinks that laches forbids the Cayugas from making a claim because the Supreme Court said so, you're going to find other courts saying so."

In Washington, Alexandra Page, an attorney with the Indian Law Resource Center, agrees. "There are tribes in the West who have boundary disputes on their reservations; there are water-law cases where you've got people looking back at what happened years ago, so the Supreme Court decision could have significant practical impact. The danger is that those with an interest in limiting Indian rights will do everything they can to expand the decision and use it in other circumstances."

## OUTLOOK:

### Who Is an Indian?

If advocates of Indian self-governance are correct, the number of tribes running their own affairs with minimal federal supervision will keep on growing. "The requests for workshops are coming in steadily," says Cyndi Holmes, self-governance coordinator of the Jamestown S'Klallam Tribe.

Others say that growth, now at a rate of about three tribes a year, may be nearing its upper limit. "When you look at the options for tribes to do self-governance, economics really drives whether they can," says LaPointe of the Rosebud Sioux, whose tribal government doesn't expect to adopt the model in the foreseeable future.

But the longstanding problems of rural and isolated reservations are not the only dimension of Indian life. People stereotypically viewed as tied to the land have become increasingly urban over the past several decades, and the view from Indian Country is that the trend will continue.

That doesn't mean reservations will empty out or lose their cultural importance. "Urban Indian is not a lifelong

label," says Susan Lobo, an anthropologist at the University of Arizona. "Indian people, like everyone else, can move around. They're still American Indians."

For Indians, as for all other peoples, moving around leads to intermarriage. Matthew Snipp, a Stanford University sociologist who is half Cherokee and half Oklahoma Choctaw, notes that Indians have long married within and outside Indian society. But the consequences of intermarriage are different for Indians than for, say, Jews or Italians.

The Indian place in American society grows out of the government-to-government relationship between Washington and tribes. And most tribes define their members by what's known as the "blood quantum" — their degree of tribal ancestry.

"I look at it as you're kind of USDA-approved," says Podlasek of the American Indian Center. "Why is no other race measured that way?"

Podlasek is especially sensitive to the issue. His father was Polish-American, and his mother was Ojibway. His own wife is Indian, but from another tribe. "My kids can be on the tribal rolls, but their kids won't be able to enroll, unless they went back to my tribe or to their mother's tribe to marry — depending on what their partners' blood quantum is. In generations, you could say that, by government standards, there are no more native people."

Snipp traces the blood-quantum policy to a 1932 decision by the Indian Affairs Commission, which voted to make one-quarter descent the minimum standard. The commissioners were concerned, Snipp says, reading from the commission's report, that thousands of people "more white than Indian" were receiving "shares in tribal estates and other benefits." Tribes are no longer bound by that decision, but the requirement — originally inserted at BIA insistence — remains in many tribal constitutions.

On the Indian side, concern over collective survival is historically well-founded. Historian Elizabeth Shoemaker of the University of Connecticut at Storrs calculated that the Indian population of what is now the continental United States plummeted from a top estimate of 5.5 million in 1492 to a mere 237,000 in 1900. Indian life expectancy didn't begin to rise significantly until after 1940.[64]

Now, Indians are worrying about the survival of Indian civilization at a time when Indians' physical survival has never been more assured.

Even as these existential worries trouble some Indian leaders, the living conditions that most Indians endure also pose long-term concerns.

Conroy Chino, New Mexico's Labor secretary and a member of Acoma Pueblo, says continuation of the educational disaster in Indian Country is dooming young people to live on the margins. "I'm out there attracting companies to come to New Mexico, and these kids aren't going to qualify for those good jobs."

Nevertheless, below most non-Indians' radar screen, the Indian professional class is growing. "When I got my Ph.D. in 1973, I think I was the 15th in the country," says Beaulieu of Arizona State University's Center for Indian Education. "Now we have all kinds of Ph.D.s, teachers with certification, lawyers." And Beaulieu says he has seen the difference that Indian professionals make in his home state of Minnesota. "You're beginning to see an educated middle class in the reservation community, and realizing that they're volunteering to perform lots of services."

In Albuquerque, the University of New Mexico's Jojola commutes to campus from Isleta Pueblo. Chairman of an advisory committee on Indians to the U.S. Census Bureau, Jojola shares concerns about use of "blood quantum" as the sole determinant of Indian identity. "A lot of people are saying that language, culture and residence should also be considered," he says.

That standard would implicitly recognize what many Indians call the single biggest reason that American Indians have outlasted the efforts of those who wanted to exterminate or to assimilate them. "In our spirituality we remain strong," says Bordeaux of the Rosebud Sioux. "That's our godsend and our lifeline."

## UPDATE

American Indians have continued their reliance on casinos as an engine of tribal economic growth. Moreover, despite moral objections from anti-gambling organizations, Indians have emerged as major political donors in Washington, where they have lobbied successfully to maintain federal spending on Indian health and education.

Revenues from the 442 so-called Indian "gaming" facilities in 30 states rose from $19.6 billion in 2004 to

Ho-Chunk, Inc.

Harvard Law School graduate Lance Morgan, a member of Nebraska's Winnebago Tribe, used seed money from his tribe's small casino to create several thriving businesses. He urges other tribes to use their casino profits to diversify. "Gaming is just a means to an end," he says.

$26.7 billion in 2008, though they declined by 1 percent in 2009, according to the National Indian Gaming Commission.

In recent years casinos in California and Oklahoma have been the most successful, and in June National Indian Gaming Association Chairman Ernie Stevens Jr. attended the annual Sovereignty Symposium in Oklahoma City to praise local tribes for their work in providing jobs and making money to pay for improvements in education, health care and transportation.[65] "Oklahoma is No. 2 in Indian gaming," said Stevens. "I think that is tremendous. Is it an accident? Is it because of luck? I don't think so. This comes from hard work. This comes from a lot of dialogue and information sharing."

"Gaming has been transformative for tribes," says Washington, D.C., attorney Alan R. Fedman, former director of enforcement for the gaming commission.

President Barack Obama, surrounded by members of the administration and Native American leaders, signs the Tribal Law and Order Act during a ceremony in the East Room at the White House on July 29, 2010.

"The experience of tribal councils successfully running their own businesses has given them the confidence to diversify into other means of economic growth," such as medical-records processing and government contracting. Only about half of the 564 federally recognized tribes are involved in gaming, Fedman adds, and the ones that are not are doing about the same economically as they were 20 years ago.

## Critics of Gambling

But the reliance on gambling is not healthy in the long term, according to Les Bernal, executive director of Stop Predatory Gambling (formerly the National Coalition Against Legalized Gambling). "The political momentum is definitely against Indian tribes relying on casinos for economic growth because gambling is the most predatory business in America," he says. Decrying "casino capitalism" that "milks existing wealth instead of creating new wealth," the anti-gambling group laments the way tribal casinos, "funded by millionaire casino investors," continue to "force their way into communities across the nation."[66]

Bernal objects to political giving by tribes, noting that six of the top 11 donors to candidates in federal and state elections are Native American interests, according to a study of the 2007-08 election cycle by the Washington-based Center for Responsive Politics.[67]

But many tribes believe that playing the Washington "pay to play" game is a political imperative. "Native American interests have already been largely ignored in Washington," said Heather Dawn Thompson, past president of the National Native Bar Association and a partner at the D.C. law firm Sonnenschein Nath & Rosenthal. "It has been an uphill battle for tribes, with corporate and union interests active in political contributing, often against tribal interests.

## Supreme Court Ruling

Indian casino expansion hit a roadblock in February 2009, when the Supreme Court ruled against an Interior Department move to acquire 31 acres in Charlestown, R.I., for the Narragansett tribe, which envisioned using the land for a gambling facility. The court ruled 7-2 in *Carcieri v. Salazar* that because the tribe had not been federally recognized before enactment of the 1934 Indian Reorganization Act, the federal government could not take the land into trust and thus exempt it from many state gambling laws and taxes.[68]

The decision affected the Mashpee Wampanoag tribe on Cape Cod. Its application to the Bureau of Indian Affairs for a casino license drew backing in a June 2010 memo from Interior Secretary Ken Salazar, who offered to give the tribe an exemption allowed under the 1988 Federal Indian Gaming Regulatory Act. The act is the chief law governing tribal casinos. It often pits revenue-hungry states against tribes seeking federal trust status in hopes of opening gambling facilities free from state taxation.[69] Salazar's memo revived the issue in the Massachusetts legislature, which is considering a gambling bill that would give a licensing preference to Indian tribes.

Nationally, Salazar and many Indian tribes are working to persuade Congress to enact legislation to overturn the *Carcieri* ruling and permit more recently recognized tribes to take land into trust. On July 13, 2010, Indian advocates representing 17 tribal organizations came to Washington and met with Sen. Byron Dorgan, D-N.D., chair of the Senate Indian Affairs Committee, which had reported out related legislation in December 2009.[70] Dorgan at the time warned that the Supreme Court's interpretation "would have the effect of creating two classes of Indian tribes — those who were recognized as of 1934, for whom land may be taken into trust, and those recognized after 1934 that would be unable to have land taken into trust." He called that an "unacceptable" decision that flew in the face of prior acts of Congress and said it would harm Indians' employment and development projects, such as the building of homes and community centers.[71]

### Government Action

On July 26, the House Interior Appropriations Subcommittee voted to add a "*Carcieri* fix" to a spending bill, but prospects for enactment this Congress appeared uncertain.

American Indians have seen new infusions of federal funds and other aid under the Obama administration. Under the economic stimulus package — the American Recovery and Reinvestment Act of 2009 — which President Barack Obama signed during his second month in office, the Indian Health Service received $500 million, including $227 million for health facilities construction and $100 million for maintenance and improvements.[72]

The landmark health care reform law signed by Obama in March 2010 included permanent reauthorization of the 1976 Indian Health Care Improvement Act. "Our responsibility to provide health services to American Indians and Alaska Natives derives from the nation-to-nation relationship between the federal and tribal governments," he said. "With this bill, we have taken a critical step in fulfilling that responsibility by modernizing the Indian health care system and improving access to health care for American Indians and Alaska Natives."

The president noted that the new law, among other effects, will allow urban Indian health programs to provide employee health benefits under the Federal Employees Health Benefits Program; exempt urban Indian health providers from licensing and registration fees; make federal medical-supply sources available to Indian clinics; and require the Indian Health Service and the Health and Human Services Department to confer with tribes before putting new policies into place.

In another sign of Native American clout in Washington, Obama on July 29 signed an anti-crime bill that will require more reporting of rapes and assaults on Indian reservations while adding federal prosecutors and toughening sentences for violators.

### Crimes against Women

American Indian and Alaska Native women are nearly three times as likely to experience a rape or sexual assault compared to white, African-American or Asian-American women, according to a 2008 federally funded study.[73]

The signing of the act is "a significant and historic moment for tribal nations and federal law enforcement officials across the country," said Jefferson Keel, president of the National Congress of American Indians. "This legislation will empower tribal nations to begin to address crime rates that have risen in our communities as a result of jurisdictional and resource limitations," he said.

Dorgan said the next big step for Native Americans would be to secure more funding to boost law enforcement on the reservations. The Bureau of Indian Affairs says that only about 3,000 police officers patrol 56 million acres of Indian land, about 48 percent below the national average.[74]

Perhaps the most pressing issue still unfolding for American Indians is the coming reauthorization of the Elementary and Secondary Education Act, commonly known as No Child Left Behind.

### Education Issues

At a June 17, 2010, hearing before the Senate Indian Affairs Committee, Chad Smith, principal chief of the Cherokee Nation, acknowledged the eight-year-old law has improved accountability measures intended to boost performance by both students and teachers. But "the Nation would specifically like to see less emphasis on testing and more flexibility in establishing our own measurables," he said. "We feel that a more diverse curriculum will better fit the needs of our students by including increased focus on native culture and language. Culturally relevant education is successful with Indian students because [our cultural strengths] have helped us to face adversity, adapt, survive, prosper and excel for generations. Our younger children, immersion students included, are also forced to take tests in English while many students in rural areas are English-language learners, meaning they arrive at school knowing little or no English, which causes them to test poorly."[75]

School safety is also an ongoing concern to American Indians. According to May 2010 testimony by Quinton Roman Nose, a board member of the National Indian Education Association, "appalling disparities exist in the levels of safety, both structural and personal, in Bureau of Indian Education-funded schools, creating educational environments that are a threat to the emotional and physical well-being of native students." He said the association is seeking funds for a deferred-maintenance backlog estimated at $500 million at nearly 4,500 Indian school buildings.

The group also called for improved youth-violence prevention programs, arguing that "tribal communities are in the best position to advise and help develop culturally relevant and appropriate methods for addressing issues like bullying prevention, substance abuse prevention, anti-gang programming and suicide prevention."[76]

Such social problems continue to drive much of the Native American agenda. The Navajo Nation in 2009 reported that the number of youth gangs among its widespread population of 250,000 in recent years has grown to 225, many of them involved in drug trafficking.[77]

Christopher Grant, former chief of detectives in Rapid City, S.D., who is now a national Native American gang specialist, said gangs and drug traffickers often take advantage of meager tribal law enforcement resources and confusion over whether federal, state, local or tribal officers have jurisdiction.[78]

Meanwhile, suicide remains a serious concern. The youth suicide rate on Indian lands is now 70 percent higher than that of the general population, according to the office of Sen. Dorgan, who on July 26 hosted a summit meeting in Washington on suicide prevention among Native Americans. Calling the situation an "urgent and pressing crisis," Dorgan said that "building partnerships between Indian Country, [the] federal government and the private sector is critical to developing better strategies and programs for reaching at-risk Native American teens."[79]

## NOTES

1. For background, see "The Administration of Indian Affairs," *Editorial Research Reports 1929* (Vol. II), at *CQ Researcher Plus Archive*, CQ Electronic Library, http://library.cqpress.com.

2. For background see Phil Two Eagle, "Rosebud Sioux Tribe, Demographics," March 25, 2003, www.rosebudsiouxtribe-nsn.gov/demographics.

3. "American Indian Population and Labor Force Report 2003," p. ii, Bureau of Indian Affairs, cited in John McCain, chairman, Senate Indian Affairs Committee, Byron L. Dorgan, vice chairman, letter to Senate Budget Committee, March 2, 2006, http://indian.senate.gov/public/_files/Budget5.pdf.

4. Jonathan B. Taylor and Joseph P. Kalt, "American Indians on Reservations: A Databook of Socioeconomic Change Between the 1990 and 2000 Censuses," Harvard Project on American Indian Economic Development, January 2005, pp. 8-13; www.ksg.harvard.edu/hpaied/pubs/pub_151.htm. These data exclude the Navajo Tribe, whose on-reservation population of about 175,000 is 12 times that of the next-largest tribe, thus distorting comparisons, Taylor and Kalt write.

5. *Ibid.*, p. 41.

6. McCain and Dorgan, *op. cit.*

7. "Injury Mortality Among American Indian and Alaska Native Youth, United States, 1989-1998," *Morbidity and Mortality Weekly Report*, Centers for Disease Control and Prevention, Aug. 1, 2003, www.cdc.gov/mmwr/preview/mmwrhtml/mm5230a2.htm#top.

8. Robert McSwain, deputy director, Indian Health Service, testimony before Senate Indian Affairs Committee, April 5, 2006.

9. *Ibid.*, p. xii.

10. Taylor and Kalt, *op. cit.*

11. *Ibid.*, pp. 28-30.

12. *Ibid.*, pp. 22-24.

13. The decision is *Cherokee Nation v. Georgia*, 30 U.S. 1 (1831), http://supreme.justia.com/us/30/1/case.html.

14. Alan Meister, "Indian Gaming industry Report," Analysis Group, 2006, p. 2. Publicly available data can be obtained at, "Indian Gaming Facts," www.indiangaming.org/library/indian-gaming-facts; "Gaming Revenues, 2000-2004," National Indian Gaming Commission, www.nigc.gov/TribalData/GamingRevenues20042000/tabid/549/Default.aspx.

15. The ruling is *California v. Cabazon Band of Mission Indians*, 480 U.S. 202 (1987), http://supreme.justia.com/us/480/202/case.html.

16. For background, see Susan Schmidt and James V. Grimaldi, "The Rise and Steep Fall of Jack Abramoff," *The Washington Post*, Dec. 29, 2005, p. A1. On March 29, Abramoff was sentenced in Miami to 70 months in prison after pleading to fraud, tax evasion and conspiracy to bribe public officials in charges growing out of a Florida business deal. He is cooperating with the Justice Department in its Washington-based political-corruption investigation. For background see Peter Katel, "Lobbying Boom," *CQ Researcher*, July 22, 2005, pp. 613-636.

17. Meister, *op. cit.*, pp. 27-28. For additional background, see John Cochran, "A Piece of the Action," *CQ Weekly*, May 9, 2005, p. 1208.

18. For background, see, "A Quiet Crisis: Federal Funding and Unmet Needs in Indian Country," U.S. Commission on Civil Rights, July, 2003, pp. 32, 113. www.usccr.gov/pubs/na0703/na0731.pdf.

19. Ryan Wilson, "State of Indian Education Address," Feb. 13, 2006, www.niea.org/history/SOIE Address06.pdf.

20. For background see, Barbara Mantel, "No Child Left Behind," *CQ Researcher*, May 27, 2005, pp. 469-492.

21. McCain and Dorgan, *op. cit.*, pp. 14-15.

22. According to the Health and Human Services Department's budget proposal, recommended funding of $2 billion for the health centers would allow them to serve 150,000 Indian patients, among a total of 8.8 million patients. For background, see "Budget in Brief, Fiscal Year 2007," Department of Health and Human Services, p. 26, www.hhs.gov/budget/07budget/2007BudgetInBrief.pdf.

23. Peter Whoriskey, "A Tribe Takes a Grim Satisfaction in Abramoff's Fall," *The Washington Post*, Jan. 7, 2006, p. A1.

24. Meister, *op. cit.*, p. 15.

25. Whoriskey, *op. cit.*

26. For background see Fred Carstensen, *et al.*, "The Economic Impact of the Mashantucket Pequot Tribal National Operations on Connecticut," Connecticut Center for Economic Analysis, University of Connecticut, Nov. 28, 2000, pp. 1-3.

27. "Gambling Revenues 2004-2000," National Indian Gaming Commission, www.nigc.gov/TribalData/GamingRevenues20042000/tabid/549/Default.aspx.

28. Schmidt and Grimaldi, *op. cit.*

29. Alaina Potrikus, "2nd Land Hearing Packed," *The Post-Standard* (Syracuse, N.Y.), Jan. 12, 2006, p. B1.

30. For background see "Profile of the Navajo Nation," Navajo Nation Council, www.navajonationcouncil.org/profile.

31. Leslie Linthicum, "Navajos Cautious About Opening Casinos," *Albuquerque Journal*, Dec. 12, 2004, p. B1.

32. For background, see "Fourth Annual State of Indian Nations," Feb. 2, 2006, www.ncai.org/News_Archive.18.0.

33. For background see Theodore H. Haas, *The Indian and the Law* (1949), p. 2; thorpe.ou.edu/cohen/tribalgovtpam2pt1&2.htm#Tribal%20Power%20Today.

34. Except where otherwise noted, material in this section is drawn from Angie Debo, *A History of the Indians of the United States* (1970); see also, Mary H. Cooper, "Native Americans' Future," *CQ Researcher*, July 12, 1996, pp. 603-621.

35. W. Dale Mason, "Indian Gaming: Tribal Sovereignty and American Politics," 2000, p. 13.

36. *Cherokee Nation v. Georgia*, *op. cit.*, 30 U.S.1, http://supct.law.cornell.edu/supct/html/historics/USSC_CR_0030_0001_ZO.html.

37. Robert A. Williams Jr., *Like a Loaded Weapon: the Rehnquist Court, Indians Rights, and the Legal History of Racism in America* (2005), p. 63.

38. *Johnson v. M'Intosh*, 21 U.S. 543 (1823), www.Justia.us/us21543/case.html; *Worcester v. State of Ga.*, 31 U.S. 515 (1832), www.justia.us/us/31/515/case.html.

39. *Johnson v. M'Intosh*, *op. cit.*

40. *Worcester v. State of Ga.*, *op. cit.*

41. Quoted in Debo, *op. cit.*, pp. 219-220.

42. Quoted in *ibid.*, p. 303.

43. The specified states were Wisconsin, Minnesota (except Red Lake), Nebraska, California and Oregon

(except the land of several tribes at Warm Springs). For background, see Debo, *op. cit.*, pp. 304-311.

44. Cited in Debo, *op. cit.*, p. 344.

45. For background see Troy R. Johnson, *The Occupation of Alcatraz Island: Indian Self-Determination and the Rise of Indian Activism* (1996).

46. For background, see Mary H. Cooper, "Native Americans' Future," *CQ Researcher*, July 12, 1996, pp. 603-621.

47. For background see "History of the Tribal Self-Governance Initiative," Self-Governance Tribal Consortium, www.tribalselfgov.org/Red%20Book/SG_New_Partnership.asp.

48. Cochran, *op. cit.*

49. For background see Paul Shukovsky, "Lummi Leader's Had It With Drugs, Sick of Substance Abuse Ravaging the Tribe," *Seattle Post-Intelligencer*, March 16, 2002, p. A1.

50. "Fourth Annual State of Indian Nations," *op. cit.*

51. Many Alaskan villages have joined collective compacts, so the total number of these agreements is 91.

52. For background see Alexandra J. McClanahan, "Alaska Native Claims Settlement Act (ANCSA)," Cook Inlet Region Inc., http://litsite.alaska.edu/aktraditions/ancsa.html; "The Permanent Fund Dividend," Alaska Permanent Fund Corporation, 2005, www.apfc.org/alaska/dividendprgrm.cfm?s=4.

53. For background see Eric Henson and Jonathan B. Taylor, "Native America at the New Millennium," Harvard Project on American Indian Development, Native Nations Institute, First Nations Development Institute, 2002, pp. 14-16, www.ksg.harvard.edu/hpaied/pubs/pub_004.htm.

54. Michael Coleman, "Jemez Casino Proposal At Risk," *Albuquerque Journal*, March 10, 2006, p. A1; Jeff Jones, "AG Warns Against Off-Reservation Casino," *Albuquerque Journal*, June 18, 2005, p. A1.

55. For background see testimony, "Off-Reservation Indian Gaming," House Resources Committee, Nov. 9, 2005, http://resourcescommittee.house.gov/archives/109/full/110905.htm.

56. Jerry Reynolds, "Gaming regulatory act to lose its 'two-part test,' " *Indian Country Today*, March 8, 2006.

57. Testimony before House Resources Committee, Nov. 9, 2005.

58. Matt Kelley, "Government asks for secrecy on its lawyers' role in concealing document shredding," The Associated Press, Nov. 2, 2000.

59. "Memorandum and Order," Civil Action No. 96-1285 (RCL), Feb. 7, 2005, www.indiantrust.com/index.cfm?FuseAction=PDFTypes.Home&PDFType_id=1&IsRecent=1.

60. "Memorandum Opinion," Civil Action 96-1285 (RCL), July 12, 2005, www.indiantrust.com/index.cfm?FuseAction=PDFTypes.Home&PDFType_id=1&IsRecent=1.

61. Glenn Coin, "Supreme Court: Oneidas Too Late; Sherrill Declares Victory, Wants Taxes," *The Post-Standard* (Syracuse), March 30, 2005, p. A1.

62. *Ibid.*

63. *City of Sherrill, New York, v. Oneida Indian Nation of New York*, Supreme Court of the United States, 544 U.S._(2005), pp. 1-2, 6, 14, 21.

64. Elizabeth Shoemaker, *American Indian Population Recovery in the Twentieth Century* (1999), pp. 1-13.

65. "Indian Gaming Update," National Indian Gaming Association, June 2010, www.indian gaming.org/info/newsletter/2010/NIGA_NEWSLETTER_06-10.pdf.

66. Stop Predatory Gambling, blog, www.stop predatorygambling.org, June 15, 2010.

67. For the study, see www.opensecrets.org/orgs/list_stfed.php?order=A. For related commentary, see "Guess who is among the top lobbying spenders in D.C.-Indian gaming," *San Jose Mercury News*, editorial, Feb. 11, 2010.

68. Matthew L. M. Fletcher, "Decision's in. 'Now' begins work to fix Carcieri," guest editorial, *Indian Country Today*, Feb. 25, 2009; Casey Ross, "A Crapshoot for Mass.," *The Boston Globe*, May 26, 2010, www.boston.com/business/articles/2010/05/26/indian_gaming_debate_has_mass_in_limbo?mode=PF.

69. George Brennan, "Tribe's Casino Odds Improve," *Cape Cod Times*, June 30, 2010.

70. John E. Mulligan, "Tribal-Rights Advocates Seek Fix in Washington," *Providence Journal-Bulletin*, July 14, 2010.

71. Gale Courey Toensing, "Most Negative Impact," *Indian Country Today*, Dec. 30, 2009, www.indiancountrytoday.com/home/content/40290987.html.

72. Indian Health Service, www.ihs.gov/ recovery/.

73. Ronet Bachman, *et al.*, "Violence Against American Indian and Alaska Native Women and the Criminal Justice Response: What is Known," National Criminal Justice Reference Service, August 2008, www.ncjrs .gov/pdffiles1/ nij/grants/223691.pdf, p. 33.

74. Michael W. Savage, "Obama to sign bill targeting violent crime on Indian reservations," *The Washington Post*, July 29, 2010, p. A21.

75. Chad Smith, testimony before Senate Committee on Indian Affairs oversight hearing on Indian education, June 17, 2010.

76. Quinton Roman Nose, testimony before Senate Indian Affairs Committee oversight hearing on Indian school safety, May 13, 2010.

77. "Gang Violence on the Rise on Indian Reservations," "Tell Me More," NPR, Aug. 25, 2009.

78. *Ibid.*

79. *Red Lake Net News*, July 27, 2010, www.rlnn.us/ Art012010DorganHostsSummitPartnerAid Indian YouthSuicidePrevEfforts.html.

# BIBLIOGRAPHY

## Books

**Alexie, Sherman,** *The Toughest Indian in the World,* **Grove Press, 2000.**
In a short-story collection, an author and screenwriter draws on his own background as a Spokane/Coeur d'Alene Indian to describe reservation and urban Indian life in loving but unsentimental detail.

**Debo, Angie,** *A History of the Indians of the United States,* **University of Oklahoma Press, 1970.**
A pioneering historian and champion of Indian rights provides one of the leading narrative histories of the first five centuries of Indian and non-Indian coexistence and conflict.

**Deloria, Vine Jr.,** *Custer Died For Your Sins: An Indian Manifesto,* **University of Oklahoma Press, 1988.**
First published in 1969, this angry book gave many non-Indians a look at how the United States appeared through Indians' eyes and spurred many young Native Americans into political activism.

**Mason, W. Dale,** *Indian Gaming: Tribal Sovereignty and American Politics,* **University of Oklahoma Press, 2000.**
A University of New Mexico political scientist provides the essential background on the birth and early explosive growth of Indian-owned gambling operations.

**Williams, Robert A.,** *Like a Loaded Weapon: The Rehnquist Court, Indians Rights, and the Legal History of Racism in America,* **University of Minnesota Press, 2005.**
A professor of law and American Indian Studies at the University of Arizona and tribal appeals court judge delivers a detailed and angry analysis of the history of U.S. court decisions affecting Indians.

## Articles

**Bartlett, Donald L., and James B. Steele, "Playing the Political Slots; How Indian Casino Interests Have Learned the Art of Buying Influence in Washington,"** *Time,* **Dec. 23, 2002, p. 52.**
In a prescient article that preceded the Jack Abramoff lobbying scandal, veteran investigative journalists examine the political effects of some tribes' newfound wealth.

**Harden, Blaine, "Walking the Land with Pride Again; A Revolution in Indian Country Spawns Wealth and Optimism,"** *The Washington Post,* **Sept. 19, 2004, p. A1.**
Improved conditions in many sectors of Indian America have spawned a change in outlook, despite remaining hardships.

**Morgan, Lance, "Ending the Curse of Trust Land,"** *Indian Country Today,* **March 18, 2005, www .indiancountry.com/content.cfm?id=1096410559.**
A lawyer and pioneering tribal entrepreneur lays out his vision of a revamped legal-political system in which Indians would own their tribal land outright, with federal supervision ended.

**Robbins, Ted, "Tribal cultures, nutrition clash on fry bread," "All Things Considered," National Public Radio, Oct. 26, 2005, transcript available at www .npr.org/templates/story/story.php?storyId=4975889.**
Indian health educators have tried to lower Native Americans' consumption of a beloved but medically disastrous treat.

**Thompson, Ginger, "As a Sculpture Takes Shape in New Mexico, Opposition Takes Shape in the U.S.,"** *The New York Times*, **Jan. 17, 2002, p. A12.**
Indian outrage has clashed with Latino pride over a statue celebrating the ruthless Spanish conqueror of present-day New Mexico.

**Wagner, Dennis, "Tribes Across Country Confront Horrors of Meth,"** *The Arizona Republic*, **March 31, 2006, p. A1.**
Methamphetamine use and manufacturing have become the scourge of Indian Country.

### Reports and Studies

**"Indian Health Service: Health Care Services Are Not Always Available to Native Americans," Government Accountability Office, August 2005.**
Congress' investigative arm concludes that financial shortfalls combined with dismal reservation conditions, including scarce transportation, are stunting medical care for many American Indians.

**"Strengthening the Circle: Interior Indian Affairs Highlights, 2001-2004," Department of the Interior (undated).**
The Bush administration sums up its first term's accomplishments in Indian Country.

**Cornell, Stephen,** *et al.,* **"Seizing the Future: Why Some Native Nations Do and Others Don't," Native Nations Institute, Udall Center for Studies in Public Policy, University of Arizona, Harvard Project on American Indian Economic Development, John F. Kennedy School of Government, Harvard University, 2005.**
The authors argue that the key to development lies in a tribe's redefinition of itself from object of government attention to independent power.

# For More Information

**Committee on Indian Affairs**, U.S. Senate, 838 Hart Office Building, Washington, DC 20510; (202) 224-2251; http://indian.senate.gov/public. A valuable source of information on developments affecting Indian Country.

**Harvard Project on American Indian Economic Development**, John F. Kennedy School of Government, 79 John F. Kennedy St., Cambridge, MA 02138; (617) 495-1480; www.ksg.harvard.edu/hpaied. Explores strategies for Indian advancement.

**Indian Health Service**, The Reyes Building, 801 Thompson Ave., Suite 400, Rockville, MD 20852; (301) 443-1083; www.ihs.gov. One of the most important federal agencies in Indian Country; provides a wide variety of medical and administrative information.

**National Coalition Against Legalized Gambling**, 100 Maryland Ave., N.E., Room 311, Washington, DC 20002; (800) 664-2680; www.ncalg.org. Provides anti-gamblingmaterial that touches on tribe-owned operations.

**National Indian Education Association**, 110 Maryland Ave., N.E., Suite 104, Washington, DC 20002; (202) 544-7290; www.niea.org/welcome. Primary organization and lobbying voice for Indian educators.

**National Indian Gaming Association**, 224 Second St., S.E., Washington, DC 20003; (202) 546-7711; www.indian gaming.org. Trade association and lobbying arm of the tribal casino industry.

**Self-Governance Communication and Education Tribal Consortium** 1768 Iowa Business Center, Bellingham, WA 98229; (360) 752-2270, www.tribalselfgov.org. Organizational hub of Indian self-governance movement; provides a wide variety of news and data.

**Upstate Citizens for Equality**, P.O. Box 24, Union Springs, NY 13160; http://upstate-citizens.org. Opposes tribal land-claim litigation.

# 9

# Racial Profiling

Kenneth Jost

Demonstrators in Los Angeles on July 16, 2013, protest the acquittal of white neighborhood watch volunteer George Zimmerman in the shooting death of Trayvon Martin, an unarmed black Florida 17-year-old. The verdict touched off a nationwide debate on racial profiling, which minority groups say is widespread. Two major court cases target the New York Police Department's stop-and-frisk policy and Arizona Sheriff Joe Arpaio's controversial immigration-related profiling.

From *CQ Researcher*, November 22, 2013.

Twice within less than a year, David Floyd was stopped and frisked by New York City police officers while on his way home — once while walking on the street and once while fumbling with keys at the front door to his building. Officers found no weapons or contraband and filed no charges in either incident, the first in April 2007 and the second in February 2008.

Five years after the second incident, however, Floyd, an African-American now 33 years old, was still seething. "The whole experience, it's humiliating, it's embarrassing," Floyd told a reporter for *Colorlines*, a New York City-based online magazine on race issues. "It doesn't matter what kind of person you are, how tough you are. It's a scary thing because you don't know what's going to happen with your life, you don't know what's going to happen with your freedom."[1]

Floyd, now a medical student in Havana, Cuba, made the comments in late March after testifying as the lead plaintiff in a major class action against the New York City Police Department (NYPD). The suit, *Floyd v. City of New York*, charges the NYPD, the nation's largest police force, with using racial profiling as part of an aggressive stop-and-frisk policy maintained for 10 years under Mayor Michael Bloomberg and Police Commissioner Raymond W. Kelly.*

Bloomberg and Kelly credit the city's declining crime rate under their watch to a sevenfold increase in the number of police stops of pedestrians during Bloomberg's tenure, especially in high-crime,

---

*The widely used term "racial profiling" in this report encompasses the targeting of an individual based on either race or ethnicity.

## Majority of States Address Racial Profiling

At least 30 states have passed laws addressing racial profiling, according to the National Conference of State Legislatures. The laws vary widely. About half explicitly prohibit profiling. Others require law enforcement agencies to compile data on the race and ethnicity of drivers and pedestrians stopped by police and to develop policies and train officers on how to avoid profiling.

### States with Racial Profiling Laws

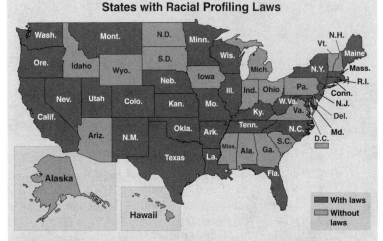

*Sources:* National Conference of State Legislatures, from unpublished compilation provided on request; Alejandro del Carmen, Racial Profiling in America (2008)

the city's request and — in an extraordinary action — removed her from the case. On Oct. 31, a panel of the Second U.S. Circuit Court of Appeals in New York City said Scheindlin had violated judicial ethics by steering the *Floyd* case to her court and by giving interviews to journalists while the case was before her. The appeals court's stay was to remain in effect until after the appeal is heard, sometime after mid-March.[3]

Scheindlin's ruling represents the most dramatic court decision on an issue that has simmered and occasionally boiled over since the 1990s.[4] African-Americans have long complained of what they regard as unwarranted traffic and pedestrian stops by police, seemingly prompted by nothing other than their race. More recently, Hispanics and people of Arab or South Asian backgrounds have registered similar complaints about being targeted by police because of their ethnicity as suspected immigration violators or as terrorists.

predominantly African-American and Hispanic neighborhoods. In a blockbuster decision, however, U.S. District Judge Shira Scheindlin ruled on Aug. 12 that such stop-and-frisk tactics violated the constitutional rights of minorities in New York City.

Scheindlin called the disproportionate number of blacks and Hispanics stopped by police "indirect racial profiling" that violates the Constitution's Equal Protection Clause and faulted police for violating Supreme Court guidelines under the Fourth Amendment on when such stops are allowed. Scheindlin emphasized that nearly 90 percent of the persons stopped were neither arrested nor given summonses. The veteran, Democratic-appointed judge named Peter Zimroth, a prominent New York lawyer and a former top counsel to the city, to serve as an "independent monitor" to oversee, with community input, reform of the use of the tactic.[2]

Two-and-a-half months later, however, a federal appeals court panel put a hold on Scheindlin's order at

Racial profiling is not only unfair to the individuals stopped but also unhealthy for police-community relations, experts say. "If the people you serve think you are going about it illegitimately, then there are going to be problems," says Jim Bueermann, president of the Police Foundation, a Washington-based think tank, and a former police chief in Redlands, Calif.

Anecdotal and statistical evidence indicating that police disproportionately stop and ticket African-American motorists compared to white drivers helped popularize the cynical phrase "driving while black." More substantively, that evidence has figured in court cases and legislation requiring law enforcement agencies to collect racial and ethnic data on traffic stops to identify possible racial profiling.

Today, minority-rights groups say racial profiling by police is widespread in the United States. "Absolutely," says Hilary Shelton, director of the Washington office of the NAACP, the century-old civil rights organization.

"We still get reports from our folks who say they cannot find any good reason why they were stopped."

Profiling of Latinos also has become "quite extensive," according to Thomas Saenz, president of the Mexican American Legal Defense and Educational Fund (MALDEF), especially now that police in some jurisdictions have been asked to engage in immigration enforcement.[5] "They are forced to rely on stereotypes," Saenz explains, "and stereotypes in immigration particularly rest on ethnicity and race."

Immigration-related enforcement is at the heart of a second closely watched profiling case in Arizona against Sheriff Joe Arpaio, the controversial head of the chief law enforcement agency in Maricopa County, which includes Phoenix. U.S. District Judge Murray Snow ordered an array of reforms on Oct. 2, including expanded use of video cameras in police stops, after having found the sheriff's office guilty in late May of discriminatory targeting of Latinos without adequate cause. Arpaio has repeatedly denied the allegations.[6]

## Most Police Stops Viewed as Legitimate

Police stopped about 31 million drivers or pedestrians in the U.S. in 2011, according to a triennial Justice Department survey. Most of those stopped said police had legitimate grounds and behaved properly during the encounter. Black and Hispanic drivers, however, were less likely than white drivers to view the stop as legitimate and more likely to be ticketed. The survey found no statistical difference in the race or ethnicity of pedestrians in street stops.

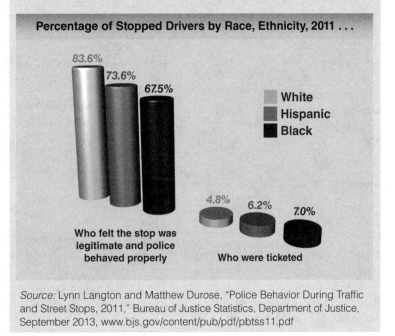

**Percentage of Stopped Drivers by Race, Ethnicity, 2011 . . .**

- 83.6% White
- 73.6% Hispanic
- 67.5% Black

Who felt the stop was legitimate and police behaved properly

- 4.8%
- 6.2%
- 7.0%

Who were ticketed

*Source:* Lynn Langton and Matthew Durose, "Police Behavior During Traffic and Street Stops, 2011," Bureau of Justice Statistics, Department of Justice, September 2013, www.bjs.gov/content/pub/pdf/pbtss11.pdf

Likewise, Bloomberg and Kelly stoutly deny improper racial profiling by the NYPD, even while acknowledging the evidence plaintiffs cited from the department's own detailed record-keeping. Of 4.4 million stops logged from 2004 to 2012, 53 percent involved African-Americans and 32 percent Hispanics. The city's overall population is only 26 percent African-American and 29 percent Hispanic.

Bloomberg and Kelly say the stops reflect the demographics of criminal offenders. "It's not a disproportionate percentage of those who witnesses and victims describe as committing the murders," Bloomberg contended in his weekly program on radio station WOR in late June.[7]

Heather Mac Donald, a senior fellow at the conservative Manhattan Institute think tank who has followed the racial profiling controversy for more than a decade, agrees the city is concentrating police resources where it should. "Given the racial distribution of crime, any police department, at least in an urban environment, that is targeting crime is going to produce racially disproportionate activity," she says. "But that is not the same as racial profiling."[8]

Nationally, experts who have studied the issue from different perspectives agree that racial profiling is difficult to measure and the extent of the practice unknown. "There's a lot of noise, but not a lot of proof that people are actually being profiled," says Brian Withrow, a professor of criminal justice at Texas State University in San Marcos who was a Texas state trooper from 1981 to 1993.

"I don't think anybody knows the answer to that particular question," says Bueermann with the Police

Foundation. "Some people believe it's prevalent," he says. "Others will tell you that it's not."

"It's a very difficult question to answer," says David Harris, a professor at the University of Pittsburgh Law School and a leading critic of racial profiling since the late 1990s. "It certainly exists. In some departments it may have a large role; in some, less so; in some, not at all."

Public concern about the issue is also hard to measure. In a recent report, the Department of Justice found that most people subjected to traffic or pedestrian stops in 2011 believed the stops were legitimate and police acted properly. But African-Americans and Hispanics were somewhat more likely to disagree and were somewhat more likely to be ticketed after traffic stops than white drivers.[9]

Lawyers from the Center for Constitutional Rights, a New York-based public interest law firm that represents the plaintiffs in the New York City case, hailed Scheindlin's ruling. "The NYPD is finally being held to account for its longstanding illegal and discriminatory policing practices," Darius Charney, a senior staff attorney with the center, said. "The city must now stop denying the problem and partner with the community to create a police department that protects the safety and respects the rights of all New Yorkers."

Appearing together on the day of the ruling, Bloomberg and Kelly defended the department's practices as lawful and effective. "Our crime strategies and tools — including Stop-Question-Frisk — have made New York City the safest big city in America," Bloomberg declared. Kelly labeled the racial-profiling finding "recklessly untrue. We do not engage in racial profiling," Kelly continued. "It is prohibited by law. It is prohibited by our own regulations."[10]

Scheindlin stressed that she was not prohibiting use of stop-and-frisk altogether. Beyond ordering the appointment of a monitor, she instructed the department only to institute a pilot project equipping officers in one precinct in each of the city's five boroughs with body-worn video cameras to record stops and arrests.

Bloomberg nevertheless warned that the judge's order threatens public safety in New York, promised to appeal and instructed the city's lawyers to seek to delay the order pending an appeal. Scheindlin on Sept. 17 rejected the city's motion for a stay. The city's lawyers then sought a stay in the Second Circuit, where an appeals panel heard arguments on Oct. 29 and issued the stay two days later.[11]

Meanwhile, the impact of stop-and-frisk on crime in New York emerged as an issue in the race to succeed Bloomberg, an Independent who was barred by term limits from seeking re-election. His policies were criticized by several candidates in the Democratic primary on Sept. 11, including the eventual winner, Bill de Blasio, the city's public advocate. De Blasio was elected mayor by a landslide on Nov. 5.

As de Blasio prepares to take office and police and law enforcement experts around the country watch developments in New York and Arizona, here are some of the major questions being debated:

## Are racial and ethnic profiling prevalent in U.S. law enforcement today?

As executive director of a community organization in the predominantly black Northside neighborhood of Kalamazoo, Mich., Mattie Jordan-Woods helps people fill out complaints against the city's police force about racial profiling. She herself feels she has been stopped because of her race several times in the past. Now, Kalamazoo officials and the city's African-American community have evidence on the issue.

A statistical study, released in September, shows that black motorists were twice as likely as white drivers to be stopped by Kalamazoo officers at 11 intersections studied over a 12-month period ending in February 2013. The study, conducted by John Lamberth, a pioneer of racial profiling research, also shows that black motorists were more likely to be searched after having been stopped, but that white drivers were more likely to be found with contraband.[12]

In submitting the report, Lamberth praised city leaders for requesting the study and promising to act on its findings. "The leadership of KPDS [Kalamazoo Department of Public Safety] and the City of Kalamazoo has made it clear to us that targeting of Black motorists is unacceptable and must change," Lamberth wrote. Jordan-Woods said she had "high hopes" but stressed that "systematic" changes were needed. "It's going to take long term," she told the *Kalamazoo Gazette*.

Lamberth, a social psychologist and former professor and chairman of the Department of Psychology at Temple University in Philadelphia, conducted path-breaking studies on racial profiling in two court cases in the 1990s. In

New Jersey, a judge relied on Lamberth's finding of apparent racial profiling by state troopers on the New Jersey Turnpike in throwing out evidence in drug cases against a group of 17 African-American defendants. Three years later, the New Jersey attorney general's office acknowledged that the state police had maintained a practice of targeting black motorists as suspected drug violators.

Lamberth had produced a similar study in Maryland that a black lawyer, Robert Wilkins, relied on in a civil suit against the state police after he was stopped without any charges being brought.* In settling the suit, the state paid Wilkins and his family $50,000 in damages and, more important, agreed to compile racial data on traffic stops and to change training and policies in order to prevent racial profiling.[13]

In the New York City case, Judge Scheindlin relied on a comparable statistical study by Jeffrey Fagan, a professor of criminal justice at Columbia Law School, which found police stops are "significantly more frequent" for blacks and Hispanics than for whites. In addition, Fagan found that police were more likely to use force against blacks and Hispanics than against whites. Experts retained by the city disputed Fagan's findings, but Scheindlin said Fagan's evidence was "more reliable."[14]

Lamberth and Fagan both took pains to make the studies statistically valid, but Mac Donald, the racial profiling skeptic at the Manhattan Institute, finds the studies generally worthless. "The cost of these studies is completely a total waste of money," she says.

Mac Donald — who had not seen the Kalamazoo study — faults traffic studies in general on the ground that they use as a benchmark all drivers instead of drivers committing traffic offenses. "It's absurd to look at who's being stopped without looking at who's speeding," she says. In a like vein, she says Fagan's study fails to account for the fact that blacks and Hispanics commit a larger percentage of crimes in New York than whites. In fact, she says, "Whites commit just 1 percent of the shootings but they're 9 percent of the stops."

Researchers agree that census data — commonly used for comparisons in news coverage — should not be used

New York City Mayor Michael Bloomberg, left, and Police Commissioner Raymond W. Kelly defend the city's aggressive stop-and-frisk policy, which they say has helped keep the city's crime rate down. They were responding to a blockbuster ruling on Aug. 12 by U.S. District Judge Shira Scheindlin that the policy violated the constitutional rights of minorities. An appeals court later removed Scheindlin from the case and put a temporary hold on her ruling, pending an appeal.

as a benchmark to compare police stops by race. "It's free, easy and it's the lowest common denominator," says Geoffrey Alpert, a professor of criminal justice at the University of South Carolina in Columbia. "And it's not worth its weight in anything in major cities and complex environments."

Creating the right baseline — for example, for traffic studies — can be "very difficult," Alpert explains. "We know who they pull over, we know to whom they give tickets, we know how long they keep them, but the problem is we don't know who the average driver is," he says. Alpert oversaw a study in Florida's Miami-Dade County that found what he termed "adverse results" at two of the eight intersections covered.

"Benchmarks are notoriously inaccurate and unreliable," says Withrow, the Texas State University professor. As another methodological problem, he notes that it is unclear how often police know the race of a driver before making a stop.

In their studies, both Lamberth and Fagan dealt with the benchmark issue. Lamberth reasoned that virtually all drivers are so likely to be committing some traffic violation as to give police broad discretion in determining what cars to stop. In his report, Fagan said he found a racial disparity after controlling for crime, the concentration of police and local social conditions.

*Wilkins is currently a federal district court judge in Washington, D.C.; President Obama nominated him for the U.S. Court of Appeals for the District of Columbia Circuit, but the Senate on Nov. 18 blocked his confirmation by failing — on a 53-38 vote, short of the 60 votes required — to close debate on the nomination.

## Blacks, Hispanics More Likely to Be Stopped

Of the approximately 1.6 million pedestrians stopped and questioned by New York City police officers during the period 2010-2012, more than half were African-American and nearly one in three were Hispanic. The statistics were compiled on behalf of the plaintiffs in the federal lawsuit *Floyd v. City of New York.*

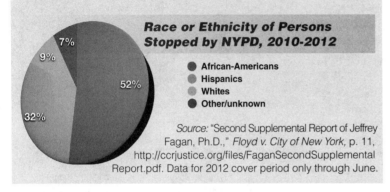

### Race or Ethnicity of Persons Stopped by NYPD, 2010-2012

- African-Americans
- Hispanics
- Whites
- Other/unknown

7%
9%
52%
32%

*Source:* "Second Supplemental Report of Jeffrey Fagan, Ph.D.," *Floyd v. City of New York,* p. 11, http://ccrjustice.org/files/FaganSecondSupplemental Report.pdf. Data for 2012 cover period only through June.

Alejandro del Carmen, chair of the Department of Criminology and Criminal Justice at the University of Texas at Arlington and a frequent instructor at police academies in Texas, says aggregate studies are useful but fail to identify individual officers who engage in racial profiling. Overall, he believes racial profiling exists but is exaggerated.

"Racial profiling as a whole doesn't have the prevalence that the media would lead the public to believe, but it happens more often than the folks on the other spectrum say," del Carmen says. "Racism continues to be a problem in the law enforcement community."

### Do aggressive stop-and-frisk tactics help reduce crime?

New York City police officers logged 97,296 stops in 2002, Bloomberg's first year as mayor and Kelly's first year as police commissioner. A decade later, in 2011, the number of stops peaked at 685,724 — a sevenfold increase. And all the while the city's overall crime rate and individual rates for murder and other crimes were falling. The murder rate, for example, fell from 4.8 to 3.9 per 100,000 inhabitants — a decline in absolute numbers from 909 in 2002 to 769 in 2011, even as the city's population rose.[15]

To Bloomberg and Kelly, the statistics prove the success of a law enforcement strategy that included increased

police stops as a significant component. "There is just no question that Stop-Question-Frisk has saved countless lives," Bloomberg said on the day of Scheindlin's decision in the stop-and-frisk case. "And we know that most of the lives saved, based on the statistics, have been black and Hispanic young men."[16]

Mac Donald, the Manhattan Institute fellow, agrees. She says stepped-up on-the-street enforcement has had "a remarkable effect," contributing to a steep decline in the state's total prison population. "Felony crime is so far down in New York City," Mac Donald says, "because they are able to intervene in suspicious behavior before it rises to the level of a felony crime."

Overlooked in the claims is the fact that New York City's crime rate began declining in the early 1990s — a decade before Bloomberg and Kelly took office. The number of murders per year, for example, peaked at 2,605 in 1990 and had declined by nearly two-thirds before Bloomberg took office. Moreover, the crime rate nationwide has been falling sharply since the 1990s. The FBI's "Uniform Crime Reports" show that the murder rate has fallen by half since 1993 — from 9.5 to 4.7 per 100,000 inhabitants.[17]

Criminologists generally play down the potential impact of specific police tactics on the overall crime rate. "I'm not certain that a specific program has that much of a benefit to the overall reduction of crime in New York City," says del Carmen, the University of Texas professor. "Crime is affected by numerous perspectives, most of which have nothing to do with police practices — for instance, the economy."

"New York City is not the only city that has had a healthy drop in crime," says Harris, the racial-profiling critic. "Other cities have done pretty well, and they have not made stop-and-frisk such an aggressive part of what they're doing."

Critics of the NYPD tactics also emphasize that the vast majority of stops resulted in no arrests or summonses. In its compilation, the New York Civil Liberties Union said the percentage of "completely innocent" persons who were stopped — meaning no arrest or summons ensued — had risen from 82 percent in 2002 to as high as 90 percent in 2006. An analysis of 150,000 stop-and-frisk arrests between 2009 and 2012 by the New York attorney general's office shows that only half resulted in convictions and only one-fourth of the total resulted in any prison time.[18]

The Supreme Court established guidelines for police stops in a 1968 decision, *Terry v. Ohio.*[19] Under *Terry*, police can stop an individual if an officer has a "reasonable suspicion" the individual is committing or is about to commit a crime. Police can conduct a limited pat-down for weapons based on a "reasonable belief" that the individual may be armed and dangerous. In both cases, the officer's belief must be based on "specific and articulable facts," not an officer's hunch. "A focus on a person's race or ethnicity does not satisfy that standard," says Tracey Maclin, a law professor at Boston University who has written briefs on Fourth Amendment issues for the American Civil Liberties Union (ACLU).

In his report, Fagan estimated that 6 percent of the stops were unjustified under the *Terry* standard. The most frequent basis for stops listed in the officers' reports was "furtive movements." In her decision, Scheindlin said Fagan underestimated the number of unjustified stops.

Both South Carolina professor Alpert and former Texas state trooper Withrow say New York City officers appear to have gone too far. "They pushed the envelope too far as to what a *Terry* stop is supposed to do," Withrow says. Alpert sees evidence of unwarranted racial profiling. "It sure seems overwhelming that they stop people of color, and they don't get hits," he says.

Maclin and others also warn that over-enforcement alienates people in the community and reduces their willingness to cooperate with police. "You're going to scoop a lot of innocent people that you may need down the road to get information," Maclin says.

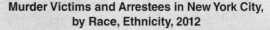

## Most Victims, Arrestees Are Minorities

African-Americans and Hispanics were victims in nearly 90 percent of the murders or non-negligent manslaughters in New York City in 2012, according to the NYPD.

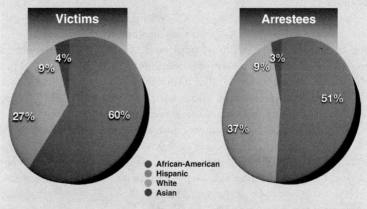

**Murder Victims and Arrestees in New York City, by Race, Ethnicity, 2012**

*Source:* "Crime and Enforcement Activity in New York, Jan. 1-Dec. 31, 2012," New York Police Department, www.nyc.gov/html/nypd/downloads/pdf/analysis_and_planning/2012_year_end_enforcement_report.pdf

Shelton, with the NAACP, agrees. "They are misusing resources when they use them so blanketly," Shelton says. "You end up losing a lot of your effectiveness."

Mac Donald dismisses that concern. People in high-crime neighborhoods want more, not less, police presence, she says. "Police should be fighting crime," she says. "The most important thing is to bring safety to law-abiding residents of poor neighborhoods."

## Should courts take a leading role in combating police racial and ethnic profiling?

When lawyer Robert Wilkins complained of racial profiling after being stopped while driving with his family in western Maryland, he filed a civil suit against the state police, the first case in which evidence was presented that showed police were targeting African-Americans. In settling the suit in 1995, the state agreed to prohibit racial profiling, institute training to combat the practice and file racial data on stops with a federal magistrate to help monitor compliance.[20]

Four years later, the New Jersey attorney general's office sought to deflect a U.S. Justice Department investigation of racial profiling by the state police with a package of similar reforms. Besides data collection, the new procedures also required a trooper to inform a dispatcher of the reason for a stop before interrogating any driver or passengers. The changes, still in place, were not enough, however, to forestall a Justice Department suit and eventual federal court settlement that included ongoing monitoring of the state police.[21]

In contrast to those cases, New York City officials have been fighting tooth-and-nail against the racial profiling allegations that are part of the broad attack on the NYPD's stop-and-frisk tactics. On the day of Scheindlin's decision, Mayor Bloomberg complained that the judge "wants to put the NYPD into receivership based on the flimsiest of evidence in a handful of cases. . . . No federal judge has ever imposed a monitor over a city's police department following a civil trial," Bloomberg said. Moreover, he noted, the Justice Department — under Presidents Clinton, George W. Bush and Obama — had "never, not once, found reason to investigate the NYPD."[22]

Bloomberg's criticism understates the role played by the courts in combating racial profiling. The Justice Department suit against New Jersey was one of several brought during the Clinton administration and served as the template for more than half a dozen suits or investigations initiated under President Obama.[23]

Racial profiling critics say the courts' role in combating the practice is useful and necessary. "That's what courts are set out to do, to determine whether police are acting within constitutional bounds," says Dennis Parker, director of the ACLU's Racial Justice Program. Withrow and del Carmen — law professors who have studied and work with police on race-related issues — both agree. "Courts have the obligation and the moral and legal duty to intervene and to dissect, analyze and respond to concerns that the community may have with respect to racial profiling," says del Carmen, the University of Texas professor.

"In some cases it's necessary," says Withrow, the Texas State professor and former state trooper. "In New Jersey, they had had a massive consent decree for 10 years — quite onerous — but that department had gotten into the position where practices were ingrained to the very bowels of the department."

Mac Donald — who criticized the New Jersey settlement in her book *Are Cops Racist?* — also criticizes Schleindin's decision in the New York City case. "A monitor is unnecessary," she says. "If the monitor adopts Scheindlin's methodology for racial profiling, it's going to signal the end of New York's record-breaking crime drop."

She also calls the appointment of a monitor a "tragic waste of resources" and sees body-worn video cameras as a waste. "I'm just not certain they would resolve the issues that are allegedly at stake here," she says of the cameras.

Even while supporting the courts' role on the issues, some racial profiling critics say remedies may be more effective if crafted by law enforcement agencies themselves. "Courts have an important role to play, but they cannot be the sole enforcer of constitutional obligations to avoid racial discrimination," says MALDEF president Saenz. "It's important to have administrative processes short of going to court," he says, including an adequate opportunity to file complaints.

Harris, the University of Pittsburgh professor, says police react negatively to court supervision. "It's perceived as a judge who knows nothing, who's never done anything on the street, telling a police department what to do," he says.

"What I would like to see is the change coming primarily from law enforcement itself, from mayors and city governments, from state legislatures," Harris continues. "They are best positioned to know what's going on on the ground around them. They are in the best position to make changes that are likely to be accepted in the departments affected. That's where reform would be best hatched. And many police departments do things like that."

## BACKGROUND

### A "Difficult" History

The term "racial profiling" is of recent coinage, but bias-based policing in the United States dates as far back as the revolutionary era with the religious profiling of Quakers seen as disloyal to the cause of independence. African-Americans have been subject to racial profiling from the days of slavery through the so-called Jim Crow era and up to modern times. Mexicans and other Latinos have been singled out for rough treatment by law enforcement since the time of Texas' independence. And immigration laws dating from the late 19th century amounted to racial or ethnic profiling against, among others, Asians and southern and eastern Europeans. "It's a very difficult history," says del Carmen, the University of Texas professor.[24]

The Continental Congress ordered the arrest and imprisonment of dozens of Pennsylvania Quakers suspected of disloyalty to the revolutionary cause in August 1777, according to an account by Emory University law professor Morgan Cloud.[25] No evidence was offered, no hearings were held and some of those arrested were exiled to imprisonment in Virginia. The captives were released by April 1778, in part, Cloud says, because of objections to the procedures not only from their families but also from some political leaders.

African-Americans comprised around one-sixth of the country's population in the pre-Civil War era, the vast majority of them held in slavery, mainly but not exclusively in the South. Those who escaped —"runaway" slaves, as they were called — could be captured by private slave hunters under the Fugitive Slave Act, a 1793 law (strengthened in 1850) that offered few procedural protections. Free blacks had no immunity from capture, as dramatized in the new movie "12 Years a Slave"; courts generally recognized a presumption that a black person was a slave.

The end of slavery merely transformed the legally and socially enforced profiling of African-Americans. The racial segregation laws of the Jim Crow era reflected the prevailing assumption that blacks were different from — and inferior to — whites. African-Americans suspected or accused of committing crimes could be subjected to abusive treatment by police or sheriffs' officers and to patently unjust proceedings in court. Worse was the threat of racially profiled vigilante justice: More than 3,400 African-Americans were lynched from the 1880s to 1950, according to a compilation by the Tuskegee Institute, the historically black college in Tuskegee, Ala (renamed Tuskegee University in 1983).[26]

Mexicans and Mexican-Americans were also the victims of ethnic profiling from the time of Texas' independence from Mexico and its subsequent annexation by the United States. The Texas Rangers, founded in 1845 and the nation's first statewide police organization, was known, according to the University of Texas' del Carmen, for "brutal acts against Comanche tribes and thousands of Mexicans."[27] Mexican-Americans in Texas and the Southwest were subjected to the same kind of residential and educational segregation as African-Americans elsewhere. And in the 1930s as many as 2 million people of Mexican descent were forced or pressured to leave the United States.

Federal immigration laws dating from the late 19th century reflected ethnic profiling at the national level. The first of the laws, passed in 1875, barred entry to "undesirables," who included Asians brought to the United States for forced labor or prostitution. Seven years later, the Chinese Exclusion Act prohibited all immigration of Chinese laborers. In the ensuing decades immigration officers enforced admission requirements, such as literacy tests, in ways that favored northern and western Europeans, del Carmen explains. The quota system enacted in the 1920s wrote those preferences into law.

The most notorious episode of ethnic profiling occurred during World War II with the internment of more than an estimated 110,000 persons of Japanese descent, most of them U.S. citizens. President Franklin D. Roosevelt authorized the internment in an executive order issued on Feb. 19, 1942, two-and-a-half months after Japan attacked Pearl Harbor, based on warnings from the military that the Japanese represented a national security threat. Today, those warnings are widely viewed as unfounded, the internment in ramshackle concentration camps in remote areas as shameful and the Supreme Court decision, *Korematsu v. United States* (1944), upholding the action as disgraceful.

Still, the court's decision in *Korematsu* established the principle that race-based restrictions in the law are "immediately suspect." Courts "must subject [such restrictions] to the most rigid scrutiny," Justice Hugo L. Black wrote for the 6-3 majority. "Pressing necessity may sometimes justify the existence of such restrictions," he continued. "Racial antagonism never can."[28] That principle laid the basis for courts, legislatures and law enforcement agencies later in the 20th century to give greater scrutiny to racial and ethnic profiling.

## An "Indefensible" Practice

Racial and ethnic profiling emerged as an important issue late in the 20th century because of a confluence of factors. The civil rights revolution embodied the demand of African-Americans for equal treatment under the law, including by police. The rapid increase in the Latino

# CHRONOLOGY

## 1960s-1970s *Civil rights movement targets racial inequality; Supreme Court forces changes in criminal justice systems.*

**1968** The National Advisory Commission on Civil Disorders (Kerner Commission), charged with examining the causes of urban riots, urges more sensitive, diverse police forces (Feb. 29). . . . Supreme Court approves limited "stop-and-frisk" authority (*Terry v. Ohio*, June 10).

**1970s** FBI develops "profiles" of airplane hijackers, serial killers.

**1975, 1976** Supreme Court limits use of race or ethnicity in roving Border Patrol stops but allows it at border checkpoints.

## 1980s-1990s *Racial profiling emerges as issue.*

**1989** Supreme Court approves use of drug courier profiles (April 3).

**1995** Maryland State Police agree to prohibit stops based on racial drug courier profiles (Jan. 4).

**1996** Supreme Court allows traffic stops even if real purpose is drug enforcement (June 10).

**1999** N.Y. police officers kill Amadou Diallo, Guinean immigrant, (Feb. 4), triggering widespread protests, racial profiling suit; officers prosecuted, acquitted. . . . N.J. attorney general finds racial profiling by state troopers despite official policies prohibiting it (April 20); Justice Department appoints monitor. . . . President Bill Clinton orders law enforcement agencies to compile race, ethnicity data to guard against profiling (June 10). . . . New York attorney general finds New York City police guilty of racial profiling (Dec. 1).

## 2000-Present *Racial profiling litigation increases; states pass laws addressing issue.*

**2001** President George W. Bush promises to help end racial profiling (Feb. 27). . . . Al Qaeda hijackers attack United States (Sept. 11); Muslims, Arabs rounded up in immigration sweeps, singled out in airport security checks, face widespread public suspicion.

**2003** Bush administration bans racial, ethnic profiling in all federal law enforcement agencies, but allows exception for national security-related investigations (June 17). . . . New York City settles racial profiling suit (*Daniels v. City of New York*) (Sept. 18); settlement approved by District Judge Shira Scheindlin (Dec. 12).

**2008** Center for Constitutional Rights files new stop-and-frisk suit against New York Police Department (NYPD) (*Floyd v. City of New York*), claiming violations of 2003 settlement in the *Daniels* case (Jan. 31); new suit is assigned to Scheindlin as "related" case.

**2009** Obama becomes first African-American president (Jan. 20); Eric Holder becomes first black attorney general. . . . African-American studies scholar Henry Louis Gates Jr. arrested at his home in Cambridge, Mass., by white police officer (July 16); Obama later hosts "beer summit" between Gates and the arresting officer to soothe feelings.

**2012** White community-watch volunteer George Zimmerman kills unarmed black teenager Trayvon Martin in Sanford, Fla., touching off a nationwide debate on racial profiling (Feb. 26); Zimmerman, charged with second-degree murder, is later acquitted. . . . Muslim plaintiffs file federal suit to halt NYPD surveillance of mosques, Muslim neighborhoods (June 6); case, with two others, still pending. . . . Federal judge dismisses FBI suit over informant's surveillance of mosques in Southern California (Aug. 14).

**2013** Federal judge finds Maricopa County Sheriff Joe Arpaio guilty of ethnic profiling of Latinos (May 24); orders appointment of monitor, other steps. . . . Scheindlin finds NYPD guilty of racial profiling, Fourth Amendment violations in stop-and-frisk policies; orders appointment of monitor, test of body-worn cameras (Aug. 12). . . . Federal appeals panel stays Scheindlin's order; removes her from case (Oct. 31). . . . Bill de Blasio, who opposes stop-and-frisk policies, elected New York City mayor (Nov. 5).

**2014** De Blasio to become New York City mayor (Jan. 1); new police commissioner expected; changes in stop-and-frisk policies expected.

population, especially from the 1980s, prompted analogous demands from Latino advocacy groups to eliminate discriminatory treatment. And the criminal law revolution wrought by the Supreme Court under Chief Justice Earl Warren subjected local and state law enforcement to greater scrutiny to comply with constitutional norms. Meanwhile, public concern about crime and, in particular, about illegal drugs led police and law enforcement agencies to adopt tactics often disproportionately aimed at African-Americans and Latinos — sometimes consciously.[29]

The Warren Court's major criminal law decisions — such as the *Miranda* ruling on police interrogation guidelines — benefited white and minority suspects and defendants alike. Despite criticism for supposedly "handcuffing" police, the Warren Court also gave police an important tool in its 1968 *Terry* decision upholding — with only one dissenting vote — the stop-and-frisk procedure. The court noted complaints of "harassment" by African-Americans, however, in stressing the need to limit the procedure to "the legitimate investigative sphere." Meanwhile, the so-called Kerner Commission, appointed by President Lyndon B. Johnson in response to urban riots of the mid-'60s, had issued a comprehensive report in 1968 recommending, among other steps, the hiring of more diverse and more sensitive police forces.[30]

The Supreme Court's initial encounter with the profiling issue came in a pair of immigration-related cases in the mid-1970s. In the first, the court in 1975 ruled that a roving Border Patrol car could not stop a vehicle solely because the driver or passengers appeared to be of Mexican ancestry. Appearance was a "relevant factor," Justice Lewis F. Powell Jr. wrote, but not enough to "justify stopping all Mexican-Americans to ask if they are aliens." A year later, however, the court ruled that agents at a border checkpoint could select motorists for secondary inspection based solely on apparent Mexican ancestry.[31]

The formal art of "profiling" began in the 1970s, as police and the FBI tried to identify characteristics to spot in potential serial killers or airline hijackers. From those rare offenses, the practice expanded to the so-called war on drugs with the federal Drug Enforcement Administration's (DEA) development of a drug courier profile in the 1980s. The DEA never published the profile, but evidence in some cases showed that profiles sometimes specifically referred to African-Americans or Hispanics. In any event, the open-ended characteristics gave agents broad discretion in selecting individuals to stop. The Supreme Court green-lighted the use of such profiles in a 1989 decision stemming from the search of a deplaning passenger at the Honolulu airport. By a 7-2 vote, the court found the combination of six listed factors justified the stop and search; the dissenters countered that none of the factors specifically pointed to criminal activity.[32]

Through the 1990s, evidence mounted that African-Americans were far and away the majority of motorists stopped in drug-related enforcement. Wilkins' suit in Maryland was the first to uncover hard evidence of targeting of African-Americans, as recounted by Harris, the University of Pittsburgh professor. A state police "Criminal Intelligence Report," disclosed during the suit and dated only days before Wilkins was stopped, included an explicit profile targeting African-Americans.

The data gathering that resulted from the settlement of Wilkins' suit showed that 72 percent of those stopped in Maryland were African-Americans. The litigation and newspaper investigations in New Jersey produced similar evidence that the vast majority of motorists stopped on the state's turnpikes were African-Americans.

Despite such evidence, the Supreme Court declined in 1996 to question the use of traffic stops as a pretext for drug enforcement. The decisions stemmed from the convictions of two African-Americans who had been found with drugs after police officers patrolling a "high-drug" area in Washington, D.C., stopped them ostensibly because of a taillight violation. Unanimously, the court said the officers' "ulterior motives" did not matter as long as they had probable cause for the stop.[33]

President Bill Clinton cited the evidence of racial profiling in traffic stops, however, when he ordered federal law enforcement agencies in June 1999 to begin collecting data on the race or ethnicity of individuals they question, search or arrest.[34] The Justice Department was to use the data to determine whether federal officers were engaging in racial profiling and, if so, what should be done to stop the practice. Clinton said he hoped state and local law enforcement agencies would adopt similar steps to try to eliminate what he called a "morally indefensible" practice. Racial profiling, he said, "is wrong, it is destructive and it must stop."

## "Deliberate Indifference"?

The issue of racial and ethnic profiling gained new importance after the Sept. 11 terrorist attacks on the

# Profiling Seen in "Shopping While Black" Incidents

*"It's disappointing that it still happens today."*

Trayon Christian was excited after getting a paycheck from his work-study job on April 29, because he could finally afford the expensive designer belt he had his eye on at Barneys, the upscale Manhattan department store.

Christian, 19, a student at New York City College of Technology, paid for the $349 Ferragamo belt with a debit card and left the store headed down Madison Avenue. Less than a block later, however, two undercover New York City police detectives stopped Christian and, according to a later lawsuit, questioned the purchase, handcuffed him and took him to the nearby station house.

Christian, who is African-American, was released without charges. But six months later he filed a civil rights suit against Barneys and the city, claiming he was in effect stopped for "shopping while black." News of the suit, first reported by the *Daily News* on Oct. 23, apparently struck a chord. Within a week, three more black New Yorkers emerged with allegations of having been racially profiled as possible credit-card scammers while shopping at New York City stores.[1]

"You still have undercover officers out there judging people on the basis of what they look like," says Kenneth Meeks, a producer at Black Enterprise Broadcast Media and author of the book *Driving While Black*, published in 2000. "It's disappointing that it still happens today, but I can't say I'm surprised."[2]

Barneys, confronted with a similar accusation from a 21-year-old black nursing student over her purchase of a $2,500 handbag in February, is denying any wrongdoing and blaming the undercover police officers for selecting shoppers to investigate. After the news of Christian's lawsuit, Barneys declared in a statement on Facebook that no employee was involved in pursuing any action against the teenager. In the second incident, a Barneys executive called the student's mother with a similar disclaimer of responsibility.[3]

"Barneys New York has zero tolerance for any form of discrimination, and we stand by our long history in support of all human rights," the company said in the Facebook statement.

Kayla Phillips, the woman in the second incident at Barneys, is planning to sue the company, according to her attorney. The actor Rob Brown, one of those who accused Macy's of racial profiling in a mistaken arrest at the store in June, filed a class action suit against the company in federal district court in Manhattan on Nov. 13. Macy's declined to comment directly on the suit, but said in a statement: "We do not tolerate discrimination of any kind, including racial profiling."[4]

Brown filed a separate class action against the NYPD for its part in the arrest even though police apologized for the mistake afterward.

Despite the denials, the New York attorney general's office initiated an investigation of the two incidents with a letter sent to Barneys on Oct. 28. The office sent a similar letter to Macy's, the huge New York City department store, after two black shoppers had emerged with similar accounts of alleged profiling. "The alleged repeated behavior of your employees raises troubling questions," wrote Kristen Clarke, head of the attorney general's Civil Rights Bureau.[5]

New York police sources confirmed to the *Daily News* that the NYPD stations undercover officers at Barneys and other stores to try to nab credit card fraud perpetrators. Police have gotten 53 grand larceny complaints this year for credit card fraud at Barneys' Madison Avenue store and have made more than 47 arrests, the department said. It did not provide a racial breakdown of those arrested.

In a subsequent story, *The New York Times* reported that Barneys' security management team had responded "several months ago" to an increase in shoplifting and credit card fraud by instructing store personnel to "take chances" in spotting suspicious customers even at the risk of intercepting innocent people.[6]

The New York City episodes surfaced only two months after Oprah Winfrey, the television mogul and one of the world's richest women, encountered a kind of racial profiling herself while trying to purchase a $38,000 handbag in a high-end women's store in Zurich, Switzerland. The store clerk declined to show Winfrey the handbag she wanted and suggested a less expensive one instead.[7]

Racial profiling is a fact of life for African-Americans in any number of public settings, according to Meeks, notably when trying to hail a cab. "I've seen it dozens of times in the past year," Meeks says. "The driver will pass the black person and take the white person instead."

President Obama himself has spoken about his own experiences of being followed while in department stores, hearing car doors lock as he passed by parked vehicles on the street or having women clutch their purses tightly when sharing an elevator. "That happens to me, at least before I was a senator," Obama said in unscheduled remarks on July 19 following the acquittal of white community volunteer George Zimmerman in the February 2012 shooting death of black teenager Trayvon Martin.[8]

The apparent profiling of black shoppers affects who gets arrested for retail theft, according to one expert, but the underlying assumption that blacks account for most store thefts is unsubstantiated. Jerome Williams, a business professor at Rutgers University who has studied marketplace discrimination, told The Associated Press that white women in their 40s engage in more shoplifting than other demographic groups. "The reason they don't show up in crime statistics is because people aren't watching them," Williams was quoted as saying.[9]

Meeks, who has three teenage children, says he wrote his book to show how to fight back against racial profiling. "You have to make a stand, so the person who profiles you thinks twice before doing it to the next person," he says. But he also warns his children to expect it to happen to them.

"They are very much aware of the ways that society looks on them," Meeks says. "They are black, and they will be profiled at some point in their lives."

— *Kenneth Jost*

New York City college student Trayon Christian, 19, filed a civil rights suit against Barneys after he was stopped, handcuffed and taken to a police station after buying a $349 belt at the upscale department store. He was released without charges.

[2]Kenneth Meeks, *Driving While Black: Highways, Shopping Malls, Taxicabs, Sidewalks. What to Do if You Are a Victim of Racial Profiling* (2000).

[3]Tina Moore and Ginger Adams Otis, "Bagged by 'Racism,'" *Daily News*, Oct. 24, 2013, p. 5.

[4]"Macy's slapped with federal class action lawsuit over racial-profiling shopping case," WPIX-11, Nov. 14, 2013, http://pix11.com/2013/11/13/macys-slapped-with-federal-class-action-lawsuit-over-racial-profiling-shopping-case/#axzz2l16fMJzE.

[5]See Kenneth Lovett, "New York attorney general targeting Barneys, Macy's over racial profiling claims," *Daily News* (New York), Oct. 29, 2013.

[6]J. David Goodman, "Profiling Complaints by Black Shoppers Followed Changes to Stores' Security Policies," *The New York Times*, Oct. 30, 2013, p. A24.

[7]See Christine Hauser, "Oprah Winfrey and the Purse She Couldn't Have," *The Lede* (*New York Times* blog), Aug. 9, 2013, http://thelede.blogs.nytimes.com/2013/08/09/oprah-winfrey-and-the-handbag-she-couldnt-have/; Tim Newcomb, "A Lot of People 'Sorry' About Oprah Winfrey Purse Incident," *Time*, Aug. 13, 2013, http://entertainment.time.com/2013/08/13/a-lot-of-people-sorry-about-oprah-winfrey-purse-incident/.

[8]For transcript, see "Obama Recalls Getting Followed, People Locking Doors On Him — In other Words, Being A Black Man In America," *The Huffington Post*, July 19, 2013, www.huffingtonpost.com/2013/07/19/obama-racial-profiling_n_3624881.html.

[9]Washington, *op. cit.*

[1]Kerry Burke, Mark Morales, Barbara Ross and Ginger Adams Otis, "How could YOU afford a belt like THIS?" *Daily News* (New York), Oct. 23, 2013, p. 5. For an overview, see Jesse Washington, "Barneys case stirs talk of 'Shopping While Black,' " The Associated Press, Oct. 29, 2013.

# Muslims Challenge "Religious Profiling"

*"We should not be singled out simply because of religion."*

Sarah Abdurrahman was in a festive mood as she returned to the United States with friends and family earlier this year after attending a friend's wedding in Canada.

But the good feelings died at the border as she and her traveling party, all U.S. citizens and all Muslims, suffered what the radio journalist later described as a painful and humiliating six-hour ordeal at the hands of U.S. Customs and Border Patrol (CPB) agents.

Abdurrahman, an assistant producer with the NPR program "On the Media," said the agents detained the traveling party without explanation, refused to identify themselves and questioned at least one of the travelers, Abdurrahman's husband, about his religious practices. She described the experience — and her fruitless efforts to get an explanation afterward — in a 20-minute report on the program on Sept. 20.[1]

The episode typifies the seeming religious profiling that advocates for the United States' 6 million Muslims say has been common since al Qaeda's September 2011 attacks on the United States. Because of terrorism-inspired scrutiny at the federal, state and local levels, many Muslims today worry that they may be monitored, interrogated, detained or even arrested for no reason other than religion, according to officials with the San Francisco group Muslim Advocates.

"We're not saying mosques or Muslims should be off limits," explains Glenn Katon, the group's legal director.

"It's that mosques should not be singled out, Muslims should not be singled out simply because of religion."

The complaints extend beyond individual anecdotes such as Abdurrahman's. Muslims are currently challenging in court broad surveillance programs maintained by the New York Police Department (NYPD) and by the FBI in Southern California. Both law enforcement agencies are accused of infringing religious liberties by infiltrating mosques without adequate justification. But so far none of the law enforcement practices has been ruled improper.

In California, Craig Monteilh posed as a Muslim convert under an assumed name for more than a year as a paid FBI informant, using audio and video recording devices to gather information. The American Civil Liberties Union (ACLU) of Southern California and the Council on American-Islamic Relations (CAIR) filed a civil rights suit against the FBI on behalf of Muslim community members in Orange County in regard to Monteilh's acknowledged infiltration of approximately 10 Southern California mosques. The government claimed the "state secrets" privilege in refusing to disclose details of Monteilh's surveillance in so-called Operation Flex. In August 2012, U.S. District Judge Cormac Carney dismissed the government as a defendant but allowed the suits against individual FBI agents and officials to proceed. ACLU lawyers appealed the decision.[2]

In New York, the NYPD is facing three separate suits challenging its surveillance of mosques and Muslims as

United States in 2001 as Muslims and people of Arab or South Asian background came under heightened attention — and suspicion — from law enforcement and the general public. Meanwhile, critics of racial profiling of African-Americans and Latinos continued efforts in court and legislative bodies to combat the practice and drew important support from the Obama administration's stepped-up scrutiny of local police forces. And two incidents made racial profiling issues front-page news: the arrest of the prominent African-American scholar Henry Louis Gates Jr. at the door of his Cambridge, Mass., home in 2009 and the killing of

Trayvon Martin, an unarmed black teenager, by a white community-watch volunteer in a gated community in Florida in 2012.

Just one month after taking office, President George W. Bush followed Clinton's example by promising in his State of the Union address on Feb. 27, 2001, that his administration would work to end racial profiling. Attorney General John Ashcroft echoed Bush's promise, describing the practice as "unconstitutional."[35] After 9/11, however, the government evidently focused attention on Muslims, Arab nationals and Arab-Americans in investigating possible links to al Qaeda — the group

Fourth Amendment violations both in New York and across the state line in New Jersey. Lawyers for the New York-based Center for Constitutional Rights and the Muslim Advocates filed the first of the suits in federal district court in New Jersey in June 2012; the ACLU, along with the New York Civil Liberties Union (NYCLU) and a police accountability project at the City University of New York Law School, filed a comparable suit in federal district court in Brooklyn in June.[3]

In a third case, lawyers from the NYCLU are charging the police with violating their own court-approved guidelines for initiating surveillance of political or religious organizations. The guidelines date back to a court-approved settlement of anti-spying litigation in the 1970s, but the NYPD got the rules eased in 2003 after claiming they hampered counterterrorism work.[4]

Separately, the ACLU has sued the FBI under the Freedom of Information Act to try to obtain the agency's guidelines for counterterrorism investigations. In a ruling on Oct. 23, the federal appeals court in Philadelphia upheld the FBI's decision to limit disclosure of the requested documents because it would reveal investigative techniques.[5]

Abdurrahman was also stymied in her efforts to determine why her traveling party was detained when they re-entered the United States earlier this year. On the radio program, Abdurrahman said she filed a complaint about the incident with the Department of Homeland Security's Office of Civil Rights and Civil Liberties. The office rejected the complaint, she said, but the reasons for upholding the agents' actions were redacted in the notice of the decision.

The program quoted Munia Jabbar, an attorney with CAIR, that Muslims are often asked "really invasive" questions about religious practices when re-entering the United States. She says the questioning, as Abdurrahman's husband described, is improper. "You're singling people out because of their religion and then subjecting them to longer detentions and to humiliating questioning about stuff that they're allowed to do legally," she says.

Abdurrahman says the episode left her shaken. "I came out of the experience wondering what our rights are," she said.

— *Kenneth Jost*

[1] See "My Detainment Story: Or How I learned to Stop Feeling Safe in My Own Country and Hate the Border Agents," NPR, Sept. 20, 2013, www.wnyc.org/radio/#/ondemand/319368. For print coverage, see Harrison Jacobs, "American Muslim Reporter Describes 'Dehumanizing' Treatment at US Border," *Business Insider*, www.businessinsider.com/sarah-aburrhman-detained-at-us-border-2013-9.

[2] The case is *Fazaga v. FBI*. For background and materials, see the ACLU of Southern California's website: www.aclusocal.org/fazaga/. For news coverage, see Victoria Kim, "Spying suit against FBI is rejected," *Los Angeles Times*, Aug. 15, 2012, p. A1.

[3] The cases are *Hassan v. City of New York*, www.ccrjustice.org/hassan, and *Raza v. City of New York*, www.aclu.org/national-security/raza-v-city-new-york-legal-challenge-nypd-muslim-surveillance-program filed in June 2013. For coverage, see Chuck McCutcheon, "U.S. Muslims Seek to End Surveillance," in "Government Surveillance," *CQ Researcher*, Aug. 30, 2013, pp. 730-731. See also Matt Apuzzo and Adam Goldman, *Enemies Within: Inside the NYPD's Secret Spying Unit and Bin Laden's Final Plot Against America* (2013).

[4] The case is *Handschu v. Special Services Division*, www.nyclu.org/case/handschu-v-special-services-division-challenging-nypd-surveillance-practices-targeting-politica.

[5] *ACLU v. FBI*, 12-4345 (3d Cir., Oct. 23, 2013), www2.ca3.uscourts.gov/opinarch/124345p.pdf; for coverage, see Jason Grant, "ACLU denied access to FBI files on profiling," *The Star-Ledger* (Newark, N.J.), Oct. 24, 2013, p. 11.

responsible for the Sept. 11 attacks — within the United States. Immigration authorities rounded up hundreds of Middle Easterners.

Despite official denials, airport screeners appeared to be giving special attention to Muslims and Arabs; and some prominent commentators — including the Manhattan Institute's Mac Donald — forthrightly defended profiling as common-sense law enforcement.[36] When the Bush administration issued racial profiling guidelines in June 2003, it included an exception for national security-related investigations.[37] A decade later, Arab-American and Muslim groups continue to complain of heightened and unwarranted scrutiny from law enforcement — including a controversial special counterterrorism unit within the NYPD.

The New York City force had come under intense scrutiny for alleged racial profiling beginning in February 1999 with the shooting death of a Guinean immigrant, Amadou Diallo, at his front door in an ethnically diverse Bronx neighborhood. Plainclothes officers in the department's Street Crime Unit thought Diallo matched the description of a suspected rapist; when Diallo reached for his wallet as identification, the officers mistook it as a weapon and fired 41 rounds, killing him. The incident sparked raucous demonstrations and an unsuccessful prosecution of the four officers in a trial moved to Albany, N.Y., because of pretrial publicity.

The episode also led to a lawsuit by the Center for Constitutional Rights, accusing the NYPD of racial profiling and unlawful stop-and-frisk practices. The suit cited, among other evidence, a report by the New York attorney general's office that showed Street Crime Unit officers stopped 16 African-Americans for every arrest made. After lengthy discovery, the city disbanded the Street Crime Unit and, in September 2003, agreed to settle the suit — called *Daniels v. City of New York* — by promising to institute policies aimed at eliminating racial profiling. District Judge Scheindlin approved the settlement in December.[38]

Obama's election as the nation's first African-American president five years later was seen by some as marking a new era in race relations, but the Gates episode only six months after Obama's inauguration underlined the continuing points of contention between law enforcement and black Americans. Gates was charged with disorderly conduct on July 16, 2009, after a white Cambridge, Mass., police officer mistook him for a possible burglar. The charges were later dropped, and Obama hosted Gates and the officer for a so-called beer summit at the White House on July 30 to smooth things over.[39]

The killing of Martin by the white community-watch volunteer, George Zimmerman, on Feb. 26, 2012, touched off a more protracted nationwide debate over possible racial profiling. Zimmerman, concerned about a rash of home burglaries in the largely white gated community in Sanford, Fla., tailed Martin as the unarmed teenager was returning to his father's home and fatally wounded him during a scuffle.

Zimmerman was charged with second-degree murder and acquitted on July 13, 2013, under Florida's controversial so-called Stand Your Ground law, which eases rules for self-defense in criminal trials. The verdict prompted widespread protests by African- Americans.[40]

Meanwhile, NYPD's stop-and-frisk litigation had resumed in 2008, after the Center for Constitutional Rights accused the city of failing to comply with the 2003 settlement. Judge Scheindlin assumed jurisdiction over the new case, *Floyd*, since it was related to the *Daniels* case that she had previously tried. The assignment would underlie later complaints of bias by the city and others,

including the Manhattan Institute's Mac Donald, and the appeals court's subsequent decision to order the case reassigned. The trial in the new case began on March 18 and closed two months later on May 20 after sharp arguments over the implications of opposing statistical studies and testimony from police officials.

Scheindlin issued her ruling on Aug. 12. Out of the 4.4 million stops logged by police, Scheindlin found that at least 200,000 — about 5 percent — were unconstitutional, and that the actual figure was probably higher. She went on to find that blacks and Hispanics were more likely to be stopped than whites after controlling for other variables, that blacks were more likely to be arrested and that blacks and Hispanics were more likely to be subjected to use of force. In all, Scheindlin concluded the data showed "deliberate indifference" on the city's part toward constitutional rights — a necessary finding to establish liability under federal civil rights law. Bloomberg vowed to appeal.

## CURRENT SITUATION
### Patterns and Practices

Police and sheriffs' departments around the country are dealing with questions of racial profiling under pressure from civil liberties and minority rights groups, community organizations, the Justice Department and federal courts.

Apart from New York City, the biggest pending controversy appears to be in Maricopa County, Ariz., where Arpaio — who styles himself as the nation's toughest sheriff — is planning to appeal a federal judge's order to place the department under a court-appointed monitor for at least four years. In other cities, including Philadelphia, New Orleans and Seattle, police departments have agreed to changes aimed at eliminating racial profiling but continue to face questions about compliance.

Despite the controversies, police organizations insist that the accusations of widespread racial profiling are unsubstantiated. "Most police departments base their stops on reasonable suspicion or probable cause, not on the basis of their race," says Darrel Stephens, executive director of the Major Cities Chiefs Association and former police chief in several metropolitan areas, including most recently Charlotte-Mecklenburg County, N.C.

# Is racial profiling by police a serious problem in the United States?

## YES

**Dennis Parker**
*Director, Racial Justice Program,*
*American Civil Liberties Union*

Written for *CQ Researcher*, November 2013

In their 2009 report, "The Persistence of Racial and Ethnic Profiling: A Follow-Up Report to the U.N. Committee on the Elimination of Racial Discrimination," the American Civil Liberties Union and the Rights Working Group concluded that despite "overwhelming evidence of its existence, often supported by official data, racial profiling continues to be a prevalent and egregious form of discrimination in the United States."

Time has not altered that conclusion. Numerous studies, data collection and individual anecdotes confirm that law enforcement agents continue to rely on race, color or national or ethnic origin as a basis for subjecting people to criminal investigations.

The cost of this reliance on race or ethnicity as a supposed indicator of likely criminal activity is high for individuals and society. Examples of the practice abound. After analyzing hundreds of thousands of police stops, a federal judge concluded that African-Americans and Latinos in New York City were far more likely than whites to be stopped by police when there was no reasonable suspicion of criminal activity and were less likely than whites to be found in possession of illegal items. Meanwhile, a federal court in Arizona found the Maricopa County Sheriff's Office relied on ethnicity in enforcing immigration laws in a way that was clearly unconstitutional. In both cases, the courts were so concerned about future violations that they ordered the use of impartial monitors to track compliance with remedies intended to stop the illegal practices.

Reliance on racial profiling is not limited to local law enforcement. Six states have adopted immigration enforcement laws that invite the profiling of Latinos. The federal government routinely relies on programs and practices that delegate immigration enforcement authority to state and local agencies, resulting in the unfair targeting of Latino, Arab, South Asian and Muslim people in the name of immigration control and national security.

Despite overwhelming evidence that racial profiling persists, the End Racial Profiling Act continues to languish in Congress. Until appropriate action is taken to address discriminatory profiling, people will continue to be subjected to the humiliation of repeated, unwarranted and intrusive stops and investigations, depriving them of their individual rights and undermining support for our criminal justice system.

The idea of basing law enforcement on actions rather than on race, ethnicity or religion is long overdue.

## NO

**Heather Mac Donald**
*Fellow, Manhattan Institute*

Written for *CQ Researcher*, November 2013

There is no credible evidence that racial profiling is a serious problem among police forces. Studies that purport to show the contrary inevitably assume that police activity should match population ratios, rather than crime ratios. But urban policing today is driven by crime data: Officers are deployed to where city residents are most victimized by violence. Given the racial disparities in crime commission, the police cannot provide protection to neighborhoods that most need it without generating racially disproportionate enforcement numbers.

In New York City, for example, the per capita shooting rate in predominantly black Brownsville, Brooklyn, is 81 times higher than in Bay Ridge, Brooklyn, which is largely white and Asian. That disparity reflects Brownsville's gang saturation, which affects policing in myriad ways. Police presence will be much higher in gang-infested neighborhoods, and officers deployed there will try to disrupt gang activity with all available lawful tools, including the stopping and questioning of individuals suspected of criminal activity. Each shooting will trigger an intense police response, as officers seek to avert a retaliatory gang hit. Given the difference in shooting rates, it is no surprise that Brownsville's per capita police stop rate is 15 times higher than Bay Ridge's. If it were not, the police would not be targeting their resources equitably, according to need. Yet some advocates cite such stop disparities as prima facie proof of profiling.

Community requests for protection are the other determinant of police tactics. Last fall, I spoke with an elderly cancer amputee in the South Bronx. She was terrified to go down to her lobby to get her mail because of the youths hanging out there, smoking marijuana. Only when the police had been by to conduct trespass stops would she venture out: "When you see the police, everything's A-OK," she said. Police cannot respond to such requests for public order without producing racially disparate enforcement data that can be used against them in the next racial profiling lawsuit.

Young, black males are murdered at 10 times the rate of whites and Hispanics combined, usually killed by other minority males. The New York Police Department has brought the homicide victimization rate among the city's minorities down nearly 80 percent, yet young, black men are still 36 times more likely to be murdered than young, white males. Proactive policing is the best protection poor, minority neighborhoods have against violence and fear.

Civil liberties and minority rights groups disagree. Racial profiling is "happening in states all across the country," says the ACLU's Parker. "The indications are that it's prevalent."

The sweeping order in Maricopa County comes in a case, *Ortega Melendres v. Arpaio*, that accuses Arpaio of a pattern and practice of targeting Latino drivers and passengers for traffic stops, investigations and arrests. The suit was filed in 2007 on behalf of Manuel Ortega Melendres, a Mexican national residing legally in the United States, who was questioned and held for several hours after the car in which he was riding was stopped supposedly for speeding. The white driver was not ticketed, but Melendres was held until U.S. authorities verified his immigration status.

The suit was later broadened into a class action and litigated by private attorneys and lawyers from the ACLU of Arizona, the ACLU's national Immigrants Rights Projects and MALDEF. After presiding over a four-week trial in July 2012, District Judge Snow, a Republican appointee, issued a 142-page decision on liability on May 24, finding the sheriff's office guilty of Fourth Amendment violations for making suspicionless stops and of equal protection violations for targeting Latinos on the basis of their ancestry.[41] Snow followed with an Oct. 2 order requiring installation of cameras in all deputies' cars, increased data collection and reporting and creation of a community advisory board. To ensure compliance with the order, Snow is to appoint a monitor. The order is to stay in effect for at least three years after full compliance is shown.

In other cities, the Philadelphia Police Department remains under a 2011 consent decree negotiated with ACLU lawyers that requires data collection on stop-and-frisk incidents and analysis of the data by an independent court-appointed monitor. The most recent report, issued in March, found that the number of stops had decreased, but that 45 percent of the stops were unjustified; African-Americans and Hispanics were the subjects of 76 percent of the stops and 85 percent of the frisks.[42]

Court-supervised consent decrees in New Orleans and Seattle stem from reports issued by the Justice Department's Civil Rights Division in 2011, which criticized both departments on use-of-force policies and "bias-based" policing — including, in the case of New Orleans, directed at lesbian, gay, bisexual or transgender persons. In Seattle,

a survey released in September and commissioned by the court-appointed monitor, attorney Merrick Bobb, found that nearly two-thirds of Seattle residents believe police routinely discriminate against people of color.[43] In New Orleans, the police department has hired a new deputy superintendent to oversee implementation of the federal court decree, but the court has yet to appoint the independent monitor to check on compliance.[44]

Meanwhile, Congress is being urged to strengthen federal efforts to combat racial profiling by passing legislation introduced in the wake of Zimmerman's acquittal in the Trayvon Martin killing. The End Racial Profiling Act, introduced by Democrats Sen. Ben Cardin of Maryland and Rep. John Conyers of Michigan, would prohibit racial profiling by federal or federally funded state law enforcement agencies. It would also authorize civil suits by the United States or any individual injured by racial profiling for a declaratory judgment or injunction, but not damages.[45]

No hearings are scheduled on the racial profiling bills. But the Senate Judiciary Committee did hear from Trayvon Martin's mother, Sybrina Fulton, in an Oct. 29 hearing on Stand Your Ground laws. Florida is one of 22 states with such laws, which generally eliminate the duty to retreat from an attacker threatening serious bodily harm or death. Fulton told the panel that the law "did not work" in her son's case, but other witnesses said there was no reason for Congress to act.

"This is about the right of everyone to protect themselves and protect their families," said Sen. Ted Cruz, R-Texas.[46]

## NYPD Changes?

The fate of New York City's stop-and-frisk case is up in the air after the landslide election on Nov. 5 of a new mayor who opposed the NYPD policies while campaigning and promised, if elected, to drop the appeal in the case.

As the city's public advocate, mayor-elect de Blasio had sided with the plaintiffs in the *Floyd* case, criticized the Bloomberg-Kelly stop-and-frisk policies and promised if elected to withdraw the city's appeal of Judge Scheindlin's order.

De Blasio, who will take office on Jan. 1, did not repeat that promise in the immediate aftermath of his election. Instead, he stressed on election night that public safety and respect for civil liberties are both important for the city. In a press conference the next day, de Blasio said only that he plans to decide on a new police commissioner soon.

Among several possibilities mentioned as new commissioner, William Bratton, a former chief in New York City and Los Angeles, is drawing the most attention. Bratton headed the LAPD from 2002 to 2009 after having served as head of the New York City Transit Police for four years and as New York City police commissioner from 1994 to 1996. Currently working as a security consultant, Bratton is known to want his old job back.

De Blasio's campaign website praised Bratton for having reduced crime in Los Angeles without the "unconstitutional" use of stop-and-frisk. De Blasio was reported to have met with Bratton several times during the campaign. Others mentioned as possible appointees include Philip Banks III, an African-American who is the NYPD's top department chief, and Joseph Dunne, leader of the Port Authority Police Department.[47]

Despite de Blasio's vow to drop the city's appeal in the *Floyd* case once in office, the future of the case is dividing interest groups. City Councilman Jumaane Wilson, a Democrat from Brooklyn, led a rally at City Hall the day after the election, urging the Bloomberg administration to drop the appeal. The next day, however, unions representing 29,000 of New York's 35,000 officers filed papers with the Second U.S. Circuit Court of Appeals asking to keep the appeal alive even if the city drops it. The union argues that Scheindlin's order unfairly taints the integrity of the force and changes operational rules for officers.

Meanwhile, Scheindlin remains removed from the case after the three-judge appellate panel reaffirmed its Oct. 31 order that it be reassigned randomly to another district court judge. The unexpected decision, issued just two days after hearing the city's request for a stay, said Scheindlin "ran afoul" of the Code of Judicial Conduct by guiding plaintiffs' lawyers to file the *Floyd* case in her court and by giving media interviews while the case was pending.

Scheindlin denied any wrongdoing and stressed that she had made no direct comment about the *Floyd* case in the interviews. A few days later, lawyers representing her asked that either the three-judge panel or the full Second Circuit reverse the action. The legal team, headed by New York University law professor Burt Neuborne, argued the action was substantively unwarranted and

procedurally flawed because Scheindlin had no opportunity to respond. In a separate letter, Neuborne said the "unseemly dispute" was a distraction from the merits of the case.

The next day the city filed a motion urging the panel to vacate Scheindlin's order altogether. New York City corporation counsel Michael Cardozo said the ruling would undermine the police department's "ability to carry out its mission effectively." The city also urged the court to speed up the appeal so that it could be ruled on before Bloomberg leaves office.

Lawyers from the Center for Constitutional Rights countered on Nov. 11 with a filing that argued reassigning the case to a new judge would result in an "undue waste of judicial resources and potential prejudice" to the plaintiffs.

On Nov. 13 the panel reaffirmed its decision in an expanded 17-page opinion.[48] In granting the stay, the judges said that "in the interest of judicial efficiency" it would also hear the appeal on the merits next spring.

By then, however, de Blasio will have had time to decide whether to drop the appeal.

## OUTLOOK:

### Mean Streets

Life can be hard for a police officer patrolling the streets of a major U.S. city. But life can be hard, too, for young black men walking those streets if they run into a cop like Philip Nace of the Philadelphia Police Department.

Nace, who is white, is under disciplinary investigation after a damning video of his racially abusive, obscenity-laced encounter on Sept. 27 with two young black men went viral on YouTube. The 16-minute video, shot on a cell phone by one of the men, shows Nace and an unidentified partner stopping the men solely because they had greeted someone as they were walking in predominantly African-American North Philadelphia.

After one of the men asks the reason for the stop, Nace scoffs at the request, tells the men to go back to New Jersey, describes them as "freeloaders" and accuses one of them of dealing in marijuana before letting them both go. "We can assure the public that he [Nace] is off the street," Lt. John Stanford told the *Philadelphia Daily News* after a second video showed Nace destroying a neighborhood basketball hoop. "What you see in those two videos is certainly not what we teach."[49]

Nace's conduct shows the underbelly of stop-and-frisk racial profiling. "There's no place for that kind of attitude and behavior in a professional law enforcement agency in this country," the NAACP's Shelton remarked after viewing the video. But the investigations and lawsuits challenging racial profiling go after the practice more broadly with statistical evidence, not just anecdotes, and aim at broad policy changes, not simply discipline of individual officers.

On the surface, the statistics seem to support accusations of racial profiling, but skeptics such as the Manhattan Institute's Mac Donald are unconvinced by what she calls "circumstantial" evidence. "It's a very complicated issue," says Alpert, the University of South Carolina professor, "and we don't know very much because it tests the boundaries of social science research."

The New York City case could influence further developments on the issue, but the appeals court's decision to stay Judge Scheindlin's order makes speculation perilous. Before the stay, Harris, the University of Pittsburgh professor and racial profiling critic, was predicting the case could encourage police departments around the country to rethink stop-and-frisk. After news of the stay, he saw a possible impact in an opposite direction. "If the case is not upheld on appeal, many people will take from that that the NYPD style of aggressively using stop-and-frisk is the right thing to do after all," Harris said.

Other experts, however, say police chiefs are already working to combat racial profiling. "Virtually all healthy, competent, well-functioning departments have policies against it," says Bueermann, the Police Foundation president. Del Carmen, the University of Texas professor, agrees that police chiefs are addressing the issue, but says policies are not always followed in the field. "There are always officers in some departments who believe that racism is part of the job," he says.

Advocacy groups that have raised the profiling issue are optimistic that police departments are moving in their direction. "Many police departments are taking the issues very seriously," says Parker with the ACLU. Saenz, the MALDEF president, foresees "a broader understanding of how inappropriate profiling is" and "a broader array of protections against the practice nationwide." Shelton agrees. "We're going to continue to move forward," he says.

From an opposite perspective, however, Mac Donald sees the racial profiling debate as interfering with good policing. "The police cannot go after crime if they're held to a population benchmark," she says. "Unless black crime goes down," she adds, "the story is not going to go away."

## NOTES

1. See Seth Freed Wessler and Jay Smooth, "David Floyd on Why He Sued NYPD," *Colorlines*, March 25, 2013, http://colorlines.com/archives/2013/03/watch_david_floyd_main_plaintiff_in_historic_nyc_stop_and_frisk_case_tell_his_story_video.html . See also Matt Sledge, "David Floyd, Lead Stop And Frisk Plaintiff, Takes Stand In First Day Of Trial," *The Huffington Post*, March 18, 2013, www.huffingtonpost.com/2013/03/18/david-floyd-stop-and-frisk-trial_n_2903682.html.

2. Scheindlin's 195-page "liability order" and 39-page "remedies order" can be found here: http://s3.documentcloud.org/documents/750446/stop-and-frisk-memoranda.pdf. The orders, along with other documents and materials, also can be found on the website of the Center for Constitutional Rights, the New York City public interest law firm that litigated the case: www.ccrjustice.org/floyd. For coverage, see Joseph Goldstein, "Judge Rejects New York's Stop-and-Frisk Policy," *The New York Times*, Aug. 13, 2013, p. A1.

3. The order is here: www.ca2.uscourts.gov/decisions/isysquery/bc15d9e2-1f1a-4611-9d0c-678bbaff704c/1/doc/13-3123_13-3442_post.pdf#xml=http://www.ca2.uscourts.gov/decisions/isysquery/bc15d9e2-1f1a-4611-9d0c-678bbaff704c/1/hilite/. For coverage, see Joseph Goldstein, "Ruling Against Frisking Tactics by New York's Police Is Blocked," *The New York Times*, Nov. 1, 2013, p. A1.

4. For background on police accountability issues, see these *CQ Researcher* reports by Kenneth Jost: "Police Misconduct," April 6, 2012, pp. 301-324; "Policing the Police," March 17, 2000, pp. 209-240.

5. For background, see Kenneth Jost, "Immigration Conflict," *CQ Researcher*, March 9, 2012, pp. 229-252.

6. The decisions and other materials in *Ortega Melendres v. Arpaio* are available on the website of the American Civil Liberties Union, which represented the plaintiffs: https://www.aclu.org/immigrants-rights-racial-justice/court-places-limits-sheriff-arpaio-prevent-future-racial-profiling. For coverage, see JJ Hensley, "U.S. judge orders MCSO oversight," *The Arizona Republic*, Oct. 3, 2013, p. A1.

7. Quoted in "Bloomberg Says Whites Are Stopped and Frisked Too Much," *Infowars.com*, July 3, 2013, www.infowars.com/bloomberg-says-whites-are-stopped-and-frisked-too-much/. See also Yoav Gonen, "Bloomberg: NYC Police 'Stop Whites Too Often and Minorities Too Little' — And 'Nobody Racially Profiles,' " *New York Post*, June 28, 2013.

8. See Heather Mac Donald, "Sorry, No Debunking of Racial Profiling Allowed," in *Are Cops Racist?* (2002).

9. Lynn Langton and Matthew Durose, "Police Behavior During Traffic and Street Stops, 2011," Bureau of Justice Statistics, Department of Justice, September 2013, www.bjs.gov/content/pub/pdf/pbtss11.pdf.

10. The Center for Constitutional Rights press release is at http://ccrjustice.org/newsroom/press-releases/judge-rules-floyd-case; Bloomberg's and Kelly's statements are on the website of the Office of the Mayor: www1.nyc.gov/office-of-the-mayor/news/275-13/statements-mayor-bloomberg-commissioner-kelly-federal-court-ruling.

11. Scheindlin's decision to deny the stay is here: www.ccrjustice.org/files/9%2017%2013%20Order%20re%20Denying%20Def%20Stay%20Motion%20in%20District%20Court.pdf.

12. See Lamberth Consulting, "Traffic Stop Data Analysis Project, The City of Kalamazoo, Department of Public Safety," September 2013, www.kalamazoopublicsafety.org/images/pdf/Racial_Profiling_Study.pdf; background drawn from coverage in *The Kalamazoo Gazette*: Emily Monacelli, "Black leaders hope study brings changes," Sept. 8, 2013; Rex Hall Jr., "KDPS officers target black drivers, racial profiling study says," *mlive.com*, Sept. 4, 2013.

13. For a summary of the two cases, see David A. Harris, *Profiles in Injustice: Why Racial Profiling Cannot Work* (2002), pp. 53-60 (New Jersey), pp. 60-64 (Maryland). The trial court ruling in the New Jersey case is *People v. Soto*, www.leagle.com/decision/19961084734A2d350_11076.

14. The full 146-page report is on the Center for Constitutional Rights website: http://ccrjustice.org/files/FaganSecondSupplementalReport.pdf. For a good summary, see John Cassidy, "The Statistical Debate Behind the Stop-and-Frisk Verdict," *The New Yorker*, Aug. 13, 2013, www.newyorker.com/online/blogs/johncassidy/2013/08/scheindlin-stop-and-frisk-verdict-new-york-statistical-debate.html.

15. "Stop and Frisk Data," New York Civil Liberties Union, www.nyclu.org/content/stop-and-frisk-data; "New York Crime Rates," Disaster Center, www.disastercenter.com/crime/nycrime.htm. Disaster Center is a Federal Emergency Management Administration site.

16. Office of the Mayor, *op. cit.*

17. "Crime in the United States 2012," Federal Bureau of Investigation, www.fbi.gov/about-us/cjis/ucr/crime-in-the-u.s/2012/crime-in-the-u.s.-2012/tables/1tabledatadecoverviewpdf/table_1_crime_in_the_united_states_by_volume_and_rate_per_100000_inhabitants_1993-2012.xls. For background, see Sarah Glazer, "Declining Crime Rates," *CQ Researcher*, April 4, 1997, pp. 289-312.

18. See Chris Francescani, "Half of New York's stop-and-frisk arrests yield convictions, report says," Reuters, Nov. 14, 2013, www.reuters.com/article/2013/11/15/us-usa-newyork-stopandfrisk-idUSBRE9AE00I20131115.

19. The citation is 392 U.S. 1 (1968).

20. See Tanya Jones, "Race-based searches prohibited," *The Baltimore Sun*, Jan. 5, 1995, p. 1B; Paul W. Valentine, "Md. Settles Lawsuit Over Racial Profiles," *The Washington Post*, Jan. 5, 1995, p. B1.

21. See David Kocieniewski, "U.S. Will Monitor New Jersey Police on Race Profiling," *The New York Times*, Dec. 22, 1999, p. B1; Jerry Gray, "New Jersey Plans to Forestall Suit on Race Profiling," *ibid.*, April 30, 1999, p. A1.

22. Office of the Mayor, *op. cit.*

23. See Jost, "Police Misconduct," *op. cit.*

24. Historical background drawn in part from Morgan Cloud, "Quakers, Slaves and the Founders: Profiling to Save the Union," *Mississippi Law Journal*, Vol. 73 (2003), pp. 369-421; Alejandro del Carmen, *Racial Profiling in America* (2008).

25. Cloud, *op. cit.*, pp. 374-390.

26. The statistics are available online as part of a law professor's page on the trial of Sheriff Joseph Shipp in connection with a lynching in Tennessee in 1906: http://law2.umkc.edu/faculty/projects/ftrials/shipp/lynchingsstate.html.

27. Del Carmen, *op. cit.*, p. 35.

28. The citation is 323 U.S. 214 (1944).

29. Background drawn in part from Harris, *op. cit.*, chs. 2, 3.

30. For background, see Helen B. Shaffer, "Negro Power Struggle," *Editorial Research Reports*, Feb. 21, 1968, available at *CQ Researcher* Plus Archive.

31. The cases are *United States v. Brignoni-Ponce*, 422 U.S. 873 (1975); *United States v. Martinez-Fuerte*, 428 U.S. 543 (1976).

32. The case is *United States v. Sokolow*, 490 U.S. 1 (1989).

33. The decision is *Whren v. United States*, 517 U.S. 806 (1996).

34. See Steven A. Holmes, "Clinton Orders Investigation on Possible Racial Profiling," *The New York Times*, June 10, 1999.

35. See Thomas B. Edsall, "Black Caucus, Ashcroft Have Tense Meeting," *The Washington Post*, March 1, 2001, p. A6.

36. See "How the Racial Profiling Myth Helps Terrorists," in *Are Cops Racist?*, *op. cit.*

37. "Fact Sheet: Racial Profiling," Department of Justice, June 17, 2003, www.policeforum.org/library/racially-biased-policing/supplemental-resources/RPFactSheet%5B1%5D.pdf. For coverage, see Curt Anderson, "Federal Agencies Get Racial Profiling Ban," The Associated Press, June 18, 2003.

38. See Center for Constitutional Rights, "Daniels v. City of New York," http://ccrjustice.org/ourcases/past-cases/daniels%2C-et-al.-v.-city-new-york. For coverage, see Greg B. Smith, "NYPD Yields on Stop-Frisk," *Daily News* (New York), Sept. 18, 2003, p. 26. The New York attorney general's report is here: www.oag.state.ny.us/sites/default/files/pdfs/bureaus/civil_rights/stp_frsk.pdf.

39. See Ben Feller, "Obama, Gates, policeman pledge to try and move on," The Associated Press, July 31, 2009.

40. See Adam Nagourney, "Prayer, Protests and Anger Greet Florida Verdict," *The New York Times*, July 15, 2013, p. A1. For background on Stand Your Ground laws, see Kenneth Jost, "Police Misconduct," *CQ Researcher*, April 6, 2012, pp. 301-324.

41. The decision on liability in *Ortega Melendres v. Arpaio* (May 24, 2013) is on the website of the ACLU Immigrant Rights Project, https://www.aclu.org/files/assets/arpaio_decision.pdf. For coverage, see Jacques Billeaud and Walter Berry, "Judge: Ariz. Sheriff's office profiles Latinos," The Associated Press, May 25, 2013.

42. See Larry Miller, "Stop and Frisk Cases Down, Still Too Many," *Philadelphia Tribune*, March 21, 2013, www.phillytrib.com/newsarticles/item/8277-stop-and-frisk-cases-down,-still-too-many.html.

43. See Mike Carter and Steve Miletich, "Survey finds racial disparity in views toward Seattle police," *The Seattle Times*, Sept. 19, 2013, p. B1.

44. See Helen Freund, "Attorney to oversee NOPD decree," *Times-Picayune* (New Orleans), Oct. 27, 2013, p. B1.

45. The companion bills are S. 1038 and H.R. 2851, H.R. 2851/S. 1038, http://beta.congress.gov/bill/113th-congress/house-bill/2851?q={%22search%22%3A[%22end+racial+profiling+act%22]}.

46. Account from Laurie Kellman, "Senate looks at 'stand your ground' laws," *The Washington Post*, Oct. 30, 2013, p. A17.

47. See J. David Goodman and Joseph Goldstein, "For Police Commissioner, the Next Mayor Has a Wide Array of Options," *The New York Times*, Oct. 18, 2013, p. A21.

48. The order is here: www.ca2.uscourts.gov/decisions/isysquery/0344cef2-358a-401a-a888-8b442ae03fe9/6/doc/13-3123_13-3088_complete_amended.pdf.

49. William Bender, Ronnie Polaneczky and Morgan Zalot, "YouTube cop Philip Nace pulled off the street as second video surfaces," *The Philadelphia Daily News*, Oct. 17, 2013, p. 3; the *Daily News* broke the story on Oct. 11. For an account with a link to the video, see Andrew Kirell, "Cops Caught on Tape Harassing Minorities: 'You Weaken the F*cking Country,' " *Mediaite*, Oct. 14, 2013, www.mediaite.com/tv/cops-caught-on-tape-harassing-minorities-you-weaken-the-fcking-country/.

## BIBLIOGRAPHY

### Selected Sources

### Books

**Del Carmen, Alejandro, *Racial Profiling in America*, Pearson/Prentice Hall, 2008.**

The chairman of the Department of Criminology and Criminal Justice at the University of Texas-Arlington examines the historical and contemporary perspectives on racial and ethnic profiling in the United States. Includes chapter notes.

**Glover, Karen S., *Racial Profiling: Research, Racism, and Resistance*, Rowan & Littlefield, 2009.**

An assistant professor in the Department of Sociology, Criminology and Justice Studies at California State University-San Marcos examines racial profiling from the perspective of critical race theory through interviews with minority group subjects who had been stopped by police officers. Includes chapter notes.

**Harris, David A., *Profiles in Injustice: Why Racial Profiling Cannot Work*, New Press, 2002.**

A professor at the University of Pittsburgh School of Law, who was one of the first to comprehensively cover racial profiling, provides examples and continues with critical arguments on the purported justifications of the practice, as well as its costs and recommendations for reforms. The paperback edition issued in 2003 includes a chapter on post-9/11 ethnic profiling. Includes detailed notes.

**Mac Donald, Heather, *Are Cops Racist? How the War Against Police Harms Black Americans*, Ivan R. Dee, 2002 [ebook issued 2010].**

A senior fellow at the Manhattan Institute, a conservative think tank, argues in a collection of magazine-length pieces that police do not engage in racial profiling and that the controversy hurts black Americans by impeding policing in minority neighborhoods.

**Meeks, Kenneth, *Driving While Black: Highways, Shopping Malls, Taxicabs, Sidewalks. What to Do if You Are a Victim of Racial Profiling*, Broadway Books, 2000.**

An editor/producer at Black Enterprise Broadcast Media describes the phenomenon of racial profiling of African-Americans not only in policing but also in ordinary daily life.

**Rice, Stephen K., and Michael D. White (eds.), *Race, Ethnicity, and Policing: New and Essential Readings*, New York University Press, 2010.**

The 22 separate essays on racial and ethnic profiling are divided into four parts: context, methods, research and future. Rice is an associate professor in the Department of Criminal Justice, Seattle University; White is an associate professor at Arizona State University School of Criminology and Criminal Justice.

### Articles

**Harris, David A., "Picture This: Body-Worn Video Devices (Head Cams) as Tools for Ensuring Fourth Amendment Compliance by Police," *Texas Tech Law Review*, Vol. 43, No. 1 (2010), pp. 357-372, http://texastechlawreview.org/wp-content/uploads/Picture_This_Body_Worn_Video_Devices_Head_Cams_As_Tools_For_Ensuring_Fourth_Amendment_Compliance_By_Police.pdf.**

A University of Pittsburgh law professor proposes making video and audio recording of search-and-seizure incidents, as is done already in several cities, a routine police practice.

**Meyer, Deborah L., "The SPOT Program: Hello Racial Profiling Goodbye Fourth Amendment," *University of Maryland Law Journal of Race, Religion, Gender, and Class*, Vol. 10, No. 2 (2010), pp. 289-339, http://digitalcommons.law.umaryland.edu/rrgc/vol10/iss2/5/.**

The author critically examines the Transportation Security Administration's so-called SPOT program

("Screening of Passengers by Observation Technique") to identify potential terrorists.

**Withrow, Brian L., and Jeffrey D. Dailey, "Racial Profiling and the Law," in Craig Hemmens (ed.), *Current Legal Issues in Criminal Justice* (Oxford University Press, forthcoming 2014).**
The 11,000-word chapter gives a comprehensive, up-to-date account of law and litigation over racial profiling from the 1960s to the present. Withrow, a former Texas state trooper, is a professor of criminal justice at Texas State University in San Marcos; Dailey is an assistant professor of homeland and border security at Angelo State University, in San Angelo.

## Reports and Studies

**"Racial Profiling and the Use of Suspect Classifications in Law Enforcement Policy,"** *Judiciary* *Subcommittee on the Constitution, Civil Rights, and Civil Liberties, U.S. House of Representatives,* **June 17, 2010, serial no. 111-131, http://judiciary.house.gov/hearings/hear_100617_1.html.**
The hearing included testimony and statements from six witnesses, including representatives of the American Civil Liberties Union, Sikh Coalition and Muslim Advocates. The committee website includes video and print transcript.

## On the Web

**"If Police Encounters Were Filmed,"** *Room for Debate* **(*New York Times* blog), Oct. 22, 2013, www.nytimes.com/roomfordebate/2013/10/22/should-police-wear-cameras.**
A former police officer endorses body cameras for police, but two civil liberties-minded advocates warn against the practice because of privacy concerns.

# For More Information

**American Civil Liberties Union**, 125 Broad St., New York, NY 10004; 212-549-2500; www.aclu.org. Monitors and sometimes brings lawsuits in cases involving racial profiling, use of force and other police-practices issues.

**Fraternal Order of Police, Grand Lodge**, 1410 Donelson Pike, A-17, Nashville, TN 37217; 615-399-0900; www.grandlodgefop.org. Largest membership organization representing rank-and-file law enforcement officers.

**International Association of Chiefs of Police**, 515 North Washington St., Alexandria, VA 22314; 703-836-6767; www.theiacp.org. Represents operating chief executives of international, federal, state and local law enforcement agencies of all sizes.

**Major Cities Chiefs Police Association**, https://majorcitieschiefs.com/about.php. Represents chiefs from 63 large American city or county police organizations.

**Mexican American Legal Defense and Educational Fund**, 634 S. Spring St., Los Angeles, CA; 213-629-2512; www.maldef.org. A leading civil rights organization for Latinos.

**Muslim Advocates**, 315 Montgomery St., 8th floor, San Francisco, CA 94104; 415-692-1484; www.muslimadvocates.org. Civil rights organization for Muslims, Arab and South Asian Americans.

**NAACP**, 4805 Mt. Hope Dr., Baltimore MD 21215; 410-580-5777; www.naacp.org. Century-old civil rights organization for African-Americans.

**National Sheriffs' Association**, 1450 Duke St., Alexandria, VA 22314; 1-800-424-7827; www.sheriffs.org. Represents and assists sheriffs' offices nationwide through education, training and information resources.

**Police Foundation**, 1201 Connecticut Ave., N.W., Washington, DC 20036-2636; 202-833-1460; www.policefoundation.org. Established by the Ford Foundation in 1970; sponsors research to support innovation and improvement in policing.

# 10

# Affirmative Action

Peter Katel, Charles S. Clark, and Kenneth Jost

Law student Jessica Peck Corry, executive director of the Colorado Civil Rights Initiative, supports Constitutional Amendment 46, which would prohibit all government entities in Colorado from discriminating for or against anyone because of race, ethnicity or gender. Attorney Melissa Hart counters that the amendment would end programs designed to reach minority groups.

From *CQ Researcher*, October 17, 2008 (updated August 5, 2010 and June 19, 2012).

JESSICA PECK CORRY
Colorado Civil Rights Initiative

MELISSA HART
Coloradans for Equal Opportunity

TV screenshot courtesy "DemocracyNow"

No white politician could have gotten the question George Stephanopoulos of ABC News asked Sen. Barack Obama. "You said . . . that affluent African-Americans, like your daughters, should probably be treated as pretty advantaged when they apply to college," he began. "How specifically would you recommend changing affirmative action policies so that affluent African-Americans are not given advantages and poor, less affluent whites are?"[1]

The Democratic presidential nominee, speaking during a primary election debate in April, said his daughters' advantages should weigh more than their skin color. "You know, Malia and Sasha, they've had a pretty good deal."[2]

But a white applicant who has overcome big odds to pursue an education should have those circumstances taken into account, Obama said. "I still believe in affirmative action as a means of overcoming both historic and potentially current discrimination," Obama said, "but I think that it can't be a quota system and it can't be something that is simply applied without looking at the whole person, whether that person is black, or white or Hispanic, male or female."[3]

Supporting affirmative action on the one hand, objecting to quotas on the other — Obama seemed to know he was threading his way through a minefield. Decades after it began, affirmative action is seen by many whites as nothing but a fancy term for racial quotas designed to give minorities an unfair break. Majority black opinion remains strongly pro-affirmative action, on the grounds that the legacy of racial discrimination lives on. Whites and blacks are 30 percentage points apart on the issue, according to a 2007 national survey by the nonpartisan Pew Research Center.[4]

## Americans Support Boost for Disadvantaged

A majority of Americans believe that individuals born into poverty can overcome their disadvantages and that society should be giving them special help (top poll). Fewer, however, endorse race-based affirmative action as the way to help (bottom).

| | Agree | Disagree |
|---|---|---|
| We should help people who are working hard to overcome disadvantages and succeed in life. | 93% | 6 |
| People who start out with little and work their way up are the real success stories. | 91 | 7 |
| Some people are born poor, and there's nothing we can do about that. | 26 | 72 |
| We shouldn't give special help at all, even to those who started out with more disadvantages than most. | 16 | 81 |

**If there is only one seat available, which student would you admit to college, the high-income student or the low-income student?**

| | Percentage selecting: | |
|---|---|---|
| | Low-income student | High-income student |
| If both students get the same admissions test score? | 63% | 3% |
| If low-income student gets a slightly lower test score? | 33 | 54 |
| If the low-income student is also black, and the high-income student is white? | 36 | 39 |
| If the low-income student is also Hispanic, and the high-income student is not Hispanic? | 33 | 45 |

*Source:* Anthony P. Carnevale and Stephen J. Rose, "Socioeconomic Status, Race/ Ethnicity, and Selective College Admissions," The Century Foundation, March 2003

admissions to top-tier state schools, such as the University of California at Los Angeles (UCLA) based on race, gender or ethnic background. Graduating from such schools is seen as an affordable ticket to the good life, but there aren't enough places at these schools for all applicants, so many qualified applicants are rejected.

Resentment over the notion that some applicants got an advantage because of their ancestry led California voters in 1996 to ban affirmative action in college admissions. Four years later, the Florida legislature, at the urging of then-Gov. Jeb Bush, effectively eliminated using race as an admission standard for colleges and universities. And initiatives similar to the California referendum were later passed in Washington state and then in Michigan, in 2006.

Race is central to the affirmative action debate because the doctrine grew out of the civil rights movement and the Civil Rights Act of 1964, which outlawed discrimination based on race, ethnicity or gender. The loosely defined term generally is used as a synonym for advantages — "preferences" — that employers and schools extend to members of a particular race, national origin or gender.

"The time has come to pull the plug on race-based decision-making," says Ward Connerly, a Sacramento, Calif.-based businessman who is the lead organizer of the Colorado and Nebraska ballot initiative campaigns, as well as earlier ones elsewhere. "The Civil Rights Act of 1964 talks about treating people equally without regard to race, color or national origin. When you talk about civil rights, they don't just belong to black people."

Connerly, who is black, supports extending preferences of some kind to low-income applicants for jobs — as long as the beneficiaries aren't classified by race or gender.

But affirmative action supporters say that approach ignores reality. "If there are any preferences in operation in our society, they're preferences given to people with white skin and who are men and who have financial and other advantages that come with that," says Nicole Kief,

Now, with the candidacy of Columbia University and Harvard Law School graduate Obama turning up the volume on the debate, voters in two states will be deciding in November whether preferences should remain in effect in state government hiring and state college admissions.

Originally, conflict over affirmative action focused on hiring. But during the past two decades, the debate has shifted to whether preference should be given in

New York-based state strategist for the American Civil Liberties Union's racial justice program, which is opposing the Connerly-organized ballot initiative campaigns.

Yet, of the 38 million Americans classified as poor, whites make up the biggest share: 17 million people. Blacks account for slightly more than 9 million and Hispanics slightly less. Some 576,000 Native Americans are considered poor. Looking beyond the simple numbers, however, reveals that far greater percentages of African-Americans and Hispanics are likely to be poor: 25 percent of African-Americans and 20 percent of Hispanics live below the poverty line, but only 10 percent of whites are poor.[5]

In 2000, according to statistics compiled by *Chronicle of Higher Education* Deputy Editor Peter Schmidt, the average white elementary school student attended a school that was 78 percent white, 9 percent black, 8 percent Hispanic, 3 percent Asian and 30 percent poor. Black or Hispanic children attended a school in which 57 percent of the student body shared their race or ethnicity and about two-thirds of the students were poor.[6]

These conditions directly affect college admissions, according to The Century Foundation. The liberal think tank reported in 2003 that white students account for 77 percent of the students at high schools in which the greatest majority of students go on to college. Black students account for only 11 percent of the population at these schools, and Hispanics 7 percent.[7]

A comprehensive 2004 study by the Urban Institute, a nonpartisan think tank, found that only about half of black and Hispanic high school students graduate, compared to 75 and 77 percent, respectively, of whites and Asians.[8]

Politically conservative affirmative action critics cite these statistics to argue that focusing on college admissions and hiring practices rather than school reform was a big mistake. The critics get some support from liberals who want to keep affirmative action — as long as it's

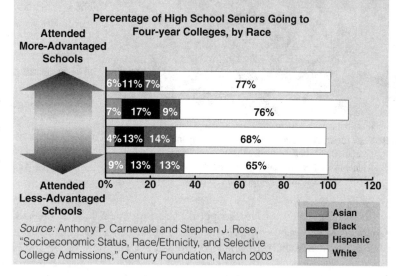

### Elite Schools Graduate Fewest Minorities

Among college-bound blacks and Hispanics, larger percentages graduated from "less advantaged" high schools than from the "most advantaged" schools.

**Percentage of High School Seniors Going to Four-year Colleges, by Race**

Attended More-Advantaged Schools

| Asian | Black | Hispanic | White |
|---|---|---|---|
| 6% | 11% | 7% | 77% |
| 7% | 17% | 9% | 76% |
| 4% | 13% | 14% | 68% |
| 9% | 13% | 13% | 65% |

Attended Less-Advantaged Schools

*Source:* Anthony P. Carnevale and Stephen J. Rose, "Socioeconomic Status, Race/Ethnicity, and Selective College Admissions," Century Foundation, March 2003

based on socioeconomic status instead of race. "Affirmative action based on race was always kind of a cheap and quick fix that bypassed the hard work of trying to develop the talents of low-income minority students generally," says Richard D. Kahlenberg, a senior fellow at The Century Foundation.

Basing affirmative action on class instead of race wouldn't exclude racial and ethnic minorities, Kahlenberg argues, because race and class are so closely intertwined.

President Lyndon B. Johnson noted that connection in a major speech that laid the philosophical foundations for affirmative action programs. These weren't set up for another five years, a reflection of how big a change they represented in traditional hiring and promotion practices, where affirmative action began. "You do not take a person who, for years, has been hobbled by chains and liberate him, bring him up to the starting line of a race and then say, 'You are free to compete with all the others,' and still justly believe that you have been completely fair," Johnson said in "To Fulfill These Rights," his 1965 commencement speech at Howard University in Washington, D.C., one of the country's top historically black institutions.[9]

Asian-American enrollment at the University of California at Berkeley rose dramatically after California voters in 1996 approved Proposition 209, a ballot initiative that banned affirmative action at all state institutions. Enrollment of African-American, Hispanic and Native American students, however, plunged.

By the late 1970s, a long string of U.S. Supreme Court decisions began setting boundaries on affirmative action, partly in response to white job and school applicants who sued over "reverse discrimination." The court's bottom line: Schools and employers could take race into account, but not as a sole criterion. Setting quotas based on race, ethnicity or gender was prohibited. (The prohibition of gender discrimination effectively ended the chances for passage of the proposed Equal Rights Amendment [ERA], which feminist organizations had been promoting since 1923. The Civil Rights Act, along with other legislation and court decisions, made many supporters of women's rights "lukewarm" about the proposed amendment, Roberta W. Francis, then chair of the National Council of Women's Organizations' ERA task force, wrote in 2001).[10]

The high court's support for affirmative action has been weakening through the years. Since 1991 the court has included Justice Clarence Thomas, the lone black member and a bitter foe of affirmative action. In his 2007 autobiography, Thomas wrote that his Yale Law School degree set him up for rejection by major law firm interviewers. "Many asked pointed questions unsubtly suggesting that they doubted I was as smart as my grades indicated," he wrote. "Now I knew what a law degree from Yale was worth when it bore the taint of racial preference."[11]

Some of Thomas' black classmates dispute his view of a Yale diploma's worth. "Had he not gone to a school like Yale, he would not be sitting on the Supreme Court," said William Coleman III, a Philadelphia attorney who was general counsel to the U.S. Army in the Clinton administration.[12]

But that argument does not seem to impress Thomas, who was in a 5-4 minority in the high court's most recent affirmative action ruling, in which the justices upheld the use of race in law-school admissions at the University of Michigan. But even Justice Sandra Day O'Connor, who wrote the majority opinion, signaled unease with her position. In 25 years, she wrote, affirmative action would "no longer be necessary."[13]

Paradoxically, an Obama victory on Nov. 4 might be the most effective anti-affirmative action event of all.

"The primary rationale for affirmative action is that America is institutionally racist and institutionally sexist," Connerly, an Obama foe, told The Associated Press. "That rationale is undercut in a major way when you look at the success of Sen. [Hillary Rodham] Clinton and Sen. Obama."

Asked to respond to Connerly's remarks, Obama appeared to draw some limits of his own on affirmative action. "Affirmative action is not going to be the long-term solution to the problems of race in America," he told a July convention of minority journalists, "because, frankly, if you've got 50 percent of African-American or Latino kids dropping out of high school, it doesn't really matter what you do in terms of affirmative action; those kids are not getting into college."[14]

As critics and supporters discuss the future of affirmative action, here are some of the questions being debated:

## Has affirmative action outlived its usefulness?

In the United States of the late 1960s and '70s, even some outright opponents of race-based affirmative action conceded that it represented an attempt to deal with the consequences of longstanding, systematic racial discrimination, which had legally ended only shortly before.

But ever since opposition to affirmative action began growing in the 1980s, its opponents themselves have invoked the very principles that the civil rights movement had embraced in its fight to end discrimination. Taking a job or school applicant's race or ethnicity into account is immoral, opponents argue, even for supposedly benign purposes. And a policy of racial/ethnic preferences, by definition, cannot lead to equality.

In today's United States, critics say, minority applicants don't face any danger that their skin color or ethnic heritage will hold them back. Instead, affirmative-action beneficiaries face continuing skepticism from others — and even from themselves, that they somehow were given an advantage that their academic work didn't entitle them to receive.

Meanwhile, opponents and supporters readily acknowledge that a disproportionate share of black and Latino students receive substandard educations, starting in and lasting through high school. Affirmative action hasn't eliminated the link between race/ethnicity and poverty and academic deprivation, they agree.

## Few Poor Students Attend Top Schools

Nearly three-quarters of students entering tier 1 colleges and universities come from the wealthiest families, but only 3 percent of students from the bottom quartile enter top schools. Far more students from poorer backgrounds enroll in less prestigious schools, and even more in community colleges.

### Socioeconomic Status of Entering College Classes

| School prestige level | First quartile (lowest) | Second quartile | Third quartile | Fourth quartile (highest) |
|---|---|---|---|---|
| Tier 1 | 3% | 6% | 17% | 74% |
| Tier 2 | 7 | 18 | 29 | 46 |
| Tier 3 | 10 | 19 | 36 | 35 |
| Tier 4 | 16 | 21 | 28 | 35 |
| Community Colleges | 21 | 30 | 27 | 22 |

Source: Anthony P. Carnevale and Stephen J. Rose, "Socioeconomic Status, Race/ Ethnicity, and Selective College Admissions," The Century Foundation, March 2003

Critics of race preferences, however, say they haven't narrowed the divide that helped to trigger affirmative action in the first place. Affirmative action advocates favor significantly reforming K-12 education while simultaneously giving a leg up to minorities who managed to overcome their odds at inadequate public schools.

And some supporters say affirmative action is important for other reasons, which transcend America's racial history. Affirmative action helps to ensure continuation of a democratic political culture, says James E. Coleman Jr., a professor at Duke University Law School.

"It's not just about discrimination or past discrimination," says Coleman, who attended all-black schools when growing up and then graduated from Harvard College and Columbia Law School in the early 1970s, during the early days of affirmative action. "It's in our self-interest. We want leaders of all different backgrounds, all different races; we ought to educate them together."

But Connerly, the California businessman behind anti-affirmative action ballot initiatives, says that race and gender preferences are the wrong tool with which to promote diversity, because they effectively erode academic standards. "Excellence can be achieved by any group of people," says Connerly, a former member of the University of California Board of Regents. "So we will keep the standards where they ought to be, and we will expect people to meet those standards."

But legislators interested in a "quick fix" have found it simpler to mandate diversity than to devise ways to improve schools. "There are times when someone has to say, 'This isn't right. We're going to do something about it,' " Connerly says. "But in the legislative process, I can find no evidence of leadership anywhere."

Like others, Connerly also cites the extraordinary academic achievements of Asian-American students — who haven't benefited from affirmative action. Affirmative action supporters don't try to dispute that point. "At the University of California at Berkeley, 40 percent of the students are Asian," says Terry H. Anderson, a history professor at Texas A&M University in College Station. "What does that say about family structure? It makes a big statement. Family structure is so important, and it's something that affirmative action can't help at all."

But if encouraging minority-group enrollment at universities doesn't serve as a social and educational cure-all, says Anderson, who has written a history of affirmative

## Few Poor Students Score High on SAT

Two-thirds of students who scored at least 1300 on the SAT came from families ranking in the highest quartile of socioeconomic status, compared with only 3 percent of students from the lowest-income group. Moreover, more than one-fifth of those scoring under 1000 — and 37 percent of non-test-takers — come from the poorest families.

**SAT Scores by Family Socioeconomic Status***

| Score | First Quartile (lowest) | Second Quartile | Third Quartile | Fourth Quartile (highest) |
|---|---|---|---|---|
| >1300 | 3% | 10% | 22% | 66% |
| 1200–1300 | 4 | 14 | 23 | 58 |
| 1100–1200 | 6 | 17 | 29 | 47 |
| 1000–1100 | 8 | 24 | 32 | 36 |
| <1000 | 21 | 25 | 30 | 24 |
| Non-taker | 37 | 30 | 22 | 10 |

* The maximum score is 1600

*Note:* Percentages do not add to 100 due to rounding.

*Source:* Anthony P. Carnevale and Stephen J. Rose, "Socioeconomic Status, Race/ Ethnicity, and Selective College Admissions," The Century Foundation, March 2003

action, the policy still serves a valuable purpose. "It's become part of our culture. On this campus, it's been 'out' to be racist for years and years. I'm looking at kids born in 1990; they just don't feel self-conscious about race or gender, they just expect to be treated equally."

Standing between the supporters and the enemies of affirmative action's racial/ethnic preferences are the affirmative action reformers. "I don't think it's time to completely abolish all forms of affirmative action," says the Century Foundation's Kahlenberg. "But it's clear there are strong legal, moral and political problems with relying solely on race."

And at the practical level, race isn't the only gauge of hardship that some students must overcome, even to be capable of competing for admission to a top-tier school. "There are students from low-income backgrounds," Kahlenberg says, "who aren't given the same opportunities as wealthier students are given, and they deserve a leg up in admissions. Someone's test scores and grades are a reflection not only of how hard they work and how talented they are, but what sorts of opportunities they've had."

## Does race-based affirmative action still face powerful public opposition?

At the state and federal level, affirmative action has generated enormous conflict over the decades, played out in a long chain of lawsuits and Supreme Court decisions, as well as the hard-fought ballot initiatives this year in Arizona, Missouri and Oklahoma — all three of which ended in defeat for race, ethnic and gender preferences.

But today's political agenda — dominated by the global financial crisis, the continuing downward slide of real estate prices, the continuing conflict in Iraq and escalated combat in Afghanistan — would seem to leave little space for a reignited affirmative action conflict.

Nevertheless, supporters and opponents of affirmative action fought hard in five states over proposed ballot initiatives, two of which will go before voters in November.

Nationally, the nonpartisan Pew Research Center reported last year that black and white Americans are divided by a considerable margin on whether minority group members should get preferential treatment. Among blacks, 57 answered yes, but only 27 percent of whites agreed. That gap was somewhat bigger in 1991, when 68 percent of blacks and only 17 percent of whites favored preferences.[15]

Obama's statement to ABC News' Stephanopoulos that his daughters shouldn't benefit from affirmative action reflected awareness of majority sentiment against race preference.[16]

Still, the exchange led to some predictions that it would resurface. "The issue of affirmative action is likely to dog Sen. Obama on the campaign trail as he seeks to win over white, blue-collar voters in battleground states like Michigan," *The Wall Street Journal* predicted in June.[17]

Just two and a half weeks before the election, that forecast hadn't come to pass. However, earlier in the year interest remained strong enough that campaigners for state ballot initiatives were able to gather 136,589 signatures in Nebraska and about 130,000 in Colorado to require that the issue be put before voters in those states.

Meanwhile, the initiative efforts in Arizona, Missouri and Oklahoma were doomed after the validity of petition signatures was challenged in those states. Connerly, the chief organizer of the initiatives, blames opponents' tactics and, in Oklahoma, an unusually short, 90-day window during which signatures must be collected. But once initiatives get on ballots, he says, voters approve them. "There is something about the principle of fairness that most people understand."

Without congressional legislation prohibiting preferences, Connerly says, the initiatives are designed to force state governments "to abide by the moral principle that racial discrimination — whether against a white or black or Latino or Native American — is just wrong."

But reality can present immoral circumstances as well, affirmative action defenders argue. "Racial discrimination and gender discrimination continue to present obstacles to people of color and women," says the American Civil Liberties Union's (ACLU) Kief. "Affirmative action is a way to chip away at some of these obstacles."

Kief says the fact that Connerly has played a central role in all of the initiatives indicates that true grassroots opposition to affirmative action is weak in states where initiatives have passed or are about to be voted on.

However, The Century Foundation's Kahlenberg points out that pro-affirmative action forces work hard to block ballot initiatives, because when such initiatives have gone before voters they have been approved. And the most recent successful ballot initiative, in Michigan in 2006, passed by a slightly bigger margin — 57 percent to 43 percent — than its California counterpart in 1996, which was approved by 54-46.[18]

Further evidence that anti-affirmative action initiatives are hard to fight surfaced this year in Colorado, where the group Coloradans for Equal Opportunity failed to round up enough signatures to put a pro-affirmative action initiative on the ballot.

Kahlenberg acknowledges that affirmative action politics can be tricky. Despite abiding public opposition to preferences, support among blacks is so strong that Republican presidential campaigns tend to downplay affirmative action, for fear of triggering a huge turnout among black

Democratic presidential candidate Sen. Barack Obama, speaking in Philadelphia on Oct. 11, 2008, represents the new face of affirmative action in the demographically changing United States: His father was Kenyan and a half-sister is half-Indonesian.

voters, who vote overwhelmingly Democratic. In 1999, then-Florida Gov. Jeb Bush kept a Connerly-sponsored initiative out of that state largely in order to lessen the chances of a major black Democratic mobilization in the 2000 presidential election, in which his brother would be running.[19]

"When you have an initiative on the ballot," Kahlenberg says, "some Republicans think that it increases minority turnout, so they're not sure whether these initiatives play to their party or not." Republican opposition to affirmative action goes back to the Reagan administration. Reagan, however, passed up a chance to ban affirmative action programs throughout the federal government, displaying a degree of GOP ambivalence. However, Connerly is an outspoken Republican.[20]

Nevertheless, an all-out Republican push against affirmative action during the past decade failed to catch on at the national level. In 1996, former Republican Senate Majority Leader Bob Dole of Kansas was running for president, and the affirmative action initiative was on the same ballot in California. "The initiative passed, but there was no trickle-down help for Bob Dole," says Daniel A. Smith, a political scientist at the University of Florida who has written on affirmative action politics.

This year, to be sure, anxieties growing out of the financial crisis and economic slowdown could rekindle passions over preferences. But Smith argues the economic environment makes finger-pointing at minorities less likely. "Whites are not losing jobs to African-Americans," he says. "Whites and African-Americans are losing jobs to the Asian subcontinent — they're going to Bangalore. The global economy makes it more difficult to have a convenient domestic scapegoat for lost jobs."

## Has affirmative action diverted attention from the poor quality of K-12 education in low-income communities?

If there's one point on which everyone involved in the affirmative action debate agrees, it's that public schools attended by most low-income students are worsening.

"The educational achievement gap between racial groups began growing again in the 1990s," Gary Orfield, a professor of education and social policy at Harvard University, wrote. "Our public schools are becoming increasingly segregated by race and income, and the segregated schools are, on average, strikingly inferior in many important ways, including the quality and experience of teachers and the level of competition from other students. . . . It is clear that students of different races do not receive an equal chance for college."[21]

The decline in education quality has occurred at the same time various race-preference policies have governed admission to the nation's best colleges and universities. The policies were designed to provide an incentive for schools and students alike to do their best, by ensuring that a college education remains a possibility for all students who perform well academically.

But the results have not been encouraging. In California alone, only 36 percent of all high school students in 2001 had taken all the courses required for admission to the state university system, according to a study by the Civil Rights Project at Harvard University. Among black students, only 26 percent had taken the prerequisites, and only 24 percent of Hispanics. Meanwhile, 41 percent of white students and 54 percent of Asians had taken the necessary courses.[22]

In large part as a result of deficient K-12 education, decades of race-preference affirmative action at top-tier colleges and universities have yielded only small percentages of black and Hispanic students. In 1995, according to an exhaustive 2003 study by The Century Foundation, these students accounted for 6 percent of admissions to the 146 top-tier institutions.[23]

Socioeconomically, the picture is even less diverse. Seventy-four percent of students came from families in the wealthiest quarter of the socioeconomic scale; 3 percent came from families in the bottom quarter.[24]

For race-preference opponents, the picture demonstrates that efforts at ensuring racial and ethnic diversity in higher education would have been better aimed at improving K-12 schools across the country.

"If you've tried to use race for 40-some years, and you still have this profound gap," Connerly says, "yet cling to the notion that you have given some affirmative action to black and Latino and American Indian students — though Asians, without it, are outstripping everybody — maybe the way we've been doing it wasn't the right way to do it."

Meanwhile, he says, making a point that echoes through black, conservative circles, "Historically black colleges and universities (HBCUs) — if you look at doctors and pharmacists across our nation, you'll find them coming from schools that are 90 percent black. These schools are not very diverse, but they put a premium on quality."

But not all HBCUs are in that class, affirmative action supporters point out. "A lot of people who come out with a degree in computer science from minority-serving institutions know absolutely no mathematics," says Richard Tapia, a mathematics professor at Rice University and director of the university's Center for Equity and Excellence in Education. "I once went to a historically black university and had lunch with a top student who was going to do graduate work at Purdue, but when I talked to her I realized that her knowledge of math was on a par with that of a Rice freshman. The gap is huge."

Tapia, who advocates better mentoring for promising minority students at top-flight institutions, argues that the effect of relegating minority students to a certain defined group of colleges and universities, including historically black institutions, limits their chances of advancement in society at large. "From the elite schools you're going to get leadership."

Still, a question remains as to whether focusing on preferential admissions has helped perpetuate the very conditions that give rise to preferences in the first place.

"At the K-12 level you could argue that affirmative action has led to stagnation," says Richard Sander, a professor of law at UCLA Law School. "There's very little forward movement, very little closing of the black-white gap of the past 20 to 30 years."

Coleman of Duke University agrees that public education for most low-income students needs help. But that issue has nothing to do with admissions to top-drawer universities and professional schools, he says. "Look at minority students who get into places like that," he says. "For the most part, they haven't gone to the weakest high schools; they've often gone to the best."

Yet the affirmative action conflict focuses on black students, who are assumed to be academically under-qualified, Coleman says, while white students' place at the best schools isn't questioned. The classroom reality differs, he says. "We have a whole range of students with different abilities. All of the weak students are not minority students; all of the strong students are not white students."

## BACKGROUND

### Righting Wrongs

The civil rights revolution of the 1950s and '60s forced a new look at the policies that had locked one set of Americans out of most higher-education institutions and higher-paying jobs.

As early as 1962, the Congress of Racial Equality (CORE), one of the most active civil-rights organizations, advocated hiring practices that would make up for discrimination against black applicants. "We are approaching employers with the proposition that they have effectively excluded Negroes from their work force a long time, and they now have a responsibility and obligation to make up for their past sins," the organization said in a statement from its New York headquarters.[25]

Facing CORE-organized boycotts, a handful of companies in New York, Denver, Detroit, Seattle and Baltimore changed their hiring procedures to favor black applicants.

In July 1964, President Lyndon B. Johnson pushed Congress to pass the landmark Civil Rights Act, which had been championed by President John F. Kennedy since his 1960 presidential election campaign.

The law's Title VII, which prohibits racial, religious or sexual discrimination in hiring, said judges enforcing the law could order "such affirmative action as may be appropriate" to correct violations.[26]

Title VII didn't specify what kind of affirmative action could be decreed. But racial preferences were openly discussed in the political arena as a tool to equalize opportunities. Official working definitions of affirmative

action didn't emerge until the end of the 1960s, under President Richard M. Nixon.

In 1969, the administration approved the "Philadelphia Plan," which set numerical goals for black and other minority employment on federally financed construction jobs. One year later, the plan was expanded to cover all businesses with 50 or more employees and federal contracts of at least $50,000. The contracts were to set hiring goals and timetables designed to match up a firm's minority representation with the workforce demographics in its area. The specified minorities were: "Negro, Oriental, American Indian and Spanish Surnamed Americans."[27]

The sudden change in the workplace environment prompted a wave of lawsuits. In the lead, a legal challenge by 13 black electric utility workers in North Carolina led to one of the most influential U.S. Supreme Court decisions on affirmative action, the 1971 *Griggs v. Duke Power Co.* case.[28]

In a unanimous decision, the high court concluded that an aptitude test that was a condition of promotion for the workers violated the Civil Rights Act. Duke Power may not have intended the test to weed out black applicants, Chief Justice Warren E. Burger wrote in the decision. But, he added, "Congress directed the thrust of the Act to the consequences of employment practices, not simply the motivation."[29]

If the point of the Civil Rights Act was to ensure that the consequences of institutions' decisions yielded balanced workforces, then goals and timetables to lead to that outcome were consistent with the law as well. In other words, eliminating racial discrimination could mean paying attention to race in hiring and promotions.

That effort would produce a term that captured the frustration and anger among white males who were competing with minority-group members for jobs, promotions or school admissions: "reverse discrimination."

The issue went national with a challenge by Allan Bakke, a white, medical school applicant, to the University of California. He'd been rejected two years in a row while minority-group members — for whom 16 slots in the 100-member class had been set aside — were admitted with lower qualifying scores.

After the case reached the Supreme Court, the justices in a 5-4 decision in 1978 ordered Bakke admitted and prohibited the use of racial quotas. But they allowed race to be considered along with other criteria. Representing the University of California was former Solicitor General

## CHRONOLOGY

1960s *Enactment of civil rights law opens national debate on discrimination.*

**1964** Civil Rights Act of 1964 bars discrimination in employment and at federally funded colleges.

**1965** President Lyndon B. Johnson calls for a massive national effort to create social and economic equality.

**1969** Nixon administration approves "Philadelphia Plan" setting numerical goals for minority employment on all federally financed building projects.

1970s-1980s *Affirmative action expands throughout the country, prompting legal challenges and growing voter discontent, leading to new federal policy.*

**1971** The U.S. Supreme Court's landmark *Griggs v. Duke Power Co.* decision, growing out of a challenge by 13 black electric utility workers in North Carolina, is seen as authorizing companies and institutions to set out goals and timetables for minority hiring.

**1978** Supreme Court's decision in *University of California Regents v. Bakke,* arising from a medical-school admission case, rules out racial quotas but allows race to be considered with other factors.

**1980** Ronald W. Reagan is elected president with strong support from white males who see affirmative action as a threat.

**1981-1983** Reagan administration reduces affirmative action enforcement.

**1985** Attorney General Edwin Meese III drafts executive order outlawing affirmative action in federal government; Reagan never signs it.

**1987** Supreme Court upholds job promotion of a woman whose advancement was challenged by a male colleague claiming higher qualifications.

1990s *Ballot initiatives banning race and gender preferences prompt President Bill Clinton to acknowledge faults in affirmative action.*

**1994** White voter discontent energizes the "Republican revolution" that topples Democrats from control of Congress.

**1995** Supreme Court rules in *Adarand Constructors v. Peña* that affirmative action programs must be "narrowly tailored" for cases of extreme discrimination. . . . Clinton concedes that affirmative action foes have some valid points but concludes, "Mend it, but don't end it." . . . Senate votes down anti-affirmative action bill.

**1996** California voters pass nation's first ballot initiative outlawing racial, ethnic and gender preferences. . . . 5th U.S. Circuit Court of Appeals rules that universities can't take race into account in evaluating applicants.

**1998** Washington state voters pass ballot initiative identical to California's.

2000s *Affirmative action in university admissions stays on national agenda, leading to major Supreme Court ruling; Sen. Barack Obama's presidential candidacy focuses more attention on the issue.*

**2003** Supreme Court's *Gratz v. Bollinger* ruling rejects University of Michigan undergraduate admission system for awarding extra points to minority applicants, but simultaneous *Grutter v. Bollinger* decision upholds UM law school admissions policy, which includes race as one factor among many. . . . Justice Sandra Day O'Connor writes in 5-4 majority opinion in *Grutter* that affirmative action won't be necessary in 25 years. . . . Century Foundation study finds strong linkage between socioeconomic status, race and chances of going to college.

**2006** Michigan passes nation's third ballot initiative outlawing racial, ethnic and gender preferences.

**2008** Opponents of affirmative action in Arizona, Missouri and Oklahoma fail to place anti-affirmative action initiatives on ballot, but similar campaigns succeed in Colorado and Nebraska. . . . U.S. Civil Rights Commission opens study of minority students majoring in science and math. . . . Saying his daughters are affluent and shouldn't benefit from race preferences, Obama endorses affirmative action for struggling, white college applicants.

**2008** Colorado voters reject ballot initiative to enact state bans on race-conscious selection methods in employment and college admissions.

**November 4** — Colorado voters reject ballot initiative to enact state bans on race-conscious selection methods in employment and college admissions.

## 2009

**June** — Arizona legislature approves putting a proposed plan to outlaw affirmative action on the November 2010 ballot. . . . On June 29, Supreme Court rules 5-4 in favor of white firefighters from New Haven, Conn., in Ricci v. DeStefano. The firefighters had challenged the city's decision to discard a competency test for determining promotions after black firefighters taking the test had underperformed. A Quinnipiac University poll shows American voters favor abolishing affirmative action, 55-36 percent.

**June 29** — Supreme Court favors white firefighters in New Haven, Conn., reverse-discrimination case; 5-4 ruling limits government employers' ability to favor minorities in hiring, promotion to avoid discrimination claims.

## 2010

Education Secretary Arne Duncan announces in Selma, Ala., that his department is launching new desegregation compliance investigations around the country. Obama administration's departments of Education and Justice together file a friend-of-the-court brief on behalf of the University of Texas at Austin, which is defending its use of race as part of its process of achieving diversity. . . . Russlynn H. Ali, Assistant Education Secretary for Civil Rights, says she anticipates more civil rights activity in her office. . . . Study finds drop in percentage of black and Mexican-American law students.

**March 8** — Education Secretary Arne Duncan announces in Selma, Ala., that his department is launching new desegregation compliance investigations around the country.

**November 2** — Arizona voters approve measure to ban affirmative action in public education, public employment, government contracting.

## 2011

**January 18** — University of Texas admissions policy upheld by federal appeals court; rehearing denied (June 17).

**July 1** — Michigan ban on affirmative action struck down by federal appeals court.

**July 28** — White firefighters in New Haven, Conn., agree to accept $2 million in damages in reverse-discrimination suit after Supreme Court victory.

**September 30** — Jefferson County (Louisville), Ky., pupil assignment plan struck down by state court; school district appeals to state high court; arguments heard April 18, 2012.

**December 2** — Obama administration lists steps for colleges, universities to increase diversity.

## 2012

**February 21** — Supreme Court agrees to hear University of Texas case; arguments in fall 2012, decision by June 2013.

**April 2** — California ban on affirmative action upheld by federal court.

**June 11** — Supreme Court allows black New Haven firefighter to pursue discrimination claim against city over scoring of promotion test.

**November 6** — Oklahoma to vote on affirmative action ban.

# "Percent Plans" Offer Alternative to Race-Based Preferences

*But critics say approach fails to level playing field.*

In recent years, voters and judges have blocked race and ethnicity preferences in university admissions in three big states with booming minority populations — California, Florida and Texas. Nonetheless, lawmakers devised a way to ensure that public universities remain open to black and Latino students.

The so-called "percent plans" promise guaranteed admission based on a student's high school class standing, not on skin tone. That, at least is the principle.

But the man who helped end racial affirmative action preferences in two of the states involved argues affirmative action is alive and well, simply under another name. Moreover, says Ward Connerly, a black businessman in Sacramento, Calif., who has been a leader in organizing anti-affirmative action referendums, the real issue — the decline in urban K-12 schools — is being ignored.

"Legislatures and college administrators lack the spine to say, 'Let's find the problem at its core,' " says Connerly, a former member of the University of California Board of Regents. "Instead, they go for a quick fix they believe will yield the same number of blacks and Latinos as before."

Even Connerly's opponents agree "percent plans" alone don't put high schools in inner cities and prosperous suburbs on an equal footing. "In some school districts in Texas, 50 percent of the graduates could make it here easily," says Terry H. Anderson, a history professor at Texas A&M University in College Station. "Some school districts are so awful that not one kid could graduate here, I don't care what race you're talking about."

All the plans — except at selective schools — ignore SAT or ACT scores (though students do have to present their scores). The policy troubles Richard D. Kahlenberg, a senior fellow at The Century Foundation, who champions "class-based" affirmation action. "The grade of A in one high school is very different from the grade of A in another," he says.

Texas lawmakers originated the percent plan concept after a 5th U.S. Circuit Court of Appeals decision in 1996 (*Hopwood v. Texas*) prohibited consideration of race in college admissions. Legislators proposed guaranteeing state university admissions to the top 10 percent of graduates of the state's public and private high schools. Then-Gov. George W. Bush signed the bill, which includes automatic admission to the flagship campuses, the University of Texas at Austin and Texas A&M.[1]

In California, the impetus was the 1996 voter approval of Proposition 209, which prohibited racial and ethnic preferences by all state entities. Borrowing the Texas idea, California lawmakers devised a system in which California high school students in the top 4 percent of their classes are eligible for the California system, but not necessarily to attend the two star institutions, UC Berkeley and UCLA. (Students in the top 4 percent-12.5 percent range are admitted to community colleges and can transfer to four-year institutions if they maintain 2.4 grade-point averages.)[2]

Connerly was active in the Proposition 209 campaign and was the key player — but involuntarily — in Florida's adoption of a percent plan. In 1999, Connerly was preparing to mount an anti-affirmative action initiative in Florida. Then-Gov. Jeb Bush worried it could hurt his party's standing with black voters — with possible repercussions on his brother

Archibald Cox, the Watergate special prosecutor who was fired on orders of President Nixon in 1973. Cox's grand-daughter, Melissa Hart, helps lead the opposition to an anti-affirmative action ballot initiative in Colorado.[30]

In 1979 and 1980, the court upheld worker training and public contracting policies that included so-called set-asides for minority-group employees or minority-owned companies. But in the latter case, the deciding opinion specified that only companies that actually had suffered discrimination would be eligible for those contracts.[31]

Divisions within the Supreme Court reflected growing tensions in the country as a whole. A number of white people saw affirmative action as injuring the educational

George's presidential campaign. Instead Gov. Bush launched "One Florida," a percent plan approved by the legislature.

In Florida, the top 20 percent of high school graduates are guaranteed admission to the state system. To attend the flagship University of Florida at Gainesville they must meet tougher standards. All three states also require students to have completed a set of required courses.

Percent plan states also have helped shape admissions policies by experimenting with ways to simultaneously keep academic standards high, while ensuring at least the possibility that promising students of all socioeconomic circumstances have a shot at college.

In Florida, the consequences of maintaining high admissions standards at UF were softened by another program, "Bright Futures," which offers tuition reductions of 75 percent — or completely free tuition — depending on completion of AP courses and on SAT or ACT scores.

The effect, says University of Florida political scientist Daniel A. Smith, is to ensure a plentiful supply of top students of all races and ethnicities. "We have really talented minorities — blacks, Latinos, Asian-Americans — because 'One Florida' in combination with 'Bright Futures' has kept a lot of our talented students in the state. We have students who turned down [partial] scholarships to Duke and Harvard because here they're going for free."

At UCLA, which also has maintained rigorous admission criteria, recruiters spread out to high schools in low-income areas in an effort to ensure that the school doesn't become an oasis of privilege. The realities of race and class

Courtesy of Ward Connerly

"The time has come to pull the plug on race-based decision-making," says Ward Connerly, a Sacramento, Calif., businessman who spearheaded anti-affirmative action ballot initiatives in Colorado, Nebraska and other states.

mean that some of that recruiting work takes place in mostly black or Latino high schools.

"It's the fallacy of [Proposition] 209 that you can immediately move to a system that doesn't take account of race and that treats everybody fairly," said Tom Lifka, a UCLA assistant vice chancellor in charge of admissions. He said the new system meets legal standards.[3]

Consciously or not, Lifka was echoing the conclusion of the most thorough analysis of the plans' operations in the three states. The 2003 study, sponsored by Harvard University's Civil Rights Project, concluded that the states had largely succeeded in maintaining racial and ethnic diversity on their campuses.

But the report added that aggressive recruitment, academic aid to high schools in low-income areas and similar measures played a major role. "Without such support," wrote Catherine L. Horn, an education professor at the University of Houston, and Stella M. Flores, professor of public policy and higher education at Vanderbilt, "the plans are more like empty shells, appearing to promise eligibility, admission and enrollment for previously excluded groups but actually doing very little."[4]

---

[1] Catherine L. Horn and Stella M. Flores, "Percent Plans in College Admissions: A Comparative Analysis of Three States' Experiences," Civil Rights Project, Harvard University, 2003, pp. 20-23, www.civil rightsproject.ucla.edu/research/affirmativeaction/tristate.pdf.

[2] *Ibid.*

[3] Quoted in David Leonhardt, "The New Affirmative Action," *The New York Times Magazine*, Sept. 30, 2007, p. 76.

[4] Horn and Flores, *op. cit.*, pp. 59-60.

---

and career advancement of people who hadn't themselves caused the historical crimes that gave rise to affirmative action.

## Reversing Course

President Ronald W. Reagan took office in 1981 with strong support from so-called "Reagan Democrats"

— white, blue-collar workers who had turned against their former party on issues including affirmative action.[32]

Initially, Reagan seemed poised to fulfill the hopes of those who wanted him to ban all preferences based on race, ethnicity and gender. The latter category followed an upsurge of women fighting to abolish limits on their education and career possibilities.

Supporters of affirmative action in Lansing, Mich., rally against a proposed statewide anti-affirmative action ballot initiative in September 2006; voters approved the proposal that November. The initiative followed a 2003 U.S. Supreme Court ruling upholding the use of race in law-school admissions at the University of Michigan. Justice Sandra Day O'Connor, who wrote the majority 5-4 opinion, predicted, however, that in 25 years affirmative action would "no longer be necessary."

Yet Reagan's appointees were divided on the issue, and the president himself never formalized his rejection of quotas and related measures. Because no law required the setting of goals and timetables, Reagan could have banned them by executive order. During Reagan's second term, Attorney General Edwin Meese III drafted such an order. But Reagan never signed it.

Nevertheless, the Reagan administration did systematically weaken enforcement of affirmative action. In Reagan's first term he cut the budgets of the Equal Employment Opportunity Commission and the Office of Federal Contract Compliance — the two front-line agencies on the issue — by 12 and 34 percent, respectively, between 1981 and 1983. As a result, the compliance office blocked only two contractors during Reagan's two terms, compared with 13 that were barred during President Jimmy Carter's term.

The Justice Department also began opposing some affirmative action plans. In 1983, Justice won a partial court reversal of an affirmative action plan for the New Orleans Police Department. In a police force nearly devoid of black supervisors, the plan was designed to expand the number — a move considered vital in a city whose population was nearly one-half black.

Affirmative action cases kept moving through the Supreme Court. In 1984-1986, the court overturned plans

that would have required companies doing layoffs to disregard the customary "first hired, last fired" rule, because that custom endangered most black employees, given their typically short times on the job.

And in 1987, a 5-4 Supreme Court decision upheld an Alabama state police plan requiring that 50 percent of promotions go to black officers. The same year, the court upheld 6-3 the promotion of a woman employee of Santa Clara County, Calif., who got promoted over a male candidate who had scored slightly higher on an assessment. The decision marked the first court endorsement of affirmative action for women.

In the executive branch, divided views persisted in the administration of Reagan's Republican successor, George H. W. Bush. In 1990 Bush vetoed a pro-affirmative action bill designed to reverse recent Supreme Court rulings, one of which effectively eased the way for white men to sue for reverse discrimination.

The legislation would have required "quotas," Bush said, explaining his veto. But the following year, he signed a compromise, the Civil Rights Act of 1991.[33] Supported by the civil rights lobby, the bill wrote into law the *Griggs v. Duke Power* requirement that an employer prove that a job practice — a test, say — is required for the work in question. A practice that failed that test could be shown to result in discrimination, even if that hadn't been the intention.

Bush also reversed a directive by his White House counsel that would have outlawed all quotas, set-asides and related measures. The administration's ambivalence reflected divided views in American society. Local government and corporate officials had grown appreciative of affirmative action for calming racial tensions. In 1985, the white Republican mayor of Indianapolis refused a Justice Department request to end affirmative action in the police department. Mayor William Hudnut said that the "white majority has accepted the fact that we're making a special effort for minorities and women."[34]

Yet among white males, affirmative action remained a very hot-button issue. "When we hold focus groups," a Democratic pollster said in 1990, "if the issue of affirmative action comes up, you can forget the rest of the session. That's all . . . that's talked about."[35]

## Mending It

From the early 1990s to 2003 race-based affirmative action suffered damage in the political arena and the courts.

In 1994, white male outrage at preferences for minority groups and women was a key factor in congressional elections that toppled Democrats from control of both houses. As soon as the Congress changed hands, its new leaders targeted affirmative action. "Sometimes the best-qualified person does not get the job because he or she may be one color," Majority Leader Dole said in a television interview. "That may not be the way it should be in America."[36]

The following year, the U.S. Supreme Court imposed limits on the use of preferences, ruling on a white, male contractor's challenge to a federal program that encouraged general contractors to favor minority sub-contractors. Justice O'Connor wrote in the 5-4 majority opinion in *Adarand Constructors v. Peña* that any racial or ethnic preferences had to be "narrowly tailored" to apply only to "pervasive, systematic and obstinate discriminatory conduct."[37]

Some justices had wanted all preferences overturned. Though that position failed to win a majority, the clear unease that O'Connor expressed added to the pressure on politicians who supported affirmative action.

In that climate, President Bill Clinton gave a 1995 speech at the National Archives in Washington in which he acknowledged that critics had a point. He said he didn't favor "the unjustified preference of the unqualified over the qualified of any race or gender." But affirmative action was still needed because discrimination persisted, Clinton added. His bottom line: "Mend it, but don't end it."[38]

The slogan seemed to match national politicians' mood. One day after Clinton's speech, the Senate voted down a bill to abolish all preferences, with 19 Republicans siding with Democrats in a 61-36 vote.

But in California, one of the country's major affirmative action laboratories, the "end it" argument proved more popular. Racial/ethnic preferences had become a major issue in a state whose minority population was booming. California's higher-education system also included two of the nation's top public institutions: the University of California at Berkeley (UCB) and UCLA.

Among many white, Anglo Californians, affirmative action had come to be seen as a system under which black and Latino applicants were getting into those two schools at the expense of whites or Asians with higher grades and SAT scores.

By 1996, the statewide university system's majority-Republican Board of Regents voted to end all race, ethnic and gender preferences in admissions. The board did allow universities to take applicants' socioeconomic circumstances into account.

And in the same year, California voters approved Proposition 209, which outlawed all race, ethnicity and gender preferences by all state entities. Connerly helped organize that referendum and followed up with successful campaigns in Washington state in 1998 and in Michigan in 2003.

Meanwhile, the "reverse discrimination" issue that had been decided in the *Bakke* case flared up in Texas, where Cheryl Hopwood and two other white applicants to the University of Texas law school challenged their rejections, pointing to the admissions of minority students with lower grades and test scores. In 1996, the 5th U.S. Circuit Court of Appeals decided for the plaintiffs, ruling that universities couldn't take race into account when assessing applicants.

The appeals judges had overruled the *Bakke* decision, at least in their jurisdiction of Texas, Mississippi and Louisiana, yet the Supreme Court refused to consider the case.

But in 2003, the justices ruled on two separate cases, both centering on admissions to another top-ranked public higher education system: the University of Michigan. One case arose from admissions procedures for the undergraduate college, the other from the system for evaluating applicants to the university's law school.[39]

The Supreme Court decided against the undergraduate admissions policy because it automatically awarded 20 extra points on the university's 150-point evaluation scale to blacks, Latinos and American Indians. By contrast, the law school took race into account in what Justice O'Connor, in the majority opinion in the 5-4 decision, called a "highly individualized, holistic review" of each candidate aimed at producing a diverse student population.[40]

## CURRENT SITUATION

### "Formal Equality"

In the midst of war and the Wall Street meltdown, affirmative action may not generate as many headlines as it used to. But the issue still packs enough punch to have put anti-affirmative action legislation up for popular vote in Colorado and Nebraska this year.

# The Preference Program Nobody Talks About

*How "legacies" get breaks at top colleges.*

Many critics say race-based affirmative action gives minority college applicants an unfair advantage. But reporter Peter Schmidt found an even more favored population — rich, white kids who apply to top-tier schools.

"These institutions feel very dependent on these preferences," Schmidt writes in his 2007 book, *Color and Money: How Rich White Kids Are Winning the War Over College Affirmative Action.* "They throw up their hands and say, 'There's no other way we can raise the money we need.' "

Colleges admit these students — "legacies," in college-admission lingo — because their parents are donation-making graduates. Offspring of professors, administrators or (in the case of top state universities) politically influential figures get open-door treatment as well.

"Several public college lobbyists, working in both state capitals and with the federal government in and around Washington, have told me that they spend a significant portion of their time lobbying their own colleges' admissions offices to accept certain applicants at the behest of public officials," Schmidt writes.[1]

Especially in regard to legacies and the families' donations, Schmidt says, "There is a utilitarian argument that the money enables colleges to serve students in need. But there isn't a correlation between how much money they're bringing in and helping low-income students."

As deputy editor of the *Chronicle of Higher Education*, Schmidt has been covering affirmative action conflicts since his days as an Associated Press reporter writing about protests over racial tensions at the University of Michigan in the mid-1990s.

His book doesn't deal exclusively with applicants from privileged families — who, by the nature of American society, are almost all white and academically well-prepared. But Schmidt's examination of privileged applicants frames his reporting on the more familiar issues of preferences based on race, ethnicity and gender.

According to Schmidt, Harvard as of 2004 accepted about 40 percent of the legacies who applied, compared to about 11 percent of applicants overall. In the Ivy League in general, children of graduates made up 10-15 percent of the undergraduates.

Though the issue is sensitive for college administrators, Schmidt found some members of the higher-education establishment happy to see it aired.

"Admissions officers are the ones who are finding the promising kids — diamonds in the rough — and getting emotionally invested in getting them admitted, then sitting down with the development officer or the coach and finding that these kids are knocked out of the running," he says.

Some education experts dispute that conclusion. Abigail Thernstrom, a senior fellow at the conservative Manhattan Institute and vice-chair of the U.S. Commission on Civil Rights, opposes "class-based" affirmative action (as well as racial/ethnic preferences), calling it unnecessary. She says that when top-tier schools look at an applicant from a disadvantaged background "who is getting a poor education — a diamond in the rough but showing real academic progress — and compare that student to someone from Exeter born with a silver spoon in his mouth, there's no question that these schools are going to take that diamond in the rough, if they think he or she will be able to keep up."

But some of Schmidt's findings echo what affirmative action supporters have observed. James E. Coleman Jr., a law professor at Duke University, argues against the tendency to focus all affirmative action attention on blacks and Latinos. "The idea is that any white student who gets here deserves to be here. They're not questioned. This has always been true."

At the same time, Coleman, who is black, agrees with Schmidt that those who start out near the top of the socioeconomic ladder have access to first-class educations before they even get to college. Coleman himself, who graduated from Harvard and from Columbia Law School, says he never had a single white classmate in his Charlotte, N.C., schools until he got accepted to a post-high school preparatory program at Exeter, one of the nation's most prestigious prep schools. "I could tell that my educational background and preparation were woefully inadequate compared to students who had been there since ninth grade," he recalls. "I had to run faster."

Schmidt says the politics of affirmative action can give rise to tactical agreements between groups whose interests might seem to conflict. In one dispute, he says, "Civil rights groups and higher-education groups had a kind of uneasy alliance: The civil rights groups would not challenge the admissions process and go after legacies as long as affirmative action remained intact."

But, he adds, "There are people not at the table when a deal like that is struck. If you're not a beneficiary of one or the other side of preferences, you don't gain from that agreement."

---

[1] Peter Schmidt, *Color and Money: How Rich White Kids Are Winning the War Over College Affirmative Action* (2007), p. 32.

# Would many black and Latino science and math majors be better off at lesser-ranked universities?

## YES    Rogers Elliott
*Professor Emeritus, Department of Psychology and Brain Sciences, Dartmouth College*

From testimony before U.S. Civil Rights Commission, Sept. 12, 2008

Race preferences in admissions in the service of affirmative action are harming the aspirations, particularly, of blacks seeking to be scientists.

The most elite universities have very high levels in their admission standards, levels which minorities — especially blacks — don't come close to meeting.

[Thus], affirmative action in elite schools, which they pursue vigorously and successfully, leaves a huge gap, probably bigger than it would be for affirmative action at an average school. That is what constitutes the problem.

At elite schools, 90 percent of science majors [got] 650 or above on the SAT math score. About 80 percent of the white/Asian group are 650 or above, but only 25 percent of the black group have that score or better. The gaps that are illustrated in these data have not gotten any better. They have, in fact, gotten a little bit worse: The gap in the SAT scores between blacks and whites, which got to its smallest extent in about 1991 — 194 points — is back to 209.

The higher the standard at the institution, the more science they tend to do. But the [lower-ranking schools] still do science, and your chances of becoming a scientist are better. Now, obviously, there are differences. The higher institutions have eliteness going for them. They have prestige going for them, and maybe getting a degree from Dartmouth when you want to be a doctor will leave you better off in this world even though you're not doing the thing you started with as your aspiration.

Seventeen of the top 20 PhD-granting institutions for blacks in this country, are HBCUs [historically black colleges and universities].

Elite institutions are very performance-oriented. They deliberately take people at a very high level to begin with — with a few exceptions — and then they make them perform, and they do a pretty good job of it. If you're not ready for the first science course, you might as well forget it. Some of these minority students had mostly A's . . . enough to get to Dartmouth or Brown or Cornell or Yale. They take their first course, let's say, in chemistry; at least 90 percent of the students in that course are bright, motivated, often pre-med, highly competitive whites and Asians. And these [minority] kids aren't as well-prepared. They may get their first C- or D in a course like that because the grading standards are rigorous, and you have to start getting it from day one.

## NO    Prof. Richard A. Tapia
*Director, Center on Excellence and Equity, Rice University*

From testimony before U.S. Civil Rights Commission, Sept. 12, 2008

The nation selects leaders from graduates and faculty of U.S. universities with world-class science, technology, engineering and math (STEM) research programs. If we, the underrepresented minorities, are to be an effective component in STEM leadership, then we must have an equitable presence as students and faculty at the very top-level research universities.

Pedigree, unfortunately, is an incredible issue. Top research universities choose faculty from PhDs produced at top research universities. PhDs produced at minority-serving schools or less-prestigious schools will not become faculty at top research universities. Indeed, it's unlikely they'll become faculty at minority-serving institutions. A student from a research school with a lesser transcript is stronger than a student from a minority-serving institution with all A's.

So are the students who come from these minority-serving institutions incompetent? No. There's a level of them that are incredibly good and will succeed wherever they go. And usually Stanford and Berkeley and Cornell will get those. Then there's a level below that you can work with. I produced many PhDs who came from minority-serving institutions. Is there a gap in training? Absolutely.

We do not know how to measure what we really value: Creativity. Underrepresented minorities can be quite creative. For example, the Carl Hayden High School Robotic Team — five Mexican-American students from West Phoenix — beat MIT in the final in underwater robotics. They were not star students, but they were incredibly creative.

Treating everyone the same is not good enough. Sink or swim has not worked and will not work. It pays heed to privilege, not to talent. Isolation, not academics, is often the problem. We must promote success and retention with support programs. We must combat isolation through community-building and mentoring.

Ten percent of the students in public education in Texas are accepted into the University of Texas, automatically — the top 10 percent. They could have said look, these students are not prepared well. They're dumped at our doorstep, let's leave them. They didn't. The Math Department at the University of Texas at Austin built support programs where minorities are retained and succeed. It took a realization that here they are, let's do something with them.

Race and ethnicity should not dictate educational destiny. Our current path will lead to a permanent underclass that follows racial and ethnic lines.

"This is a progressive approach," said Jessica Peck Corry, executive director of the Colorado Civil Rights Initiative, which is campaigning for proposed Constitutional Amendment 46. The amendment would prohibit all state government entities from discriminating for or against anyone because of race, ethnicity or gender. "America is too diverse to put into stagnant race boxes," she says.

Melissa Hart, a co-chair of "No On 46," counters that the amendment would require "formal equality" that shouldn't be confused with the real thing. She likens the proposal to "a law that says both the beggar and the king may sleep under a bridge." In the real world, she says, only one of them will spend his nights in a bedroom.

Unlike California, Michigan and Washington — the states where voters have approved initiatives of this type over the past 12 years — the Colorado campaign doesn't follow a major controversy over competition for university admissions.

To be sure, Corry — a libertarian Republican law student, blogger and past failed candidate for state Senate — has publicly opposed affirmative action for several years.[41] But Corry, who is also a policy analyst at the Denver-based Independence Institute, a libertarian think tank, acknowledges that the referendum campaign in Colorado owes its start to Connerly. He began taking the ballot initiative route in the 1990s, after concluding that neither state legislatures nor Congress would ever touch the subject.

"They just seem to lack the stomach to do what I and the majority of Americans believe should be done," Connerly says. "Clearly, there's a disconnect between elected officials and the people themselves."

Connerly's confidence grows out of his success with the three previous initiatives. But this year, his attempts to get his proposal before voters in Arizona, Missouri and Oklahoma all failed because his campaign workers didn't gather enough valid signatures to get the initiatives on the ballot.

Connerly blames what he calls an overly restrictive initiative process in Oklahoma, as well as organized opposition by what he calls "blockers," who shadowed signature-gatherers and disputed their explanations of the amendments.

Opponents had a different name for themselves. "Our voter educators were simply that — voter educators," said Brandon Davis, political director of the Service Employees International Union in Missouri. "Ward Connerly should accept what Missourians said, and he should stop with the sore-loser talk."[42]

The opposition began deploying street activists to counter what they call the deliberately misleading wording of the proposed initiatives. In Colorado, Proposition 46 is officially described as a "prohibition against discrimination by the state" and goes on to ban "preferential treatment to any individual or group on the basis of race, sex, color, ethnicity or national origin."[43]

"We want an acknowledgement that disadvantage cannot be specifically determined based on looking at some race data or gender data," Corry says. But tutoring, counseling and other activities should be extended to all who need help because of their socioeconomic circumstances, she contends.

Likewise, a project to interest girls in science and math, for instance, would have to admit boys. "In a time when America is losing its scientific advantage by the second, why are you excluding potential Nobel prize winners because they're born with the wrong biology?" she asks rhetorically.

Hart says that many tutoring and similar programs tailored to low-income students in Colorado already welcome all comers, regardless of race or ethnicity. But she questions why a math and science program tailored for girls should have to change its orientation. Likewise, Denver's specialized public schools for American Indian students would have to change their orientation entirely. "Class-based equal opportunity programs are not substitutes for outreach, training and mentoring on the basis of race and gender," she says.

The issue of class comes up in personal terms as well. Corry portrays herself as the product of a troubled home who had to work her way through college and graduate school. Though her father was a lawyer, her mother abandoned the family and wound up living on the streets. And Corry depicts Hart as a member of the privileged class, a granddaughter of former Solicitor General Cox and a graduate of Harvard University and Harvard Law School. "People like Melissa, I believe, are well-intentioned but misguided," Corry says. "The worst thing you can do to someone without connections is to suggest that they can't make it without preferences."

Hart, rapping Corry for bringing up personal history rather than debating ideas, adds that her father and his part of the family are potato farmers from Idaho.

"I am proudly the granddaughter of Archibald Cox, proud of the fact that he argued the *Bakke* case for the

University of California, and proud to be continuing a tradition of standing up for opportunity in this country," she says.

The Nebraska campaign, taking place in a smaller state with little history of racial or ethnic tension and a university where competition for admission isn't an issue, has generated somewhat less heat. But as in Colorado, college-preparation and other programs of various kinds that target young women and American Indians would be threatened by the amendment, says Laurel Marsh, executive director of the Nebraska ACLU.

## Over Their Heads?

The U.S. Civil Rights Commission is examining one of the most explosive issues in the affirmative action debate: whether students admitted to top universities due to racial preferences are up to the academic demands they face at those institutions.

Math and the hard sciences present the most obvious case, affirmative action critics — and some supporters — say. Those fields are at the center of the commission's inquiry because students from high schools in low-income areas — typically minority students — tend to do poorly in science and math, in part because they require considerable math preparation in elementary and high school.

Sander of UCLA, who has been studying the topic, testified to the commission that for students of all races who had scored under 660 on the math SAT, only 5 percent of blacks and 3.5 percent of whites obtained science degrees. But of students who scored 820 or above on the SAT, 44 percent of blacks graduated with science or engineering degrees. Among whites, 35 percent graduated with those degrees — illustrating Sander's point that that issue is one of academic preparation, not race.

Abigail Thernstrom, the commission's vice-chair, says that most graduates of run-of-the-mill urban schools labor under a major handicap in pursuing math or science degrees. "By the time they get to college they're in bad shape in a discipline like math, where all knowledge is cumulative," she says. "The colleges are inheriting a problem that, in effect, we sweep under the rug."

Thernstrom, a longtime affirmative action critic, bases her views both on her 11 years of service on the Massachusetts state Board of Education and on data assembled by academics, including Sander. "Test scores do predict a lot, high school grades predict a lot," Sander says in an interview, disputing critics of his work

TV cameramen in Lincoln, Neb., shoot boxes of signed voter petitions that qualified a proposed initiative to be put on the ballot in Nebraska this coming November calling for a ban on most types of affirmative action.

who say students from deficient high schools can make up in college what they missed earlier.

Testifying to the commission on Sept. 12, Sander presented data showing that black and Hispanic high school graduates tend to be more interested than their white counterparts in pursuing science and math careers, but less successful in holding on to majors in those fields in college. Lower high school grades and test scores seem to account for as much as 75 percent of the tendency to drop out of those fields, he says.

Sander added that a student's possibilities can't be predicted from skin color and that the key factor associated with inadequate academic preparation is socioeconomic status. "We ought to view that as good news, because that means there's no intrinsic or genetic gap," he testified.

Rogers Elliott, an emeritus psychology and brain sciences professor at Dartmouth College, told the commission that the best option for many black and Hispanic students who want to pursue science or math careers is to attend lower-rated universities. Among institutions that grant the most PhDs to blacks, 17 of the top 20 are HBCUs, Elliott said, "and none of them is a prestige university."

Richard Tapia, a Rice University mathematician, countered that consigning minority-group students who aren't stars to lower-ranking universities would be disastrous. Only top-tier universities, he argued, provide their graduates with the credibility that allows them to assert leadership. "Research universities must be responsible for providing programs that promote success," he said, "rather than be let off the hook by saying that minority students should go to minority-serving institutions or less prestigious schools."

Tapia directs such a program — one of a handful around the country — that he says has helped Rice students overcome their inadequate earlier schooling. But he accepts Sander's and Elliott's data and says students with combined SAT scores below 800 would not be capable of pursuing math or science majors at Rice.

Tapia, the son of Mexican immigrants who didn't attend college, worked at a muffler factory after graduating from a low-achieving Los Angeles high school. Pushed by a co-worker to continue his education, he enrolled in community college and went on to UCLA, where he earned a doctorate. He attributes his success to a big dose of self-confidence — something that many people from his background might not have but that mentors can nurture.

A commission member sounded another practical note. Ashley L. Taylor Jr., a Republican lawyer from Richmond, Va., who is black, argued that colleges have a moral obligation to tell applicants if their SAT scores fall within the range of students who have a shot of completing their studies. "If I'm outside that range, no additional support is going to help me," he said.

Sander agrees. "African-American students and any other minority ought to know going into college the ultimate outcomes for students at that college who have their profile."

Tapia agreed as well. "I had a student that I was recruiting in San Antonio who had a 940 SAT and was going to Princeton. I said, 'Do you know what the average at Princeton is?'" He said, "Well, my teachers told me it was about 950.' I said, 'Well, I think you'd better check it out.'"

In fact, the average combined math and verbal SAT score of students admitted to Princeton is 1442.[44]

## OUTLOOK:

### End of the Line?

Social programs don't come with an immortality guarantee. Some supporters as well as critics of affirmative action sense that affirmative action, as the term is generally understood, may be nearing the end of the line.

"I expect affirmative action to die," says Tapia. "People are tired of it. And if we had to depend on affirmative action forever, then there was something wrong. If you need a jump-start on your battery, and you get it jumped, fine. If you start needing it everywhere you go, you'd better get another battery."

Tapia's tone is not triumphant. He says the decline in public school quality is evidence that "it didn't work, and we didn't do a good job." But he adds that the disparities between the schooling for low-income and well-off students is what makes affirmative action necessary. "Sure, in an ideal world, you wouldn't have to do these things, but that's not the world we live in."

UCLA's Sander, who favors reorienting affirmative action — in part by determining an academic threshold below which students admitted by preference likely will fail — sees major change on the horizon. For one thing, he says, quantities of data are now accessible concerning admission standards, grades and other quantifiable effects of affirmative action programs.

In addition, he says, today's reconfigured Supreme Court likely would rule differently than it did on the 2003 University of Michigan cases that represent its most recent affirmative action rulings.

Justice O'Connor, who wrote the majority decision in the 5-4 ruling that upheld the use of race in law-school admissions, has retired, replaced by conservative Justice Samuel A. Alito. "The Supreme Court as it stands now has a majority that's probably ready to overrule" that decision, Sander says. A decision that turned on the newly available data "could lead to a major Supreme Court decision that could send shockwaves through the system."

For now, says Kahlenberg of The Century Foundation, affirmative action has already changed form in states that have restricted use of racial and ethnic preferences. "It's not as if universities and colleges have simply thrown up their hands," he says. "They now look more aggressively at economic disadvantages that students face. The bigger picture is that the American public likes the idea of diversity but doesn't want to use racial preferences to get there."

Anderson of Texas A&M agrees that a vocabulary development marks the shift. "We've been changing affirmative action and quotas to diversity," he says. "Diversity is seen as good, and has become part of our mainstream culture."

In effect, diversity has come to mean hiring and admissions policies that focus on bringing people of different races and cultures on board — people like Obama, for example. "Obama's talking about merit, and keeping the doors open for all Americans, and strengthening the middle class," Anderson says.

Obama, whose father was Kenyan and whose half-sister is half-Indonesian, also represents another facet of the changing face of affirmative action. "Our society is becoming a lot more demographically complicated," says Schmidt, of *The Chronicle of Higher Education* and author of a recent book on affirmative action in college admissions. "All of these racial groups that benefit from affirmative action as a result of immigration — they're not groups that have experienced oppression and discrimination in the United States. And people are marrying people of other races and ethnicities. How do you sort that out? Which parent counts the most?"

All in all, Schmidt says, the prospects for affirmative action look dim. "In the long term, the political trends are against it," he says. "I don't see a force out there that's going to force the pendulum to swing the other way."

At the same time, many intended beneficiaries — African-Americans whose history set affirmative action in motion — remain untouched by it because of the deficient schools they attend.

The catastrophic state of public schools in low-income America remains — and seems likely to remain — a point on which all sides agree. Whether anything will be done about it is another story.

Top schools will continue to seek diverse student bodies, says Coleman of Duke law school. But the public schools continue to deteriorate. "I haven't seen any effort by people who oppose affirmative action, or people who support it, to do anything to improve the public school system. We ought to improve the quality of education because it's in the national interest to do that."

## 2010 UPDATE

The Supreme Court's June 29, 2009, ruling in favor of white firefighters in New Haven, Conn., was perhaps the key event in affirmative action over the past two years. The firefighters had challenged the city's decision to discard a competency test for determining promotions after black firefighters taking the test had underperformed. The 5-4 decision in *Ricci, et al. v. DeStefano, et al.* prompted Fordham University law professor Sheila Foster to declare that it "will change the landscape of civil rights law."[45]

The court majority ruled against New Haven's action to discard the performance results. It did, however, say an employer can invoke fear of litigation — suits that might be brought by either the white or the black firefighters citing disparate impact — as a defense against the white firefighters' charge that discarding the competency test was unlawful discrimination. But the lead opinion, written by Justice Anthony Kennedy, said such a defense is available only where the employer has "strong . . . evidence" that it would be held liable, which the New Haven Fire Department did not have.[46]

In a dissent, Justice Ruth Bader Ginsburg wrote that the white firefighters "understandably attract this court's sympathy. But they had no vested right to promotion. Nor have other persons received promotion in preference to them."[47]

Notably, the ruling overturned an earlier appeals court ruling signed by then-federal Judge Sonia Sotomayor in the midst of the confirmation process for her elevation to the U.S. Supreme Court. Opinion polls just before the ruling showed some public skepticism toward affirmative action. American voters, by 55-36 percent, said that affirmative action should be abolished, and 71 percent disagreed with Sotomayor's ruling in the New Haven firefighters' case, according to a June 2009 Quinnipiac University poll.

### Poll Results Differ

But The Associated Press, using different phrasing in poll questions, got a different result: 56 percent of Americans favor affirmative action, it reported, with 36 percent opposed. An NBC News-*Wall Street Journal* poll showed 63 percent agreeing that "affirmative action programs are still needed to counteract the effects of discrimination against minorities, and are a good idea as long as there are no rigid quotas."

The election of the first African-American president focused additional attention on Americans' attitudes about using affirmative action as a tool to ease racial disparities. President Barack Obama displayed his approach to such change in his Supreme Court appointments of Sotomayor and Elena Kagan, in the naming of an assertive chief of civil rights at the Education Department, and his administration's switch away from Bush-era litigation priorities in the area of race-conscious legal remedies.

Congratulating Obama for his 2008 victory, ReNee Dunman, president of the Washington-based American Association for Affirmative Action, said, "Where there is inequality and exclusion, affirmative action remains essential in promoting equal opportunity in the workplace, higher education and contracting." She went on to blast what she called the "scorched-earth campaign to end equal opportunity in America" waged in several states by longtime affirmative action critic Ward Connerly.[48]

Connerly's Sacramento-based American Civil Rights Institute continued its efforts to enact state bans on race-conscious selection methods in employment and college admissions. In November 2008, voters in Colorado narrowly rejected a ballot initiative to that effect, and proposed bans were kept off the ballots by opponents in Arizona, Missouri and Oklahoma. That left Connerly's group with one victory, in Nebraska, to add to existing bans in California, Michigan and Washington State.

## Obama Criticized

"Obama is hostile to my effort to end race-based preferences," Connerly said in a recent interview, recalling that Obama as a presidential candidate "mentioned me by name and called my efforts 'divisive.' That is what you say if you can't disagree on the merits of an issue." Connerly said Obama will rely on the "disparate-impact theory to argue ipso facto that if minorities" are shown to be in fewer numbers in universities and public employment, "then that is the same as discrimination, forgetting that the level of preparation is not where it needs to be."

A key player in Obama's handling of affirmative action is Education Secretary Arne Duncan. In March 2010 he journeyed to Selma, Ala., site of an historic civil rights march in 1965, and announced that his department was launching new desegregation-compliance investigations around the country. He also said the Education Department's Office for Civil Rights "has not been as vigilant as it should have been" in confronting discrimination over the past 10 years.[49]

On April 15, 2010, the Duncan-appointed assistant Education secretary for civil rights, Russlynn H. Ali, told *The Chronicle of Higher Education* she saw a more active civil rights office in the future. When she first arrived on the job, she said, "what we found [were] some tireless civil-rights pioneers that are hungry and eager, in their words, 'to do civil rights again.'"[50]

The government's muscular approach to litigation reflects a new emphasis on civil rights. On March 12, 2010, the Obama administration's departments of Education and Justice together filed a friend-of-the-court brief on behalf of the University of Texas at Austin, which is defending its race-conscious methods "to achieve the educational benefits of diversity."[51]

By contrast, George W. Bush administration policy sided with the Supreme Court's 2003 decision in *Gratz v. Bollinger* striking down a University of Michigan law school affirmative action plan as too mechanistic. The current Texas litigation was brought by white students Abigail Noel Fisher and Rachel Multer Michalewicz, who said the denial of their applications for admission as undergraduates violated the 14th Amendment's Equal Protection Clause.

The university permits the use of race as one factor in an index in applying efforts to use "top 10 percent" admission plans based on a 1996 Texas law that guarantees admission to state universities to all high-school seniors in the top 10 percent of their class. After that law was implemented, minority representation at the University of Texas dropped sharply. The case is pending in the Fifth U.S. Circuit Court of Appeals.

Universities and think tanks, meanwhile, published new studies on the impact of race-conscious methods and efforts at diversity in the workplace and on campus. According to a study by Columbia Law School Professor Conrad Johnson, from 1993 to 2008 the percentage of black and Mexican-American law students nationwide fell, despite the opening of 3,000 new places and clear improvements in the aggregate Law School Admission Test scores of the two groups.[52]

## Research Claims Challenged

The study's results were challenged by scholars organized at the UCLA Law School under the banner of Project SEAPHE (Scale and Effects of Admissions Preferences in

Higher Education). In a Feb. 16, 2010, critique, it said the claims by the researchers were not borne out by the data. "Using the same reference period as the article, (1993 to 2008), accurate statistics show that absolute numbers of black matriculants are up, and Hispanic matriculants are way up," SEAPHE wrote. "Meanwhile, improvements in the average credentials of minority law school applicants have been trivial or non-existent over this same period."[53]

In preparation for elections in fall 2010, friends and foes of affirmative action studied lessons from the 2008 victory for the affirmative action ban in Nebraska and the defeat of the one in Colorado. Some 58 percent of largely white Nebraska voters backed the ban, even though the University of Nebraska Board of Regents had opposed it. Roger Clegg, president of the Center for Equal Opportunity, which opposes consideration of race in admissions, said that part of the legal defense of considering race involves public colleges saying that they have no alternative ways to promote diversity. As more states eliminate the consideration of race — and many of them find ways to still have diverse classes — how plausible is it to make that claim? he asked.[54]

In Colorado, opinion polls showed voters initially appeared to favor the proposal to amend the state constitution to ban preferential treatment to individuals based on race, color, sex, ethnicity or national origin. But a door-to-door campaign against it helped turn the tide (final tally 51 percent to 49 percent), and opponents, such as Democratic Gov. Bill Ritter, called the measure deceptive, saying it would jeopardize outreach programs for minority children.[55]

The chief organizer of Colorado's proposed ban, Jessica Corry, said voters were confused by too many items on the ballot and that the ban would have passed any other year.

Those seeking to outlaw affirmative action were cheered when the Arizona legislature in June 2009 approved a plan to put a proposed ban on the November 2010 ballot. It was the first time a state legislature had enacted a ballot referendum as opposed to citizens' groups gathering signatures, noted Connerly. His group has hopes for Utah taking up a ban next year.

Over the long term, Connerly says, he is working to get rid of race-based classifications as legal categories, such as those on the 2010 census forms, by encouraging Americans to decline to fill out such information.

## 2012 UPDATE

The Supreme Court is set to re-examine the contentious issue of whether colleges and universities can consider an applicant's race in a selective admission process.

The justices will hear arguments in fall 2012 in a challenge to admissions policies at the University of Texas' flagship campus in Austin brought by an unsuccessful white applicant. Nancy Fisher contends that the school's use of race as a factor in the admissions process violated her constitutional rights by disadvantaging her in comparison to minority applicants.

The case, Fisher v. University of Texas, will mark the first time the court under Chief Justice John G. Roberts Jr. revisits the issue since the 2003 decision in Grutter v. University of Michigan allowed universities to make limited use of racial preferences in admissions.[56]

The Roberts court's other race-related rulings on K-12 pupil-assignment systems and government hiring and promotion policies cheered critics of racial preferences and dismayed traditional civil rights groups. Roberts and Justice Samuel A. Alito Jr., both appointed by President George W. Bush, cast pivotal votes in the 5-4 rulings. Advocates and experts on both sides of the affirmative action debate expect the Texas case also to be closely divided, with Justice Anthony M. Kennedy viewed as likely to hold the decisive vote.

Under President Obama, the administration has cheered traditional civil rights groups by endorsing steps to promote racial diversity in K-12 and higher education and challenging use of standardized tests and other employment practices that may limit hiring of minorities. But critics of race-based policies say their views are advancing in lower-court rulings, local school board decisions and two new statewide bans on affirmative action in public education, public employment and government contracting.

### College Admissions

The Texas case involves a challenge to changes adopted by the University of Texas Board of Regents after Grutter for the entering class of 2005 that allowed race to be considered as one factor in an applicant's Personal

Achievement Index (PAI). Other factors include an applicant's essays, leadership experience and extracurricular activities. Applicants continued to be qualified for automatic admission to the flagship Austin campus if they graduated in the top 10 percent of their high school class.

Fisher, who failed to qualify under the top-10 percent rule, was denied admission to the Austin campus for the entering class of 2008. She contended that the rejection violated her right to equal protection because she had academic credentials superior to those of minority applicants who were admitted. The university countered that its admissions process conformed to the limited use of race allowed under Grutter and had resulted in a marked increase in African-American students needed for racial diversity.

A three-judge panel of the Fifth U.S. Circuit Court of Appeals upheld the admissions policies in a lengthy opinion on Jan. 18, 2011. "UT undoubtedly has a compelling interest in obtaining the educational benefits of diversity," Judge Patrick E. Higginbotham wrote for the court, "and its reasons for implementing race-conscious admissions . . . mirror those approved by the Supreme Court in Grutter." Five months later, the full court voted 7-5 against rehearing the case, but four of the dissenters joined an opinion by Judge Edith Jones that said the ruling went beyond Grutter and called on the Supreme Court to review the decision.[57]

The high court agreed to review the decision on Feb. 21, setting the stage for arguments likely in October or November. Fisher, who went on to graduate from Louisiana State University in June 2012, said in a statement that she hoped the court would decide that future applicants "will be allowed to compete for admission without their race or ethnicity being a factor." UT-Austin President William Powers countered that the university needs "to weigh a multitude of factors when making admissions decisions about the balance of students who will make up each entering class."[58]

Meanwhile, two federal appeals courts have differed on the validity of statewide ballot measures banning racial preferences in university admissions as well as employment and government contracting. A Michigan measure approved by voters in 2006 was struck down by the Sixth U.S. Circuit Court of Appeals in July 2011.[59] In April 2012, however, the Ninth U.S. Circuit Court of

Appeals reaffirmed an earlier decision upholding California's similar measure adopted by voters in 1996.[60] In related developments, similar measures were approved by Arizona voters in November 2010 and by the New Hampshire legislature in 2011.[61] Oklahoma voters will decide on a similar ballot measure on Nov. 6.

For its part, the Obama administration issued companion policy memos in December 2011 setting out steps that public schools, colleges and universities can take to promote racial diversity. The memos, issued jointly by the Education and Justice departments, differed from Bush administration directives that cautioned against race-conscious pupil assignment or admissions policies.[62]

The Texas case will be heard by only eight justices. Justice Elena Kagan recused herself; she was U.S. solicitor general when the government filed a brief supporting the university before the Fifth Circuit. A 4-4 vote would affirm the Fifth Circuit's decision, thus leaving the university's policy in place.

## Public Schools

Local school systems are also evaluating pupil enrollment policies in light of the Roberts court's 2007 decision that generally prohibits the use of race as a determinative factor in assigning individual students to schools. The 5-4 ruling in Parents Involved in Community Schools v. Seattle School District No. 1 struck down pupil-assignment policies in Seattle and Jefferson County, Ky., which includes Louisville.[63]

In the main opinion, Roberts appeared to condemn any use of race in pupil assignments or in other government policies. "The way to stop discrimination on the basis of race," Roberts wrote, "is to stop discriminating on the basis of race." In a pivotal concurring opinion, however, Kennedy called diversity a "compelling interest" for school systems and listed permissible "race-conscious mechanisms," including redrawing attendance zones and "strategic" site selection, to further the goal.

The Seattle school board had already suspended the use of its so-called racial tie breaker for pupil assignments during the litigation. Today, school spokeswoman Teresa Wippel says the system uses a neighborhood assignment system. "We don't base it on race at all anymore," Wippel says.

In Louisville, the school system is now in court defending the pupil-assignment system adopted after the court ruling. An intermediate state court of appeal ruled in October 2011 that the plan violated a state law allowing parents to enroll their children in the school closest to their home. In arguments in April on the school system's appeal, however, justices of the Kentucky Court of Appeal, the state's highest court, were reported to appear inclined toward upholding the policy.[64]

The Supreme Court's decision appears to have moved school systems away from explicit use of race in pupil assignments. Controversies continue to flare, however. The Wake County, N.C., school system, which includes the state capital of Raleigh, had an income-based plan for promoting diversity in place for several years until it was scrapped by a newly elected, majority Republican school board in 2010; civil rights groups protested the decision.[65] A suit currently under way in Nashville, Tenn., challenges a 2009 redistricting plan that African-American families allege zoned black children away from higher-achieving schools in predominantly white neighborhoods; the suit also seeks to bar the startup of new charter schools that are racially isolated.[66]

### Employment, Contracting

The court's ruling in the New Haven firefighters case is creating problems for government personnel administrators and lawyers in determining what steps if any can be taken to avoid charges of discriminating against minorities without risking reverse-discrimination claims by white employees or applicants. "It's damned if you do and damned if you don't," says Roger Clegg, president of the Center for Equal Opportunity, a Washington area-based advocacy group that opposes racial preferences.

The subsequent developments in the New Haven case illustrate the problem. The city agreed in July 2011 to pay $2 million in damages to the plaintiffs — all of them white, including one Hispanic — who had been denied promotions. The city also was to pay $3 million in attorneys' fees and court costs.[67]

Meanwhile, however, some black firefighters were continuing to challenge the test-scoring system used in determining promotion as racially biased against minorities. A federal district court judge threw out the suit, but the Second U.S. Circuit Court of Appeals ruled in August 2011 that one of the plaintiffs could proceed with his suit. The appeals court said the high court's decision did not prevent Michael Briscoe from trying to

prove that the city's decision to give greater weight to the written instead of the oral portion of the promotion exam had a "disparate impact" on minority applicants in violation of federal civil rights law.[68]

The Obama administration has been "aggressive," according to Clegg, in using disparate-impact theories in civil rights litigation in employment, housing and lending. As one example, the Justice Department filed a suit on April 23, 2012, against the Jacksonville, Fla., Fire and Rescue Department challenging the use of a written promotion exam for supervisory positions as discriminatory against minority firefighters.[69]

Minority preferences in government contracting also appear to be drawing more critical scrutiny from courts, both federal and state. In one important case, the U.S. Court of Appeals for the Federal Circuit in 2008 struck down a Defense Department program that gave preferences to minority-owned contractors. The court said the program was unconstitutional without any evidence that it was needed to remedy past discrimination by the Pentagon.[70]

## NOTES

1. See "Transcript: Obama and Clinton Debate," ABC News, April 16, 2008, http://abcnews.go.com/Politics/DemocraticDebate/story?id=4670271&page=1.

2. *Ibid.*

3. *Ibid.*

4. See "Trends in Political Values and Core Attitudes: 1987-2007," Pew Research Center for People and the Press, March 22, 2007, pp. 40-41, http://people-press.org/reports/pdf/312.pdf.

5. See Alemayehu Bishaw and Jessica Semega, "Income, Earnings, and Poverty Data from the 2007 American Community Survey," U.S. Census Bureau, August 2008, p. 20, www.census.gov/prod/2008pubs/acs-09.pdf.

6. See Peter Schmidt, *Color and Money: How Rich White Kids Are Winning the War Over College Affirmative Action* (2007), p. 47.

7. See Anthony P. Carnevale and Stephen J. Rose, "Socioeconomic Status, Race/Ethnicity, and Selective College Admissions," The Century

Foundation, March 2003, pp. 26, 79, www.tcf.org/Publications/Education/carnevale_rose.pdf.

8. See Christopher B. Swanson, "Who Graduates? Who Doesn't? A Statistical Portrait of High School Graduation, Class of 2001," The Urban Institute, 2004, pp. v-vi, www.urban.org/UploadedPDF/410934_WhoGraduates.pdf.

9. Quoted in Ira Katznelson, *When Affirmative Action Was White: An Untold History of Racial Inequality in Twentieth-Century America* (2005), p. 175.

10. See Roberta W. Francis, "Reconstituting the Equal Rights Amendment: Policy Implications for Sex Discrimination," 2001, www.equalrightsamendment.org/APSA2001.pdf.

11. See Clarence Thomas, *My Grandfather's Son: A Memoir* (2007), p. 126.

12. Quoted in "Justice Thomas Mocks Value of Yale Law Degree," The Associated Press, Oct. 22, 2007, www.foxnews.com/story/0,2933,303825,00.html. See also, Coleman profile in Berger&Montague, P.C., law firm Web site, www.bergermontague.com/attorneys.cfm?type=1.

13. See Linda Greenhouse, "Justices Back Affirmative Action by 5 to 4, But Wider Vote Bans a Racial Point System," *The New York Times*, June 24, 2003, p. A1.

14. "Barack Obama, July 27, 2008, Unity 08, High Def, Part II," www.youtube.com/watch?v=XIoRzNVTyH4&eurl= http://video.google.com/videosearch?q=obama%20UNITY&ie=UTF-8&oe=utf-8&rls=org.mozilla:enUS:official&c.UNITY is a coalition of the Asian-American Journalists Association, the National Association of Black Journalists, the National Association of Hispanic Journalists and the Native American Journalists Association, www.unityjournalists.org.

15. See "Trends in Political Values . . .," *op. cit.*, pp. 40-41.

16. See http://abcnews.go.com/Politics/Democratic Debate/story?id=4670271.

17. See Jonathan Kaufman, "Fair Enough?" *The Wall Street Journal*, June 14, 2008.

18. See Christine MacDonald, "Ban lost in college counties," *Detroit News*, Nov. 9, 2006, p. A16; and "1996 General Election Returns for Proposition 209," California Secretary of State, Dec. 18, 1996, http://vote96.sos.ca.gov/Vote96/html/vote/prop/prop-209.961218083528.html.

19. See Sue Anne Pressley, "Florida Plan Aims to End Race-Based Preferences," *The Washington Post*, Nov. 11, 1999, p. A15.

20. See Walter Alarkon, "Affirmative action emerges as wedge issue in election," *The Hill*, March 11, 2008, http://thehill.com/campaign-2008/affirmative-action-emerges-as-wedge-issue-in-election-2008-03-11.html.

21. *Ibid.*, p. viii.

22. Catherine L. Horn and Stella M. Flores, "Percent Plans in College Admissions: A Comparative Analysis of Three States' Experiences," The Civil Rights Project, Harvard University, February 2003, pp. 30-31, http://eric.ed.gov/ERICDocs/data/ericdocs2sql/content_storage_01/0000019b/80/1a/b7/9f.pdf.

23. See Carnevale and Rose, *op. cit.*, pp. 10-11.

24. *Ibid.*

25. Quoted in Terry H. Anderson, *The Pursuit of Fairness: A History of Affirmative Action* (2004), p. 76. Unless otherwise indicated, material in this subsection is drawn from this book.

26. For background, see the following *Editorial Research Reports:* Richard L. Worsnop, "Racism in America," May 13, 1964; Sandra Stencel, "Reverse Discrimination," Aug. 6, 1976; K. P. Maize and Sandra Stencel, "Affirmative Action Under Attack," March 30, 1979; and Marc Leepson, "Affirmative Action Reconsidered," July 31, 1981, all available in *CQ Researcher Plus Archive.*

27. Quoted in Anderson, *op. cit.*, p. 125. For more background, see Richard L. Worsnop, "Racial Discrimination in Craft Unions," *Editorial Research Reports*, Nov. 26, 1969, available in *CQ Researcher Plus Archive.*

28. *Griggs v. Duke Power*, 401 U.S. 424 (1971), http://caselaw.lp.findlaw.com/scripts/getcase.pl?court=US&vol=401&invol=424. For background, see Mary H. Cooper, "Racial Quotas," *CQ Researcher*, May 17, 1991, pp. 277-200; and Kenneth Jost, "Rethinking Affirmative Action," *CQ Researcher*, April 28, 1995, pp. 269-392.

29. *Ibid.*

30. See *University of California Regents v. Bakke*, 438 U.S. 265 (1978), http://caselaw.lp.findlaw.com/scripts/getcase.pl?court=US&vol=438&invol=265.

31. See *United Steelworkers of America, AFL-CIO-CLC v. Weber, et al.*, 443 U.S. 193 (1979), http://caselaw.lp.findlaw.com/scripts/getcase.pl?court=US&vol=443&invol=193; and *Fullilove v. Klutznick*, 448 U.S. 448 (1980), www.law.cornell.edu/supct/html/historics/USSC_CR_0448_0448_ZS.html.

32. Unless otherwise indicated, this subsection is drawn from Anderson, *op. cit;* and Jost, *op. cit.*

33. For background, see Cooper, *op. cit.*

34. Anderson, *op. cit.*, p. 186.

35. *Ibid.*, p. 206.

36. Quoted in *ibid.*, p. 233. Unless otherwise indicated this subsection is drawn from Anderson, *op. cit.*

37. *Ibid.*, p. 242.

38. *Ibid.*, p. 244.

39. For background, see Kenneth Jost, "Race in America," *CQ Researcher*, July 11, 2003, pp. 593-624.

40. Quoted in Greenhouse, *op. cit.*

41. "Controversial Bake Sale to Go On at CU, College Republicans Protesting Affirmative Action," 7 News, Feb. 10, 2004, www.thedenverchannel.com/news/2837956/detail.html.

42. Quoted in Kavita Kumar, "Affirmative action critic vows he'll try again," *St. Louis Post-Dispatch*, May 6, 2008, p. D1.

43. "Amendment 46: Formerly Proposed Initiative 2007-2008 #31," Colorado Secretary of State, undated, www.elections.colorado.gov/DDefault.aspx?tid=1036.

44. College data, undated, www.collegedata.com/cs/data/college/college_pg01_tmpl.jhtml?schoolId=111.

45. Adam Liptak, "Supreme Court Finds Bias Against White Firefighters," *The New York Times*, June 30, 2009.

46. Michael C. Dorf, "The Supreme Court Decides the New Haven Firefighter Case," July 1, 2009, *Findlaw*, http://writ.news.findlaw.com/dorf/20090701.html.

47. Edmund H. Mahony and Josh Kovner, "U.S. Supreme Court Rules in Favor of New England Firefighters." *Hartford Courant*, June 30, 2009.

48. Press release, Nov. 30, 2008, www.affirmative action.org/news.html.

49. Paul Basken, "Education Department Promises Push on Civil-Rights Enforcement," *The Chronicle of Higher Education*, March 8, 2010.

50. Libby Sander and Peter Schmidt, "Stepping Up the Pace at the Office of Civil Rights," *The Chronicle of Higher Education*, April 15, 2010.

51. See the joint brief at www.justice.gov/crt/briefs/fisher_appellee_brief.pdf.

52. Tamar Lewin, "Law School Admissions Lag Among Minorities," *The New York Times*, Jan. 6, 2010.

53. See SEAPHE.org.

54. Scott Jaschik, "Nebraska Bars Use of Race in Admissions," *Inside Higher Ed*, Nov. 5, 2008, www.insidehighered.com/news/2008/11/05/ affirm.

55. Colleen Slevin, "Colorado voters reject affirmative action ban," *Colorado Gazette*, Nov. 7, 2008.

56. Materials on the case can be found on SCOTUSBlog, www.scotusblog.com/case-files/cases/fisher-v-university-of-texas-at-austin/?wpmp_switcher=desktop.

57. See Fisher v. University of Texas, 631 F.3d 213 (5th Cir., 2011), www.ca5.uscourts.gov/opinions%5Cpub%5C09/09-50822-CV0.wpd.pdf (as revised Feb. 1, 2011). The denial of rehearing is found at www.ca5.uscourts.gov/opinions%5Cpub%5C09/09-50822-CV1.wpd.pdf. For coverage, see articles by Ralph K. M. Haurwit: "UT admission policy upheld," Austin American-Statesman, Jan. 19, 2011; "Court won't review UT admissions guidelines," ibid., June 22, 2011.

58. Quoted in Monica Rhor, "Top court to take up UT policy on race," The Houston Chronicle, Feb. 22, 2012, p. A1. See also Adam Liptak, "Justices Take Up Race as a Factor in College Entry," The New York Times, Feb. 22, 2012, p. A1.

59. The decision is Coalition to Defend Affirmative Action v. University of Michigan (6th Cir., July 1, 2011), www.ca6.uscourts.gov/opinions.pdf/11a0174p-06.pdf. See David Ashenfelter and Dawson

Bell, "Michigan ban on race in college admissions is illegal," Detroit Free Press, July 1, 2011; Tamar Lewin, "Michigan Rule on Admission to University Is Overturned," The New York Times, July 2, 2011, p. A10.

60. The decision is Coalition to Defend Affirmative Action v. Brown (9th Cir., April 2, 2012), www.ca9 .uscourts.gov/datastore/opinions/2012/04/ 02/11-15100.pdf. See Carol J. Williams, "Racial policy ban is upheld," Los Angeles Times, p. AA4.

61. See "Arizona approves anti-affirmative action measure," The Associated Press, Nov. 2, 2010; Peter Schmidt, "New Hampshire Ends Affirmative-Action Preferences at Colleges," The Chronicle of Higher Education, Jan. 4, 2012.

62. See U.S. Departments of Education, Justice, "Guidance on the Voluntary Use of Race to Achieve Diversity and Avoid Racial Isolation in Elementary and Secondary Schools," www2.ed.gov/about/ offices/list/ocr/docs/guidance-ese-201111.html; "Guidance on the Voluntary Use of Race to Achieve Diversity in Postsecondary Education," www.justice .gov/crt/about/edu/documents/guidancepost.pdf. The undated documents were released on Dec. 1, 2011.

63. The citation is 551 U.S. 701 (2007). For coverage of background and ruling, see Kenneth Jost, Supreme Court Yearbook 2006-2007.

64. See articles by Chris Kenning: "Court strikes down JCPS student-assignment plan," The Courier-Journal (Louisville), Oct. 1, 2011, p. A1; "Ky. Justices may favor JCPS," ibid., April 19, 2012, p. A1.

65. See Stephanie McCrummen, "In N.C., a new battle on school integration," The Washington Post, Jan. 12, 2011, p. A1.

66. See Julie Hubbard, "Metro Nashville schools rezoning lawsuit could echo far," The Tennessean (Nashville), April 30, 2012.

67. See Abbe Smith, "Firefighters get $2 million," New Haven Register, July 29, 2011, p. A1.

68. The decision is Briscoe v. New Haven, 10-1975-cv (2d Cir., Aug. 15, 2011), www.ca2.uscourts .gov/decisions/isysquery/2a558a1b-8e49-4693- 80fe-73210ac25bd3/2/doc/10-1975_opn .pdf#xml=www.ca2.uscourts.gov/decisions/isys query/2a558a1b-8e49-4693-80fe-73210 ac25bd3/2/hilite/. For coverage, see Luther Turnelle, "Firefighter case is reinstated," New Haven Register, Aug. 16, 2011, p. A3. The Supreme Court declined to hear the city's appeal on June 11, 2012.

69. Press release, April 23, 2012, www.justice.gov/opa/ pr/2012/April/12-crt-517.html. For coverage, see Steve Patterson, "U.S. sues city over firefighter tests," Florida Times-Union (Jacksonville), April 24, 2012, p. B3.

70. The case is Rothe Development Corp. v. Department of Defense (Fed. Cir., Nov. 4, 2008). For coverage, see Elise Castelli, "Court: DoD minority contracting program unconstitutional," Federal Times, Nov. 10, 2008, p. 6. See also Jody Feder and Kate M. Manuel, "Rothe Development Corporation v. Department of Defense: The Constitutionality of Federal Contracting Programs for Minority-Owned and Other Small Businesses," Congressional Research Service, March 16, 2009, www.fas.org/sgp/crs/misc/ R40440.pdf.

# BIBLIOGRAPHY

## Books

**Anderson, Terry H.,** *The Pursuit of Fairness: A History of Affirmative Action,* **Oxford University Press, 2004.**
A Texas A&M historian tells the complicated story of affirmative action and the struggles surrounding it.

**Kahlenberg, Richard D., ed.,** *America's Untapped Resource: Low-Income Students in Higher Education,* **The Century Foundation Press, 2004.**
A liberal scholar compiles detailed studies that add up to a case for replacing race- and ethnic-based affirmative action with a system based on students' socioeconomic status.

**Katznelson, Ira,** *When Affirmative Action Was White: An Untold History of Racial Inequality in Twentieth-Century America,* **Norton, 2005.**
A Columbia University historian and political scientist argues that affirmative action — favoring whites — evolved as a way of excluding Southern blacks from federal social benefits.

Schmidt, Peter, *Color and Money: How Rich White Kids are Winning the War Over College Affirmative Action*, Palgrave Macmillan, 2007.
An editor at *The Chronicle of Higher Education* explores the realities of race, class and college admissions.

Sowell, Thomas, *Affirmative Action Around the World: An Empirical Study*, Yale University Press, 2004.
A prominent black conservative and critic of affirmative action dissects the doctrine and practice and its similarities to initiatives in the developing world, of which few Americans are aware.

## Articles

Babington, Charles, "Might Obama's success undercut affirmative action," The Associated Press, June 28, 2008, www.usatoday.com/news/politics/2008-06-28-3426171631_x.htm.
In a piece that prompted a debate question to presidential candidate Barack Obama, a reporter examines a possibly paradoxical consequence of the 2008 presidential campaign.

Jacobs, Tom, "Affirmative Action: Shifting Attitudes, Surprising Results," *Miller-McCune*, June 20, 2008, www.miller-mccune.com/article/447.
A new magazine specializing in social issues surveys the long-running debate over university admissions. (*Miller-McCune* is published by SAGE Publications, parent company of CQ Press.)

Leonhardt, David, "The New Affirmative Action," *New York Times Magazine*, Sept. 30, 2007, p. 76.
A journalist specializing in economic and social policy explores UCLA's efforts to retool its admissions procedures.

Liptak, Adam, "Lawyers Debate Why Blacks Lag At Major Firms," *The New York Times*, Nov. 29, 2006, p. A1.
A law correspondent airs a tough debate over affirmative action's success, or lack of it, at big law firms.

Matthews, Adam, "The Fixer," *Good Magazine*, Aug. 14, 2008, www.goodmagazine.com/section/Features/the_fixer.
A new Web-based publication for the hip and socially conscious examines the career of black businessman and affirmative-action critic Ward Connerly.

Mehta, Seema, "UCLA accused of illegal admissions practices," *Los Angeles Times*, Aug. 30, 2008, www.latimes.com/news/local/la-me-ucla30-2008aug30,0,6489043.story.
Mehta examines the latest conflict surrounding the top-tier university's retailored admissions procedures.

## Reports and Studies

Coleman, James E. Jr. and Mitu Gulati, "A Response to Professor Sander: Is It Really All About the Grades?" *North Carolina Law Review*, 2006, pp. 1823-1829.
Two lawyers, one of them a black who was a partner at a major firm, criticize Sander's conclusions, arguing he overemphasizes academic deficiencies.

Horn, Catherine L. and Stella M. Flores, "Percent Plans in College Admissions: A Comparative Analysis of Three States' Experiences," The Civil Rights Project, Harvard University, February 2003.
Educational policy experts with a pro-affirmative action perspective dig into the details of three states' alternatives to traditional affirmative action.

Prager, Devah, "The Mark of a Criminal Record," *American Journal of Sociology*, March 2003, pp. 937-975.
White people with criminal records have a better chance at entry-level jobs than black applicants with clean records, an academic's field research finds.

Sander, Richard H., "The Racial Paradox of the Corporate Law Firm," *North Carolina Law Review*, 2006, pp. 1755-1822.
A much-discussed article shows that a disproportionate number of black lawyers from top schools leave major law firms before becoming partners.

Swanson, Christopher B., "Who Graduates? Who Doesn't? A Statistical Portrait of Public High School Graduation, Class of 2001," The Urban Institute, 2004, www.urban.org/publications/410934.html.
A centrist think tank reveals in devastating detail the disparity in high schools between races and classes.

# For More Information

**American Association for Affirmative Action**, 888 16th St., N.W., Suite 800, Washington, DC 20006; (202) 349-9855; www.affirmativeaction.org. Represents human resources professionals in the field.

**American Civil Liberties Union**, 125 Broad St., 18th Floor, New York, NY 10004; www.aclu.org/racialjustice/aa/index.html. The organization's Racial Justice Program organizes legal and voter support for affirmative action programs.

**American Civil Rights Institute**, P.O. Box 188350, Sacramento, CA 95818; (916) 444-2278; www.acri.org/index.html. Organizes ballot initiatives to prohibit affirmative action programs based on race and ethnicity preferences.

**Diversity Web, Association of American Colleges and Universities**, 1818 R St., N.W., Washington, DC 20009; www.diversityweb.org. Publishes news and studies concerning affirmative action and related issues.

**www.jessicacorry.com.** A Web site featuring writings by Jessica Peck Corry, director of the Colorado campaign for a racial preferences ban.

**Project SEAPHE (The Scale and Effects of Admissions Preferences in Higher Education)**, UCLA School of Law, Box 951476, Los Angeles, CA 90095; (310) 267-4576; www.seaphe.org. Analyzes data on the effects of racial and other preferences.

**U.S. Commission on Civil Rights**, 624 Ninth St., N.W., Washington, DC 20425; (202) 376-7700; www.usccr.gov. Studies and reports on civil rights issues and implements civil rights laws.

# 11

# Racial Diversity in Public Schools

Kenneth Jost and Charles S. Clark

White enrollment at Seattle's Ballard High School is above previous guidelines five years after a racial-diversity plan was suspended because of a legal challenge. The Supreme Court's June 28 decision invalidating racial-balance plans in Seattle and Louisville, Ky., bars school districts from using race for student-placement decisions but may permit some race-conscious policies to promote diversity.

AP Photo/Ted S. Warren

From *CQ Researcher*,
September 14, 2007 (updated August 12, 2010).

Hannah MacNeal's parents were glad to learn of an opening at the popular magnet elementary school near their upscale neighborhood in eastern Louisville, Ky. When they applied in mid-August for Hannah to enroll as a fourth-grader at Greathouse/Shryock Elementary, however, school system officials said she could not be admitted.

The reason: Hannah is white.

Only six weeks earlier, the U.S. Supreme Court had ruled that Jefferson County Public Schools (JCPS) — which includes Louisville — was violating the Constitution by assigning students to schools on the basis of their race.

Hannah's stepmother, Dana MacNeal, was surprised and upset when she learned Hannah would have been admitted to the school if she had been black. And she was all the more upset when JCPS Student Placement Director Pat Todd insisted on Aug. 14 that the Supreme Court ruling allowed the school system to continue maintaining separate attendance zones for black and white students for Greathouse/Shryock and two of the system's other three magnet elementary schools.

The school system's lawyers were surprised as well to learn of the policy. After the MacNeals decided to fight the decision keeping Hannah in her regular elementary school, officials agreed to enroll her at Greathouse/Shryock and scrap the racially separate boundary zones beginning in 2008.[1]

"Of course, they backed off from the position, knowing they were wrong," says Louisville attorney Ted Gordon, who represented the MacNeals in the latest round in his long-running battle to overturn Jefferson County's school racial-diversity policies. "They have to follow the law."

# School Racial-Balance Plans in Louisville and Seattle

The Supreme Court's June 28, 2007, ruling on the school racial-diversity plans in Seattle and Jefferson County (Louisville) bars the use of racial classifications in individual pupil assignments but appears to permit some "race-neutral" policies aimed at racial diversity.

### Jefferson County (Louisville) (98,000 students; 35 percent African-American)

**History:** County was racially segregated before *Brown v. Board of Education* ruling; court-ordered desegregation plan in 1975 called for crosstown busing between predominantly African-American West End and mainly white neighborhoods in eastern suburbs; court order dissolved in 2000; school board adopts pupil-assignment plan with use of racial classifications to promote diversity; assignment plan still in effect after Supreme Court decision, pending new plan expected for 2009-2010 academic year.

**Details:** Plan classifies students as "black" or "white" (including Asians, Hispanics and others); guidelines call for each elementary, middle or high school to have between 15 percent and 50 percent African-American enrollment; residence-based system assigns students to school within residential "cluster"; most West End neighborhoods assigned to schools outside area; student applications for transfer from assigned school evaluated on basis of several factors, including effect on racial makeup; under Supreme Court decision, individual transfer requests will no longer be denied on basis of race.

### Seattle (45,000 students: 58 percent "non-white")

**History:** No history of mandatory segregation, but racially identifiable neighborhoods: predominantly black south of downtown, predominantly white to the north; racial-balance plan with crosstown busing voluntarily adopted in 1978; school choice introduced in 1990s, with race as one "tiebreaker" to distribute students among oversubscribed schools; school board suspended the plan in 2002 because of legal challenge; Supreme Court ruling held plan invalid.

**Details:** Ninth-graders permitted to apply to up to three of district's 10 high schools; tiebreakers used for applications to oversubscribed schools; sibling preference was most important factor, race second; race used if school's enrollment deviated by specified percentage from overall racial demographics: 40 percent white, 60 percent non-white.

The Supreme Court's fractured ruling struck down pupil-assignment policies adopted in 2000 limiting African-American enrollment at any individual school in Jefferson County to between 15 percent and 50 percent of the student body. The ruling also rejected the Seattle school system's use of race as a "tiebreaker" for assigning students to high schools; the plan had been suspended in 2002 because of the litigation.[2]

In response to the MacNeals' case, Todd's office drew up new boundary zones for the four magnet elementary schools that were approved by the school board on Sept. 10. For the longer term, officials are trying to find ways to maintain a measure of racial balance in the 98,000-student school system under the Supreme Court decision, which bars the use of racial classifications in individual pupil assignments but appears to permit some "race-neutral" policies aimed at racial diversity.

"We are going to do our best to achieve it," says JCPS Superintendent Sheldon Berman. "We are deeply committed to retaining the qualities of an integrated environment."

The court's June 28 decision dealt a blow to hundreds of school systems around the country that have adopted voluntary race-mixing plans after court-ordered desegregation plans lapsed in recent years.

Five of the justices — led by Chief Justice John G. Roberts Jr. — said using racial classifications in pupil assignments violated the Equal Protection Clause of the 14th Amendment. That is the same provision the court cited a half-century earlier in the famous *Brown v. Board of Education* (1954) ruling that found racial segregation in public schools unconstitutional.[3]

In a strong dissent, the court's four liberal justices — led by Stephen G. Breyer — said the ruling contradicted previous decisions upholding race-based pupil assignments and would hamper local school boards' efforts to prevent "resegregation" in individual schools. But one of the justices in the majority — Anthony M. Kennedy — joined the liberal minority in endorsing racial diversity as a legitimate goal. Kennedy listed several "race-neutral" policies, such as drawing attendance zones or building new schools to include students from different racial neighborhoods, that schools could adopt to pursue the goal.

The ruling drew sharp criticism from traditional civil rights advocates. "It's preposterous to think the 14th Amendment was designed to permit individual white parents to strike down a plan to help minority students have better access to schools and to prevent school districts from having integrated schools that are supported by a majority of the community," says Gary Orfield, a longtime civil rights advocate and director of the Civil Rights Project at UCLA's Graduate School of Education and Information Sciences.

Ted Shaw, president of the NAACP Legal Defense Fund, said the ruling blocks school boards from using "one of the few tools that are available" to create racially diverse schools. "The court has taken a significant step away from the promise of *Brown*," says Shaw. "And this comes on top of the reality that many school districts are highly segregated by race already."

Conservative critics of race-based school policies, however, applauded the ruling. "I don't think school districts should be drawing attendance zones or building schools for the purpose of achieving a politically correct racial mix," says Roger Clegg, president of the Center for Equal Opportunity, which joined in a friend-of-the-court brief supporting the white families that challenged the Seattle and Louisville school policies.

"A lot of parents out there don't like it when their students are treated differently because of race or ethnicity," Clegg adds. "After these decisions, the odds favor those parents and those organizations that oppose school boards that practice racial or ethnic discrimination."

School officials in Louisville and Seattle and around the country are generally promising to continue race-mixing

## Racial Classifications Barred But Diversity Backed

The Supreme Court's June 28 decision in Parents Involved in Community Schools v. Seattle School District No. 1 invalidating pupil-assignment plans in Seattle and Louisville bars school systems from assigning individual students to schools based on their race. In a partial concurrence, however, Justice Anthony M. Kennedy joined with the four dissenters in finding racial diversity to be a legitimate government interest and in permitting some race-conscious policies to achieve that goal.

### Roberts (plurality opinion)

Scalia  Thomas  Alito

"Racial balancing is not transformed from 'patently unconstitutional' to a compelling state interest simply by relabeling it 'racial diversity.'"

### Kennedy (concurring in part)

". . . [A] district may consider it a compelling interest to achieve a diverse student body. Race may be one component of that diversity. . . . What the government is not permitted to do . . . is to classify every student on the basis of race and to assign each of them to schools based on that classification."

### Breyer (dissenting)

Stevens  Souter  Ginsburg

"The plurality . . . undermines [*Brown v. Board of Education's*] promise of integrated primary and secondary education that local communities have sought to make a reality. This cannot be justified in the name of the Equal Protection Clause."

*Credits:* AFP/Getty Images/Paul J. Richards (Alito, Kennedy, Roberts, Souter, Scalia, Thomas); Getty Images/Mark Wilson (Ginsburg, Stevens); AFP/Getty Images/ Brendan Smialowski (Breyer)

policies within the limits of the court's decision. "School boards are going to have to do the hard work to find more tailored ways of approaching diversity in their schools," says Francisco Negrón, general counsel of the National School Boards Association.

The evidence in Louisville and nationally suggests, however, that the goal will be hard to achieve. In

## Southern Schools Least Segregated, but Slipping

Schools in the South were the least segregated in the nation in the 1970s and '80s, a distinction they maintained in the 2005 school year. But Southern schools have been resegregating steadily since 1988.

### Change in Black Segregation in Southern Schools, 1954-2005

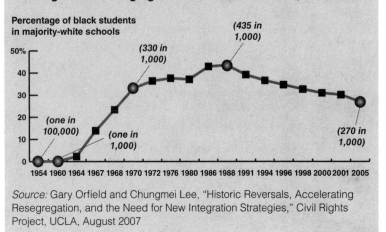

Source: Gary Orfield and Chungmei Lee, "Historic Reversals, Accelerating Resegregation, and the Need for New Integration Strategies," Civil Rights Project, UCLA, August 2007

Supporters of racial-balance plans argue that diversity in the classroom helps boost academic achievement for minority students without adversely affecting achievement for white students. Opponents dispute those claims.

The debate over diversity also highlights a secondary dispute over the widespread practice of "tracking" — the offering of separate courses for students based on ability or previous achievement. Supporters say the practice matches curriculum to students' needs and abilities, but critics say it results in consigning already disadvantaged students — including a disproportionate number of African-Americans — to poor-quality education.

Meanwhile, some experts and advocates are calling for shifting the focus away from race and instead trying to promote socioeconomic integration — mixing low-income and middle- and upper-class students. Richard Kahlenberg, a senior fellow with the left-of-center Century Foundation who is most closely associated with the movement, says policies aimed at preventing high concentrations of low-income students will produce academic gains along with likely gains in racial and ethnic diversity.

"Providing all students with the chance to attend mixed-income schools can raise overall levels of achievement," Kahlenberg writes in a report released on the day of the Supreme Court decision.[6]

As the debate over diversity in public-school classrooms continues, here are the major questions being considered.

### Should school systems promote racial diversity in individual schools?

School officials in Lynn, Mass., a former mill town 10 miles northeast of Boston, take pride in a pupil-assignment system that has helped maintain racial balance in most schools even as the town's Hispanic population has steadily increased over the past decade. "We work very hard to promote integration and cultural diversity so that our children are able to get along with each other," says Jan Birchenough, the administrator in charge of compliance with the state's racial-balance law.

Louisville, nine schools are now outside the district's 15/50 guidelines, with several having more than 55 percent African-American enrollment, according to Todd. "If the board wants to continue to maintain diversity, we've already had some significant slippage at some selected schools," he says.[4]

Nationally, a new report by the UCLA Civil Rights Project concludes that African-American and Latino students are increasingly isolated from white students in public schools. Overall, nearly three-fourths of African-American students and slightly over three-fourths of Latino students attend predominantly minority schools. Both figures have been increasing since 1980, the report says.[5]

Critics of race-based pupil assignments are unfazed by the trends. "We're past guidelines, we're past quotas and we need to move on," says Gordon of the Louisville statistics. He calls instead for an array of reforms focused on schools with high concentrations of low-income students.

"All other things being equal, I like racially diverse schools," says Abigail Thernstrom, a senior fellow at the conservative Manhattan Institute and a former member of the Massachusetts Board of Education. "But I do not think it works from any angle to have government entities — whether they are federal courts or local school boards — try to engineer diversity."

## White Students Are Racially Isolated

Segregation remained high in 2005-06 for all racial groups except Asians. White students remained the most racially isolated, although they attended schools with slightly more minority students than in the past. The average white student attended schools in which 77 percent of their peers were white. Meanwhile, more than half of black and Latino students' peers were black or Latino, and fewer than one-third of their classmates were white.

### Racial Composition of Schools Attended by the Average . . .

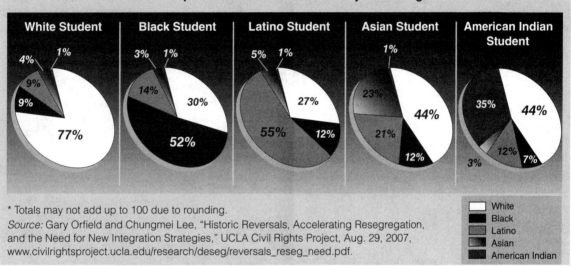

| White Student | Black Student | Latino Student | Asian Student | American Indian Student |

White Student: 77%, 4%, 1%, 9%, 9%
Black Student: 3%, 1%, 14%, 30%, 52%
Latino Student: 5%, 1%, 27%, 55%, 12%
Asian Student: 1%, 23%, 21%, 44%, 12%
American Indian Student: 35%, 44%, 3%, 12%, 7%

\* Totals may not add up to 100 due to rounding.
*Source:* Gary Orfield and Chungmei Lee, "Historic Reversals, Accelerating Resegregation, and the Need for New Integration Strategies," UCLA Civil Rights Project, Aug. 29, 2007, www.civilrightsproject.ucla.edu/research/deseg/reversals_reseg_need.pdf.

Legend: White, Black, Latino, Asian, American Indian

But attorney Chester Darling says Lynn's policy of denying any transfer requests that would increase racial imbalance at an individual school "falls squarely within" the kinds of plans prohibited by the Supreme Court decision in the Louisville and Seattle cases. "It can't be race-neutral if you use the word race," says Darling, who is asking a federal judge in Boston to reopen a previously unsuccessful suit filed by parents challenging the policy.[7]

Critics of race-based assignment plans hope the Supreme Court decision will persuade or force school districts like Lynn's to drop any use of racial classifications in pupil placement. "Most school districts will look at the decision's bottom line, will consider that the Louisville and Seattle plans were not sloppily done, and yet at the end of the day were declared unconstitutional," says Clegg of the Center for Equal Opportunity. "This cost the school boards a lot of time and money, and they're going to have to pay the other side's lawyer."

But school board officials say the court's fractured ruling leaves room for local systems to consider race in trying to create racial and ethnic mixing in individual schools.

"Race is still not out of the question," says Negrón of the school boards' association. "A plurality of the court said certain things that are not the law of the land. What the majority has done is invalidate these particular programs, but certainly left the door wide open to the use of race — which continues to be a compelling government interest."

Apart from the legal issue, supporters and opponents of racial-diversity plans also disagree on their educational and other effects. "There's a consensus in the academic world that there are clear educational benefits, and the benefits aren't just for minority students," says UCLA Professor Orfield.

Conversely, "racial isolation leads to reduced achievement," says Negrón.

Critics of racial-diversity policies, however, say those benefits are unproven and the logic of the claimed cause-effect relationship unconvincing. "There is very little empirical evidence," says Thernstrom, the Manhattan Institute fellow.

"I don't think how well you learn or what you learn depends on the color of the skin of the person sitting

## Non-Racial Approaches to Integration

Some 40 school districts around the country are seeking to diversify enrollment in individual schools through socioeconomic integration — typically, by setting guidelines for the percentage of students eligible for free or reduced-price lunch. Here are some of the districts taking such approaches, as drawn from a report by the Century Foundation's Richard Kahlenberg, a strong advocate of the policies.

**School District** *Enrollment: Percentage of whites (W), African-Americans (B), Hispanics (H), Asian-Americans (A)*

**Berkeley, Calif. ( 9,000: 31% W, 29% B, 17% H, 8% A )**
Socioeconomic and racial diversity guidelines were adopted in 2004 to replace a voluntary racial-integration plan; plan being phased-in one grade at a time; in 2005-06, eight of 11 elementary schools were within 15% of the districtwide average of 40% of students receiving subsidized lunches; most parents (71%) still receive first choice of schools.

**Brandywine, Del. ( 11,000: 54% W, 39% B, 3% H, 4% A )**
The district — comprising parts of Wilmington and surrounding suburbs — was granted an exception in 2001 by state Board of Education to law mandating neighborhood schools; plan limits subsidized-lunch enrollment to between 16% and 73%; plan credited with maintaining racial diversity; some evidence of academic gains in higher grades.

**Cambridge, Mass. ( 6,000: 37% B, 35% W, 15% H, 11% A )**
Plan adopted in 2001 to replace race-conscious "controlled choice" system says individual schools should be within 15 percentage points of districtwide percentage of free/reduced lunch students; race remains a potential factor in assignments; racial diversity maintained, socioeconomic diversity increased; limited evidence finds academic gains for low-income students, no negative effect on middle-income students.

**Charlotte-Mecklenburg, N.C. ( 129,000: 42% B, 36% W, 14% H, 4% A )**
School board dropped racial-desegregation effort, adopted public school choice plan after school system was declared "unitary" in 2001, or no longer a dual system based on race; plan gives some priority to low-income students in schools with concentrated poverty, but transfers to higher-performing schools are permitted only if seats are available; plan seen as unsuccessful in creating racial or socioeconomic integration.

**La Crosse, Wis. ( 7,000: 20% minority )**
Was first district to adopt socioeconomic integration policy in 1991-92 in response to influx of Hmong refugees; plan used redrawn attendance zones and busing to spread low-income students among elementary schools and two high schools; plan largely survived political battle in 1992-93 that included recall of several school board members; plan touted as success, but enrollments at most elementary schools have been and still are outside guidelines.

next to you," says Clegg. "Students in overwhelmingly white schoolrooms in Idaho and in overwhelmingly African-American classrooms in Washington, D.C., can each learn."

Critics cite as one concrete disadvantage the time spent on buses when students are transported out of their neighborhoods for the sake of racial balance.

"There's no educational benefit there, and it's a waste of their very precious time," says Thernstrom. The travel burdens also hamper student participation in extracurricular activities and parental involvement, the critics say.

In traditional desegregation plans, those burdens typically fell for the most part on African-American students, who were transported out of their neighborhoods to schools in predominantly white areas. Busing was "usually a one-way street" for African-Americans, says James Anderson, head of the department of educational-policy studies at the University of Illinois, Champaign-Urbana.

In recent years, however, school-choice policies in some communities have meant increased busing for whites as well as minority students. Negrón cites the example of Pinellas County (Clearwater), Fla., which has a universal-choice program allowing students to enroll in any school in the county and providing transportation if requested. "It is a cost," Negrón says. "But school districts are finding that it depends on the facts and circumstances."

Civil rights advocates counter that racial isolation imposes much more serious costs for minority students. "The consequences of segregation of African-American students in public schools — and it is increasingly true for Latino students — have been concentration of poverty, deprivation of resources and a host of other problems that do impact on the quality of education," says the Legal Defense Fund's Shaw.

Like many of the critics, Thernstrom stops short of absolute opposition to any race-conscious school policies. "I don't mind" redrawing attendance zones for racial mixing, she says, "but I don't think we should be starry-eyed about what it's going to achieve."

Michael Rosman, president of the Center for Individual Rights, says schools should try to prevent "racial isolation" in individual schools "if it is shown to have deleterious educational effects."

But Illinois Professor Anderson says school boards should take affirmative steps to "take advantage" of diversity. "We could build wonderful, intellectually rich environments where kids really do have an exchange of ideas and an exchange of cultures and come out of that with a cosmopolitan sense of culture that is unique," he says. "How can you be global," he adds, "yet at the same time so parochial?"

## Should school systems seek to promote socioeconomic integration in individual schools?

The consolidated school system in Wake County, N.C. — encompassing the rapidly growing Research Triangle Park area (near Raleigh and Durham) — made nationwide news in 2000 by dropping the use of racial guidelines in favor of socioeconomic-integration policies. The "Healthy School" assignment guidelines call for limiting individual schools to no more than 40 percent enrollment of students receiving free or reduced-price lunches or 25 percent enrollment of students performing below grade level.

Seven years later, the policies are a bragging point for the school system and exhibit No. 1 for advocates of socioeconomic integration. "Classrooms that are balanced from a diversity point of view are important to maintaining academic performance," says Michael Evans, the school system's communications director, citing the district's declining achievement gap for African-American, Hispanic and low-income students.

Some Wake County parents are not sold, however. Dave Duncan, the one-time president of the now largely inactive advocacy group Assignment by Choice, discounts the claimed academic gains by pointing to the relatively small percentage of students assigned under

| School District  *Enrollment: Percentage of whites (W), African-Americans (B), Hispanics (H), Asian-Americans (A)* |
| --- |
| **Manatee County, Fla. (** *42,000: 60% W, 20% H, 15% B, 4% other* **)** |
| District south of Tampa Bay has had limited success with a plan adopted in 2002 admitting students to schools based on maintaining socioeconomic balance: Only 10 elementary schools were within guidelines in 2005-06; among 14 schools with above-average low-income enrollment, only four showed adequate academic gains. |
| **McKinney, Tex. (** *20,000: 64% W, 21% H, 11% B, 3% other* **)** |
| Dallas suburb adopted socioeconomic-balance policy in 1995 by redrawing attendance zones; low-income students perform better on statewide tests than low-income students statewide; some opposition to longer bus rides, but plan said to have broad support. |
| **Minneapolis, Minn. (** *36,000: 41% B, 28% W, 16% H, 10% A* **)** |
| Desegregation suit settled in state court in 2000 with agreement to adopt four-year experiment to encourage socioeconomic integration; plan provides transportation for low-income students to suburban schools; also requires wealthier magnet schools in Minneapolis to set aside seats for low-income students; 2,000 low-income students attended suburban schools over four-year period; legislature voted to extend program after end of experiment. |
| **Omaha, Neb. (** *47,000: 44% W, 32% B, 21% H* **)** |
| School board adopted plan aimed at socioeconomic integration after system was declared unitary in 1999; low-income students given preference in weighted lottery for admission to magnet schools; 2006 proposal to expand plan to recently annexed neighborhoods prompted backlash in state legislature, but education groups won passage of 2007 bill to establish goal of socioeconomic diversity throughout metropolitan area. |
| **Rochester, N.Y. (** *33,000: 64% B, 22% H, 13% W* **)** |
| Managed-choice plan adopted in city in 2002 includes socioeconomic-fairness guidelines; vast majority of elementary school students (83%) are economically disadvantaged; plan seen as likely to have limited effect unless interdistrict choice program is established between city and suburbs. |
| **San Francisco, Calif. (** *55,000: 32% Asian, 22% H, 13% B, 9% W* **)** |
| Student-assignment plan adopted in 2001 replaced racial-desegregation scheme with plan aimed at socioeconomic diversity; seven-part definition includes SES (socioeconomic status), academic achievement, language, other factors; plan seen as fairly successful in balancing schools by SES, less so in producing racial diversity; district is consistently top-performing urban district in state. |
| **Wake County (Raleigh), N.C. (** *136,000: 54% W, 27% B, 10% H, 5% A* **)** |
| Guidelines adopted in 2000 replacing racial guidelines limit schools to 40% free/reduced lunch, 25% reading below grade level; policies credited with maintaining racial diversity; role in academic gains questioned; school-zone changes due to growth draw criticism from some families. |

*Sources:* Richard D. Kahlenberg, Century Foundation, "Rescuing *Brown v. Board of Education:* Profiles of Twelve School Districts Pursuing Socioeconomic School Integration," Century Foundation, June 28, 2007, www.tcf.org; news accounts.

the guidelines and the comparable academic gains statewide. The school system "used the diversity issue as a smoke screen when there is criticism or opposition to the way they do the student-assignment process," Duncan says.

As the most prominent advocate of socioeconomic integration, the Century Foundation's Kahlenberg acknowledges varied results in districts with such policies. But he strongly argues that the policy of mixing students by socioeconomic background offers educational benefits in its own right and practical advantages for districts trying to promote racial diversity without running afoul of the Supreme Court's new limits on race-based assignments.

"There's a wide body of research that the single, best thing you can do for low-income kids is to give them the opportunity to attend a middle-class school," says Kahlenberg. Despite some well-publicized exceptions, schools with "concentrated levels of poverty" tend to have more student-discipline problems, lower caliber teachers and principals and less parental involvement than predominantly middle- or upper-class schools, he explains. Socioeconomic integration, he says, results in higher academic achievement for low-income students and no adverse effect on others as long as there is "a strong core of students with middle-class background."

Kahlenberg says socioeconomic integration is also likely to produce some racial and ethnic mixing since the poverty rate among African-Americans and Latinos is higher than among whites. In educational terms, however, he says socioeconomic diversity is more valuable than racial diversity because the academic gains of mixing by class and income appear to be well established, while the claimed gains of race mixing are in dispute.

Traditional civil rights advocates like the Legal Defense Fund's Shaw do not quarrel with socioeconomic integration but insist that it is "not an adequate substitute for racial integration."

Orfield agrees that socioeconomic integration is "a good idea" but quickly adds, "You can't achieve racial integration very well by using social and economic integration."

"If you talk to districts that have relied solely on that, it doesn't reach all of the students that they need to reach," says Negrón at the school boards association.

For their part, conservatives raise fewer objections to mixing students by socioeconomic background than by race, but they worry the practice may merely be a pretext for racial classifications. "It has fewer constitutional problems," says Thernstrom. "It is less politically controversial."

"It's better than race-based student assignments," says Clegg at the Center for Equal Opportunity. "But if you're using socioeconomic status simply as a proxy for race, many of the same policy and legal problems remain."

Thernstrom is unconvinced, however, of the claimed academic benefits. "There are no proven results from it," she says. She scoffs at what she calls "the notion that if you sit next to somebody, differences [in values] are going to somehow melt away."

In any event, Clegg says he opposes either racial or socioeconomic mixing if it requires assigning students to schools distant from their homes. "Neighborhood schools are the preferable means of assignment," he says, "because you're not having to pay for busing and you're not having to put children on long bus rides, which keep them from engaging in extracurricular activities."

Kahlenberg disagrees. "I haven't heard anyone make a convincing case that from an educational perspective the best way to assign students is the place where their parents can afford to live," he says. "That's the way we do it, but there's no argument that's the best way to educate kids in our society."

From opposite perspectives, however, both Orfield and Thernstrom agree that socioeconomic integration engenders some of the same kinds of opposition that racial integration does. "You do have a lot of middle-class flight as a result," Thernstrom says. "It's not really more popular than racial integration," Orfield says.

Despite the resistance, Kahlenberg believes the policy would fulfill a fundamental goal of public education in the United States. "Most people believe at least in theory that education is the way for kids of any background to do well," he says. "As long as we have economically segregated schools, that promise is broken."

### Is the focus on diversity interfering with efforts to improve education in all schools?

As he wrapped up his legal challenge to the Louisville pupil-assignment plan before the Supreme Court, attorney Gordon depicted the case as a choice between "diversity" and "educational outcome."

"For me," Gordon told the justices during the Dec. 4 arguments, "I would use all these millions of dollars. I would reduce teacher-student ratio. I would give incentive pay to the better teachers. I would [build] more magnet schools, more traditional schools."

"We presuppose that we're going to have bad schools and good schools in this country," he continued. "I don't think we can no [sic] longer accept that."

Gordon describes himself as a civil rights liberal, but his argument parallels the views of conservatives like

Clegg. "School districts should be worrying less about the racial and ethnic mix than about improving the education that's offered at all schools," Clegg says.

"If you're just focusing on racial diversity, as it's called, for its own sake without trying to assess whether you're improving the educational outcomes," says Rosman, "then you're detracting from the overall goal of achieving educational excellence. In some instances, that's happened."

"The solution is to reduce the gap, the racial gap, the ethnic gap, the socioeconomic gap," says Thernstrom. "Then kids will be looked at as just kids without any kind of assumptions made about, you know, are they like me?"

Traditional civil rights groups and advocates insist that diversity and educational reform complement rather than conflict with each other. In any event, they say, the push for diversity is neither so strong nor so extensive as the critics contend.

"We haven't had any federal policy of promoting diversity since 1981," says Orfield, referring to the first year of Ronald Reagan's presidency. "We haven't had any new lawsuits to integrate schools for a long time. Ever since 1980, most desegregation plans have had voluntary choice and magnet schools, and almost all of them are part and parcel of educational reform plans."

John Trasviña, president and general counsel of the Mexican American Legal Defense and Educational Fund (MALDEF), calls the claimed conflict between diversity and educational quality "a diversion." Referring to educational reform, he says, "We aren't doing that either. It's always easy to say let's address some other issue. When it comes to do that, it's not done."

Diversity advocates dispute critics' suggestion that racial or economic integration has been pursued solely for its own sake with no attention to improving educational quality. "I don't think anybody ever thought that school integration by itself was a sufficient policy," Orfield says.

"The whole reason for economic integration is to promote academic achievement and raise the quality of schooling," says Kahlenberg. "No one has figured out how to make separate schools for rich and poor work well, certainly not for poor kids."

Orfield and Kahlenberg also dismiss concerns that the transportation costs entailed in some diversity plans take scarce dollars from other, more promising school-improvement initiatives. "We've spent billions and billions of dollars on low-income schools, which hasn't produced a lot of results," Kahlenberg says.

Orfield is even blunter about recent efforts to reduce the racial gap. "It's been a failure," he says. Desegregation and anti-poverty programs of the 1960s and '70s did narrow the racial-achievement gap, Orfield writes in the recent UCLA Civil Rights Project report. But he says "most studies" find that President Bush's No Child Left Behind law — which specifically calls for narrowing the achievement gap between white and minority pupils — has had "no impact" on the disparities so far.[8]

From opposite perspectives, Thernstrom and Trasviña lay out demanding agendas for schools to try to close the racial gap. "I want more learning going on," says Thernstrom. "You need really good schools. The day should be longer, the teachers should be better, the principals should have more authority.

"Our kids aren't learning enough in school," she continues. "That will level the playing field."

"We clearly need to improve the quality of our schools," says Trasviña. He calls for steps to reduce the dropout rate and to channel more students into so-called STEM courses (science, technology, engineering and math). But diversity helps, not hurts reform efforts, he says.

"While it is true that simply putting children of different backgrounds in seats in the same classroom does not necessarily improve the classroom experience by itself, [diversity] adds to it," Trasviña says. "And it adds to the political will to make sure that people understand that these are our schools."

## BACKGROUND

### The "Common School"

The idea of free, universal public education has been espoused in the United States since the Revolutionary Era and still holds a central place in American thought as a tool for personal development and social cohesion. But the ideal of equal educational opportunity for all has never obtained in practice. Even as education became more nearly universal in the 20th century, African-Americans and other racial and ethnic minorities faced blatant discrimination that was only partly alleviated by landmark court rulings outlawing legally mandated segregation.[9]

George Washington and Thomas Jefferson were among the nation's early leaders to call in general terms for mass

## CHRONOLOGY

**Before 1950** *Free, universal public education is enshrined as American ideal and advances in practice, but African-Americans, Hispanics and Asian-Americans are consigned to separate and unequal schools in much of the country.*

**1950s-1960s** *Racial segregation in public schools is ruled unconstitutional, but desegregation is slow.*

**1954, 1955** Supreme Court's unanimous decision in *Brown v. Board of Education* (1954) outlaws mandatory racial segregation in public schools; a year later court says school districts must dismantle dual systems "with all deliberate speed" (*Brown II*). "Massive resistance" in South stalls integration.

**1964, 1965** Civil Rights Act of 1964 authorizes Justice Department to file school-desegregation suits; Title I of Elementary and Secondary Education Act provides targeted aid to school districts for low-income students.

**1968** Supreme Court tells school districts to develop plans to dismantle dual systems "now."

**1970s-1980s** *Busing upheld as desegregation tool but draws strong protests in North and West as well as South; Supreme Court, Justice Department withdraw from desegregation cases.*

**1971** Supreme Court unanimously upholds federal courts' power to order crosstown busing to desegregate schools.

**1973** Supreme Court rejects federal constitutional right to equal school funding; one month later, New Jersey supreme court is first to sustain funding-equity suit under state constitution.

**1974** U.S. Supreme Court, 5-4, bars court-ordered desegregation between inner cities and suburbs; decision is first in series of closely divided rulings that limit desegregation remedies.

**1983** U.S. Department of Education report "A Nation at Risk" paints critical picture of rising mediocrity in U.S. schools, shifts agenda away from equity issues.

**1990s** *Racial isolation increases for African-Americans, Latinos; "reverse discrimination" suits by white students backed in some federal courts, fail in others.*

**1991** LaCrosse, Wis., becomes first school district to aim to balance enrollment by students' income status: "socioeconomic integration."

**1995** Supreme Court signals federal courts to wrap up desegregation cases; lower courts respond by generally granting "unitary" status to school systems seeking to be freed from desegregation orders.

**1998, 1999** Federal appeals courts in Boston, Richmond, Va., bar racial preferences in public school admission.

**2000-2007** *Socioeconomic integration advances; Latinos become largest ethnic minority; Supreme Court ruling bars racial classifications in pupil assignments.*

**2000** Wake County (Raleigh), N.C., becomes largest school district to try socioeconomic integration.

**2001** President George W. Bush wins congressional approval of No Child Left Behind Act, requiring school districts to meet achievement benchmarks, including closing racial gap.

**2001-2005** White families challenge racial-diversity plans in Seattle and Louisville, Ky; federal courts back school districts, ruling plans are "narrowly tailored" to achieve "compelling" interest in diversity.

**2005, 2006** Bush nominates John G. Roberts Jr. and Samuel A. Alito Jr. to Supreme Court; both win Senate confirmation, strengthening conservative majority on court.

**2007** Supreme Court ruling in Louisville and Seattle cases limits use of race in pupil assignments, but five justices say race-neutral measures can be used to promote compelling interest in diversity; school boards vow to try to maintain racial diversity; advocates push socioeconomic integration on legal, political grounds.

## 2008

**February 23** — Federal judge lifts 1974 desegregation order for Mark Twain Intermediate School in Brooklyn, N.Y., effectively eliminating racial quotas.

**November 4** — Nebraska votes to ban affirmative action; Colorado rejects a proposed ban.

## 2009

**June 11** — California Supreme Court rejects challenge to the Berkeley Unified School District's policy of considering the racial composition of students' neighborhoods in deciding where pupils will enroll.

## 2010

**March 8** — Education Secretary Arne Duncan speaks on the state of minorities in education in Selma, Ala.

**March 26** — Department of Justice signs consent agreement with Monroe School District in Louisiana to level offerings of advanced-placement and gifted-and-talented courses with predominantly white and predominantly black schools.

**March 29** — Delaware and Tennessee named first winners of Department of Education's Race to the Top competition, designed to spur reforms in state and local K-12 education.

**June 20** — Boston College launches $20 million program to improve urban education and better prepare low-income students from the area for college.

**July 20** — Nineteen arrested in protest of Wake County (Raleigh, N.C.) School Board's decision to dismantle a decade-old policy of busing students to achieve diversity.

---

public education, but the educational "system" of the early 19th century consisted of private academies, rural district schools and a handful of "charity" schools in cities. Horace Mann, the so-called father of American public education, used his appointment as Massachusetts' first commissioner of education in 1837 to advocate the "common school" — publicly supported and open to all. As University of Wisconsin educational historian William Reese explains, Mann saw education as a way to restore social harmony at a time of social tensions between rich and poor and between native-born and immigrants. Others saw the same connection. His fellow New Englander Alpheus Packard wrote in the 1840s of the "sons of wealth and poverty" gaining mutual respect by sitting side by side in a public school.[10]

Abolitionist Mann's vision had no practical meaning, however, for African-American slaves before the Civil War and only limited significance for their descendants for decades after slavery was abolished. Both before and after the Civil War, the vast majority of African-Americans "lived in states that were openly and explicitly opposed to their education," according to the University of Illinois' Anderson.

After emancipation slaves who had learned to read and write became teachers in rudimentary schools, aided by Northern missionaries and philanthropists and some sympathetic white Southerners. With the end of Reconstruction, however, Southern leaders "pushed back the gains that had been made," Anderson says. In a racially segregated system in the early 20th century, per capita spending for black pupils in the South amounted to one-fourth to one-half of the amount spent on whites.[11]

Education was becoming nearly universal for white Americans, even as racial segregation became entrenched for African-Americans and, in many places, for Mexican- and Asian-Americans.[12] Elementary school attendance was nearly universal by the 1920s. High schools — once viewed as fairly selective institutions — began doubling in enrollment each decade after 1890 thanks to a declining market for child labor and the growing enforcement of new compulsory education laws. Secondary school enrollment increased from 50 percent of 14-17-year-olds in 1920 to nearly 95 percent of that age group by the mid-1970s. Meanwhile, the average school year was also

# "Tracking" Leads to Racial Separation in Classes

*But grouping students by ability has wide support.*

Ballard High School sits on a spacious campus in an overwhelmingly white suburban neighborhood in the eastern end of Jefferson County, Ky. As part of Jefferson County Public Schools' racial balance policies, however, Ballard's attendance zone includes neighborhoods on the opposite side of the county in Louisville's predominantly African-American West End section.

By drawing students from the West End, the school achieved around 25 percent black enrollment in the 2006-07 academic year. But despite the measure of racial balance in overall enrollment, Ballard students say blacks and whites are less than fully integrated inside. "Kids naturally separate," remarks Ben Gravel, a white 12th-grader, as he arrives at school on Aug. 13 for the opening of a new school year.

At Ballard — and in schools around the country — the racial separation is especially pronounced in the classroom itself. African-American students are disproportionately enrolled in less challenging, "low-track" classes and under-represented in higher-track classes, such as advanced placement (AP) courses and international baccalaureate (IB) programs. In 2006, for example, African-Americans comprised about 13 percent of graduating high school seniors but only 6 percent of the total number of students who took advanced placement exams administered by the College Board.[1]

The widespread practice of tracking — or "ability grouping" as supporters prefer to call it — has been a contentious issue within education circles for more than two decades. "Detracking" advocates have had occasional success in pushing reforms, but the practice has persisted — in part because of strong resistance from parents of students enrolled in higher-track courses.[2]

Supporters say the practice matches curricular offerings to students' abilities and achievement level. "It doesn't make sense to the average person that you would put a non-reader in the same English classroom as some kid who's reading Proust," says Tom Loveless, director of the Brown Center on Educational Policy at the Brookings Institution in Washington.

Critics say the practice simply keeps already-disadvantaged students on a path to lower academic achievement. "If you have classes that are structured to give kids less of a challenge, those kids tend to fall farther behind," says Kevin Welner, an associate professor at the University of Colorado's School of Education in Boulder.

Civil rights advocates say the enrollment patterns reflect what they call "segregation by tracking." In her critique of the practice, Jeannie Oakes, director of urban schooling at UCLA's Graduate School of Education and Information Studies, cited research evidence indicating that African-American and Latino students were more likely to be assigned to low-track courses than white students even when they had comparable abilities or test scores.[3]

increasing — from 144 days in 1900 to 178 days in 1950. And per capita investment in education rose during the same period from 1.2 percent of national income to 2 percent.

The Supreme Court's 1954 decision in *Brown* outlawing racial segregation in public schools capped a half-century-long campaign by the NAACP to gain a measure of equal educational opportunity for African-Americans.[13] The legal campaign — directed by the future Supreme Court justice, Thurgood Marshall — was waged at a deliberate pace even as many black students and families were agitating for better schools at the local level. The eventual decision seemed far from inevitable beforehand.

Only after 1950 did the NAACP decide to ask the court to abolish segregation rather than try to equalize the separate school systems. And the justices were closely divided after the first round of arguments in 1952; they joined in the unanimous ruling in 1954 only after a second round of arguments and shrewd management of the case by the new chief justice, Earl Warren.*

---

*California, home to the nation's largest concentration of Asian-Americans and the secondlargest concentration of Mexican-Americans after Texas, had abolished racial segregation in schools by law in 1947.

"I wouldn't use the phrase 'segregation by tracking.' A lot of it is self-tracking," counters Abigail Thernstrom, a senior fellow at the conservative Manhattan Institute and co-author of a book on the educational gap between white and minority students. "Is it terrible that we have so few Latino and black students who are prepared to take the most educationally rigorous courses?" she adds. "Of course, it's terrible."

Welner acknowledges minority students often choose low-track courses, but faults school systems instead of the students. Minority parents and students often lack the information needed to understand the different course offerings, he says. And students "sometimes don't want to be the only minority in the high-track class," he says.

Loveless acknowledges the critics' complaints about low-track classes, but says the solution is to reform not to abolish them. "Let's fix the low-track classes," he says. Despite the critics' doubts, he says many private, charter and parochial schools have developed low-track curricula that more effectively challenge students than those often found in public schools.

"If we know how to create a high-track class, why would we then create a separate set of classes that don't have those opportunities?" Welner asks. "Why would we let students opt for a lesser education?"

Loveless says under a random-assignment system, high-achieving students "would lose quite a bit," middle-range students "would lose a bit" and lowest-achieving students "would probably benefit a little bit" — mainly by reducing the concentration of students with behavioral issues in low-track classes.

Welner disagrees that high-achieving students are necessarily harmed by reforms. "Good detracking doesn't take

Sixth-graders study science as part of the international baccalaureate curriculum at Harbour Pointe Middle School in Mukilteo, Wash.

anything away from these kids," he says. "The high achievers are not only holding their own but are doing better after the reform."

Despite the recurrent clashes at the local level, Loveless predicts that tracking will continue to be a widespread practice. "Polls are very clear," he says. "Parents, teachers and students favor ability grouping. Those are three important constituency groups."

---

[1]College Board, "Advanced Placement: Report to the Nation 2006," p. 11 (www.collegeboard.com). For background, see Marcia Clemmitt, "AP and IB Programs," *CQ Researcher*, March 3, 2006, pp. 193-216.

[2]For opposing views, see Tom Loveless, *The Tracking Wars: State Reform Meets School Policy* (1999); Jeannie Oakes, *Keeping Track: How Schools Structure Inequality* (2d ed.), 2005.

[3]*Ibid.*, pp. 230-231.

---

The high court's "remedial" decision one year later in *Brown II* directed school districts to desegregate "with all deliberate speed." Many Southern politicians lent support to a campaign of "massive resistance" to the ruling by diehard segregationists. A decade after *Brown*, fewer than 5 percent of black students in the South were attending majority-white schools; more than three-fourths were attending schools with 90 percent minority enrollment.[14] In 1968, an evidently impatient Supreme Court declared that school districts had to develop plans to dismantle dual systems that promised "realistically" to work — and to work "now." Three years later, a new chief justice, Warren E. Burger, led a unanimous court in upholding

the authority of local federal courts to order school districts to use cross-neighborhood busing as part of a desegregation plan.[15]

### "Elusive" Equality

The campaign to desegregate schools stimulated broader efforts in the late 20th century to equalize educational opportunity at national, state and local levels. Initially, desegregation advanced in the South and to a lesser extent in other regions. But integration eventually stalled in the face of white opposition to busing, ambivalence among blacks and Supreme Court decisions easing pressure on

## More Blacks and Latinos Attend Poorest Schools

The vast majority (79 percent) of white students attend schools where less than half the student body is poor, compared with 37 percent of black students and 36 percent of Hispanics. For schools where at least 91 percent of the students are poor, whites made up just 1 percent of the student body compared with 13 and 15 percent, respectively, for blacks and Hispanics.

### Distribution of Students in Public Schools by Percentage Who Are Poor, 2005-2006

| Percent Poor | Percentage of each race | | | | |
|---|---|---|---|---|---|
| | White | Black | Latino | Asian | American Indian |
| 0-10% | 20 | 5 | 7 | 23 | 17 |
| 11-20% | 17 | 5 | 5 | 14 | 6 |
| 21-30% | 16 | 7 | 7 | 12 | 8 |
| 31-40% | 14 | 9 | 8 | 11 | 9 |
| 41-50% | 12 | 11 | 9 | 9 | 11 |
| 51-60% | 9 | 11 | 10 | 8 | 11 |
| 61-70% | 6 | 12 | 11 | 6 | 11 |
| 71-80% | 3 | 13 | 12 | 6 | 10 |
| 81-90% | 2 | 14 | 14 | 6 | 8 |
| 91-100% | 1 | 13 | 15 | 4 | 9 |

* Totals may not add up to 100 due to rounding.

*Source:* Gary Orfield and Chungmei Lee, "Historic Reversals, Accelerating Resegregation, and the Need for New Integration Strategies," Civil Rights Project, UCLA, August 2007

### Total number of students (in millions)

| | |
|---|---|
| White | 28 |
| Black | 8 |
| Latino | 10 |
| Asian | 2 |
| American Indian | 1 |

suburban districts. Three years later, the court essentially freed school districts from any obligation to prevent resegregation after adopting a racially neutral assignment plan. The decisions coincided with widespread opposition to busing for racial balance among white families in many communities, most dramatically in Boston in the 1970s, where police escorts were needed for buses taking pupils from predominantly black Roxbury to predominantly white South Boston.

African-American students and families, meanwhile, had mixed reactions to desegregation generally and busing in particular, according to Professor Anderson. In many districts, desegregation meant the closing or transformation of historically black schools that had provided a good education for many students. In the South, desegregation also often meant the loss of black principals and teachers. And busing was a "one-way street" for African-Americans: most plans entailed the transportation of black students away from their neighborhoods to a mixed reception at best in predominantly white communities.

From the start, the NAACP and other civil rights groups had viewed desegregation not only as a goal in its own right but also — and perhaps more importantly — as an instrument to equalize educational opportunities for black and white pupils. In the heady days of the civil rights era, Congress had put educational equality on the national agenda in 1965 by passing a law as part of President Lyndon B. Johnson's "war on poverty" to provide federal aid targeted to poor children.[17] By the end of the century, however, Title I of the Elementary and Secondary Education Act was seen as having produced mixed results at best — in part because allocation formulas shaped by the realities of congressional politics directed much of the money to relatively well-to-do suburban districts.

local school districts to take affirmative steps to mix white and black students. School funding reform efforts produced some results, but as the 21st century began educational equality remained — in Professor Reese's word — "elusive."[16]

The Supreme Court's unanimity in school race cases broke down in the 1970s, and a continuing succession of closely divided decisions reduced districts' obligations to develop effective integration plans. In one of the most important rulings, the justices in 1974 divided 5-4 in a case from Detroit to bar court-ordered desegregation between predominantly black inner cities and predominantly white

# Do Racial Policies Affect Academic Achievement?

*Most studies find beneficial effects from integration.*

When the Supreme Court outlawed racial segregation in schools in 1954, it relied heavily on research by the African-American psychologist Kenneth Clark purporting to show that attending all-black schools hurt black students' self-esteem. Over time, the court's reliance on Clark's study drew many critics, who questioned both the research and its prominent use in a legal ruling.

A half-century later, as they considered challenges to racial-diversity plans in Seattle and Louisville, Ky., the justices were deluged with sometimes conflicting research studies on the effects of racial policies on educational achievement. Among 64 friend-of-the-court briefs, nearly half — 27 — cited social science research. Most found beneficial effects from racial integration, but a minority questioned those claims.

The National Academy of Education, a select group of education scholars, created a seven-member committee to evaluate the various studies cited in the various briefs. Here are the committee's major conclusions from the research, released on June 29 — one day after the court found the school districts' plans unconstitutional:

**Academic achievement.** White students are not hurt by desegregation efforts or adjustments in racial composition of schools. African-American student achievement is enhanced by less segregated schooling, although the magnitude of the influence is quite variable. The positive effects for African-American students tend to be larger in the earlier grades.

**Near-term intergroup relations.** Racially diverse schools and classrooms will not guarantee improved intergroup relations, but are likely to be constructive. The research identifies conditions that need to be present in order for diversity to have a positive effect and suggests steps schools can take to realize the potential for improvement.

**Long-term effects of school desegregation.** Experience in desegregated schools increases the likelihood over time of greater tolerance and better intergroup relations among adults of different racial groups.

**The critical-mass question.** Racial diversity can avoid or mitigate harms caused by racial isolation, such as tokenism and stereotyping, particularly when accompanied by an otherwise beneficial school environment. Some briefs suggest a minimum African-American enrollment of 15 percent to 30 percent to avoid these harms, but the research does not support specifying any particular percentage.

**Race-neutral alternatives.** No race-neutral policy is as effective as race-conscious policies for achieving racial diversity. Socioeconomic integration is likely to marginally reduce racial isolation and may have other benefits. School choice generally and magnet schools in particular have some potential to reduce racial isolation, but could also increase segregation.

*Source*: Robert L. Linn and Kevin G. Welner (eds.), "Race-Conscious Policies for Assigning Students to Schools: Social Science Research and the Supreme Court Cases," National Academy of Education, June 29, 2007 (www.naeducation.org/Meredith_Report.pdf).

Meanwhile, advocates of educational equity had turned to the courts to try to reduce funding disparities between school districts — with mixed results.[18] The Supreme Court ruled in 1973 that funding disparities between districts did not violate the federal Constitution. One month later, however, the New Jersey Supreme Court became the first state tribunal to find differential school funding to run afoul of a state constitutional provision. Over the next three decades, school funding suits resulted in court rulings in at least 19 states finding constitutional violations and ordering reforms. But funding disparities persisted. In a wide-ranging survey in 1998, *Education Week* gave 16 states a grade of C- or below on educational equity between school districts.[19]

At the same time, school policymakers were focusing on clamorous calls to improve educational quality stimulated by the publication in 1983 of a report by the Reagan administration's Department of Education sharply criticizing what was depicted as rising mediocrity in U.S. schools. The debate generated by "A Nation at Risk" brought forth all manner of proposals for imposing educational standards, revising curricula or introducing competition within public school systems or between public and private schools. The debate diverted policymakers' attention to some extent from diversity issues and led many white parents to worry more about their own children's education than about educational equity or diversity.[20]

Minnijean Brown, 15, one of the Little Rock Nine, arrives at Central High School on Sept. 25, 1957, guarded by soldiers sent by President Dwight. D. Eisenhower. Brown and eight other African-American students desegregated the Arkansas school three years after the Supreme Court's landmark *Brown v. Board* of *Education* ruling.

By the end of the 1990s, federal courts were all but out of the desegregation business, and racial isolation — "resegregation" to civil rights advocates — was on the rise. In a trio of cases in 1991, 1993 and 1995, the Supreme Court gave federal courts unmistakable signals to withdraw from superintending desegregation plans. School districts that sought to be declared "unitary" — or no longer dual in nature — and freed from desegregation decrees, like Jefferson County, invariably succeeded. By 2001, at least two-thirds of black students and at least half of Latino students nationwide were enrolled in predominantly minority schools. And after narrowing in the 1980s, the educational-testing gaps between white and black students began to widen again in the 1990s. In 2000, the typical black student scored below about 75 percent of white students on most standardized tests.[21]

## "Diversity" Challenged

Even as courts reduced the pressure on school districts to desegregate, hundreds of school systems adopted voluntary measures aimed at mixing students of different racial and ethnic backgrounds. Some plans that made explicit use of race in pupil assignments drew legal challenges from white families as "reverse discrimination." Meanwhile, several dozen school systems were adopting — and achieving some success with — diversity plans tied to socioeconomic status instead of race. Support for socioeconomic integration appeared to increase after the Supreme Court's June 28 decision in the Seattle and Louisville cases restricting the

use of race in pupil assignments but permitting race-neutral policies to achieve diversity in the classroom.

School boards that voluntarily sought to achieve racial and ethnic mixing claimed that the policies generally improved education for all students while benefiting disadvantaged minorities and promoting broad political support for the schools. Many plans — like those in Seattle and Louisville — explicitly considered race in some pupil assignments, and several drew legal challenges. In November 1998 the federal appeals court in Boston struck down the use of racial preferences for blacks and Hispanics for admission to the prestigious Boston Latin School. Then in fall 1999, the federal appeals court in Richmond, Va., ruled in favor of white families challenging race-based policies in two districts in the Washington, D.C., suburbs. The rulings struck down a weighted lottery that advantaged blacks and Hispanics in Arlington County, Va., and a transfer policy in Montgomery County, Md., that limited students from changing schools in order to maintain racial balance.[22]

The idea of socioeconomic integration first gained national attention when the midsized town of La Crosse, Wis., redrew attendance zones in the early 1990s to shift students from an overcrowded, predominantly affluent high school to the town's second high school in the blue-collar section with a growing Hmong population. In Kahlenberg's account, the plan survived concerted political opposition, produced measurable educational progress and now enjoys widespread support. Cambridge, Mass., substituted socioeconomic integration policies for racial busing in 1999 after the federal appeals court ruling in the Boston Latin case. Wake County, N.C., similarly dropped its racial balancing plan in 2000 in favor of an assignment plan tied to free or reduced-lunch status to comply with the rulings by the Richmond-based appeals court in the Arlington and Montgomery County cases. By 2003, Kahlenberg claimed some 500,000 students nationwide were enrolled in school systems that used economic status as a factor in pupil assignments.[23]

In the main, however, school districts that had adopted racial balancing plans stuck with them despite legal challenges. Seattle adopted its "open choice" plan in 1998 — some two decades after it had become the largest school district in the nation to voluntarily adopt a racial busing plan. The ad hoc group Parents Involved in Community Schools filed its suit challenging the use of race as a "tiebreaker" in pupil assignments in July 2000. That same year, Jefferson County Public Schools adopted its controlled choice plan after a federal judge freed the system from a desegregation decree dating to 1975. Parent Crystal Meredith challenged the race-based assignments in April 2003. Federal district judges upheld the plans — in April 2001 in the Seattle case and in June 2004 in the Jefferson County case. The 4th U.S. Circuit Court of Appeals in Cincinnati then upheld the Jefferson County plan in July 2005. The Seattle case followed a more complicated appellate route. The school district suspended the plan after an initial setback in 2002, but eventually the 9th U.S. Circuit Court of Appeals in San Francisco upheld the plan in October 2005.

The Supreme Court's decision to hear the two cases immediately raised fears among civil rights advocates that the conservative majority fortified by President George W. Bush's appointments of Chief Justice Roberts and Justice Samuel A. Alito Jr. would strike down the plans. Questions by Roberts and Alito during arguments on Dec. 4, 2006, left little doubt about their positions. The high-drama announcement of the decision on June 28 lasted nearly 45 minutes with Roberts, Kennedy and Breyer each delivering lengthy summaries of his opinion from the bench.

"The way to stop discrimination on the basis of race," Roberts declared as he neared his conclusion, "is to stop discriminating on the basis of race."

Breyer was equally forceful in his dissent. "This is a decision that the court and this nation will come to regret," he said.

Almost immediately, however, Kennedy's pivotal concurrence began to draw the closest scrutiny as advocates and observers tried to discern what alternatives remained for school boards to use in engineering racial diversity. The National School Boards Association urged local boards to continue seeking diversity through "careful race-conscious policies." Administrators in Seattle and Louisville said they planned to do just that.

But Clegg of the Center for Equal Opportunity said school systems would be better off to drop racial classifications. "At the end of the day, these two plans didn't pass muster," he said. "And the impact will be to persuade other school districts that this is not a good idea."[24]

## CURRENT SITUATION

### "Resegregation" Seen

The Louisville and Seattle school systems are in the opening weeks of a new academic year, with few immediate effects from the Supreme Court decision invalidating their previous pupil-assignment plans. Officials in both districts are working on new pupil-assignment plans to put into effect starting in fall 2009, with racial diversity still a goal but race- or ethnic-based placements no longer permitted.

Both school systems, however, are reporting what civil rights advocates call "resegregation" — higher percentages of African-American students in predominantly minority schools. Critics of racial-diversity policies object to the term, arguing that segregation refers only to legally enforced separation of the races. Whatever term is used, a new report documents a national trend of "steadily increasing separation" in public schools between whites and the country's two largest minority groups: Latinos and African-Americans.

The report by the UCLA Civil Rights Project shows, for example, that the percentage of black students in majority-white schools rose from virtually zero in 1954 to a peak of 43.5 percent in 1988 before beginning a steady decline. In 2005 — the most recent year available — 27 percent of black students attended majority-white schools.

Meanwhile, the proportion of African-Americans attending majority-minority schools has been slowly increasing over the past two decades — reversing gains in integration in the 1960s and '70s — while the percentage of Latino students in majority-minority schools has grown steadily since the 1960s. In 2005, 73 percent of black students were in majority-minority schools, and more than one-third — 38 percent — were in "intensely segregated" schools with 90 to 100 percent minority enrollment. For Latinos, 78 percent of students were in majority-minority schools.

By contrast, Asian-Americans are described in the report as "the most integrated" ethnic group in public schools. In 2005, the average Asian student attended a school with 44 percent white enrollment — compared to 30 percent white enrollment for the average black student and 27 percent white enrollment for the average Latino. The report attributed the higher integration for Asians to greater residential integration and relatively small numbers outside the West.

Seattle was already experiencing increasing racial isolation after suspending its previous placement plan, which included race as one "tiebreaker" in pupil assignments. "There has been a decline in racial diversity since suspension of the plan," says Seattle Public Schools spokeswoman Patti Spencer.

**AT ISSUE**

# Is racial diversity in the classroom essential to a good education?

 **YES** Janet W. Schofield
*Professor of Psychology, University of Pittsburgh*

 **NO** Abigail Thernstrom
*Senior Fellow, Manhattan Institute*
*Co-author,* No Excuses: Closing the Racial Gap in Learning

Written for *CQ Researcher,* September 2007

Written for *CQ Researcher,* September 2007

Education in a democratic society serves three basic purposes. It provides students with workforce skills, prepares them to function as thoughtful and informed citizens in a cohesive country and enriches their lives by awakening them to new knowledge, perspectives and possibilities. Racial diversity in schools and classrooms enhances the attainment of each of these goals.

The ability to work effectively with individuals from diverse backgrounds is a fundamental workplace skill, as the well-known report "What Work Requires of Schools," issued by President George H.W. Bush's administration, points out. Yet, many students never develop this skill because our country's neighborhoods, social institutions and religious organizations are often highly segregated. Racially diverse schools provide a milieu essential to the development of this crucial skill.

Racially diverse schools also have a vital role to play in developing fair-minded citizens and in promoting social cohesion. Research demonstrates that in-school contact with individuals from different backgrounds typically reduces prejudice, a fundamentally important outcome in our increasingly diverse society. In addition, students who attend diverse schools are more likely than others to choose diverse work and residential settings as adults, thus promoting social cohesion.

Racially diverse schools also enrich students' understanding and expand their perspectives by placing them in contact with others whose views and life experiences may be very different. Just as visiting a foreign country is a much richer and more powerful experience than reading about it, interacting with students from different backgrounds brings their perspectives and experiences alive in a way not otherwise possible.

Even individuals who discount the arguments above must acknowledge that heavily segregated minority schools disadvantage the very students most in need of an excellent educational environment. Such schools typically have relatively impoverished curricular offerings, great difficulty recruiting experienced teachers and high teacher-turnover rates, all of which may help to explain why research suggests that attending such schools typically undermines students' achievement relative to similar peers in more diverse schools.

Racial diversity in and of itself does not guarantee a good education, but as a recent report by the National Academy of Education suggests, it creates preconditions conducive to it. In our increasingly diverse democracy, the educational cost of segregated schools is too high for majority and minority students alike.

Racially diverse classrooms are desirable — of course. But are they essential to a good education? Absolutely not. If they were, big-city school districts would be stuck providing lousy educations for America's most disadvantaged children into the indefinite future. A large majority of students in 26 out of the 27 central-city districts with a public school population of at least 60,000 are non-white. The white proportion in these districts averages 16 percent. Thus, big-city schools will not be racially "diverse" unless we start flying white kids from Utah into, say, Detroit.

Or rather, they will not be racially "diverse" according to the Seattle school board's definition in the racial balancing plan the Supreme Court condemned last term. Seattle had divided students into only two racial groups: white and non-white. If schools were half-Asian, half-white, that was fine; if they were 30 percent white with the rest Asian, they weren't sufficiently "diverse," and educational quality would be somehow lacking.

What racial stereotyping! Do all non-white students express the same non-white views — with all white students having a "white" outlook? In fact, why is racial diversity the only kind that counts for those concerned about the group clustering in certain schools? What about a social class or religious mix?

And on the subject of racial stereotyping, do we really want to embrace the ugly assumption that black kids are incapable of learning unless they're hanging around some white magic? Good inner-city schools across the country are teaching the children who walk through the door. In excellent schools, if every one of the students is black — reflecting the demography of the neighborhood — the expectations for educational excellence do not change. And happily, there are no compelling studies showing enormous positive gains for black students when they attend schools with large numbers of whites.

Good education is not confined to academic learning. But there is no evidence that schools engaging in coercive racial mixing build a lifelong desire to "socialize with people of different races," as Seattle assumed. Visit a school lunchroom! Racial and ethnic clustering will be very much in evidence.

Those who insist school districts should turn themselves inside out to engineer racial diversity haven't a clue as to the limits of social policy. And they demean the capacity of non-Asian minority kids to learn, whatever the color of the kid in the seat next to them.

In Louisville, nine schools now have African-American enrollment above the previous guideline limit of 50 percent — most of them in predominantly black neighborhoods in Louisville's West End or the heavily black areas in southwestern Jefferson County. Black enrollment in some schools in the predominantly white East End has declined, though not below the minimum figure of 15 percent in the previous guidelines.

The 15/50 guidelines remain "a goal," according to Student Placement Director Todd. "We're trying to prevent as much slippage as possible."

In Seattle, outgoing Superintendent Raj Manhas told reporters after the Supreme Court ruling that the school district would look at "all options available to us" to try to preserve racial diversity in the schools.[25] The new superintendent, Maria Goodloe-Johnson, is an African-American who was sharply critical of racial policies in her previous position as superintendent in Charleston, S.C. Since taking office in Seattle in July, however, Goodloe-Johnson has not addressed racial balance, according to Spencer.[26]

Opponents of the race-based policies say school districts should refocus their efforts. "Where school districts should focus is on education standards, not creating a specific racial mix of students," says Sharon Browne, a staff attorney with the Pacific Legal Foundation, the conservative public interest law firm that supported the legal challenges in Louisville and Seattle.

"The guidelines are gone," says attorney Gordon in Louisville. "They're past tense."

In Seattle, Kathleen Brose, the longtime school activist who founded Parents Involved in Community Schools to challenge the use of race for high school placements, says diversity is "important," but parental choice is more important. "The school district has been so focused on race," she adds, "that, frankly, I think they forgot about academics."

## Legal Options Eyed

School boards around the country are re-examining their legal options for promoting diversity. At the same time, they are bracing for new legal challenges to their diversity plans that, so far, have not materialized.

The National School Boards Association plans to provide local boards with advisories on what policies can be used under the Supreme Court's decision to promote

racial balance. But General Counsel Negrón expects few changes as a result of the ruling.

"School districts are not going to be changing their policies drastically to the extent that they will be abandoning their choices of diversity or integration as their goal, if that's what they've chosen to do," Negrón says. "School districts are going to comply with the law as they understand it. And there's a lot of room in Justice Kennedy's concurrence for school districts to be creative and innovative."

Barring any consideration of race, Negrón adds, "was just not what the decision stood for."

Pacific Legal Foundation attorney Browne, however, worries that school districts are not complying with the ruling. "We are very disappointed that there are school districts who are ignoring the decision by the U.S. Supreme Court and continuing to use race [in pupil assignments]," she says.

Browne says school districts should have begun developing contingency plans for assigning students on a non-racial basis after the oral arguments in the Seattle and Louisville cases in December indicated the court would find both plans unconstitutional.

The Louisville and Seattle cases themselves are still pending in lower federal courts, with winning lawyers in both cases asking the courts to order the school boards to pay attorneys' fees.

In Seattle, the firm of Davis Wright Tremaine is seeking $1.8 million in attorneys' fees despite having previously said that it was handling the parents' case pro bono — for free. "Congress specifically and explicitly wrote into the law that if the government is found to have violated citizens' civil rights, then the prevailing party should seek fee recovery," explained Mark Usellis, a spokesman for the firm. The school system reported spending $434,000 in legal fees on the case.[27]

Louisville solo practitioner Gordon is asking to be paid $200 per hour for the "hundreds of hours" he devoted to the case plus a bonus for the national impact of the case. Without specifying a figure, he also wants to be reimbursed for spending his own money on expenses and court costs. Meanwhile, plaintiff Crystal Meredith is asking for $125,000 in damages, which she attributes to lost wages, invasion of privacy and emotional distress.[28]

Gordon says he received several complaints from parents whose applications for transfers for their children had been denied on the basis of limited capacity at the school they had chosen. Gordon says he suspected school officials were actually denying the transfers on racial grounds, but the MacNeals' case was the only "smoking gun" he found.

The Pacific Legal Foundation is following up on "many inquiries" received from parents since the Supreme Court ruling, according to Browne, but no new cases have been filed. She declined to say where the complaints originated. The foundation has suits pending in California courts against the Los Angeles and Berkeley school districts over race-based policies.

If any new legal challenges are filed, Negrón expects federal courts will defer to local school boards' decisions, for the most part. The [Supreme Court] didn't tell us exactly what to do," he explains. "School districts will be trying their best to come up with something that meets the requirements of the law and at the same time meets their educational interest in regard to diversity."

## OUTLOOK:

### "Minimal Impact"?

In striking down the Seattle and Jefferson County racial-balance plans, Chief Justice Roberts cited figures from the two school districts showing that the policies actually affected relatively few students — only 52 pupils in Seattle and no more than 3 percent of the pupil assignments in Jefferson County. The "minimal impact," he wrote, "casts doubt on the necessity of using racial classifications."

Writing for the dissenters, however, Justice Breyer cast the stakes in broader terms by citing the growing percentage of black students in majority non-white schools nationwide. The Louisville and Seattle school boards, Breyer said, were asking to be able to continue using tools "to rid their schools of racial segregation." The plurality opinion, he concluded, was "wrong" to deny the school boards' "modest request."

Two months after the ruling, civil rights advocates are continuing to voice grave concerns that the decision will hasten what they call the resegregation of public schools nationwide. "We're going to have a further increase in segregation of American schools," says UCLA's Orfield. "School districts are going to have to jump through a whole series of hoops if they want to have some modest degree of integration."

Legal Defense Fund President Shaw fears new challenges not only to pupil-assignment plans but also to mentoring and scholarship programs specifically targeting racial minorities. "Our adversaries are not going to go away," says Shaw. "They're going to continue to attack race-conscious efforts to address racial inequality."

Opponents of racial-balance plans either discount the fears of increased racial isolation or minimize the harms of the trend if it materializes.

"I don't think there will be dramatic consequences from these decisions," says Rosman of the Center for Individual Rights. School systems with an interest in racial diversity "will find a way to do that legally," he says. "For schools that use race explicitly, it will still be a contentious matter."

"There's going to be less and less focus on achieving politically correct racial and ethnic balance and more focus on improving education," says the Center for Equal Opportunity's Clegg. "That's where the law's headed, and that's where policy's headed. We ought to be worrying less about integration anyhow."

For his part, the Century Foundation's Kahlenberg stresses that the number of school districts with race-conscious policies — guesstimated at around 1,000 — is a small fraction of the nationwide total of 15,000 school systems. Many of the districts that have been seeking racial balance will likely shift to socioeconomic integration, he says, "because that's a clearly legal way to raise academic achievement for kids and create some racial integration indirectly."

In Louisville, the county school board did vote on Sept. 10 to broaden its diversity criteria to include socioeconomic status. "Race will still be a factor," Superintendent Berman said, "but it will not be the only factor."[29] Meanwhile, Student Placement Director Todd says Jefferson County's use of non-contiguous school-attendance zones to mix students from different racially identifiable neighborhoods is likely to be continued.

In his concurring opinion, Justice Kennedy suggested "strategic site selection" as another permissible policy to promote racial diversity — placing new schools so they draw students from different racial neighborhoods. The suggestion may prove impractical in many school districts. Jefferson County opened one new school this fall — in the rapidly growing and predominantly white eastern end, far removed from the African-American neighborhoods in the West End. As Breyer noted in his opinion, many urban school systems are unlikely to be building new schools because they are losing not gaining enrollment.

Changing demographics and changing social attitudes are inevitably bringing about changes in the schools. Within a decade or so, demographers expect white students will no longer comprise a majority of public school enrollment. And, as Abigail Thernstrom notes, young people have different attitudes toward race than their parents or grandparents.

"In terms of racial attitudes, we're on a fast track," Thernstrom says. "Young kids are dating across racial and ethnic lines. America is changing in very terrific ways and has been for some time. I expect that change to continue."

But University of Wisconsin educational historian Reese cautions against expecting racial issues to disappear. "It's like a never-never land to imagine that racial issues can somehow disappear," he says. "It's a nice thing to say that we should live in a kind of perfect world, but we don't. I can't imagine that it will disappear. It couldn't have disappeared in the past, and it won't disappear in the future."

## UPDATE

"Hey, hey, ho, ho, resegregation has got to go." So echoed the 1960s-style chant of protesters at a July 20, 2010, meeting of the school board in North Carolina's Wake County (Raleigh). Police arrested 19 for disrupting discussion of a new neighborhood school-busing plan that dismantles existing school assignments intended to achieve racial diversity. A rally earlier in the day in Raleigh drew 1,000 people. They heard speakers invoke memories of separate water fountains for blacks and whites and compare the Wake controversy to the early 1950s school-desegregation battle that culminated in the Supreme Court's landmark ruling in *Brown v. Board of Education*.[30]

Such fear of public school "resegregation" has haunted some American communities ever since the Supreme Court's June 28, 2007, decision in *Parents Involved in Community Schools v. Seattle School District No. 1* invalidating race-conscious pupil-assignment plans in Seattle and metropolitan Louisville, Ky. And despite active national school-reform efforts by the nation's first African-American president, many families and policy

advocates who wish to preserve racial diversity in schools express disappointment in the Obama administration's priorities in this area.

"Obama is emphasizing charter schools, which are racially isolating, and firing teachers at high-poverty schools," says Richard Kahlenberg, a senior fellow at the Century Foundation and longtime student of the racial make-up of schools. "As far as I can tell, he's been silent on the Wake County situation."

Scholars at the University of California at Los Angeles Civil Rights Project also scolded the Obama team for failing to deliver on promised guidance on how voluntary integration of schools should proceed in the wake of the 2007 high-court ruling. The complex, 5-2 decision "confused many educators, and it was somewhat unclear what did remain legal," they wrote in a recent report reviewing the response to the ruling.[31] "In 2008, the Bush administration sent a letter to school districts misguidedly interpreting the *Parents Involved* decision in a way that suggested only race-neutral means of pursuing integration would be legal. This was an inaccurate description of [Justice Anthony] Kennedy's controlling opinion and suggested that school authorities should abandon all efforts to intentionally pursue integration."

The UCLA researchers were also responsible for recent research stating that the increasingly popular movement to create more parental choices in charter schools continues "to stratify students by race, class, and possibly language, and [charter schools] are more racially isolated than traditional public schools in virtually every state and large metropolitan area in the country." Nationally, 70 percent of black charter students attend schools where at least 90 percent of students are minorities, double the figure for traditional public schools, the researchers found.[32]

Others, however, found clarity in the Supreme Court ruling. "Any fair reading of the decision is that any kind of race consciousness by school boards in assignment of students is legally very dangerous," says Roger Clegg, president and general counsel of the Center for Equal Opportunity, a Falls Church, Va., think tank opposed to racial preferences. "And it wouldn't be politically wise for Obama to mount any kind of counter-crusade."

Clegg discourages the term "resegregate," which he says calls to mind the period in history when schools

U.S. Secretary of Education Arne Duncan listens to students, teachers and former students describe their educational experience as he visits Robert E. Lee High School in Montgomery, Ala., during brief stops at schools in Montgomery and Selma, Ala., in March.

*AP Photo/Montgomery Advertiser/David Bundy*

were deliberately segregated by law. "We're talking [now] about racial imbalances due to student choice and residential living patterns," he says. "Reasonable people can disagree about the best way to achieve balance. But those who believe that competition and choice are essential have the better argument. The overwhelming majority of parents and students of all racial groups would prefer to have better schools and more choices rather than some politically correct racial and ethnic mix."

Education Secretary Arne Duncan in March 2010 made a much-publicized visit to Selma, Ala., to speak on the state of minorities in education at the Edmund Pettus Bridge, site of a dramatic confrontation between billy club-wielding police and civil rights marchers in 1965. Duncan promised to reinvigorate his department's Office of Civil Rights, reduce resource disparities among schools and confront continuing barriers to achieving the Rev. Martin Luther King Jr.'s vision of a colorblind society.

Yet Duncan also suggested that modern times call for a more individualistic approach. "The civil rights struggle has grown more complex since the days of Selma," he said. "Freedom, it turns out, is not only the right to sit in the front of the bus, or cast a ballot. It's not even just the opportunity to purchase a home without fear of discrimination, as essential as that is. . . . No, freedom is also the ability to think on your own and to pursue your own path as far as your gifts can take you — and only education can give you that freedom, can open those doors."[33]

Specifically, Duncan's department has pursued school integration with two competitive-grant programs. One provides technical assistance to districts preparing pupil-placement policies that don't run afoul of the Supreme Court ruling, one of which is being used by Kentucky's Jefferson County (Louisville), a party to the *Parents Involved* suit. Another is new funding for the Magnet Schools Assistance Program (MSAP), a long-standing effort that encourages creation of attractive voluntary programs that draw students from many neighborhoods. The department's description mentions reducing racial isolation as a priority.

The overall trend since the *Parents Involved* ruling, says Kahlenberg, is to assign school zones with an eye on minimizing concentrations of children of low socioeconomic status. "There's no legal problem with it, and it accomplishes a fair amount of racial integration," he says. Back in 2000, only two or three school districts were using such methods, he adds, while in the year the Supreme Court ruled there were 40, and now there are more than 70. "A lot of school districts after the ruling could have walked away and said, 'Our hands are tied,'" Kahlenberg says. "Instead, some said, 'we value racial integration, so let's come up with a legally permissible way to integrate.'" Research confirms that low-income children achieve more when they're in school with middle-class children, he says.

The main arena for diversity issues, of course, is in school districts around the country. In Seattle, where the Supreme Court case originated, a new school boundary set to take effect this fall is based on neighborhood proximity and does not mention race as a factor in a decision-making process that included public hearings. A Seattle secondary school, Cleveland High, is set to open as a citywide magnet school focusing on math, science, engineering and technology, though, as in many districts reeling from the recession, funding is shaky.

And in Jefferson County (the second party to the suit), school officials are considering the percentage of minority students in the greater Louisville area as well as the education and income of adults in the area when weighing admissions, said Pat Todd, director of student assignment for Jefferson County schools. "This gives us more racial, ethnic and economic diversity," she said.[34]

Louisville school officials are using an analytical tool called "opportunity mapping," which was developed at Ohio State University's Kirwan Institute for the Study of Race and Ethnicity.[35]

In Chicago, a city with neighborhoods long divided along racial lines whose school system was previously run by Secretary Duncan, a recent plan to use students' social and economic profiles instead of race to increase classroom diversity is raising fears that it will set back the modest progress toward integration achieved in recent decades. Amanda Orellano, whose daughter is the third generation in her family to attend a prominent Chicago magnet school that is moving away from a race-based enrollment policy, said, "Somebody's going to feel that they're the only one here that's this way or that way, and feel isolated."[36]

The Justice Department, as it has since the birth of the civil rights movement in the 1950s, continues to monitor racial discrimination in more than 200 mostly Southern school districts on their compliance with decades-old court desegregation orders. Recently, the department sued the school board in Walthall, Miss., for a policy that permitted white students to transfer out of a predominantly black high school to a majority-white school. In April, a federal judge ruled that the policy created "racially identifiable" schools in violation of a 1970 desegregation order.[37]

In some cases, the department focuses not just on school demographics or attendance zones but on equal availability of quality academic programs and clean, modern physical plants. In March 2010, Justice announced it had signed a consent agreement with the Monroe City School District in Louisiana to equalize the offering of advanced placement and gifted-and-talented courses between the predominantly black and white high schools. Subject to court approval, the settlement was based on agreement that the unequal offerings under the existing system violated the equal protection provisions of the 1964 Civil Rights Act.

The new focus on pursuing diversity using socioeconomic status has not prevented one of the oldest civil rights organizations, the NAACP Legal Defense Fund, from continuing to emphasize race-based disparities even in what some had hoped would be President Obama's "post-racial America." In its recommendations for the still-in-progress reauthorization of the No Child Left Behind law, the group proposed that parents receive progress reports from the Education Department's Office of Civil Rights and that schools designate a point-of-contact to receive parental complaints about racial discrimination.

"Some have articulated a belief that our nation is unable to garner the resources to provide a high-quality education for all students, and therefore we should just save those we can," the group wrote. "But as civil rights advocates, our objective is not to support prescriptions that only have the capacity to change a few schools for a few students. . . . Securing equal access to high-quality education is the civil rights battle of this generation."[38]

## NOTES

1. For coverage, see Chris Kenning, "Separate attendance zones voided," *The* [Louisville] *Courier-Journal*, Aug. 29, 2007, p. 1A.

2. The decision is *Parents Involved in Community Schools v. Seattle School District No. 1*, 552 U.S. ___ (2007); the companion case was *Meredith v. Jefferson County Public Schools*. For a detailed chronicle of the cases, see Kenneth Jost, "Court Limits Use of Race in Pupil Assignments," in *The Supreme Court Yearbook 2006-2007*, http://library.cqpress.com/scyb/.

3. For background, see Kenneth Jost, "School Desegregation," *CQ Researcher*, April 23, 2004, pp. 345-372.

4. See Chris Kenning, "JCPS sees change in racial makeup," *The* [Louisville] *Courier-Journal*, Sept. 2, 2007, p. 1A.

5. Gary Orfield and Chungmei Lee, "Historic Reversals, Accelerating Resegregation, and the Need for New Integration Strategies," UCLA Civil Rights Project (formerly based at Harvard University), August 2007, pp. 29, 35.

6. Richard D. Kahlenberg, "Rescuing *Brown v. Board of Education*: Profiles of Twelve School Districts Pursuing Socioeconomic School Integration," June 28, 2007, p. 3.

7. For coverage, see Peter Schworm, "AG Urges Court to Uphold Lynn Plan," *The Boston Globe*, July 18, 2005, p. B4.

8. Orfield and Lee, *op. cit.*, pp. 7-8. For background, see Barbara Mantel, "No Child Left Behind," *CQ Researcher*, May 27, 2005, pp. 469-492.

9. Background drawn in part from William J. Reese, *America's Public Schools: From the Common School to "No Child Left Behind"* (2005); R. Freeman Butts, *Public Education in the United States: From Revolution to Reform* (1978).

10. Reese, *op. cit.*, pp. 10-11, 25-26.

11. For background, see James Anderson, *The Education of Blacks in the South, 1860-1935* (1988). See also Heather Andrea Williams, *Self-Taught: African American Education in Slavery and Freedom* (2003).

12. For background, see "School Desegregation," *op. cit.*, p. 350 (Latinos), pp. 356-357 (Asian-Americans), and sources cited therein.

13. Some background drawn from James T. Patterson, Brown v. Board of Education: *A Civil Rights Milestone and Its Troubled Legacy* (2001).

14. For data, see *ibid.*, pp. 228-230.

15. The decisions are *Green v. County School Board of New Kent County*, 391 U.S. 430 (1968), and *Swann v. Charlotte-Mecklenburg County Board of Education*, 402 U.S. 1 (1971).

16. Reese, *op. cit.*, p. 246. For background on later school desegregation cases, see Patterson, *op. cit.*

17. For background, see H. B. Shaffer, "Status of the War on Poverty," in *Editorial Research Reports*, Jan. 25, 1967, available at *CQ Researcher Plus Archive*, http://library.cqpress.com.

18. Background drawn from Kathy Koch, "Reforming School Funding," *CQ Researcher*, Dec. 10, 1999, pp. 1041-1064.

19. The decisions are *San Antonio Independent School District v. Rodriguez*, 411 U.S. 1 (1973), and *Robinson v. Cahill*, 62 A.2d 273 (N.J. 1973).

20. For background, see Charles S. Clark, "Attack on Public Schools," *CQ Researcher*, July 26, 1996, pp. 649-672.

21. See Patterson, *op. cit.*, p. 214 n.19, p. 234.

22. The decisions are *Wessmann v. Gittens*, 160 F.3d 790 (1st Cir. 1998); *Tuttle v. Arlington County School Board*, 195 F.3d 698 (4th Cir. 1999), *Eisenberg v. Montgomery County Public Schools*, 197 F.3d 123 (4th Cir. 1999). For coverage, see Beth Daley, "Court Strikes Down Latin School Race Admission Policy," *The Boston Globe*, Nov. 20, 1998, p. A1; Jay Mathews, "School Lottery Loses on Appeal," *The Washington Post*, Sept. 26, 1999, p. C1 (Arlington County); Brigid Schulte, "School Diversity Policy Is Overruled," *ibid.*, Oct. 7, 1999, p. A1 (Montgomery County).

23. See Richard D. Kahlenberg, *All Together Now* (2003 ed.)., p. xiii.

24. Quoted in Andrew Wolfson, "Desegregation Decision: Some Find 'Sunshine' Amid Rain," *The [Louisville] Courier-Journal*, June 29, 2007, p. 6K.

25. Quoted in Jessica Blanchard and Christine Frey, "District Vows to Seek Out Diversity Answers," *Seattle Post-Intelligencer*, June 29, 2007, p. A1.

26. See Emily Heffter, "First Day of School for Chief," *Seattle Times*, July 10, 2007, p. B1.

27. See Emily Heffter, "Law firm wants school district to pay $1.8M," *Seattle Times*, Sept. 6, 2007, p. B5.

28. Chris Kenning and Andrew Wolfson, "Lawyer in schools case seeks fees, bonus," *The* [Louisville] *Courier-Journal*, July 29, 2007, p. 1A.

29. Quoted in Antoinette Konz, "Schools adopt guidelines for assignment plan," *The* [Louisville] *Courier-Journal*, Sept. 11, 2007.

30. Mike Baker, "Racial Tensions Roil NC School Board; 19 arrests," The Associated Press, July 20, 2010.

31. Adai Tefera, Genevieve Siegel-Hawley and Erica Frankenberg, "School Integration Efforts Three Years After 'Parents Involved,'" The Civil Rights Project/Proyecto Derechos Civiles, University of California, Los Angeles, June 28, 2010.

32. Howard Blume, "Charter Schools' Growth Promoting Segregation, Studies Say," *Los Angeles Times*, Feb. 4, 2010.

33. Sam Dillon, "Officials Step Up Enforcement of Rights Laws in Education," *The New York Times*, March 7, 2010, p. A11.

34. Tefera, *et al.*, UCLA Civil Rights Project, *op. cit.*

35. See Susan Eaton and Steven Rivkin, "Is Desegregation Dead?" *Education Next*, fall 2010. See also

http://kirwaninstitute.org/research/gismapping/opportunity-mapping/.

36. Crystal Yednak and Darnell Little, "City Schools' New Criteria for Diversity Raise Fears," Chicago News Cooperative, Dec. 20, 2009.

37. Stephanie McCrummen, "Ruling on Racial Isolation in Miss. Schools Reflects Troubling Broader Trend," *The Washington Post*, April 20, 2010.

38. "Framework for Providing All Students an Opportunity to Learn through Reauthorization of the Elementary and Secondary Education Act," NAACP Legal Defense Fund, July 26, 2010, www.naacpldf.org.

## BIBLIOGRAPHY

### Books

**Frankenberg, Erika, and Gary Orfield (eds.), *Lessons in Integration: Realizing the Promise of Racial Diversity in American Schools*, University of Virginia Press, 2007.**
Twelve essays by 19 contributors examine the educational and social effects of desegregation and the disadvantages to students in segregated schools. Orfield is co-director of the Civil Rights Project, UCLA Graduate School of Education and Information Studies (formerly, the Harvard Civil Rights Project); Frankenberg is a study director for the project. Includes notes, 46-page bibliography.

**Loveless, Tom, *The Tracking Wars: State Reform Meets School Policy*, Brookings Institution Press, 1999.**
The director of the Brown Center on Educational Policy at Brookings depicts tracking as a traditional educational practice and detracking as "a gamble" that may hurt rather than help students in low-achievement schools. Includes detailed notes.

**Oakes, Jeannie, *Keeping Track: How Schools Structure Inequality* (2d ed.), Yale University Press, 2005.**
The director of urban schooling at UCLA's Graduate School of Education and Information Studies updates the landmark critique of tracking that launched a detracking reform movement after its publication in 1985. Includes detailed notes.

**Patterson, James T., *Brown v. Board of Education: A Civil Rights Milestone and Its Troubled Legacy*, Oxford University Press, 2001.**
An emeritus professor of history at Brown University gives a compact account of the landmark school desegregation case and a legacy described as "conspicuous achievement" along with "marked failures."

**Reese, William J., *America's Public Schools: From the Common School to "No Child Left Behind,"* Johns Hopkins University Press, 2005.**
A professor of educational-policy studies at the University of Wisconsin-Madison provides an accessible overview of the history of U.S. public education from Horace Mann's advocacy of the "common school" through 20th-century developments.

**Thernstrom, Abigail, and Stephan Thernstrom, *No Excuses: Closing the Racial Gap in Learning*, Simon & Schuster, 2003.**
The authors decry the persistent achievement gap between white and black students but discount the importance of racial isolation in schools as a cause. Includes extensive statistical information, notes. Both authors are senior fellows with the Manhattan Institute; Abigail Thernstrom is vice chair of the U.S. Civil Rights Commission, Stephan Thernstrom a professor of history at Harvard.

### Articles

**Simmons, Dan, "A Class Action: Leaders Tried to Rein In Effects of Poverty in Public Schools; Voters Were in No Mood for Busing," *La Crosse* (Wis.) *Tribune*, Jan. 21, 2007, p. 1.**
The story and an accompanying sidebar ("Balance by Choice") examine the history and current status of the La Crosse school district's 15-year experiment with socioeconomic integration.

### Reports and Studies

**Kahlenberg, Richard D., "Rescuing *Brown v. Board of Education*: Profiles of Twelve School Districts Pursuing Socioeconomic School Integration," Century Foundation, June 28, 2007, www.tcf.org.**
The 42-page report describes the mixed results of socioeconomic integration in 12 school systems, with lengthy

treatment of three: La Crosse, Wis.; Cambridge, Mass.; and Wake County (Raleigh), N.C. For a book-length treatment, see Kahlenberg, *All Together Now: Creating Middle-Class Schools through Public School Choice* (Brookings Institution Press, 2001).

**Linn, Robert L., and Kevin G. Welner (eds.), "Race-Conscious Policies for Assigning Students to Schools: Social Science Research and the Supreme Court Cases," National Academy of Education, June 29, 2007, www.naeducation.org/Meredith_Report.pdf.**

The 58-page report details social-science research on the effects of racial diversity in schools and finds "general support" for the conclusion that the overall academic and social effects of increased racial diversity are "likely to be positive."

**Orfield, Gary, and Chungmei Lee, "Historic Reversals, Accelerating Resegregation, and the Need for New Integration Strategies," UCLA Civil Rights Project, Aug. 29, 2007, www.civilrightsproject.ucla.edu.**

The 50-page report finds "accelerating isolation" of African-American and Latino students in public schools and recommends a variety of measures to counter the trend, including an attack on housing segregation, socioeconomic integration of schools and congressional initiatives "to require and/or to support racial progress."

### On the Web

The *Courier-Journal* has an extensive compilation of articles, photographs and information on the course of school desegregation in Louisville and Jefferson County (www.courier-journal.com/desegregation). Current coverage can be found on the Web sites of Seattle's two newspapers, the *Seattle Times* (http://seattletimes.nwsource.com/html/education/) and the *Seattle Post-Intelligencer* (http://seattlepi.nwsource.com/).

# For More Information

**American Educational Research Association**, 1430 K St., N.W., Suite 1200, Washington, DC 20005; (202) 238-3200; www.aera.net. National research society encouraging scholarly research in efforts to improve education.

**Center for Individual Rights**, 1233 20th St., N.W., Suite 300, Washington, DC 20036; (202) 833-8400; www.cir-usa.org. Nonprofit public-interest law firm opposed to racial preferences.

**Center for Equal Opportunity**, 7700 Leesburg Pike, Suite 231, Falls Church, VA 22043; (703) 442-0066; www.ceousa.org. Think tank devoted to equal opportunity and racial harmony.

**Century Foundation**, 41 E. 70th St., New York, NY 10021; (212) 535-4441; www.tcf.org. Public-policy institution promoting methods for socioeconomic integration in education.

**Mexican American Legal Defense and Educational Fund**, 634 S. Spring St., Los Angeles, CA 90014; (213) 629-2512; www.maldef.org. Protects and promotes the civil rights of Latinos living in the United States.

**NAACP Legal Defense and Educational Fund**, 99 Hudson St., Suite 1600, New York, NY 10013; (212) 965-2200; http://naacpldf.org. Serves as legal counsel on issues of race, with emphasis on education, voter protection, economic justice and criminal justice.

**National School Boards Association**, 1680 Duke St., Alexandria, VA 22314; (703) 838-6722; www.nsba.org. Seeks to foster excellence and equity in public education by working with school board leadership.

*Here is contact information for the school districts involved in the Supreme Court decision,* Parents Involved in Community Schools v. Seattle School District No. 1:

**Jefferson County Public Schools**, VanHoose Education Center, 3332 Newburg Rd., P.O. Box 34020, Louisville, KY 40232-4020; (502) 485-3011; www.jefferson.k12.ky.us.

**Seattle School District No. 1**, 2445 Third Ave. South, Seattle, WA 98134; (206) 252-0000; www.seattleschools.org.

# 12

# Fixing Urban Schools

Marcia Clemmitt and Charles S. Clark

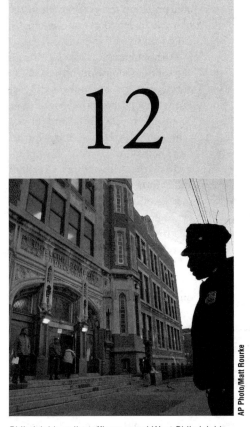

Philadelphia police officers guard West Philadelphia High School on March 12, 2007, where a teacher was attacked by three students three days earlier. Experts suggest that a "behavior gap" between black and white students parallels the academic achievement gap between high- and low-performing students.

From *CQ Researcher*,
April 27, 2007 (updated June 5, 2012, and June 29, 2014).

"I didn't go to school much in elementary, and they saw me as a bad girl" who skipped class, says Jeanette, a Houston high-school student who dropped out several times but is struggling to get a diploma. After her parents divorced when she was in grade school, she fell into a pattern typical of urban students, repeatedly "switching schools," sometimes living with her mother, sometimes her father and sometimes with an aunt who "didn't make us go to school" at all.[1]

In middle school, Jeanette began taking drugs but later got involved in sports, which motivated her to try, sometimes successfully, to keep up her grades and stay off drugs. Some teachers have tried hard to help her, but like many troubled urban kids, she pulls back. "If I need help . . . I don't say anything. . . . They have to ask me." Still, Jeanette is determined to avoid the fate of her parents, who dropped out of school when they had her. At the time, her mother was only 13. "I don't want to live like them. I want to have a better life," she says.

Jeanette typifies the daunting challenge that urban schools face in promoting academic achievement among children whose lives have been disordered and impoverished.

Most middle-class families with children have moved to the suburbs, leaving urban schools today overwhelmingly populated by low-income, African-American and Hispanic students. "Nationally, about 50 percent of all black and Latino students attend schools in which 75 percent or more of the students are low-income, as measured by eligibility for free and reduced-price lunch," according to the Center for Civil Rights at the University

## Minority Districts Often Get Less Funding

In 28 states, school districts with high-minority enrollments received less per-pupil funding (shown as a negative number, top map) than districts with low-minority levels. For example, in Illinois, the highest-minority districts received an average of $1,223 less per student than the lowest-minority districts. In 21 states, the highest-minority districts received more per pupil (shown as a positive number, bottom map), than the districts with the lowest-minority enrollments. For example, in Georgia, the highest-poverty districts received $566 per student more than the lowest-poverty districts.

### Minority Funding Gaps by State, 2004

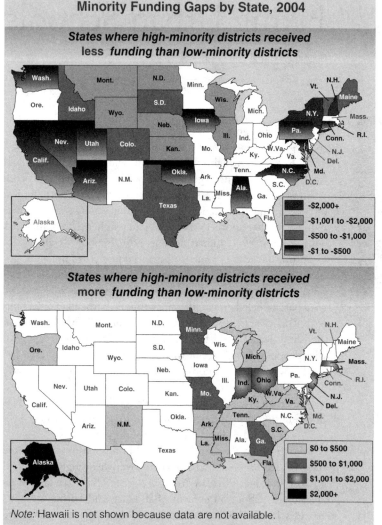

**States where high-minority districts received less funding than low-minority districts**

-$2,000+
-$1,001 to -$2,000
-$500 to -$1,000
-$1 to -$500

**States where high-minority districts received more funding than low-minority districts**

$0 to $500
$500 to $1,000
$1,001 to $2,000
$2,000+

*Note:* Hawaii is not shown because data are not available.

*Source:* Funding Gaps 2006, The Education Trust, 2006

of North Carolina. Only 5 percent of white students attend such high-poverty schools.[2]

These schools, mostly urban, aren't making the grade, even in the context of lagging achievement in American schools overall.

Although states show significant variations, nationwide "71 percent of eighth-graders are not reading at grade level," and the percentage shoots up to between 80 and 90 percent for students of color, says former Gov. Bob Wise, D-W.Va., now president of the Alliance for Excellent Education, a broad-based coalition that advocates for academically stronger high schools.

Furthermore, of the approximately 15,000 U.S. high schools, 2,000 — mostly in cities — account for half of the nation's school dropouts, says Wise.

When President George W. Bush joined Massachusetts Sen. Edward M. Kennedy and other congressional Democrats to enact the No Child Left Behind Act (NCLB) in 2002, a key aim was requiring states to report achievement scores for all student groups. That ensured that lagging scores of low-income and minority students wouldn't be masked by having only state or district overall average scores reported.[3]

This year, Congress is expected to provide funding to keep the law in operation, but there's considerable disagreement about where federal education law should go next, and lawmakers may wait until next year to consider revisions.

NCLB's test-score reporting requirements "make it more possible to look at whether schools are doing well just for more affluent students or for poor students" as well, and that's valuable, says Jeffrey Henig, professor of political science and education at Columbia University's Teachers College.

But some supporters, including President Bush, say the NCLB has done more than just improve data-gathering, arguing that the law itself has pushed achievement upward. "Fourth-graders are reading better. They've made more progress in five years than in the previous 28 years combined," he said on March 2.[4]

Many education analysts disagree with that rosy assessment. The small improvement in fourth-grade reading and mathematics scores is part of a long-term trend, which began years before NCLB was even enacted, said Harvard University Professor of Education Daniel M. Koretz. "There's not any evidence that shows anything has changed" since NCLB, he said.[5]

And for urban schools, the post-NCLB picture is especially grim.

Of the non-achieving schools in New York state, for example, 90 percent are in cities and 80 percent in the state's five biggest cities, says David Hursh, an associate professor of teaching and curriculum at the University of Rochester's Margaret Warner Graduate School of Education.

The gap between average reading scores of black and white fourth-graders narrowed by only one point on the 500-point National Assessment of Educational Progress test (NAEP) between 2002 and 2005, and the narrowing appears to be part of a long-term trend, since it narrowed by three points between 1998 and 2005. Between 2002 and 2005, the reading-score gap between white and black eighth-graders actually widened, from 25 points to 28 points.[6]

The continuing severe achievement gap, newly highlighted by NCLB's data-reporting requirements, leaves lawmakers and educators scratching their heads about what to do next.

Some analysts say lagging achievement in urban schools demonstrates that poor families in poor communities require much more intense interventions than middle-class students, including better teachers and longer school days as well as improved health care, nutrition and parenting education.

A public school enrolling mainly middle-class white students has a one-in-four chance of producing good test scores, across years and in different subject matter, according to Douglas N. Harris, assistant professor of education policy at the University of Wisconsin, Madison. A school with a predominantly low-income minority population has a 1-in-300 chance of doing so.[7]

Experts blame the poor outcome on the fact that urban schools, like all schools, are staffed and organized to provide substantial extra help to only 15 percent of students and curriculum enrichment to another 15, while "the students in the middle are supposed to take care of themselves," says Robert Balfanz, associate research scientist at the Johns Hopkins University Center on the Social Organization of Schools and associate director of the Talent Development High School program, a reform initiative in 33 schools nationwide. The formula for extra help fits most suburban schools, "but in urban schools 50 to 60 percent, and sometimes up to

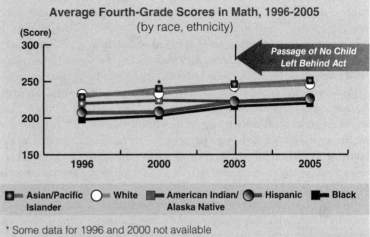

## All Racial/Ethnic Groups Improved on Test

Fourth-graders in all racial and ethnic groups began modestly improving in math on the National Assessment for Educational Progress several years before passage of the No Child Left Behind Act.

**Average Fourth-Grade Scores in Math, 1996-2005**
(by race, ethnicity)

Passage of No Child Left Behind Act

Legend: Asian/Pacific Islander — White — American Indian/Alaska Native — Hispanic — Black

\* Some data for 1996 and 2000 not available

*Source:* U.S. Department of Education, National Center for Education Statistics

80 percent, of the kids are 'high-needs,' defined as English-as-a-second-language students, special-education students or students below grade level or with severe attendance problems.

"We're not set up to respond when that many kids need one-on-one tutoring, monitoring of their attendance on a daily basis, [or] people calling up to say, 'Glad you came today,' " Balfanz says.

One of the biggest problems is the kind of "student mobility" experienced by Jeanette, the Houston dropout.

"Homelessness is much underreported," says James F. Lytle, a professor at the University of Pennsylvania and former school superintendent in Trenton, N.J. "Statistics are based on who's in shelters and on the streets. But 20 to 30 percent of our kids were living in 'serial households' on a day-to-day basis," or moving about from parents to grandparents to relatives to friends — not living in the same house all the time.

Inner-city schools have a 40 to 50 percent student-mobility rate, which means up to half the students change schools at least once a year because of parents losing or changing jobs, evictions and other factors, says Columbia University's Henig. That disrupts students' ability to keep up with work and build relationships with the adults in a school.

In addition, city students miss school for a wide range of reasons, including high asthma rates; lack of school buses, forcing kids to get to school on their own, often through unsafe neighborhoods; and family responsibilities, like caring for younger siblings.

"Imagine the teacher's dilemma in a classroom where the population is different every day," says Balfanz.

But some conservative analysts argue that a large proportion of high-needs students is still no reason for schools to fail.

"Schools frequently cite social problems like poverty . . . and bad parenting as excuses for their own poor performance," said Jay P. Greene, a senior fellow at the Manhattan Institute, a conservative think tank. "This argument that schools are helpless in the face of social problems is not supported by hard evidence. . . . The truth is that certain schools do a strikingly better job than others," including public, private and charter schools.[8]

Some educators say one solution for low-quality urban schools is establishing publicly funded "charter" schools and awarding vouchers for private-school tuition.[9] When choice is expanded, "urban public schools that once had a captive clientele must improve the education they provide or else students . . . will go elsewhere," said Greene.[10]

But others argue that lessons from successful urban schools, including charters, demonstrate that raising low-income students' achievement requires resources and staff commitment that may be tough for the nation to muster.

"Teachers in high-poverty urban schools are as much as 50 percent more likely to . . . leave than those in low-poverty schools," in part because of the intensity of the work, according to researchers at the University of California, Santa Cruz.[11]

A second-grade teacher fluent in Spanish who reported working 10 hours a day, six days a week said she'd probably stop teaching when she had children: "It's too time-consuming and energy-draining," she said.[12]

"None of the teachers in our sample could conceive of being a successful urban teacher without an extra-ordinary — perhaps unsustainable — commitment to the work," the researchers commented.[13]

Not just schools but communities must help in the effort to improve students' performance.

"There ought to be a parade through the heart of town" every time a student achieves an academic goal, says Hugh B. Price, a fellow at the Brookings Institution, a liberal think tank. "We need to wrap and cloak kids in this message of achievement." That's how the military successfully trains soldiers, Price says. "They will praise anything that's good."

Schools and communities also have a role in helping parents better equip their children for school, says Mayor Douglas H. Palmer of Trenton, N.J., president of the National Conference of Democratic Mayors. "You don't have to be rich to talk to your child, help her build vocabulary and learn to reason and negotiate," as psychologists recommend, he says. "We can help parents with these skills."

As educators and lawmakers debate the next steps to improving urban schools, here are some of the questions being asked:

### Has the No Child Left Behind law helped urban students?

NCLB was intended to improve overall academic achievement and raise achievement for minority and low-income students, in particular, mainly by requiring more student testing, getting schools to report test data separately for student groups including minorities and the poor and requiring schools to employ better-qualified teachers.

The law, scheduled for reauthorization this year, gets praise for focusing attention on the so-called achievement gap between minority and low-income students and their middle-class counterparts. But critics say the legislation doesn't do enough to assure that low-performing urban schools get the excellent teachers they need.

Student achievement also has improved slightly under the law, some advocates point out. "Is NCLB really paying off? The answer is yes," U.S. Chamber of Commerce Senior Vice President Arthur J. Rothkopf told a joint House-Senate committee hearing on March 13. While current testing data is still "abysmal," it nevertheless "represents improvement from where this nation was" before the law.

The law has benefited urban schools by raising reading scores for African-American and Hispanic fourth- and eighth-graders and math scores for African-American and Hispanic fourth-graders to "all-time highs." Achievement gaps in reading and math between white fourth-graders and African-American and Hispanic fourth-graders also have diminished since NCLB, he noted.[14]

NCLB's data-reporting requirements have "lifted the carpet" to reveal two previously unrecognized facts about American education — "the continuing underperformance of the whole system and the achievement gap" for low-income and minority students, says Daniel A. Domenech, senior vice president and top urban-education adviser for publisher McGraw-Hill Education and former superintendent of Virginia's vast Fairfax County Public Schools.[15]

And while some critics complain that NCLB gave the federal government too much say over education — traditionally a state and local matter — "there needs to be a strong federal role for these kids" in low-income urban schools "because they have been left behind," says Gary Ratner, a public-interest lawyer who is founding executive director of the advocacy group Citizens for Effective Schools. "States and localities have not stepped up."

Now NCLB "has got the country's attention," and when Congress reauthorizes the law, "the federal role can be redirected to focus on Title I schools" — those serving a large proportion of disadvantaged students — "and do more of the things that professional educators support," Ratner says.

NCLB's requirement that every school "have very qualified teachers is good," says Gary Orfield, a professor of social policy at the Harvard Graduate School of Education and director of The Civil Rights Project.

But critics argue that NCLB doesn't put muscle behind the high-quality teacher requirement and sets unrealistic goals and timetables for school progress.

NCLB actually "incentivizes teachers to leave failing schools," the last thing lawmakers intended, says Jennifer King-Rice, an economist who is associate professor of education policy at the University of Maryland, College Park. "Teachers say, 'I can't produce the AYP [average yearly progress] results' " the law calls for in low-performing schools with few resources and, frustrated, go elsewhere, she says. Nevertheless, it's still unclear whether and how the government can enforce the qualified-teacher rule.

The law provides no additional funding to help schools meet the teacher-quality goal, said Richard J. Murnane, professor of education and society at the Harvard Graduate School of Education. "Teaching in these schools is extremely difficult work," and "very few school districts provide extra pay or other inducements to attract talented teachers to these schools.[16]

"As a result, all too often these schools are left with the teachers other schools don't want," he continued. "And the teachers who do have options exercise seniority rights to leave . . . as soon as they can."[17]

The achievement targets set by NCLB are panned by many. The main goal schools must meet is moving kids over a standardized-testing threshold from "basic" or "below basic" understanding of reading and math to a "proficient" level or above. But focusing on that narrow goal as the key measure by which schools are judged created bad incentives to game the system, many analysts say.

Rather than concentrating on raising overall achievement or trying to give the most help to students who score lowest, many schools concentrate "on students who are on the bubble" — those who need to raise their scores by only a few points to move into the "proficient" range — and "forget the others," says Patrick McQuillan, an associate professor of education at Boston College's Lynch

## Minority Enrollment and Teacher Quality

In Illinois, 88 percent of the schools that were virtually 100 percent minority ranked in the lowest quartile of the state's Teacher Quality Index (graph at left). By comparison, only 1 percent of the all-minority schools ranked in the highest quartile (right). High-quality teachers have more experience, better educations and stronger academic skills. Similar patterns are found in most other states.

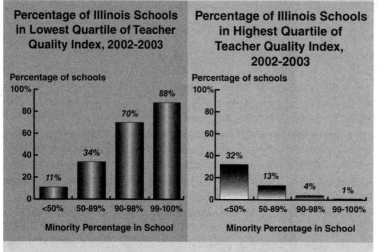

**Percentage of Illinois Schools in Lowest Quartile of Teacher Quality Index, 2002-2003**

Percentage of schools
- <50%: 11%
- 50-89%: 34%
- 90-98%: 70%
- 99-100%: 88%

Minority Percentage in School

**Percentage of Illinois Schools in Highest Quartile of Teacher Quality Index, 2002-2003**

Percentage of schools
- <50%: 32%
- 50-89%: 13%
- 90-98%: 4%
- 99-100%: 1%

Minority Percentage in School

*Source:* "Teaching Inequality: How Poor and Minority Students Are Shortchanged on Teacher Quality," The Education Trust, June 2006

School of Education. Schools that succeed at pushing the scores of "bubble" students up by a few points are deemed successful, according to current NCLB standards, even if they leave the neediest students even farther behind, he says.

The law's pronouncement that 100 percent of U.S. students will test at the "proficient" level is simply unrealistic, some critics say.

"We've never fully funded education in the United States," and achievement continues to lag far below the "proficient" level, especially for low-income students, says Domenech. So "let's not kid around and say that by 2014" all students will be academically proficient, he says. "That's like saying, 'I'm going to push you out the window, and I know you can fly.'"

Furthermore, NCLB's focus on a handful of standardized tests as the sole measures of children's progress puts teachers in an ethical bind that "definitely lowers their morale," says Marshalita Sims Peterson, an associate professor of education at Atlanta's Spelman College,

an historically black school for women.

Teachers in training are taught that students are individuals with a wide variety of learning styles, and that no single assessment can define a student, says Peterson. The NCLB's excessive focus on a single measurement of achievement "leaves the teacher in an awful position" she says. "You need to keep the job, but when you are actually completing that form" stating the single score "for a third-grader, you're asking, 'Is that all there is to this child?'"

### Should governments make schools more racially and economically diverse?

Today, most African-American and Latino students attend urban schools with a high concentration of low-income students and very few white classmates.

Some advocates argue that the country has backtracked to an era of separate but unequal schools and say government programs aimed at creating more racially and socioeconomically diverse schools are good tools for narrowing the achievement gap. Opponents of government interference with children's attendance at neighborhood schools argue that with residential neighborhoods increasingly segregated by race and income, school integration is unrealistic, and that governments should focus instead on improving achievement in urban schools.[18]

"The effort to get the right racial balance is misguided" and represents a kind of "liberal racism — a belief that black children need to be in school with white children to learn," says Stephan Thernstrom, a history professor at Harvard University and a fellow at the conservative Manhattan Institute.

If integration "can be managed naturally, that's fine, but there is no clear correlation that can be drawn from data" showing it's important for closing the achievement gap, Thernstrom says. He rejects as incomplete and flawed studies that suggest integration does make a big difference. Furthermore, "if you need a white majority to learn," learning will soon be impossible in America, since Hispanic, Asian and African-American populations are growing faster than the current white majority, he notes.

Racial concentration is not the same as segregation and doesn't stand in the way of achievement, said his wife, Manhattan Institute Senior Fellow Abigail Thernstrom. School districts are powerless to change housing demographics, making it highly unlikely that racial concentration of students ever could be ended, she said.[19]

Some school districts are attempting to integrate lower-income and higher-income students, rather than integrating schools based on race. But Abigail Thernstrom argued that giving children a longer commute to schools outside their neighborhoods, for any reason, simply wastes time better spent in the classroom. "Busing doesn't raise the level of achievement," she told C-SPAN. "Now they're going to start busing on the basis of social class. And I have a very simple view of that. Stop moving the kids around and teach them."[20]

Meanwhile, some charter schools — such as the Knowledge Is Power Program (KIPP), begun in Houston — are making great strides in reducing the urban achievement gap, and for the most part those schools are not racially integrated, wrote *New York Times Magazine* features editor Paul Tough last year.

Most of the 70 schools that make up the three charter networks he observed have "only one or two white children enrolled, or none at all," he noted. Leaders of the networks, all of them white, actually intend to educate their students separately from middle-class students, according to Tough. However, unlike those who've argued that schools can be "separate but equal," the successful high-intensity charter schools aim for "separate but better." Their founders argue that

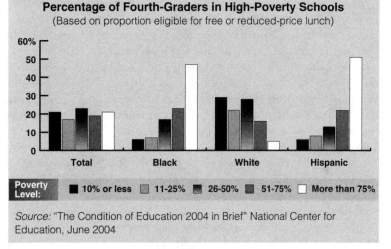

**Blacks, Hispanics Attend High-Poverty Schools**

Black and Hispanic students are more likely to be concentrated in high-poverty schools than white students. Forty-seven percent of black and 51 percent of Hispanic fourth-graders were in the highest-poverty schools in 2003 vs. 5 percent of white fourth-graders. By contrast, only 6 percent of black and Hispanic fourth-graders were in the lowest-poverty schools compared with 29 percent of whites.

**Percentage of Fourth-Graders in High-Poverty Schools**
(Based on proportion eligible for free or reduced-price lunch)

Poverty Level: ■ 10% or less ▨ 11-25% ▨ 26-50% ▨ 51-75% □ More than 75%

*Source:* "The Condition of Education 2004 in Brief" National Center for Education, June 2004

"students who enter middle school significantly behind grade level don't need the same good education that most American middle-class students receive; they need a better education," he said.[21]

But many advocates argue that data show a proven way to improve education for thousands of low-income students rather than for the handful that attend the highly successful charter schools is integration of minority and poor students with middle-class children.

School desegregation by race "has clear academic benefits," wrote R. Scott Baker, an associate professor of education at Wake Forest University. Data from Charlotte, N.C., show that the longer both black and white students spent in desegregated elementary schools, the higher their standardized test scores in middle and high school. Research also suggests that "where school desegregation plans are fully and completely implemented," local housing also becomes more integrated.[22]

In the 1960s and '70s some federal courts mandated programs to help urban minority families move to middle-class white suburbs. Long-term data from those cases show that children who moved did better than those who stayed behind, according to Howell S. Baum, a professor of urban studies and planning at the University of Maryland. In St. Louis, 50 percent of the black students who moved to the suburbs graduated from high school, compared to 26 percent of those who remained in the high-minority, low-income urban schools.[23]

Many policy analysts agree that segregating low-income children in some public schools "perpetuates failure," wrote the Century Foundation's Task Force on the Common School. Nevertheless, there is an "equally durable political consensus that nothing much can be done about it." The panel argued that this must change: "Eliminating the harmful effects of concentrated school poverty is the single most important step that can be taken for improving education in the United States."[24]

"Dozens of studies" dating back to the 1960s "find that low-income children have . . . larger achievement gains over time when they attend middle-class schools," said the panel.[25]

"The tragedy right now is that places that were once forced to [integrate their schools] now aren't allowed to," says Orfield of The Civil Rights Project. "That will be seen as a cosmic blunder" for white Americans as well, he said. "We're not preparing ourselves for the multiracial society and world" of the 21st century.

## Are teachers prepared to teach successfully in urban classrooms?

Urban schools have high teacher turnover, low test scores and many reported discipline problems. Furthermore, most of America's teaching force still consists of white, middle-class women, while urban schoolchildren are low-income minorities, creating a culture gap that may be hard to bridge.

Consequently, some analysts argue that today's teachers aren't prepared to teach successfully in urban classrooms for a variety of reasons, from discipline to second-language issues. Others, however, point to sterling examples of teachers and schools that do succeed and argue that the real problem is teachers not following good examples.

Fifth-grade teacher Rafe Esquith, at the Hobart Elementary School in central Los Angeles, routinely coaches his urban Korean and Central American-immigrant students to top standardized-test scores. Furthermore, his classes produce Shakespearean plays so impressive they've been invited to perform with Britain's Royal Shakespeare Company, said Abigail Thernstrom.[26]

But despite Esquith's success, "nobody copies him," even in his own school, said Thernstrom. "I went to the fifth-grade [classroom] next door [to Esquith's] one day," and "it was perfectly clear nothing was going on." When Thernstrom suggested the teacher might copy Esquith's methods — which include beginning class as early as 6 a.m. and working with students at his home on weekends — he remarked that "it's an enormous amount of work."[27]

Today, around the country, "we do have shining examples" of schools that succeed at urban education, says Timothy Knowles, executive director of the University of Chicago's Center for Urban School Improvement and a former deputy school superintendent in Boston.

Ratner, of Citizens for Effective Schools, agrees. "I spent time in an elementary school in Chicago a few years ago where all the teachers were teaching reading," even at the upper grades, equipping students with the vocabulary and comprehension skills needed for future academic work, he says. "They had a good principal, and they were showing that it can be done."

But while successful urban schools and classrooms are out there, many education analysts say the know-how and resources needed to spread that success to millions of students are sorely lacking.

Some individual schools are closing the achievement gap for needy students, but "very few, if any" entire school districts have had equivalent success, says Knowles.

Charter schools also haven't seen their successes spread as widely as many hoped.

Out of Ohio's "300-plus charter schools," for example, "some . . . are indeed excellent, but too many are appalling," wrote analysts Terry Ryan and Quentin Suffran of the conservative Thomas B. Fordham Foundation in a recent report.[28]

There are reasons for that, said Mark Simon, director of the Center for Teacher Leadership at Johns Hopkins University, in Baltimore. "Teaching lower-class kids well is tougher than teaching middle-class kids." Furthermore, "it is surprising how little we know about teaching practices that cause students to succeed, particularly in high-poverty schools."[29]

"You have poverty in many districts, but in urban schools you have a concentration of it" that makes teaching successfully there much harder than in middle-class suburbs, says Timothy Shanahan, professor of urban education at the University of Illinois at Chicago and president of the International Reading Association. Schools are traditionally set up to deal with 15 to 20 percent of a student body having very high needs, says Shanahan. But urban schools usually have 50 percent or more of their students needing special attention of some kind, "and that's a huge burden on the teachers," he says.

"Literally, we have 5-year-olds who come into the Chicago school system not knowing their own names," he says. "I know local neighborhoods with gang problems, where the kids are up all night. Their mothers are hiding them under the bed to protect them from shootings in the street. Then teachers can't keep them awake in class."

The nation's rapidly growing Hispanic population is heavily concentrated in urban schools. That new phenomenon presents another tough obstacle for the urban teaching force, because "older teachers know nothing about working with non-native English speakers," says McQuillan of Boston College.

Not just language but race complicates urban-school teaching. As many as 81 percent of all teacher-education students are white women.[30]

"Those most often entering teaching continue to be white, monolingual, middle-class women," wrote Jocelyn A. Glazier, assistant professor of education at the University of North Carolina at Chapel Hill.[31]

Many teachers, especially white women, shy away from making tough demands on African-American students, according to a survey of urban community leaders by Wanda J. Blanchett, associate professor of urban special education at the University of Wisconsin, Milwaukee. "Especially with African-American males, you hear the teachers say, 'Oh, he is such a nice kid.' But . . . this irks me when teachers baby their students to death instead of pushing. . . . I get that a lot when you have white teachers who have never worked with black students from the urban environment."[32]

Many entering education students at Indiana University-Purdue University, in Indianapolis, balked at the school's fieldwork and student-teaching venues,

which were in urban schools, wrote Professor Christine H. Leland and Professor Emeritus Jerome C. Harste. "They saw our program's urban focus as an obstacle to their career goals" of teaching in schools like the suburban ones most had attended.[33]

Some viewed urban students as an alien race they didn't want to learn to know. "Students rarely felt the need to interrogate their underlying assumption that poor people deserve the problems they have" or "spent any time talking or thinking about issues such as poverty or racism," Leland and Harste wrote. After student teaching, however, some students changed their plans and applied to become urban teachers.[34]

Race is a taboo subject in America, which some analysts say compounds urban teachers' difficulties. Many teacher-preparation programs center on an effort not to see or at least not to acknowledge race differences, according to Glazier. But "by claiming not to notice [race], the teacher is saying that she is dismissing one of the most salient features of a child's identity."[35]

"Many teachers believe that if they recognize a student's race or discuss issues of ethnicity in their classroom, they might be labeled as insensitive and racist," wrote Central Michigan University graduate student in education Dreyon Wynn and Associate Dean Dianne L. H. Mark. But white teachers' deliberate color-blindness ignores students "unique culture, beliefs, perceptions, [and] values," blocking both learning and helpful student-teacher relationships, Mark and Wynn argue.[36]

## BACKGROUND
### Educating the Poor

American education has long struggled with providing equal education for the poor, racial minorities and non-English-speaking immigrants. Until recently, however, even people who never made it through high school could usually find a good job. A new, global, technical economy may be changing that.

In the earliest years in the United States, schooling wasn't widespread. A farm-based economy made extensive education unnecessary for most people. In 1805, more than 90 percent of Americans had completed a fifth-grade education or less, and education for richer people was often conducted by private tutors.[37]

# CHRONOLOGY

**1950s-1960s** *Concerns grow over student achievement and racially segregated schools.*

**1954** Supreme Court rules in *Brown v. Board of Education* that separate schools are inherently unequal.

**1965** Title I of the new Elementary and Secondary Education Act (ESEA) targets the largest pool of federal education assistance to help schools serving disadvantaged students.

**1966** Sociologist James S. Coleman's "Equality of Educational Opportunity" report concludes that disadvantaged African-American students do better in integrated classrooms.

**1969** National Assessment of Educational Progress (NAEP) tests launched but report statewide average scores only, allowing states to mask lagging achievement among poor and minority students.

**1970s-1980s** *Latinos are becoming most segregated minority in U.S. schools. "Magnet schools" are established. School integration efforts gradually end.*

**1973** Supreme Court rules in *San Antonio Independent School District v. Rodriguez* the Constitution does not guarantee equal education for all children. . . . In *Keyes v. School District No. 1*, the court bans city policies that segregate Denver schools.

**1990s-2000s** *Steady gains in African-American students' test scores over the past two decades begin to taper off by decade's end. . . . Poverty concentrates in cities. . . . Governors lead efforts to raise education standards.*

**1990** New Jersey Supreme Court rules in *Abbott v. Burke* the state must provide more funding for poor schools than for richer ones.

**1991** Minnesota enacts first charter-school law.

**1994** In reauthorizing ESEA, Congress requires states receiving Title I funding for disadvantaged students to hold them to the same academic standards as all students.

**1995** Knowledge Is Power Program charter schools launched in Houston and New York City. . . . Boston

creates Pilot School program to research ideas for urban-school improvement.

**1999** Florida establishes first statewide school-voucher program.

**2000** Countywide, income-based school integration launched in Raleigh, N.C.

**2002** Cambridge, Mass., schools begin integration based on income.

**2002** No Child Left Behind Act (NCLB) requires states to report student test scores "disaggregated" by race, income and gender to avoid masking the failing scores of some groups. . . . U.S. Supreme Court rules in favor of Ohio's school-voucher program, which allows public funding for tuition at Cleveland parochial schools. . . . State takes over Philadelphia's bankrupt school system, allows private companies to run some schools.

**2005** Hoping to halt isolation of the lowest-income students in inner-city schools, Omaha, Neb., tries but fails to annex neighboring suburban districts.

**2006** Department of Education admits that few students in failing city schools receive the free tutoring NCLB promised and that no states have met the 2006 deadline for having qualified teachers in all classrooms. . . . Government Accountability Office finds that nearly one-third of public schools, most in low-income and minority communities, need major repairs.

**2007** Gov. Deval L. Patrick, D-Mass., puts up $6.5 million to help schools lengthen their hours. . . . Democratic Mayor Adrian Fenty, of Washington, D.C., is the latest of several mayors to take control of schools. . . . New York City Schools Chancellor Joel Klein says he will fire principals of schools with lagging test scores. . . . Teachers' unions slam report calling for all high-school seniors to be proficient in reading and math by 2014. . . . Houston school district calls for state to replace NCLB-related standardized periodic testing on math and reading with traditional end-of-course subject-matter exams.

**June 2007** U.S. Supreme Court invalidates school-attendance-zone plans used in Seattle and Louisville to achieve greater racial diversity. The 5-4 ruling in *Parents Involved in Community Schools v. Seattle Dist. No. 1* said the Seattle School District's plan to use race as a consideration in student assignments was unconstitutional.

**Nov. 26, 2008** Washington, D.C., School Chancellor Michelle Rhee appears on the cover of Time.

**2009-2010** *Educational reforms have been made by 28 states under the administration's $4 billion state grant education initiative, Race to the Top. The number of reforms is triple that of the previous two years.*

**2009** Education Secretary Arne Duncan rescinds pending scholarships under the D.C. Opportunity Scholarship Program, and Congress declines to reauthorize.

**2010** Obama administration unveils its blueprint to overhaul No Child Left Behind Act. . . . In the District of Columbia in June, school officials and the teachers' union finalize a contract that, in addition to granting a retroactive pay increase, requires all teachers in the system to be evaluated in part on whether their students' test scores improve, and offers sizable pay increases to teachers who opt for and succeed in a special new pay-for-performance arrangement. . . . Civil Rights Project at UCLA reviews school integration efforts and calls on the Obama administration to issue guidance on how race can be considered in public education. . . . Washington, D.C., School Chancellor Rhee dismisses 241 teachers.

## 2011

*Thirty-seven states provide less funding to local schools than in the 2010-2011 school year.*

**January** — Newly elected Republican governors and legislators in states including Wisconsin, Ohio, Indiana, Idaho, New Jersey and Florida propose bills to lower costs and improve education by ending teacher tenure, limiting teachers' collective bargaining rights, instituting merit pay and firing teachers based on student-achievement test results.

**March** — *USA Today* reports possible evidence of cheating on standardized tests at Washington, D.C., schools.

**May** — Georgia Bureau of Investigation reports that 178 teachers and principals in Atlanta conspired to change student-achievement test scores.

**November** — U.S. Department of Education data show that many districts don't provide high-poverty schools with resources equal to those provided to schools in wealthier neighborhoods.

## 2012

**March** — For the fourth consecutive year, many teachers in the Los Angeles and San Francisco school districts receive warnings that their jobs are at risk.

**May** — A committee of the Illinois legislature supports requiring school districts to provide more funding for charter schools; Chicago Teachers Union campaigns against the proposal. . . . Schools nationwide perform poorly on a science-achievement test, but black and Hispanic students slightly narrow the gap between their scores and those of white students. . . . Federal Communications Commission announces it will inform phone companies that they must follow a 15-year-old rule requiring them to give schools bargain prices so more can afford good Internet access.

## 2013

**January 1** — Urban schools could face major cuts in federal Title I funds if Congress doesn't resolve a budget stalemate.

**October 4** — Members of Chicago Teachers Union, ending a month-long walkout, overwhelmingly approve a new three-year contract that includes pay increases and new evaluation system.

**March** — After months of short-term funding bills, Congress passes omnibus measure that includes 5 percent cut to federal education programs.

**September** — Time magazine reports that Kentucky, first to adopt Common Core, saw its high school graduation rate increase from 80 percent in 2010 to 86 percent in 2013.

**November** — Bill de Blasio, elected mayor of New York City, plans to back off predecessor's pursuit of charter schools.

## 2014

**January 1** — The year the original goals of the 2001 No Child Left Behind law were to have been met; the law's reauthorization is stalled in Congress.

**May** — Overall federal funding levels for education set with Title I apt to receive small increase.

# Dropouts' Problems Often Begin Early

*Clear warning signs appear, such as skipping class*

With the baby-boom generation on the verge of retirement, sustaining the American workforce and economy depends on having a cadre of new young workers to replace them, says former Gov. Bob Wise, D-W.Va., now president of the Alliance for Excellent Education. But with jobs in the fastest-growing economic sectors now requiring at least a high-school diploma and, often, two years or more of post-high-school training, coming up with an adequately trained new workforce won't be easy, Wise says.

The annual graduation rate has risen from a little over 50 percent per year in the late 1960s to 73.9 percent in 2003. If it's to rise higher, however, the improvement must come among poor and minority students, mostly in urban schools, who are far less likely than others to earn diplomas.[1]

For example, while about two-thirds of all students who enter ninth grade graduate four years later, on-time graduation rates for minority and low-income students, especially males, are much lower. In 2001, for example, only about 50 percent of African-American students and 51 percent of Latino students graduated on time, compared to 75 percent of white students and 77 percent of Asian and Pacific Islanders.[2]

Students with family incomes in the lowest 20 percent dropped out of school at six times the average rate of wealthier students.[3]

In about a sixth of American high schools, the freshman class routinely shrinks by 40 percent or more by the time students reach senior year. For the most part, those schools serve low-income and minority students. Nearly half of African-American students, 40 percent of Latino students and 11 percent of white students attend high schools where graduation is not the norm. A high school with a majority of students who are racial or ethnic minorities is five times more likely to promote only 50 percent or fewer freshmen to senior status within four years than a school with a white majority.[4]

Meanwhile, the earning power of dropouts has been dropping for three decades. For example, the earnings of male dropouts fell by 35 percent between 1971 and 2002, measured in 2002 dollars. Three-quarters of state prison inmates and 59 percent of federal inmates are dropouts. In 2001, only 55 percent of young adult dropouts were employed. Even the death rate is 2.5 times higher for people without a high-school education than for people with 13 years or more of schooling.[5]

But if the consequences are known, the cures may be harder to pinpoint.

Many educators say dropping out starts early. "Disengagement doesn't start in the ninth grade. It starts in fifth," says James F. Lytle, a University of Pennsylvania professor and former superintendent of the Trenton, N.J., public schools. For on-track students in middle-class schools, "middle school has the most interesting, exciting stuff in class" — science experiments, readings about interesting people in history and studies "of how the world works" — he says.

But once students are judged to be reading behind grade level, as happens with many urban fifth-graders, middle schools turn to "dumbed-down remedial work" that's below students' real intellectual level and leaves them bored and dispirited, Lytle says. It doesn't have to be that way, he says. "But I wish that educational courseware was farther down the road" of providing ways to combine skills teaching with subject matter that is at students' actual age level.

State legislatures were just beginning to debate whether to establish free tax-funded schools for all children.[38] Nevertheless, even in those early days, some religious and other charitable groups considered it a moral duty to educate the poor. In New York City, for example, the Association of Women Friends for the Relief of the Poor opened a charity school in 1801. By 1823 the group was providing free elementary education for 750 children, with some public assistance. Similar charity schools sprang up in most other major cities.

But as all states began establishing public education systems — between the late 18th and the mid-19th century — questions over equality in education arose, first for black students and later for immigrants. "When public schools opened in Boston in the late 18th century, black children were neither barred nor segregated,"

"Kids disengage early," says Lalitha Vasudevan, an assistant professor at Columbia University's Teachers College who works in an education program for young African-American males who've been diverted from jail and are mostly dropouts. "Often, early on, they've had teachers say things to them that they interpret as, 'You don't really care that I'm here,' " she says.

Dropping out "is not a decision that is made on a single morning," says a report from the Bill & Melinda Gates Foundation. In an extensive survey of dropouts, researchers found that "there are clear warning signs for at least one-to-three years" before students drop out, such as frequently missing school, skipping class, being held back a grade or frequently transferring among schools.[6]

Some key factors cited by the dropouts in the Gates study: Schools don't respond actively when students skip class and don't provide an orderly and safe environment. "In middle school, you have to go to your next class or they are going to get you," said a young male dropout from Philadelphia. "In high school, if you don't go to class, there isn't anybody who is going to get you. You just do your own thing."[7]

Lytle says cities could also establish post-dropout academies, like the Dropout Recovery High School he started in Trenton, which helped increase that city's graduation numbers.

"Rather than defining the whole problem as stopping dropouts, we can also reach out to those who already have," he says. "There are a slew of people around" who are out of school and would like to go back, from teenage mothers caring for their children to 60-year-olds, he says. "They need a school that is built around their lives. I simply don't understand why urban districts haven't been more imaginative" about this.

## Majority of Dropouts Are Hispanic, Black

More than 50 percent of 20-year-old male high-school dropouts are Hispanic or African-American (graph at left). By comparison, 55 percent of the females are black or Hispanic (graph at right).

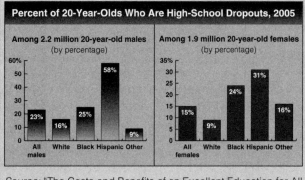

**Percent of 20-Year-Olds Who Are High-School Dropouts, 2005**

Among 2.2 million 20-year-old males (by percentage)

All males 23% · White 16% · Black 25% · Hispanic 58% · Other 9%

Among 1.9 million 20-year-old females (by percentage)

All females 15% · White 9% · Black 24% · Hispanic 31% · Other 16%

Source: "The Costs and Benefits of an Excellent Education for All of America's Children," Teachers College, Columbia University, January 2007

[1] Nancy Martin and Samuel Halperin, *Whatever It Takes: How Twelve Communities are Reconnecting Out-of-School Youth,* American Youth Policy Forum, www.aypf.org/publications/WhateverItTakes/WITfull.pdf.

[2] *Ibid.*

[3] *Ibid.*

[4] Robert Balfanz and Nettie Legters, "Locating the Dropout Crisis," Center for Social Organization of Schools, Johns Hopkins University, June 2004.

[5] Martin and Halperin, *op. cit.*

[6] John M. Bridgeland, John J. DiIulio, Jr. and Karen Burke Morison, *The Silent Epidemic: Perspectives of High School Dropouts,* Bill & Melinda Gates Foundation, March 2006.

[7] Quoted in *ibid.*

wrote Derrick Bell, a visiting professor at the New York University School of Law. "But by 1790, racial insults and mistreatment had driven out all but three or four black children."[39]

Later, some black families joined with white liberals to form black-only schools in Massachusetts and in other states. But complaints about poor conditions and poor teaching in those schools led others to sue for integrated education.

Even in the early 19th century, some courts were bothered by race-based inequities in education, said Bell. A federal court struck down a Kentucky law directing that school taxes collected from white people would maintain white schools, and taxes from blacks would operate black schools. "Given the great disparities in taxable resources" this would result in an inferior education for black children, the court said.[40]

# The "Behavior Gap" Between Black and White Students

*Many educators blame a system that's middle-class and white-centered*

Data from around the country indicate that black students, especially males, are cited much more often for disciplinary infractions than whites. The resulting "behavior gap" parallels the much-talked-about academic achievement gap.

Many analysts blame the phenomenon in part on a "culture clash" between black students, many poor, and an education system that's white-centered and middle-class. But there's little agreement about exactly what the gap means and what to do about it.

"You find the gap in all schools," including wealthy ones, says Clara G. Muschkin, a researcher at the Duke University Center for Child and Family Policy. Nevertheless, some evidence suggests there may also be a behavior gap between richer and poorer students, which accounts for just under a third of the black-white gap, Muschkin says.

In North Carolina schools, the racial gap "is persistent at all the grades" but is widest in seventh grade, says Muschkin. About 30 percent of black seventh-graders and 14 percent of whites have at least one disciplinary infraction reported during the school year.

African-American male students have the highest rates of suspensions and expulsions in most metropolitan areas around the country, according to Denise L. Collier, a doctoral candidate in education at California State University, Los Angeles. In New York, for example, where African-American males are 18 percent of the student population, they account for 39 percent of school suspensions and 50 percent of expulsions. In Los Angeles, black males make up 6 percent of the population but account for 18 percent of suspensions and 15 percent of expulsions.[1]

Some educators say that many urban African-American students don't learn at home the kinds of communication behaviors that are the norm for the middle class, and that this lack of background accounts for much of the gap.

"Americans of a certain background learn . . . early on and employ . . . instinctively" techniques like sitting up straight, asking questions and tracking a speaker with their eyes in order to take in information, said David Levin, a founder of the Knowledge Is Power Program (KIPP) charter schools, which serve mainly black and Hispanic students in several cities.[2]

When students in one Levin class were asked to "give us the normal school look," they responded by staring off into space and slouching, recounted *New York Times Magazine* editor Paul Tough in an article last year on successful urban charter schools. "Middle-class Americans know intuitively that 'good behavior' is mostly a game with established rules; the KIPP students seemed to be experiencing the pleasure of being let in on a joke," Tough observed.[3]

Behavior like a proper in-school work ethic has to be taught "in the same way we have to teach adding fractions with unlike denominators," said Dacia Toll, founder of the Amistad Academy charter school in New Haven, Conn. "But once children have got the work ethic and the commitment to others and to education down, it's actually pretty easy to teach them."

The academic gap that puts many black students in remedial instruction as they move through school may worsen the problem, says Robert Balfanz, associate research scientist at the Johns Hopkins University Center on the Social Organization of Schools. "In traditional remedial

---

Around the 1820s, waves of non-English immigration began, raising new controversies over educating poor children of sometimes-despised ethnicities.

Before 1820, most U.S. immigrants were English, and a few were Dutch. But between 1820 and 1840 Irish immigrants became the first in a long parade of newcomers

judged inferior by the predominantly English population. A rising tide of immigration in the late 19th and early 20th centuries included many non-English-speakers — Italians, Germans, Chinese, Russians, Poles and many others — who posed new challenges for schools and were looked down on by many citizens.

instruction, I assume you know nothing, so I teach the times table" and basic reading skills like letter sounds, he says. "But the majority of kids behind can actually read at a basic level. What they're missing is comprehension skill, vocabulary. So they get bored and frustrated."

Middle-class education majors student-teaching in urban schools found that using books about topics their students personally had encountered — including homelessness, racism and poverty — decreased discipline problems, even though the teachers initially resisted the books as inappropriate for children, according to Professor Christine H. Leland and Professor Emeritus Jerome C. Harste of Indiana University-Purdue University, Indianapolis. Once the student teachers broached the tough subject matter, they began reporting "fewer discipline problems . . . the children listened carefully and engaged in thoughtful discussions when they perceived that the issues being discussed were worth their attention."[4]

Many African-American student discipline problems involve "defiance" issues such as acting threatening or making excessive noise rather than activities like drug use or leaving the classroom without permission, according to University of Virginia Assistant Professor Anne Gregory.[5]

Seventy-five percent of African-American disciplinary referrals were for "defiance" behaviors in a study Gregory cites, many more than for other ethnic groups. That may suggest that teachers judge African-American students' behavior more "subjectively" than that of other students, Gregory says. Based on their past feelings of being restricted and excluded, some African-American students may be more likely to act out when they perceive that teachers are being unfair, Gregory suggests.

"If I was this little Caucasian boy or this preppy girl, she wouldn't talk with me that way. I am like the opposite. I am this little thug . . . I mean, she don't know," one student in Gregory's study said of a teacher perceived to be unfair.[6]

Avoiding excessive discipline battles in urban schools requires a seemingly contradictory set of characteristics that not everyone can muster, said Franita Ware, a professor of education at Spelman College, a historically black school for women in Atlanta. Teachers who succeed tend to be "warm demanders," those whom "students believed . . . did not lower their standards" but also "were willing to help them."[7]

"Sometimes I mean-talk them in varying degrees of severity," one teacher told Ware. But "sometimes you have to go back and say, 'What was really going on with you when I yelled at you? I'm just so sorry.' "[8]

Often the adult is the provocateur in the behavior situation, even if they don't realize it, such as when a student finds the nurse's office door locked at 3:02 and starts pounding on it, says James F. Lytle, a professor at the University of Pennsylvania and former school superintendent in Trenton, N.J.

"A lot of it is just the way you talk to people — respect," Lytle says. "Many are so accustomed to being denigrated. The kids have so little that the protection of one's ego is very important."

[1]Denise L. Collier, "Sally Can Skip But Jerome Can't Stomp: Perceptions, Practice, and School Punishment (Preliminary Results)," paper presented at the American Educational Research Association annual meeting, San Francisco, Calif., April 2006.

[2]Quoted in Paul Tough, "What It Takes To Make a Student," *New York Times Magazine*, Nov. 26, 2006, p. 51.

[3]*Ibid.*

[4]Christine H. Leland and Jerome C. Harste, "Doing What We Want to Become: Preparing New Urban Teachers," *Urban Education*, January 2005, p. 67.

[5]Anne Gregory, "Justice and Care: Teacher Practices To Narrow the Racial Discipline Gap," paper presented at the American Educational Research Association annual conference, San Francisco, Calif., April 2006.

[6]Quoted in *ibid.*

[7]Franita Ware, "Warm Demander Pedagogy: Culturally Responsive Teaching that Supports A Culture of Achievement for African-American Students," *Urban Education*, July 2006, p. 427.

[8]Quoted in *ibid.*

The new immigrants generally clustered in cities, the economic engines of the time, and overcrowded city schools were charged with integrating them into American life. Critics charged that the urban schools used rigid instruction and harsh discipline to control classrooms bursting with 60 or more children, many of whom spoke no English.

## Two Tracks

In the economy of the early 20th century, however, there remained little need for most students to learn more than basic reading and writing, so the failure of poor urban schools to produce many graduates wasn't seen as a problem.

In current debates over U.S. education, "people aren't looking at education historically" and therefore expect American schools to do things they were never designed to do, says Ratner of Citizens for Effective Schools.

"We consciously decided to have a two-track system," he says. In the early 20th century, education experts generally agreed that "in the industrial age there are lots of immigrants and poor people, and most are going to work on the assembly line, so how about if we create an academic track and a general/vocational track" mostly for the poor?

The school system that we have "was never set up to educate all students to the levels of proficiency now being asked for," Ratner says.

"I graduated exactly 40 years ago, and then about half the kids — 52 percent — were graduating," says Wise of the Alliance for Excellent Education. "And the non-graduates could still get good jobs."

But today "the fastest-growing sectors of the economy require two years of post high-school training," says Daniel J. Cardinali, president of Communities In Schools, a dropout-prevention group that helps school districts bring services like tutoring and health care to needy students.

Calls in the 1990s for higher academic standards by groups like The Business Roundtable brought widespread attention to the problems of low student achievement, especially in low-income schools.

Today few question the premise that all students should attain higher levels of literacy, mathematical problem-solving and critical thinking. Many who work in schools argue that simply setting higher standards isn't nearly enough, however, especially for urban schools where most students already are behind grade level.

As standards rise, for example, "ninth-graders are increasingly placed in introductory algebra classes . . . despite skill gaps in fundamental arithmetic," wrote Balfanz and Ruth Curran Neild, research scientists at the Johns Hopkins University Center on the Social Organization of Schools.

But few resources exist to help kids catch up, "nor are there many curriculum materials that specifically target the spotty skills of urban ninth-graders," the Johns Hopkins researchers said. And when students reading behind grade level enter middle and high school, their "secondary-certified English teachers" — educated to teach high-school-level literature and composition — "are generally unprepared" to diagnose reading problems or to teach comprehension strategies and background vocabulary they need. Science and history teachers are even less prepared to help, Balfanz and Neild said.[41]

Retooling the school system to support higher standards may seem daunting, but "a quick walk through history" shows that it wouldn't be the first time the United States has made heroic efforts on education, says Wise. For example, "after World War II, you had soldiers coming home in need of better skills, and you had the GI Bill" to help them continue their educations.

Then "in the civil rights era we said, 'We believe that every child should be able to enter school,' and that happened," Wise says. "Now we're saying that every child should graduate."

For a time, the civil rights era seemed to be accelerating growing academic parity in learning, at least between black and white students. Following World War II, standardized test scores for black students began moving closer to white students' scores. The years from the 1960s to the '80s saw fully half of the black-white academic achievement gap eliminated, says The Civil Rights Project's Orfield.

In the late '80s, however, the progress of African-American students in closing the gap stalled, and between 1988 and 1994, average test scores for black students actually began falling.[42]

## Minority Schools

U.S. schools briefly became more integrated after the civil rights battles of the 1950s and '60s, but shifting housing patterns have caused the concentration of poor, minority and non-English-speaking students in urban schools to rise for the past 25 years.

"One thing that's not fully understood is that, through a long historical process, we've concentrated our most needy students in a small subset of schools and districts" in rural and, mostly, urban areas, vastly increasing the burden those schools face in raising academic achievement, says Balfanz.

In its landmark 1954 *Brown v. Board of Education* ruling, the Supreme Court declared it illegal to intentionally segregate schools by race.[43] In 1964, Congress passed the Civil Rights Act, outlawing discrimination in any institution that received federal funds, including schools.[44] As a result, more schools accommodated lower-income students along with middle-class students, white students and students from other ethnic groups.

The civil rights era lasted a scant 20 years, however, and housing patterns and new waves of immigration soon led to concentrations of poor and minority students in many urban school districts again.

As early as 1974, the Supreme Court effectively set limits on how far racial integration of students could go. The court ruled in *Milliken v. Bradley* that the remedy to racial segregation in Detroit could not include moving children to schools in the surrounding suburbs.[45]

Then, in the 1980s, federal efforts to desegregate schools effectively ended. During the presidency of Ronald Reagan (1981-1988), the U.S. Justice Department backed off forcing states to comply with desegregation mandates. Two Supreme Court decisions in the early 1990s effectively declared the goal of black-white school integration had been addressed, as the court ruled that school districts could be excused from court-ordered busing if they had made good-faith efforts to integrate, even if they had not fully complied with court orders.[46]

At the same time, however, Hispanic students were becoming a new minority that concentrated in schools with bigger academic challenges than others, such as teaching English-language learners.

The segregation of Latino students soared during the civil rights era. In 1973, in *Keyes v. School District No. 1,* the Supreme Court outlawed policies in Denver that had the effect of segregating Hispanic and African-American children into separate schools. In ensuing years, however, this somewhat complex ruling was only spottily enforced, according to civil rights advocates.[47]

Today Latinos "are America's most segregated minority group," said Orfield. The average Latino student goes to a school that is less than 30 percent white, has a majority of poor children and an "increasing concentration" of students who don't speak English.[48]

## Poor in School

Until around the 1970s, children of all races and classes attended urban schools, and their average achievement levels didn't draw the same alarmed attention as today. Urban sprawl and white flight from cities over the past three decades have not only increased the number of urban schools with high minority populations but also

AP Photo/Mike Derer

Edwin Bradley listens to his fifth-grade daughter Antoinette read at the South Street School library in Newark, N.J. One of the poorest in the state, the school district has been encouraged under a new program to support parental involvement in an attempt to improve student performance.

increased the concentration of urban poverty as well, increasing the burden on urban schools.

"Sprawl is a product of suburban pulls and urban pushes," said the University of Maryland's Baum. "Families move to the suburbs for good housing, open space. They leave cities to avoid bad schools, threats to safety . . . contact with other races and poor public services."[49]

Furthermore, minority children are more concentrated in urban areas than the general population, largely because white families with children move to suburbs while childless whites are more likely to remain in the city, said Baum. Nationally, in nearly all school districts with more than 25,000 students, interracial contact has declined since 1986.[50]

Even more than ethnic minorities, poor people have concentrated in cities, says Balfanz. Over the past 20 years, even in periods when overall poverty has dropped, "the cities have gotten poorer and the concentration of poverty there deeper."

Between 1960 and 1987, the national poverty rate for people in central cities rose from 13.4 percent to 15.7 percent. At the same time, the poverty rate for rural residents fell by one-half and for suburban residents by one-third. By 1991, 43 percent of people with incomes below the federal poverty line lived in central cities.[51]

# Would raising teacher pay help struggling schools?

## YES
**Patty Myers**
*Technology Coordinator,*
*Great Falls (Montana) Public Schools*

From testimony on behalf of the National Education Association before U.S. Senate Committee on Finance, March 20, 2007

Ensuring a highly qualified teacher in every classroom is critical to closing achievement gaps and maximizing student learning. No single factor will make a bigger difference in helping students reach high academic standards. . . .

Unfortunately, difficulty in attracting quality teachers and high turnover rates severely hamper the ability to maintain a high-quality learning environment. Approximately one-third of the nation's new teachers leave the profession during their first three years, and almost one-half leave during their first five years. And turnover in low-income schools is almost one-third higher than the rate in all schools.

The teaching profession has an average national starting salary of $30,377. Meanwhile, computer programmers start at an average of $43,635, public accounting professionals at $44,668 and registered nurses at $45,570.

Annual pay for teachers has fallen sharply over the past 60 years in relation to the annual pay of other workers with college degrees. The average earnings of workers with at least four years of college are now over 50 percent higher than the average earnings of a teacher. Congress should reward states that set a reasonable minimum starting salary for teachers and a living wage for support professionals working in school districts. NEA recommends that all teachers in America enter the classroom earning at least $40,000 annually.

NEA also supports advancing teacher quality at the highest-poverty schools by providing $10,000 federal salary supplements to National Board Certified Teachers. Congress also should fund grants to help teachers in high-poverty schools pay the fees and access professional supports to become certified.

Often schools with the greatest needs and, consequently, the most challenging working conditions have the most difficulty retaining talented teachers. . . . Many hard-to-staff schools are high-poverty inner-city school or rural schools that, as a consequence of their location in economically depressed or isolated districts, offer comparatively low salaries and lack [the] amenities with which other districts attract teachers.

NEA strongly supports federal legislation with financial incentives for teaching in high-poverty schools, such as the Teacher Tax Credit Act introduced in the 109th Congress. The bill would provide a non-refundable tax credit to educators who work at schools that are fully eligible for federal Title I funds for disadvantaged students and would help hard-to-staff schools retain the quality teachers they need to succeed.

## NO
**Jay P. Greene**
*Senior Fellow, Manhattan Institute*

Posted on the Web, 2006

The common assertion that teachers are severely underpaid is so omnipresent that many Americans simply accept it as gospel. But the facts tell a different story.

The average teacher's salary does seem modest at first glance: about $44,600 in 2002 for all teachers. But when we compare it to what workers of similar skill levels in similar professions are paid, we find that teachers are not shortchanged.

People often fail to account for the relatively low number of hours that teachers work. Teachers work only about nine months per year. During the summer they can either work at other jobs or use the time off however else they wish. Either way, it's as much a form of compensation as a paycheck.

The most recent data indicate that teachers average 7.3 working hours per day, and that they work 180 days per year, or about 1,314 hours. Americans in normal 9-to-5 professions who take two weeks of vacation and another 10 paid holidays put in 1,928 hours. This means the average teacher's base salary is equivalent to a full-time salary of $65,440.

In 2002, elementary-school teachers averaged $30.75 per hour and high-school teachers $31.01 — about the same as architects, civil engineers and computer-systems analysts. Even demanding, education-intensive professions like dentistry and nuclear engineering didn't make much more per hour.

Some argue that it's unfair to calculate teacher pay on an hourly basis because teachers perform a large amount of work at home — grading papers on the weekend, for instance. But people in other professions also do off-site work.

Many assume that teachers spend almost all of the school day teaching. But in reality, the average subject-matter teacher taught fewer than 3.9 hours per day in 2000. This leaves plenty of time for grading and planning lessons.

It is well documented that the people drawn into teaching these days tend to be those who have performed least well in college. If teachers are paid about as well as employees in many other good professions, why aren't more high performers taking it up?

One suspects that high-performing graduates tend to stay away because the rigid seniority-based structure doesn't allow them to rise faster and earn more money through better performance or by voluntarily putting in longer hours. In any case, it's clear that the primary obstacle to attracting better teachers isn't simply raising pay.

"The nation's student population is two-thirds middle class (not eligible for federally subsidized lunches), yet one-quarter of American schools have a majority of students from low-income households," according to The Century Foundation.[52]

Among the burdens urban schools bear are poverty-related learning deficiencies children bring to school with them, regulations and economic barriers that limit urban-school resources, and a historical role as job providers in inner cities.

A large body of research shows that many low-income parents interact with their children in ways that hinder them in school, wrote Tough last year in *The New York Times Magazine*. For example, professional parents speak to their young children about two-and-a-half more times in an hour than poor parents do and encourage them verbally about six times more often than they discourage them; low-income parents discourage their children about three times as often as they encourage them, he said.

Unlike poor parents, middle-class parents also encourage their children to question, challenge and negotiate. In short, "in countless ways, the manner in which [poor children] are raised puts them at a disadvantage" in a school culture, Tough noted.[53]

For a variety of reasons, urban schools also have a much harder time keeping good teachers. "Many thousands — perhaps millions — of urban students don't have permanent, highly qualified teachers, ones with the skill to communicate important stuff to kids," says Kitty Kelly-Epstein, a professor of education at the Fielding Graduate University in Santa Barbara, Calif. In California, at least, state rules force some urban school districts to rely on temporary teachers because not enough applicants have required certifications, she says. "There never has been a time when low-income schools were fully staffed," she says.

With joblessness high in cities, especially for minority applicants, it's also "not uncommon" for school districts to be the major job source in the area, according to Johns Hopkins University Associate Professor of Education Elaine M. Stotko and colleagues. In a tradition that dates back to patronage systems in the early 20th century, urban politicians often interfere with schools' hiring the best managerial and teaching candidates by pressuring them to hand out jobs "as political favors."[54]

The Supreme Court is due to rule by the end of June in two race-based integration cases. With a new conservative majority, the court is widely expected to rule in favor of the white parents who are seeking to end race-based school integration in Seattle and Louisville, Ky. Decisions against the school districts could end many similar programs around the country, many of which were court-ordered in the past.[55]

But some school districts still worry that schools with high concentrations of minority and poor students harm achievement. Over the past several years, a few districts, including Raleigh, N.C., and Cambridge, Mass., have experimented with integrating students by socioeconomic status. In 2000, for example, the school board in Wake County, N.C., which includes Raleigh and its suburbs, replaced its racial integration system with the goal that no school should have 40 percent of students eligible for free or reduced-price lunch.[56]

Raleigh's effort was simpler politically than most, because the school district contains both the area's low-poverty and high-poverty schools. If the higher-income suburbs had been outside the district, political push-back would have made the program a tougher sell.

Some early Raleigh results look promising. On the state's 2005 High School End of Course exams, 63.8 percent of the low-income students passed, as did 64.3 percent of its African-American seniors, compared to pass rates in the high-40 and low 50-percent range for the state's other urban districts.[57]

## CURRENT SITUATION

### Congress Divided

The No Child Left Behind Act (NCLB), enacted in 2002, is intended to push American schools to raise achievement for all students, including low-income and minority children. As such, it represents one more step down a road that Congress embarked on in its 1994 reauthorization of the Elementary and Secondary Education Act — exerting federal influence to ensure that all students meet higher academic standards.

With NCLB up for reauthorization, Congress is struggling to figure out its next steps, with little apparent agreement on the horizon. With the press of other business, and strong disagreements in Congress about the education law, it's not clear that it will be reauthorized this year. The new congressional Democratic majority has already begun to hold hearings, however.

Newsmakers/Getty Images/Chris Hondros

The Knowledge Is Power Program (KIPP) charter school in the Bronx, N.Y., boasts the highest test scores in the area. Although most KIPP schools are not racially integrated, they are reducing achievement gaps between black and white students.

U.S. businesses have become increasingly involved in education policy, and many business leaders are urging Congress to continue and strengthen federal efforts to raise academic standards and provide incentives for states and localities to extensively retool their school systems to improve student achievement.

"Unless we transform the American high school, we will limit economic opportunities for millions of Americans," declared Microsoft Chairman Bill Gates at a Senate Health, Education, Labor and Pensions Committee hearing on March 7.[58]

Meanwhile, a group of conservative congressional Republicans has introduced legislation that would replace most of the NCLB achievement and reporting requirements that determine funding with block-grant funding that states could get whether they met NCLB standards or not. The measure would restore states and localities to their traditional role as prime overseers of schools, said Rep. Peter Hoekstra, R-Mich., who sponsored the legislation. "President Bush and I just see education fundamentally differently," he said. "The president believes in empowering bureaucrats in Washington, and I don't."[59]

But many congressional Democrats argue that a strengthened federal hand in education is warranted, partly because NCLB data now clearly reveal that the state-run systems of old have left so many poor and minority children disastrously behind.

Rep. George Miller, D-Calif., and Sen. Kennedy, key supporters of NCLB and chairs of the House and Senate committees that govern it, have both held pre-authorization hearings this year. Both say they're committed to increasing resources for struggling schools in a new bill, especially by supporting the hiring and training of more and better teachers.

"We know the law has flaws, but we also know that with common-sense changes and adequate resources, we can improve it by building on what we've learned," said Kennedy in a statement.

### Retooling NCLB?

Education analysts have no shortage of changes to suggest.

President Bush is looking at "tinkering" with NCLB in a reauthorization, but Democrats are "interested in something broader," says Cardinali of Communities in Schools. "The [current] law is too fixated on academics," he says. After 30 years of experience helping students get additional services they need like tutoring and health care, "we've learned that student services are a critical component," he says.

"The brutal truth is that there is only one institution in America where you can get to kids in a thoughtful way — the school," he says. "Let's make that the center" where parents and children can get needs met that are critical for learning. "Are we trying to make public education something it's not? No. It's a holistic view" of what it takes to educate a child.

One gap the University of Chicago's Knowles would like to see rectified: In NCLB's reporting requirements "the unit of analysis is the kid, the school and the district, and there's a stunning absence there if we really believe that instruction is at the heart of learning." Research indicates, he says, that individual classroom teachers may be the strongest in-school influence on student achievement.

However, "Democrats' strong ties to labor" helped keep teacher accountability out of the bill, he says.

In addition, "higher ed has been given pretty much a free pass," Knowles says. A future bill should focus attention on which education schools are producing the best-quality teachers.

Low-achieving schools shouldn't be punished, but given the tools to do better, says Knowles. Supports like teacher development and well-integrated extra services like social workers, closely targeted on high-need schools, are a "precondition" for improvement, he says.

Another key: additional flexibility for leaders of low-achieving schools to hire and fire and set policy and schedules. Principals say, "Yeah, you give me the hiring and firing of teachers and I'll give you the better results," and they're correct, says Knowles.

Reporting data for accountability isn't the problem. It's the very narrowly focused reporting requirement, many analysts say.

"Replace the overreliance on standardized testing with multiple measures," such as attendance figures and accurate dropout rates, says the University of Rochester's Hursh.

The federal government should also support strong, unbiased research on what improves instruction, especially in the middle- and high-school years, which are federally funded at a tiny fraction of the level of elementary schools and colleges, says Wise of the Alliance for Excellent Education. "No state or local district has the money for this," he says.

## OUTLOOK

### Agreeing to Disagree

There's growing agreement that schools should be educating all students to a higher standard. However, there's still disagreement about how much and what kind of help schools would need to do it.

An ideal outcome would be for institutions that are the most lasting presence in cities, such as business groups like the Chamber of Commerce, local hospitals and colleges to take ownership of urban education to drive change, says Balfanz of Johns Hopkins. A movement in that direction may be beginning, he says. "For awhile, there were mainly rhetorical reports," but today groups like the Chamber of Commerce are producing more potentially useful policy work, he says.

"The climate is shifting" toward the conclusion that everyone needs a diploma, says Balfanz. "You can't even find an employer who says, 'I'll hire people who aren't high-school graduates.' " So when students drop out, "it just feeds the next generation of poverty," he says.

There's currently an opportunity to revise NCLB in a way that helps low-achieving schools, says the University of Chicago's Knowles. Nevertheless, "people have already formed hard opinions," and debate could turn solely partisan, he says.

Lawmakers must aim for a delicate balance on federal initiatives, says Columbia's Henig. Federal interventions must aim at "making local processes work," since local on-the-ground actions are ultimately what make or break schools, he says.

The University of Pennsylvania's Lytle fears that privatization may be on the verge of overwhelming education, with potentially disastrous consequences for low-income families.

"I think the K-12 education business is in the process of deconstructing," he says. "The middle class is looking outside the schools" to private tutoring companies and Internet learning for academics. "More and more, for them, schools are amounting to expensive child care." Some states are aggressively pioneering "virtual" online charter schools and charters granted to home-schoolers, he says.

"The cost side and the efficacy side of education are on a collision course, and I think Congress will end up endorsing fairly radical experimentation" with vouchers, for example, Lytle says. "They'll say, 'There's no evidence that reducing class size or other expensive measures helps, so let's let American ingenuity work. Where does that leave urban kids? Out of luck," Lytle says. "You've got to be pretty sophisticated to make market forces work for you."

But "there's been progress in the last decade with whole-school reform," says Balfanz. "The big question now is how we [change] whole school districts. "It's a big job but within human capacity," he says.

## 2010 UPDATE

An array of forces has slowed long-sought progress in narrowing the minority-student achievement gap among urban schools. Those forces include mixed results in nationwide test scores, three years of delay in reauthorizing the federal No Child Left Behind Act and a pivotal 2007 Supreme Court ruling on school desegregation that, combined with a severe recession, has steered the education debate toward favoring economic considerations over racial equity.

"As a nation we decided long ago against separate but equal, but the reality is we're moving fast to becoming a majority-minority population," former West Virginia Gov. Bob Wise, president of the Alliance for Excellent

Davis Guggenbeim, director of "Waiting Superma," a documentary about the public school in Amercia, and Michelle Rhee, D.C. Public Schools Chancellor, attend the Silverdocs Festival in Silver Spring, Md.

Education, said in a recent interview. "So we need to focus on each child having a quality school no matter where they live." Because the modern economy now requires success by poor children as well as by those bound for higher-paying jobs, Wise said, education reform must link both economic performance and social justice.

The economic pressure on schools continues. A recent study by labor economist Anthony Carnevale of Georgetown University found that two-thirds of the 47 million new jobs he expects the U.S. economy to create between 2008 and 2018 will require workers who have at least some college education.[60] That is a sea change from a half-century ago when nearly two-thirds of jobs were filled by those with only a high school diploma.

The latest student test scores from the nation's urban K-12 schools show some noteworthy but unspectacular improvements. According to a new experimental index of urban student performance in the reading portion of the National Assessment of Educational Progress (NAEP), average reading scores for students in large-city school districts in grades four and eight rose by several points on the proficiency scale between 2003 and 2009, a change that narrowed the achievement gap to 10 points when compared with the national sampling.[61]

## Lagging in Math

In math, according to a March analysis of NAEP scores and state tests by the Council of the Great City Schools, 79 percent of districts increased the percentage of fourth-graders who scored at or above proficient between 2006 and 2009, with a fourth of the districts raising scores by more than 10 percent.[62] Yet "despite significant gains in performance and faster rates of improvement than their states," the assessment said, "the majority of urban school districts continue to score below state averages on fourth- and eighth-grade mathematics assessments."

The decades-old assumption that school districts should actively pursue racial integration was challenged by a June 2007 U.S. Supreme Court ruling that invalidated school-attendance-zone plans used in Seattle and metropolitan Louisville to achieve greater diversity. In a 5-4 ruling in *Parents Involved in Community Schools v. Seattle Dist. No. 1*, the majority, in an opinion written by Chief Justice John G. Roberts Jr., said, "The way to stop discrimination on the basis of race is to stop discriminating on the basis of race."[63] Roberts deplored what he saw as an "ends justify the means" approach to achieving integration. "[R]acial classifications," he argued, "are simply too pernicious to permit any but the most exact connection between justification and classification."

The dissent by the court's liberal justices argued that Roberts' opinion undermined the promise of integrated schools the court set down in its 1954 landmark decision in *Brown v. Board of Education*, a change that Justice John Paul Stevens called "a cruel irony." Justice Anthony Kennedy, in a concurring opinion, left open the possibility of a more modest consideration of race in drawing school boundaries.

The court's ruling was hardly the last word, however. In a June 2010 review of school integration efforts since the Supreme Court decision, the Civil Rights Project at UCLA said the "divided decision confused many educators and it was somewhat unclear what did remain legal."[64] It noted that "economic pressure is forcing school districts to make deep cuts in services, which is another potential constraint for integration efforts," and it called on the Obama administration to issue new guidance on how race can be considered.

One of the nation's most troubled urban districts, the District of Columbia, in spring 2010 became the scene for ratification of a highly innovative teachers' contract.

For nearly three years, national attention had focused on the controversial tenure of D.C. Public Schools Chancellor Michelle Rhee. Her efforts at reforming the system's bureaucracy and sweeping away incompetent teachers — she appeared on the Nov. 26, 2008, cover of *Time* holding a broom — had put her at odds with the local branch of the American Federation of Teachers. Her reputation for tough management has attracted private foundation money to help the D.C. schools, and her future in the job became an issue in the current mayoral race.

Further roiling the waters was Rhee's firing of 241 teachers this summer, including 165 who received poor appraisals under a new evaluation system based in part on students' standardized test scores.[65]

## Paying for Success

But in June 2010, school officials and the teachers' union finalized a contract that, in addition to granting a retroactive pay increase, requires all teachers in the system to be evaluated in part on whether their students' test scores improve, and it offers sizable pay increases to teachers who opt for and succeed in a special new pay-for-performance arrangement.[66]

D.C.'s special constitutional status that gives Congress a major say in its education policies continued to play a role in the district's efforts to improve results. Since 2004, Congress has funded the D.C. Opportunity Scholarship Program, a unique, federally funded voucher option favored by many conservatives that has given some 3,700 students $7,500 per year to attend any accredited private school that will accept them.[67]

But the Democratic takeover of Congress and the election of President Obama brought a change in priorities. Education Secretary Arne Duncan in 2009 rescinded the pending scholarships, and Congress declined to reauthorize them. An Education Department report found that the voucher program had not demonstrated much impact on test scores, though graduation rates for students in the program topped those of other students in D.C. Public Schools.[68]

Virtually every tool in the school reform grab bag — from charter schools to new teacher-accountability rules to dropout-prevention efforts — will be affected by the long-delayed reauthorization of the Elementary and Secondary Education Act (ESEA), known since 2002 as No Child Left Behind. The law has long been the center of disputes over reliance on student test scores. Its deadlines for improving student proficiency are seen by many as unrealistic, and critics have considered its funding levels inadequate. The bill has run into a new set of obstacles in the Obama era.

## A Call for Flexibility

In a March 15, 2010, "blueprint" to overhaul No Child Left Behind, the Obama team argued that the law had "created incentives for states to lower their standards; emphasized punishing failure over rewarding success; focused on absolute scores, rather than recognizing growth and progress; and prescribed a pass-fail, one-size-fits-all series of interventions for schools that miss their goals." It called for greater flexibility in methodology to turn around some 5,000 schools labeled as underperforming.

But the reauthorization, though the subject of a dozen or more hearings this year in the House and Senate, has continued to divide Congress. One reason is the attention devoted to Obama's competitive $4 billion state grant education initiative, called Race to the Top. It is viewed by some as highly successful in providing incentives to states to enact reforms. Though only Delaware and Tennessee have won grants so far, 28 states have made reforms in 2009 and 2010, or triple the number during the previous two years, according to *Education Week*.[69] Yet in a surprise twist, the ravages to state and local budgets wrought by the current recession prompted the House to pass an emergency jobs bill that would shift funds from Race to the Top to preserve current teacher salaries.

In another division among education reformers, the teachers' unions want to make the rewrite of the law less "punitive" toward teachers and more cognizant of family income disparities. "Today, students' success in school depends in large part on the zip code where they live," National Education Association president Dennis Van Roekel told Congress. "Students who struggle the most in impoverished communities too often don't attend safe schools with reliable heat and air conditioning; too often do not have safe passage to and from school; and far too often do not have access to great teachers on a regular and consistent basis."[70]

Former Gov. Wise worries that if the reauthorization is not completed this year, the nation must continue with the existing No Child Left Behind, which he sees as inflexible and short on help for high schools. The law "focused on where the problems are, and a light has been shined on the fact that students of color or low economic status are not making it," Wise says. "But the law does not have adequate remedies. It's like a compact disc in an iPod world."

## 2012 UPDATE

As state and local governments continue to grapple with crippling funding shortages — and draconian cuts in federal spending loom — lawmakers and school districts look for economical ways to boost student achievement. Some argue for competition-based strategies such as closing schools and firing teachers based on test scores and allowing privately run charter schools to vie for public funding. Critics of such market-oriented reforms, however, argue that such measures won't solve the problems facing high-poverty urban schools.

Many states have cut their contribution to local school districts since the economic crisis began four years ago.

In the 2011-2012 school year, 37 states were providing less funding per student to local schools than they did in 2010-2011, according to the Center on Budget and Policy Priorities (CBPP), a liberal, nonprofit research group. Thirty states provide less local-school funding than they did four years ago, and 17 have cut per-student funding by more than 10 percent since the recession began in 2008. Four states — South Carolina, Arizona, California and Hawaii — cut per-student funding by more than 20 percent, according to the CBPP.[71]

Next year, the U.S. Department of Education (DOE) could suffer a 7.8 percent cut in its funding — most of which supports state and local education initiatives — unless Congress resolves a budget stalemate that began in 2011. Last fall, with congressional Republicans and Democrats unable to agree on a combination of spending cuts and tax increases to reduce the federal deficit, Congress agreed to allow the hefty DOE cut and other budget reductions to take effect on Jan. 1, 2013, if the legislative standoff continues. With House Republicans, in particular, continuing to declare that tax increases are

off the table for deficit reduction, a deal to avoid the mandatory cuts — including at least a $3.5 billion reduction in education funding — seems out of reach for now.[72]

More than a third of those cuts — about $1.3 billion — would come directly from federal funds for schools in low-income areas — known as Title I schools. Most Title I schools, which have large numbers of economically disadvantaged students and others at high risk of dropping out, are in urban areas.[73]

### Funding Cuts

A DOE study concluded last year that Title I funds are being used to compensate for cuts in state and local education funding for high-poverty schools instead of merely supplementing those funds. As a result, the DOE concluded, poor school districts are spending substantially less per student than wealthier districts.[74]

For example, DOE found that in districts with both Title I and non-Title I schools, more than 40 percent of Title I schools spent less money per student on staffing than non-Title-I schools did.[75]

The "findings confirm an unfortunate reality in our nation's education system," said Education Secretary Arne Duncan. "Many schools serving low-income children aren't getting their fair share of funding," and "in far too many places Title I dollars are filling budget gaps rather than being extra."[76]

As a result of the financial crisis and related government budget struggles, severe financial troubles have plagued many urban schools.

In Ypsilanti, Mich., for example, schools face a debt expected to reach $9.4 million by the end of this school year, despite previous spending cuts. Reductions in school support staff, for example, have already gone "beyond a point where work can be completed effectively," according to a deficit-elimination plan prepared by district officials.[77]

While many states promised to restore the education funding once the financial crisis waned, some have decided instead to use the money for tax cuts.

Lawmakers in Kansas, for instance, slashed school funding by nearly $700 per student since 2008, resulting in — among other things — large-scale layoffs and school closures in Wichita and other urban schools. "We couldn't take another year like the last three," Wichita

Public Schools Superintendent John Allison said recently.[78]

So when he heard that the state would have a $300 million surplus this year, he said, "We thought, 'Finally, things are going to start getting back to normal.' " Instead, lawmakers last month used the surplus to reduce the top tax rate from 6.45 percent to 4.9 percent — the largest tax cut in state history. Critics said that by 2018 the tax cut would convert this year's surplus into long-term budget deficits totaling $2.5 billion. Education spending was increased by only $58 per student for next year.[79]

In some districts, staff and resource cuts are accompanied by a continuing atmosphere of worry and uncertainty that has eroded morale. In the San Francisco and Los Angeles school districts, for example, state law requires teachers who are at risk of being laid off within the next year to receive advance warning in March. By 2012, as budget woes continue, some teachers had received a warning for four years running.

Uncertainty saps energy needed to operate schools properly, teachers and administrators say. "I've seen teachers who have cried," said Phyllis Bradford, senior director of human resources for the Los Angeles Unified School District. "Others have moved out of state. . . . It's a very depressing time."[80]

## Alternatives Sought

Looking for budget savings and an alternative to what they view as failing urban public schools, some lawmakers have embraced proposals to boost charter schools and other alternatives, such as vouchers to help families place their children in private schools, including religious schools. A wave of Republican governors and state legislators who swept into office in 2010 have been the principal, but not sole, backers of such plans.

In 2011, for example, newly elected Wisconsin Gov. Scott Walker, a Republican, shepherded a substantial expansion of Wisconsin's school-voucher program through the legislature. The program began as a low-income-only program for Milwaukee but was subsequently expanded to include Racine, the state's fifth-largest city. Among other changes, the expanded voucher program eliminated an enrollment cap; raised the income cap for eligible families to 300 percent of the federal poverty level while allowing families to continue receiving voucher support if their income rises after a student enrolls; and allows Milwaukee students to use vouchers at schools in the surrounding county.[81]

In Pennsylvania, newly elected Republican Gov. Tom Corbett tried but failed last year to form a statewide voucher program. Pennsylvania school-choice proponents, who have advocated for vouchers for the last two decades, expressed frustration after the state's Republican-controlled House of Representatives failed to approve Corbett's plan. "It's beyond disappointing," said Dawn Chavous, executive director of Students First PA, a nonpartisan group pushing to provide more alternatives to traditional schools. "We're going to keep fighting. I'm not going to go anywhere."[82]

In Philadelphia, school-system leaders announced this year that looming "severe, long-term deficits" estimated at $1.1 billion by 2017, plus slow progress in improving learning, make it imperative to close many neighborhood schools, restructure school-district administration and promote charter schools over the next five years.[83]

"In spite of progress" in academics," we are not improving nearly fast enough" compared to cities such as San Diego and Boston, school district leaders said in a report.[84] And while "efforts to reduce violence are paying off" — with violent incidents dropping from 3.7 per 100 students in 2007-08 to 2.6 in 2001-2011 — violence "continues to plague our schools."[85] One key to improving the schools while balancing the budget, the leaders said: "Promote equal access to quality choices for parents by expanding high-performing district and charter programs."[86]

But many local activists dub the proposal a stealth maneuver to privatize public schools and diminish the district's power under the guise of saving it. "No one would debate that there are financial problems in the district," said the Rev. Mark Kelly Tyler, pastor of Mother Bethel AME Church, in South Philadelphia. "But is it so bad that the only answer is to shutter 64 schools and remove the remaining 20 percent to charter schools?"[87]

In Illinois, a legislative committee backed a plan in May 2012 to require school districts to direct more money to charter schools. The measure, which has not yet been voted on by the full legislature, is intended to provide "equal funding for our charter schools, equal funding with the public schools," which is "an issue of fairness," said Rep. Daniel Burke, D-Chicago, the measure's sponsor.[88]

The Chicago Teachers Union has strongly opposed the legislation, however, arguing that traditional public schools, "funded almost entirely by taxes," may actually have fewer available resources than the many charter schools that "receive private money from corporate privatization proponents."[89]

Meanwhile, researchers continue to examine whether promoting measures such as charter schools and vouchers makes budgetary sense or improves learning. Findings are mixed. For example, statewide achievement scores in Illinois, released in December 2011, showed that one chain of nine charter schools in Chicago beat the district average, but scores at other charter chains fell well below district averages.[90]

By contrast, in one of the largest studies of its kind, the Center for Research on Education Outcomes (CREDO) at Stanford University found in 2009 that Chicago and Denver charter-school students outpaced their public-school counterparts on the National Assessment of Student Progress (NAEP), which is often called the "nation's report card." In Arizona, Ohio and Texas, charter-school students lagged public-school students' achievement, while in Washington, D.C., public- and charter-school students showed similar achievement levels, the study found.[91]

Groups such as the conservative Thomas B. Fordham Institute, an education-policy think tank in Washington, support charter schools partly because, theoretically, they are more likely to operate like businesses, facing bankruptcy and quick closure if they fail in their educational mission. However, a 2010 Fordham analysis found that 72 percent of the charter schools — and 80 percent of traditional public schools — that were low-achieving in 2004-2004 were still operating, and still performing poorly, five years later.[92]

Critics of urban public schools often charge that public school systems siphon money that could be used for student learning and that charter schools can reverse that pattern. However, Michigan State University Professor of Educational Administration David Arsen and University of Utah Assistant Professor of Educational Leadership and Policy Yongmei Ni, found that, at least in Michigan, charter schools spend twice as much per student on administration as traditional public schools and 20 percent less on instruction.[93]

## Cheating Scandals

In the current wave of school reform plans that began about a decade ago — including the federal No Child Left Behind Act (NCLB), signed into law in 2002 — many seek to hold schools and, increasingly, individual teachers accountable for low student achievement by imposing sanctions if test scores or other measures don't improve.

Under NCLB, sanctions include expanded opportunities for parents to move their children to higher-performing schools. And if students' standardized-test scores continue to lag, schools could experience mass staff firings and reorganization.

How well such methods work is a matter of increasing debate, however, especially in the wake of several administrative scandals in which schools in several cities were suspected of altering students' test scores, presumably to avoid sanctions.

Throughout the 2000s, the Atlanta school system had gained nationwide attention for repeatedly raising test scores. But in 2008 and 2009, the *Atlanta Journal-Constitution* reported that, based on the paper's statistical analysis, many of the increases were so unlikely that they raised suspicions that the district had manipulated test results.

In July 2011, the Georgia Bureau of Investigation accused 178 Atlanta teachers and principals of engaging in a "conspiracy" to change students' test answers. In what has been called the biggest school-cheating scandal in U.S. history, 82 of the people named in the Bureau report confessed to the scheme, in which teachers and administrators erased students' wrong test answers and replaced them with correct responses.[94]

The Georgia Bureau of Investigation found that administrators rather than teachers were apparently the driving force behind most of the cheating. Several teachers who tried to blow the whistle on the scandal found themselves the subject of intimidation and, in one case, even an ethics investigation led by school administrators.[95]

Opponents of basing high-stakes decisions about schools and teachers primarily on standardized-test scores argue that the practice itself invites cheating. "When test scores are all that matter, some educators feel pressured to get the scores they need by hook or by crook," said Robert Shaeffer, a spokesman for National Center for Fair & Open Testing, which opposes heavy reliance on standardized tests for school decision making. "The higher the stakes, the greater the incentive to manipulate, to cheat."[96]

While Atlanta remains the most heavily substantiated case of widespread cheating, various analyses in the past two years have suggested that other districts also have cheated on the tests.

A March 2011 *USA Today* investigation, for example, concluded that patterns of erased-then-replaced test answers at some Washington, D.C., schools suggested that teachers and administrators may have changed students' answers to produce higher scores. At some D.C. schools that had been touted as nationwide models for learning improvement, students' tests had astonishingly high numbers of erasures in which wrong answers were changed to right answers — far more than would be likely to occur by chance, according to the paper.[97] Questions about the D.C. tests remain unresolved.

Investigations, mainly by newspapers, have turned up possible evidence of cheating in Baltimore, Dallas, Detroit, Houston and Los Angeles, as well as some non-urban districts.[98]

### Adding Values

Meanwhile, efforts are expanding to hold individual teachers accountable for students' academic improvement, such as by offering merit pay based in whole or in part on standardized test scores.

In April 2011, for example, the Los Angeles Unified School District publicly released school-by-school results of its new so-called value-added measure of school and teacher performance and announced that it would soon take the more controversial step of telling individual teachers how they'd performed on the new measurement system. The value-added system compares progress of an individual student in a given year to the student's progress in previous school years, as measured by standardized tests. Teachers are then scored on how well their current students perform, compared to how those same students performed in

Thousands of teachers, school workers, students and parents participate in a "state of Emergency" rally in downtown Los Angeles on May 13, 2011, to protest proposed education budget cuts.

past years. By comparing each student only to his or her own past achievements, the method takes into account such factors as poverty or learning disabilities, which an individual teacher can't control, supporters of value-added rankings say.[99]

Many other analysts, as well as teachers' unions, argue that the test-based value-added measures are too narrow to use as a basis for evaluating teacher pay and promotions. In Los Angeles and New York City, for example, tense negotiations continue between the school districts and teachers and their unions over whether the measures should be used as a primary evaluation tool.[100]

### Test Results

Recent test scores on student achievement show mixed results, both for the nation as a whole and for low-income and minority students, who make up a large part of the urban-school population.

On the most recent NAEP, only 32 percent of eighth-graders scored at a "proficient" level in science and only 2 percent at an "advanced" level, for example. However, a longstanding science achievement gap between white eighth-graders and black and Hispanic eighth-graders has slightly narrowed recently, as black and Hispanic students have raised their scores at a slightly faster rate than white students. Between 2009 and 2011, white students raised their average science score on the biannual test by 1 point, compared to three points for black students and five for Hispanics.[101]

Meanwhile, NAEP has undertaken an experimental, voluntary program that gathers detailed data from a group of urban districts as part of a project to determine whether NAEP can be used for district-to-district comparisons. In the experimental program, math scores in participating districts — all of them urban — improved somewhat in 2011 compared with 2009, but reading scores did not. Urban districts continue to lag far behind rural and suburban districts in NAEP scores, however, and most of the math-score increase in urban areas came from higher-income students. Still, most of the urban districts have improved in both math and reading since the early 2000s.[102]

"We've been able to close the gap between [large cities] and the nation by between 25 percent and 36 percent" since 2003, said Michael Casserly, executive director of the Council of the Great City Schools, a coalition of the city's largest urban school districts. "It says to us that many urban school districts in aggregate appear to be moving in the right direction."[103]

But progress is far too slow, said other analysts. "There's nobody who's performing at advanced levels," said Mark Schneider, a vice president of the American Institutes for Research, a Washington-based social-science research group that has been involved in NAEP and other federal education programs. "This is just really, really, really depressing."[104]

One surprise in the findings was Atlanta's results. While Atlanta cheated on the state tests, its performance on the national test — untainted by cheating — was well above average. On NAEP, Atlanta schools made significant continuing gains throughout the past decade, including in 2011, demonstrating that — despite the scandal —"what you saw by way of reform in the school district was real," said Casserly.[105]

## 2014 UPDATE

On June 18, 2014, Louisiana governor Bobby Jindal became the first governor to overrule state education officials and begin pulling out of the nationwide movement to outfit schools with the Common Core State Standards. "The federal government would like to assert control of our educational system," the conservative Jindal said in explaining his shift from previous support for the private-public effort that began before the Obama Administration took office. "We're very alarmed about choice and local control of curriculum being taken away," Jindal said.[106]

Jindal's move was limited—focused on blocking a test he considers expensive—and the Louisiana legislature and state school board may outflank him. But he made national headlines by joining several conservative governors who've soured on a once-bipartisan program to boost classroom rigor, a campaign being pushed by governors and state education chiefs with backing in 44 states and District of Columbia.

But Common Core is also under fire from the opposite end of the political spectrum. American Federation of Teachers president Randi Weingarten in a May 2014 op-ed warned of dire consequences of proliferating high-stakes tests—noting more than 100 different tests within schools in New York City. "Implementing the standards will not be accomplished by targets and sanctions," she wrote. "It will require more adequate and equitable resources and greater investments in professional capacity, especially for currently underfunded schools that serve the highest-need students."[107]

Nonetheless, the National Governors Association and Council of Chief State School Officers are coordinating two consortia of states crafting sets of assessments aligned with Common Core standards that were field tested during the 2013–2014 school year and will be widely used in 2014–2015.

Many urban school systems are embracing Common Core. The Council of Great City Schools, a network of 67 districts serving seven million students, in a 2013 survey of curriculum directors found the majority said their district's progress in implementing Common Core was either good or excellent.

For individual educators, Common Core may prompt both hope and fear. In Washington, D.C., schools chancellor Kaya Henderson in June 2014 announced that anxiety among teachers had led to her to postpone using test scores in teacher evaluations while the city adjusts to exams based on the Common Core.[108]

In Albuquerque, veteran school administrator Denise Brigman welcomed the movement's effect on innovation. "We are doing Common Core just as every other elementary school in the district, but the benefit we have is the extra time to come together, on a daily basis, to have deep conversations about our teaching and learning and supporting our students," she said.[109]

More to the liking of conservatives are the choices offered parents by charter schools. Jindal touts the New Orleans charters—which have served 90 percent of the city's students since the public system was demolished by Hurricane Katrina in 2005—as a national model. The Cresent City's Recovery School District will begin the 2014–2015 year as the nation's first all-charter district.[110]

Nationally, a recent Stanford University study of charters found that public charters in Washington, D.C., and New York clearly outperformed comparable district schools, even as public charters in Nevada and Texas underperformed the traditional schools.[111]

The politics of the publicly funded but independently run charters, however, remain divisive. No sooner had New York City mayor Bill de Blasio taken office in January 2014 than he began challenging his predecessor Michael Bloomberg's encouragement of charters. Objecting to charters' "free ride," he began withdrawing building space the charters were sharing, along with food and janitorial services.[112]

Perhaps a wider reform impacting urban schools is the nonpartisan, state and city push to better prepare children for elementary school by funding preK programs. President Obama has proposed such a program federally, but Congress has not acted. In San Antonio, Texas, the city government in 2013 launched an early childhood program using a dedicated tax. The program is run by educators, with certified teachers in the key roles of management and instruction. Similar programs are cropping up in Boston, Cleveland, and Seattle. "A meta-analyses spanning five decades and more than 120 studies conducted by researchers at the University of Chicago and Rutgers," according to the *San Antonio Express-News*, found that quality preschool has "a substantial impact on children's cognitive, social, and emotional development and school outcomes."[113] Laurie Posner, "Pre-K Poses Great Hope for Texas, It's Students," *San Antonio Express-News*, June 15, 2014, http://digital. olivesoftware.com/Olive/ODE/SanAntonioExpress News/LandingPage/LandingPage.aspx?href=U0FFTi8y MDE0LzA2LzE1&pageno=NzE.&entity=QXIwNzEw MA..&view=ZW50aXR5.

Among the promising management reforms in urban schools are the formation of new networks within such large cities as those in New York, Baltimore, Chicago, and Denver, groupings of a more manageable size than large-scale centralized authorities, according to a May 2014 study by the liberal-leaning Center for American Progress. "As districts struggle to improve their supports for schools, especially those serving large numbers of disadvantaged students," wrote Maureen Kelleher, "school networks show promise as an emerging strategy to help schools improve student learning and to solve the operational problems that can suck time and energy away from a focus on instruction."[114]

The private sector is also involved in urban school improvements. The McLean, Virginia-based wireless provider Kajeet, for example, partners with districts to supply school-managed Wi-Fi hotspots using the Sprint 4G LTE network to keep students connected to educational resources on the Internet at home or during summer.

On the funding front, urban schools—like many public programs—are doing more with less. "At least 35 states are providing less funding per student for the 2013-14 school year than they did before the [2008] recession hit," writes the liberal-leaning Center for Budget and Policy Priorities. "At least 15 states are providing less funding per student to local school districts in the new school year than they provided a year ago."[115]

Federally, Obama's fiscal 2015 budget proposed $69 billion for education, which, if Congress approved, would be a 2 percent increase over last year's level. Nearly 90 percent of that money would go toward disadvantaged, poor, and minority students, those with disabilities and English learners, the Education Department said.

Education Secretary Arne Duncan heralded good news for urban schools in the 2013 National Assessment of Education Progress. Of 21 urban districts that took part, Los Angeles Unified "achieve the highest gains over two years on fourth-grade reading scores for African American students, white students and those from low-income families," the *Los Angeles Times* reported. Los Angeles is among the school systems that are "examples for the rest of the country of what can happen when schools embrace innovative reforms," Duncan said.[116]

Elsewhere, "The 2013 NAEP results show gains in large city schools over this last decade that are statistically significant and educationally significant," said Michael Casserly, executive director of the Council of the Great City Schools. "We estimate that nearly 100,000 more of our fourth-graders score at or above the proficient level in math than 10 years ago."[117]

# NOTES

1. Quoted in Judy Radigan, "Reframing Dropouts: The Complexity of Urban Life Intersects with Current School Policy," paper presented at the Texas Dropout Conference, Houston, Oct. 6, 2006.

2. "The Socioeconomic Composition of the Public Schools: A Crucial Consideration in Student Assignment Policy," University of North Carolina Center for Civil Rights, Jan. 7, 2005, www.law.unc.edu/PDFs/charlottereport.pdf.

3. For background, see Barbara Mantel, "No Child Left Behind," *CQ Researcher*, May 7, 2005, pp. 469-492.

4. Quoted in David J. Hoff and Kathleen Kennedy Manzo, "Bush Claims About NCLB Questioned," *Education Week*, March 9, 2007, www.edweek.org.

5. Quoted in *ibid.*

6. "The Nation's Report Card: Reading 2005," U.S. Department of Education Institute of Education Sciences, www.nationsreportcard.gov.

7. Douglas N. Harris, "Ending the Blame Game on Educational Inequity: A Study of 'High-Flying' Schools and NCLB," Education Policy Studies Laboratory, Arizona State University, March 2006.

8. Jay P. Greene, "Education Myths," The American Enterprise Online, American Enterprise Institute, August 2006.

9. For background, see Charles S. Clark, "Charter Schools," *CQ Researcher*, Dec. 20, 2002, pp. 1033-1056; Kenneth Jost, "School Vouchers Showdown," *CQ Researcher*, Feb. 15, 2002, pp. 121-144.

10. Greene, *op. cit.*

11. Brad Olsen and Lauren Anderson, "Courses of Action: A Qualitative Investigation Into Urban Teacher Retention and Career Development," *Urban Education*, January 2007, p. 5.

12. Quoted in *ibid.*, p. 14.

13. *Ibid.*

14. Arthur J. Rothkopf, "Elementary and Secondary Education Act Reauthorization: Improving NCLB To Close the Achievement Gap," testimony before the Senate Committee on Health, Education, Labor, and Pensions and the House Committee on Education and Labor, March 13, 2007.

15. For background, see Kenneth Jost, "Testing in Schools," *CQ Researcher*, April 20, 2001, pp. 321-344.

16. Richard J. Murnane, "Improving the Education of Children Living in Poverty," unpublished paper, Jan. 25, 2007.

17. *Ibid.*

18. For background, see Kenneth Jost, "School Desegregation," *CQ Researcher*, April 23, 2004, pp. 345-372.

19. Quoted in "Center on Race and Social Problems Commemorates *Brown v. Board of Education*," University of Pittsburgh School of Social Work, May 7, 2004.

20. Quoted in Brian Lamb, "No Excuses: Closing the Racial Gap in Learning," transcript, "Booknotes," C-SPAN, Feb. 1, 2004.

21. Paul Tough, "What It Takes To Make a Student," *The New York Times Magazine*, Nov. 26, 2006, p. 70.

22. R. Scott Baker, "School Resegregation: Must the South Turn Back?" *Journal of Southern History*, November 2006, p. 993.

23. Howell S. Baum, "Smart Growth and School Reform: What If We Talked About Race and Took Community Seriously?" *Journal of the American Planning Association*, winter 2004, p. 14.

24. "Divided We Fail: Coming Together Through Public School Choice," Task Force on the Common School, The Century Foundation Press, 2002, p. 3.

25. *Ibid.*, p. 13.

26. Quoted in Lamb, *op. cit.*

27. *Ibid.*

28. Terry Ryan and Quentin Suffren, "Charter School Lessons from Ohio," *The Education Gadfly*, Thomas

B. Fordham Foundation, March 15, 2007, www.edexcellence.net.

29. Mark Simon, "What Teachers Know," *Poverty & Race*, September/October 2004, www.prrac.org.

30. Dreyon Wynn and Dianne L. H. Mark, "Book Review: Educating Teachers for Diversity: Seeing With a Cultural Eye," *Urban Education*, May 2005, p. 350.

31. Jocelyn A. Glazier, "Moving Closer to Speaking the Unspeakable: White Teachers Talking About Race," *Teacher Education Quarterly*, winter 2003.

32. Wanda J. Blanchett, "Urban School Failure and Disproportionality in a Post-*Brown* Era," *Remedial and Special Education*, April 2005, p. 70.

33. Christine H. Leland and Jerome C. Harste, "Doing What We Want to Become: Preparing New Urban Teachers," *Urban Education*, January 2005, p. 60.

34. *Ibid.*, p. 62.

35. Glazier, *op. cit.*

36. Wynn and Mark, *op. cit.*

37. For background, see Wayne J. Urban and Jennings L. Wagoner, *American Education: A History* (2003); Stanley William Rothstein, *Schooling the Poor: A Social Inquiry Into the American Educational Experience* (1994).

38. For background, see Kathy Koch, "Reforming School Funding," *CQ Researcher*, Dec. 10, 1999, pp. 1041-1064.

39. Derrick Bell, *Silent Covenants:* Brown v. Board of Education *and the Unfulfilled Hopes for Racial Reform* (2004), p. 88.

40. *Ibid.*, p. 91.

41. Ruth Curran Neild and Robert Balfanz, "An Extreme Degree of Difficulty: The Educational Demographics of Urban Neighborhood High Schools," *Journal of Education for Students Placed at Risk*, spring 2006, p. 135.

42. V. W. Ipka, "At Risk Children in Resegregated Schools; An Analysis of the Achievement Gap," *Journal of Instructional Psychology*, December 2003, p. 294.

43. The case is *Brown v. Board of Education of Topeka*, 347 U.S. 483 (1954).

44. For background, see Jost, "School Desegregation," *op. cit.*; Gary Orfield and John T. Yun, "Resegregation in American Schools," The Civil Rights Project, Harvard University, June 1999, www.civilrightsproject.harvard.edu/research/deseg/reseg_schools99.php.

45. The case is *Milliken v. Bradley*, 418 U.S. 717 (1974).

46. Ipka, *op. cit.* The cases are *Board of Education of Oklahoma City v. Dowell*, 498 U.S. 237 (1991) and *Freeman v. Pitts*, 498 U.S. 1081 (1992).

47. Gary Orfield and Chungmei Lee, "Racial Transformation and the Changing Nature of Segregation," The Civil Rights Project, Harvard University, January 2006, www.civilrightsproject.harvard.edu; *Keyes v. School District No. 1*, Denver, Colorado, 413 U.S. 189 (1973).

48. Gary Orfield and Susan E. Eaton, "Back to Segregation," *The Nation*, March 3, 2003, p. 5.

49. Baum, *op. cit.*

50. *Ibid.*

51. Neild and Balfanz, *op. cit.*, p. 126.

52. "Divided We Fail," *op. cit.*, p. 17.

53. Tough, *op. cit.*

54. Elaine M. Stotko, Rochelle Ingram and Mary Ellen Beaty-O'Ferrall, "Promising Strategies for Attracting and Retaining Successful Urban Teachers," *Urban Education*, January 2007, p. 36.

55. Patrick Mattimore, "Will Court Put Integration on Hold?" *San Francisco Examiner*, Dec. 8, 2006, www.exaaminer.com. The cases — argued on Dec. 4, 2006 — are *Meredith v. Jefferson County Board of Education*, 05-915; and *Parents Involved in Community Schools v. Seattle School District No. 1*, 05-908.

56. Richard Kahlenberg, "Helping Children Move from Bad Schools to Good Ones," The Century Foundation, 2006, www.tcf.org/list.asp?type=PB&pubid=565.

57. *Ibid.*

58. Quoted in Michael Sandler, "Minding Their Business," *CQ Weekly*, April 2, 2007, p. 952.

59. Quoted in Jonathan Weisman and Amit R. Paley, "Dozens in GOP Turn Against Bush's Prized 'No Child' Act," *The Washington Post*, March 15, 2007, p. A1.

60. Written testimony of Anthony P. Carnevale, director, Georgetown University Center on Education and the Workforce, U.S. Senate Committee on Health, Education, Labor and Pensions, Feb. 24, 2010, http://help.senate.gov/imo/media/doc/Carnevale.pdf.

61. Council of the Great City Schools, press release, May 20, 2010, www.cgcs.org/pressrelease/TUDA_Reading2010.pdf.

62. "Beating the Odds: Analysis of Student Performance on State Assessments and NAEP," Council of the Great City Schools, March 2010.

63. Linda Greenhouse, "Justices Limit the Use of Race in School Plans for Integration," *The New York Times*, June 28, 2007, p. A1.

64. Civil Rights Project, University of California at Los Angeles, www.civilrightsproject.ucla.edu/research/deseg/school-integration-three-years-after-parents-involved.pdf.

65. Bill Turque, "Rhee dismisses 241 D.C. teachers; union vows to contest firing," *The Washington Post*, July 24, 2010, p. A1, www.washingtonpost.com/wp-dyn/content/article/2010/07/23/AR20100 72303093.html.

66. Bill Turque, "D.C. Teachers' Contract Passes Its Final Hurdle; Council Unanimously Approves Pact that Bases Pay on Results," *The Washington Post*, June 30, 2010.

67. "Opportunity Denied," editorial, *The Washington Post*, June 23, 2010.

68. "Evaluation of the DC Opportunity Scholarship Program: Final Report," U.S. Department of Education, June 2010, http://ies.ed.gov/ncee/pubs/20104018/pdf/20104018.pdf.

69. Chad Adelman, "How Race to the Top Could Inform ESEA Reauthorization," *Education Week*, June 28, 2010.

70. Testimony before Senate Health, Education, Labor and Pensions Committee, March 9, 2010.

71. Phil Oliff and Michael Leachman, "New School Year Brings Steep Cuts in Funding for Schools," Center on Budget and Policy Priorities, Oct. 7, 2011, www.cbpp.org/files/9-1-11sfp.pdf.

72. Jamie Baxter, "We Must Avoid Sequestration: Savage Cuts in Education Funding Would Cripple Our Schools," *Post-Gazette.com* (Pittsburgh), May 3, 2012, www.post-gazette.com/stories/opinion/perspectives/we-must-avoid-sequestration-savage-cuts-in-education-funding-would-cripple-our-schools-634125.

73. *Ibid.*

74. Ruth Heuer and Stephanie Stullich, "Comparability of State and Local Expenditures Among Schools Within Districts: A Report from the Study of School-level Expenditures," U.S. Department of Education, 2011, www2.ed.gov/rschstat/eval/title-i/school-level-expenditures/school-level-expenditures.pdf; "The Potential Impact of Revising Title I Comparability Requirement to Focus on School-level Expenditures," U.S. Department of Education, November 2011, www2.ed.gov/rschstat/eval/title-i/comparability-requirement/comparability-policy-brief.pdf.

75. "The Potential Impact of Revising Title I Comparability," *ibid.*, p. 3.

76. Quoted in Alyson Klein, "Poor Schools Shortchanges on Funding, Ed Dept. Says," *Education Week blogs*, Nov. 30, 2011, http://blogs.edweek.org/edweek/campaign-k-12/2011/11/for_years_advocates_for_poor.html.

77. "Narrative Section, Deficit Elimination Plan," School District of Ypsilanti, December 2011, www.ypsd.org/downloads/financial/2011-2012_deficit_elimination_plan_20111214_111811_7.pdf.

78. Mike Alberti, "States to residents, localities: forget promises to restore funding," Remapping Debate, www.remappingdebate.org/article/states-residents-localities-forget-promises-restore-funding.

79. *Ibid.*

80. Quoted in Christina Hoag, "California's Fourth Year of Teacher Layoffs Spurs Concerns," The Associated Press/ABC News, May 5, 2012, http://abcnews.go.com/US/wireStory/califs-4th-year-teacher-layoffs-spur-concerns-16285889#.T616a1JzaUk.

81. "2011-2013 Legislative Session," "Accurate Information About School Choice," School

ChoiceWI.org, www.schoolchoicewi.org/stgov/detail.cfm?id=10; Patrick Marley and Jason Stein, "Senate OK'd Budget Goes to Walker," *Journal Sentinel online* (Milwaukee), June 16, 2011, www.jsonline.com/news/statepolitics/124004679.html, and Amy Hetzner and Erin Richards, "Budget Cuts $834 Million from Schools," *Journal Sentinel online* (Milwaukee), March 1, 2011, www.jsonline.com/news/statepolitics/117192683.html.

82. Quoted in Jan Murphy and Charles Thompson, "State House Rejects School-voucher Proposal," PennLive.com/ *The Patriot-News* (Harrisburg), Dec. 14, 2011.

83. "A Blueprint for Transforming Philadelphia's Public Schools" (Draft), School District of Philadelphia, http://thenotebook.org/sites/default/files/BlueprintPublicPresentation_4_22_12.pdf.

84. *Ibid.*, p. 4.

85. *Ibid.*, p. 5.

86. *Ibid.*

87. Quoted in Julianne Hing, "The Remaking of Philadelphia Public Schools: Privatization or Bust," *Color Lines*, May 11, 2012, http://colorlines.com/archives/2012/05/the_remaking_of_philadelphia_public_schools_privatization_or_bust.html.

88. Jim Broadway, "Bill to Give More Cash to Charters Moves Forward," State School News Service/Catalyst Chicago, May 9, 2012, www.catalyst-chicago.org/notebook/2012/05/09/20105/bill-give-more-cash-charters-moves-forward.

89. Quoted in *ibid.*

90. Rosalyn Rossi and Art Golab, "Chicago Charter Schools Produce Wildly Uneven Results on State Tests," *Chicago Sun-Times*, Jan. 1, 2012, www.suntimes.com/news/education/9145306-418/story.html.

91. "Multiple Choice: Charter School Performance in 16 States," Center for Research on Education Outcomes, 2009, http://credo.stanford.edu/reports/MULTIPLE_CHOICE_CREDO.pdf.

92. David A. Stuit, "Are Bad Schools Immortal?" Thomas B. Fordham Institute, December 2010, www.edexcellencemedia.net/publications/2010/20101214_AreBadSchoolImmortal/Fordham_Immortal.pdf.

93. Emily Pfund, "Study Finds Michigan Charter Schools Spend Twice as Much as Public Schools," *Central Michigan Life*, Central Michigan University, April 26, 2012, www.cm-life.com/2012/04/26/study-focuses-on-michigan-charter-schools-finds-charter-schools-spend-twice-as-much-as-public-schools.

94. Patrik Jonsson, "America's Biggest Teacher and Principal Cheating Scandal Unfolds in Atlanta," *The Christian Science Monitor*, July 5, 2011, www.csmonitor.com/USA/Education/2011/0705/America-s-biggest-teacher-and-principal-cheating-scandal-unfolds-in-Atlanta; and "School Cheating Investigation: Atlanta Journal-Constitution Flags Improbable Test Scores in Analysis," Associated Press/ *Huffington Post*, March 25, 2012, www.huffingtonpost.com/2012/03/24/schools-cheating-investig_n_1377767.html.

95. Jonsson, *ibid.*

96. Quoted in *ibid.*

97. Jack Gillum and Marisol Bello, "When Standardized Test Scores Soared in DC, Were the Gains Real?" *USA Today*, March 30, 2011, www.usatoday.com/news/education/2011-03-28-1Aschooltesting28_CV_N.htm.

98. "School Cheating Investigation: Atlanta Journal Constitution Flags Improbable Test Scores in Analysis," *op. cit.*

99. Jason Song and Jason Felch, "L.A. Unified Releases School Ratings Using 'Value-added' Method," *Los Angeles Times*, April 12, 2011, http://articles.latimes.com/2011/apr/12/local/la-me-0413-value-add-20110414; for background, see Marcia Clemmitt, "School Reform," *CQ Researcher*, April 29, 2011, pp. 385-408.

100. Fernanda Santos and Anna M. Phillips, "With Release of Teacher Data, Setback for Union Turns Into Rallying Cry," *The New York Times*, Feb. 26, 2012, www.nytimes.com/2012/02/27/nyregion/teacher-ratings-produce-a-rallying-cry-for-the-union.html.

101. Sarah D. Sparks, "Most 8th Graders Fall Short on NAEP Science Test," *Education Week*, May 10, 2012, www.edweek.org/ew/articles/2012/05/10/31naep_ep.h31.html?tkn=VPXFO3wzO2s%2Bbex2WwFqNNnCfYtzrpCNzSmA&cmp=ENL-EU-NEWS1,k, and "The Nation's Report Card: Science 2011," National Center for Education Statistics, May 2012, http://nces.ed.gov/nationsreportcard/pubs/main2011/2012465.asp.

102. Christina Samuels, "Urban NAEP Scores Show Math Scores Up, Reading Mostly Flat," *Education Week blogs*, Dec. 7, 2011, http://blogs.edweek.org/edweek/District_Dossier/2011/12/urban_naep_scores_show_math_up.html; and Joy Resmovits, "City-level National Tests Show Slight Math Growth, No Change in Reading," *Huffington Post*, Dec. 7, 2011, www.huffingtonpost.com/2011/12/07/urban-schools-test_n_1132775.html.

103. Quoted in Resmovits, *ibid.*

104. Quoted in *ibid.*

105. Quoted in *ibid.*

106. Julia O'Donoghue and Danielle Dreilinger, "Bobby Jindal announces plans to get Louisiana out of Common Core," *The Times Picayune*, http://www.nola.com/politics/index.ssf/2014/06/bobby_jindal_gets_out_of_commo.html#incart_river

107. Linda Darling-Hammond and Randi Weingarten, "It's Time for a New Accountability in American Education," *The Huffington Post Blog*, http://www.huffingtonpost.com/linda-darlinghammond/its-time-for-a-new-accoun_b_5351475.html?utm_hp_ref=education&ir=Education.

108. Emma Brown, "Schools Take Hiatus From Test-Based Teacher Evaluations As City Moves to Common Core Exams," *The Washington Post*, June 19, 2014, http://www.washingtonpost.com/local/education/dc-public-schools-takes-hiatus-from-test-based-teacher-evaluations-as-city-moves-to-common-core-exams/2014/06/19/184b8b44-f7c2-11e3-8aa9-dad2ec039789_story.html.

109. Lesli A. Maxwell "N.M. School Builds Bridge to Standards for ELLs." *Education Week*, Nov. 13, 2012, http://www.edweek.org/ew/articles/2012/11/14/12cc-ell.h32.html

110. Lyndsey Layton, "In New Orleans, Traditional Public Schools Close for Good." *The Washington Post,* May 28, 2014, http://www.washingtonpost.com/local/education/in-new-orleans-traditional-public-schools-close-for-good/2014/05/28/ae4f5724-e5de-11e3-8f90-73e071f3d637_story.html.

111. See, The Center for Research on Education Outcomes, http://credo.stanford.edu/documents/NCSS%202013%20Final%20Draft.pdf.

112. Conor P. Williams, "Why Is Progressive Mayor Bill de Blasio Throwing Charter Schools Out of New York City?" *Daily Beast*, March 4, 2014, http://www.thedailybeast.com/articles/2014/03/04/why-is-progressive-hero-bill-de-blasio-throwing-charter-schools-out-of-new-york-city.html.

113. Laurie Posner, "Pre-K Poses Great Hope for Texas, It's Students," *San Antonio Express-News*, June 15, 2014, http://digital.olivesoftware.com/Olive/ODE/SanAntonioExpressNews/LandingPage/LandingPage.aspx?href=U0FFTi8yMDE0LzA2LzE1&pageno=NzE.&entity=QXIwNzEwMA..&view=ZW50aXR5.

114. Maureen Kelleher, "The Rise of Networks," May 2014, Center for American Progress, http://americanprogress.org/issues/education/report/2014/05/27/90377/the-rise-of-networks/.

115. Michael Leachman and Chris Mai, "Most States Funding Schools Less Than Before the Recession," The Center on Budget and Policy Priorities, http://www.cbpp.org/cms/?fa=view&id=4011.

116. Howard Blume, "LAUSD Gains in Reading, Math Proficiency Praised," *Los Angeles Times*, Dec. 22, 2013.

117. Ann Doss Helms, "CMS tops urban districts on national math, reading tests,"

## BIBLIOGRAPHY

### Books

**Kozol, Jonathan,** *The Shame of the Nation: The Restoration of Apartheid Schooling in America,* **Three Rivers Press, 2006.**
A longtime education writer and activist reports on his five-year journey to closely observe 60 schools in 11

states. He describes almost entirely resegregated urban schools with dilapidated buildings, dirty classrooms and a dearth of up-to-date textbooks.

**Rothstein, Richard, *Class and Schools: Using Social, Economic, and Education Reform to Close the Black-White Achievement Gap, Economic Policy Institute,* 2004.**

A research associate at a think tank concerned with low- and middle-income workers and families argues that raising the achievement of urban students requires public policies that address students' multiple social and economic needs.

**Thernstrom, Abigail, and Stephan Thernstrom, *No Excuses: Closing the Racial Gap in Learning, Simon & Schuster,* 2004.**

A husband and wife who are senior fellows at the conservative Manhattan Institute for Public Policy Research argue that charter schools and the No Child Left Behind Act's focus on holding schools accountable for poor student achievement can close the achievement gap for urban students.

## Articles

**Boo, Katherine, "Expectations," *The New Yorker,* Jan. 15, 2007, p. 44.**

A reform-minded superintendent closes Denver's lowest-achieving high school, hoping its students will accept the offer to enroll in any other city school, including some with mainly online classes. Mostly Latinos from the city's poorest families, the displaced students struggle with losing their old school, which has provided many with a sense of community, and with new choices that confront them, as well as the ever-present choice of dropping out.

**Moore, Martha T., "More Mayors Are Moving To Take Over School System," *USA Today,* March 21, 2007, p. A1.**

Albuquerque's mayor is among those who believe they could run schools better than their local school boards.

**Saulny, Susan, "Few Students Seek Free Tutoring or Transfers From Failing Schools," *The New York Times,* April 6, 2006, p. 20.**

The No Child Left Behind Act promises free tutoring for many students in low-achieving schools, but few of those students' families know about the option or have been able to enroll their children in good-quality tutoring programs.

**Tough, Paul, "What It Takes To Make a Student," *The New York Times Magazine,* Nov. 26, 2006, p. 44.**

A handful of charter schools are making strides against the achievement gap. But largely because low-income and minority students arrive at school with smaller vocabularies and far less knowledge about how to communicate with adults and behave in a learning situation, the work requires extra-long school hours and intense teacher commitment.

## Reports and Studies

***Beating the Odds: An Analysis of Student Performance and Achievement Gaps on State Assessments: Results from the 2005-2006 School Year, Council of the Great City Schools,* April 2007.**

A group representing 67 of the country's largest urban school districts examines in detail the recent performance of urban students on state tests.

***Divided We Fail: Coming Together Through Public School Choice, Task Force on the Common School, The Century Foundation,* 2002.**

Basing its discussion on the idea that race- and class-segregated schools have proven a failure, a nonpartisan think tank explores the possibility of encouraging cross-district integration of low-income and middle-income students by methods like establishing high-quality magnet schools in cities.

***Engaging Schools: Fostering High School Students' Motivation to Learn, Committee on Increasing High School Students' Engagement and Motivation to Learn, National Research Council,* 2003.**

A national expert panel examines methods for re-engaging urban high-school students who have lost their motivation to learn, a problem they say is widespread but solvable.

**Bridgeland, John M., John J. DiIulio, Jr., and Karen Burke Morison, *The Silent Epidemic: Perspectives of High School Dropouts, Bill & Melinda Gates Foundation,* March 2006.**

Nearly half of high-school dropouts say they left school partly because they were bored. A third of the students left because they needed to work, and more than a fifth said they left to care for a family member.

**Levin, Henry, Clive Belfield, Peter Muennig and Cecilia Rouse, "The Costs and Benefits of an Excellent Education for All of America's Children,"** *Teachers College, Columbia University,* **January 2007; www .cbcse.org/media/download_gallery/Leeds_Report_ Final_Jan2007.pdf.**

A team of economists concludes that measures to cut the number of school dropouts would pay for themselves with higher tax revenues and lower government spending.

# For More Information

**Achieve, Inc.,** 1775 I St., N.W., Suite 410, Washington, DC 20006; (202) 419-1540; www.achieve.org. An independent bipartisan group formed by governors and business leaders to promote higher academic standards.

**Alliance for Excellent Education,** 1201 Connecticut Ave., N.W., Suite 901, Washington, DC 20036; (202) 828-0828; www.all4ed.org. A nonprofit research and advocacy group seeking policies to help at-risk high-school students.

**The Center for Education Reform,** 1001 Connecticut Ave., N.W., Suite 204, Washington, DC 20036; (202) 822-9000; www.edreform.com. A nonprofit advocacy group that promotes school choice in cities.

**The Century Foundation,** 41 E. 70th St., New York, NY 10021; (212) 535-4441; www.tcf.org. Supports research on income inequality and urban policy.

**Citizens for Effective Schools,** 8209 Hamilton Spring Ct., Bethesda, MD 20817; (301) 469-8000; www .citizenseffectiveschools.org. An advocacy group that seeks policy changes to minimize the achievement gap for low-income and minority students.

**Council of the Great City Schools,** 1301 Pennsylvania Ave., N.W., Suite 702, Washington, DC 20004; (202) 393-2427; www.cgcs.org. A coalition of 67 urban school systems dedicated to improving urban schools.

*Education Next,* Hoover Institution, Stanford University; www.educationnext.org. A quarterly journal on education reform published by a conservative think tank.

**The Education Trust,** 1250 H St., N.W., Suite 700, Washington, DC 20005; (202) 293-1217; www2.edtrust .org. Dedicated to closing the achievement gap in learning and college preparation for low-income and minority students.

**National Center for Education Statistics,** 1990 K St., N.W., Washington, DC 20006; (202) 502-7300; http:// nces.ed.gov. A Department of Education agency that provides statistics and analysis on U.S. schools, student attendance and achievement.